THE TWENTIES

American Writing in the Postwar Decade

Also by Frederick J. Hoffman

Freudianism and the Literary Mind

The Little Magazine: A History and Bibliography
(with Charles Allen and Carolyn F. Ulrich)

The Modern Novel in America: 1900–1950

Edited by Frederick J. Hoffman

William Faulkner: Two Decades of Criticism
(with Olga W. Vickery)

The Achievement of D. H. Lawrence
(with Harry Thornton Moore)

The Growth of American Literature
(with Edwin Harrison Cady and Roy Harvey Pearce)

THE TWENTIES

American Writing in the Postwar Decade

BY FREDERICK J. HOFFMAN

New York · THE VIKING PRESS · Mcmlv

PS/21

H/N

Library of Congress catalog number: 55-7379

PRINTED IN THE U.S.A. BY VAIL-BALLOU PRESS, INC.

To E.C. and C.E.

CONTENTS

PREFACE

THE 1920s are a decade especially susceptible to the image-making and stereotyping of historians, literary or otherwise. The reason for this tendency to give the easiest definition of the decade's character lies partly in the special place it has had in our century. Bounded as it was by a war and a depression, it very early acquired an isolated position in cultural history. The peculiarities of the decade, or of the large minority who articulated its feelings, were put under an especially narrow scrutiny, from which they emerged in several kinds of distortion. For the most part, the story of the decade has been told with an improper emphasis upon the most sensational of its effects.

The Twenties is, at least in part, a corrective of the most extreme forms of distortion. When I began writing it I was convinced that a period of years responsible for so many distinguished products in the arts, one capable of holding the interest of subsequent generations so fully, must have been more substantial than it is usually represented as being. It seemed to me that there were several reasons why the 1920s had not so far been fairly portrayed. The most important was that the methods used, while not dishonest or improper, were inadequate to the task of giving the full quality of the decade. A chronological presentation of events does not really give more than their surface. Emphasis upon historical and social matters leaves much that is either ignored or insufficiently realized. The most popular method so far used in studies of the 1920s has been the journalistic one of searching out and featuring prominently the sensational events or characteristics of the time. This approach, while it entertained readers, did so at a considerable sacrifice of perspective and of what I insist is the truth of the decade. The real value lies, not merely in newspaper copy or in public event, but in the ways in which the literature expressed, formally, climactically, and meaningfully, the several impor-

ix

tant preoccupations, modes of thought, and attitudes of the times.

I did not want to write either a political or a literary history of the decade; I needed an approach that revealed the value of the thousands of documents one finds in the popular and semi-popular writings of the period but at the same time subordinated them to the central values they suggested. I encountered several problems in my search for the center of the decade's value. Not the least of these was the need to give a sense of the proper balance of the literary work with its documentary environment. How valuable were the hundreds of statements, arguments, editorials, charges, and countercharges, concerned with essential matters but not in any real sense literature? What was the true relationship of these documents to works of acknowledged literary value? Most important of all, what insights into the major issues of the decade were available in the literature, and how could one best represent them? It has often seemed to me that quarrels over the importance of the formal as opposed to the social values of literature ignore (sometimes quite arbitrarily) the genuine opportunities for seeing the true virtues of a literature, which are neither purely formal nor exclusively documentary but—in achieving a balance of both—moral. The aesthetic forms employ the evidence which the journals of the age accumulate; the social, the political, and the journalistic responses to issues of the time are responsible for a vast, often undifferentiated mass of detail which in its crude form is the "raw material" of a literature.

If literature is important to history, it is not because it serves as a social document or as a footnote to political or intellectual history, but primarily because it is a culmination, a genuine means of realizing the major issues of its time. With this truth in mind, I tried to see the 1920s from the perspective of its literature; and I selected for each of the book's eight chapters a literary text which I felt would serve best to present in a sharp and meaningful way the issues, concerns, and points of view discussed in it. These texts thus serve as "representative anecdotes" of the matter found in the chapters. In selecting them I took into account three important matters: the artist's sense of form, his appreciation of the special emotional tone of his subject, and his grasp of its "reality." These, in their various kinds of balance and integration, constitute the "anecdote" that illustrates, formulates, and represents the subject of the chapter. The artist has at his disposal certain qualities of form—he has been educated in them, or has educated himself; he has also, in his personal view of the reality of the subject, access to certain theories, moral and social forms, and conventions; and his use of these is qualified by his way of seeing and judging the subject.

The reality itself can be seen in an informal and often an unenlightened state in hundreds of documents of the time: editorials, feature articles, and minor works of literature. Ultimately the value of any idea rests not merely in the fact that it is talked about at length and in detail, but rather in its having been realized formally, given meaning by an artist sensitive to both its formal and its moral implications. The importance of literature as text and anecdote, therefore, is that it gives the subject of its time back to us in one or another form of heightened, enriched, and sensible realization. Literature is not valuable simply because it "uses" the matter of the time, nor merely because it has degrees of formal excellence, but because it helps us to see the reality of any idea in a full, clear, and meaningful form; the form *is* the matter, the matter is *in* the form, and the reality which is thus formally given is a moral and aesthetic anecdote of one or another aspect of the time. I have selected texts neither because they are "great works" (some of them are not) nor because they are "interesting social evidence"; I have tried, however, to choose those works of literature that come nearest to being the best of their kind and at the same time the most representative of the preoccupations and attitudes discussed in the chapters.

The selection of texts is, therefore, a major principle of this book's organization. In every chapter the discussions of the subject, the use of secondary material, the quotations from documents are all presented with two principal aims: to give a sense of the *abundance* of detail and illustration which the subject of the chapter possesses (that is, to show its *complicated* nature); and to move toward the concluding text, as representative anecdote, by one or several strategies of development (in other words, to show the *complexity* of the subject).

Perhaps I can explain my method further by discussing the development of one of the chapters—Chapter II will serve. I begin on a note of contrast: certain writers presented World War I as a culminating test of man's loyalties and his moral responsibility; their work is colored and controlled by an appreciation of, a devotion to, standards which they had accepted long before. But this was *not* the most important view of the war taken in the 1920s; the major writings of the decade presented it in quite a different manner. I proceed to discuss this difference, to explain it, to show what precedent for it existed in earlier literature. I examine in some detail certain works of the 1920s that present the new perspective upon the war; at the same time I return (sometimes briefly, once or twice at some length) to the contrast with which the chapter began. In section iv (called "The Unreasonable Wound") I try to gather together the matter of the chapter, to examine once again what I have so far said, but this time in the work of Ernest Hemingway, the most articulate and the best writer on the subject of the chapter. Section iv anticipates the text of the chapter, prepares the way for it; section v is an additional preparation; again, minor works, what I have called "documents," are used. The final section is an analysis of the text, in this case Hemingway's *The Sun Also Rises*. If the reader will bear in mind that the chapter is called "The War and the Postwar Temper," he will appreciate that novel (in my discussion of it) as the culmination of the chapter's meaning, suggesting and realizing as it does its full matter and its many details in several central images.

This is an example of the kinds of strategy I have used throughout the book. The specific development of each chapter depends, of course, upon its subject, the kinds of document related to it, and the kinds of presentation best suited to it. It is quite impossible in a work of this kind to give full summaries, detailed information, concerning everything discussed; the chronology and the biographical notes in the appendix should help the reader to fill in details if he wants to do so. In general, the progress of the chapters is of this order: from non-literary document to literary treatment to text. It is a development beginning with a multiplicity of detail, gradually moving toward the stressing of important themes, and culminating in a critical analysis of the text's value as literature and as representative anecdote.

There are critics, of course, who reject the idea of decade study, or of the study of any period of time isolated from its past and its future. I do not deny the importance of origins, the influence of past upon present. The area of concentration in the book is America of the years 1918 to 1932; the first date the end of World War I, the second the year when a full realization of the depression caused many men to think of the decade as "definitely finished." My principal excursions outside of these years have been in the time before 1918; I have moved back as early as 1900, and have at times devoted considerable space to the second decade of the century, but always with the single object of illuminating, explaining, and realizing the years of the postwar decade. For the same reason I have discussed occasionally the work of English and other European writers, when they have an important bearing upon the subject at hand. In other words, I have tried to make the 1920s in

THE TWENTIES

American Writing in the Postwar Decade

I

THE TEMPER OF THE 1920S

1. The Old Gang and the New

HOW MAY one properly re-enter a phase of history, or appreciate and understand the nuances of its culture, without entirely distorting or merely exploiting them? Men may carefully preserve their memories, but these are mere fragments of any whole or accurate picture. The reality of a past is almost invariably strange; one finds it hard to share vanished enthusiasms or to tolerate what now seem to be the most childish of prejudices.

Backward glances at the 1920s are especially marked by limited perspectives. But certain documents, no longer significant for our own time perhaps, help to direct us to the quality of the decade. They are not necessarily true, or free from distortion, in themselves, and may even be gross exaggerations of the truth; but their prejudices sometimes indicate a common disposition, help us to realize the decade in at least one of its aspects and to appreciate some of its peculiarities of mind and spirit. In the 1920s there were many documents of this kind, though none was so rich in suggestions about the time as the symposium magisterially entitled *Civilization in the United States,* edited by one of the decade's literary vagabonds, Harold Stearns.

On July 4, 1921, Stearns finished his preface to this volume; taking with him the manuscript of his own still uncompleted contribution, he fled to Paris, to escape the monster he had helped to create and to serve as an example to his readers. In its own way the book, which appeared early in 1922, was a historical landmark of the post-World War I years, a curious document of disaffection, pointing to and reiterating the failure of culture, entertainment, family life, religion—of everything but

3

science, and even it scored only a partial success in the survey of American life and institutions.

It was scarcely a surprise to those who knew the work of the contributors—among them, H. L. Mencken, Stearns himself, Van Wyck Brooks, and George Jean Nathan. Nor was it an outcry of pained youth, rebelling against an older generation. The average age of the thirty-three contributors was almost thirty-six; the oldest was fifty-seven, the youngest twenty-seven. It is not unreasonable to think of them as a middle generation encouraging a younger to reject its heritage and to look to other lands and other cultures.[1]

The incriminating details appear with monotonous regularity on page after page of the symposium: the city is an index of our material success and our spiritual failure (Mumford); on every hand we can observe "the incurable cowardice and venality of the normal American politician" (Mencken); the press is corrupt and controlled by advertisers, and the public accepts uncritically what the newspaper provides (John Macy); in the American university the general student becomes a "specialist in the obvious" (R. M. Lovett); our cultural interests and activities have been turned over to the almost exclusive custody of women and the only hopeful sign in "The Intellectual Life" is the disrespect the younger people have for their elders (Stearns); in such a setting the literary life will inevitably be "a very weak and sickly plant" and talents will scarcely find nourishment in such a soil (Brooks); in our business life we no longer have an ethic; "business morality" is a term without meaning. Business is neither moral nor immoral. It represents "man's acquisitive instinct acting outside of humanistic motives" (Garet Garrett); finally, in his family life, the American husband, overcome by mother-worship, "becomes everything in his business and nothing in his home, with an ultimate neurotic breakdown or a belated

[1] The contributors to Stearns' survey were not the "young generation" of the 1920s. They formed a transitional generation, midway between the elders whose point of view was so summarily dismissed and the so-called "lost generation" of Gertrude Stein's Paris.

The problem of chronology and generations is a vexing one. In the 1920s there was much crossing of lines. The men and women most responsible for the decade's distinguished record in literature averaged 24 years in 1922. Hemingway was 23, Cummings 28, Wescott 21, Kay Boyle 19. Pound was 37, and Gertrude Stein 48, but neither belonged in any way but chronologically to the generation that flourished in the second decade. The Old Gang might in a few cases be younger than the "young man," because the latter's private realization or public recognition had been delayed.

plunge into promiscuity. The wife, on her part, either becomes hysterical or falls a victim of religious reformatory charlatanism" (Alfred Kuttner).

Very few of the essays discovered any means to mitigate or to vary the indictment. Stearns commented in his Preface on the underlying unity of the opinions expressed. This was especially surprising, he said, "in view both of the fact that every contributor has full liberty of opinion and that the personalities and points of view finding expression in the essays are all highly individualistic." He could only suggest that the contributors had independently come to their conclusions because these were the only conclusions available to an impartial board of review.

With such guides as this to a world fashioned and made intolerable by the prewar generation (the Old Gang, as it was scornfully labeled), the men and women who took over in the postwar decade could have had little confidence in either the precepts or the conveniences of their country. A pattern of rejection was soon established, abundantly supported by an accumulation of prejudices and views. However distorted and exaggerated, it followed rather closely the lines of a threefold criticism of the prewar generation and of the civilization it had made: there was, first, a failure of communication; second, a failure of social meaning and value; and third, a failure of morality. These failures—in each case crucial because they touched closely the dominating emotional and aesthetic needs of the younger generation—while not caused by the war, were revealed by the events of the war. Faith in the older generation, not unmixed with criticism of its enormities, persisted through what Van Wyck Brooks has called "the confident years" (1885–1915); but when the war had ended, this generation discovered that it had lost most of its influence.

Long before, especially during the latter half of the nineteenth century, many Americans had felt uncomfortably inferior in their attainments of mind and had quite naturally assumed the need to search in Europe (if the chance occurred) for a cultural "finish"; they either went themselves to Europe or had their agents send as much of Europe to them as they could afford. They apologized for their own country on the grounds that it had had no time to develop a culture; or that culture was after all only a secondary matter, to be added later; or that they possessed a high degree of moral probity, which they might trade to Europe for its art.

This recognition of cultural immaturity was only one aspect of American self-criticism. As for the moral failure, they were aware of that too, but never quite so sharply as was the generation that sought its way out in the 1920s. Criticism of public venality and corruption, never so strong as in the days when Edward Bellamy, Mark Twain, and Robert Herrick attended to it, was, however, generally softened by the hope that men of good will would eventually change all that; that man, who is naturally good, has also a natural inclination to improve his status. The naïve utopian zeal of Bellamy's novels was not unique. The extreme form of naturalistic theory, of course, defined man as hopelessly depraved, invariably doomed, incapable of the least effort to dignify his brief stay on this earth. But even the darkest and the gloomiest of the naturalists had accesses of optimism and tenderness; the naturalist thesis almost never triumphed entirely. And while the naturalists wrote in partial or total commitment to that thesis, parallel with their writings were the findings of the muckracking journalists and novelists. In a very reassuring way, all of them shared the "veritist" confidence of Hamlin Garland and the serene (one is tempted to say the genteel) assurance of William Dean Howells. The myth of improvement held them all in the years leading up to World War I; and even the most intransigent American of them all, Ezra Pound, spoke of the hope, perhaps of the imminence, of a Risorgimento, an awakening, as he described it in 1912 (in *Patria Mia*), that "will make the Italian Renaissance look like a tempest in a teapot."

Pound, looking across the ocean at the America he had first left four years before, appreciated his country's tremendous energy but failed to find in it a "guiding sense," a "discrimination in applying the force." That "the force" was there everyone who had looked at the country, whether with sympathy or indignation, agreed, whatever his interpretation; and that the means existed to redirect it was seldom denied. For some this meant a change of government; for others, a defeat of taboos and the restoration of "healthy common sense" to social and family life; for a few, the sharpening of instruments of communication, a move toward greater precision and "classicism" and away from the vague, meaningless deception of the romantic point of view.

Before 1915 the liberal, the dissident, the progressive member of society hoped for a moral, intellectual, and aesthetic resurgence: literature could bring about a better society, and a better society would help establish a better literature—or so men like Upton Sinclair felt.

Sinclair's *The Jungle* (1906) was itself a testimony to the reasonableness of the hope.

These hopes, which were not only indefinite but subject to frequent
abuse and disappointment, were all but abandoned at the end of World
War I. Socialism seemed a lost cause, at least for the moment. It had
never really held out more than a slender hope, kept alive by the wishful
thinking of a number of men and women of good will. Their thought
was largely a continuation of an earlier socialism, and they felt little
need for hastening the process of social change, though Emma Goldman wished the time of change were near, and sometimes thought it
was; and her friend Alexander Berkman had thought to perform a
caesarean operation upon the old world. In 1919 both Miss Goldman
and Berkman sailed, with more than two hundred other undesirable
citizens, on the S. S. *Buford,* as punishment for their hopes. Events had
discouraged most radicals from hoping for a change in social values
and had forced the extremists overseas or underground.

For those who contributed to *Civilization in the United States* there
was no longer any hope on which to pin a faith, and in the volume there
is no program or pattern of constructive suggestion. Though Carl Van
Doren (*Nation,* February 22, 1922) saw in it a "guiding confidence"
in the worth of the intellectual, and George Santayana (*Dial,* June
1922) thought the presence of thirty [2] such spirits was scarcely evidence
that civilization was lacking in the United States, the document was
nonetheless a grim and melancholy index of failure in almost every
field of human activity and expression.

In many respects this failure may best be defined as a loss of precision
in the communication of basic ideas—in the university and in education in general; in the morality of public life; in the arts themselves.
Ezra Pound spoke in 1912 of this crisis in communication:

> When a young man in America, having the instincts and interiors of
> a poet, begins to write he finds no one to say to him: "Put down ex-
> actly what you feel and mean! Say it as briefly as possible and avoid
> all sham of ornament. Learn what technical excellence you can from a
> direct study of the masters, and pay no attention to the suggestions
> of anyone who has not himself produced notable work in poetry."

This was what Pound repeated to the young men and women who even
then were coming from America to hear him say it. And, indeed,

[2] There were actually thirty-three authors, three of them foreign "observers"
whose cavils possessed a specious geographical advantage over the majority.

Pound was to go on, in London, and later in Paris and Rapallo, guiding young poets and prose writers alike, as no one else had been able or willing to do. Harriet Monroe, who had many reasons to respect, admire, and hate Pound, said in her autobiography that America, in letting him go to Europe, lost a great teacher. But that part of America which wanted to learn followed him to Europe—and there, with his aid and that of Gertrude Stein and Ford Madox Ford, helped to inaugurate twentieth-century literature.

Meanwhile, in Pound's view, for one, the Old Gang was doing its best to keep that literature from coming alive. Writing to Margaret Anderson in January 1918, Pound said, apropos of his failure to find any worth-while writing in his own country, "There appears to be nothing in America between professors and Kreymborgs and Bodenheim. . . . Anemia of guts on one side and anemia of education on the other." Though Pound appreciated what Whitman had done, he felt that the "barbaric yawp" was not enough—"we can't stop with the 'yawp.' We have no longer any excuse for not taking up the complete art." In his "Pact" with Walt Whitman (1915), he acknowledged that Whitman had helped to make the break from the past ("It was you that broke the new wood"), but wanted now to go on to the task of refining the language and making it more precise ("Now is a time for the carving"). He had found nothing but timidity in writers and critics, and intimidating, dogmatic force on the part of those who might have made an artist's life tolerable.

Pound was very conscious of his role in Europe, which was neither to restore Europe nor efficiently to admire its cathedrals (like Christopher Newman of Henry James's *The American*), but to encourage the "helpless few in my country,/O remnant enslaved!"—those other Americans who felt intimidated or stifled in Davenport or Philadelphia or Crawfordsville. "The Rest" states melodramatically what many of Pound's contemporaries felt:

> Artists broken against her,
> A-stray, lost in the villages,
> Mistrusted, spoken-against,
>
> Lovers of beauty, starved,
> Thwarted with systems,
> Helpless against the control;—

And he begged those who could not adjust themselves to the success pattern of American business to take heart:

> You who can not wear yourselves out
> By persisting to successes,
> You who can only speak,
> Who can not steel yourselves into reiteration; . . .

He might serve as their example; he had, after all, come through:

> I have weathered the storm,
> I have beaten out my exile.

The failure in communication had long before disturbed Howells, who himself had almost failed of precise honesty and courage. Many of the writers whom Howells sponsored did seem aware of the need to smash the barriers to honest expression; but, despite their earnest study and dedication, they were too often careless of their art, not clear about its necessary limits and decorum. They would not have appreciated Pound's call for precision, for they thought themselves precise enough. Frank Norris, Stephen Crane, Jack London, and Theodore Dreiser suffered from one or another imprecision in style, form, or vision. While they had conquered timidity and arrogance in one way, they had failed to master them in another; and their work, for all its thrilling newness and audacity, was scarcely the ideal attack on the Old Gang and its hold on American cultural life.

One thing they had early succeeded in doing: they had again and again pointed to the contradictions in social values and to the hypocrisies underlying the preaching and practice of democracy. The social and moral criticism of the 1920s was largely concerned with the failure of society to provide breathing space for its independent spirits. The "flight from democracy" was described in dozens of minor novels, from Floyd Dell's *Moon-Calf* to Ben Hecht's *Erik Dorn;* it was provided with a rationale in scores of books and magazines, which emphasized the absurdities as well as the dangers of a leveling society.

In the *Dial* (1918) and the *Freeman* (1920 and 1921), Harold Stearns published a group of essays, subsequently gathered under the title *America and the Young Intellectual* (1921), which was, for its time at least, a crucial statement of the failure of social definition of which the generation of the 1920s accused the Old Gang. The danger, as Stearns saw it, was that the young men, seeing with what fear and hostility any distinction was treated, would themselves "subscribe to the conventions and traditions." The "reforming zeal" of the years 1885–1915 had not sufficed to reduce this danger; for such zeal was too often of a piece with the large-scale effort to make everyone alike in mind and manner. Nor could they hope to escape through false sophistication, which denied the problem and debased the arts, so that these became mere ornaments of a futile life.

This range of argument, while it gave Stearns' contemporaries immense gratification, was scarcely the equivalent of Pound's criticism of democracy. In fact, Pound so severely judged the evidences of democratic practice that what he proposed seemed at times not to be democracy at all. He had a sharp sense of urgency in his criticism that was all but absent from the documentation found every month in Mencken's *American Mercury*. Pound was not simply or solely interested in the ludicrous. He was not just comfortably amused by human foibles but sincerely and honestly concerned about the democratic social position —about the efforts to deceive its citizens, to mold them falsely, to teach them mediocrity as a virtue and thus deny them the chance to prove themselves worthy of something better. " 'Tis of my country that I would endite," he wrote in "L'Homme Moyen Sensuel," not to prove himself the wiser, but "In hope to set some misconceptions right." Radway, the model democratic Christian of the poem, has learned early to respect and obey his tutors; and his mind is formed by

> These heavy weights, these dodgers and these preachers,
> Crusaders, lecturers and secret lechers,
> Who wrought about his "soul" their stale infection.

From them he finds a guide to proper manners, though the first-rate artists of his country have had to seek their recognition abroad. At the same time Radway is stimulated by what he reads in the daily press; "So he 'faced life' with rather mixed intentions." But in his country all must be alike (at least in public) until the day will come

> . . . when man
> Will long only to be a *social function*,
> And even Zeus' wild lightning fear to strike
> Lest it should fail to treat all men alike.

Having enjoyed his pleasures secretly, Radway atones by joining "an organization for the suppression of sin," and notes how profitable it is to be known publicly as a crusader against vice:

> For as Ben Franklin said with such urbanity:
> "Nothing will pay thee, friend, like Christianity."

This is the portrait of "l'homme moyen sensuel": taught by inferior editors and preachers to loathe the improper life, he seeks out his private opportunities while announcing publicly his vigorous Christian virtue, "as a business asset pure an' simple."

The deception and hypocrisy that America's artists saw in their society endangered democracy, which, as Whitman had often said, ought to protect the individual as well as further the cause of the mass. Whether because of inherent weaknesses in democracy or because men had long since strayed from its principles, by the end of World War I the air was full of criticism, cavil, and denunciation.

The failure of the Old Gang to please the young gave rise to another form of criticism, directed against a moral failure—which is to say, a failure to achieve and to permit others to achieve a normal, healthy life. As men and women worked toward a definition of the American type, they had also to search in America's past for its history. From November 1916 to October 1917 *The Seven Arts* severely but hopefully pursued its researches into present definitions and past causes. One of its associate editors, Van Wyck Brooks, had in 1915 published the first of his examinations of the moral imbalance of the American man. In *America's Coming-of-Age* he pointed to a most unfortunate division in American cultural life, the two irreconcilable opposites of its character, which had led to the worst forms of cultural depression and illness: idealism (an impractical idealism fostered by Emerson) and "catchpenny opportunism . . . originating in the practical shifts of Puritan life, becoming a philosophy in Franklin, passing through the American humorists, and resulting in the atmosphere of our contemporary business life."

An entire (though often a quick) survey of the American past served only to reinforce the conviction that the Puritan, who had dominated history and was now fully in command of American life, was responsible for an intolerable situation. What Brooks wrote in *Letters and Leadership* (1918) was echoed in a score of other places: the new generation of writers "find themselves born into a race that has drained away all its spiritual resources in the struggle to survive and that continues to struggle in the midst of plenty because life itself no longer possesses any meaning."

This conviction all but dominated American criticism throughout the 1920s. The American was an industrial giant, an emotional dwarf; having repressed his love of life (that is, his emotional predisposition to things, animals, fellow creatures), he came through with ingenious inventions, processes, methods; he built bigger, better, and faster locomotives, and was experimenting with automobiles and playing with airplanes; but the nearer India seemed, the more difficult the passage to it became.

The phenomenon of America's industrial wealth and its spiritual poverty was the subject of one of the most exhaustive examinations in the history of modern criticism. Europeans often inordinately admired the giant and were puzzled to see so many Americans fleeing from him. Americans, closer to a knowledge of the sacrifices needed to make him so enormous, insisted on pointing to the devastating division in the moral economy caused by his growth. Ezra Pound, in one of his frequent expressions of view (*Nation,* April 18, 1928), spoke of the "Fordian" tendency in American life:

> This is admirable as far as it goes, but Ford's world is the world of the hired man. Ford himself is the hired man, raised to the thousandth degree, a titanic but by no means gargantuan figure, a revolutionist to such a degree that the bickering of impotent reds concerning him is almost comic. . . . But where does this get us? For everything above comfortable brute existence there is a vacuum.

Both the past history and the present condition of the American industrialist were thoroughly examined and accounted for before the decade began. The most important documents in the research were Randolph Bourne's "The Puritan's Will to Power" (1917), H. L. Mencken's "Puritanism as a Literary Force" (1917), and Waldo Frank's *Our America* (1919). This last was a "command performance" to explain America to the French and presumably also to Americans in Europe. Two members of the French High Commission, in America to observe their allies, asked Frank to write the book, "Not because I was an authority. . . . Merely because it seemed reasonable to these cultural envoys to spice the mass of American conformist utterance abroad with a statement that could not even remotely be suspected of an official stamp." What Frank wrote was an extreme expression of the *Seven Arts'* point of view regarding the moral failure of the Old Gang, complete with a history of the stereotyped figure responsible for that failure. The Puritan, in this account, forced himself to repress vital ranges of feeling, emotion, desire; or he was forced by the circumstances of a raw, new, dangerous, and exploitable continent to "do violence upon himself."

> Whole departments of his psychic life must be repressed. Categories of desire must be inhibited. Reaches of consciousness must be lopped

off. Old, half-forgotten intuitions must be called out from the buried depths of his mind, and made the governors of his life.

In view of these necessities, the Puritan-pioneer had successfully eliminated pleasures, in favor of things and technical processes. By the time there were more than enough of "things" to go around he had lost his capacity to feel life as a whole, and his spiritual energy flowed in only one direction, "that of utilitarian ethics." So the Puritan in history had created not only giants but monsters; a genius of invention and method, he was a lost child in a maze of ill-considered and unanswered questions regarding "the full life." Desire repressed, as every editor of *The Seven Arts* knew, must somehow be satisfied; in this case it "sickened and shriveled and grew perverse. It sought expression in neurotic arts, in obversely sensual religions, in sadistic interference with Desire in others. . . . But it *went on*. For it *is* life." For the ordinary man, "l'homme moyen sensuel," this public repression of desire led to "the hypocrisy of the American who goes to church on Sunday and bleeds his brother on Monday, who leads a sexually vicious life and insists on 'pure' books, draped statues, and streets cleared of prostitutes, who preaches liberty and democracy and free speech and supports the subtlest oligarchy of modern times."

What could a young man do? Exposed to this criticism, how could he hope to preserve himself, to keep his selfness pure? The documents provided by Stearns, Brooks, Frank, Mencken, and others coincided with the opening of new opportunities for escape. For the most part parents were still financially solvent. The young man could go to Paris; or he could try, in isolated refuges, to set up a life of his own, become an artist, and live the bohemian life, whatever that may have meant. Whether he went to Paris or stayed in Greenwich Village, his criticism of the Old Gang persisted, even though he grudgingly accepted and quickly spent the checks sent to him by his elders in Cleveland or Omaha or Dubuque.

The young generation of the 1920s had two boards of advisers: those represented in Stearns' volume, and those who dedicated their efforts to refining and sharpening the arts. The first group did not unanimously advise Paris as a cure for Dubuque. In fact, it very often condemned the young for fleeing its problems and wasting its talents —though Stearns himself could hardly wait for his boat to sail. The second group not only advised Paris but considered it indispensable as "the laboratory of the spirit," and they were better qualified to answer the question, "What can a young man do?" in a way the young man could appreciate. Above all else, the activities of the young man (born in 1900, in Europe at the age of seventeen or eighteen, twice removed from his American heritage through college and war) were literary activities, sponsored and encouraged by the conviction that of all forms of activity the literary was least pitiful or ludicrous. He was taken in neither by his commercial fathers nor by the boisterous anti-Americanism of the Mencken-Boyd-Nathan *Mercury,* but was impressed by the intransigence of Pound, the taste of Gertrude Stein, and the intelligence of Ford Madox Ford.

The 1920s were a time least likely to produce substantial support among intellectuals for any sound, rational, and logical program. What had earlier been respected for its appearance of stability was now condemned because all evidences of stability seemed illusory and artificial. The very lively and active interest in science was perhaps the decade's most substantial contribution to modern civilization. Yet in this case as well, achievement became a symbol of disorder and a source of disenchantment. Pragmatism and liberalism were important preoccupations among the enlightened elders of the decade. But, together with their radical poor relation, Marxism, these relied too much upon a clear view of society as progressing in a straight line toward a perfection both of means and ends; and this view the young intellectuals refused to accept. Recent history had failed to support such an assurance.

Perhaps the most striking quality of the postwar intellectual was his attitude of refusal—refusal of the comfortable platitudes of the middle class, refusal of the desperate assurances of liberal tacticians, and finally refusal of the suggestion that the war had provided an opportunity for renewing tradition, reviving it, or changing it without destroying it. This negative attitude was confined for the most part to the decade: it did not survive the debacle of October 1929; nor could it continue once the middle class, the source of its financial support and the object of its derision, had temporarily lost its hold upon public confidence. But while it lasted there was widespread and free experimenting with social and aesthetic forms. The 1920s were marked by a disrespect for tradition and an eager wish to try out any new suggestions regarding the nature of man—his personal beliefs, convictions, or way to salvation.

2. The Bohemian

THE NINTH WARD in Manhattan, Greenwich Village, begins approximately at West 14th Street and Fifth Avenue and courses southward in a maze of streets and alleyways, a jumble of impressive apartment buildings, small old shops, redecorated and repainted stone fronts, churches, night clubs, and slums. As in some other parts of Manhattan, real-estate developments have in places caught up with the disintegration of properties, and there polished brass alternates with rusted iron. There are security and privacy in this confusion of cross streets and alleyways. Though the Village is served by the subway system, it is possible to live in a place that seems fairly remote from the worst of Manhattan's urban confusion because the maze often protects from all but accidental interference. It is as though the overgrown city at one time encountered a barrier to its planning and, in its haste to develop at any cost, decided to bypass rather than solve another engineering problem. After a while the city discovered it had made a delightful mistake, had unwittingly preserved one of its districts against the irritations of progress. The Village became a haven from the City; it protected those who lived there against the horrors and the nervous efficiency of urban life.

In the early years of the nineteenth century the independent Village of Greenwich was an almost neglected rural section of the thriving metropolitan rock to the south. Then, in 1819, 1822, and 1823, there were yellow-fever epidemics in the city, during which people flocked to the country, anxious to escape the disease. These were boom times for the Village; at the end of each epidemic there was an increase in population. Permanent buildings were constructed along the lanes and bypaths that had been laid out in a pattern diagonal to that of the city's streets. What had once been a potter's field was turned into a park and became Washington Square; on each side of it were the homes of Manhattan's elect. Except for the streets near the Hudson River, the Village remained for many years a residential area.

But toward the end of the last century the City caught up with the Village; though it never seriously wished to make a city of it, it did use it as a depository for some of its excess baggage of the poor. The

Village was bordered on the west and on the south by tenements, and these invaded the Village itself. The Negroes to the south, and eventually the Italian immigrants, settled in the tenements. The fine old mansions degenerated into slums. Factories, particularly along the waterfront but also in the heart of the Village, radically altered its appearance; there seemed every chance that this part of Manhattan would soon be hard to distinguish from other downtown sections. Industry moved off the island, or much of it did, leaving the tenements without occupants. After 1910 no more tenements were built in this area. In 1916 the heart of the Village was officially made a residential district. And though the waterfront continued to be dependent upon economic changes, the slums of the Village itself were an inexpensive haven for impoverished writers, artists, clerks, and teachers. Here was a place both picturesque and inexpensive, a place that neither landlord nor tycoon would disturb too much.

In the second decade of the twentieth century the Village became a bohemia. The new immigrants lived with the old, both held there by poverty; but the Villagers—the artists and their fellow travelers—paid almost no attention to the local people, except, after 1920, to buy their raw wine and to keep their speakeasies going during Prohibition years. The Italians had their political organizations and their religion, both of which the Villagers largely ignored. The Italians were somehow beneath the Villagers' notice; the Villagers were often above the Italians' —the one seemed stupid, the other immoral. As Caroline Ware has put it, "To the Italians, living among the Villagers was almost like living in a large-scale disorderly house; to the Irish and others it was only somewhat less so. No wonder the local people regarded the Villagers as a menace to the decency of their neighborhood and to the morals of their children." The invasion of the Villagers meant a constant threat of increased rents and of eviction. Their "ungodliness" contrasted sharply with the Catholicism of the Italians and the Irish. One of the Italian women guessed that the Village girls were "kept women," for "how else could they live in these apartments? You know what a girl can earn." An Irish woman complained, "How can I bring [my children] up decent with that sort of goings-on right under their eyes and those nuts that call themselves artists not even taking the trouble to close the blinds."

To the struggling artist, poverty was endurable if the environment was right. "In the Village there were to be rented, for thirty dollars a month, whole floors in old houses, each with two enormous rooms—

high-ceilinged rooms with deep-embrasured windows and fireplaces—
and a hall bedroom, a kitchen with a gas range, and a bathroom," says
Floyd Dell in one of his chronicles of Village life and love. And John
Reed, in his doggerel "The Day in Bohemia, or Life among the Artists,"
spoke of

> Inglorious Miltons by the score,
> And Rodins, one to every floor.
> In short, those unknown men of genius
> Who dwell in third-floor-rears gangreneous,
> Reft of their rightful heritage
> By a commercial, soulless age.
> Unwept, I might add—and unsung,
> Insolvent, but entirely young.

The happy isolation of the Village from uptown, responsible for so
much of the casual freedom of New York's bohemia, did not long outlast America's entrance into World War I. In 1917 the West Side subway was opened. Other improvements in traffic followed. The Village
became accessible; and thanks to the scarehead journalism of some uptown newspapers and commercial magazines, it became a tourist spot.
Tea shops with fake atmosphere (some of them hired "bohemians" to
display their eccentricities), curio shops, night clubs, and speakeasies
—all these seemed to suggest the end of privacy for the artist who had
originally come to the Village because it was inexpensive and secluded.
Caroline Ware's study (*Greenwich Village, 1920–1930*) points out
that real-estate values went up, between 1920 and 1930, from 40 per
cent in such districts as Barrow Street and Christopher Street, to as
much as 199 per cent on the Grove-Bleecker block and around West
4th Street and Charles Street. In 1920 the population of the Village was
54,643, more than 90 per cent of whom might be classed as tenement
dwellers, only 10 per cent belonging to high-income groups. By 1930
the population had dropped, the income had risen: out of 38,045 inhabitants, fewer than 80 per cent were tenement dwellers. In 1922 the
rise in rents caused the American League of Artists to protest that "the
poor artist who is struggling to make a start is being driven out." In
the twenties the Village acquired several reputations it had only infrequently enjoyed earlier: it became known as "a charming place,"
a good residential district, a haunt of homosexuals, a continuous carnival, and an artists' colony.

Of these changes the veterans of the second decade were quite re-

sentful. They watched rather helplessly what seemed to them a vulgar-
ization of the place—its reduction to what Floyd Dell called "a sideshow for tourists." But Dell thought that his generation possessed one
advantage over the intrusive uptowners: "We had something which it
seemed all bourgeois America—sick to death of its machine-made
efficiency and scared respectability—wistfully desired to share with us:
we had freedom and happiness." The influx of young men as colleges
held commencement exercises or troops were demobilized, wrote
Malcolm Cowley in *Exile's Return* (1934, 1951), displeased and
rather bored the older Villagers:

> We had fresh faces and a fresh store of jokes and filthy songs collected
> in the army; we were nice to take on parties, to be amused by and to
> lecture. Sometimes they were cruel to us in a deliberately thoughtless
> way. Sometimes they gave us advice which was never taken because
> it was so obviously a form of boasting. I don't believe they thought
> much about us at all.

In 1919 the Prohibition Amendment changed the character of Village
meetings and altered the general decorum of the Village itself. Here
as elsewhere, this law was responsible for a considerable increase in
the consumption of alcohol; it also served as another excuse for the
exodus to Paris during the postwar decade. Its effect upon the intellectual life was severe: from being a mild accompaniment to dining and
conversation, alcohol became almost a primary and constant necessity. As in many other places in America, liquor sales in the Village were
thinly disguised; no longer restricted to the corner saloon, they proved
in many cases the most profitable source of revenue for Italian grocers,
barbers, bootblacks, and tobacconists.

There were other "villages," either isolated places within cities,
suburban retreats from cities, or remote colonies of artists. For a few
years in the second decade Chicago had been an important center of
bohemian life, and the route taken by the young, untried Midwesterner
from Apex City, Nebraska, or Maple Valley, Iowa, to New York City
often included a stop of some months or years in Chicago. In the
1920s writers and artists in the East often went to isolated places in
upstate New York, in Connecticut, along Cape Cod, and elsewhere; and
the decision of D. H. Lawrence to settle in the Southwest helped to
establish or at least to publicize the artists' colony at Taos, New Mexico.
The Far Westerners found Carmel and Monterey in California to their
liking. Greenwich Village, however, was the most consistently attractive

place for writers and artists from all parts of the United States, partly because the important publishers were within easy reach (several of them had been Villagers before they moved uptown to establish their firms) and the art galleries and critics were nearby, but mainly because it retained much of its charm and continued to tolerate eccentric behavior. The Hotel Brevoort was the point of departure for the brave voyagers who left for Europe, but it was also the port of call for those who returned.

The year 1919 can be used to suggest important differences of temperament, interest, and achievement between the bohemians of one time and those of the next. In that year events tested the political allegiances of every good American in Greenwich Village: the Palmer anti-Red crusade, the arrest of anarchists (followed, in 1920, by the arrest of Sacco and Vanzetti) and the deportation of many, and the breakdown in leftist loyalties and organizations in the Chicago meetings of leftist parties. Villagers were forced to decide one way or another with regard to what, precisely, their anarchism, their liberalism, or their communism meant; or, as Malcolm Cowley put it, to determine once and for all "what kind of rebels they were: if they were merely rebels against puritanism they could continue to exist safely in Mr. Wilson's world. The political rebels had no place in it."

Though the Village still attracted America's writers and artists, it had difficulty holding them because of the much greater attraction of Paris, Pound, and Stein. The present nature and future history of literature were being made abroad and not in the Village. One of the minor curiosities in the history of American literature is that Greenwich Village retained its literary (though not its intellectual) allegiance to England even at a time when Hugh Selwyn Mauberley was saying a bitter good-bye to that country. For the most part the aesthetic forms of literary behavior, weak as they were, borrowed from the British 1890s; and even symbolism, which was largely a French monopoly, came to the Village in forms devised by Arthur Symons and Walter Pater.

Guido Bruno, who published several short-lived and ill-clad magazines in the Village, was an extreme case of the Villager wholly committed to the *fin de siècle*. Except for the accident of having printed Hart Crane's first published poem (in *Bruno's Weekly* in 1915), Bruno is chiefly interesting because of his sponsorship of Wilde, Beardsley, Pater, Symons, and the other British "saints condemned to life in the crude hard world," as he called them. Bruno's American contributors soon moved to their own magazines: *The Rogue, Glebe,* then *Others,* and Margaret Anderson's *The Little Review.*

Most critics of Village life (Sinclair Lewis among them) took the faded signs of tea-room symbolism to be the marks of its art; but the Wildean Villager was by no means the most vital artist America was to produce. The Harvard Aesthete, as Cowley called him, usually did not get to the Village until he had fought in the war and had had his taste of French culture at the Sorbonne and the Left Bank of the Seine; he was not more than mildly amused by the efforts of Bruno to perpetuate an 1890s decadence. Ezra Pound (in *Pavannes and Divisions,* 1918) characterized the "pallid pilgrim" to English shores in this fashion:

> This little American went to Oxford. He rented Oscar's late rooms. He talked about the nature of the Beautiful. He swam in the wake of Santayana. He had a great cut-glass bowl full of lilies. He believed in Sin. His life was immaculate. He was the last convert to Catholicism.[3]

F. O. Matthiessen said in 1922 (*Yale Literary Magazine*) that the Villagers wrote too much: "Quantities of what they produce strike us as being mere feeling, fragmentary thoughts, which they have scribbled down just as they occurred, as though fearful of losing some part in the transition." The usual criticism of the Villagers and their contemporaries in the 1920s was not that they spent too little time with the discipline and the form of the art, but that they spent altogether too much, and that content mattered too little. The "Reviewer" of the *Freeman*'s pages paid insistent attention to this criticism. How can a writer assume for one moment, he said in effect, that attention to form is an acceptable substitute for responsibility to life? Isn't this art divorced from humanity, and doesn't it spring from "a fear of life, a disgust with life, a disillusionment with life . . . ?"

Ernest Boyd's portrait of "Aesthete, Model 1924" acidly suggested that the Villager had shifted from one set of inaccurate ideas to another; that he had scarcely waited to acquire even competence on the way; that he had picked up only a smattering of sophistication on the way back from the Argonne Forest to the Brevoort Hotel; that he was

[3] The collapse of American *fin-de-siècle*-ism is no better seen than in the decline and fall of Vance Thompson, who had tried so hard at the turn of the century to become the American Arthur Symons, and who, when he died at Nice in 1924, was remembered by the press not as the editor of *M'lle New York* and the author of *French Portraits,* but as the author of the self-help text *Eat and Grow Thin.*

a victim of early and easy success ("He writes a competent book review and awakes to find himself famous"), and that he dreaded solid information and well-digested facts as endangering his position as a true aesthete. Other critics (most of them in the *New Republic, Saturday Review of Literature, Saturday Evening Post, New Masses, Bookman,* and *Modern Monthly*) regretted the loss of what one of them called a sense of "the values of life," or claimed that a preoccupation with form was decadent, as are all attempts to appraise "the values of life chiefly as aesthetic values"; several complained that the Villager spent most of his time drinking and only pretended to be an artist; the spirit of the time was called Byronic by one, nihilistic by another; many critics disdained to dignify it by any label except exhibitionist, escapist, and defeatist. A British observer offered this definition:

> Bohemianism was understood to mean a gay disorderliness of life, cheerful bad manners, and no fixed hours or sexual standards.

Whatever the foundation for these criticisms and caricatures (they are a small fraction of the total sum), there were often more reasonable and more thorough explanations of the bohemian life: 1) It was a rebellion against authority: the bohemian preferred to become a literary anarchist rather than endure an authority he did not respect; 2) it was an attempt, however poor, to find the ideal life and the free one—that is, when the attempt was genuine and not mere faking; 3) it was a natural result of the defeat of respect and propriety that the war had caused.

Of each of these, and especially of the last, there were numerous examples. The novels of the 1920s repeatedly blamed the war for whatever was abhorred in the behavior of the young generation: the war years "shattered our illusions"; the young have every right to say to their elders, "You lied to us. Your ideas were vicious, and we reject them and we reject you"; or they could argue that "if you massacre ten million people . . . it is not easy to return to a morality that regards it as wrong to pocket a salt-cellar."

Most compelling of the bohemian's defenses, perhaps, was that which pointed out that he was not in all this for a good time, that he was not a "small-time hedonist," but was rather desperately searching for a way of life that he could tolerate. So the hero of Edmund Wilson's play, *Beppo and Beth,* explained his life:

> When you're in Galesburg, Illinois, you want to get to Chicago; then when you get to Chicago, you want to make good in New York. Then

when you do put it over in New York, what in God's name have you
got? the thoroughly depressing companionship of a lot of other poor
small-towners like yourself who don't know what the hell to do with
themselves either! . . . You think it would be better in Paris, but then
when you get to Paris, you find the same old fizzed-out people and you
decide that they're worse than the ones at home because they haven't
got even their small-town background to make fools of themselves
against.

There was, after all, something to be said for the Village as a place
where young men and women from the prairie states and the factories
found it possible, in the words of another Wilson hero (Hugo Bamman,
in the novel *I Thought of Daisy*), "to leave behind them the constraints
and self-consciousness of their homes, the shame of not making
money."

There was no single explanation of bohemian virtues, no easy exten-
uation of bohemian vices. The liberals of the *Freeman* and the *New
Republic* most often regretted the waste of talent and the concern with
an empty aesthetic ritual; the leftists of the *New Masses* condemned
what they thought was a criminal escape from civic responsibilities.
But, apart from the regrets and vituperations, there was the very real
sense of achievement. Even the mediocre artists of the decade had an
exciting sense of creating something new; even though the newness were
proved false tomorrow, it was not a shabby imitation of something too
old to be respected. There was the additional hope that, by keeping
alive and disciplining the desire to create, the artists of the decade
might produce something quite good. The energies of the young generation, no longer directed by Garland's veritism or Howells' advice to
"tell the truth, however commonplace," about society, were turned to
problems directly relevant to literature.

Upon what resources could the bohemians of the 1920s depend? In
what ways did they try to shape new patterns from their experience?
First, they turned to the substantial body of literature that explained,
exploited, and justified the irrational in human behavior. With Dostoevski, Baudelaire, and Rimbaud, acceptance of the irrational had been
based on their demand that Christianity once more recognize evil as
an important and effective part of the human soul; they protested against
the facile separation of good from evil. This was in direct opposition
to the cheerful optimism of the theorists of progress, who assumed
that the world was getting better and that evil would inevitably disap-
pear.

Middle-class manners and customs, governed by certain tribal edicts against abnormal behavior, denied those guilty of it the privileges of their society. While a democratic middle class often allowed defenses of religious freedom, and sometimes of economic freedom, it refused to allow any kind of conduct that could not be defended as normal or socially acceptable. The work of Freud, Havelock Ellis, and others toward the end of the nineteenth century and at the beginning of the twentieth was published and distributed at a convenient time; and mildly and vaguely romanticized versions of sexual behavior and sex relationships, such as Edward Carpenter's *Love's Coming of Age* (1896), helped to justify attacks upon the lines that Victorian morality had drawn.

The young artists of the decade gained confidence in their own importance as a group. They criticized and distrusted the middle-class conventional man as an insensitive and incompetent person who could never be aware entirely of vital realities because he had trained himself to ignore them. Hence the belief that the artist possessed exclusive insights and a sensibility denied to the non-artist. This attitude was often defended by reference to the work of Nietzsche, not because Nietzsche consistently supported it, but because he from time to time made statements that, taken from their context, could easily be made to support the artist's point of view.

More important perhaps for the 1920s, the cutural panic following the debasement of the liberal point of view in World War I re-established the significance of art itself. Often the artist's search for values was entirely subjective; the respect of artists for the work of Flaubert, for example, was attached chiefly to the discipline of his art and his insistence upon the value of the artist's life. As one editorial of the 1920s put it, Flaubert "saw that moral power and spiritual significance inhere in the material, in the personal vision which is identical with style, and in the interpenetration of these two. Thus he eliminated at once both the pointing of morals and the adorning of tales, and exemplified the organic character of the truth and the beauty of his art." Underlying each of the many generalizations about the life of art was the conviction that the artist's way is different from that of the non-artist; that the artist has explored a complex world of sense and feeling which the non-artist restricts, at least during his working day, in the interests of supporting and profiting from a narrower interpretation of values.

There was also the extensive body and variety of scientific discovery and invention. The *method* of science was welcomed not for its rigorous discipline or its habit of excluding extraneous facts, but because of its prestige value in the world at large. In a sense, science supported the bohemian in his attack upon respectability by questioning all non-verifiable conclusions, thus encouraging skeptical attitudes toward traditional religion and morality. The bohemians respected Freud as a scientist, for example, but did not often use him as one. They were excited by the speculations of Bertrand Russell and A. N. Whitehead, but these were usually extra-scientific gestures of men whose reputations had originally been made as scientists and mathematicians. Neglecting the disciplines of systematic research, the bohemians thought themselves free to appropriate whatever suggestion was offered by those whose very prestige had been founded upon a respect for system.

To the degree that bohemians were political radicals they were interested in Marxist theory and in the many forms of socialism suggested and developed in the century or so preceding the 1920s. They linked capitalist oppression with middle-class stupidity and often thought of the capitalist as inhuman and insensitive even though crudely competent in his limited world. But the bohemian was rarely an active revolutionary in the field of politics; he welcomed change, but his support of it was haphazard. He was generously tolerant of the Marxists' sponsorship of economic revolution but was not vitally interested in the tactics of class struggle. He was an anarchist who resented all forms of systematic intrusion upon his private life. This explains the very real difficulty that proletarian writers encountered in the 1920s in their efforts to enlist the aesthetic radicals in a political cause; and it should also help to explain the debate that persisted in such magazines as the *New Masses* before the financial panic of 1929–30 gave great additional support to leftist argument and persuasion.

These were the principal resources of intellectual life in the 1920s. It would be unwise to assume that any one of them acted directly as a simple or pure influence upon the bohemian, or to imagine that he always understood clearly what any one of them actually meant. They were casual and accidental for the most part, with little clear definition of their separate importance or original value.

Though there were dissension and bitterness enough in the decade, and open conflicts as well, there was seldom any fear of the consequences of free discussion. From 1915 to 1930 the writer seemed at home in his world; even the interference of World War I did not long discourage him in his freedom. He was afraid of little because he saw

little to fear. Least of all was he afraid of seeming inconsistent or illogical in his exchange of ideas. Fear of ideas, of their consequences for
persons and personalities, seems to have begun in 1930, when ideas
became weapons.

3. The Expatriate

" AFTER all everybody, that is, everybody who writes," said Gertrude Stein in *Paris France* (1940), "is interested in living inside
themselves in order to tell what is inside themselves. That is why writers
have to have two countries, the one where they belong and the one in
which they live really. The second one is romantic, it is separate from
themselves, it is not real but it is really there." The second of these countries, the country of the imagination, is the fortunate place to which
they go, prepared to think well of it. In a sense it is an unreal place,
and it remains an unreal place no matter how often one goes there or
how long one stays. For most of the expatriates this second country
was France, partly because of the tradition of Paris, which they had
read about in romanticized novels and in histories of modern art. The
French traditionally accepted foreigners with little stir or curiosity.
"Their tradition kept them from changing," said Miss Stein, "and yet
they naturally saw things as they were, and accepted life as it is, and
mixed things up without any reason at the same time. Foreigners were
not romantic to them, they were just facts, nothing was sentimental,
they were just there, and strangely enough it did not make them make
the art and literature of the twentieth century but it made them be the
inevitable background for it." Writers came from America to write, and
they could not do that at home. They could be dentists at home, because that was practical, and America was above all practical. For the
Americans had invented and perfected "the characteristic thing of the
twentieth century," which was "the idea of production in a series, that
one thing should be like every other thing, and that it should all be
made alike and quantities of them."

The young American artist found Paris a congenial place for the
development of his talents, or at least for the pretense of a talent that
may not always have been there. The Left Bank was a more exciting
place than Greenwich Village. True, there was the same easy and care-
free atmosphere, but here drinking was in the open, at the sidewalk

cafés—interesting and new drinks with a predictable alcoholic content and an honest label. The Village, though it tried bravely and with some success to be what Joseph Freeman has called "The Happy Island," was still in the United States and subject to the irritation if not the enforcement of its laws.

The older Paris on the Left Bank of the Seine had long been the dwelling place of artists, students, and hangers-on who enjoyed living and working in this large and complex bohemia. Where the boulevard Montparnasse crosses the boulevard Raspail was one of the centers of Paris's bohemian life. The Sorbonne and the Beaux Arts contributed hundreds of students and artists to its population. The Americans of Henry James's novels were accustomed to more gentility than *le rive gauche* could provide; the wealthy tourist-Americans, like Sinclair Lewis's Dodsworth and some of Fitzgerald's expatriates, lived in the expensive hotels on the Right Bank, drank American cocktails at the Ritz bar and the Café de la Paix, and occasionally slummed in the Latin Quarter.

The expatriated Americans, such as those described in Hemingway's *The Sun Also Rises,* lived, ate, drank, made love, and tried or pretended to write, on the Left Bank (the Fifth and Sixth Arrondissements). It was Greenwich Village on a very large scale with the Village's attractions extended and more varied. There was the same mixture of the genuine and struggling artist with the eccentric, the wastrel, the opportunist, and the egomaniac. On the compact little streets off the boulevard Saint Michel and the boulevard Saint Germain were the small, inexpensive hotels where rooms might be rented for very little in American money (like the Hotel du Caveau on the rue de la Huchette, described in Elliott Paul's *The Last Time I Saw Paris*). Here scores of American expatriates stayed during the 1920s—wrote, painted, or merely lived. Almost all the bars and cafés described in *The Sun Also Rises* were in the Quarter; some of them, like the Café du Dôme, had over many decades of bohemian life established reputations as gathering places for artists and writers.

Americans who worked, as distinguished from those who came chiefly to spend money they had brought with them, went to the Place de l'Opéra on the Right Bank to do their daily stint in the Paris offices of American newspapers; or they stayed in their small, cheap rooms and worked at translations; or they turned out articles and essays for American commercial magazines; or, in the much less certain economy of haphazard patronage and amateur business enterprise, they attempted to make a go of the little magazines. In studio apartments they gathered to talk, searching for some vagrant clue to "the word" in its various and significant disguises. Among these informal salons were the apartments of Ford Madox Ford and Stella Bowen, of Bill and Mary Widney ("where one was always likely to find some of the *transition* crowd or the monocled Tristan Tzara, founder of dada, and a young French surrealist or two"), the home of Professor Bernard Fäy of the Sorbonne, and the salon of Nathalie Barney in the rue Jacob.

The favorable rate of exchange brought over many of the writers and editors of little magazines, who moved from one place to another in the hope of finding better and better values for their American money: Berlin, where one's dollar was worth twenty times its value in other places; Vienna, where the first issue of Gorham Munson's *Secession,* twenty-two leaves in all and printed on excellent paper, cost twenty dollars to produce; Rome, where the more ambitious and lavish *Broom* of Alfred Kreymborg and Harold Loeb cost five hundred dollars an issue, including payment to contributors. In Paris, though the rate of exchange was somewhat less favorable to the American dollar,[4] living was less expensive than in New York.

[4] It is a mistake to overemphasize this fact in considering expatriation in the 1920s. The dollar was worth much more in Germany, Italy, Austria, and other European countries than in France. Yet, and in spite of the relatively high cost of living in Paris, the exchange rate did definitely favor those who had dollars to bring with them. Below are typical values during the 1920s (information given me by Professor Warren I. Susman of Reed College):

Date	the dollar in francs
September 14, 1919	7.98
September 16, 1920	15.18
September 5, 1922	12.84
July 1, 1923	16.395
July 1, 1924	18.94
July 1, 1925	22.16
July 1, 1926	35.84
July 1, 1927	25.545
July 1, 1928	25.40
July 1, 1929	25.5425
July 1, 1930	25.46
July 1, 1931	25.465
July 1, 1932	25.5125
July 1, 1933	20.02
July 1, 1934	15.1425

One might point out that, except for 1920 and 1926, the franc was relatively stable in the decade, with nothing like the inflationary fluctuations of some other European currencies.

A study of Americans who went abroad in the years 1915–1930 reveals some very interesting facts. Choosing some eighty-five writers who were known to have spent time in Europe during those years, I have consulted such books as Peter Neagoe's anthology, *Americans Abroad* (1932), for information about them. Of the number, 58 were from twenty to thirty years of age in 1920, 12 from thirty to forty, and 15 from fifteen to twenty; the great majority were in their twenties in the postwar decade. They had been born in the East (29) and the Midwest (25) for the most part; 8 came from New England, 11 from the South, 2 from the Southwest, and 4 from the Northwest. A large percentage (almost a third of them) was from the Midwest. As for kinds of places to which they owed their origins, 28 had come from large cities (12 from New York, 7 from Chicago), and 38 (or almost half of them) from small towns or farms.

The facts about their education are at first glance surprising. Of the 61 for whom this information was available, only 5 had no college education at all; 15 of those who had gone to college had not finished, the remainder had received at least a B. A. degree, and 20 had done postgraduate work. The large Eastern universities, privately endowed, proved the principal sources of their education: Harvard graduated 12, Yale 9, Princeton 4, and Columbia 7; state universities (usually Midwestern) were responsible for 10 degrees, and small colleges for 11. Almost a third of the young men saw war service directly after their college experience or before graduation; of these, 16 had enlisted and 22 had served overseas. The ambulance service and the military transport (which Cowley rightly called, in *Exile's Return*, "college-extension courses for a generation of writers") were the most popular forms of war service for those (10) who had enlisted before the United States came into the war.

It follows that the years of expatriation should have begun at some date between 1920 and 1930, since the war experience usually led to a return to Europe after a brief attempt at repatriation. Of the 85 men and women checked, 34 began their European sojourns between 1920 and 1925, 25 between 1925 and 1930; only 11 had started before 1915, and 11 from 1915 to 1920.[5] Most important of all is the length of their stay. Some few (10) can be called only "visitors," since they remained for less than two years, and in several cases the total time was made up of more than one short trip abroad. But 32 of them were abroad for

[5] These figures do not include the actual years of fighting: serving in the war is not considered "expatriation."

more than five years, and 21 from 2 to 5 years. At least the first of these latter two groups can be called the "genuine expatriates" of the decade. More than half (45) chose France as their "second country" and Paris as its center (only 3 chose to go to the Soviet Union).

The problem of finding a means of support was solved in various ways: 7 were lucky enough to have established reputations before they came and could rely upon royalties for at least part of their incomes; 11 had private incomes, or married those who had; 6 were supported by foundation grants. But of the 65 about whom it was possible to get information, the large majority (almost two-thirds) resorted to editing, writing, or day-to-day journalism to make a living: 6 were regular correspondents for European editions of American newspapers (the Paris edition of the *Chicago Tribune* was the most important of these); [6] at least 12 received more than an occasional check for feature stories and articles from American newspapers and magazines; and 8 tried to make a go of editing little magazines and reviews, sponsored sometimes by wealthy patrons, sometimes supported by collections and subscriptions. To stay in Europe, in spite of the advantage of the exchange, often proved to be a much more difficult task than getting there had been.

In his autobiography, *Being Geniuses Together* (1938), Robert McAlmon describes his personal investigations of statements made in American newspapers and magazines about the "dissolute" and "wastrel" expatriates; he discovered that the men were writers or painters who worked hard, lived simply, and scarcely ever spent lavishly. There were parasites and drunks, of course; but these one could find anywhere, and "the hangers-on might as well go to hell in Paris as become equally spineless, futile, and distressing specimens in their home villages. A Parisian drunk is not nearly so sad to watch as the small-town down-and-outer. He isn't alone or lonely." McAlmon himself published his friends' books at the Contacts Editions Press. Pound, Mary Butts, Robert Coates, Gertrude Stein, Ernest Hemingway ("his first two books to appear anywhere"), H. D., Ford Madox Ford, William Carlos Williams, and other writers were represented on his lists.

Americans in exile wrote, painted, composed, sculpted—or, as editors, sponsors, or select audience, encouraged those who did. Most of them were conscious of being quite at the center of important, exciting events. In small or large groups, they were to be seen at the home

---

[6] There were many others who used this way occasionally for making up deficits or meeting bills.

of Gertrude Stein, at 27 rue de Fleurus; in the offices of Ford's *trans-atlantic review* or Samuel Putnam's *New Review;* in Joyce's apartment; and, perhaps most important of all, at 12 rue de l'Odéon, Sylvia Beach's shop. William Carlos Williams, in his *Autobiography,* speaks of her and of Adrienne Monnier's unfailing efforts to encourage and to help modern writers:

> At the slightest invitation from Sylvia she [Adrienne Monnier] would close her shop door, on the opposite side of the rue de l'Odéon, to see a writer from abroad. To conserve and to enrich the literary life of her time was her unfailing drive. They conspired to make that region of Paris back of the old theatre a sanctuary for all sorts of writers: Joyce, of course, and many of the younger Americans found it a veritable home.

Midwesterners were so prominent among the expatriates, especially in Paris, that Ford Madox Ford, editing the *transatlantic review* with Hemingway's "assistance," asserted that almost all the new writers seemed to have come from the Midwest, though he was rather unsure of his geography. In *It Was the Nightingale,* Ford wrote:

> The Middle West was seething with literary impulse. It is no exaggeration to say that 80 per cent of the manuscripts in English that I received came from west of Altoona, and 40 per cent of them were of such a level of excellence that one might just as well close one's eyes and take one at random as try to choose between them.

Ford cited for special mention the work of Hemingway (Illinois), McAlmon (Kansas), Katherine Anne Porter (Texas), Glenway Wescott (Wisconsin), Elizabeth Madox Roberts (Kentucky), and Caroline Gordon (Tennessee). However wide of Hamlin Garland's "middle border" his idea of the Midwest was, the list is an impressive indication of what Ford underscored in the title of another of his books, that *New York Is Not America.*

No less surprising than the quantity was the subject matter of the literature submitted: it was almost invariably concerned with life in the Midwest, in the small towns and on the farms—as though the authors, having physically removed themselves to Paris, returned to the Midwest in imagination, there being no other place in their experience or their minds. Summing up the content of the manuscripts "that came pouring in from all over the Middle Wests of three continents," Ford tells us in his Preface to *Transatlantic Stories* that he "was appalled at the sheer boredom of the lives rendered."

You had women going mad after thunderstorms in solitudes; women becoming screaming hysteriacs after long parental subjection in excruciatingly dull towns; . . . the men, on the whole, took it out in drink; but now and then you would have a small English suburban grocer represented as getting the only thrill of his life out of the announcement that his wife, in hospital, was about to die of cancer.

Of the Americans in Europe, Glenway Wescott is perhaps most notable for the pursuit of this theme: not a few of his works of fiction are an explanation for his having left Wisconsin, though he eventually revealed himself (especially in *The Grandmothers*) more in love with the Midwest than he seemed earlier willing to admit. In the title story of *Good-Bye, Wisconsin* (1928), Wescott speaks of the Midwesterners roaming the world, "a sort of vagrant chosen race like the Jews." The small Wisconsin town to which the narrator returns for a Christmas visit is in every respect (its churches, its architecture, its people) a documentary explanation of the title: "There is the sluggish emotional atmosphere, the suavity of its tedium, the morbid grandeur of its meanest predicaments." The grim cold, "German gothic" midwinters, the timid, conformist denominational college, all remind him that he must go back to New York and from there once more to Europe, where he hopes some day to escape from his Wisconsin and himself, into a style of "rapid grace for the eye rather than sonority for the ear, in accordance with the ebb and flow of sensation rather than with intellectual habits, and out of which myself, with my origins and my prejudices and my Wisconsin, will seem to have disappeared."

The strength of these "origins" is as great as the power of the "prejudices." Wescott's *The Apple of the Eye* (1924) grimly retails the terrors of Midwestern orthodoxy; but *The Grandmothers* (1927), while it is largely a portrait of failures and frustrations, is prompted more by nostalgia than by hatred for his Wisconsin past. He says of Alwyn Tower, the expatriate hero of that novel:

> For a moment, all Europe seemed less significant than the vicissitudes of pioneers, men who were anonymous unless they were somebody's relatives. He did not quite like their sufferings, their illiterate mysticism, their air of failure; but he understood them, or fancied that he did. It did not matter whether he liked them or not—he was their son.

In their several degrees and levels of excellence, Wescott and his fellow Midwesterners committed their memories and their bitterness to paper—with such results as might have recalled the realism of such nineteenth-century Americans as Joseph Kirkland and Ed Howe, were it not that the style and the art were usually of a vastly superior quality. "You could not go back," says Hemingway's Lieutenant Henry (*A Farewell to Arms*, 1929) as he recalls his youth in the Midwest:

> The hay smelled good and lying in a barn in the hay took away all the years in between. We had lain in hay and talked and shot sparrows with an air-rifle when they perched in the triangle cut high up in the wall of the barn. The barn was gone now and one year they had cut the hemlock woods and there were only stumps, dried tree-tops, branches and fireweed where the woods had been.

You could not go back because the wound suffered on the Isonzo and the confusion of Caporetto had intervened; except, of course, in your art, which fixed the memory and reshaped it, sometimes into literature of some merit and importance.

The avid, sometimes nostalgic interest shown by Americans writing in Paris on American subjects helped to disprove the suggestion that "the country does not matter," as one critic put it. Whatever perspective on their own country Paris afforded, it provided a milieu they found lacking at home. They still love America, said one observer (L. J. Thomson, *American Mercury*, May 1925), but "they prefer to love it at a distance," in a place where they generally find "a keener, fuller, more satisfying intellectual life than there is at home." It is possible, said another (Louis Bromfield, *Saturday Review of Literature*, March 19, 1927), for a writer to see America more clearly from the vantage point of a Paris café, and the experience only makes him more American. The tempo of life slows down for him; he becomes relaxed, more calm; he is not constantly reminded that he must get ahead, and he begins to realize that perhaps there are values not measurable in terms of money. A minor character in a Dos Passos novel (*Manhattan Transfer*, 1925) summed it up this way: "It's all the same, in France you are paid badly and live well; here you are paid well and live badly."

A number of expatriate Americans, asked by *transition* magazine, "Why do Americans Live in Europe," replied in the May 1928 issue: because an artist needs a place away from home (Gertrude Stein); because in America there are "no facilities for the enjoyment of leisure" (Hilaire Hiler); because in Europe there is less interference with one's private life (McAlmon); because in America "each citizen functions with pride in the American conspiracy against the individual" (Kay Boyle).

Though Americans went to Paris because it was cheaper to live and because the living was more casual and open, the two principal reasons for the migration were more profound and more complex: France was to them a great center of literature and art, and its nineteenth-century achievements were as fascinating to the American writer and artist as the Russians had found them at an earlier time; and, second, the withdrawal of young writers to Paris was part of the general strategic retreat from what they called puritanism.

As for the first, the reputation of French writers and artists had been known to almost all young Americans long before they thought of seeking out their "second country." Some years before, T. S. Eliot, Ezra Pound, and several of their contemporaries had read and been influenced by French poets; young Americans read Eliot and Pound, followed the Imagist discussions and Pound's several "crusades" in the early years of *Poetry* and *The Little Review,* read translations of Rimbaud and Baudelaire in the reviews, and then searched enthusiastically for the French masterpieces of the nineteenth century.[7] When they landed in Paris they were prepared not only to follow the older masters but to seek out new masters in contemporary French literature. It was often not so much the *art* of the French but their attitude toward it that impressed the American visitors. They admired, for one thing, the preoccupation of the French artist with the life of art, the search for *le mot juste,* what appeared to them to be the artist's neglect of more mundane matters. "Art is vast enough," Flaubert had written in one of his letters, "to occupy the whole man."

The examples set by Rimbaud in his life and his art were enviously observed and often consciously imitated. The violence and splendor of the poet's life, together with his attack upon formal Christianity, gave Americans a romanticized version of life for art's sake. For them, Baudelaire's appeal lay partly in his having pointed out indirectly the weaknesses of a theory of moral progress; as Eliot put it ("Baudelaire," 1929), "the possibility of damnation is so immense a relief in a world of electoral reform, plebiscites, sex reform and dress reform, that damnation itself is an immediate form of salvation—of salvation from the ennui of modern life, because it at least gives some significance to living." In short, the nineteenth-century tradition in France attracted the young American intellectual of the twenties because it had done earlier and more successfully what he seriously thought needed to be done.

[7] The only extensive scholarly study of this phenomenon is René Taupin's *L'Influence du symbolisme français sur la poésie américaine de 1910 à 1920* (1929).

The exodus from America was also part of the strategy in fighting American puritanism. The scorn of Americans for America was a very real emotion; it had had a long and substantial history. It was evident in the cartoons and caricatures of the *Masses* and the *Liberator;* it made up a good share of the documentation of the American scene in *The Seven Arts;* it was found in the editorials and contributions of all exile magazines. The insistent refrain of criticism, both native and expatriate, was that America lacked taste, was crude, vulgar, pretentious; that it crushed the sensitive soul, rewarded the unscrupulous and the thick-skinned, drove its artists and writers into retreats on the margins of its prosperous cities and towns.

For this the Puritan was blamed: first for having overrated morality and suppressed art; then (in his historic role as pioneer) for having exalted ambition and suppressed a normal life; and finally (as a modern businessman), for having made both morality and art servants of financial success. Everything not done on schedule, not measurable in terms of practical, tangible results, was considered a form of idleness—the writing of poetry, the painting of pictures, education, if it became "impractical." This portrait of the American businessman was drawn again and again. From the big men with the black cigars of Art Young's cartoons to Kenneth Fearing's "Portraits," there is a steady development of scorn for the heavy-paunched managers of America's horn of plenty.

Of the general reaction against puritanism Malcolm Cowley gave an amusing analysis in the sketch "Young Mr. Elkins" (*Broom,* December 1922): "Mr. Elkins, being an American intellectual, belongs to the professionally young. At sixty he will retain the discouraged deep skepticism of adolescence. . . . He wanted so to be Free and he wanted to be urbane; he wanted to be English and Continental; he hardly understood what he wanted or how his new idea was born, but already before he graduated from college he was declaiming against American grossness and American puritanism in one breath and as if they were the same thing." Mr. Elkins gathers disciples and publishes magazines that print statistics to prove the depravity of American civilization. His thesis is simple, and the evidence to prove it endless. "Young Mr. Elkins places an evident value on his facts and yet he collates them around a simple, almost childish thesis; a single thesis concerning America and puritanism: puritanism is bad; America is puritan; therefore America is bad." He dreams of a depuritanized America: "A broad leisurely America without machines and Method-

ism . . . [with] open urinals and racetrack gambling; the works of
Freud and Boccaccio and D. H. Lawrence sold at newsstands openly."
And as he broods over the crassness of his world he writes down his
thought "on a typewriter which is the most finished product of a
mechanical civilization."

In an essay published in the volume *Foreign Influences in American
Life,* R. P. Blackmur explains expatriation as the product of a divorce
of cultural and political powers from economic and scientific powers.
He sets aside as counterfeit the expatriates of the inflationary twenties,
who took advantage of the opportunity afforded by economic conditions in Europe—"the run-of-the-mill *valuta* expatriates of the arts and
the bars who joined movements and lived lives which were deliberately
forced to a maximum unavailability to the society which produced
them." These people, in his view, were expatriates only because of an
economic accident; implicit in this characterization is the feeling that
genuine expatriation is a matter of more importance than can be shown
in this case. Which is to say that a radical instance of expatriation is
an inaccurate case. One would think rather that it demonstrates *in
extremis* the genuine imbalance between the monetary and cultural
interests of a country. The great move of our artists from one shore to
another suggests a violent outburst of doubt and rejection; and it seems
also that *valuta* was not the only opportunity these artists saw; a more
pressing obligation was evident in their reaction against a system of
values in democratic, industrial society.

The artist often hopes for an ideal, an aesthetic way of life, which
is in part a result of his intense self-confidence and his distrust of the
wisdom of his compatriots. Any bohemia is an expression of the utopian
wish; but it can be realized only as a very small community, dependent
economically on the very society from which it has withdrawn. Since
the artist often tries to reject summarily his own social order, it is difficult for him to remain an independent economic being. He must either
romanticize his poverty, take advantage of whatever mistakes the "other
world" makes, or accept the economic support offered occasionally by
that world. In none of these cases is he entirely a free agent.

Expatriation is often a necessary expression of bohemianism. The
bohemian who leaves his native country is not forcibly exiled but with-
draws of his own free will. What Blackmur calls "ingrown expatriation" is a normal reaction against circumstances on the part of a person who either has no means of escape or does not wish to leave. In

such a case the bohemian retires rather than flees; he may build his defenses skillfully enough if they are richly fortified by reserves of irony and other devices through which isolation is always possible without physical uprooting. When opportunity for actual flight does occur, as it did because of the postwar inflation in Europe, the attraction of a "second country" has in it some of the quality of the utopian myth; freedom from one's native world suggests freedom from responsibility, a chance to criticize that world, and to make over one's life according to personal taste. The physical fact of expatriation is, of course, an important event in the history of the bohemian; and the expatriation of the 1920s had a profound effect upon the quality and the nature of the decade's life and art.

4. The Text: Ezra Pound's
Hugh Selwyn Mauberley *

THE IDEAL literary translation of the problems and tensions described in this chapter would be a work with these qualities: a sharp realization of the older generation, of its loss of prestige during and immediately after World War I; an abundance of realistic detail and image which serve to define that condition; a satire and an irony that are profound as well as flexible and can be maneuvered to give a rich surface as well as a full depth to the cultural scene; an aesthetic humility—that is, a quality of self-realization that goes beyond and beneath mere quibbling over circumstances, that *places* the artist within them instead of assuming that he is entirely free of blame or weakness. Such a work must show a vivid awareness of circumstance, must reveal it for what it is, and must include its author in the general censure.

Ideally such a work does not exist. It calls for an artist who can see the faults both in the world and in himself. There are a great many texts, ranging from elaborate expressions of self-pity to sharp but limited glimpses. Eliot's evocations of Prufrock and the Lady, sharply set in a world of "short, square fingers stuffing pipes" and sawdust-covered floors, give their own special insights. Kay Boyle's *Year Before Last* is a representative portrayal of the avant-gardist devotee to the arts, braving and suffering all for literature; but in the end it proves to be sentimental and insufficiently self-critical. As we have seen, there are many documentary views of the world rejected and of the Old Gang

* See p. 435 for the complete text.

responsible for it; inventory follows melancholy inventory of the evidence justifying the rejection.

Except for Ezra Pound's *Hugh Selwyn Mauberley,* we have no really satisfactory exploration of the artist's situation at the beginning of the 1920s; it was published in 1920, when Pound, thirty-five years of age, prepared to leave England for the Continent. The poems in this sequence are superficially a commentary upon the cultural scene. There are the crimes against taste committed by the Old Gang; there is the literary world itself, the professional "game" of writing as opposed to the isolated and obstinate search for an honest style; there is the war itself, which was responsible for numerous ironies as well as for profound tragedies of the human spirit; there is the battle of artist against critic and public opinion—or, public neglect and scorn. The necessary elements are here. The poet has a praiseworthy devotion to his art; he admires the artists who suffered neglect in the recent past, and he resents their abuse. He sees the history of art, of the public reception of art, in a rather sentimental way. In a more remote past, there were times when the arts flourished, when they were good and their goodness was understood. These times sometimes contrast directly with the present: past beauty *versus* present cheapness; past sincerity *versus* present hypocrisy; past dedication *versus* present superficiality. The war is a major symbol of the destructive change in cultural attitudes. The monuments are reduced to rubble; promising young artists are destroyed before they can begin to realize their promise; worse, the war is managed by a cynical and corrupt world (an "old bitch gone in the teeth").

It is necessary to see these developments in terms of their meaning for the man of letters, the young man who was struggling to gain a reputation, the older artist who was fighting to save his integrity. The great difficulty lay in the temptation merely to rant and rave against the circumstance; all but a few of the writings of the postwar years did no more than just that. *Hugh Selwyn Mauberley* saves itself because of its complex range of ironic statement. Without this it would simply have been a clever but one-sided indictment of contemporary culture. The poems in the sequence condemn their subject from a doubly ironic vantage point—the world of England (and of the Western alignment of World War I, including the "yankee" world that had driven Pound to England), and Pound's own estimate of himself as of 1920. The latter view involves a brilliant union of self-deprecation and insight into the misconceptions of his critics and reviewers.

Of the eighteen poems, the first thirteen are a unified sequence in themselves, and the last five provide a redaction and a revaluation of what they have said. The first poem sums up conservative opinion; directed against Mauberley, this opinion provides a tomb for "E. P." [8] and a shroud for those who would bury him. The quatrains must therefore be thought of as an expression of impatient dismissal: the conservators burying this strange person "born/In a half savage country, out of date," who had come to England and refused to accept or understand it. He is "out of key with his time" and refuses to understand what the age requires; it is fitting, therefore, that the Old Gang select his tomb.

In stanza four the line, "His true Penelope was Flaubert," underscores the main point of disaffection. Flaubert's guidance and influence are foreign, as is the poet himself; he has "fished by obstinate isles," gone far afield for his models in an attempt to make his art pure, free of the taint of all cheapness and superficiality. The "obstinate isles," if we may see the victim commenting ironically for a moment on those who are burying him, are also the British Isles, obstinate in the sense of resisting change or refusing to understand it. The poet's journey to perfection is as perilous in its way as that of Odysseus toward his "true Penelope." The poet wasted his time on elegances instead of attending to the "real issues"; he ignored "the mottoes on sun-dials." He was "Unaffected by the 'march of events' " and therefore deservedly

> He passed from men's memory in *l'an trentiesme*
> *De son eage* . . .

It is best that his case be closed, since it "presents/No adjunct to the Muse's diadem."

The next eleven poems touch upon the matters with which the bohemian and the expatriate concerned themselves. Read with a full understanding of the history of rebellion in the 1920s, they are illuminating annotations upon the cultural scene. They provide another perspective, neither Mauberley's nor the Old Gang's, but Pound's. In a succession of images and portraits he attacks the cultural defection of the conservators as well as the failure of the British 1890s to provide a compelling example for Mauberley to follow in his opposition to them. In

---

[8] The "E.P." of the title of the first poem is a mask of Pound and Mauberley; the poet rejected by his society is both Mauberley and his creator. Pound would prefer that Mauberley represent an aspect of himself which he wants to dismiss, as subsequent poems in the series demonstrate.

spite of Pound's warning in his footnote that "the sequence is so distinctly a farewell to London that the reader who chooses to regard this as an exclusively American edition may do well to omit it," what is said is as relevant to America as it is to England; for, after all, it is what "the *age* demanded," and not exclusively what England demanded, that Pound so profoundly condemns in poems II through XII. The age was impatient of careful workmanship, of studious and painful striving for *le mot juste* or the right image; it needed something cheap, quickly made. It scorned "the obscure reveries/Of the inward gaze"; it abhorred not only Mauberley but also Joyce and Ford Madox Ford, and was quick to show its contempt, as the careers of both men, self-exiled on the Continent, clearly show.

A brief look at three phrases in poem II will help to see the irony of Pound's view. The phrase "obscure reveries/Of the inward gaze" refers to the profound reflections found in the art and thought of the past. But the "inward gaze" reveals *"obscure* reveries"; they are not precise, even though they are not superficial. Their vagueness is a result of a failure on the artist's part to communicate with precision; it is a vagueness infinitely preferable, however, to that which comes from the superficiality of quick modern glimpses of the human condition. Such effects as the rhyming of "plaster" with "alabaster" and the contrast of "prose kinema" with "the 'sculpture' of rhyme" (last quatrain) give a direct view of the difference between past and present. In each case the quality of the object in the past is lasting, solid, carefully realized; the balancing and contrasting quality of the present is soft, cheaply imitative, quickly representative of the surfaces of its object.

In poem III Pound gives us varied evidence of what the age preferred and of what it rejected. The tea-room and drawing-room circle is the place where art is now discussed, replacing the ruder settings where men of the arts once talked seriously of their work. The jangling of a mechanical piano replaces the lute of Sappho. The pathos of change is clear: Christ having supplanted Dionysus, and Caliban, Ariel, there is now no room for beauty, nothing but a "tawdry cheapness"; for even the beauty of Christianity (that is, the beauty of religion sincerely practiced) is no longer possible. The age has neither the charm of "Faun's flesh" nor "the saint's vision." For its beliefs it has "the press for wafer"; the deep illusory belief of past Christian rituals is now replaced by reverence for the journalistic "word." In the same mode there is a substitution of "Franchise for circumcision."

The fourth poem moves straightway to the problem of heroism in the modern world, to a commentary upon war and courage. It is one of the most brilliant, most deeply moving of the poems written about World War I. It differs from scores of literary reactions to the war only in its extreme of pathos and bitterness, in its sharp economy and justness of poetic image and effect. The war was bad, disillusioning, disastrous in its consequences for the loyalties and allegiances of those fighting it. It was, in short, not heroic. In this war it was *not* "sweet and proper" to die for one's country; the casualties were not heroic sacrifices for a sacred cause but losses bitterly regretted. Worse, those who did not die returned disabused and disillusioned about great causes, confused over their future course of action. The pathos and bitterness are quite appropriately expressed through Pound's use of the Horatian line, "Dulce et decorum est pro patria mori." Why did men fight in this war? Pound asks. "These fought in any case": these men fought anyway, in any case or cause, they knew not quite what—"pro domo" at least, and officially "pro patria," but "non 'dulce' non 'et decor' . . ." In a few quick lines the reasons are cited: some from love of fighting, of adventure, from fear of being called cowards, "from fear of censure," some from a misconception of what killing was, some from very fear of what they later learned to love. These fought, then returned home "to a lie."

In the next four lines the "disenchantment" on both sides of the Atlantic is superbly given in summary:

> home to many deceits,
> home to old lies and new infamy;
> usury age-old and age-thick
> and liars in public places.

After they had "walked eye-deep in hell," their belief in "old men's lies" is understandably shattered: "then unbelieving/came home." These lines say strikingly what it often took reams of copy and scores of books to describe, concerning the failures of the Old Gang to sustain and assure the young.

It is important to identify poem IV with World War I, and to see the order in its self-committed historical sequence of specific events and persons. The concluding lines give with great force the special intensity of the war's disenchantment: a great "wastage as never before" of youth and promise, leading perhaps inevitably to "frankness as never before," to the uninhibited and frank denunciation one sees in all literature of the 1920s that speaks from memory of "the fraud."

Poem V enforces this conviction and lends to it the power of Pound's own sharp phrasing: the best of them died

> For an old bitch gone in the teeth,
> For a botched civilization.

The shattered remnants of that civilization ("two gross of broken statues," "a few thousand battered books") recall our attention to the "aesthetic issue" to which Pound now returns (if, indeed, it can be said that he has left it).

Between poems V and VI there is a shift in time as well as in subject. The war was, after all, one in a chain of events; there was a "before" as there is or will be an "after." Pound fixes upon the 1890s as the locus of the prewar world. He says little about the economic causes of the war, or the political maneuvers leading to it. His concern, here as elsewhere, is with the public attitude toward native talent and the forms that talent assumed, was forced to assume, because of that attitude. Poems VI and VII serve a double purpose: to show the obtuseness of "Fœtid Buchanan" and his crowd regarding the aesthetes, and to raise the issue of the aesthetes' own weaknesses. The pale-green eyes of Cophetua's maid in the Burne-Jones painting stare "with a vacant gaze" in an age when "The English Rubaiyat was still-born." The criticism in VI is largely directed against the world of Gladstone, Ruskin, Buchanan, who preferred Tennyson to Burne-Jones and Swinburne, though Pound's own preference is not without its irony.

The feeling that the 1890s are after all outmoded (in addition to their having been destroyed by inner weakness) is brought sharply into focus in the melancholy portrait of Monsieur Verog of poem VII. He has talked for hours of that past time: of the French Gallifet, who suppressed the Paris commune in 1870; of Lionel Johnson, whose drinking made him forget the confusions of this world as his late conversion to Catholicism prepared him for another; of Ernest Dowson, who "found harlots cheaper than hotels"; of the Reverend Stewart Headlam, a curious amalgam of "devotions," for "uplift" and for art. By his reveries Monsieur Verog proves himself "out of step with the decade," "Neglected by the young." Not only is the reminiscence melancholy because of Victorian opposition to the artists of that time; "the young" themselves who possess "Frankness as never before" find his preoccupations with the past boring and out of place; as indeed Pound found the gift of Dowson, Johnson, and others no longer to his taste.

The criticism of Mauberley in the last five poems of the sequence puts poems VI and VII into a correct perspective: many artists of the 1890s were deficient in courage and unsound. They were made so because of great errors of taste committed by the genteel arbitrators of the aesthetic conscience. The war was a culminating enormity, which wiped out both the critics who disliked the arts and the artists who had so inadequately practiced them. But the world is still uncomfortable for the dedicated poet, the heir of Flaubert, the "stylist." He is led, driven, compelled into exile; he cultivates his own garden, not from choice but from necessity, and he risks the loss of his importance to a society that very much needs him if only it would realize its need.

Poems VIII to XII describe the circumstances leading to a self-imposed exile; again the evidence is as American as it is British. "Brennbaum"—"The stiffness from spats to collar/Never relaxing into grace" —is akin partly to Eliot's Prufrock, partly to his Bleistein. In any event, Brennbaum's only real identification with a culture—"The heavy memories of Horeb, Sinai and the forty years"—makes of him a kind of exile as well. Mr. Nixon of poem IX is the genuine portrait of the businessman of letters, the success, who offers "the cream gilded cabin of his steam yacht" as conclusive testimony of his shrewdness in negotiating for royalties, in buttering reviewers, in pushing his work. Nixon has ideally found the "prose kinema" that the "age demanded," and it is *prose:*

> "And give up verse, my boy,
> There's nothing in it."

In sharp contrast to the cream gilded cabin of his steam yacht is the sagging roof where "the stylist" of poem X has taken shelter, escaping false "sophistications" and jarring "contentions." In *The Poetry of Ezra Pound* (1951) Hugh Kenner suggests Ford Madox Ford as the best candidate for the life "Beneath the sagging roof." In fact, Kenner maintains, Ford's "detailed account of the cultural state of postwar London in the first third of *It Was the Nightingale* can be made to document *Mauberley* line by line." A shrewd observation; and several references—"He exercises his talents/And the soil meets his distress"; "He offers succulent cooking"—almost make of X a *poème à clef.* But it is the contrast in poems IX, X, XI, and XII that is most important to *Mauberley*'s exactness of statement.

The image in XI and XII is the most conventional of satirical visions of the arts. The young poet, naïve and expectant, views the public drawing-room, considers the matter of patronage. Just how well and how profoundly do these sponsors know and like the arts they profess to admire? How much have time and manners corrupted appreciation of the arts? The poet thinks of "Daphne with her thighs in bark," a sentimental recall of ancient myth; but he is actually waiting upon the graces of a patroness of the arts, the Lady Valentine, and his appearance is ludicrously inappropriate in this "stuffed-satin drawing-room." This woman, for whose support he timidly waits, has played about with the idea of patronizing the arts; she is "Conservatrix of Milésien," though she possesses no inheritance that can make her equal to either the tales of Daphne or the "Milésien":

> No instinct has survived in her
> Older than those her grandmother
> Told her would fit her station.[9]

Nevertheless it is her "vocation" to know and help artists. The fourth and fifth quatrains of XII are again Pound's mockery at its best:

> Poetry, her border of ideas,
> The edge, uncertain, but a means of blending
> With other strata
> Where the lower and higher have ending;
>
> A hook to catch the Lady Jane's attention,
> A modulation toward the theatre,
> Also, in the case of revolution,
> A possible friend and comforter.

In each of these lines there is an image of the uses to which Wyndham Lewis's "Apes of God" (patrons of the arts) put their poets; and XII ends with another of those Corbièrean "brutalities"—in this case the severely proper integrity of Dr. Johnson is evoked as commentary on the Fleet Street of today, where "the press is wafer" and commodity, and

> The sale of half-hose has
> Long since superseded the cultivation
> Of Pierian roses.

"Envoi (1919)," poem XIII of the sequence, is a doubly ironic conclusion of the major group of Mauberley poems. It is an appeal to his poem, to offer to his "lady" ("that sang me once that song of Lawes")

---

[9] It has been suggested that this personality is based upon Hilda Doolittle ("H.D."), but Pound must have had more than one person in mind. At any rate, it is more profitable to consider the women of XI and XII as a composite.

this undying testimony to the glory of Song: *this* testimony, above all, this criticism of the stupidities in both drawing-room and editorial office, of all that prevents true understanding of the beauty of Song. The lines have a tone and diction ("And build her glories their longevity") directly imitative of Elizabethan song. Beauty has its own means of surviving; and this "dumb-born book"

> *Might, in new ages, gain her worshippers,*
> *When our two dusts with Waller's shall be laid,*
> *Siftings on siftings in oblivion,*
> *Till change hath broken down*
> *All things save Beauty alone.*

These lines are a deliberate reversal of the tone exhibited previously. They are not only a testimony of Pound's great skill as an adapter of languages and rhythms; they are also a transitional mode, moving from the major diagnosis of Pound's departure for Paris to a final estimate (in the last five poems) of Mauberley's still imperfect art. The survey of elegances, the striving for a "profile" sharpness of delineation, the pale gold and the porcelain—all suggest that, though Flaubert may be his true Penelope, he has not found the true way to her. The porcelain medallion and the abstraction are the two conflicting concepts in the concluding sequence. The crucial issue is not the virtue of the stylist under his sagging roof but the question of the poet's own right sense of the use of his poetry:

> Nothing, in brief, but maudlin confession,
> Irresponse to human aggression,
> Amid the precipitation, down-float
> Of insubstantial manna,
> Lifting the faint susurrus
> Of his subjective hosannah.

Not that the Old Gang was right in thus abusing him: the succession of harsh-sounding "ation" words in all this "neo-Nietzschean clatter" is sufficient guarantee that the poet hasn't revised his view there; but that, given his fundamental—that is, his sound, right—passion, his urge to integrity—

> This urge to convey the relation
> Of eye-lid and cheek-bone
> By verbal manifestations;
>
> To present the series
> Of curious heads in medallion—

is this quite enough? Or are the results somehow not sufficiently "real"; is there not something lacking? He is right to be "Quite out of place" in the world of pompous "clatter," but does he not remove himself too far?

> "I was
> And I no more exist;
> Here drifted
> An hedonist."

Thus, as the "Envoi" ironically proposes that his indictment be a new song, to rise from his and Waller's dust, the "Medallion" concludes the second and closing phase of "Mauberley" with ironic self-deprecation; except, of course, that Mauberley has not permitted the Old Gang the satisfaction of being right (other than in a thoroughly "wrong way") about him. The medallion is, after all, not entirely satisfactory as a work of art:

> The grand piano
> Utters a profane
> Protest with her clear soprano.

Eliot's "La Figlia che Piange" and, in another sense, his "Portrait of a Lady" express a comparable doubt with respect to the use made in his art of emotion: should the "arrangement" defeat the reality, will it reward the effort? *Hugh Selwyn Mauberley* is, if its total pattern be seen, a farewell not only to the conservators of a tradition but also to a form of rebellion against it, a means of exclusion from the "neo-Nietzschean clatter."

The age demanded not only that poets like Mauberley be forgotten —as inconsequential triflers—but also that the issues of today's Fleet Street (not Dr. Johnson's) be faced directly and not fumbled gracelessly in the barbaric jargon parodied in the very language Pound uses in the sixteenth poem of the sequence. Pound is himself not satisfied with Mauberley's kind of poet, though he most certainly resents his isolation as well as that suffered by his predecessors of the 1890s. Pound had begun the Cantos as early as 1916; and his many discussions of "communication" in the arts, of their vital relations to a civilization different from that misconceived by the Old Gang, show what he wanted his poetry to become. Mr. Kenner is most acutely right when he speaks of the question of Mauberley's relationship to Pound:

> It would be misleading to say that he is a portion of Mr. Pound's self whom Mr. Pound is externalizing in order to get rid of him (like

Stephen Dedalus); it would be a more accurate exaggeration to say that he is a parody of Pound the poet with whom Mr. Pound is anxious not to be confounded.

As a whole, *Hugh Selwyn Mauberley* provides a complex analysis of the ills that disturbed culture at the beginning of the decade. Briefly, simply, they were these: artists were forced, because of several failures of taste, into a reduced world and consequently produced works of art that were perfect in only a limited sense. They were not vital, not precise in the sense that the arts communicate and formulate most exactly the problems and the nature of humanity. The conservators of tradition, who wished art to be a servant of their proper views, made artists of integrity withdraw from the public world and practice their art in small, fine, limited expressions of a pale unvital beauty. The public was thus guilty, but the artists were themselves regrettably inadequate to the need. The true artist would perfect his "style" and restore the arts to their proper role. Mauberley cannot do this, but another Pound (another *kind* of Pound) can and will. He must overcome the temptation to become a "soft Bohemian"; he must deal directly with the problems of communication in the arts and in criticism; he must do more than satirize the Nixons and the Lady Valentines. These are the surface meanings of *Hugh Selwyn Mauberley;* they must be considered always with a full appreciation of the qualities and nuances of statement which the texture of the poem itself gives.

Hugh Selwyn Mauberley is, in this sense, quite well suited to the American scene. While it most eloquently denounces "what the age demanded" and ironically portrays a state of culture deplored more prosaically and less subtly by the contributors to *Civilization in the United States,* it also rejects two of the principal ways of opposing it: the Shavian, Wellsian "reform" literature (as being too superficial and too pompous), and the *fin de siècle* preciosity, which too often led to an attenuated vision of alternatives. Of course, the "stylist" remains, but he is not a bohemian in his pose, and he accepts rather than forces his exile, seeking a suitable "haven," not a drawing-room of "sophistications and contentions." Perhaps a more strictly American analogue of Mauberley's plight is that of Lambert Strether, of James's *The Ambassadors* (1903). But Strether is, after all, "too old" to renounce his native town entirely for Paris; he returns to the Massachusetts mill town, rather chastened in spirit and somewhat enlightened in mind. Strether's successors, two generations later, were not so easily dissuaded.

II

THE WAR AND
THE POSTWAR TEMPER

1. The War to Save Ideals

THE DECLARATION of war in August 1914 came as a profound
shock to certain persons of a generation too old to fight in it. Such
novelists as Edith Wharton, Dorothy Canfield, and Willa Cather were
deeply distressed when France and Germany resumed the quarrel of
1870. Yet all three felt the fight was a necessary, perhaps even a vital,
challenge to our devotion. For Mrs. Wharton the war served as a form
of education in ultimate responsibility. At the beginning of the novel
A Son at the Front (1923), John Campton tries in every way to save
his son from military duty, but he discovers that his son does not want
to be saved from what he thinks is a "precious responsibility," and that
he himself wants the fight to go on against the German menace:

> Yet in one respect all were agreed: the "had to be" of the first day
> was still on every lip. The German menace must be met: chance willed
> that theirs should be the generation to meet it.

To her great love of French taste and integrity (both of which she
described in some detail in *French Ways and Their Meaning,* 1919),
Mrs. Wharton added a profound disapproval of German vulgarity—
which, she said, was abundantly evident in the German way of life,
form of government, and architecture. Teutonic sensitivity there was,
no doubt, but for her it was a rare exception; to save the French from
a Gothic invasion far worse than that suffered by her New Yorkers at
the hands of Nebraskans was her task, and should be the task of every
grateful American.

47

The war was a mission for her; and though she was not unaware of "fathomless mud, rat-haunted trenches, freezing nights under the sleety sky, men dying in the barbed wire between the lines," there was an inevitability, a *rightness,* in the proceedings, which sustained her in her own Red Cross work in Paris and sustained Campton in his most poignant grief. Art and religion on the one side, vulgarity and militarism on the other: this was, in all its bare simplicity of meaning, the issue. Mrs. Wharton, who for decades had had experience with the arts and with a proper measure of good taste, was not ignorant of their opposites. Her point of view had been sustained through most of her fiction by a precise knowledge of what was there, at the core of discretion. While Lawrence Selden (of *The House of Mirth,* 1905) had remained largely inactive, and Ralph Marvell (*The Custom of the Country,* 1913) had killed himself, these men had experienced only fragments of "the invasion." In the all-out "Teutonic migration" vulgarity made efficient was threatening her entire world. She knew the Germans less well than she did the invaders—like the Spraggs—from the Midwest; and she had only a limited knowledge of the Americans who came to fight the enemy in France. George Campton, the son at the front, was too good, too eager, too sensitively aware of the fundamental "goodness" of Paris, Reims, and the Sorbonne to be quite real. He was a quite different spirit from Dos Passos' Martin Howe (of *One Man's Initiation,* 1920); and he bore scarcely any resemblance to the soldiers of Thomas Boyd's fiction, or Hemingway's. There was always something "clean" about George's wounds; and his death was both hallowed and meaningful. When his first serious wound was healed he awaited the chance to go back " 'as soon as ever I'm patched up.' " For, after all, he was needed: "If France went, Western civilization went with her; and then all they had believed in and been guided by would perish."

Undoubtedly age had something to do with this attitude; though George was of military age, he had been born old in Mrs. Wharton's imagination. She herself was fifty-two when the war began (sixty-one, when *A Son at the Front* was published). Her love of France had been nourished by years abroad; since 1907 she had made her home in France. She was but one member of an older generation that thought as she did about the war: non-participants, women for the most part, they saw the issues of the war much more simply (and therefore more "clearly") than did the writers of the so-called war generation. They did experience some doubt, even a measure of disillusionment. Mrs. Wharton spoke of the loss of precision suffered by such words as *honor:*

" 'I was considering how the meaning had evaporated out of lots of our old words, as if the general smash-up had broken their stoppers.' " The heroine of Dorothy Canfield's *The Deepening Stream* (1930) has her eyes opened several times during the war, but never so wide as after it, while the Peace Conference is under way. When she has had her fill of news concerning behind-the-scenes maneuvers, she walks along the Place de la Concorde, bitter and unhappy:

> She had not reached the sidewalk at the edge of the Place before she began to cry. She felt her way to a bench and sat on it, burying her face in her hands, and sobbing as she had not . . . since the night of her father's death. . . .
>
> She felt a hand on her shoulder. . . . A gaunt old man, shabbily dressed, a refugee. . . . "Pardon . . . I see that Madame is in trouble. Madame is a refugee?"
>
> "No," said Matey, and then, *"Yes!"*

This is the deepest measure of Miss Canfield's doubt of the campaign for Western civilization. Yet the heroine has given everything to save what, during her father's sabbatical years in France, she had come to love as the best life of all.

Miss Cather's feeling about the war (in *One of Ours,* 1922), though less intense, was less simple. Her hero, Claude Wheeler, finds in France what he had always missed in Nebraska; and he dies the death of one of the last "pure heroes" of American fiction. The mobility of Miss Cather's soldiers is nothing short of amazing; Claude, as an enlisted officer in the American Army, finds time in a few weeks to educate himself in the amenities, the culture, and the arts of France sufficiently well so that his death seems a natural tribute and sacrifice to a newly found way of life. Most of *One of Ours* is devoted to an exhaustive account of what Nebraska lacks, but for her, as for her hero, the final chapters provide a definition of values. If one must die, death should have meaning; it should be suffered not as a leave-taking from things one despises but as a sacrifice for things one loves. Miss Cather is not so deluded as her hero; she saves herself, but not him, from the charge of simple-mindedness. In the last chapter Claude's mother, seeing through his illusions, reflects: "He died believing his own country better than it is, and France better than any country can ever be." He was safe, beautifully safe, from disillusion: "Perhaps it was well to see that vision, and then to see no more."

Whatever the differences of detail, these three American women were in agreement on the meaning of the war; their view, however, was not the popular one—in fact, proved untenable on several counts. It was hard to see—as Miss Canfield had herself pointed out—that a civilization had actually been saved; and as for the "spiritual definition" achieved by Miss Cather's and Mrs. Wharton's heroes before their deaths, it was so remote from other contemporary accounts that the fiction describing it seemed the worst kind of contrivance. Since they had not fought the war (though Mrs. Wharton and Miss Canfield had done the next best thing—toiled unceasingly at Red Cross work), their descriptions of battle were secondhand. This need not have been a fatal deficiency, for wars had been brilliantly described before by non-combatants. The second failure was more serious: they could not possibly have had an experience similar *in kind* to Hemingway's; they were older by at least two decades; the shock of war could not have been the same, for theirs was a shock suffered by noncombatants well behind the lines, and in one case across the Atlantic. In this sense it was scarcely a shock at all, and it led to results almost antithetically different from those seen in another war fiction. Mrs. Wharton, especially, rushed to the aid of an ideal, a culture, a history of good taste; she deeply felt the threat to these, and her two contemporaries saw it as profoundly, each in her own way. But at worst it was a cultural and not a physical or a psychological trauma. Finally, not only years but intellectual experience separated the two attitudes toward the war. To the older generation the war was fought to sustain their convictions that America's only hope of a tradition lay in the survival of France, of the "old France," and of England; that here was the culture Americans must imitate.

For the most part the young men went into the war without a sense of tradition, except for what they had found in a few years at Harvard or elsewhere. Hemingway, of course, did not even have Harvard to sustain him; and Harvard scarcely contributed to anyone's sense of an *American* tradition. The work of Mrs. Wharton, Miss Canfield, and Miss Cather served primarily to show how far the traditional evaluation of the war was from the view of the 1920s. It had recourse to traditional sympathies scarcely ever felt by the postwar generation (if felt at all, as in the case of Dos Passos, applied in an entirely different way). It led to only occasional and partial glimpses of the personal tragedy of the war, of death, shock, rain, and mud, and of the psychological imbalance that affected so many soldiers. In all the fiction of Dos Passos, Hemingway, and Boyd there is no hero like Mrs. Wharton's "son at

the front"; his "splendid death" would have been dismissed scornfully
by John Andrews or Lieutenant Henry. The 1920s had no room for
such heroics, as Miss Cather soon realized in her postwar search for
verities to replace Ántonia's (*My Ántonia,* 1918). Miss Cather had to
move a considerable distance away from the present before she was satisfied with what she found.[1] Those who faced the present and described
the war for the decade gave it a meaning alien to hers in almost every
particular.

2. The Nightmare

M OST of the writers of war fiction went into the war before the
United States officially declared its intentions in April 1917.
In much of the literature of the 1920s there is an untidy eagerness to
"get into the thick of it," to be doing something, to push up toward
the front before the excitement is over. Since 1865 Americans had had
no real opportunity to test themselves on fields of battle; the Spanish-
American War, for all Stephen Crane had made of it, was really only
an incident. Young men at Harvard, at Princeton, or in Kansas City
were anxious to get to France where guns were booming and armies
maneuvering. Some of them, like Dos Passos, were already in Europe.
Open to them were the ambulance service and the military transport.
The American Ambulance Service—the Norton-Harjes on the French
front, the Red Cross ambulance sections on the Italian—claimed the
loyalty of many young Americans.

Malcolm Cowley, in *Exile's Return,* lists some twelve future American writers who drove ambulances or camions; there were many more.[2]

---

[1] Mrs. Wharton's experience was in many ways comparable. She had started
A Son at the Front in 1917 but put it away, for a novel (*Summer*), "as remote
as possible in setting and subject from the scenes about me"; then, after the war,
she postponed her war novel once more, for *The Age of Innocence,* "a momentary
escape in going back to my childish memories of a long-vanished America." Mrs.
Wharton did return, many times, to the present—no aspect of the 1920s failed
to get her attention—but the results did not remotely equal her earlier work.

[2] For full documentation of these matters, see Charles A. Fenton, "Ambulance
Drivers in France and Italy, 1914–1918," *American Quarterly,* Winter 1951. Fenton lists some 693 volunteer drivers from Harvard, Yale, and Princeton, almost
half of them from Harvard, from which Richard Norton had been graduated in
1914. Most of these young men joined the service because they wished to do

Others, like William Faulkner and Ernest Walsh, joined the air force of one ally or another. They were all either very close to, or right in, the thick of the fighting. Most of them went in for very vague reasons at best. Hemingway's Lieutenant Henry, when asked why he, an American, was fighting in an Italian war, gave evasive answers: he had studied architecture in Rome, he spoke Italian, he had nothing better to do. In any event, this war "did not have anything to do with me. It seemed no more dangerous to me than war in the movies." [3]

Of these young men, almost no one was precisely aware of his motives for being in Europe. A sense of the need to experience danger (or observe it), a vague feeling that in a time of war all other activities (such as going to college or earning a living in the States) were unimportant, a great curiosity about matters of courage, injury, and death—these were for the most part the prevailing motives. In scarcely any case was there a clear, pure reason such as compelled George Campton to the front in a war to which he had no legal or official attachment.

Whatever it was that led to participation or near-participation, not a few young Americans met with violence, came close to death, and suffered one or another kind of shock. Cowley suggests that the war "created in young men a thirst for abstract danger, not suffered for a cause but courted for itself." The danger in many cases became real, and thus quickly changed the dispositions of many Americans. Hemingway's wound from a shell burst on the northern Italian front has been well publicized; Faulkner suffered from a plane crash while training in Canada with the RCAF; Walsh had a similar accident and suffered a punctured lung; Laurence Stallings was seriously wounded serving with the American Marines. In each case the war experience profoundly influenced the writing subsequently done in the 1920s.

their part in "defending civilization"; like one of the Princeton undergraduates, they said "we were going to France to help make the world a little better if we could." But they did not establish or influence the postwar attitude toward the war; the important writers who served as volunteers came out with a quite different impression of their experience. The general response to the war can be seen in such titles as these: *At the Front in a Flivver; The White Road of Mystery; An American Crusader at Verdun.*

[3] In Chapter IV of *A Farewell to Arms,* Catherine Barkley says to Lieutenant Henry:

"What an odd thing—to be in the Italian army."

"It's not really the army. It's only the ambulance."

"It's very odd though. Why did you do it?"

"I don't know," I said. "There isn't always an explanation for everything."

"Oh, isn't there? I was brought up to think there was."

The shock was not always physical. E. E. Cummings was falsely arrested and for over four months detained in "The Enormous Room" at La Ferté Macé, a hundred miles west of Paris. Harry Crosby, ready to drive an ambulance full of wounded, saw a shell burst in the road and the boy next to him go down, badly hurt. He was merely a spectator, yet the experience so changed him that he became haunted by the thought of death.

Crosby's *War Letters,* published by his Black Sun Press (in 1932, more than two years after his suicide), are the testimony of a naïve young patriot slowly becoming aware of the war's realities. On August 16, 1917, he reports having seen a church destroyed: "The only thing left untouched was a beautiful statue of Christ just behind the altar. His hands were out-stretched in such a fashion that he seemed to say to the congregation: 'Look and see what the Germans have done to my temple!' " On November 5, 1917, he writes that "God ordained this war . . . and when it's over the world will be a finer, cleaner, and squarer place." But he is both horrified and fascinated by the images of death and destruction he observes daily. These, he thinks, are "European"; they have little to do with America ("Oh you Statue of Liberty!"): "Shell-gutted ravines, pock-marked hillocks, frightful roads, masses of debris, dead horses, smashed, overturned wagons, vegetation and general ghastliness pervade the whole ungodly, awful scenery" (November 14, 1917). In a letter to his sister, November 23, 1917, he describes the accident which had happened in a night attack: as he is driving what is left of his friend back to the field hospital, "They were shelling the road and it was very unpleasant." The letters following are religious in tone, but he still clings to the simple distinction that has so far sustained him: the war (Europe) is a horror, but the peace (America) will be clean, white, "normal." The details of his reports become increasingly, obsessively horrifying; he is more and more interested in talking about death, the landscape of war, the lurid glare of warfare at night.

Crosby's journal (*Shadows of the Sun,* 1928) refers to the memory of his experiences "four years ago"; he revisited the battlefields, "And how I have changed but the land itself is little changed since the war and it is still the Waste Land." There is much talk of suicide in the journal; he plans it, reads extensively in books on suicide, thinks he will go to his death in a plane, as befits a sun-worshiper. The two books reveal starkly the effect of Crosby's war shock. The letters describe it and give his immediate reactions to it; he "adjusts" to the horror by referring to prewar securities, those he brought with him to the war scene. *Shadows of the Sun* reveals his obsessive, compulsive search for other kinds of adjustment. Throughout, the weird horror of the night attack remains with him, and he turns to the sun as "the only thing in life that does not disillusion." But the memory of death remains, to force him to the final act of adjustment, his suicide.

Whatever the actual experience, these men were introduced to a world of violence, an irrational world in which vulgarity, filth, confusion, and unreason were the rule instead of the unpleasant exception. And yet, the Americans, even after April 1917, had a curious sense of isolation from the causes. The large underlying purposes of the war were not real to them, as so many novels and plays of the 1920s testify. Unlike Cummings' "clean upstanding well dressed boy," these men did not have

> one thought alone: to do or die
> for God for country and for Yale

In fact, if they were decisive about anything, it was their disapproval of American propaganda and of the oppressive routine and discipline the war had required. For every one of the American volunteers who later wrote in terms of his experience a sharp distinction was drawn, whether explicitly or implicitly, between words used vaguely to inspire or coerce and words used to designate objects, persons, and acts. Never before in American history was there such a sharp "nominalistic" examination of the reasons for using words and phrases, or of the kinds of persons who used them. That is why, among other reasons, they could not trust—could not tolerate—such writers as Edith Wharton, whose naïve good intentions made the words sound meaningful, who *tried* to give them their former meaning at a time when their meaning was being nullified.

Consider the literary consequences. The worst victims among our language habits were the abstraction and the capitalized noun. The time-worn psychological values lying behind words were either canceled out or distorted, at the least revised. Broad and profane ironies marked the responses to slogans. The change in attitudes toward what the words stood for led to a minor revolution in style. The letter "i" often became lower case as the point of view of the narrator was lost in the general, reductive terror. Lower-case spellings—in the titles of magazines, in poetry, and in interior monologue—were as much a testimony of human doubt as they were literary novelties. Certain words were avoided, because they had too often been used by men who turned out to be either stupid or brutal, in speeches, directives, and the prose defenses of "ideals." The public personality, because he *was* public and spoke in platitudes, became ridiculous; and, along with him, the sponsors of "ideals" and "values"—the orator, the priest, the head of the YMCA and his assistants—were thrown into the discard.

What was left was the isolated person, who had in almost every case to start anew. No one could *tell* him about death or advise him what to do until the surgeon came, or the priest, to cut off an offending limb or administer spiritual comfort. He was forced into himself, was shocked into a painful suspicion of the words and acts of others; he retreated into embarrassed silence and suspicious disapproval when he encountered any public display of formal emotion or belief.

Such a person could scarcely know what the word "courage" meant, since his earlier notion of it had not really survived his war participation. For writers like Hemingway, only Stephen Crane's *The Red Badge of Courage* (1895), of all the naturalist descriptions of violence and courage, made sense. It was Crane too who, of all naturalists, had most earnestly and intently sought to answer the riddle of violence and death. His instinct had been entirely right when he selected the Civil War as the only genuine large-scale demonstration of violence in American history as he knew it; when, as if to check his intuitions in the matter, he went far afield, to Cuba and to Greece, to get as close to war and death as possible, he took a course that was followed a few decades later by Hemingway.

Crane's *Wounds in the Rain* (1900) foreshadowed, in its details at least, the preoccupation of postwar novelists. Crane was the only genuine predecessor of the 1920s generation of writers. He was obsessed by death and saw it in a way decisively different from the customary vision. His description of death was scarcely ever heroic or pompous. He did not treat corpses as the remains of heroes dead in glorious battle but took them for what they seemed literally to be. For all that, he was not entirely free from the habit of viewing them romantically; but his romanticism, instead of either glorifying death or weeping excessively over it, turned to ironic contemplation of its causes. In this he was immature; and the schoolboyish tone of many of his *War Is Kind* (1899) verses demonstrates only too well his imperfect grasp of what after all was a phenomenon much more closely identified with the twentieth than with the nineteenth century.

The disarming honesty in Crane's examination of Henry Fleming was attractive to Hemingway, Dos Passos, and Thomas Boyd. But it was his exhaustive, almost obsessive, examination of courage that compelled the later novelists to respect and admire his best work of fiction. Crane described courage as the consequence of an accident, wholly removed from the glamorous circumstances traditionally supposed to accompany it. For Hemingway and the others, courage was a word used to signify an instinctive move toward or away from the center of violence, with self-preservation and self-respect the mixed motives. It was not, in fact, an emotion at all—certainly not in the sense of governing an act or preparing a man for the performance of one. For this reason, the last chapters of *The Red Badge of Courage* seemed to ring false, and especially the rescue of the battle flag. Further, Crane's novel, while it disabused its readers of the validity of conventional military virtues, actually turned cowardice into courage, however ironical the occasion. For postwar novelists human acts on the battlefield often began and ended in cowardice; flight and nausea were the principle reactions to the experience, and there was no warm flow of resignation and self-assurance born of them.

The peculiarities of America's participation in World War I are of first importance to an understanding of the postwar years. The strangeness of the war is perhaps the most relevant of these: in one sense, France and Germany were engaged in the most recent phase of an old quarrel. The sympathies of America were largely, though not entirely, with France. But, despite Henry James's indignation and Mrs. Wharton's impatience over America's delayed entrance, France was an ocean's distance away, and coming to her support was not an act that could entirely enlist the sympathy of young Americans. However close to the war they were, it still seemed an affair they were not quite genuinely committed to sharing. They were spectators, gazing curiously at Paris and the French countryside, not entirely sure of what it was all about. What happened, therefore, was never quite so closely linked with *"la gloire française"* as Mrs. Wharton would have us believe.

In short, for men like Hemingway a wound in 1918 was a wound personally suffered and not in any way to be interpreted as a contribution to the cause—though thirty-two years later, in *Across the River and into the Trees,* Hemingway was, pardonably perhaps, to think differently. The shock was immediate and for a long time irremediable. Danger, violence, battle chaos, death, were in every case dissociated from both geography and culture. The postwar American was almost abnormally sensitive to a form of experience that may best be described by the term "violation," a term that indicates what happened to their sense of dignity and security as the result of events that had little or nothing to do with them.

3. "I Had Seen Nothing Sacred"

THAT sense of violation is present in each of the principal works of American war literature. (English writers were "disenchanted," disabused of their sacrifices *pro patria,* but in only a few cases had a comparable feeling of outrage.) Among the forms taken by the feeling of outrage, three reactions are prominent in the war literature of the 1920s: the war as a monstrous hoax, an unendurable outrage committed by the elders, who were brutal, insensitive, and stupid; the war as a violent re-education of the soldier in the ugliness and the scatological realities underlying the surface of decorum; the war as a means of testing the true nature of men and of reclassifying them morally. In each of these cases the reactions or discoveries come as more of a surprise than one suspects they normally should, and the heroes who awake to these truths seem a little too naïve in their expectations. The young *naïf,* like the provincial coming to the brilliant confusion of the great city for the first time, is overwhelmed by an experience he half expects and partly hopes to find, but which stuns him by being so much more unpleasantly true than he had bargained for.

In the first of the war novels, Dos Passos' *One Man's Initiation: 1917* (1920), the hero, Martin Howe, and his friend Randolph watch German shells destroying an abbey:

> When the cloud of dust blew away, they saw the lantern had fallen in on the roof of the apse, leaving only one wall and the tracery of a window of which the shattered carving stood out cream-white against the reddish evening sky.

The heroes of Dos Passos' first two war novels seem always to be observing such climactic ironies: the military destroying what had been considered permanent in art, thought, human pretension. Dos Passos' thesis was simple enough: the war was absurd; it led not only to the destruction of abbeys but to the collapse of trust in the noble thoughts of adventurous minds of the past. One of the ambiguities the Dos Passos *naïf* could never puzzle out for himself was the fact that the war was obviously absurd and yet it persisted, and men continued to fight without more than ineffectual protest. Martin Howe, looking at his glass of Chartreuse, "green like a stormy sunset," recalls the talk of his friends: "No, they had been saying, it could not go on." It was too absurd, and someday "people everywhere . . . would jump to their feet and bust out laughing at the solemn inanity, at the stupid, vicious pomposity of what they were doing." [4]

The stupidity is usually symbolized by the disintegration of religious properties: [5] Howe, walking in the streets of Paris at night, looks at the Cathedral of Notre Dame and remembers the quick destruction of the abbey, the almost surgical cleanness with which the shells had all but wiped it out. A church seemed to him the most enduring monument to man's civilized history; yet it could not stand in the way of military need. American interest in European churches underwent a spectacular revision in the war years. In the days of Henry James's Christopher Newman the churches had been the most reassuring testimony of permanence; but Howe watches the abbey dissolve, Nick Adams, hit in the spine, leans against an Italian church, and the narrator of Cummings' war book passes through the forbidding prison chapel on his way to "the enormous room."

For Dos Passos especially the defeat of art and civilized thought was a terrifying aspect of postwar reality. John Andrews, of *Three Soldiers* (1921), lying on a hospital cot, reflects upon the pathetic loss of value in our intellectual tradition, as Martin Howe had measured the war's destruction of our artistic past. When he returns to consciousness after his injury on the battlefield, Andrews finds he has been transferred to a hospital, formerly a spacious hall, perhaps part of a Renaissance palace:

> In the yellow glow of the electric lights, looking beyond the orderly's twisted face and narrow head, he could see very faintly, where the beams of the ceiling sprung from the wall, a row of half-obliterated shields supported by figures carved out of the grey stone of the wall. . . . He felt at home in that spacious hall, built for wide gestures and stately steps, in which all the little routine of the army seemed unreal,

[4] Note difference in use of word "absurd": Dos Passos and World War I, Existentialists and World War II.

[5] Dos Passos had joined the war from Spain, where he had been studying architecture.

and the wounded men discarded automatons, broken toys laid away in rows.[6]

Against this background of architectual verities, the absurdity of the war overrules its brutality, and the behavior of nurses, YMCA attendants, and other persons of skill and good intention seems ridiculous and paltry. Andrews is unwilling to accept the illusion that the monuments of our civilization will outlast the tiny men and women who are carrying on and justifying this war. It seems fitting, therefore, that in this Renaissance hall he should make explicit his loss of trust in all the nobility and wisdom of the past.

The immediate cause of his disillusioning reflection is the appearance of a Y man, come to cheer him, "a puffy, middle-aged face, with a lean nose and grey eyes, with dark rings under them." Among the gay, reassuring remarks the Y man offers are these: "I guess you're in a hurry to get back at the front and get some more Huns"; and, "It's great to feel you're doing your duty"; and, the Huns "are barbarians, enemies of civilization." To these clichés, thinks Andrews, the "best that had been thought" is now reduced. "Furious, hopeless irritation consumed him." But surely "There must be something more in the world than greed and hatred and cruelty. . . . He thought of all the long procession of men who had been touched by the unutterable futility of the lives of men, who had tried by phrases to make things otherwise, who had taught unworldliness." But these men had not survived: "Democritus, Socrates, Epicurus, Christ; so many of them, and so vague in the silvery mist of history that he hardly knew that they were not of his own imagining; . . . And he felt a crazy desire to join the forlorn ones, to throw himself into inevitable defeat, to live his life as he saw it in spite of everything, to proclaim once more the falseness of the Gospels under the cover of which greed and fear filled with more and yet more pain the already unbearable agony of human life."

The only gesture that would match the acts of the world's great dissidents was desertion; once he has decided to desert, he is excited

[6] Cf. Malcolm Cowley's "Château de Soupir: 1917," in *Blue Juniata* (1929), which describes an eighteenth-century château and gardens destroyed by trenches, machine-guns, and shell fire:

> An enemy machine-gun mocks
> this ante-bellum comedy
> and then falls silent, while a bronze
> Silenus, patron of these lawns,
> stands riddled like a pepper-box.

and exhilarated over his decision. The figures on the wall "seemed to be wriggling out of their contorted position and smiling encouragement to him." It is significant that, when Andrews does make his "separate peace," he plans a composition he will call "The Body and Soul of John Brown," to put "all that misery in music" and to salute the one heroic individual in his memory whose individualism had led to the performance of an act of meaningful rebellion.

No postwar novel expressed so fully its author's hatred of the army and the war as did *Three Soldiers*. In its exposition of the army's oppressive disciplines, in its detailed portrayals of war tedium and vulgarity, the theme is reiterated. The dominating symbolism is the machine, which rules over the individual and reduces to nothing all his pretensions and hopes. The training-camp incidents are entitled "Making the Mould"; description of the war itself is called "Machines"; the hospital scenes, "Rust"; and the final description of desertion and capture "Under the Wheels." These chapter titles suggest what the novel's details support: that the war was for Dos Passos brutal, vulgar, cruel, but inevitable; that the brutality was part of a world-wide plan to discredit every decent human virtue; and that the world was becoming —had become, in fact—a machine for which traditional values no longer had a meaning.

Dos Passos' first two war novels are a continuous loud expression of indignation, the center of which is a young man, a *naïf*, taught to respect himself and his past and horrified by the total, calamitous, and absurd ways in which he as person and the past are thrown to the scrap heap. This is a position antithetical to that taken by the heroes of Mrs. Wharton's and Miss Cather's war fiction. Yet there is a great measure in his novels of raw naïveté. The abbeys, the cathedrals, and the "great thoughts" are no more adequate scapegoats than the Germans themselves. Dos Passos' occasional demonstrations of a very real talent, of a literary sense of the proper and the useful, are inhibited by his obsessive and driving need to show the monster at work wrecking the world.

Whatever his weaknesses, Dos Passos scored a great popular success, especially with *Three Soldiers*. It was the kind of portrayal of World War I that the majority of readers wanted to have. The melancholy and apologetic withdrawal of "decency" was described with devastating irony; and the details of war itself were real enough to satisfy anyone who had been there or had wondered what it was like. Each of his heroes was an ardent, sensitive young man who came to his war expecting danger and experienced an unexpected quantity of it; he left as immature as he had been when he arrived. He responded to the shock of the violation in long passages of rhetorical indignation. He trusted his taste and his love of the "little things," such as colors, nuances of conversation, lights and shadows. And he himself never abandoned his ambition, which was to prove the war false *to himself,* or—as one of Martin Howe's friends puts it—to show it as unreal, "like Alice in Wonderland, like an ill-intentioned Drury Lane pantomime, like all the dusty futility of Barnum and Bailey's circus."

Other war novelists were content to portray the stark simplicity of trenches, huts, barbed wire, and gangrenous corpses. Thomas Boyd satisfied the reader's curiosity for scatological detail and stimulated his mind only to the point of accepting simple ironies that seem literally taken over from Stephen Crane. A passage such as this, from *Through the Wheat* (1923), shows clearly Crane's influence and is also representative of what Boyd offered the decade's readers:

> Three bodies, motionless as the rocks themselves, were stretched at length. One had fallen face forward, an arm thrown over the stock of the weapon. His back, that swelled under the gray coat, was turned reproachfully toward the sky. Another was sprawled on his back, his hands and legs frozen in a gesture of complete negation. His chin had fallen heavily on his breast, and upon his head his small trench cap was tilted forward at a rakish angle. The other man's face was a clot of blood. Death, camera-like, had caught and held him fast, his body supported by the rocks, his face like a battered sunflower in the evening.[7]

Everything is there but a guiding talent: the boredom of the drill, the misery and danger of the attack, the proper disarray of bodies, the stench, even the refugee carts moving toward the rear. ("Outside the city they met an old man with a patriarchal beard, seated upon his household goods, which were piled upon a little cart driven by a mule.")[8] Readers could at least say that Boyd had been through it, that he had some skill in describing what it was like, and that he was sufficiently indignant over "the ambitious who cause the wars and the financiers who grow fat on them." His hatred of financiers gave him a kind of distinction; a decade later this view of wars was to dominate the leftist interpretation of World War I, as well as wars in general—at

[7] Cf. *The Red Badge of Courage,* end of chapter 7.
[8] The prevailing images of this war fiction were the ruined abbey (or cathedral), the refugee cart, the big guns, the prostitute.

least until the Spanish Civil War suggested that wars might have to be fought, no matter who provided the weapons.[9]

Those who had arranged the war and had publicly declared their dedication to its aims were portrayed as personal enemies. It was the distinction of E. E. Cummings that he should have described them exhaustively, and that he should have provided a means of classifying them. This view of the "officials" and their underlings has remained consistent throughout his career. His world is run by the officials; it is sanctioned by naïve well-wishers and diligent nincompoops like "my sweet old etcetera/aunt lucy" and

> my sister
>
> isabel [who] created hundreds
> (and
> hundreds) of socks not to
> mention shirts fleaproof earwarmers . . .

It seems dedicated to a periodic explosion of cannon, whose bigness is "skilful," "death's clever enormous voice," which leaves "all the silence/filled with vivid noiseless boys." The cannon themselves are blunt instruments that in their own way reduce humanity to quiet acquiescence in the war's acts and purposes; those who object too conscientiously are given another treatment by "kindred intellects" who argue for "allegiance per blunt instruments."

In any future appraisal of the war's peculiar influence, two of Cummings' books will perhaps be considered essential documents: *The Enormous Room* (1922) and *Eimi* (1933). The latter also describes an enormous room, but enlarged by eleven years of perceptive observation and altered in that not only the officials but their victims now lived in it—the latter either not aware or unwilling to admit they had made a prison over into a way of life. Cummings himself has said, in the introduction to the 1934 edition of *The Enormous Room,* that *Eimi* describes "a more complex individual, a more enormous room."

Cummings spent a little over four months (from the latter part of August 1917 to January 11, 1918) in the first "enormous room," a detention camp a hundred miles west of Paris, called La Ferté Macé.

[9] Boyd became a Communist in 1934, a year before his death. He was not the only one to inveigh against the military and the munitions-makers: see also Henri Barbusse, *Under Fire* (1928); Andreas Latzko, *Men in War* (1918); Arnold Zweig, *The Case of Sergeant Grischa* (1928); Bernhard Kellerman, *The Ninth of November* (1921).

With his friend William Slater Brown ("B" of the account), he had been apprehended on suspicion of "treasonable correspondence." After a preliminary examination before "six eyes which sat at a desk," he was introduced to French jails, French railways, and the *gendarmerie*. This sudden and apparently irrevocable confinement, which in a few hours had cut him off from that other world, where "the air must be beautifully cool," was Cummings' traumatic experience of World War I. Unlike Hemingway's shock, Cummings' shock forced him unreasonably into a private, dark hole in which bestiality and filth were the accustomed order and men were reduced to the least attractive of strategies merely to remain alive. In these circumstances he was amazed by the quickness of adjustment to the vulgarities of this world. Indeed, through the months of his detainment he became aware of a "decorum of vulgarity" in which physical details not ordinarily mentioned were absorbed by the routine of living.

On the way to La Ferté Macé he is not informed of his destination, thinks it likely that he is being deported. Gradually the journey to the enormous room is symbolically realized, if not actually understood. Walking the last miles, he comes upon "a little wooden man hanging all by itself in a grove of low trees."

> The wooden body clumsy with pain burst into fragile legs with absurdly large feet and funny writhing toes; its little stiff arms made abrupt, cruel, equal angles with the road. About its stunted loins clung a ponderous and jocular fragment of drapery. On one terribly brittle shoulder the droll lump of its neckless head ridiculously lived. There was in this complete silent doll a gruesome truth of instinct, a success of uncanny poignancy, an unearthly ferocity of rectangular emotion.

He had seen himself, "the coarse and sudden sculpture of his torment" —this martyr to God knew what terrible mystery was the present revival of "some medieval saint with a thief sagging at either side, surrounded with crisp angels." Only, in this case, he was alone in his torture, silent, doll-like, ridiculous. The victim of whatever suspicion the war had invoked to protect itself from whatever danger, the narrator of *The Enormous Room* suffered the torture of an unreal and unreasonable experience—to no purpose, and with scarcely any determinable outlines to guide him.

When he is examined by his first official at La Ferté, he confronts a man of middle age, whose "face was seedy, sallow and long. He had bushy, semicircular eyebrows which drooped so much as to reduce his eyes to mere blinking slits. . . . He had no nose, properly speaking, but a large beak of a preposterous widthlessness, which gave his whole face the expression of falling gravely downstairs." This is the beginning of the caricature gallery of officials and their underlings whose acts are either demonic or absurd or both. They behave with a truculent, often a desperate, ignorant strategy, the object of which is to keep "things in line at any cost," to prevent or to quell disturbances, and to see that their victims are improperly fed, housed, and clothed.

The hero's course to the enormous room leads him first into a chapel where he is to find his mattress: "Staring ahead, I gradually disinterred the pale carrion of the darkness—an altar, guarded with the ugliness of unlit candles, on which stood inexorably the efficient implements for eating God." The prison room itself is "unmistakably ecclesiastical in feeling—two rows of wooden pillars, spaced at intervals of fifteen feet, rose to a vaulted ceiling 25 or 30 feet above the floor."

Here, in this tale of a perverted, modern "pilgrim's progress," Cummings was to spend his months. From the experiences and persons minutely described, he was to reformulate certain important points of view. The room and the enforced occupancy within it altered his sense of time and place and sharpened his appreciation of the eccentric details which make persons individuals. In this second phase of his progress he discovered the "Delectable Mountains"—the men who were "cursed with a talent for thinking" at the very time when the "great governments . . . demanded of their respective peoples the exact antithesis of thinking." In terms of what he knew about them, he concluded that treason must mean "any little annoying habits of independent thought or action which *en temps de guerre* are put into a hole and covered over, with the somewhat naïve idea that from their cadavers violets will grow whereof the perfume will delight all good men and true and make such worthy citizens forget their sorrows."

Of all the officials only one was decent: he "did not enjoy being cruel." The orderlies who kept guard were merely stupid, "the next to the lowest species of human organism; the lowest, in my experienced estimation being the *gendarme* proper." Not all the good was inside, nor all the bad outside, the enormous room; but when a man inside it proved repulsive, it was not unreasonable to suppose, as in the case of "the Spy," that he had been corrupted by the outside. The interesting persons within the room were there because they thought for themselves, had admirable eccentricities of character that threw the world outside into confusion, or were "guilty of who knows what gentleness, strength and beauty."

These men were Cummings' principal sources of what in all his work he was to establish as points of reference and judgment: a gentility accessible to no measure of taste or custom previously established. For Cummings the "Delectable Mountains" contributed a definition of "ISness" to put against the "world of un." Their major virtues were their soft animal natures, their reasonableness, their lack of cunning, and the absence of bombast or rhetoric; in fact, for such a man as Zulu, whom "I must perforce call an IS," silence was a form of communication infinitely more meaningful than the noise of speech harshly ordered. They were children, whose minds and tastes had not been perverted by adult ambitions, greeds, cruelties. Their innocence, having survived years of torture and unreasonableness, was a means of judging the world of adults. They were the first of the graceful, guileless, charming innocents whom Cummings continued to defend and to describe, along with the flowers of the "mud-luscious spring," the prostitutes of Paris, and the moon's soft and gentle light.

The world that Cummings presented in *The Enormous Room* was a mouse's world as it might have appeared in a cat's mind. His characters had a mouse's opportunities to evade the cat's purpose and, meanwhile, to make something of its short life. But, as the chaplain of the prison was fond of saying on Sundays at mass, *"toujours l'enfer";* and always, in this account of captive innocents, there is the expectation of disaster and the suffering of continuous dirt and inconvenience. "In the course of the next ten thousand years," Cummings remarked, "it may be possible to find Delectable Mountains without going to prison"—that is, if the "intelligent revolution" succeeds in wiping out "The Great Mister Harold Bell Wright and The Great Little Miss Pollyanna." But in the end, when Cummings approached New York and saw "The tall, impossibly tall, incomparably tall, city shouldering upward into hard sunlight" and the "hurrying dots which are men and which are women," the hope seemed slight if not altogether vain.

Cummings' war education radically altered and rearranged his views of human nature; they became genuinely "unconventional"—that is, antipodal to conventional appraisals of men and their occupations and beliefs. The USSR of *Eimi* proved to be an infinite extension of the enormous room, from which the Delectable Mountains had all but disappeared; there were hundreds of "minuteless minutes" of Marxian dialectic, and the geometry of Lenin's tomb replaced the unmistakably "ecclesiastical" feeling of La Ferté. What there had been of revolution had not had the results Cummings hoped for.

The Enormous Room contains many things, not the least of which is its picture of a life from which all decorum and artifice have gone. The protective disguises that enable men to stand straight, talk with confidence, and act shrewdly in their own interest are lacking. In their place are the consequences of unhealthful, close contact, the necessary vulgarities of bodily functions, the unnecessary vulgarities of brash and ignorant cruelty. Hemingway described the psychological results of the battlefield; Cummings portrayed the terrors and pointed to the survivors of the concentration camp. In each case, there was a suspension of time and a modification of customary space; in each case, conditions governing life were reduced to the borderline of consciousness; in each case, fundamental changes took place in the formation of the postwar attitude toward those who continued to live and to believe "conventionally." The two, more than any others, gave the 1920s the most complete rationalization of its postwar attitudes.

4. The Unreasonable Wound

IN HER novel Death Comes for the Archbishop (1927), Willa Cather made several observations about human death and the circumstances in which it takes place. On one occasion a Father Lucero receives his last sacrament, after confession: "The ceremony calmed the tormented man, and he lay quiet with his hands folded on his breast." This ceremony is significant not only for him but for those who attend him in his last moments: "Watching beside a death-bed was not a hardship for them, but a privilege—in the case of a dying priest it was a distinction." In those days, Miss Cather says (she is speaking of the early nineteenth century and of the southwestern United States),

> death had a solemn social importance. It was not regarded as a moment when certain bodily organs ceased to function, but as a dramatic climax, a moment when the soul made its entrance into the next world, passing in full consciousness through a lowly door to an unimaginable scene. Among the watchers there was always the hope that the dying man might reveal something of what he alone could see; that his countenance, if not his lips, would speak, and on his features would fall some light or shadow from beyond.

These words, published two years before Hemingway's *A Farewell to Arms* (1929), have a source and an orientation radically different from Hemingway's. *Death Comes for the Archbishop* celebrates the triumph of a simple and serene faith over the hardships of terrain and society; elsewhere Miss Cather has spoken of her rejection of the modern world: she will have nothing to do with its crassness, its vulgarity and its violence. In 1936, looking back upon her first introduction to the widow of James T. Fields, she spoke of the passing of that gracious life in the home at 148 Charles Street. The house had since been replaced by a garage, its stark vulgarity superseding the "softly lighted drawing-room, and the dining-table where Learning and Talent met, enjoying good food and good wit and rare vintages, looking confidently forward to the growth of their country in the finer amenities of life." Somehow, "The world broke in two in 1922 or thereabouts . . ." and she thought it not unlikely that World War I had been at least partially responsible. Despite the fact that it had proved a source of renewal for one of her heroes, Claude Wheeler of *One of Ours*, it was nevertheless blamed for having radically altered twentieth-century tastes, habits, and points of view. She was not explicit about this, only vaguely resentful; she did not try to explain why the change had taken place, but rather retreated from the world which had suffered it, retiring to a place where traditional securities were still an important means of defining and governing human behavior.

To Miss Cather the modern world was one in which death and life had lost what she thought was a peculiarly precious and meaningful relationship. The extreme form of imbalance between death and life is caused by violence; but there are, of course, forms and degrees of violence. The most widely disparate forms are violence caused by "strong emotion" and that made possible by efficient technological means. Of the first Miss Cather feels that the securities have their own emotional means of combating it; but there is no real way out of the agony, the shock, the meaninglessness of the second.

One of the most radical changes in modern literary sensibility can be described as the symbolic injury. The circumstances of such an injury are almost invariably violent, and the violence, while not entirely unexpected, comes as a surprise, as a shock, to the person injured. There are some evidences of security even here, though quite superficial and not at the heart of the experience. The hero may be with soldiers whom he knows, with whom he talks and eats an improvised meal. Beyond this scene, there are the love and the religion he has left. About him there are many threatening noises, and these bear promise of violent injury or death. If one of these noises should come near, to actualize the danger, that is an accident; but the accident is the result not of mere chance but of impersonal misfortune impersonally caused. The injury, when it comes, is a form of death whether the victim survives it or not.

Hemingway once spoke of his own injury, on the night of July 8th, 1918, as a death [10] (it is important too that the injury should occur at night). "I died then," he is reported by Malcolm Cowley as having said, "I felt my soul or something coming right out of my body, like you'd pull a silk handkerchief out of a pocket by one corner. It flew around and then came back and went in again and I wasn't dead any more!" [11] According to Ezra Pound's version, told to John Peale Bishop, Hemingway "had lain four days under the debris of the trench" before he was rescued; this, adds Bishop, "is one day longer underground than Lazarus." Though the facts of this account may not be true, they do have a symbolic meaning: Hemingway's "awareness of death," his experience of it, had led to a form of rebirth, had "separated" him from his (as well as from Nick Adams') American past, from the Middle West. The experience of the wound and the circumstances in which it had happened radically altered Hemingway's entire view of the world he re-entered. He had therefore to find a different perspective from which to view and judge the world.

The most important consequence of a traumatic shock is that the experience that caused it is recalled again and again. It is not that the victim enjoys the experience and so wishes it repeated, but rather that initially it has thrown him entirely off balance and he is therefore unable to adjust to it. [12] The more violent and unexpected the experience, the more liable it is to such compulsive repetition, which is in reality a long and painful means of reaching a stage of complete adjustment. A severe injury to the body suggests a comparably severe injury to the psychic nature. The injured man will not rest until he has found what is to him a meaningful and original pattern of adjustment. The shock often has other effects: for one, it may upset his confidence in the past

[10] He was with three Italian soldiers at the time; all three of them died. Hemingway was himself all but given up for dead—237 fragments of the "Minnie" shell were extracted from one leg alone.

[11] Cf. *A Farewell to Arms:* "I went out swiftly, all of myself, and I knew I was dead and that it had all been a mistake to think you just died."

[12] Cf. Sigmund Freud, *Beyond the Pleasure Principle* (1922); see Philip Young, *Ernest Hemingway* (1953).

—his own past and the social past of which he has been a part. The experience is itself almost equivalent to a death; what follows it amounts to a new and a different life. The man who survives violence is often quite remarkably different from the man who has never experienced it.

The symbolic wound has affected a large share of Hemingway's fiction. Its distinguishing features are the shock of the actual occurrence, the sudden cutting away of past experience and securities (which do survive, but only in fragmentary form), the mystery and impersonality of its source, the anger, fear, and helplessness that are part of the reaction to it. The wound is "unreasonable"; that is, the victim cannot understand why "it has happened to *him*." It gives him a profound distrust of those who—remote from the experience itself—try to formulate explanations or assurances about it. They are obviously "faking"; they don't know what they are talking about; if they knew what it was really like, they would not talk at all, and they would most certainly not try to speak of dignity or glory or sacrifice, because these words are almost invariably betrayed when tested by reality. But some definition of a man's life is necessary if he is to care about surviving, and this definition is hard to formulate when so many useful words and expressions have defaulted.

The memory of the war haunts Hemingway's earliest fiction; many of the stories of Nick Adams' youth in *In Our Time* (1925) are given in terms of the author's own meeting with violence. The securities provided by Nick's father and mother and by the natural setting are never free of the tortured comment which the sketches of war and violence offer. In fact, these sketches act as a somber, brooding supervisory deity in the affairs of Nick Adams. His father's assurances may have been adequate before the injury occurred, but they are no longer capable of exorcising the nightmarish spirit which returns after each of the Adams stories. "There was no end and no beginning" in the Greek retreat described in Chapter II of *In Our Time,* a sketch immediately after the story "Indian Camp," in which there have been both beginning *and* end. The emotional response to birth and death is governed by Nick's own ability to accept the security of his father's competence as a doctor and of the quiet natural setting of the early morning: ". . . sitting in the stern of the boat with his father rowing, he felt quite sure that he would never die."

The "absolutely perfect barricade" of Chapter IV and the garden wall of Chapter III both lead to "perfect" deaths, containing in them elements of shock and accident and managed, through ingenuity and skill, with a total lack of emotion or passion. "It was simply priceless," and "we were frightfully put out when we heard the flank had gone and we had to fall back." These remarks are a form of compulsive repetition; in placing them in the context of *In Our Time,* Hemingway skillfully explains the meaning of his title: in our time, he says in effect, a return to the past of Nick's boyhood is never free of the shock and the wound.[13] Almost everything that happens to Nick Adams in the stories is accounted for simply; he has a way of adjusting to the horror that penetrates his world from "the outside," or he can get away from it—he can "get out of this town" or just "not think about it."

But in Chapter VI Nick himself experiences the wound: "Nick sat against the wall of the church where they had dragged him to be clear of machine-gun fire in the street. Both legs stuck out awkwardly. He had been hit in the spine." He talks to Rinaldi, who "lay face downward against the wall," about the end of his commitment to the war, about his having paid his debt, and about his "separate peace."

All of *In Our Time* is an early testimony to the powerful influence of "the unreasonable wound." Even the sparse symbolism contributes to that impression: the garden wall, the "absolutely perfect obstacle," and the wall of the church underscore the helplessness of the war's circumstance; the rain falls grimly upon the refugees as they make their way out of Adrianople, and upon the six cabinet ministers who are shot against the wall of a hospital. At the end we see not Nick Adams but the war, not tradition and the church but the wall and the rain; Nick's position against the wall of the church is an important sign of his initiation into the reality of the "outside"; a wall usually suggests protection, but "in our time" it has become an obstacle to safety and security.

A Farewell to Arms contains the fullest account of this kind of death. Lieutenant Henry is wounded in terms roughly similar to Hemingway's actual experience. Very important too are certain facts of the novel's war setting: Gorizia, the "nice" town, with its hospitals, its cafés, its two brothels (one reserved for the officers), its artillery up side streets. Dominating the town are the artillery pieces, which in the summer are "covered with green branches" to disguise them as part of the landscape.[14] In the mountains, at the front, they are hidden from

[13] Hemingway said that he had written these interchapters as "exercises" in condensation.

[14] Note also the troops, who wore cartridge boxes under their capes, so that they looked "as though they were six months gone with child"—death masquerading as life; the battlefront "no place for virgins" or for mothers.

view, and only the round puffs of smoke can be seen: "You saw the flash, then heard the crack, then saw the smoke ball distort and thin in the wind." The two important ministers to the faith and security of the soldiers are the priest and Rinaldi the surgeon. The guns, the surgeon, and the brothels all act to reduce life at the front to its secular minimum; the priest is always "five against one," as the Captain says at the officers' mess. The priest's advice is rarely taken seriously; his remarks are not quite like the patriotic phrases of the battle police, but they are heard by Lieutenant Henry with embarrassment, and sometimes with boredom.

The most crucial of all Hemingway's explorations of the military condition is his description of the retreat from Caporetto (Book Three). The retreat begins in an orderly enough fashion, but as it proceeds the sense of order dissolves. It becomes "unreasonable"; Italians fire on Italians; Germans break through the lines; the *carabinieri* suspect impartially and kill the innocent. In the landscape of unreason of which this section of the novel gives a brilliant description, Lieutenant Henry loses all sense of personal dedication to his fellow soldiers, abandons his feeling of responsibility to the army, and breaks out of the trap the war has laid for him. From then on he links his fate with only a few persons—nurses, doctors, and bartenders—and they serve his emotional needs and protect him from dangers.

This does not, however, save him from ultimate defeat; it is important to see his defeat in terms of the "unreasonable wound" received earlier. The death of Catherine Barkley, however remote its setting from that of the war, is placed in sharp equation with the defeating and confusing terror of the war itself. The long, slow, almost monotonous life of waiting in Switzerland intensifies the terror and bitterness of the final scene. The two deaths of that scene are an excruciating addition to the evidence of impersonal cruelty the novel as a whole provides. The child is stillborn and the mother dies in her attempt to give him life. Here there is no priest to speak of God and love; there are only death and the rain outside on the walk back to the hotel. Catherine's death is another example of the unreasonable wound, more pathetic really because it defeats a plan to which Lieutenant Henry has irrevocably committed himself.

A Farewell to Arms affords a remarkably complete view of the modern death about which Miss Cather was so critical. Superficially, Lieutenant Henry may be said to have had an honorable choice of two equally persuasive and practicable modes of action. Actually, the choices are neither persuasive nor practicable. The war itself gives only one kind of answer to the questions posed by those living at its center: the shock, the surprise, the helpless anger are present three times in the novel—when Lieutenant Henry is wounded, at the end of the retreat, and in Catherine's death in Switzerland. The setting of the war —the guns hidden in the mountains and dealing impersonally in death —dominates Hemingway's fiction throughout the postwar decade. To this specter priest, surgeon, and other men of skill or good intention pay futile and desperate heed, but adjustment to the violent and incalculable death which is its gift cannot be made with the help of any of them.

With the feeling that he must understand and honestly account for this condition, Hemingway came to Paris early in the 1920s to learn how to write; he found that the greatest difficulty, "aside from knowing truly what you really felt, rather than what you were supposed to feel, and had been taught to feel, was to put down what really happened in action. . . ." He wanted to begin with "the simplest things, and one of the simplest things of all and the most fundamental is violent death." The only place to see that happen, "now that the wars were over, was in the bullring."

The consequences of this interest are testified to both in *Death in the Afternoon* (1932) and in *The Sun Also Rises* (1926). In the total design of the bullfight, as in its details of risk, grace, danger, and death, Hemingway apparently found the perfect palliative to the bewilderment and terror felt by the victims of the "unreasonable wound." The key to Hemingway's interest in the bullfight seems to be the artificial nature of its design; quite aside from the very real danger of death that it poses for the matador, it is true that he creates, manipulates, and controls that danger. It is the only art, Hemingway said in *Death in the Afternoon,* "in which the artist is in danger of death and in which the degree of brilliance in the performance is left to the fighter's honor." Here there is nothing unreasonable; there are no surprises, no tragedies that cannot be explained as the result of fear, ignorance, or mere gracelessness. Within the limitations imposed by usage and circumstance (tradition and "present danger"), it is possible to evaluate courage and virtue, "purity of line" and "grace under pressure."

The bullfight had a simplified past and a continuous, ritualized present. It was above all possible to measure, to gauge, human emotions within a set of brilliantly formed "calculated risks." There is no doubt that Hemingway was attracted to the simplicity of the matador-hero, to his lack of sophistication, and to his constant preoccupation with the concrete details of his task and craft. This simplicity of dedication—that is, among those fighters who were "the real thing"—when circumstances were right and when acts of grace and courage were sympathetically seen and understood, became for Hemingway a meaningful ritual for his time, the most meaningful he was able to find during the first postwar decade.

The strength of his interest in Spain and in the bullfights is fully seen in *The Sun Also Rises*. This novel is a brilliant improvisation of a moral point of view, largely because of that interest. That the *corrida* was a specious resolution of postwar ills and that it could not, because of its artificiality, really take the place of religion or become a substitute tradition does not necessarily nullify its importance. The bullfight contributed both a criticism and a corrective to the persons involved in the atmosphere of postwar life. It is an ideal measure of that group's inadequacy; and it profoundly influenced certain persons and certain actions. The bullfight marked an ideal unity of specific detail with formal tradition, a unity lacking in the lives of the expatriates. The past had preserved the matador's naïveté, his purity and his "honor"; the requirements of the fight itself meant that with each new appearance in the ring he had to renew his caution, his skill, and his courage. While the procedures were largely fixed by tradition, there was nothing lifeless or mechanical or meaningless in them. The motion, the emotion, and the action formed a single figure that could be seen and shared by those who had understanding. In every detail this artificial pattern of behavior, this aesthetic ordering of human risk and emotion, contrasts sharply with the lives of Jake Barnes and his friends.

The Sun Also Rises itemizes with an earnest exhaustiveness the consequences of the unreasonable wound. That the wound should in this case have deprived Jake Barnes of his virility is in one sense an example of literary and moral economy. The sterility and perversion in several Hemingway stories are intended as one insight into the postwar situation. In making Jake Barnes impotent through an "accident," Hemingway offers a comparable insight, at the same time providing a pathos and a terror like those of the last scenes of *A Farewell to Arms*. Jake tries for a consistent limitation of his behavior and judgment. In his personal and private life he must always hold himself back, subdue his resentment and his anger, by excluding all "romantic effusion" and all abstract reasoning from his attitude, and thus face his death-in-life with all the courage and grace that are his to command. In this struggle for balance Robert Cohn is an ever-present danger—a danger not unlike that risked by the "honest" matador who is tempted to give in to the "decadence" of his art. Whatever Jake Barnes or Lady Brett does must fail to achieve an entirely satisfactory adjustment, except when it touches upon the world and art of the matador. Brett's release of Romero at the end is a fine, positive moral act, the only kind of which she is capable.

Jake's private heroism and courage are admirable when put within the context of what Hemingway has described as "the real thing" in the bullfight. In the Paris scenes of the novel, this context is lacking, and Hemingway here gives us the fullest description of the postwar landscape of unreason. The three acts of the bullfight are in themselves a quite artificial pattern, an adventitious ordering of human emotion and act, but Hemingway could find no other. "The sun also ariseth, and the sun goeth down, and hasteth to the place where he arose."

From 1924 to 1932 Hemingway gave us in his writing the most compelling evidence of his concern over the "unreasonable wound," his repeated efforts to review it and its consequences, to find a balance between the inner terror caused by it and the outward need to survive. Since he could not call upon religion to provide that balance, he had to discover it in a context both secular and traditional. He has never since described the moral condition of postwar man with quite the same precision. Harry Morgan's dying (*To Have and Have Not,* 1937) was forced self-consciously into a social reference; Robert Jordan's heroics were too excessively and too deliberately placed within a context of affirmation; too much was made of his sacrifice and too little of himself. *For Whom the Bell Tolls* (1940) was, for Hemingway, an extremely important stage in the development of his point of view. In the 1920s he could not turn either to politics or to religion; but in the 1930s he found, in the Spanish Civil War, an ideal union of violence and meaning. The death of Jordan is very different from the wound suffered by Lieutenant Henry: it is not unexpected; Jordan is not unprepared for it; most important, it is given a specious meaning by Jordan's love for Maria and by his dedication to a cause. Hemingway found—to his own satisfaction at least—a significant and sufficient reason for violence and death, outside the bullring.

In *Across the River and into the Trees* (1950) there is an almost obsessive preoccupation with wounds and death. Since Hemingway had found in the 1930s and 1940s a meaning for violence, a reason for the wound, the concern of his Colonel Cantwell with death becomes both sentimental and retrospective. The kneecap he lost in the Italian war is now part of the land and has helped to make that land "sacred." He would like to be buried near it. Anyway, he reflects, after death you are of some use, "a sort of mulch, and even the bones will be of some use." He can have no affection except for those who had fought in that first war, "where it all made sense," those "who had been there and had received the castigation that everyone receives who goes there long enough." In this novel death is expected, and laborious preparations of feeling are made for it; love is pure and romantic, and the expectation of death adds a flavor of sentiment to it: food, drink, sights, and savors provide the details of the sentiment. The Colonel does not die of violence or shock or even of treachery or the misfire of stratagem. Nor does he die Robert Jordan's kind of death; he is pathetic and not patently heroic. He dies of a heart attack, for which the entire novel has provided a tedious preparation.

Among other distinctions, Hemingway can claim that of having honestly attempted an explanation of a form of death to which the twentieth century is peculiarly heir—death that comes as a violent disruption of life. It is unreasonable (that is, it is not properly "motivated," cannot be understood in terms of any ordinary system of motivation). It puts traditional securities to shame, since they cannot satisfactorily keep pace with its indiscriminate destructiveness. It demands a new form of resourcefulness and courage, and—in Hemingway's case—a new type of moral improvisation. The sudden violent injury inflicted impersonally by efficient guns or planes too remote from the victim to "hold him any special grudge" is the symbol of this type of death and of the death-in-life which is its consequence.

The problem of understanding and facing this kind of death remains unsolved. "We died on the wrong page of the almanac," says the narrator of Randall Jarrell's poem, "Losses," who then reflects upon a kind of death even more impersonalized than that suffered in the Italian retreat of *A Farewell to Arms*. "When we died they said 'Our casualties were low.' " The individual death is absorbed into a statistical estimate, the same kind of ironic official notice that Hemingway uses at the end of Chapter II of *A Farewell to Arms:* "At the start of the winter came the permanent rain and with the rain came the cholera. But it was checked and in the end only seven thousand died of it in the army."

Jarrell's poem underscores the persistence of this "unreasonable wound" in modern morality and literature. Hemingway described its circumstance and gave it its first and its most incisive literary statement and judgment.

5. "An Old Bitch Gone in the Teeth"

As THE descendant of a long line of Southern warrior-heroes, Richard Plume (of Laurence Stallings' novel *Plumes,* 1924) enlists in the war as he is expected to do. Severely wounded, he returns to America, to suffer the consequences of what he now regards as his "romantic folly." Lying for the third or fourth time in a hospital bed, he curses out the "scoundrelly orators who were not there—were not with him." It amuses him to work out a calculus of pain, "to figure on ten million men wounded in the last war . . . to total their kilowatt hours of pain." Then, his interest aroused, he works out the total "kilowatt hours of mental anguish for mothers and wives." *This* time, Richard Plume means it when he says he is the last of the Plumes to go to war in support of heroic illusions. Perhaps his son will get it in the next war, but not because he has foolishly rushed into it.

In the absence of any clearly defined reasons for having fought, the returned soldier felt hurt, ill at ease, uncertain of his future, "disenchanted." The sharpest portrait of the returning soldier is found in Hemingway's story "Soldier's Home." Harold Krebs, who had come back "much too late" to his town in Oklahoma, could not adjust to the life he had left for Belleau Wood, Soissons, the Champagne, St. Mihiel, and the Argonne. "He did not want any consequences. He did not want any consequences ever again. He wanted to live along without consequences." He loved no one, could not bring himself to enjoy or respect his family, his home. He could only make his mother weep; she would not understand. So he would go away, somewhere, to get a job.

The war had itself been so violent a departure from custom, from the "rules," that it was almost impossible to return to them. One either went away or tried to change the rules. And what were these rules? In the 1920s scores of writers tried to explain them and to understand their mood of rejection. On both sides of the Atlantic there was what C. E. Montague called "a more vigilant skepticism" (*Disenchantment,* 1922); he described it as

a new impatience of strident enunciations of vague, venerable, political principles; a rough instinctive application of something like the new philosophy of pragmatism to all questions; and an elated sense of the speed and completeness with which institutions and political creeds and powers apparently founded on rock can be scoured away.[15]

It was impossible to recapture the prewar mood or free the current mood from the images of the fighting and the dead. This was true even for those who had been noncombatants. The mood of futility, the shrugging of shoulders over questions of moral imperative, were in large part a consequence of the war. The postwar generation felt honestly that it had been victimized by a gross and stupid deception. Nothing genuine had come out of the war. American politicians had refused to accept their responsibility in a world league (which, as it was plotted at Versailles, seemed unworkable anyway) and had chosen isolation. The elders had made fools of themselves, had involved the young in murderous folly; how could they respect them? Nothing they would do in the future could be one-tenth as absurd as what their elders had done. Why, then, should they consider themselves responsible for the postwar world? They felt their only responsibility was to themselves. In much of the literature of the twenties there was a continuous statement of rejection; this was in part a naïve awakening to the existence of new forms of evil in the world, but it also served as an indignant protest against a civilization that had played a bad joke on itself.

"As for the faith lost by the intellectuals, there is room to wonder what sort it was, to continue serene from 1900 to 1914, and then so suddenly give way," said Gilbert Seldes (*New Republic*, October 21, 1925). The really creative forces of the last one hundred years had been defeated in the last ten: "Progress ended in the war, science in machinery; democracy died two deaths, in Bolshevism and KKK Fascism, either one sufficient to discredit representative government; education came to a climax in Dayton. Of the vaguer assumptions, liberty and the love of humanity remain in the cocked hat where they landed between 1914 and 1919. No one believes that these apotheoses are final, or even important. They are convenient and melodramatic excuses for not bothering any more about knowledge, politics, economics, and good works."

[15] Cf. *Hugh Selwyn Mauberley*, poem IV:
Frankness as never before,
disillusions as never told in the old days . . .

The young men who were disillusioned by the war were not completely surprised by what they believed to be its moral failure. To assume that they were would be to argue a startling naïveté on their part. The failure of the war as they saw it was proof of the absurdity of the forces that had caused it and of the propaganda which had helped to bring it to a successful conclusion. Of this absurdity the young men and women were already aware before the war started. Their disillusionment was sometimes an affectation; it was sometimes an excuse for freeing themselves from certain moral commitments. They pointed to the war as a blanket apology for their way of life. How could anyone possibly discredit the "queer things they did" when the world itself had just gone through a monstrous display of disorder and stupidity? With varying degrees of sincerity they justified their behavior as a resort to individual substitutes for a morality that had lost its prestige.

One of the most important distinctions in any society is that between the normal and the abnormal. The distinction is similar to that made between good and evil, or virtue and vice. Such adjectives as "queer," "eccentric," "unsafe," are applied to those who rebel against society or who, whether willingly or not, are guilty of transgressions. There is a norm for each aspect of life—a sexual norm, an economic norm, a norm of right opinion, a norm of social etiquette, and of course a general social correctness. There are also forms of "correct" language to express these forms of normality and to measure the exact degree of balance necessary in society.

Cases of isolated protest or exile do not discredit accepted forms but only give them the chance of vigorous defense. From time to time, however, violent upheavals against the social pattern do occur—cultural panics or crises; then the accepted view of what is normal is severely questioned. World War I was such a crisis—a crisis in moral management really, since it was largely denounced by the disillusioned generation as a succession of stupid, bungling acts. During a period of cultural crisis the line between normal and abnormal is hard to define, and harder to keep consistently in view; a free criticism of normality sets in, a profound doubt of its validity. Generations are "lost" because they dissociate themselves from custom and habit and distrust their past.

No examination of the influence of World War I is complete without at least a mention of Ford Madox Ford's four novels in the Tietjens cycle.[16] Ford proposed the series as a study of "the world as it culminated in the war." Though his hero participates in the war, has his taste of fighting, and is wounded, these are not war novels in the usual sense, primarily because Tietjens is not a naïve young man who is shocked out of all illusions by the violence of his experience. Tietjens, as Ford planned him, must be a man of the class that—in the opinion of most soldiers—had "caused the war to happen"; yet he must be severely critical of that class, sometimes insufferably so, righteous and correct to the point of exasperation. He is, therefore, not a hero in any simple sense: "My character would be deprived of any glory. He was to be just enough of a man of action to get into the trenches and do what he was told." Tietjens' overbearing conscientiousness is in itself a means of gauging the defections of his class; he is an honorable man, and his meticulous honesty makes the men of his class uncomfortable: "You see, in such a world as this an idealist—or perhaps it's only a sentimentalist—must be stoned to death."

Since Tietjens belongs to the ruling class—the men who administer affairs—the problem of responsibility for the war is inevitably associated with his unyielding and literal code. "Some do not" give in to temptations; some men *are* honorable. But they are so few that one is almost certain that Tietjens is a lone and curious survivor of an older moral type. The war itself is apparently run on no principle at all; Tietjens' behavior in it is both an exasperation and a corrective in terms of its management. It is above all an incisive commentary upon the war's role in revealing the Old Gang as finally and irremediably culpable. Tietjens' refusal to divorce his wife or to take a mistress (some do not do even this) is a commentary upon one other convention very closely related to the others. The first three novels give in sharp and awesome detail the collapse of all conventions; *The Last Post,* the fourth, is a continuation of the other three as well as a summing-up of the process begun before the war. It reveals the postwar world in a nightmare of nonsequiturs and irrational scenes. The collapse of Tietjens' system of values is complete. From the start Tietjens is doomed, but his doom is a telling epitaph for the society responsible for running the war and morally culpable for the anarchy following upon the peace.

No American literature of the 1920s came quite so close to the heart of the cultural issue that Ford's tetralogy so brilliantly documents. The

[16] *Some Do Not* (1924), *No More Parades* (1925), *A Man Could Stand Up* (1926), and *The Last Post* (1928).

interpretations given by Edith Wharton and Dos Passos were both, in their way, extremes of a naïve view. The details of Boyd's fiction, of the play *What Price Glory,* even of Erich Remarque's *All Quiet on the Western Front* (a best-seller in translation in 1929), added up to a simple—an over-simple—thesis: that war was dirty, unreasonable, and mean; that the ruling class was somehow guilty of fraud (the nature of the guilt was never quite understood; it was largely felt). The principal implication of all but a small share of the war literature, however, was that those who had come through it could not go back to their home towns, to their former way of life. The American feeling was perhaps even more desperate than the English or French. Exile, expatriation, became a necessary *mise en scène* in which to measure and describe the war's effect.

6. The Text: Hemingway's
The Sun Also Rises

The Sun Also Rises is Hemingway's best war book. In a very real sense all of Hemingway's fiction is war fiction, even *To Have and Have Not,* written when Hemingway was deeply involved in the proletarian-Loyalist issue of the Spanish Civil War. A brilliant achievement in organizing postwar tensions, pressures, and situations, *The Sun Also Rises* offers a concentrated picture of the 1920s. In its shifts of scene, its maneuvering of dramatis personae, its precision of narrative detail, it is like a dramatic poem. *The Sun Also Rises* is also a moral novel, accommodating itself to the need for moral improvisation with a remarkable sense of the correct and proper moral tone a novel written at this time (1926) about these people in these places must have.

Krebs of "Soldier's Home" is surrounded by people who remind him of his intolerable past (are, in their deeply serious way, that past), but the expatriates in Paris and Pamplona are almost entirely isolated from their pasts. Only occasionally does the "normal world" impinge on their isolation, and then only to put a seal upon it. There is the casual incident of Chapter IV, for example: Woolsey and Krum, fellow journalists in Paris, ride in a cab with Jake Barnes for a short while. They are family men; they live in the suburbs; their ambition is to live in the country and have a car. Like so many Americans in Paris in the 1920s, they are suburban middle-class husbands and fathers, mildly curious about the dives across the river ("The Dingo, that's the great place, isn't it?"), but inhabitants of another world. They and the Knights of Columbus tourists on the trip to Spain are curious specimens of normality, which serve to underscore the separateness of Jake Barnes and his friends.

The major settings are Paris and Pamplona. The tragic motif is this isolation; it is an isolation described and symbolized with such exhaustive detail that eventually its reality becomes the very medium through which the novel's idea is actualized. The isolation is, first of all, caused by the wound inflicted upon Jake in the war (" 'I got hurt in the war,' I said. 'Oh, that dirty war.' "). The wound has made him impotent; impotence in its several forms is seen in the behavior of Jake's friends. In addition to sexual deficiency, the impotence of Jake leads to other kinds of failure: Brett's failure of sexual adjustment, Mike's collapse into the vulgar and strident baiting of Robert Cohn, in general the absence or failure of normal relationships of any kind.

In the Paris scenes of the novel, the isolation of Jake and his friends from normality is portrayed in several ways. The night life of Paris, for example, whose casualness is murderous and chaotic, has no reasonable explanation; it "happens" and the events have a quality of aimless sequence.

The lack of order, of useful and meaningful event, is in itself a kind of impotence. The existence of fake expatriates is also important: Robert Prentiss, the rising young novelist, Mrs. Braddocks, Frances Clyne, Cohn himself. Jake says of them, "This whole show makes me sick, is all." [17] In one of those scenes which so brilliantly mark the novel, Jake, with a prostitute as a companion, watches Brett come in with a crowd of young homosexuals:

> I could see their hands and newly washed, wavy hair in the light from the door. The policeman standing by the door looked at me and smiled. They came in. As they went in, under the light I saw white hands, wavy hair, white faces, grimacing, gesturing, talking. With them was Brett. She looked very lovely, and she was very much with them.

These perversions are sexual paradoxes of great significance; they are a commentary on, as they are a consequence of, the impotence.

[17] Note that the writers for whom most critics have a continuing respect were able to distinguish between the fake and the real. The distinctions drawn between genuine and pretentious expatriates should quiet those who protest against expatriation as a whole.

Most conspicuous of the failures is Robert Cohn, the incurable romantic, who accepts literally words, feelings, attitudes long mistrusted by Jake and his friends. Cohn had "read and reread *The Purple Land* . . . a very sinister book if read too late in life. It recounts splendid imaginary amorous adventures of a perfect English gentleman in an intensely romantic land, the scenery of which is very well described. . . . Cohn, I believe, took every word of *The Purple Land* as literally as though it had been an R. G. Dun report." He displays the same literalness in his reaction to his affair with Brett, and his naïve ignorance of the true pathos of Brett and Jake is both amusing and irritating.

In the face of the necessities forced upon him by the several levels of isolation (forms of impotence), Jake fashions for himself a pattern of discretion and restraint. In terms antithetically opposed to Cohn's behavior (Cohn is both irritant and contrast in the design of the novel), Jake must practice a code, must suppress anger and fear, must accept his condition as though it were normal, certainly inevitable. This he does not always find it easy to do: at night, for example, it is much harder to accept his fate. Nor is it easy for him to be "on demand" when Brett needs his help because of some scrape.[18] But this is absolutely necessary. The wound has forced him into a position where survival and sanity depend on his balance and self-restraint. In Paris, therefore, he moves in a world as confused and tangled as his own "problem." He must again and again repeat the circumstances of his life and must somehow hold on:

> I had the feeling as in a nightmare of it all being something repeated, something I had been through and that now I must go through again.

The confusion of Paris is a repetition of the violence (in the scale of emotional tension, at any rate) of the war experience; he must bear the one as a reminder of the other.

This in itself makes the novel a meaningful commentary on the pathos of the postwar experience, and is a very real measure of the depth of that experience. But *The Sun Also Rises* moves out of Paris. There is a lighthearted and surface quality of the fishing trip with Bill Gorton in the Spanish Pyrenees. Here there is no Brett, no Cohn. The Burguete "interlude" is a temporary return to an idyllic childhood experience,

---

[18] "That was it. Send a girl off with one man. Introduce her to another to go off with him. Now go and bring her back. And sign the wire with love. That was it all right."

but it is a reversion of adults, not a resumption of childhood; the cold wine, the fishing, the quiet of the surroundings, the wisecracking of Gorton, all are an adult version of Nick Adams and "The Three Day Blow," complete with topical allusions, bravado, and humor brought strictly up to date.[19] But it does not last. A telegram from Cohn returns Jake to the responsibilities and the tensions of his former world.

The next scene is Pamplona, Spain. Certain differences are clear: Pamplona is a small city; the occasion is a fiesta, a religious celebration; the principal events are the fiesta itself and the bullfights that mark its close. Jake Barnes and his crowd move into a place that is to offer them both contrast and opportunity. In the course of events a Spaniard is killed in the *encierro,* or the running of the bulls. He is given a religious burial, and his friends and fellow workers march in the funeral procession. The church is open to Jake and Brett, but neither is comfortable there; Brett is in fact turned away because she does not wear a hat. In the streets again, at the height of the festival,

> Some dancers formed a circle around Brett and started to dance. . . . Brett wanted to dance but they did not want her to. They wanted her as an image to dance around.

With an almost uncanny sense of the relevance of situation, Hemingway in this novel always reduces the religious suggestions, evocations, hints, to their secular equivalents. The church is like other institutions of the past, now unacceptable, though regretted, because it no longer provides certain securities. In the final chapters the problem is to offer a secular equivalent of both morality and religion. This Hemingway finds in the dramatic, ceremonial, and traditional design of the bullfight. The bullfight does not profoundly alter the behavior of Jake's crowd. Nevertheless it gives Jake "that disturbed emotional feeling that always comes after a bullfight, and the feeling of elation that comes after a good bullfight."

There is another kind of secular ritual experience in Brett's flirtation with Romero and her final release of him. In these scenes—along with Cohn's comic-pathetic defense of his true love against Jake, "the pimp"—we have a drama played out in terms of the three-act tragedy of the *corrida.* The values of the one are matched against the character

[19] "You're an expatriate. You've lost your touch with the soil. You get precious. Fake European standards have ruined you. You drink yourself to death. You become obsessed by sex. You spend all your time talking, not working. You are an expatriate, see? You hang around cafés."

of the other; and Brett's renunciation of Romero is a positive moral act.

It is a startling thing to see Jake in the barroom in Madrid reviewing for one final time his relationship with Brett. Readers have almost always reacted with distaste to Brett's words summing up the meaning her act has for herself. But we should remember that the entire moral drama has been worked out in isolation from the decorum that engenders our distaste. Brett does not leave Madrid with all her problems happily resolved; her sense of loss is as strong as it ever was. It is a mistake to assume that her renunciation comes from or leads to a profound change in her experience. Nor is Jake any more secure after having witnessed the renunciation. In a few scenes, however, a thoroughly secular design, a traditional pattern of ritualized behavior, has touched the lives of these expatriates and passed judgment upon them, forcing them to a realization of their lot, even in a small way to an essential sacrifice. This experience—or rather, Hemingway's description of it—forces our attention once more upon the code itself, with its sources in the violence and the unreasonableness of the war, and finally upon Jake's own admirable discretion and restraint in the face of his own need.

The Sun Also Rises is not a cheap exploitation of postwar interest in immoralities, but a perceptive portrayal of the human condition within the rigorous limits of circumstance which the postwar world had imposed. It reveals the men and women who lived in this closed, secular world isolated from tradition for what they genuinely were; above all it shows them working painfully for an adjustment, with all the problems of adjustment increased and intensified.

For a moment of his career, Hemingway saw the human condition in starkly honest postwar terms. He angrily brushed aside conventional palliatives, dismissed the shams of literary explanation, and obstinately risked what seemed absurdities and obscenities to reach the naked, raw, quivering core of human fear and hysteria. His overpowering honesty produced a work of art that is at the same time a literal ordering of a historical-emotional experience. As a result his major characters, Brett and Jake, are often pathetic creatures, and almost always ridiculous to the descendants of Woolsey and Krum.

As on several other literary occasions of the decade, *The Sun Also Rises* joins art and history precisely at the point where the sensitive person is shown to be deeply and personally affected by headline event. More than *The Enormous Room,* this novel sums up the war account; it is as pathetically honest, yet as rigorously *true,* as *A Son at the Front* is wishfully false. Hemingway and Mrs. Wharton were equally insulted by history; but Hemingway did not have the comforts and mitigations that sustained her. *A Son at the Front* looks back to a time when its hero believed in sculpture and painting and other symbols of a culture; *The Sun Also Rises* looks forward to the time when man either would be existentially honest or would flagrantly disabuse his friends of his sincerity. *The Sun Also Rises* is in its essential integrity the twentieth-century development of *Ecclesiastes*, from which its title is correctly derived. It is better (in its special and limited role in the 1920s) than Hemingway was ever again to be.

III

THE VERY YOUNG

1. *Vanity Fair*: Handbook for the Sophisticate

IT IS hard to imagine a magazine more appropriate to the decade than *Vanity Fair*. Its pages were filled with pertinent references to the customs of the time, parodies of its pretensions, serious discussion of its intellectual interests (or the lack of them), and, in the advertisements, appeals to the wealthy and the snobbish. Its Hall of Fame celebrated the men and women who, in whatever field, were making life less dull and more enchanting: truculent phrasemakers like H. L. Mencken and George Jean Nathan; prophets like D. H. Lawrence ("Because in his novels he has had new and stimulating things to say about the struggle between the sexes"); critics like Ezra Pound, Aldous Huxley, Clive Bell, and Alexander Woollcott; novelists like Sinclair Lewis, Theodore Dreiser, Virginia Woolf; and humorists and cartoonists like Robert Benchley, Donald Ogden Stewart, George Herriman (creator of Krazy Kat), and John Held, Jr. ("Because as a caricaturist he invented the modern flapper").

Huxley appeared in almost every issue (beginning in January 1921), dissecting and vivisecting morals, religion, and the elementary schools. D. H. Lawrence contributed frequently, from February 1924. Sherwood Anderson wrote on everything from the need for immaturity in a writer's style to the value of the small town for the American conscience. Kenneth Burke wrote on Freud and literature, Tristan Tzara on Dada, Dorothy Richardson and Ezra Pound on Paris and London, Willa Cather on Nexö. The great wrote about each other: Gertrude Stein on Picasso and Jo Davidson; Edmund Wilson on T. S. Eliot; T. S. Eliot on Joyce and Lawrence. The book reviews were written for

86

a time by Edmund Wilson, then by John Peale Bishop; Dorothy Parker and Heywood Broun took care of the drama; Walter Lippmann explained politics and pondered over the lack of interest in them. Robert Benchley discussed a reissue of Veblen's *The Theory of the Leisure Class* in 1919, and in 1920 offered "Einstein's Theory for the Lay-Mind in Simple Terms."

The subscribers were kept informed on the latest in the arts: there were discussions of futurism, of modern music (Dorothy Richardson on George Antheil), of *vers libre*, of the symbolists, of Joyce's new "Work in Progress," of Apollinaire, of *The Waste Land*. The "lively arts" were more than adequately covered: several pertinent studies of American jazz were offered, by Edmund Wilson, Gilbert Seldes, John Peale Bishop, Carl Van Vechten, Virgil Thomson; E. E. Cummings wrote about the circus, the burlesque, the musical revue; Seldes and Patrick Kearney discussed the importance of the comic strip; Jim Tully interviewed Mack Sennett, Rudolph Valentino, Elinor Glyn, and Clara Bow; and Walter Winchell admired the girls in Broadway chorus lines.

Among the issues most frequently debated in *Vanity Fair* was the overwhelming stupidity of Prohibition (by 1928 this was a matter of political as well as of moral concern). Other topics were the American fondness for crazes and easy cures (coué-ism, mah-jong, the crossword puzzle, the marathon dance, psychoanalysis); censorship and evangelism (the "blue-nose" crusades were unanimously condemned); the "mail-order colleges"; and occasionally the vulgarity of American "spenders," both in New York and abroad ("The chief objection to [wealth] lies in the idiocy with which it is being spent").

Perhaps its most successful offerings were the parodies, the cartoons, the humorous treatment of customs and pretensions. The generally light tone of its discussion of extremes of behavior was at least less pompous than more serious and more "distinguished" studies. John Peale Bishop thought parody an effective kind of criticism (June 1922); and the examples offered usually bore him out. Donald Ogden Stewart rewrote "Bedtime Stories for Grown-Ups" (April 1921) in the styles of Sinclair Lewis, James Branch Cabell, and Theodore Dreiser; Samuel Hoffenstein contributed "Love in Lettuce, Ohio: A Drama Recounted in the Manner of the Realistic Middle-Western Novelist" (September 1924); E. E. Cummings wrote on what would happen "when Calvin Coolidge Laughed" (April 1925):

> On Wall Street . . . Coca-Cola tobogganed in eight minutes, from nine hundred decimal point three to decimal point six zeros seven

four five, wiping out at one fell swoop the solidly founded fortunes of no less than two thousand two hundred and two pillars of society.

In another issue (March 1927) Cummings added to the magazine's growing list of parodies of psychoanalysis and its practitioners; Nancy Boyd (Edna St. Vincent Millay) suggested some new turns in conversation (March 1922): " 'You have heard, perhaps, . . . Mr. S. Freud, author of the popular ballad entitled, "Tell Me What You Dream and I Will Tell You What You Want"?' " Edgar Dalrymple Perkins offered, in the manner of Lowell Schmaltz, a defense of American culture: "Well, a noted savant has already pointed out that the good old U.S.A. is way ahead in the three great A's, Architecture, Advertising, and Athletics, as well as in another department that gets two initials all to itself, Musical Revues." Another sketch (June 1925), by "Myrtle Mapelet," discussing the work of Oswald Brockle, "America's Latest Greatest Artist," described a "great dada composition":

> . . . 14" x 7¾", Beaver Board, painted pink, to which is appliquéd 3 sprays of pussy willow, a razor blade, a snapshot of Gilda Gray taken in 1918, page 3 of the *Congressional Record,* and a teaspoonful of Worcestershire sauce.

John Riddell parodied fashions in the American short story, as these were displayed in E. J. O'Brien's annual anthologies (April 1929). Among his parodies was the "gloomy Midwestern story," which concluded, "She broke her arm at the elbow, just to hear it snap."

The magazine skillfully combined a spirit of mockery with a proper attention to its publisher's worries about what "that old lady in Dubuque might think." [1] It was sophisticated and philistine, and its advertisements appealed to both tastes.

No aspect of the decade was more thoroughly burlesqued or more seriously considered than the behavior and affectations of the younger generation. They lived all over Manhattan, at both ends of Fifth Avenue, and disported themselves in a manner that amused *Vanity Fair*'s humorists, impressed its book reviewers, and provoked replies and analyses from its sophisticated journalists. Hoffenstein, parodying the "advanced" thought of the Village in "You Know Me, Neurosis" (January 1925), gave some examples:

> IRMA: Ah, pure thought in music! Wonderful! Do you think we shall ever have it in sex—the pure idea without the emotion?

---

[1] This was publisher Crowninshield's phrase which *The New Yorker* later amended to "Not for the lady from Dubuque."

BUBESCO: Why not? The child of the future will be the sum of two concepts.

*   *   *

[An almost nude nude woman enters]
IPSHINSKI: Have you a lover?
WOMAN: No, he is an intellectual. He has talked me out of everything.

Dr. I. L. Nascher, writing on "Esthesiomania" (April 1919), described it as "a form of insanity marked by deranged moral feeling and by purposeless eccentricities," but was most concerned to condemn the fake bohemians, the faddists of the avant garde, who

> imitate and exaggerate the eccentricities of well-known characters to attract attention to themselves. . . . They are readily swayed by argument or threat, are not inherently vicious or immoral, but like the high-grade moron, they lack a sense of responsibility and obligation to society. They are studiously negligent in their appearance; talk volubly on art, music, and literature . . . their whole life is a sham.

The age of the "new generation" ranged from twelve to thirty; it was best that the flapper be from seventeen to twenty-one (one of Fitzgerald's notes described the ideal flapper as "lovely and expensive and about nineteen"); the young man should be in his twenties. He might be a bit younger, even an undergraduate in an Ivy League college (few if any of the flappers' escorts attended anything less); at worst, he should remember his college experience as something quite recently past. Older people "joined the dance" but were a bit ludicrous in their performances.

The most precocious member of the younger generation, young even for *its* youth, was Elizabeth Benson, who at twelve and thirteen wrote three essays for *Vanity Fair* (November 1926, April and September 1927). The first was "A Child's Impressions of Lewis, Mencken, Cabell, Arlen, and Other Literary Figures." In the second, she offered "The Truth about the Younger Generation" and her defense of it:

> When boys and girls of the adolescent and post-adolescent age are granted an audience with their elders, they deliberately manufacture evidence of their wildness merely to hold the attention of their elders.

"We can scarcely be blamed," she said in the third essay, if we profit from the examples set by our elders:

> We studied Freud, argued Jung, checked our dreams by Havelock Ellis, and toyed lightly with Adler. And all these authorities warned

us of the danger in repressing our normal instincts and desires. . . .
Nature, and war, and prohibition, and feminism, and psychoanalysis
and new fashions in dress; a tottering religion, imitation of our elders,
automobiles, radios and free money, the industrial era and a new physical education—these forces have had their hand in baking the pie out
of which, like the four and twenty blackbirds, has sprung the younger
generation of today.

With which brilliant metaphor the thirteen-year-old essayist concluded
her explanation of the strange behavior of her contemporaries.

Floyd Dell, more than three times her age but not out of sympathy
with the generation, spoke of the "moon-calf," or "The Imaginative
Young Man" (February 1921):

He never quite conforms to the current conventions of male attire.
. . . For his contemptuous difference in appearance is only the outward sign of his contemptuous difference in thought and belief and
ambition to all the rest of the world. . . . [Moon-calves] despise democracy. Besides, they don't want the world made safe. They want
it made dangerous. They have a poor opinion of the world, and the
faster it goes to the devil, the better they are pleased.

Older citizens of Vanity Fair, casting a not unkind eye upon the behavior of the youngsters, generally forgave them for having been born
into a decade and a world to which the oldsters had only too eagerly
conformed. "Society seems to be going through a process of reconstruction," said Richard Le Gallienne (January 1924), "and the process, as
it has always been, is disquieting. But the modern woman and man
alike may eventually come out of it, none the worse for having kicked
over the traces and jazzed around the Maypole with unbecoming and
ostentatious levity."

Occasionally there were peevish complaints about the waste of talent
and youth. "The Smart-Aleck," said Walter Prichard Eaton (June
1927), ignores "the entire contribution of the church to Western civilization, the foundation of America, or the religious stability of the
Puritans, the whole psychological mystery of Man, who has always
demanded some sort of religious outlet." (The Smart-Aleck who inspired this peevish retort was Sinclair Lewis, who, while not a member
of the younger generation, encouraged many to leave Main Street for
New York.) "Only ignorant passions and recriminations," wrote
Eaton, could come from Lewis's attack upon institutions because "he
doesn't really know the thing he is attacking, doesn't understand it,
hasn't the necessary sympathy and seriousness to criticize it effectively."

Both the attacks on and defenses of the very young were superficial in the extreme. Their adventures were often good copy, especially when experienced by one of their more articulate and talented spokesmen. Fitzgerald had, of course, the most glittering reputation of them all; in 1920, when *This Side of Paradise* was published, he was twenty-three. The book "makes us feel very old," said Heywood Broun in the *New York Herald Tribune*. It had actually been written a few years earlier, then revised and refurbished; and some of its pages (especially the poems) dated from Fitzgerald's Princeton years. He described an early version of it (called "The Romantic Egotist") in a letter to Edmund Wilson (January 10, 1918):

> It rather damns much of Princeton but its [*sic*] nothing to what it thinks of men and human nature in general. I can most nearly describe it by calling it a prose, modernistic Childe Harolde and really if Scribner takes it I know I'll wake some morning and find the debutantes have made me famous over night. I really believe that no one else could have written so searchingly the story of the youth of our generation.

The true portrait of the debutantes and their escorts that came from his pen made him famous overnight; and in the novels and short stories that followed, every conceivable issue, trait, dilemma of the very young was explored. He always wrote about himself or about his friends, and his vision of the young showed them in a hundred poses, from ludicrous to pathetic. As his work progressed it became more mature, sharper, freer of the slickness that had first made him popular; until, when *The Great Gatsby* appeared (1925), critics were caught in the act of regretting the very deficiencies that had all but disappeared. Paul Rosenfeld's penetrating criticism of Fitzgerald was printed in February 1925, two months before Gatsby arrived on the scene; what Rosenfeld said was true for the most part of Fitzgerald's work prior to *Gatsby:*

> What one does affirm, however, and affirm with passion, is that the author of *This Side of Paradise* and of the jazzy stories does not sustainedly perceive his girls and men for what they are, and tends to invest them with precisely the glamour with which they in pathetic assurance rather childishly invest themselves.

John Peale Bishop, Fitzgerald's "artistic conscience," wrote (*Vanity Fair*, October 1921):

> He has an amazing grasp of the superficialities of the men and women about him, but he has not yet a profound understanding of

their motives, either intellectual or passionate. Even with his famous flapper, he has as yet failed to show that hard intelligence, that intricate emotional equipment upon which her charm depends, so that Gloria [of *The Beautiful and Damned*] . . . remains a little inexplicable, a pretty, vulgar shadow of her prototype.

These were the very qualities of Fitzgerald's work that endeared him to his readers. The women, from Isabelle Borgé (*This Side of Paradise*) to Daisy Fay (*The Great Gatsby*) and Nicole Warren (*Tender Is the Night*), improved in portraiture, but Rosalind Connage (*This Side of Paradise*)—the first of Fitzgerald's attempts to write off the nightmare of his near-failure to marry the girl—appealed to his public, and Gloria Gilbert (*The Beautiful and Damned*) did too, perhaps *because* she was superficially (though accurately) drawn. He had only a few things to say, or to repeat, about each of his young women, but they were almost always the things they wanted to hear. They were lovely; they were expensive; they were nineteen.[2]

This is not to say that Fitzgerald monopolized the province of the very young and its interests. There were many variants of the young man and the young woman in the literature of the decade. Some were self-consciously serious or even morbid; in revolt against Davenport or Omaha, they went to Chicago, and there they eventually rebelled against the rawness of that city and moved on to New York, where they found some refuge from civilization in the United States. Others were cynical and overbearing, dreading and despising the middle class with a hatred strong enough to destroy it. Still others were sophisticated and bored in the manner of a latter-day Huysmans or Wilde. In every case the young man or woman was fresh and naïve; freed of the preconceptions of their elders, he or she experimented, whether in utmost seriousness or extravagant frivolity, with new modes of action and attitude.

The novels may well have had for their subtitle "The Young Cynic as Hero." The characters became cynics very early in their lives, long before they had had time to get over being naïve. They read many books, all but a few of them too difficult for them to understand but not beyond their talent for quoting and using. They were, in short, not infrequently ridiculous and a bit pathetic.

[2] See "Descriptions of Girls," in Fitzgerald's Note-Books, *The Crack-Up*, edited by Edmund Wilson (1945).

2. The Young Cynic and the Moon-Calf

THE HERO of Ben Hecht's novels is a disgusted young man; everywhere he sees people and institutions designed to trap him, to cut him down to their size. He is a "philosopher," fond of commenting upon the dreary stupidity of his inferiors and of quoting the "best authorities" he has read. The authorities he knows best are Nietzsche and Veblen, though he also remembers the titles of many books. He likes only himself and is afraid only that the people who come near him will prevent his self-realization. Everything that happens in a society is a barrier to the completion of that self-realization. He takes pride in his talent for shocking people. He is a writer, an artist of sorts, and is therefore entitled to a life different from that of the ordinary man.

Having decided upon his unique and precious identity as a soul set apart, the young man acts and talks out his role. It is mostly talk, epigrams fashioned from his rejection of the customs of his inferiors. Since he believes in nothing, these epigrams come easily; he has only to pervert ordinary truth. He has an enemy who both symbolizes and literally believes in everything the cynical hero despises.

The cheap Nietzschean polarity of *Erik Dorn* (1921) is a typical device for dramatizing the young hero's situation. Erik is actually thirty at the novel's beginning, but his age only makes him more "tired" than the younger Dell or Fitzgerald hero. George Hazlitt is the enemy. In him are to be found, in their extreme forms, all the conventional virtues; and he literally hates anyone who does not practice them. Virtue hardens into convention; convention is the basis for legal action and social order. To Hazlitt, the unvirtuous are disorderly:

> Disorder he thought not only illegal, but debasing. . . . His intelligence, clinging like some militant parasite to the stability of life, resented all agitations, material or spiritual, all violators who violated the equilibrium to which he was fastened.

This upstanding knight of conventional virtue, of order, and of unquestioning faith pursues the hero, until, in Germany after the war, Hazlitt and Dorn fight it out. Hazlitt, in uniform, defends the virtue of his woman against Dorn, a vile seducer. Hazlitt is killed, Dorn exonerated.

But it is characteristic of the Hecht protagonist that he takes no joy from his escape from death. Believing in nothing, he corrupts those who are attracted to him. The women who sleep with him are offended by his quick accesses of boredom; his cynicism has made him emotionally impotent. Invariably the hero suffers isolation because he cannot tolerate close contact.

The cynic comes full circle. He returns to the city he has left, and he is left alone in it. In the end the spectacle he has so often rejected and scorned is all he has left. The meek will inherit the earth; all social organizations are planned to protect the weak against the strong:

> The race must protect its weak, so it invents laws to curb the instincts and power of its strong. And we obey the laws—a matter of adjusting ourselves ludicrously to our weaknesses and endowing these adjustments with high names.

It is the task of the young cynic as hero persistently to ridicule his enemy. There is much of this kind of rhetoric in Hecht's novels. None of it equals so much as a line from *Prufrock,* but it is an index of the pain of self-adjustment. Take, for example, the struggle of Kent Savaron, hero of *Humpty Dumpty* (1924); his only enemy is the stupidity of others, whose "life-denying codes" protect them. If he cannot destroy them, he can at least try to prevent them from destroying him. Meanwhile the enemy provides him with an amusing spectacle: pretense of virtue, affectation of culture, rituals of love, marriage, christenings, funerals. It is dramatically fitting that Savaron, hating all this, should risk defilement by it. He falls in love with the daughter of one of the most pompous of conventional men. He must, to save himself, get her away from her family, force her to renounce them in his presence, "their ideas, their attitudes, their little half-decayed souls, their smugness." This she does, and Savaron makes off with her in triumph. But in her great love for him she begins to work against his deep hatred; she is convinced that "His invective was a hangover, an adolescent characterization which her love would eventually dispel." Gradually, insidiously, her family returns; worse, she herself is secretly trying to make him "normal":

> She dreamed of the day when his violent points of view would vanish and when his contempt for the things she inwardly accepted as the necessary standards and furniture of life would also go.

The "Rotarian ritual" of a baby shower proves the culminating indignity. After it, he is determined to leave the woman who has tried to

reform him, to "make him a stranger to his thoughts." Early one morning, after having walked the snow-covered streets all night, he kills
himself.

The young cynic in Hecht's novels must always come to the shocking
realization that he is in danger of becoming normal. This is the only
wisdom he acquires. His heroics are otherwise entirely negative; his
enemy is invariably a caricature of normality and convention, ugly and
ludicrous, after the manner of George Grosz's postwar drawings of Ber-
liners. The hero himself has nothing really significant to offer; he distrusts affection, resents love, is wary of flattery, denies everything. At
the same time he possesses nothing really except his "cleverness," a
knowledge of men and women borrowed from a shelf of books that
only in the 1920s could be found together. His energy is utilized to
reject, to destroy, the only social forms he knows. He attacks them
from a position that is a weird mixture of Nietzsche, Wilde, Freud, and
Huysmans. When he loves—as occasionally he does—his thoughts become "poetic" ("Your breasts are white birds dreaming under the stars.
Your body is like the Queens of China parading through the moon").
In the end he is pathetically amoral, stupidly "witty," aggressively
bitter, and a *poseur* of the worst kind. As one of his acquaintances puts
it:

> "This Dorn, what is he? His writing is amusing, sometimes violent, but
> always empty. He doesn't like life much, eh? . . . He hates us all
> —reds and whites, radicals and bourgeoisie. Yet he can write in a big
> way. But he isn't a big man. He has no faith."

There were probably more Erik Dorns than Amory Blaines or Felix
Fays among the younger generation. Men of little talent but of an all-
consuming hatred, they fought both their enemies and themselves and
provided those who read about them with the thrill of vicarious cynicism. Like Kent Savaron, readers were ensnared by rituals of conformity blessed by the church and protected by law. They submitted with
some show of resignation to the social forms or shrewdly found ways of
circumventing them for their pleasure; they did not commit suicide, but
they were grateful to Savaron for having done so, in the role of their
scapegoat.

> They had come to Greenwich Village, both of them, less than a year
> ago; he from Ohio and she from Oregon. . . . They had heard—as
> who has not?—of the Village, and had come here, looking for the
> realization of some vague idea of adventure, of beauty, of joy, of free-
> dom.

Floyd Dell's Midwestern heroes and heroines go to the great cities to
find refuge from small-town, middle-class absurdities; it is a pattern
of pilgrimage common enough in the 1920s. The efforts to achieve
self-definition result in several kinds of journey: the physical one of
departure (how many dramatic scenes take place at railroad stations
in these novels!); the intellectual process of "reading one's way out"
(Nietzsche, Pater, Wilde, Shaw, Ibsen, perhaps even Baudelaire and
Rimbaud, in translation); [3] the "passionate pilgrimage," by means of
which the young man and woman find the right answer after several
experiments in properly unconventional experience. Whatever the way,
there is always the one persistent desire, to defeat the older generation
and condemn its institutions. Since for Dell these are more obviously
and painfully unholy in the smaller towns, the heroism of his characters begins at the railroad station: this is the act of physical renunciation, for which an agent provides a one-way ticket to Chicago. The
progress is almost invariably eastward, to New York or Paris if possible, to Chicago at least.

Felix Fay of *The Moon-Calf* (1920) is a bookish young man; his
first discovery is that the books do not match the real people in his
real town; this is a "rude shock." Then he encounters bigotry and intolerance, which he associates with religion; they seem invariably to
accompany the practice of religion. As he enters adolescence (for
Dell's heroes always the most exhilarating and important stage of life),
he begins his active campaign against his elders. He reads the lectures
of Robert G. Ingersoll and becomes an atheist and a nonconformist.

In time Fay meets the heroine, his female counterpart; she is an
anarchist first, a woman second. They read *Leaves of Grass* together;
then he reads her his own poetry. Not much later they begin discussing
the Girl Question; she resists his attempts to make her a "modern
woman." He is, of course, writing a novel; not surprisingly, it is to be
the story of "a revolutionary young hero [who] was dealing masterfully
with circumstances in general, and with a young woman of the bourgeoisie in particular, in just the way that Felix was finding it impossible
to do in real life."

Completion of this first stage of the young man's education is presented in the image of the railway station:

He saw again in his mind's eye, as he tramped the road, a picture of
the map on the wall of the railway station—the map with a picture of

[3] See Dell's *Intellectual Vagabondage* (1926), especially Part Two.

iron roads from all over the Middle West centering in a dark blotch
in the corner. . . . "Chicago," he said to himself.

To Chicago he goes (in *The Briary-Bush,* 1921), and here he is forced
once again to revise his views on love, marriage, and the conventional
life. He will try a "free" marriage; he will give up being a village Ingersoll, but this marriage must be different. He settles with his new-found
companion in a twelve-dollar-a-month apartment in Chicago's version
of Greenwich Village. But the arrangement does not work; the revolt
ends in unhappiness; they are not the brave, bright spirits they had
hoped to be but instead are possessive male and unhappy female.
Eventually everything is straightened out; Felix and his woman are
finally joined in the conventional bonds. They will "build their house."

Timidity dominates the young hero as Dell sees him; his distrust of
his elders is part of his fear of himself; he takes up advanced ideas because he is afraid of conventional ones. He must live in a bohemia and
talk with the other rebellious young in his effort to overcome his fears.
Some of Dell's characters go beyond this stage. In *Janet March* (1923),
for example, the heroine, heavy with child, goes to New York and
registers at the Brevoort (no prettier picture of rebellious youth than
that). Here, at the entrance to Greenwich Village, Janet finds people
"who care," who are neither dogmatic oldsters nor foolish youngsters:
"there must be some middle ground where the natural human instincts
held sway." For Dell, the revolt of the young generation was senseless
if it led merely to a rejection of the past, with nothing to replace it.
Janet and her friends will "not be like that." They will be intelligent in
their interests, not hidebound; but they will also be "very much interested in life." There is no more really conventional portrait than this.

Felix Fay and Janet March come to a conventional life in a round-
about way, the phase of rebellion being indispensable to the conclusion.
They must despise their elders before they submit to the social forms.

In most of Dell's novels the young exhaust themselves in talk; their
flirtation with the new and their revolt against the old are managed
largely on the level of words and fancies. There are, of course, crises,
when they courageously leave the place they have rejected so often in
their talk. Whatever they may do, in whatever place, the result is a
sentimental and romantic adjustment to the society which they began
by despising. The Dell story is a mild interlude in the tale of the very
young. The cynicism of his characters is quite superficial, and soon
wiped out by their eagerness to capture a conventional happiness. They

share with the people of other novels only their distrust of the forms, and that only briefly.

The young of Carl Van Vechten's novels are old before their time, have run through experiences and made adjustments with remarkable speed. "We're here because we're here, and we should be extremely silly not to make the worst of it." The father of one young man runs an advertisement:

> Wanted: a young man of good character but no moral sense. Must know three languages and possess a sense of humor. Autodidact preferred, one whose experience has led him to whatever books he has read. It is absolutely essential that he should have been the central figure in some public scandal.

One of Van Vechten's representative figures (the author smiling at himself) is Gareth Johns, the novelist of *Firecrackers* (1925).[4] He is frankly engaged in writing novels about the futility of life:

> "It doesn't seem to occur to the crowd that it is possible for an author to believe that life is largely without excuse, that if there is a God he conducts the show aimlessly, if not, indeed, maliciously, that men and women run around automatically seeking escapes from their troubles and outlets for their lusts."

It is of the utmost importance, however, to be amusing about it; the worst sin is to be serious, which is the equivalent of being stupid. Naturally enough, the most amusing incidents occur at the parties and the salons. To these Van Vechten devotes much attention; and his favorite heroine, Campaspe, witty hostess on many occasions, provides the best formula for avoiding the tedium and bad taste of being serious.

> The tragedies of life, she reflected, were either ridiculous or sordid. The only way to get the sense of this absurd, contradictory, and perverse existence into a book was to withdraw entirely from reality. . . . *On n'apprend qu'en s'amusant,* according to Sylvestre Bonnard.

If you would stay alive and continue living graciously, avoid Theodore Dreiser like the plague. If you cannot be witty yourself, at least appreciate the wit of others. The worst enemies of society are those who try to reform it or who too soberly and pessimistically make literature out of its obvious but amusing inequities.

Van Vechten had an especial fondness for Scott and Zelda Fitzgerald, who figured importantly in *Parties* (1930) as David and Rilda

[4] See Chapter VII:iii, for a discussion of his Midwestern origins.

Westlake. "They cling to each other like barnacles cling to rocks," says one of their friends. "But they want to hurt each other all the time to test their feeling." The public performances of these two were retold in the fiction of the time; the hero and heroine of both fiction and fact were held up to the public gaze as exemplary and superbly appropriate.

Fitzgerald's public self warred constantly with his writer's conscience. In his public life he accumulated debts that could be paid off only by the kind of stories his public expected of him. At one time, after a series of Long Island weekends, he owed five thousand dollars; that winter he wrote eleven stories and sold them for seventeen thousand. "I really worked hard as hell last winter," he wrote Edmund Wilson, "but it was all trash and it nearly broke my heart as well as my iron constitution." It was nearly all trash; and the wonder is that he managed so often to penetrate beneath the superficial (and horrifying) gaiety of the decade's brightest youths, to speak so well of their genuine distress.

He was not alone, except in the superiority of his talent. The problems of his youth were, with many variations, those of many other writers. Most heroes were drawn, with some directness, from life. Only Fitzgerald's life seemed to provide him with the variety and—as the decade drew to a close—the complexity of experience necessary to make something moderately good out of it. The strains and pressures of that life yielded more and more to the understanding and the integrity of the artist who sincerely wanted to find its meaning. Fitzgerald *is* representative of the decade, but not, certainly, in having clowned for its amusement. He was able, when he felt comparatively free, to see his experience as both symbolic and symptomatic. The young men and the flappers in his stories grew perceptibly older, hardened, and eventually became representative images of a class. Most important, perhaps, he wrote gracefully of them; they were not tedious egotists like Erik Dorn or self-conscious *naïfs* like Felix Fay. Fitzgerald was a successful novelist during the twenties because, as he said, he told "people that he felt as they did." In the thirties he continued to tell them, but they no longer felt that way and were not pleased to be told that they ever had.[5]

So many reflections upon the "meaning of Fitzgerald" are full of the scorn that an old grad has for the man who (like Tom Buchanan) cannot admit that he has been graduated. They neglect to consider the fact that the 1920s were a brilliant opportunity for evaluating under-

[5] Cf. "Babylon Revisited" (written in 1931): Marion Peters' feeling about Charlie Wales, a reformed sinner of the 1920s.

graduate experience. In its freedom from any too systematic or im-
perious moral scruple and in view of a most remarkable succession of
national absurdities, the decade offered Fitzgerald one of the greatest
literary chances a good writer has ever had. In his best work he judged
and defined with the utmost clarity the decade's worst errors of taste
as well as its most sincere moral gestures.

3. "Her Sweet Face and My New Clothes"

As an undergraduate at Princeton in 1916, Fitzgerald became interested in modern literature. He read "voraciously in Tarkington, Shaw, Wells, Butler, and, above all, Compton Mackenzie," says
Arthur Mizener in *The Far Side of Paradise.* "He was enchanted by
Youth's Encounter and *Sinister Street* [6] and began a period of seeing
himself as Michael Fane and all his friends as appropriate subsidiary
figures. Wilson and his other New York friends fitted in admirably,
as did Father Fay, who took him to dine in suave splendor at the
Lafayette, and got confused in Fitzgerald's exuberant imagination with
Mr. Viner."

Edmund Wilson and John Peale Bishop, college friends of Fitzgerald,
both pointed out the similarities of *This Side of Paradise* to *Sinister
Street.* "We have read your delicate burlesque of Compton Mackenzie's
Sinister Street and feel that you have a gift in this direction," Bishop
wrote (March 23, 1920); Wilson, writing (November 21, 1919) before its publication, said that Fitzgerald's novel "ought to be a classic
in a class with *The Young Visiters* [by Daisy Ashford]. . . . Your
hero is an unreal imitation of Michael Fane who was himself unreal.
. . . As an intellectual Amory is a fake of the first water and I read
his views on art, politics, religion, and society with more riotous mirth
than I should care to have you know. . . . Cultivate a universal irony
and do read something other than contemporary British novelists."
Though the criticisms of *This Side of Paradise* were entirely warranted,
the novel achieved great popularity; like *Sinister Street* and Stephen
Vincent Benét's *The Beginning of Wisdom,* it took the undergraduate
scene seriously, or at least gave a detailed description of campus life.

There are obvious parallels with Mackenzie's novel: Michael Fane's
youth, his experiences at Oxford, his growing dissatisfaction with his

[6] In England, the two volumes of Compton Mackenzie's novel were published
under the title *Sinister Street.*

elders and with those of his own generation who still believed in them, his romantic flirtations, his experiences with "evil," and his own descent into the "dark night of the soul." [7] Unlike Amory Blaine, Michael has little trouble adjusting to the preparatory school to which he goes, but otherwise there are many similar details: Michael dances fourteen times in one evening with his "first love, Muriel," and he is enchanted by her "porcelain-blue eyes and the full bow of her lips and the slimness and girlishness of her"; the Anglican Father Viner consults with Michael over religion and the need for faith, with apparently as much and as little success as Monsignor Darcy has with Amory: Michael Fane "could acquire nothing more positive than a gentle skepticism of the value of every other form of thought."

In the undergraduate life at Oxford the parallel is most clear; Oxford and Princeton are scarcely alike, though the undergraduates have similar views of the extracurricular life and of classroom examinations. There are many pauses in each novel for contemplation and debate upon the intellectual and spiritual life, though Michael's friends seem to have a clearer notion than Amory's of what they are talking about.

In the final section of *Sinister Street* the parallels seem slight and remote, though Fitzgerald must have had them well in mind when he described Amory's vision of the devil in the harlot's room in New York. There are similarities in the early disillusion that comes to both young men; and in each case the college experience serves frequently as a point of reference. They share a fascination with the *Satyricon* of Petronius.[8] One of Michael's friends asks him if he knows the book, then speaks glowingly of it.

> "It's the only book in which anyone in my position with my brains could behold myself. Oh, it is such a nightmare. And life is a nightmare

[7] When Katherine Faraday, of Frances Newman's *The Hard-Boiled Virgin* (1926), visited Oxford, "she was distressed because the porter of Magdalen College was unable to point out the room in which Compton Mackenzie had eaten the bread and cheese of his first lunch as a member of the college."

[8] Amory Blaine includes Petronius among the "misty side streets of literature" he has explored, though it is doubtful that Fitzgerald read the *Satyricon* when he was at Princeton, at least not at the time he was writing *This Side of Paradise*. The reference to the *Satyricon* in *Sinister Street* may have been his first acquaintance with Petronius. The pathos of the heroine's use of the book, especially as it accords with Michael's own reflections on "the moral economy of the world," must have fascinated Fitzgerald. He probably read the *Satyricon* when it appeared in translation in a Modern Library edition. He was certainly interested in it when he came to the writing of *The Great Gatsby*. (See Paul L. MacKendrick, "The Great Gatsby and Trimalchio," *Classical Journal*, April 1950.)

too. After all, what is life for me? Strange dross in strange houses. Strange men and strange intimacies. Scenes incredibly grotesque and incredibly beastly. The secret vileness of human nature flung at me. Man revealing himself through individual after individual as utterly contemptible."

In the end Michael is far more mature, far less muddled, than is Amory. He has had a series of experiences with the "lower depths" quite different from Amory's descent to poverty; but both young men have needed to find a definition of human life more closely associated with human experience than that encountered as undergraduates. In each case the charm of the campus is great, as is the beauty of college associations and friends. The novels attracted their public because their authors described undergraduate life with loving care and tried to define experience and to give it meaning in terms of the very young. In their books the undergraduate becomes a young man of some interest, whose behavior merits a degree of attention.

This Side of Paradise is more striking than other novels of its kind because of its literal attention to the particulars of its youth. Stephen Vincent Benét's novel, *The Beginning of Wisdom* (1921), in its earlier chapters, seems almost an imitation.[9] Philip Sellaby's experiences at Yale are not unlike Amory Blaine's at Princeton. He enjoys undergraduate friendships, is involved in campus politics, admires a few teachers, reads continuously in the library stacks, and has his loves:

> The Stillman girl is as different as country strawberries are from soda-fountain strawberry syrup. . . . She cannot be more than seventeen, she has all the pride and witchcraft of first youth still upon her—youth ever flamboyantly wasteful in its giving when it has so inexhaustively much still to spend.

The love-making leads to an undergraduate marriage, and Sellaby ages quickly. The young bride dies suddenly before he has finished his undergraduate work, and the novel abruptly leaves Yale, to take its hero far away from the Ivy League, to Arizona and the Pacific Coast. His experiences there include a strike, film-making in Hollywood, an army training camp (like a "rigid outdoor boarding-school with reformatory manners"), and end with his job on a truck-garden ranch. He has learned "to see all things without shame or fear in the mind

[9] See page 357: " 'We're a portent and an astonishment and a horror to all the rocking-chair people who shivered over *This Side of Paradise*.' "

or sentimentality. To test by irony as one tests with burning acid for counterfeit coin." *The Beginning of Wisdom* gives only a half-memory of Yale; Benét is not at his best in those early chapters, and there is a division of purpose in the novel that makes it much less successful than *This Side of Paradise* as a record of undergraduate life.

Dos Passos' novel of Harvard, *Streets of Night* (1923), is even less like Fitzgerald's; the people in it are not undergraduates, and they are used primarily to discredit campus life. Fanshawe Macdougan, an instructor in the history of art, is a caricature of the campus aesthete, who finds that culture was, after all, more charming in Renaissance Italy than it is now, though even now it is helping us to "live less ugly, money-grabbing lives." The tragic suicide of Macdougan's friend is in its way a commentary on the failure of such a view of culture, a final rejection of the *vita contemplativa,* which the friend has so melodramatically despised. College life was never presented less attractively, nor its people with less respect, than in this parody of the Harvard aesthetes.

In the novels of the 1920s the campus was often the setting (in Percy Marks's *Flaming Youth,* for instance) for the antics and superficial debates on the morality of the college set. These were somewhat less than subtle imitations of *This Side of Paradise,* written, perhaps, in the hope that the financial success of Fitzgerald's novel might be repeated if only its subject were.

The division of *This Side of Paradise* into two books was designed to show a process of growth (in the manner of what Amory Blaine calls the "quest" books) from the "egotist" to the "personage." Amory's good friend and counselor, Monsignor Darcy ("a pagan Swinburnian young man" who had joined the Catholic Church when Amory's mother refused him), describes for him the necessary distinction between the *personality* and the *personage:*

A personality is what you thought you were. . . . Personality is a physical matter almost entirely; it lowers the people it acts on—I've seen it vanish in a long sickness. . . . Now a personage, on the other hand, gathers. He is never thought of apart from what he's done. He's a bar on which a thousand things have been hung—glittering things sometimes, as ours are; but he uses those things with a cold mentality back of them.

At one point in Amory's Princeton life he "loses his personality," loses his desire to *be* a personality, but it is not until the very end of the novel that he becomes a personage. Meanwhile he has to live through many years of wanting things and of desiring desperately to gain one or another kind of juvenile distinction. His favorite dreams (at age thirteen) are "the one about becoming a great halfback, or the one about the Japanese invasion, when he was rewarded by being made the youngest general in the world." After his first view of a musical comedy, he wants to become "an habitué of roof-gardens, to meet a girl . . . whose hair would be drenched with golden moonlight, while at his elbow sparkling wine was poured by an unintelligible waiter." In his prep-school days at St. Regis, he realizes one of his dreams: as quarterback in the game with Groton, "falling behind the Groton goal with two men on his legs, in the only touchdown of the game." He is a personality, a Big Man, before he leaves St. Regis for Princeton, a university he chooses because of "its atmosphere of bright colors and its alluring reputation as the pleasantest country club in America."

From the first, Amory falls in love with Princeton for its "lazy beauty," its sense of easy and handsome prosperity—most of all, for its struggle for social prominence, in which he engages immediately and vigorously. His literary enthusiasms (he has failed to make the freshman football team) are largely stimulated by the classmates who edit and write for the *Nassau Lit.*, almost never by his professors. He is very impressionable; for a while he and Tom D'Invilliers read Swinburne and Oscar Wilde, and "the world became pale and interesting, and he tried hard to look at Princeton through [their] satiated eyes." The beginning of World War I fails to arouse him, "beyond a sporting interest in the German dash for Paris." But the death of two of his classmates in an auto accident does stir him—"so useless, futile . . . the way animals die." After this incident Amory loses interest in undergraduate excitements, takes to reading a wide and odd assortment of books. In New York he sees the devil in a hallucinatory scene, the first realization of the evil that he has half-suspected underlies the calm surface of his life. He turns to "quest books," like *Sinister Street* and H. G. Wells's *The Research Magnificent,* novels that describe an autobiographical search for personal meaning; he respects the radicalism of a classmate, Burne Holiday, and especially admires him because "he doesn't believe that public swimming pools and a kind word in time will right the wrongs of the world."

The education of the personage goes far beyond graduation, involves a much more complex life than the campus usually provides. True maturity of the hero comes only after he has attended carefully to the facts of love and money. Of these two, and of their corruptive relationship, Fitzgerald has had more to say than any other American novelist. In *This Side of Paradise* he was as close to his own experience as he was ever to get. He had not quite succeeded in getting Zelda Sayre's consent to their marriage because he was too poor; the rewriting of *This Side of Paradise* and Scribner's acceptance of it saved him from Amory's fate. The portrayal of Amory's one great love, for Rosalind Connage, is charged with the horror of a fate the author had barely escaped. Rosalind is "very youthful, thank God—and rather beautiful, thank God—and happy, thank God," and her love for Amory has changed everything for them, in those "intangibly fleeting, unrememberable hours" before the collapse of their plans. She *must* marry a wealthy man:

> "I can't be shut away from the trees and flowers, cooped up in a little flat waiting for you. You'd hate me in a narrow atmosphere. I'd make you hate me." [10]

The great love ends "at exactly twenty minutes after eight on Thursday, June 10, 1919," as Amory meticulously observes in his rounds of the bars, where he puts his grief on public display. Gradually, after many attempts to forget that "first flush of pain," Amory gives an interpretation of his experience, projects it away from himself and into the world of his own generation: the war, for example "certainly ruined the old backgrounds, sort of killed individualism out of our generation." [11]

The final pages of *This Side of Paradise* provide what seems a necessary search for a larger meaning. The excesses of grief for the loss of Rosalind have been alleviated. Amory's change from egotist to personage is now complete. His experience is used as a lesson that his generation may examine. The major reflections of the book's conclusion occur while Amory is on his way back to Princeton. It was at Princeton, after all, that the education of a personage had begun.[12]

[10] Cf. "The Bridal Party" (in *Taps at Reveille,* 1935): Michael had "lost her, slowly, tragically, uselessly, because he had no money and could make no money; because, loving him still, Caroline had lost faith and begun to see him as something pathetic, futile and shabby, outside the great, shining stream of life toward which she was inevitably drawn."

[11] It had scarcely any effect on Amory himself, though he had served in it.

[12] Before that conclusion, however, Amory has to lose the last hope of regaining Rosalind and is informed of the death of Monsignor Darcy. He is left with nothing but "himself as personage."

The popularity of *This Side of Paradise* is a fascinating but puzzling fact. Much of its appeal was due to the love scenes (which made a glamorous thing of a kiss and developed an elaborate code concerning it) and to its representation of undergraduate life. But perhaps the *formula* of disenchantment, which Amory Blaine makes out of his experiences in the concluding pages, was most responsible for the book's success; there was something very touching about the sad young man, whose youth made the sadness acute and pertinent, and who said so many things that were so conveniently true.

Amory had "grown up to a thousand books, a thousand lies; he had listened eagerly to people who pretended to know, who knew nothing." In the novel's conclusion, for the first time, he genuinely distrusts generalizations, epigrams, as too easy, too dangerous for the public mind. He becomes interested in "people," in "others"; as he rides to Princeton with two businessmen who have picked him up, he announces himself a socialist. Wealthy men, he says, are "the keepers of the world's intellectual conscience." He suggests government control of all industry, argues that there are other incentives for men than money. But he admits that he is arguing socialism because "I'm sick of a system where the richest man gets the most beautiful girl if he wants her."

This is a personalized social conscience, and it is followed—when he is left alone, near Princeton—by an appeal to fearless self-dependence of a sort quite likely to give the young a fine glowing sense of their own rebellion. This new generation were a chosen people, "the chosen youth from the muddled, unchastened world, still fed romantically on the mistakes and half-forgotten dreams of dead statesmen and poets."

Here was a new generation,[13] shouting the old cries, learning the old creeds, through a revery of long days and nights; destined finally to go out into that dirty gray turmoil to follow love and pride; a new generation dedicated more than the last to the fear of poverty and the worship of success; grown up to find all Gods dead, all wars fought, all faiths in man shaken.

He himself is "safe now, free from all hysteria," and though he cannot say why he wants to go on, he is secure in his own mind:

He stretched out his arms to the crystalline, radiant sky.
"I know myself," he cried, "but that is all."

[13] It was this generation, "just younger than me," that Fitzgerald described in most of the fiction following *This Side of Paradise*—not quite his own class at Princeton, but, perhaps, the class of 1922 or 1923.

Fitzgerald himself was a long way from knowing what all this meant. The "intellectual" matter of the reformed "personage" was not far short of ridiculous. Though full of clichés and scraps of attitudes picked up from an assortment of second-rate books, the novel saved itself again and again by its ingratiating accuracy of detail. As Bishop and Rosenfeld pointed out, Fitzgerald scrupulously spoke for the experiences of the very young, gave them importance—at the very least provided an excuse for their worst errors in taste, at best credited to their protest a value beyond its actual merit.

In every subsequent book Fitzgerald was to revalue what he had said here, to tighten his saying of it and penetrate beneath the surface of life here presented, to clear the modern scene of trash that cluttered the formulations of attitude in *This Side of Paradise*. To use a conspicuous example, he was blessed over and over again by her grateful contemporaries for having given them the decade's young girl, the bright and beautiful flapper with a sure sense of what to do with and for her men. In her very youth he found charm, glamour. Other novelists of the decade had not nearly so much respect for her: Faulkner, for example, in *Soldiers' Pay* (1926), portrayed her kind (in Cecily Saunders) in a number of poses ludicrous and pathetic.

For Fitzgerald, the flapper was a genuine center of young life; she helped him to pose a major question and served as its evidence and text. Early illustrations of juvenile charm were Amory's loves—Isabelle Borgé, for example:

> Her education, or, rather, her sophistication, had been absorbed from the boys who had dangled on her favor; her tact was instinctive, and her capacity for love-affairs was limited only by the number of the susceptible within telephone distance. *Flirt* smiled through her intense physical magnetism.

With her, Amory felt that "everything was hallowed by the haze of his own youth. . . . Silently he admired himself. How conveniently well he looked, and how well a dinner coat became him." The kiss was "the high point of vanity, the crest of his young egotism."

The tragedy of youth was age, as Michael Fane had come to realize; and in Fitzgerald's stories of the young girl there is always a sense of foreboding; almost any day one might find oneself twenty-four instead of twenty-three. The passing of time is itself an ominous event, to be feared for what it might bring of furrows, wrinkles, a slower step, and other jarring intrusions upon the sophomore spring. In "Winter

Dreams" (1922) the fabulously beautiful Judy Jones ("a continual impression of flux, of intense life, of passionate vitality") does in time become middle-aged and ordinary, and Dexter Green is crushed by the thought of this immitigable calamity:

> For the first time in years the tears were streaming down his face. But they were for himself now. He did not care about mouth and eyes and moving hands. He wanted to care, and he could not care. For he had gone away and he could never go back any more. The gates were closed, the sun was gone down, and there was no beauty but the gray beauty of steel that withstands all time.

For Fitzgerald's young the moment of beauty and serene self-confidence was short indeed. In his world of debutantes and young college men time was always reduced to a pinpoint present, and the task of maturing was a hard one, involving the need to give up that present. The opportunity for the moment of "high vanity" might easily be lost—if one were poor, or if the war intervened, or if the lovely one proved to have too expensive tastes. His heroes were constantly threatened with the danger not only of losing their youth but also of never realizing it. Faulkner looked upon the conduct of his Miss Cecily Saunders with sardonic amusement; for Fitzgerald, there was always a touch of disaster, or of the fear of it, in his bright young women with their pretty faces.

4. "The Rich Are Different"

FROM Rosalind Connage to Nicole Warren, the lives of Fitzgerald's heroines were associated with the facts of money, with having it or needing it. They were often quite fabulously wealthy themselves ("The Martin-Jones fortune of seventy-five millions had been inherited by a very little girl on her tenth birthday"), and therefore bought what they needed—as much love as they could want, or a psychiatrist for a husband; or they waited, like Gloria Gilbert of *The Beautiful and Damned* (1922), for wealth to release them from the tedium of poverty; or they married the wrong man or failed to marry the right one because he was too poor and poverty was too ugly to bear.

The problem of wealth was the major concern of Fitzgerald's work for other reasons as well. He hated the poor for their helplessness, the extraordinary inferiority of their bargaining position. Nevertheless he

THE VERY YOUNG 109

could not see that the wealthy were quite worthy of their advantage. Wealth seemed to him not infrequently associated with a lack of taste, a coarseness and raw ostentation, a sense of privilege existing outside the reach of moral responsibility. In the beginning Fitzgerald resented wealth because it could "buy the girl," and some of his early work is haunted by his sense of that horrible advantage. But he came to see that the position of the wealthy created another kind of morality, a totally different kind of person, whose social mobility and freedom from "fixed" convention put him beyond any ordinary moral calculation:

> [The Rich] possess and enjoy early, and it does something to them, makes them soft where we are hard, and cynical where we are trustful, in a way that, unless you are born rich, it is very difficult to understand. They think, deep in their hearts, that they are better than we are because we had to discover the compensations and refuges of life for ourselves.

The tragedy of the 1920s—or one of them—for Fitzgerald was the *need* of money in order to keep the moment of beauty and illusion alive, to keep it for oneself. Nowhere in his work does one find a rich man worthy of his inheritance—*with* an inheritance, in fact, of anything but money; there is no Adam Verver, no Paul Marvell, no Tom Corey— no one who, whatever his financial status, inherited taste, a sense of decorum, a real knowledge of the human decencies. Instead the wealthy are aging exhibitionists (old Adam Patch, Dan Cody) or "rich boys." James Russell Lowell had in 1884 defended a leisure class as a means of preserving taste and culture in a democracy. Fitzgerald's Tom Buchanan wanders about "wherever people are rich together," and wherever he goes is restlessly unhappy and hopelessly vulgar.

One of Fitzgerald's most acute and penetrating observations was that of the rich boy with his monopoly of privilege. He did not like the wealthy, though he refused to give up what small share of their mobility his writing success could give him. He liked to think he could use their wealth to much greater advantage than they had the sense to do. As he resented their privileges (with the "smouldering hatred of a peasant"), so he saw the decline of national morality that in the 1920s made quick accumulations of wealth possible. The fabulous successes of the days of James J. Hill—and of Cody—were in the twenties duplicated almost overnight. This fact, one of the incredible truths of the decade, was made into a convincing symbol by Fitzgerald.

Gatsby, arriving in New York from Louisville, with no money in his pocket, in three years can buy an estate at West Egg, equip it and service it, and keep it bright and noisy far into the morning. Gatsby's house is, after all, the house of James J. Hill transplanted to the Long Island of the Prohibition decade. Not less incredible are Gatsby's motives for behaving in this way. Money will buy back the girl, since money had taken her away from him; with money Gatsby slowly maneuvers his way back into Daisy Buchanan's world and succeeds, for a few months at least, in recapturing the past "moment" of beauty that Amory Blaine had lost forever.

The judgment implicit in this was incomplete, undecided. Fitzgerald did not often reach final meanings in his considerations of money and its human influences. Most often he portrayed wealth in terms of fantasy or ridicule: a ten-year-old girl inherits seventy-five millions; a diamond mountain is destroyed by its owner; a young heir collapses during a lawsuit that recovers his inheritance; a sick heiress buys her way to health by marriage to a psychiatrist. Throughout the 1920s there was in Fitzgerald's work a feeling that money after all does *not* buy anything but tragedy and remorse: "In life these things hadn't happened yet, but I was pretty sure living wasn't the reckless, careless business these people thought—this generation just younger than me." Nevertheless he was only mildly concerned over the immorality of Gatsby's means; the stupidity and amorality of the "robber baron" scarcely touched him (though in "The Diamond as Big as the Ritz" he definitively blasted him), and the bootlegger and gambler of the Prohibition era were seen in only a few brilliant, isolated images for what they were. Perhaps that was as much as he could do for them, or as much as he cared to do. He was not a moralist, and he did not care to go into the economics of American exploitation. Marx was not his redeemer.[14] But within his intellectual means Fitzgerald gave us a thorough and highly moral view of the decade, seen from the vantage point of the St. Paul boy and what he himself called the "spoiled priest."

His point of view can be given in summary. Its origins are actually the insights of Amory Blaine at Princeton, however crudely they may have been presented there. Fitzgerald begins by trying to define an undergraduate's notion of what is beautiful, together with his experience of evil. In its second phase his view requires a description of the beautiful

[14] "I have the feeling," Fitzgerald said in 1936, "that someone, I'm not sure who, is sound asleep—someone who could have helped me to keep my shop open. It wasn't Lenin, and it wasn't God."

as an experience most fully appreciated by privileged youth. That youth can be maintained for a longer time, when it is captured at all, if there is money to secure its privilege: the Fitzgerald woman prefers to worry about the tan on her legs rather than to fret over calluses on her hands. Fitzgerald's judgment of the decade finally has to do with this question of wealth and taste; this was a generation, as he put it in 1931, that "eventually overreached itself less through lack of morals than through lack of taste."

In just what ways had the most highly prized experiences—as well as even ordinary privileges and amenities—become associated with the possession of wealth or the need of it? And in what ways did the spending of that money prove vulgar, irresponsible, immoral? Was there, perhaps, a fundamental lack of substance, of depth, in the American experience and in its historical background? For Dick Diver fails, as does Gatsby, and this sense of disaster haunts most of Fitzgerald's stories. His final judgment, had he made it, would have been that the failure resulted from a fundamental lack of a clear moral sense, a lack really of cultural tact, which had caused men in the very beginning to have the wrong dreams, and which gave them no proper knowledge of the means to judge them.

5. The Text: Fitzgerald's *The Great Gatsby*

Mr. Fitzgerald [to Van Wyck Brooks]: Well, don't you think, though, that the American millionaires must have had a certain amount of fun out of their money? Can't you imagine a man like Harriman or Hill feeling a certain creative ecstasy as he piled up that power? Think of being able to buy anything you wanted . . . think of being able to give a stupendous house party that would go on for days and days, with everything that anybody could want to drink and a medical staff in attendance and the biggest jazz orchestras in the city alternating night and day! I must confess that I get a big kick out of all the glittering expensive things.

This is Edmund Wilson's version (in *Discordant Encounters,* 1926) of Fitzgerald's view of the wealthy. It is drawn partly from what Fitzgerald himself said in *The Beautiful and Damned* (1922), in his short stories, and in *The Great Gatsby* (1925). Jay Gatsby was a special type of rich man, a product of the opportunity for quick wealth offered by

Prohibition. The chance of having anything you wanted, as Wilson put it, both fascinated and appalled Fitzgerald.[15]

In spite of Gatsby's physical appearance (he is always on the verge of being just a little absurd), he is an attractive person. He has an indefinable grace and charm, a remarkable simplicity of attitude, but also an obvious vulgarity and cheapness, which have come from achieving too early the success he finds indispensable to his purpose. Fitzgerald's crucial strategy in this novel is to put the two men, Nick Carraway and Gatsby, in relation to each other and in the course of the narrative to "prove" Gatsby to Carraway.

The narrator, Nick Carraway, had first to get used to Gatsby's fabulous estate and to what went on there nightly:

> It was a factual imitation of some Hôtel de Ville in Normandy, with a tower on one side, spanking new under a thin beard of raw ivy, and more than forty acres of lawn and garden.

At this mansion, "every Friday five crates of oranges and lemons arrived from a fruiterer in New York—every Monday these same oranges and lemons left his back door in a pyramid of pulpless halves." There were other evidences of preparations for an elaborate party: the buffet tables, on which "spiced baked hams crowded against salads of harlequin designs and pastry pigs and turkeys bewitched to a dark gold." In the main hall a huge bar was stocked with all the liquors the law had forbidden. At seven in the evening the orchestra for the affair made its appearance, "a whole pitful of oboes and trombones and saxophones and viols and cornets and piccolos, and low and high drums."

Gradually the guests came to the party; and cars were "parked five deep in the drive." One day Carraway jotted down "on the empty spaces of a timetable" the names of some of the guests: "the Chester Beckers and the Leeches and a man named Bunsen, whom I knew at Yale, and Doctor Webster Civet"; besides these, the Hornbeams and the Willie Voltaires, Clarence Endive (who "came only once, in white knicker-

---

[15] In "Winter Dreams" (1922) Fitzgerald had experimented with the notion that success conferred such an inclusive privilege, and he had concluded that money bought only a limited number of things. That story, which Fitzgerald called an early attempt to work with the ideas of *The Great Gatsby,* has a few things in common with the novel: in each, the hero is slighted by a pretty girl and is determined to recapture her; both heroes know that, to do so, one must have money and must display the marks of obvious success; both are defeated in the end, the one because he fails to understand the rather simple facts of physical decay, the other because he refuses to acknowledge moral corruption and decay.

bockers, and had a fight with a bum named Etty in the garden"), the Fishguards and the Ripley Snells, S. B. Whitebait ("who was well over sixty"), the Hammerheads, Gulick the state senator, Newton Orchid ("who controlled Films Par Excellence"), G. Earl Muldoon ("brother to that Muldoon who afterward strangled his wife"), S. W. Belcher and the Smirkes and the young Quinns (later divorced), and Henry L. Palmetto (who later "killed himself by jumping in front of a subway train in Times Square"). All these, and many others, came to Gatsby's parties in the summer of 1922; they were not invited, "they just went there," and afterward "conducted themselves according to the rules of behavior associated with an amusement park."

Why the parties at all—and who is the man who gives them? Carraway goes one night to find out what he can. The guests know nothing about Gatsby but speculate that he's killed a man or been a German spy. After Nick has finally met Gatsby, he is even more mystified, by his gentleness, his "understanding" smile:

> It faced—or seemed to face—the whole eternal world for an instant, and then concentrated on *you* with an irresistible prejudice in your favor. . . . Precisely at that point it vanished—and I was looking at an elegant young roughneck, a year or two over thirty, whose elaborate formality of speech just missed being absurd.

Much of the novel is taken up by Nick's attempts to clear up the mystery of Jay Gatsby, who gives these extravagant and vulgar and apparently pointless affairs but is not really a part of them and—so far as Nick can see—has no pleasure in them or in his guests. Gatsby tells a version of his story while he and Nick drive to Manhattan in the cream-colored Rolls-Royce: he is the son of "some wealthy people in the Middle West"; he was educated at Oxford ("It is a family tradition"); after that he traveled in Europe, collecting jewels, hunting big game, "and trying to forget something very sad that happened to me long ago." In the war he had been decorated by "every Allied government . . . even Montenegro, little Montenegro down on the Adriatic Sea!" To Nick's astonishment Gatsby produces the medal from Montenegro: "then it was all true," Nick says to himself, and he thinks of the weird story as plausible in the way of romances in the slick magazines.

The real Gatsby story, scarcely less incredible, is at the core of the novel's meaning. Fitzgerald narrates Gatsby's past in isolated fragments, interrupted always by a return to the present of West Egg and

East Egg. Its beginnings concern a James Gatz who, at the age of seventeen, rowed out to Dan Cody's yacht in Lake Superior to warn its owner that "a wind might catch him and break him up in half an hour." He had spent two weeks in a small Lutheran College in southern Minnesota; "dismayed at its ferocious indifference to the drums of his destiny," he had left and drifted back to Lake Superior, waiting for the "day that Dan Cody's yacht dropped anchor in the shallows along-shore." Cody became Gatsby's symbol of greatness. Like the Harriman and Hill of Wilson's dialogue, Cody could buy anything he wanted,[17] and he appointed James Gatz to accompany him "in a vague personal capacity," largely to protect him from fortune-hunting women. From Cody, Gatsby learned much: to leave liquor alone, for example, and to smile ingratiatingly when you want a man to like you; perhaps most important of all, that the "main chance" could be had if you were persistent in looking for it. This education was put to practical use only after the war, when Gatsby needed to make a great amount of money in a very short time.

The next part of the Gatsby story is told by Jordan Baker; it concerns her friend Daisy Fay who is the most important of Fitzgerald's women and whose characterization is the most instructive of his discourses on wealth and beauty. In Louisville, in 1917, Gatsby met Daisy Fay, the first "nice" girl he had ever known. From the beginning he knew that his chance was "a colossal accident." They were several classes and several millions apart, and he took her by deceiving her about his status in life. After that "she vanished into her rich house, into her rich, full life, leaving Gatsby—nothing." When he went abroad she married Tom Buchanan of Chicago, who "came down with a hundred people in four private cars, and hired a whole floor of the Muhlbach Hotel, and the day before the wedding he gave her a string of pearls valued at three hundred and fifty thousand dollars."

Gatsby correctly guessed that it was not Tom but the money that had finally convinced her. To win her back, he would have to "buy her," to exceed in ostentation and power the wealth of Buchanan's inheritance. Of her love for him Gatsby had no doubt, and he refused to believe that it had been a moment in the past that could not be repeated. When he

---

[16] Fitzgerald had thought of including the story "Absolution" as a picture of Gatsby's early life, but "cut it because I preferred to preserve the sense of mystery." (Letter to John Jamieson, April 15, 1934.)

[17] ". . . a gray, florid man with a hard, empty face—the pioneer debauchee, who during one phase of American life brought back to the Eastern seaboard the savage violence of the frontier brothel and saloon."

returned from France, Daisy and Tom were still on their wedding trip, and Gatsby "made a miserable but irresistible journey to Louisville on the last of his army pay." But it was "no good"; he had lost his experience in the past, and the only means of recovering it was to build his fortune as quickly as possible.

The manner of narration does not permit much discussion of the means by which Gatsby finally arrived at West Egg, but in the few glimpses of Gatsby's "business" we have a remarkable view of the underworld of the 1920s. On his first trip to Manhattan with Gatsby, Nick is introduced to Wolfsheim, Gatsby's boss, the man "who fixed the World's Series back in 1919"; quite a character around New York —"a denizen of Broadway." [18] From Wolfsheim himself, Carraway learns of the association after Gatsby's death:

> "Did you start him in business?" I inquired.
> "*Start* him. I *made* him. . . . I raised him up out of nothing, right out of the gutter. I saw right away he was a fine-appearing, gentlemanly young man, and when he told me he was an Oggsford man I knew I could use him good."

Wolfsheim is Cody's successor, and the difference between the two masters suggests clearly the story of several decades of exploitation and money-gathering in the American world. Wolfsheim, friend of gamblers and crooks, was able to help Gatsby to the fortune he needed in such a hurry. You *can* repeat the past, says Gatsby indignantly to Carraway at one time; but in order to do so you must make up the difference between the penniless soldier in Louisville and the master of the West Egg estate. Tenaciously, quietly, Gatsby maneuvers his affairs to the day when, with Carraway as host, Daisy is finally returned to him. Having recaptured her, he shows her his magnificent estate and all his possessions:

> He hadn't once ceased looking at Daisy, and I think he revalued everything in his house according to the measure of response it drew from her well-loved eyes. Sometimes, too, he stared around at his possessions in a dazed way, as though in her actual and astounding presence none of it was any longer real. Once he nearly toppled down a flight of stairs.

This is the "real" Gatsby, as fabulous a person as the fake one he first described to Carraway. Underlying all the incredible accounts

[18] Based apparently on Arnold Rothstein, of whom Fitzgerald knew only gossip and rumor. (See Mizener's *The Far Side of Paradise,* page 171.)

of West Egg and of the parties there, Carraway sees the inflexible purpose of Gatsby's conduct: he is coarse, vulgar, ostentatious; he is associated with the principal leaders of New York's underworld; he has made his fortune in several illegal manipulations. But Carraway eventually forgets or condones this as he becomes convinced that Gatsby is "worth the whole damn bunch put together":

> I've always been glad I said that. It was the only compliment I ever gave him, because I disapproved of him from beginning to end.

In these remarks Carraway redresses the balance of his relationship to Gatsby. His *disapproval* of him, important in itself, has been based upon what he had been taught was a "proper" manner, the *decorum* of his Midwestern background. Gatsby has violated that manner from beginning to end; yet, to the young man from the Midwest, the coarseness and vulgarity of the man finally have come to be a matter of secondary importance. In the last pages of the novel Carraway becomes the guardian of Gatsby's illusion, is committed to it and to a defense of it against the "whole rotten," indifferent, selfish world that came to Gatsby's parties but ignored him in his agony and his death.

Against the obvious venality of Gatsby's world—the corruption of it, the collapse of all discernible limits and restraints—Fitzgerald opposes one unalterable fact. Gatsby, after all, held to his illusion to the end; his behavior was consistent from the start; he was an *interested* person, involved with and responsible to others. His dedication to his purpose and his integrity finally won Carraway to him, and at the end Carraway set aside the corruption deliberately and wishfully:

> On the last night, with my trunk packed and my car sold to the grocer, I went over and looked at that huge incoherent failure of a house once more. On the white steps an obscene word, scrawled by some boy with a piece of brick, stood out clearly in the moonlight, and I erased it, drawing my shoe raspingly along the stone.

This act symbolizes the degree of Carraway's conversion: the huge incoherent failure of a house is after all symbolic of the external structure of Gatsby's life, which must collapse when Gatsby dies. The obscenity is in itself an act of indifference, symbolic of the obscene indifference shown by the scores of people who had feasted at Gatsby's board, drunk his champagne, and disappeared when the news of his death spread. Their world is revealed in a number of other brilliant images: the old timetable on whose margins Carraway wrote down

their names; the pompous front lawn and front porch of Tom Buchanan's East Egg mansion; Tom's apartment on 158th Street, where he
keeps his mistress.

Their obscenity, which Carraway erases from the steps, consists primarily of their indifference, their abysmal failure to acknowledge either
affection or illusion. Their moral defection is pathetic as well, because
it involves a basic failure of moral "caution" and an inability "to care."
Set alongside it, Gatsby's clumsy but deep affection for one person
(and his talent for ingratiating others) is a profound virtue, in whose
interest the entire dream "of the republic" deserves to be consulted.

No person suffers more severely from Carraway's rasping indignation
than Daisy Buchanan, who expects as her right both affection and
luxury. Gatsby's insight into her nature is nowhere better seen than
when, in the Buchanan house, he talks briefly to Carraway about her:

> "She's got an indiscreet voice," I remarked. "It's full of—" I hesi-
> tated.
> "Her voice is full of money," he said suddenly.
> That was it. I'd never understood it before.

Fitzgerald always understood it; for Daisy Buchanan is Rosalind Connage once more, or any other of his heroines whose love of "beauty"
and of large, ample, luxurious settings and excitements had in it a
quality of disaster and ruin. At the end of the novel Daisy has not
proved "worth it" except as the concrete image of Gatsby's illusion.

The tragedy of Gatsby's career is not his death, which is after all the
result of an accident brought about by Tom Buchanan's belligerent
carelessness. It lies fundamentally in an error Gatsby makes at the
very beginning, when his name is still James Gatz. He is not wholly responsible for making the error; he could not really help making it. He
simply dedicates his life to what Carraway terms "the service of a vast,
vulgar, and meretricious beauty." This is the cheapened "Platonic conception of himself," and in the years following it is associated with the
particular beauty and loveliness of Daisy Fay in Louisville. What follows is a colossal waste of talent, affection, desire, and intelligence.

This is of the utmost importance in the matter of seeing Fitzgerald's
work for what it is. He had a number of times portrayed his heroines
in settings and in situations that attracted his readers and gave him
quick financial returns; but he was often depressed, and not infrequently
outraged, by his knowledge that his heroines were dishonest with themselves and with others, or "careless," as Carraway finally called the

Buchanans.[19] His judgment of Daisy was severe; as the final, particular embodiment of Gatsby's purpose, she was unequal to the task, first of understanding his love, then of realizing the effort he had made to recover the one moment in the past that seemed worth while to him.

From being the younger generation's most brilliant and charming spokesman, Fitzgerald in a few short years became its most perceptive and incisive judge. In order to assume that role, he had (or thought he had) in *The Great Gatsby* to measure the younger generation against the only person who merited his respect. Gatsby scarcely deserved the position Fitzgerald gave him, and he deserved not at all the romantic adulation Carraway offered his memory in the last paragraphs of the novel. Fitzgerald's effort to point to the "disaster" implicit in the behavior of the very young led him to an excess of admiration for Gatsby in untenable and in almost intolerable terms. For all its grace of style and tightness of structure, *The Great Gatsby* was a sentimental novel, with several fatal lapses of taste and judgment.

Fitzgerald was not quite equal to the task he set for himself. Throughout his career he sought the adequately "correct" modern hero—a man of bright promise, trying to realize himself and defeated inevitably by the indifference, the selfishness, the corruptibility of those about him, as well as by a fatal weakness within himself. But his fiction almost never escaped a sudden shift in his attitude toward his characters. His criticism, even in the best of his work, was blunted or turned aside or maneuvered into unlikely compromises with his subject.

Partly because of this his work is a revealing story of the very young in the decade. He is, in his life and in his tastes, an inseparable part of that story, a victim of the decade's own standards of judging people. He never quite makes the proper intellectual use of the disaster implicit in the behavior of the very young. Gatsby, his most remarkable creation, is judged only in terms of himself; and Gatsby's indiscretions, which are enormous, are first forgiven, then sanctified and romanticized. "One wonders whether a certain coyness toward the things of the mind is not one reason for the lack of development in most American writers," said William Troy, speaking of Fitzgerald's failure.[20] "Art is not intellect

[19] Carraway's judgment of Jordan Baker is not without its importance: "She was incurably dishonest. She wasn't able to endure being at a disadvantage and, given this unwillingness, I suppose she had begun dealing in subterfuges when she was very young in order to keep that cool, insolent smile turned to the world and yet satisfy the demands of her hard, jaunty body."

[20] In *Forms of Modern Fiction*, edited by W. V. O'Connor (University of Minnesota Press, 1948).

alone; but without intellect art is not likely to emerge beyond the plane of perpetual immaturity." This is perhaps too severe a judgment, but it does point up what are crucial failures of *control* in Fitzgerald's art. The details are presented with brilliantly accurate insight, greater than any other found in modern American fiction, but there are places where the control fails, and as in the case of Gatsby, the opportunity to judge becomes an occasion for attachment and sentimental defense.

IV

FORMS OF TRADITIONALISM

1. Using the American Past

THE FIGURE of Sweeney, T. S. Eliot's "apeneck" protagonist of the "lower world," is least likely to suggest memories of the past. The American tradition, from which Sweeney is forever cut off, haunts Eliot's mind as he portrays "Sweeney Erect" (*Poems*, 1920), "addressed full length to shave." Upon this scene, complicated by other matters peculiar to Sweeney's habits, the memory of Ralph Waldo Emerson parenthetically reflects:

> (The lengthened shadow of a man
> Is history, said Emerson
> Who had not seen the silhouette
> Of Sweeney straddled in the sun.)

The silhouette and the paraphrase of Emerson combine to produce a strange commentary upon tradition. Emerson would have been shocked to see the silhouette and could not have found a place for it in his speculations concerning the "modern" man as a hero in a once self-reliant world. Miss Nancy Ellicott rode across "the barren New England hills" scarcely aware, if at all, that

> Upon the glazen shelves kept watch
> Matthew and Waldo, guardians of the faith,
> The army of unalterable law.

These two brief glimpses of a young poet in London, looking across to New England, are of course only superficial indices to the twentieth-century uses of the American tradition. They are limited also in their reference only to a New England past, and such reference testifies to

120

one of the most thorough exploitations of historical irony ever made in American literature. New England served, more often than not, as the scapegoat of their abuse when American critics of the 1920s attended at all to the past: Puritanism and the transcendentalists, and frequently Emerson.

The question of such abuse involves many shades of meaning and usage. What is a tradition? Specifically, what is "the American tradition," and of what use is it? The American time sense in the 1920s was at best erratic; tradition meant a great many things, but least of all a chronological past. The most important formative times were the immediate present and the calculable future; of these, the immediate present appealed most to artists, who wished to attend to it or thought they were forced to because the past was empty and the future hopeless—but most of all, perhaps, because the present excited and disturbed them. The present often became a fixed spatial metaphor, a rich field for a free discussion of improvised manners and codes. The calculable future was for the most part the province of liberal-journalist speculations, but even these diminished in confidence after the conclusion of the war. The strongest statement made in the decade concerning this future and its promise was contained in James Harvey Robinson's *The Mind in the Making* (1921).[1] In it, the past, while not rejected, was held rigorously in line; it was good only insofar as it offered evidences of a future victory of the liberal intelligence. In this same spirit John Dewey wrote his *Reconstruction in Philosophy* (1920), a revision of the philosophic past to suit the terms of the liberal hope, for that foreseeable future "when the consciousness of science is fully impregnated with the consciousness of human value." There was more than a hint of utopianism in all this; the actual present, the usable past, and the definable future were combined to produce a liberal metaphor of linear progress.

As for the actual American past, writers in the 1920s were concerned for the most part to make it serve their own ends. "Positively, the new movement [2] sought to create literary history in its own image," Howard

[1] Morton G. White, in summing it up (*Social Thought in America,* 1949), also quite plausibly gives us its meaning as an intellectual document of the time: "It communicates not only the liberal critique of the past but also liberal optimism, the forward glance to the bravest of all possible worlds; it is also the sigh of an intellectual who survived a horrible war, the critical and cynical reaction of a believer in the new social science."

[2] It began with the publication of John Macy's *The Spirit of American Literature* (1913).

Mumford Jones said (*Theory of American Literature,* 1948); "that is, it deliberately sought to rewrite the story of American letters in values known only to the twentieth century. Every age, of course, remakes history in its own image, but the special mark of these iconoclasts was a refusal of historical importance as a canon of judgment"—which is to say, the uses of the past were selective and prejudicial. Many critics sought to redress a historical balance, to break the barrier of chronology and to use criteria of "neglected greatness," "genuine value as opposed to historical place," and "usefulness for our own time." Norman Foerster, introducing the volume *A Reinterpretation of American Literature* (1928), complained that national letters had up to then been "a subject attractive to facile journalists and ignorant dilettanti, and repellent to sound but timorous scholars."

There are a great many ways of explaining this reaction to the past. World War I at least temporarily put the younger writers on their guard with respect to superficial readings of the American tradition. The realist and naturalist developments in American literature, which antedated the war by several decades, had prepared the way for a general trend toward value reduction in the 1920s. Literary criticism also modified the perspective upon tradition: in its frequent emphasis upon experiment, its search for "new forms," its preference for the "object" as against sociological or historical context, its preference for analysis of the poem as against the biography or personality of the poet. In putting "first things first," criticism pushed the usual considerations of culture and history into the background. When such critics as Pound and Eliot used a past, it was a past of their own selection, a past whose literary expressions either taught them in formal matters or struck a responsive chord from them in their views of present culture. This was true of other developments in the thinking of the 1920s: Eliot and Pound were no more selective than Dewey; the expatriates often cast off Dickens and Thackeray, to take up Flaubert and other French models; the surrealists made forages into the past to suit their needs; and in American literature, Longfellow, Whittier, and other nineteenth-century greats were vigorously abused, and Melville began his slow journey to prominence in modern criticism.

Perhaps one of the most important reactions—and the one most difficult to explain—was the hatred of the American nineteenth century. It was not, for example, so much the seventeenth-century Puritan who disturbed many writers as it was the "militant Puritan" of the late nineteenth century.[3] For such critics the most distasteful of American customs and naïvetés had grown and been nourished in the previous century; and the alliance of religious sanctimony with shrewd commercial practice was condemned with all the vigor they could command. They viewed with suspicion the institutions that had enjoyed their greatest prosperity in the decades following the Civil War. Some writers were convinced that a pre-institutional life (as they saw it), a simple, primitive life, which antedated the destructive growth of industrial America, was a lost and all but irrecoverable ideal. Somehow, these men felt, the change in incentive, from the desire to live fully to the desire to become and remain prosperous, was a major force in cheapening and threatening American life.

The uses of the American past involved a number of metaphors and simplifications: the "Freudian" metaphor of a repressed nation; the metaphor of an "American myth," variously understood and used; the metaphor of a specially vivid and fixed formal "classical" past; and the metaphor of "the land" as a spiritual figuration of the human personality and its history. All these were operative in helping to establish the forms assumed by traditionalism in the 1920s.

2. Emerson, Whitman, and the Silhouette of Sweeney

SPEAKING in 1922 of the failure of some of the younger critics [4] to "connect themselves vitally" with the American tradition, Stuart Pratt Sherman confided his suspicion that this was responsible for a general lack of direction and of moral clarity in their work:

> But one cannot help asking whether this inability does not largely account for the fact that Mr. Lewisohn's group of critics are restless impressionists, almost destitute of doctrine, and with no discoverable unifying tendency except to let themselves out into a homeless happy

[3] The nineteenth-century Puritan was a revision of seventeenth-century soul-searching. Samuel Sewall became, in the unfortunate expansion of the private to public conscience, Anthony Comstock. This was a scandal of criticism, to which Sewall would have reacted with more surprise than resentment.

[4] Those included in Ludwig Lewisohn's *A Modern Book of Criticism* (1920). Sherman cites especially Lewisohn himself, Van Wyck Brooks, James Huneker, H. L. Mencken, and Randolph Bourne.

land where they may enjoy the "colorful" cosmic weather, untroubled by businessmen, or middle-class Americans, or congressmen, or moralists, or humanists, or philosophers, or professors, or Victorians, or Puritans, or New Englanders, or Messrs. Tarkington and Churchill.[5]

The great men of America's literary past were the subject of lively journalistic exchange throughout the decade. For the most part it was the conservatives (the academics, Humanists, the "angry professors," as Malcolm Cowley once called them) who insisted that the real measure of American culture was in its past. They were also the first to regret the decline in influence exerted by that past upon the younger generation.

The cases of Emerson and Thoreau were especially symptomatic. Interest in them and in transcendentalism reached a new low in the 1920s. They continued, of course, to be objects of special scholarly concern, and Sherman—in what is perhaps the key essay of his *Americans* (1922)—paid great tribute to Emerson and to his continuing and perdurable influence on Americans. But most of the few writers who attended to either Emerson or Thoreau admitted to a decline of interest in them, even pointed to an alarming ignorance of the phase of American culture represented by them. "American life has gone precisely counter to [Emerson's] dream of it," said one critic. Another regretted that Thoreau's ideal grows ever more remote from us, "with each progressive alienation from the real sources of food, clothing, and shelter." George N. Shuster thought that perhaps Emerson was too refined for us: "Our world is vulgar and he is exquisitely refined" (*Catholic World,* March 1918).

H. L. Mencken, Sherman's own special enemy, put what he thought were the finishing touches upon the farewell to the "Unheeded Lawgiver" in his first collection of *Prejudices* (1919); the obituary contains many of Mencken's most engaging absurdities of style and implication:

> What remains of him at home, as I have said, is no more than, on the one hand, a somewhat absurd affectation of intellectual fastidiousness, now almost extinct even in New England, and, on the other hand, a debased transcendentalism rolled into pills for fat women with vague pains and inattentive husbands—in brief, the New Thought—in brief, imbecility. This New Thought, a decadent end-product of American superficiality, now almost monopolizes him. One hears of him in its preposterous literature, and one hears of him in textbooks for the young, but not often elsewhere.

[5] Winston Churchill, the American novelist.

Even Paul Elmer More, who otherwise demonstrated a qualified admiration for Emerson's position in the American past, admitted that he "often loses value for his admirers in proportion to their maturity and experience. He is pre-eminently the poet of religion and philosophy for the young; whereas men as they grow older are inclined to turn from him, in their more serious needs, to those sages who have supplemented insight with a firmer grasp of the whole of human nature." Much of the defense of Emerson had the quality of Wordsworth's sonnet, "Milton, thou shouldst be living at this hour": he is needed desperately now, in "this hour of cowardice, disillusionment, and inhibition," said Bliss Perry (*In Praise of Folly,* 1923); and Sherlock B. Gass hopefully suggested that the "forgotten man," the Emersonian individual, seems finally to be "lifting his head and finding in Emerson a reminder of his birthright" (*Outlook,* September 5, 1928).

The 1920s were scarcely a time for a specific or intelligent comprehension of Emerson or of transcendentalism. Sherman's lyrical worship of him, Van Wyck Brooks's attempt to reconstruct the Concord life of the "golden age" of New England (*Emerson and Others,* 1927), Bliss Perry's editorship of *The Heart of Emerson's Journals* (1926), were among the few evidences of a continuing interest in his contribution to the American past. The major objective was to find some use for that past, and for many Emerson was scarcely usable and hardly acceptable.

In many ways Walt Whitman escaped the decade's general censure of the past. For one thing, he was himself seen as a rebel against tradition, and he had experimented in new ways of speaking; for another, his appeals for a native literary tradition, a lyrical celebration of "these United States," offered a challenge that was not ignored. He was a "modern" in ways that Emerson could not be described as being; he offered a vision of democratic man that could survive even the reductive influence of much cultural criticism. The career of Whitman's reputation in the 1920s is an interesting cross-section of the decade's views of the American past.

In 1919 many magazines published tributes to Whitman on the occasion of the one-hundredth anniversary of his birth. For the most part they contained fulsome praise of the man one journalist called "the supreme spokesman of American democracy." Edgar Lee Masters, writing in Whitman's own *Brooklyn Eagle,* said that "he has more nearly justified the ways of God to man than any writer that we have produced." Whitman was complimented also for being the principal "animating force in contemporary poetry" (P. H. Boynton); he was given credit for having inspired "Frost, Sandburg, Dreiser, Oppenheim, Anderson, Masters, Lindsay, and a score of autochthonous authors" (Louis Untermeyer); he was hailed as the modern sponsor of "the poet as prophet, and of poetry as a religion, as an ecstatic expression of faith" (Harriet Monroe). Both Emanuel Carnevali and J. R. Mc-Carthy wrote poems for the occasion. McCarthy, in "Come Down," begged Walt to "Loose your arm from Abe Lincoln's/And come down," to inspirit "this horde," to "shout forth the beauty of their dreams,/Translate their hundred tongues."

There were a number of qualifications to this eloquence. In 1921 Norman Foerster admitted that Whitman possessed great poetic power but asserted that he "fell into delusions and infatuations" and worshiped confusion, that his followers did not sufficiently explore or analyze the moral value of his utterances. Vachel Lindsay's observations were of another kind: he acknowledged Whitman's greatness but said that he "will always survive outside the main line of tradition as a gigantic lonely individual" (*New Republic,* November 5, 1923). L. W. Smith heaped calumny upon the message of Whitman, whose ideas were leading to a "proletarian and plebeian world, and all the noxious weeds of unrestrained desires may properly be left to flourish in it" (*South Atlantic Quarterly,* October 1923). John Gould Fletcher pointed out that the world Whitman had hoped for could not be realized by the "intellectuals," who were the only ones to attend to him; they are "unable to create a civilization resting on the values which he considered the sole permanent ones" (*North American Review,* March 1924).

The most thorough document of abuse was Ernest Boyd's essay (*American Mercury,* December 1925):

Walt Whitman was the first of the literary exhibitionists whose cacophonous incongruities and general echolalia are the distinguishing marks of what is regarded as poetry in aesthetic circles today. He was the herald and forerunner of that ultra-violet literature, in prose and verse, which sprawls its eccentric topography and linguistic barbarisms over the pages of reviews that make "no compromise with the public taste."

Whitman was a club for beating Boyd's special brand of enemy; he had, Boyd said, "surveyed nature from the top of a Broadway omnibus"; he is read not by the people but only by "the unhappy few to whom we owe a literature of barren aestheticism without beauty." Harvey O'Higgins contributed one of his "psychoanalyses," commenting on Whitman's mother fixation and his narcissism and concluding that such a man could never be accepted as "democracy's poet" (*Harper's*, May 1929).

Whitman was a very special case in the American tradition. He seemed closer to the 1920s than Emerson, and his work seemed less implausible, more assimilable. A group of poets—among them, Vachel Lindsay, Carl Sandburg, Edgar Lee Masters, and Stephen Vincent Benét—carried much of his message and many of his innovations of style into the twentieth century. Such magazines as *The Soil, Midland,* and *Poetry* testified to his influence. His name was frequently brought into discussions of free verse, though a few critics noted essential differences of aim and practice from the modernist forms. Ezra Pound, in "A Pact" (1912), had put fairly well both the admiration and the reservations of the younger poets and critics.[6] The great tribute to Whitman came in Hart Crane's *The Bridge* (1930), especially in the "Cape Hatteras" section.

Perhaps the greatest barrier to a proper evaluation of America's past in the 1920s was the general spirit of skepticism concerning the worth of any past; it was certainly true that developments in twentieth-century literature and criticism had encouraged a view of the present as the time of major, even of exclusive, significance. Writers suspected that American culture had suffered from various kinds of disease, or they claimed that critics had in the past misled and misinformed their readers concerning the reality of American life. One type of criticism took the form of a moral diagnosis of America's cultural ills and an attempt to discover the history of the illnesses. The principal culprit was the Puritan; examination of Puritan history was the most elaborate of all the excursions into the American past undertaken in the decade. This criticism had begun before the war, and it increased in frequency and vigor in the years following. The most suggestive term-dates of this criticism are 1908 (Van Wyck Brooks, *The Wine of the Puritans*) and 1930 (Matthew Josephson, *Portrait of the Artist as American*).

[6] Pound wrote his father in June 1913: "Whitman is a hard nutt [*sic*]. The *Leaves of Grass* is the book. It is impossible to read it without swearing at the author almost continuously." As for Sandburg's poetry, Pound discussed its failure of precision and its lack of subtlety. In a letter to Harriet Monroe (August 21, 1917), he said: "A decent system would give him time to loaf in a library, which while perhaps less important than loafing in pubs, is still a part of the complete man's loafing."

Like most of Brooks's writings, up to and including the first edition of *The Ordeal of Mark Twain* (1920), *The Wine of the Puritans* surveyed the apparent consequences of Puritan thought and discipline for contemporary America. Written in Europe, it considered also the reasons for American expatriation—men find in Europe "the premisses of an artistic life really taken for granted." Brooks sought in vain for an integrated civilization in America's past; he asserted that life in America was either too highly "polished" or simply too "rough."

This division he also discussed in *America's Coming-of-Age* (1915): the two main currents of the American mind are idealism, which stems from the transcendentalism of Emerson, and "catchpenny opportunism," which originated in "the practical shifts of Puritan life, becoming a philosophy in Franklin." These are the "highbrow" and the "lowbrow," and the young man is caught between the two: he is indoctrinated in highbrow idealism at college but finds that there is no place where it can be integrated with or applied to the practical world; the ideals therefore "end by breeding nothing but cynicism and chagrin; and, in becoming permanently catalogued in the mind as impracticable, they lead to a feeling that all ideas are unreal." Brooks maintained that there was a total divorce of the American literary past from its contemporary reality. "If my soul were set on the accumulation of dollars," he said, Thoreau, Emerson, Poe, Hawthorne, could not dissuade him—not because they had nothing to say to him, but because they were but indifferently regarded, and the only real "American hero" is the "inspired millionaire."

This diagnosis continued in *Letters and Leadership* (1918). There is a great cry for a national culture, Brooks said, because "our inherited culture has so utterly failed to meet the exigencies of our life, to seize and fertilize its roots." In his melancholy survey of a cultural waste land, Brooks cited almost every figure of the American past as either villain or victim; and in 1920 he presented his first full-length documentation of the thesis. *The Ordeal of Mark Twain* is the most complete expression of Brooks's early diagnosis of the American past.[7]

[7] While *The Ordeal of Mark Twain* was not the last of Brooks's discussions of the American malady, not long after its publication he began to reconsider his position. The principal section of *Emerson and Others* (1927) is an amiable attempt to reconstruct the "spirit" of Concord in Emerson's time; it is without criticism and it contains no implication for the thesis concerning the deadly influence of American culture upon its artists. As for the "Others," Brooks apologized in the prefatory "note" for including two of them: "Those [essays] on Randolph Bourne and the Literary Life in America contain many statements that

Mark Twain suffered from "some deep malady of the soul"; he was

> a frustrated spirit, a victim of arrested development, and beyond this
> fact, as we know from innumerable instances the psychologists have
> placed before us, we need not look for an explanation of the chagrin
> of his old age. He had been balked, he had been divided, he had even
> been turned . . . against himself; the poet, the artist in him, conse-
> quently, had withered into the cynic and the whole man had become a
> spiritual valetudinarian.

The sum total of Brooks's work from 1908 to 1920 suggests several
types of criticism: a strict bifurcation of American culture in the past;
an overemphasis upon expediency and practicality; suppression of an
interest in the arts and of the life of the mind; the resultant failure of
American culture to sustain, attract, or encourage its artists; finally,
either by suggestion or by direct analysis, fixing the primary responsibility upon the "Puritan," who is judged largely in terms of what he
is alleged to have done to the state of the national culture.[8] In a sense,
these faults serve to sum up the characteristics of the Puritan as seen
from a prejudiced and an unhistorical point of view; they are an extreme
example of the use of tradition for purposes of contemporary polemic.

The pattern of this criticism was followed very closely in the 1920s,
varying in details only as the special vocabularies and conceptions of
Nietzsche (Mencken), Freud (Waldo Frank, Harvey O'Higgins, and
many others), and Jefferson (Parrington) were brought to bear.[9] As

---

are certainly less true now than they were when they were written; but I have
thought it best to reprint them in their first form." In *The Writer in America*
(1953), Brooks looked back some thirty-nine years; in *America's Coming-of-Age*,
he said, "I was reflecting the point of view that prevailed when I was in college."
He had underrated American culture, he admitted, because his professors had
almost invariably belittled it as a "dependency" of England. *The Writer in
America* tried for a redress of balance through severe treatment of those critics
who did not follow or respect his approach to the culture.

[8] Kenneth Murdock, in his contribution to *A Reinterpretation of American
Literature* (1928), offered what is perhaps the most incisive criticism of the current
anti-puritanism; he began by objecting to both Mencken's and Brooks's views,
then pleaded for clarity of distinction: "The Puritan tradition must be that
handed down by the people historically called Puritans. If Victorianism is in
question—always assuming there is someone who can define Victorianism—or
Presbyterianism, or Methodism, or capitalism, it is better to say so rather than
to make the vague doubly vague by stretching a useful historical term to cover
what it only loosely fits."

[9] For a much more extensive discussion of these matters, see Chapter VII,
"Critiques of the Middle Class."

for Parrington's *Main Currents in American Thought* (1927–1930), it seemed strangely out of keeping with what was otherwise being done in contemporary literature.[10] Yet the work was enthusiastically received upon its appearance. It cut through many barriers of interpretation, provided a simplified explanation of the "Colonial Mind," set up an easily understandable set of evaluative terms. In spite of, or because of, Parrington's general dislike of puritanism, his thesis was presented with an apparently rational clarity that was generally admired and appreciated. For Parrington the Puritans were not so much the originators of a malaise of which men and women of the 1920s were trying to cure themselves as an authoritarian, autocratic people, who needed to be properly placed if the real American tradition, the Jeffersonian tradition, was to succeed them.

Critical reviews of the American past revealed a sense of order; that is, they followed from a fairly clear notion of what the American past was. They were neither erratic nor merely impressionistic; what was questionable, however, was the value of their initial premises, which were often clearly prejudiced or inspired by a prejudicial version of historical causes. In many cases critics began with a special view of the present, assumed because of some contemporary prejudice; they were therefore animated by a vivid sense of the current American scene and a deep wish to understand its past. They proceeded from this point to establish several assumptions as to what a culture ideally should be, and—finding that, in their estimate, American culture fell short of achieving the ideal—went on to examine the past with the aim of discovering reasons for the failure.

Most frequently cited among the shortcomings in present society were those associated with the conventional life, the serious effects of industrialism upon culture, and the strong emphasis upon the commercial life and materialist obsessions. Some of these weaknesses could, they thought, be explained by re-examining (as did Charles Beard) the economic framework of our history; this form of re-examination

[10] See Howard Mumford Jones, *Theory of American Literature* (1948): "Our search for a usable past projected an eighteenth-century temperament into the world of Freud, Einstein, Kafka, and T. S. Eliot, surely an astonishing anachronism in a literary world that has gone all out for expressionism, sublimation, and the stream-of-consciousness novel!" If one considers this "anachronism" carefully, much of what the decade has meant in the history of twentieth-century American culture becomes clear. Jefferson was the hero of the liberal interpreters of the past, the despair of the Agrarians, a lost and naïve scapegoat of "modernist" critics.

became the dominating one in the 1930s. Other weaknesses were religious defections, or moral, or spiritual, or, perhaps, psychological consequences of an overbearing and an obsessive drive for material security. The pioneer was the Puritan writ large, in this view. The exploitation of this judgment of the American past was not accidental; it was an opportunity, seized by many writers, to explain to themselves their break from the past or their rebellion against convention. To prove their contemporaries or the older generation ridiculous gave them one form of satisfaction; to see in the whole of the American past continuous evidence of absurdity was an even more satisfactory experience; finally, to convince themselves that the American past was responsible for the most unpleasant aspects of life in the present was a remarkably gratifying justification for their forms of rejection. This is not to suggest that they were frivolous in their reading of past causes for present sins. Some of them were so serious as to be ponderously exhortatory and gloomily prophetic. Nevertheless the results were a strange reading of American cultural history and a still more striking series of caricatures of ancestral figures.

3. Impressionistic Versions of American History

"IT HAS always seemed to me a rare privilege, this, of being an American," Gertrude Stein said in *The Making of Americans* (1925), "a real American, one whose tradition it has taken scarcely sixty years to create. We need only realize our parents, remember our grandparents, and know ourselves and our history is complete." This statement does more than reveal pride of country; it testifies to Miss Stein's interest in generations, in the immediacy of tradition, the simultaneity of past with present.

The Making of Americans [11] is a history of generations, of families, of persons. There is little attempt to differentiate the persons sharply; they experience and communicate with respect to their inner natures. Nor is there much reference to external event; the persons are not his-

[11] Written, she tells us, in 1906–1908; published by Robert McAlmon's Three Mountains Press (Paris, 1925). Hemingway prepared parts of the original manuscript for publication in the *transatlantic review,* an experience which, Miss Stein informs us, helped him in his own efforts to become a writer.

torical in the sense of their achieving public prominence. The book is not a history; it does not chronicle public events. It is "interior" history; as Donald Sutherland has said, it is "a history written in subjective time." The passage of time is represented largely through similarity of custom, significant repetitions of behavior, the precedents established in one generation for the limiting of acts in the next:

> Once an angry man dragged his father along the ground through his own orchard. "Stop!" cried the groaning old man at last, "Stop! I did not drag my father beyond this tree."

All Gertrude Stein's views of writing and the arts were closely associated with a theory of time. Her major assumptions were that generations are the same (that is, that many things are carried over from one generation to the next); that generations are different in what they experience and in the nature of the experiencing ("each generation has something different at which they are looking"); finally, that "big" events, such as the war, can accelerate experience, can make it "more contemporary" by adjusting the consciousness of man more rapidly:

> This then the contemporary recognition, because of the academic thing known as war having been forced to become contemporary [12] made every one not only contemporary in act not only contemporary in thought but contemporary in self-consciousness made every one contemporary with the modern composition.

Miss Stein's most important contribution to the consciousness of tradition was her sense of a "continuous present." She considered that the past, through its similarities, was contained in the present; her idea of progress in human action was that acts flow into one another and that in their successive occurrences there is more repetition than sharp differences and interruptions; her definition of the present concerned the precise nature of "the thing seen" in terms of its being immediately experienced:

> The only thing that is different from one time to another is what is seen and what is seen depends upon how everybody is doing everything.

[12] That is, war is "academic" in the beginning in the sense that it is fought according to textbooks based on past war experiences; but it is "forced to become contemporary" when the textbooks don't prepare for new experiencing. The quotation is from *Composition As Explanation*, a lecture she gave at Cambridge and Oxford Universities, published in 1926 in London by the Hogarth Press.

This is an extreme form of contemporaneity. The temporal sense is here reduced almost to a spatial one, if the space be considered that of one's consciousness, of the "thing seen," and of the relationship of the two. In writing, the objects described (or rather, realized in the act of their being described) are identified with one another as parts of a continuous, unwinding, gradually differentiating whole.

In so localizing the relevance of time, Miss Stein was doing in an extreme way what many writers of the 1920s were doing variously. Miss Stein in fact did two things to the "time sense" of modern writing: she described what the present is at the moment of its being present; she removed traditional figures from their historical context and described them as present, rearranging events and readjusting ordinary concepts of their relevance.[13] The "pastness" of people and events was not so important as their relevance, and this relevance was tested in the light of its applicability to the present. This was something more than insisting on the importance of the twentieth century in the teaching and writing of history;[14] it led to the *isolation* of historical figures and happenings from their original context and to the evaluation of each in terms of its contemporary revelance. The *nature* of that relevance was, of course, individualized with each writer who surveyed or selected from the past.

Consider the consequences for literary history of so extreme a perspective: a writer grows up in his own times; if he is young in a time when (as Miss Stein said) a war "may be said to have advanced a general recognition of the expression of the contemporary composition by almost thirty years," he is not very likely to have had a thorough grounding in a tradition. He may also have had experience with cultures not his own, and in some respects may have valued those cultures more

[13] See *Four in America* (written, 1932–33; published 1947), in which she considers Grant, Henry James, Wilbur Wright, and George Washington, giving them careers different from the ones we generally associate with their histories: Grant as a religious leader, Henry James as a general, Wright as a painter, Washington as a novelist. (See Donald Sutherland, *Gertrude Stein: A Biography of Her Work,* 1951.)

[14] See Morton G. White, *Social Thought in America* (1949), Chapter IV: James Harvey Robinson and Charles Beard "openly confessed [in their textbook, *The Development of Modern Europe,* 1907] their association with the new history by admitting that they had 'consistently subordinated the past to the present,' and that it had been their 'ever-conscious aim to enable the reader to catch up with his own times; to read intelligently the foreign news in the morning paper; to know what was the attitude of Leo XIII toward the Social Democrats, even if he has forgotten that of Innocent III toward the Albigenses.' "

than his own. His orientation with respect to the past will be both *present* and *selective:* that is, he will think for the most part in terms of the present (of what he has immediately gained by way of insight into the human condition); and he will select from tradition those persons and those events relevant to his sense of the present. He will take them out of chronological order, disregard conventional notions of their relative importance and conventional judgments of their value. The result is an "impressionistic" history, a highly personalized rearrangement of the past in the interests of explaining, justifying, and lending support to an especially contemporaneous disposition toward human fact.

Such impressionistic versions of the past rarely achieve any degree of reputation; they are often mere notes on the way to the assimilation of a tradition—as, presumably, a succession of university courses leads to the mastery of a tradition when a student has put them all in a perspective given him at the time he is graduated. Nevertheless an impressionistic reading of history sometimes does achieve prominence for the merit of its insights, however "unhistorical" these may be. This is true of D. H. Lawrence's *Studies in Classic American Literature,* first published in America in 1923. Lawrence came to American literature as a fresh, original, in many ways a naïve reader, not especially concerned with—and not very well informed about—prevailing academic or scholarly forms of ordering the subject. His appraisal was very much and very interestingly a "Studies in Laurentian Responses to the Reading of Classic American Literature." In almost every detail the insights are Laurentian and worth while for their revelation, not of the American past but of the Laurentian present. The American past gains from the exchange, but the gain can hardly be measured or evaluated.

For Benjamin Franklin, God is "the heavenly store-keeper, the everlasting Wanamaker."

Concerning the *Leatherstocking Tales,* the friendship of Natty Bumppo and Chingachgook is "A stark, stripped relationship of two men, deeper than the deeps of sex. . . . The stark, loveless, wordless unison of two men who have come to the bottom of themselves. This is the new nucleus of a new society, the clue to a new world epoch."

The Scarlet Letter: ". . . the sin in Hester and Arthur Dimmesdale's case was a sin because they did what they *thought* it *wrong* to do. If they had really *wanted* to be lovers, and if they had had the courage of their own passion, there would have been no sin: even had the desire been only momentary."

Moby Dick: "[The white whale] is the deepest blood-being of the white race. He is our deepest blood-nature.

"And he is hunted, hunted, hunted by the maniacal fanaticism of our white mental consciousness. We want to hunt him down. To subject him to our will. And in this maniacal conscious hunt of ourselves we get dark races and pale to help us, red, yellow, and black, east and west, Quaker and fire-worshipper, we get them all to help us in this ghastly maniacal hunt which is our doom and our suicide."

This is a reading of American tradition that, however remote from either the actual past or the minds of those whose works are being judged, is starkly relevant to the present created by Lawrence for himself.[15] It contains in an extreme form a personalized, individualized, localized present context of relevance—and it is only in terms of that context that the American past is permitted entry. Some element of this selectivity is to be found in almost all writing in the 1920s on the American past.[16]

[15] American reviews of the book were keenly aware of the deeply personal nature of Lawrence's responses. Conrad Aiken (*Nation and Athenaeum,* July 12, 1924), after discussing Lawrence's style, went on to say: "These paraphernalia, undefined and numerous, confuse Mr. Lawrence's book and make apparent his own confusion. One comes away with a feeling that Mr. Lawrence could perceive psychological and aesthetic causes with remarkable shrewdness, but that for the most part he is prevented from a clear view by a frenzy of excitement. Life, art, and criticism of art—all, for Mr. Lawrence, have in them something feverish and sensational. . . . His own affects, in other words (which are of a highly peculiar and tyrannous nature), are too immediately and uncontrollably engaged—he loses distance. The result, when he turns to criticism, is a kind of sensationalism—awkward, harshly jocose, violent, and often offensive—but here and there lighted with an extraordinarily fine bit of perception, beautifully given." John Macy, in the *Nation* (October 10, 1923), while he devoted much space to Lawrence's misreadings of America and Americans, admitted that "the core of the book is its tinglingly vital challenge not only to America but to all manner of human quackery and puffery." H. I. Brook (*New York Times,* September 16, 1923) found that "in spite of the extraordinary things he has to say about people whom so many commentators have seemed to make hopelessly dull . . . you are driven to conclude that at bottom D. H. Lawrence is a bore, and, like most bores, complacently concerned with himself, bent buzzingly on his own preoccupations."

[16] See, for example, Sherwood Anderson's letters; also Pound's *Indiscretions* (1923), an autobiography of sorts, and his "American" *Cantos* (xxxi to xli). On this last, cf. Hugh Kenner, *The Poetry of Ezra Pound* (1951).

Perhaps the most illuminating, and one of the most influential, of impressionistic readings of American history was William Carlos Williams' *In the American Grain* (1925). Here are many brilliant flashes of personalized insight comparable in intensity and eccentricity to Lawrence's. Williams also shares some of the preoccupations of the writers who diagnosed America's cultural weaknesses. The book is primarily lyrical in style, and vigorously assertive in its realignments of dominating and subordinate "heroes." In consequence, certain phases of the American past emerge from obscurity, others are pushed back into it, and the whole forms a symbolic reordering of the historical context, in some respects not unlike that given it in Hart Crane's *The Bridge*.[17]

Williams' "argument" is suggested in his selection of objects for examination, in the quality of his prose style as he examines them, in the emphasis he puts upon each, and in the degree to which the present is made to play upon each as it is drawn from the past for inspection. He argues, for one thing, that America has only infrequently been realized as a *place;* the original explorers only occasionally sensed it as a thing to be seen and experienced. Columbus was a notable exception, and America was for Columbus not so much a place as a symbolic reshaping of a dream that had barely been touched by reality. Others thought of America as a continent to be explored, exploited, and endured. For them, it was either a puzzling land or merely a problem in military strategy. The Indians were not considered really human; they were unformed humans ("imperfect" or unrealized Puritans), either accessible to "improvement" or beyond the hope of it. Occasionally heroes do emerge. They are persons who are fully and independently themselves, they act as themselves, as *"Americans,"* and not as transplanted Englishmen or provincial subordinates to a European culture: Daniel Boone as explorer, Aaron Burr in politics, Edgar Allan Poe in literature.

As Williams sees the American past, the major *superior* evil was puritanism: its view of America as place was from the beginning abstract and "theological"; its attitude toward persons other than Puritans, arrogant and pitifully ignorant. The Puritan stupidity was demon-

---

[17] On November 21, 1926, Crane wrote Waldo Frank: "Williams' *American Grain* is an achievement that I'd be proud of. A most important and *sincere* book. I'm very enthusiastic—I put off reading it, you know, until I felt my own way cleared beyond chance of confusions incident to reading a book so intimate to my theme. I was so interested to note that he puts Poe and his 'character' in the same position as I had *symbolized* for him in 'The Tunnel.' "

strated in the treatment of witches; in the Salem trials the Puritan failure to understand the most elementary human facts was abundantly proved.[18] The serious American weakness was that our forefathers were niggardly, not worthy of this fabulous new world; that they gave their energy to "the smaller, narrow, protective thing, and not to the great New World." The symbol for Williams of this smallness was Franklin, as he was for Lawrence: "our wise prophet in chicanery, the great buffoon, the face on the penny stamp."

Evidences of this disposition toward the American past abound in *In the American Grain*. The great image of discovery is of course the journey of Columbus to the New World. For all his brief acquaintance with the ground itself and his failure accurately to identify it, Columbus had a luminous vision of what the New World meant. Other explorers did not have this lively sense of their mission; as a result ("The Destruction of Tenochtitlan"), history began for America "with murder and enslavement, not with discovery." In a sense, the Continent avenged itself upon them, in the burial of DeSoto in the Mississippi River: "Down, down, this solitary sperm, down into the liquid, the formless, the insatiable belly of sleep."

More than the Spanish explorers, whose aim had been quick access to gold, our Puritan ancestors were responsible for the failures in the American past: "The Pilgrims, they, the seed, instead of growing, looked black at the world and damning its perfections praised a zero in themselves." This is, unfortunately, not a disadvantage confined to themselves; we have inherited it, as "a malfeasant ghost that dominates us all," an "atavism that thwarts and destroys." In an interlude ("Père Sebastian Rasles"), Williams discusses this fact with a Frenchman in Paris; the expatriate setting serves as an important quality in the judgment. The great fault was that the Puritan did not visualize or realize the Continent; it was, rather, an extension of his *concept* of place. They went to it, but it did not come to them. One result of "this abortion of the mind" is that Americans have no sense of the past as a concrete, regional, natural thing, but know it only as a place where ideas and ambitions can and must be translated into facts. It

[18] Consider this as a special index of the influence of the "time sense." The witch trials were conducted on a theological basis; Williams looks at them from a personal bias, hostile to Puritan abstractions. Theology forgave (or was ignorant of) personal errors of judgment. More than two centuries had intervened before Williams gained his perspective upon Salem. Only Samuel Sewall (who rose during a church service to confess an error) gave Williams encouragement in the seventeenth century.

is impossible in such circumstances, argues Williams, for a real morality to grow out of the past, unless the Puritan miscalculation can eventually be overcome.[19]

In the light of this major and damning factor of American history, Williams selects for special evaluation and praise a few spirits who avoided or escaped it: for example, the "great voluptuary" of the westward movement, Daniel Boone, a "lineal descendant of Columbus on the beach at Santo Domingo." [20] Boone saw the Indian, not as an "unformed Puritan," but "as a natural expression of the place, . . . the flower of his world." Boone is therefore an object lesson in Williams' indictment of the past:

> It is necessary in appraising our history to realize that the nation was the offspring of the desire to huddle, to protect—of terror—superadded to a new world of great beauty and ripest blossom that wellnigh no man of distinction saw save Boone.

Similarly, the political hero of Williams' text, Aaron Burr, was overcome by the main line of historical event, his "careless truth," spontaneous gesture, openness, gaiety, and unconstraint buried and obscured. Poe was also defeated; he too belonged to the small group of persons with something to say to the present:

> Either the New World must be *mine* as I will have it, or it is a worthless bog. There can be no concession. His attack was *from the center* out.

Longfellow had expressed the American ideal of finding a culture fully developed somewhere else and *putting it into* America. Poe, however, "was the first to realize the hard, sardonic, truculent mass of the New World," and to sense that this world should not be destroyed, "painted over, smeared." He was therefore the free independent Ameri-

[19] Cf. Williams' attacks upon the use of *place* as an object of expropriation and exploitation, in *Paterson,* leading in Part IV of that poem to the Pound-like abuse of usury, a mathematical compounding of the abstract denial of a place as a concrete object. Alexander Hamilton is a villain for both Williams and Pound.

[20] Some reflection of the spirit of Boone is to be found in Hart Crane's portrayal of the hoboes in "The River"; they find themselves at the *end* of the materializing process, in whose own judgment they are "Blind fists of nothing, humpty-dumpty clods"; but they "touch something like a key perhaps." See Crane's letter to Otto Kahn, September 12, 1927 (*Letters*): ". . . their wanderings carry the reader through an experience parallel to that of Boone and others." Crane had almost nothing directly to say about puritanism in *The Bridge,* but said a good deal by implication.

can artist, as Boone was America's natural man and Burr its spontaneous, independent man of public affairs.

Through all of its surprising insights and its unusual shiftings of historical event and relevance, *In the American Grain* demonstrates clearly the mind of the present impressionistically encountering the past. The learning demonstrated in the book is not inconsiderable; however, it is not methodologically ordered, but rather lyrically and polemically adjusted to the immediate necessities of present conviction. In these terms the book is an especially important illustration of history and tradition as "continuous present," a conscious attempt to create a series of contemporary relevances out of an accessible past.

4. Humanism: the "Classical" Past

HOWEVER much they differed among themselves in the details of their criticism, the Humanists shared several views in their survey of morality and taste in the 1920s: that the most important part of the American past was New England puritanism; that modern critics had grossly misrepresented the Puritans, for reasons of their own; that modern American literature (called variously realism, naturalism, and romanticism) deserved only the strictest censure. In an important sense, the past for Paul Elmer More and Irving Babbitt was not identifiable with any given century or period of time; they were interested in a *kind* of culture, a kind of literature, a kind of psychological and moral effect. If these could be found at all in literary history, they were perhaps best seen in eighteenth-century England, and before "romanticism" had overcome man's sense of propriety and rational decorum. They were much concerned over the presence and the exercise of a moral will, and the Puritan will most nearly represented it in the American tradition.

Upon these crucial points the Humanist judgment of tradition depended. The question of standards was closely identified with this judgment. "The real question," More said in *The Demon of the Absolute* (1928), "is not whether there are standards, but whether they shall be based on tradition or shall be struck out brand new by each successive generation or by each individual critic." These standards require a special description of the moral nature: man is both "natural" and "human"; there are a "lower" and a "higher" nature, a "bestial" and a divine. "The true artist . . . is aware indeed of the bestial in man, but sees also something else, and in that something else looks for the meaning of life." Norman Foerster (*American Criticism,* 1928) offered a description of the Humanist personality: he will be a "complete" man; he will acknowledge and value "proportion" and he will have standards; he will understand the moral "constants" that have appeared in cultures of the past; he will be a man of reason but also a man of imagination; he will above all recognize that the "ultimate ethical principle is that of *restraint* or *control.*" This Humanist personality should also be able to detect the failures of literature and thought for what they are; his moral faculty is all but identical with his critical, and the two function basically in harmony:

> The philosophy of Humanism finds its master truth not in men as they are (realism) or in men as worse than they are (naturalism) or in men as they "wish" to be (romanticism), but in men as they "ought" to be—"ought" . . . with reference to the perfection of the human type.

The problem of locating and describing the primary instrument of control was a severe challenge to the Humanist's ingenuity. More labeled it the "inner check" (*Shelburne Essays,* Eighth Series, 1913) and defined it as "that within man which displays itself intermittently as an inhibition upon this or that impulse, preventing its prolongation in activity, and making a pause or eddy, so to speak, in the stream. This negation of the flux we call the inner check. . . . What, if anything, lies behind the inner check, what it is, why and how it acts or neglects to act, we cannot express in rational terms." Babbitt preferred the term "vital control" (*frein vital*) and defined it (in *Humanism and America,* 1930) "as the higher immediacy that is known in its relation to the lower immediacy—the merely temperamental man with his impressions and emotions and expansive desires."

In addition to this discussion of inner controls, More and Babbitt both attended to the problems of "outer control." This was generally identified with some form of aristocratic society—not often, or necessarily, an economic class, but an aristocracy of taste, education, manners, and decorum. In establishing the terms of this social reference, they severely condemned humanitarianism and allied social attitudes— More in *Aristocracy and Justice* (1915), Babbitt in *Democracy and Leadership* (1924). More spoke of a "natural aristocracy," a selection of the "best" from a community as "the true consummation of a democracy." These best are not a sharply defined class but are characterized by their natural superiority.

Babbitt's book cut at the heart of modern humanitarianism, scoffing at both pretensions and love of progress; his criticism of the humanitarian was addressed chiefly to what he thought was a mistaken emphasis on "the welfare and progress of mankind in the lump" instead of on "the individual and his inner life." Material progress has been made, he said, by means of concentration on "the facts of natural law." As a consequence, the modern American admires only material things, is complacent, smug, and inactive where the moral life and its responsibilities are concerned; he is, in short, all but ridiculous. "The American reading his Sunday paper in a state of lazy collapse is perhaps the most perfect symbol of the triumph of quantity over quality that the world has yet seen." In contrast to this spectacle, Babbitt presented the figure of the Puritan, who at least possessed a moral will and sensed a responsibility to God and to himself. He proposed that we stop confusing the issue of puritanism, but he did not urge a return to a Puritan way of life:

> If we in America are not content with a stodgy commercialism, it does not follow that we need, on the one hand, to return to puritanism, or, on the other, to become "liberals" in the style of the *New Republic;* nor again need we evolve under the guidance of Mr. H. L. Mencken into second-rate Nietzscheans. We do need, however, if we are to gain any hold on the present situation, to develop a little moral gravity and intellectual seriousness.

In the many cross-currents of Humanist criticism, several interpretations of its view of tradition stand out: that the tradition should be a moral one; that the literature expressing it should demonstrate a moral restraint and discipline in its author and somehow educate and further the moral sensibility of the reader; that a faculty of good taste and a strong sense of "vital control" go into the making of the educated man, the man of control as opposed to the "merely temperamental man"; that the literature most likely to help in the cultivation of such a man is "classical" rather than romantic, and it is almost certain not to be modern. There was no general agreement about what writers or what books met the Humanist terms, but there were degrees of assent, and all but a scattered few Humanists agreed on what authors should be excluded from the list. They generally defended the Puritans (rather as persons than as writers); they were divided on the question of Emerson's value, not always sure of Thoreau, inclined to admire Longfellow as a minor poet but as an admirable scholar and personality, and severe in their judgment of Whitman, who, Babbitt said, "represents in an extreme form the substitute for vital control of expansive emotion under the name of love."

The great controversy with Humanism in the 1920s was for the most part associated with its hostility to contemporary literature. Its severe judgment of "the moderns" was almost unrelieved and uniform, including all expressions of naturalists, realists, journalists, "new critics." Occasional merits were seen (Cabell was thought "wise" in his reflections from time to time), but the Humanists were hard put to find any contemporary literature they could accept: Edith Wharton, Edwin Arlington Robinson, Robert Frost, "the fairly distinguished output of Booth Tarkington," Dorothy Canfield, whose *The Brimming Cup* gained special mention and praise. But the moderns, those who had, as More put it, "signed the new Declaration of Independence in letters," were almost universally proscribed.[21]

Only Stuart Pratt Sherman, of all Humanist critics, changed his mind about the postwar writers. In the beginning he condemned the literature; he felt, as did the other Humanists, that the attack upon puritanism was unpardonable. But he suggested that the pessimism of much modern writing was a good sign, that it was a "preliminary to the reintegration of the national spirit and its expression in literature." As an honest reappraisal of assumptions that had gone unexamined too long, this literature bespoke an earnest desire, a search for "a binding generalization of philosophy, or religion, or morals, which will give direction and purpose . . . to the languid, diffusive drift of their lives" (*The Genius of America,* 1923). Sherman deviated from Humanist policy in other ways as well: in being unreservedly enthusiastic over Emerson, in speaking vaguely of what he called a "genuinely democratic humanism," of which Whitman was of course the voice.[22]

[21] More's statements about modern literature were sometimes vigorously metaphorical: *Manhattan Transfer* "might be described in a phrase as an explosion in a cesspool." Dreiser's English, when "he tries to be literary is of the mongrel sort to be expected from a miscegenation of the gutter and the psychological laboratory." Gertrude Stein was "that adventuress into the lunar madness of literary cubism." (Quotations from *The Demon of the Absolute*.)

[22] For these departures from Humanist custom Sherman was severely judged, notably in a *Bookman* essay by G. R. Elliott (April–May, 1930). Sherman had been victimized by "The Emersonian naïveté and happy confusion," said Elliott; he had retained the influence of Babbitt and More, but he "could not or did not . . . build at once firmly and originatively upon them."

The controversy between Humanists and modernists began as early as 1910, when More's influence as editor of the *Nation* (a position he had assumed in 1909) was being felt. The newer writers resented his disapproval of them and found it hard to accept his statements of principle and belief. It became a general, open fight when Mencken began attacking the *"Nation* school" of critics.[23] Mencken and his many followers accused the Humanists of being pedants, dull scribblers, intolerant of anything new, and incapable of advising or aiding young writers.[24]

In the late 1920s, after a number of years in which, as even they admitted, the Humanists were comparatively ignored, a rise of new interest occurred. The revival of Humanism, begun in 1928 with a series of articles in the *Forum* magazine, was aided by the publication in the same year of Gorham Munson's *Destinations,* Norman Foerster's *American Criticism,* and More's *The Demon of the Absolute.* The *Bookman,* with Seward Collins as its editor, took the lead in sponsoring Humanist criticism. A series of charges and countercharges followed; Allen Tate discussed "The Fallacy of Humanism" in *The Criterion* (July 1929), and was answered by Robert Shafer's essay, "Humanism and Impudence" (*Bookman,* January 1930). In 1930 two collections of essays summed up the quarrel and added new impetus to it: *Humanism and America* (edited by Foerster) and *The Critique of Humanism* (edited by C. Hartley Grattan). The first was hailed by More as a great sign of revival, "about the most significant event that has fallen under my notice in many years of reading and reviewing" (*Bookman,* March 1930).

Opponents did not hesitate to reply: Grattan, in his introduction to the dissenting volume, asserted that Humanism opposed progress, was aristocratic and anti-democratic, and was ignorant of modern scientific theory and therefore incompetent to pass judgment upon its effects upon society. Malcolm Cowley, in "Angry Professors" (*New Republic,* April 9, 1930), asked what Humanism had to say for "the mill hands

[23] Mencken called them "the Victorians, the crêpe-clad pundits, the bombastic word-mongers of the *Nation* school—H. W. Boynton, W. C. Brownell, Paul Elmer More, William Lyon Phelps, Frederick Taber Cooper."

[24] To this last accusation Seward Collins replied (*Bookman,* June 1930) that Babbitt and More "had more important work to do than to try to stem the advance of the shallow and misguided generation that has dominated American letters for twenty years. That would have been equivalent to a teacher's spending all his time on the dunce in his class because he was popular with his fellows."

of New Bedford and Gastonia, for the beet-toppers of Colorado, for the men who tighten a single screw in the automobiles that march along Mr. Ford's assembly belt? Should it be confined to the families who draw dividends from these cotton mills, beet fields, factories, and to the professors who teach in universities endowed by them?"

On aesthetic grounds, contributors to the *Critique* questioned the critical intelligence of Humanists: R. P. Blackmur said that "either Humanism is not interested in the content of literature and the problems surrounding it, or it has had no experience therein." Yvor Winters accused Babbitt and More of failing, for all their diatribes against literature, to specify clearly the objects of their attack. They seemed, he said, always interested in condemning "journalists" like Sinclair Lewis, Mencken, and Cabell. This, he maintained, is not literary criticism; the critic must be, "in the most profound sense of the expression, a man of letters, not a man of theories." [25] Rebecca West, in her letter of resignation from the *Bookman* (August 1930), pointed out that of all the contributors to *Humanism and America,* only one (T. S. Eliot) was a "creator"—so that Humanism seemed too much "like a league of the uncreative against the creative." Suppose, she said, Humanism does become dominant in the future: what will happen to literature? The young writer "will be encouraged to convert [his] sense of inferiority into a sense of superiority, not by performance, but by subscription to a very easily held faith. One will then have a world of T. S. Eliots who have not achieved *The Waste Land,* who are utterly sterile and utterly complacent."

This battle over the control of the writing and the judging of literature hinged upon all-important issues: the matter of the past *versus* the present, to which was added the question of a sympathetic review of new literature; the matter of "standards" as opposed to what the Humanists contended was mere irresponsible yielding to impulse; the beliefs held by American liberals, progressives, and humanitarians and their views of both past and present; and the issue of formal analysis of literature as distinguished from a didactic approval or disapproval

---

[25] More occasionally discussed matters of critical evaluation, but he frankly admitted that "If you should ask me by what rhetorical devices or by what instrument of representation one poem or one work of art appeals more successfully than another to the higher faculty within us, . . . though both poems were written with equally good intentions, I would reply frankly that the solution of this problem may be beyond my powers of critical analysis" (*The Demon of the Absolute*). His judgment of Shakespeare was typically in the Humanist mode (see *Shelburne Essays,* Second Series, 1905).

of its intent and subject. In this battle of charges and countercharges, which became at times very bitter and vituperative, the Humanists tried to hold steadfastly to the image of a "classical past," neither exclusively American nor entirely European,[26] from which standards of morality and taste might be formulated and to which all questions of taste, discipline, and moral control might be referred.

The historical importance of Humanism for the 1920s was that, in formulating and defending their standards, Humanist critics were almost universally indisposed to modern literature, or hostile to it, and so new writers of the decade thought a strong, vigorous opposition to them was indispensable to survival. To the extent that Humanists did affect the dominating literature of the decade, it was to increase the interest of writers in those things the Humanists most bitterly opposed.

5. The "Southern" Past

THE PAST of the Southern "Agrarians," as they were called, is best visualized as a community—limited, particular, and intimate. Human consciousness is directed to its discrete particulars, and it infers from them a manner, a code. The place is therefore specific; the time borrows from it its specificity: it is a matter of generations inheriting practices. Most important, economic and aesthetic behavior must be identified with each other. As Allen Tate has said, "The traditional community is made up of men who are never quite making their living all the time and who never quite cease to make it: they are making their living all the time and affirming their code all the time." This union of the economic and the moral, if one assumes that it is continued in time, constitutes a tradition. At the base of the tradition there must be a land with which one is familiar, to which one refers in terms of personal situations extended to social forms, qualified and given quality by habitual repetition. This is a tradition as object; to acquaint one's self fully with such an object, one must experience it in both its general outlines and its intimate, quotidian details. Life in these circumstances involves acting in terms of rules, codes, manners, "games";[27] the rules are formed partly from the demands nature

[26] Not really identifiable with any nation or specifiable culture.

[27] Consider fishing and hunting as "games"; see Hemingway, Caroline Gordon, Lionel Trilling.

makes upon a man who wishes to conquer and use it, partly from human notions of propriety.

The Agrarians did not propose that America be made over into single plots of self-sufficient traditional units; they pointed out, however, that the industrial progress of the North had succeeded in imposing upon cultures and upon men an untraditional, abstract, and abstracting society. The cities thus created were nonentities, the people suffered from a drab repetition of uninviting circumstances, the arts did not exist except in museums, which featured objects borrowed from other cultures. There was no sanctity of precedent, no satisfactory way to believe in what one was doing, no really viable symbolic interpretation either of generations or of the present.

The Agrarians, like the Humanists, opposed the progress of industrialism, together with its liberal humanitarian gospels and its glorification of science practically realized and applied. Unlike the Humanists, they did not set up a formal past dissociated from region or specific place. Their view of tradition was unpretentious; it was, as Tate called it, "quite simply that quality of life that we have got from our immediate past, or if we are makers of tradition, the quality that we create and try to pass on to the next generation." It involved also property which one owned, to which one was responsible. One didn't have a culture or experience it in a rented house or a furnished room. Indispensable to the genuine possession of a tradition was the "higher myth" of religion (which Ransom defended in *God Without Thunder,* 1930) and what Tate called "the lower myth of historical dramatization."

These Southern poets and critics first met, as students and teachers, at Vanderbilt University, where nineteen issues of *The Fugitive* magazine were published, from April 1922 to December 1925. Among the original members of the group were Allen Tate, John Crowe Ransom, and Donald Davidson. Robert Penn Warren joined the group later; his first contribution to the magazine appeared in the issue of June–July 1923. In the beginning they were not especially interested in debating the issues of Southern regionalism; they announced themselves as "self-convicted experimentalists," and Davidson (June 1924) spoke of the "fallacy of regionalism" in poetry: "Place is incidental; it is subordinate; it may even form a definite limitation, and perhaps does in the case of much American poetry."

Tate (April 1924) spoke of the loss of the poet's status because "our time cleaves to no racial myth, its myth is the apotheosis of machinery. . . . But at least our poet is aware of his own age, barren for any art though it may be, for he can't write like Milton or Homer now; from the data of his experience he infers only a distracting complexity." [28] In his poetry of these years Tate was pondering the "myth of machinery" (in "The Subway," the psychosis of machinery), the barrenness of modern culture, the loss of a genuine capacity for belief. The configurations of *The Waste Land* haunted his mind as he spoke of the cheapening of modern culture ("Retroduction to American History," 1925) [29] or of the effect of abstraction upon man's willingness to believe ("Last Days of Alice," 1928).[30]

That these writers were concerned with the Southern tradition was nevertheless clear. As Richard Weaver has said, "it was not until about 1925 that Southern intellectuals caught up with Lee and Jackson. The latter had known in 1862 that the one chance for the South was to carry the fight to the enemy." A number of them were writing not only poetry but prose, biographies of Southern figures or discussions of matters vital to the Agrarian position: Tate's biographies of Stonewall Jackson (1928) and Jefferson Davis (1929); Warren's *John Brown* (1929), an unfavorable account; Ransom's *God Without Thunder* (1930).

The first decisive act in carrying the fight led to the publication in 1930 of *I'll Take My Stand*, by "Twelve Southerners." [31] The "State-

[28] In his poetry of the 1920s Tate used Homer and Vergil as historical critics of twentieth-century America.

[29] Narcissus is vocabulary. Hermes decorates
A cornice on the Third National Bank. Vocabulary
Becomes confusion, decoration a blight; the Parthenon
In Tennessee stucco, art for the sake of death.

[30] Being all infinite, function depth and mass
Without figure, a mathematical shroud

Hurled at the air—blesséd without sin!
O God of our flesh, return us to Your wrath,
Let us be evil could we enter in
Your grace, and falter on the stony path!

Cf. the essay, "Humanism and Naturalism" (in *Reactionary Essays on Poetry and Ideas*, 1936): "To detemporize the past is to reduce it to an abstract lump. To take from the present its concrete fullness is to refuse to let standards work from the inside." This is an attack upon the Humanist effort to create a past independent of history. The Agrarian past was essentially historical, Southern, and ante-bellum; to suggest a past that did not correspond in some imaginative reference to actual history was for Tate an amiable delusion. Moreover, Tate's poems of the 1920s were essentially "American" in their objections to prevailing images of America.

[31] This was also the year of publication of the two symposia, *Humanism in America* and *Critique of Humanism*. It was just a few months after the Wall Street

ment of Principles" introducing the volume specified the issue of "a Southern way of life against what may be called the American or prevailing way" or, otherwise phrased, Agrarian *versus* Industrial. The primary object was to define the failures of an industrial (that is, Northern) society, a society in which religion, the arts, "the amenities of life," could not flourish. The statement had its polemical objective: "The theory of agrarianism is that the culture of the soil is the best and most sensitive of vocations, and that therefore it should have the economic preference and enlist the maximum of workers."

Ransom's contribution fully defined the Southern traditionalist, the "unreconstructed Southerner," who "persists in his regard for a certain terrain, a certain history, and a certain inherited way of living." This South, said Ransom (who, like his fellows, had had experience with and reverence for the European tradition), "is unique on this continent for having founded and defended a culture which was according to the European principles of culture." Man can love an object or a form that has come from attention to objects, but he cannot love "a mere turnover" or "a credit system." [32]

Davidson attended especially to the influence of industrialism upon the arts. The arts need a certain kind of environment in which to flourish: "societies which were for the most part stable, religious, and agrarian; where the goodness of life was measured by a scale of values having little to do with the material values of industrialism; where men were never too far removed from nature to forget that the chief subject of art, in the final sense, is nature." As for industrial communities, art becomes for them a commodity, medicinal or entertaining,[33] and education in the humanities is a losing fight in the midst of a hopeless division of interests: "The product of a humanistic education in an industrial age is most likely to be an exotic, unrelated creature—a disillusionist or a dilettante."

Tate's essay pointed out the advantages of simplicity in the Southern culture. The North had "performed wonders" in breaking down the

---

crash, and history in a sense offered a full opportunity for both positions to be heard.

[32] Neither Ransom nor Tate believed that the North would turn to agrarianism, or that the South could itself resist some form of industrialization; but Ransom pointed to the danger that the South might revise its character altogether and "lose entirely her historic identity."

[33] ". . . one visualizes caravans of art, manned by regiments of lecturers, rushed hastily to future epidemic centers of barbarism when some new Mencken discovers a Sahara of the Bozart."

European culture of our ancestors. Only in the South was some sense
of unified culture retained:

> The Southern mind was single, not top-heavy with learning it had no
> need of,[34] unintellectual, and composed; it was personal and dramatic,
> rather than abstract and metaphysical; and it was sensuous because it
> lived close to a natural scene of great variety and interests.

The Southerner must take hold of his tradition "by violence." He has
inherited an unfortunate history, and he cannot in present circumstances "fall back upon his religion." He finds it necessary to use the
instrument of politics to restore his "private, self-contained, and essentially spiritual life." He "must do this."

But the Southerners of the *Fugitive* and of *I'll Take My Stand* [35]
were neither sanguine nor violent. They felt deeply the loss of prestige
suffered by the Southern tradition, and they knew that culturally the
South was neither ready nor anxious for any radical reaction. The
literature they produced was at times retrospective and bitterly caustic,
at other times concerned merely to portray the dilemma of the young
Southerner as a modern dilemma, the predicament of the modern
"solipsist" who cannot give himself to any heroic tradition or challenge. It was not quite enough to explain why the South was good or
to determine the areas in which culture and cultivation might be genuinely meaningful.

Ransom and Tate both concerned themselves with the general theme
of "lost innocence," combining it with the "dynastic wound" of a defeated tradition whenever the two naturally coalesced. They were sensitive to the very complications of man's life which qualified or even
destroyed that innocence. The only way to preserve innocence, they

[34] He is contrasting it with the culture of New England here. In an essay on
Emily Dickinson, Tate suggested that New England more than any other
Northern region possessed a unified tradition, at least into the early nineteenth
century: "It gave final, definite meaning to life, the life of pious and impious, of
learned and vulgar alike. . . . Socially we may not like the New England Idea.
Yet it had an immense, incalculable value for literature: it dramatized the
human soul" (*Reactionary Essays on Poetry and Ideas,* 1936).

[35] There were nine other essays of the volume: Frank L. Owsley, "The Irre-
pressible Conflict"; John Gould Fletcher, "Education, Past and Present"; Lyle H.
Lanier, "A Critique of the Philosophy of Progress"; H. C. Nixon, "Whither
Southern Economy"; Andrew N. Lytle, "The Hind Tit"; Robert Penn Warren,
"The Briar Patch"; John D. Wade, "The Life and Death of Cousin Lucius";
H. B. Kline, "William Remington: A Study in Individualism"; and Stark Young,
"Not in Memoriam but in Defense."

felt, is to continue it from one generation to the next. But people forget; they lose a sense of the past in listening to the persuasions of the present and the urgent (liberal and "progressive") drive toward future promise. Most important of all, the viability of tradition depends upon an ability to sustain some quality of heroic emotion from past into present. Symbols, archetypes, do continue in the present, but if the allegiance to the memory of what they originally signified is weak, they become merely quaint or are defeated altogether by "brute" realism.

The most important Southern poets were torn between deep emotional attachment to a traditional object and a naturalistic tendency to reduce it to brute and pitiful fact. This was the major preoccupation of Ransom and Tate, as it proved to be in the work of Robert Penn Warren. Southern history offered much evidence of this tension; the Southern past seemed unfortunately rich in events that threatened to destroy the poet's ideal image of a tradition.

Ransom's "Antique Harvesters" [36] is at once a recognition of the Southern present and an appeal to retain what has become a symbolic memory of the Southern past. The old men who meet to gather the harvest [37] are reminded of age and of the imminence of death by their persons ("dry, gray, spare") and the place; their primary necessity is to translate their lives into the design of another generation, to strengthen the memories of the young men. The means of doing this are first the forms of the past: the land, the field, is both present place and symbol of the past:

> One spot has special yield? "On this spot stood
> Heroes and drenched it with their only blood."
> And talk meets talk, as echoes from the horn
> Of the hunter—echoes are the old men's arts,
> Ample are the chambers of their hearts.

The aesthetic, the forms of a tradition, are their sole gift to the young. Tradition is offered to them as a unified pattern of impulse unsatisfied, economic plans postponed, selfishness qualified by a respect for the non-self. The hunters are therefore participants in a symbolic rite; the fox is a ritual figure, his acts motivated by the need for sacrifice.

[36] First published in *Two Gentlemen in Bonds* (1927).

[37] Throughout the poem, such words as *harvest* are intended analogically to unite past and present, concrete object and symbolic memory.

> And the fox, lovely ritualist, in flight
> Offering his unearthly ghost to quarry;
> And the fields, themselves to harry.

The harvest has become a memorial act, an act of worship; the yield is gathered not for profit but in worship of "the Lady":

> Bare the arm, dainty youths, bend the knees
> Under bronze burdens. And by an autumn tone
> As by a grey, as by a green, you will have known
> Your famous Lady's image . . .

The poet finally asks that the young remain within the tradition. View your own lives, he pleads, *sub specie aeternitatis;* the young will become old,

> . . . and if one talk of death—
> Why, the ribs of the earth subsist frail as a breath
> If but God wearieth.

Nowhere is so full a measure given to the Southerner's experiences of retrospective agony and to his desire for a formal security against disbelief than in Allen Tate's "Ode to the Confederate Dead." [38] The poem is not about the South, Confederate armies, or the "heroic past," though it concerns all these. Discussing this matter in an essay ("Narcissus as Narcissus"), Tate said that "the proof of the connection must be, if anywhere, in the experienced conflict which is the poem itself. Since one set of references for the conflict is the historic Confederates, the poem, if it is successful, is a certain section of history made into experience, but only on this occasion, and on these terms: even the author of the poem has no experience of its history apart from the occasion and the terms."

The situation of the poem is a man at the gate of a Confederate cemetery. The "conflict" has to do with what he makes of the circumstance. The things he sees and the vision he tries (without success) to make of them exist in his mind. Naturalistic detail is therefore essential to the effect, a supreme demonstration of the defeat of the will to entertain a belief. The headstones slowly yield their names to time; the wind provokes no image of the past; the leaves casually pile up, a natural index of the death of living matter. It is autumn, and the scene of death is enhanced by seasonal evidences of its recurrence. Into

[38] First printed in the *American Caravan* of 1927, the "Ode" underwent many revisions from the time of its first writing (1926) to the time it was printed in its present version (1936).

this scene the observer tries to project his vision: the trite notion of natural continuity ("the inexhaustible bodies that are not/Dead, but feed the grass row after rich row") is the opening move. He is first returned to the womb of death and eternity by "the brute curiosity of an angel's stare," and is plunged "to a heavier world below" where he shifts his "sea-space blindly/Heaving, turning like the blind crab." But he is returned to the naturalistic world of things *only,* in the first appearance of the refrain:

> Dazed by the wind, only the wind
> The leaves flying, plunge [39]

In the second attempt to regain the past the observer comes close to a full vision of it; but the key to his failure is in the word "know," for knowing in this case frustrates experiencing. The observer tries to imagine the pines, the sky, the leaves, as an army attacking, reckless of death, pushing toward an objective; but once again the vision is reduced to its naturalistic details:

> Here by the sagging gate, stopped by the wall.
>
> Seeing, seeing only the leaves
> Flying, plunge and expire

He is then forced to resort to echoes in his own mind of "the immoderate past": names of battles, repetition of the name of a Confederate general ("Stonewall, Stonewall" [40]). Once again, and now in desperate recognition of its truth, the refrain reiterates the defeat of the past as recoverable vision. All tradition dies before the onslaught of a present and traditionless world. The full depravity of this condition is given in the figure of

> The hound bitch
> Toothless and dying, in a musty cellar . . .

The context of the poem now changes: the observer, who has been addressed as "you," is now absorbed in a commemorial "we," who

[39] Tate explained that "the wind-leaves refrain was added to the poem in 1930, nearly five years after the first draft was written. . . . It 'times' the poem better, offers the reader frequent pauses in the development of the two themes, allows him occasions of assimilation . . . eases the concentration of imagery—without, I hope, sacrificing a possible effect of concentration" (*Reason in Madness*).

[40] An echolaic pun: the stone wall (decayed) separating him from the heroic dead contrasts with the heroic figure of Stonewall Jackson, one of the greatest and most limited geniuses of the Civil War; Tate published a biography of him in 1928.

gather "In the ribboned coats of grim felicity" to express a formal
grief. What can the mourners say of death? Only that it is inevitable
and total, a fate that awaits everyone, a process of physical dissolution.
The screech-owl momentarily recalls the past; its sound "seeds the
wind/With the furious murmur of their chivalry." The refrain seals
the protagonist's fate; the "we" now reflects upon the leaves, which
"Flying, plunge and expire."

Finally the full impact of the modern dislocation, the "solipsism," as
Tate calls it, which prevents man from communicating with the past,
is signified in the remarkable simile of the jaguar who "leaps/For
his own image in a jungle pool, his victim." The modern Narcissus seeks
to devour himself; his death is a consequence of lustful power directed
upon himself as prey. In full realization of his failure, the observer is
bidden to

> Leave now
> The shut gate and the decomposing wall . . .

The "Ode" is therefore not so much concerned with tradition as it is
with the frustrating failure to re-experience a tradition; this is the condition of modern man, as Tate saw him in the context of the 1920s.
The poem underscores the major mode of the Southerners' view of tradition, which is very much a matter of the past, and the strength of
modernism is so great as to make that past all but irrecoverable. The
writing of the Agrarians was almost entirely retrospective, though at
times (as in several essays in *I'll Take My Stand*) it became vindictive
and argumentative. The past as an ideal, and idealized, unit of experience both remembered and imagined was the primary image it
contributed to traditionalism in the 1920s. Like the Humanist past, it
was contrasted again and again with the "ugly present." Unlike the
Humanist past, it was composed of objects rather than texts, myths
rather than philosophical disquisition, specific metaphors rather than
reiterated generalizations.

6. The Text: Willa Cather's Two Worlds

TWO IMAGES are essential to an understanding of Willa Cather's
traditionalism: the garage, dread and ugly servant of a utilitarian
ethic; the "long, green-carpeted, softly lighted drawing-room," where
Learning and Taste met and where there was a lock of Keats's hair

under glass, to be seen by those who cared. She speaks of these in an essay published in a volume admonishingly called *Not Under Forty* (1936). The drawing-room, at 148 Charles Street in Boston, was owned by Mrs. James T. Fields, widow of the Boston publisher. "Today, in 1936, a garage stands on the site." How had this change come about? "When and where were the Arnolds overthrown and the Brownings devaluated? Was it at the Marne? At Versailles, when a new geography was being made on paper?"

But Willa Cather did not wait until 1936 to establish the terms of her rejection of the present. In Omaha, in October 1921, she delivered herself of her most emphatic criticism of the garage and all it stood for. Life, she said, is becoming mechanized, packaged, and tinned; taste has degenerated from the complex recipes for old-fashioned roast goose to a mere matter of selecting the proper tins in the proper amount. "We have music by machines, we travel by machines—the American people are so submerged in them that sometimes I think they can only be made to laugh and cry by machinery." This is a false life, a fake success; it upsets human rhythms, it drives out repose, it destroys the chance of beauty. "Nobody stays at home any more; nobody makes anything beautiful any more."

While she rejected the world of the garage and the modern department store, she also rebelled against the "well-furnished novel." The novel must henceforth be "démeublé"; it must be spare, dry, uncluttered. As the style "improved," the setting became more starkly simple, the problem more simply posed and more simply answered. The novel was no longer to be like *The Song of the Lark* (1915); *One of Ours* (1922) was the last of the "furnished" novels, and even it possessed furnishings of a uniform grayness and drabness.

Miss Cather had from the beginning tried for a strict definition of manners; it was partly a non-Jamesian expression of a Jamesian taste, partly a morally useful metaphor of the land. In her most famous novels of the prairie states she developed her own kind of international theme: it was the Old World that advanced into the New, settled it, fought its recalcitrance, tutored it, and eventually reduced it to neatly classical squares, triangles, and rectangles of fertile soil. The history was not without its tragedies: the too sensitive European might be overcome in the struggle, might die by his own hand. Ántonia Shimerda says (*My Ántonia,* 1918): "My father, he went much to school. He knew a great deal; how to make fine cloth. . . . He play horn and violin, and he read so many books that the priests in Bohemia come to talk to him." But fine cloth, violin, and books do not avail him; he had, when he arrived in America, been too "complete," with too little of the resiliency and tolerance necessary for coming to terms with a new, harsh, undeveloped land.

Some human pattern (some classical form of order) must rise from this union of Old World manner and New World necessity. It was a problem of "scale"—how to order a vast, uninhibited geography in human terms; how to make the European virtue responsive to the mid-American challenge. Miss Cather, in *O Pioneers!* (1913) and *My Ántonia,* offers a land myth and a land goddess to rule it: a noble creature, strong, patient, robust, sensitive, and enduring, who undergoes a symbolic courtship with the land. The land at first coerces the heroine, but at last she is able to dominate it. It then becomes metaphorically "polite," civilized, classically ordered, and religiously fertile. It acquires a "manner," and the result is a noble, creative, and productive unity of man and nature. Like most carefully wrought designs, this pattern of decorum and fertility is threatened from without. The ugly, venal, amoral cities offer another way of life, a deceptively easy and distracting one. But the cities are not communities; they are huge congested areas in which man lives and dies in isolation—dies frequently *of* isolation. The exploiter—the man who sells what other men make, the man who is interested only in calculating risks and profits—is the villain: Ivy Peters of *A Lost Lady* (1923), whose instinctive sense of business contrasts eloquently with the grand manner of Captain Forrester; Bayliss Wheeler,[41] who is merely a servant of industry and the machine.[42]

From her reflections upon the moral and religious significance of the pioneer scene, Miss Cather suggests her ideal pattern of morality and decorum. Her hero or heroine has a strong sense of what is proper: great sensitivity (which by itself, however, often leads to disaster), great strength and courage, an almost superhuman talent for

[41] See *One of Ours:* "The farmer raised and took to market those things with an intrinsic value. . . . In return he got manufactured articles of poor quality; showy furniture that went to pieces, carpets and draperies that faded, clothes that made a handsome man look like a clown. Most of his money was paid out for machinery—and that, too, went to pieces. A steam thrasher didn't last long; a horse outlived three automobiles."

[42] Cf. a similar calculus of values in John Steinbeck (*Grapes of Wrath, In Dubious Battle*), dramatically adjusted to the issues of the 1930s. Faulkner's treatment of the problem is much more complex, though there are extremes of villain and land-hero here as well.

heroic struggle and fortitude, most of all, a *faith,* which is realized in the fertility rites of the seasons on the land, the sowing and the harvest, and in ceremonials (both secular customs and religious rituals), which are accepted without question or skepticism.

The great charm of Mrs. Field's drawing-room was that it contained the past securely and protected it from the present: "it was a place where the past lived on—where it was protected and cherished, had sanctuary from the noisy push of the present." But it too had had to give way to the garage; the world "broke in two in 1922 or thereabouts." The tawdry and cheap replaced the enduring things. Miss Cather was distressed, resentful, and puzzled. She had to make her choice: should she live in the twentieth century (in this "after-war welter," as Edith Wharton called it) or should she withdraw from it, in the hope of recapturing in the past the setting and the symbol of her ideal circumstance? This was the crucial question posed for all those interested in the American past.[43]

[43] Research in the subject, principally with the assistance of Ernest E. Leisy's *The American Historical Novel* (1950), reveals that the fictional exploitation of all aspects of the American past was especially lively in the 1920s; there was no loss of interest in the American past among general readers in the decade. The following indicates the popularity of the several aspects of American history in the number of novels published from 1919 through 1932.

Journey of Columbus: 1
Colonial America, chiefly New England: 10 (The witch scare and
    trials merit three novels)
French and Indian War: 2
The Revolutionary War: 10
Pre-Civil War (Abolitionism, the Mexican War, etc.): 2
Early nineteenth-century shipping industry: 3
Pioneer, emigrant, homestead novels, dealing with extremely varied
    aspects of the Westward movement: 52 (These novels include
    movements from Connecticut to Ohio, to the "Middle Border
    States," to California; the Gold Rush, the great Western scouts,
    the Indian Wars, etc.)
Civil War: 15
Lincoln's role in the Civil War: 4
Post-Civil War and Reconstruction: 5
The Spanish-American War: 2
Others: 16 (Erie Canal, feminism, late nineteenth-century fortunes,
    "Seward's Folly," etc.)

Among the most notable historical novels published during these years are the following, listed chronologically:

1919: Joseph Hergesheimer, *Java Head*

Both the struggle and one form of its resolution are dramatically portrayed in *The Professor's House* (1925). The all-too-simple images of withdrawal and adjustment in that novel are the old house and the new. There are also ironies that associate the two. Professor Godfrey Napoleon St. Peter has won the Oxford prize for history for his eight-volume study of *Spanish Adventurers;* with the prize money the family builds a new house, fully utilitarian and convenient and horribly vulgar.[44] The Professor would rather have the old house in spite of (or perhaps because of) its ugliness and inconvenience. Nowhere is this inconvenience better demonstrated than in the study on the third floor of the old house:

> The low ceiling sloped down on three sides, the slant being interrupted on the east by a single square window, swinging outward on hinges and held ajar by a hook in the sill. This was the sole opening for light and air. Walls and ceilings alike were covered with a yellow paper which had once been very ugly, but had faded into inoffensive neutrality. The matting on the floor was worn and scratchy. Against the wall stood an old walnut table, with one leaf up, holding piles of

1922: Emerson Hough, *The Covered Wagon*
        Edgar Lee Masters, *Children of the Market Place*
1923: Margaret Wilson, *The Able McLaughlins*
1924: Joseph Hergesheimer, *Balisand*
1925: J. P. Marquand, *The Black Cargo*
        James Boyd, *Drums*
        Martha Ostenso, *Wild Geese*
1926: Stark Young, *Heaven Trees*
1927: O. E. Rölvaag, *Giants in the Earth*
        Glenway Wescott, *The Grandmothers*
1928: Esther Forbes, *Mirror for Witches*
1929: O. E. Rölvaag, *Peder Victorious*
        Evelyn Scott, *The Wave*
1930: Elizabeth Madox Roberts, *The Great Meadow*
        Kenneth Roberts, *Arundel*
        Edna Ferber, *Cimarron*
1931: Caroline Gordon, *Penhally*
        O. E. Rölvaag, *Their Father's God*
        Evelyn Scott, *A Calendar of Sin*
        T. S. Stribling, *The Forge*
1932: Leonard Ehrlich, *God's Angry Man*
        T. S. Stribling, *The Store*

[44] Note that *vulgarity* in this case is an index of *convenience:* what is convenient is vulgar because it does not challenge native resources, moral and physical.

orderly papers. Before it was a cane-backed office chair that turned on a screw. This dark den had for many years been the Professor's study.

It is, in short, a retreat in which the Professor daily performs his ritual of withdrawal from the present into the womb of time, into a historical past. The ugliness is itself set off from the smart cheapness and bright efficiency of the new house. He refuses to improve the study, fearing that any change will cause it to lose something of its value as an entrance into the past. The rusty, round gas stove with no flue he uses for heating the study is especially significant. A sudden gust of wind might easily "blow the wretched thing out altogether" and endanger his life. He does not wish to repair or replace it because it is a familiar object, part of the setting in which he has written the history; most of all, because it is unconsciously associated with death itself, which is the final withdrawal from present into past. As it turns out, he *is* almost killed by it; he all but *wills* his death, and is saved only by the timely appearance of the dressmaker Augusta, a woman of deep and practical faith. She combines the two great virtues of Miss Cather's heroines: faith and a hard practical sense (she is "seasoned and sound and on the solid earth").

The conflict of time past with time present engages another major irony. St. Peter's only memorable student, Tom Outland, had perfected a special device for use in aircraft and had died and left his possessions to Rosamond, one of the Professor's two daughters. The invention is taken over by Rosamond's husband, Lou Marsellus, and both become extremely wealthy in consequence. Properly grateful but improperly noisy and imperceptive, Marsellus builds a country house, which he proposes to call "Outland" as a sort of memorial. It is in the very worst of tastes: ". . . a Norwegian manor house, very harmonious with its setting," he says; "just the right thing for rugged pine woods and high headlands," and equipped with wrought-iron door fittings, brought all the way from Chicago, and hand-painted Spanish bedroom furniture. For this, and for all of the other new vulgarities, "the light in Outland's laboratory used to burn so far into the night!"

The problem is thus simply posed: against the old house and its memories, the new one and its smart gimcrack world; against the silent dedication of Tom Outland, the noisy pretensions of the promoter, the man of machines and practical science; against the old world, in which St. Peter has dwelt in his happiest moments, this new one, restless in its love of things and gadgets and hopelessly ignorant of beauty or value. Tradition becomes his sole refuge because the past is more credible, makes more valuable sense. In an after-hour conversation with his students, the Professor offers us Miss Cather's first overt statement of this thesis. Science has given us "a lot of ingenious toys," he tells them; "they take our attention away from the real problems, of course, and since the problems are insoluble, I suppose we ought to be grateful for distraction." Seriously, the effect of science has been to remove or to discredit essential symbols of the moral and religious life:

> "I don't think you help people by making their conduct of no importance—you impoverish them. As long as every man and woman who crowded into the cathedrals on Easter Sunday was a principal in a gorgeous drama with God, glittering angels on one side and the shadows of evil coming and going on the other, life was a rich thing.
> . . . And that's what makes men happy, believing in the mystery and importance of their own little individual lives." [45]

Ironically Tom Outland has proved the link of past with present; his genius and dedication have been translated into "chemicals and dollars and cents." It was not always so. Outland once was the real clue to the past; his representative tale reinforced St. Peter's great faith in history. It is important to see fully the manner in which this conviction is dramatized in the novel. Before he came to the Midwestern college town, Outland had a remarkable experience out West. With a friend of his, he herded cattle in the open spaces of New Mexico. The space is important, as are the silences that dominate the life; these are indices of the past, as they are characteristics of the contemplative, undisturbed reflective life. Near their camp was a mesa, which looked "like a naked blue rock set down alone in the plain, almost square, except that the top was higher at one end." This is a final, an absolute index of time arrested in a figure of tradition; as such it clearly symbolizes, in its rarefied atmosphere, Miss Cather's estimates of both virtue and time. The blue color ("Mary's color"), the brilliant isolation on the vast plain of land, the altar-shaped end of the chapel-shaped structure are all parts of the figuration fixed in the Professor's memory.

On this mesa Outland and his friend discovered the remains of a past civilization, preserved "in the dry air and almost perpetual sunlight like a fly in amber." The air, the water, above all the silence, are pure signs of the arresting of time by faith. The values are much the same as those quietly appreciated by Miss Cather's Alexandra and Ántonia; the limit-

[45] Miss Cather joined the Episcopal Church on December 27, 1922.

less horizons of the prairie land [46] are such a setting, and Alexandra and Ántonia are themselves only more recent inhabitants of a world made whole by simplicity and natural faith. "These people had been isolated, cut off from other tribes, working out their destiny, making their mesa more and more worthy to be a home for man, purifying life by religious observances, caring respectfully for their dead, protecting their children." Wherever this happens there is a civilized world: "Wherever humanity has made that hardest of all starts and lifted itself out of mere brutality, is a sacred spot. . . . They built themselves into this mesa and humanized it." So too had Alexandra and Ántonia built themselves into Nebraska and humanized it.

After an exasperating and futile journey to Washington, Outland returned to the mesa, where he spent a season entirely alone, memorizing lines from Vergil's *Aeneid,* shouting them into the lifeless, chaste, and sacred space:

> . . . blue and purple rocks and yellow-green piñons with flat tops, little clustered houses clinging together for protection, a rude tower rising in their midst, rising strong, with calmness and courage—behind it a dark grotto, in its depths a crystal spring.

This is the purest form of communion with tradition, with the peace of isolation from noisy time and cluttered space. It is a "classical" form, a religious experience, a dedicated and endowed communion with the purified essence of a world.

The significant imagery of tradition in *The Professor's House* is now clear. The old house with its denlike study leads, through a memory easily encouraged, to the mesa, with its "dark grotto" and "in its depths a crystal spring." In each place there are "remains": the grotesque outlines of human forms on the mesa recall the attack of some predatory tribe; the dressmaker's forms in the study remind the Professor that another kind of predatory society has taken away his daughters and indeed destroyed the family as he has known it in the old house; both Outland and St. Peter grow fond of the remains, almost prefer them to the human reality they ludicrously resemble. Both men experience a

---

[46] "I wanted to walk straight on through the red grass and over the edge of the world," says Jim Burden, the narrator of *My Ántonia.* "It could not be very far away. The light air about me told me that the world ended here: only the ground and sun and sky were left, and if one went a little further off, there would be only sun and sky, and one would float off into them like the tawny hawks which sailed over our heads making shadows on the grass."

religious emotion associated with the past: for Outland, with the lost tribe who had made such a beautiful world out of hard, implacable nature (only other people had destroyed them); for the Professor, with the entire, aerated past of the Southwest for which he had written his history and in which he himself found his only secure place.

The crisis of the novel is comparable to the crisis in Miss Cather's life: which world must she choose? The Professor is tempted to go to the last extreme, to translate himself into the past. The last step in a removal to the past is death, and—despite the rituals and ornaments which bespeak immortality—in death all forms are fixed, all time has stopped, and the present is level with the past. The Professor would recover Eden in his own image; at first he returns in fancy to the time of his early youth, and the memory of it is associated with the heroic endurance and patience of simple peoples. But he must decide if he will go all the way into the past or allow himself to return to his family and the new house. The opportunity offers itself—the gas stove is finally blown out in a storm—and he is on the edge of the eternity he has visualized from Tom Outland's experience. His dressmaker, a "woman of faith," saves him, and he will never know how close he has been to self-destruction: "when he was confronted by accidental extinction, he had felt no will to resist, but had let chance take its way." As the novel ends he is resigned to the new house and to the new order of things. Apparently only the hard and precious common sense of Augusta's prayer book and her natural acceptance of death in the midst of life makes the return tolerable.

Miss Cather also withdrew into the past of her imagining; she created an image of history, made of simple and primary qualities, isolated in the past, free from the complications of modern life, with standards so purified as almost to make each human act a ritual exemplar. In so doing—and in stressing the values of traditional religion—she succeeded in vanquishing, to her own satisfaction at least, the unholy modern trinity of science, invention, and war.[47]

[47] Cf. Hart Crane, "The River":

SCIENCE—COMMERCE and the HOLYGHOST
RADIO ROARS IN EVERY HOME WE HAVE THE NORTHPOLE
WALLSTREET AND VIRGINBIRTH WITHOUT STONES OR
WIRES OR EVEN RUNning brooks connecting ears
and no more sermons windows flashing roar
Breathtaking—as you like it . . . eh?

There is a continuity, in the design she chose, of essential qualities: the Nebraska plains, the deserts and mesas of the nineteenth-century Southwest, the "rock" of Quebec of the early eighteenth century. The rock, like the blue mesa, is surrounded by wilderness; there is more than a suggestion of eternity in all three geographical settings for her image of the past. The garden and the desert are finally united in an exemplum drawn from historical analogies to suit her taste.

The Professor's House serves admirably as a representative anecdote of the forms which traditionalism assumed in the 1920s. Miss Cather touches all the images of tradition evoked in the decade. She resents bitterly the defeat of taste by a growing, fretful, distracting commercial world; she presents (in *One of Ours* especially, but elsewhere as well) the "gray" tones of an inhibited "Puritan" society. Her protagonist in the struggle is an academic personage, dedicated to the moral truth and impatient to the point of exasperation with the easy and reckless formulations of the "moderns." Miss Cather's major unit of ideal human existence is a piece of land to which her favored characters are responsible, from which they draw their half-articulated patterns of meaningful life. After "the world broke in two" she moves into history, fixing upon those images of the past which best answer the terms of her judgment of the present, and demonstrate most conclusively to her the values which it denies but which must be preserved.

Like other forms of traditionalism in the decade, Miss Cather's was motivated by a firm conviction concerning the world as she saw it then, and it was shaped as she acted upon her conviction. Perhaps it was better after all, she said of both Claude Wheeler and Tom Outland, that the war destroyed them before they could suffer the disillusionment for which their ingenuity and their naïveté were responsible. She herself, having survived the war, found in her version of tradition a means of denying the postwar world. It provided an image to which she could go to escape the garage, to recover the drawing-room, extended into both space and time. Of all the forms of traditionalism, hers was the most apparently, and illusorily, precise and the most unfamiliar to those who naïvely and excitedly answered the challenge of immediacy.

V

FORMS OF EXPERIMENT
AND IMPROVISATION

1. The Image and Last Year's Magazines

EXPERIMENT in modern American literature began with the vigorous effort of a few persons to revise the status of the arts and to redefine the artist's responsibilities. Chief among these was Ezra Pound. In his critical writings, his letters, his maneuverings with magazines, he was concerned about every aspect of the writer's world: the price of books, the dispositions of publishers, the economic support of artists, censorship; above all, the formulation and defense of an aesthetic, which he wanted to make as practical and as clearly incisive as possible. His promotional activity covered a wide range: Imagism, vorticism, sponsorship of nineteenth-century and contemporary French poets, revision of literary history, and a dozen other "ideas" which he set in motion through his strategically useful relationships with magazines and the sponsors of magazines and artists.

Pound tolerated much nonsense (was responsible for some himself) if the results were in small measure good. Writing of *Poetry* magazine, of which he was "Foreign Correspondent" from 1912 to 1917, he said (to Felix Schelling, November 1916) that it was "a distressful magazine which does, however, print a few good poems written in our day along with a great bundle of rubbish." He admitted (to Harriet Monroe, April 1916) that he had "launched" Imagism "to get printed and published the work of a few poets whose aim was to write a few excellent poems, perhaps not enough for even the slenderest volume, rather than the usual magazine thousands of E—— B——, the futurist diarrhoea, rhetorical slush, etc." New writers, he felt, *must* have a place

163

in which to appear, and any strategy that gave them one was legitimate.[1] They *must* be supported; they should have financial help, but not so much that receiving it would threaten their integrity: "the point is that if I accept more than I *need* I at once become a sponger, and I at once lose my integrity. By doing the job for the absolute minimum I remain respectable and when I see something I want I can ask for it" (to Margaret Anderson, around May 1917).[2] Pound watched eagerly and critically every new development in the economics of authorship: the founding of the Literary Guild (which he condemned because the judges all represented "2nd-rate aspiration"), the *Dial* awards, establishment of the Guggenheim Foundation, the appearance of persons of means on the literary horizon.[3]

Pound was motivated by the purest of disinterested conviction: that literature was in a very bad way; that new writers, not yet established, could do much to improve it; that these writers needed every chance they could get to free themselves for the major work, the development of their talent. Nothing was more important than this, for the artist was morally and culturally the arbiter and the "savior" of a race.

Pound felt that developments in the "new poetry" and the "new literature" should have their beginnings in *moral* definition. Once responsibilities had been defined and the relationship between artist and audience clarified, there were the questions of the precise means of "communication," of determining what was good and what was false in the new writing, and of finding the best models, influences, and

[1] To Margaret Anderson (probably January 1917) he wrote, when she asked him to become "Foreign Editor" of the *Little Review:* "I want an 'official organ' (vile phrase). I mean I want a place where I and T. S. Eliot can appear once a month (or once an 'issue') and where Joyce can appear when he likes, and where Wyndham Lewis can appear if he comes back from the war."

[2] See Poems IX and X of *Hugh Selwyn Mauberley.*

[3] To Simon Guggenheim he wrote (February 24, 1925), suggesting that the Foundation be used to sponsor writers, to prevent the tragedies of men "of unusual ability hampered, infamously hampered, by financial stress, while hundreds of mediocrities swallowed up America's heavy endowments." The "Bel Esprit" plan was his most ambitious attempt to secure a steady income for deserving artists. In 1922 John Rodker printed and distributed the "Bel Esprit" circular, asking specifically for help for Eliot so that he "may leave his work in Lloyd's Bank and devote his whole time to literature." (See *Letters.*) As originally conceived, it proposed thirty guarantors at £10 per year, "for life or for as long as Eliot needs it," the support to decrease as Eliot's royalties from sales go up—this "to prevent his being penalized for suppressing inferior work. Every writer is penalized as at present for not doing bad work, penalized for not printing EVERYTHING he can sell." (Letter to W. C. Williams, March 22, 1922.)

disciplines. In these matters Pound thought that America was woefully deficient; he felt a necessity himself to search for them (in literatures not generally accepted or popular), to work out an aesthetic of his own. This fully expressed need was the primary incentive for all experiment in modern American writing, however extreme the consequences frequently were.

To begin, then, with questions of communication and integrity: the artist must communicate his thought in terms of his art; this is essential to the survival and health of a civilization. There are many barriers, moral, economic, social. If an artist has talent—if he is not from the beginning a fraud who exploits, gives in to, or shares the blame for sins against good taste—he should be encouraged to communicate (by improving his personal circumstance) and to learn *how* to communicate (through every disciplinary means available in literatures past and present). Pound presented this position as forcefully as he could in numerous places, but notably in "The Serious Artist" (1913),[4] one of the most important documents in the history of modern "experiment." Not that experiment, innovation, departure from tradition are admirable or advisable in themselves; rather, art is actually in danger of being ignored or hopelessly subordinated to lesser matters. Pound saw gloomily in 1913 that the artist, if he had an insight that did not conform, risked neglect or scorn when he tried to present it. But the question of art is a *moral* question, and the artist is, or should be, a morally responsible being. The morality of art hinges upon accuracy. "Bad art is inaccurate art. It is art that makes false reports." There are many reasons why the artist may wish to falsify, and in so doing he is committing an immoral act; Pound summed up this matter in a passage of great importance to the history of modern letters:

If an artist falsifies his report as to the nature of man, as to his own nature, as to the nature of his ideal of the perfect, as to the nature of his ideal of this, that or the other, of god, if god exist, of the life force, of the nature of good and evil, if good and evil exist, of the force with which he believes or disbelieves this, that or the other, of the degree in which he suffers or is made glad; if the artist falsifies his reports on these matters or on any other matter in order that he may conform to the taste of his time, to the proprieties of a sovereign, to the conveniences of a preconceived code of ethics, then that artist lies. If he lies out of deliberate will to lie, if he lies out of carelessness, out of

[4] Published in the *New Freewoman* for October 15, November 1, and November 15, 1913; reprinted in *Pavannes and Divisions* (1918).

laziness, out of cowardice, out of any sort of negligence whatsoever, he nevertheless lies and he should be punished or despised in proportion to the seriousness of his offence.

Such a severe admonition needs, of course, the support of terms by which truth and falsehood may be known. The moral key to his aesthetic is the term *integrity*—which, however variously defined and used in Pound's writings, means the artist's responsibility to communicate precisely, in whatever medium he has chosen, the idea, emotion, complex of ideas and emotions, with which he was originally inspired or moved. Responsibility to "audience" can be fulfilled only by an intelligent awareness of medium and its relationship to the poetic object. This is both the morality and the psychology of art. "The touchstone of an art is its precision." This is not to say that the "simplest" statement is the most accurate: "This precision is of various and complicated sorts and only the specialist can determine whether certain works of art possess certain sorts of precision." [5]

Good writing is the result, therefore, of control, accuracy, discipline in the means of communication. The writer says "just what he means. He says it with complete clarity and simplicity. He uses the smallest possible number of words." He tries to communicate "with the greatest possible dispatch, save where for any one of forty reasons he does not wish to do so." *Simplicity* and *clarity* are not easy terms to understand. There are shades and degrees of necessary clarity: "The whole thing is an evolution." As man develops, he requires "an ever increasingly complicated communication." There are pre-verbal, gestural levels; there are the levels of the "ideogram," of the "vortex," in which the object and its representation are as nearly identical with each other as they can be. Finally there is a level of complexity that requires an extremely complex representation:

> You wish to communicate an idea and its modifications, an idea and a crowd of its effects, atmosphere, contradictions. You wish to question whether a certain formula works in every case, or in what per cent of cases, etc., etc., etc., you get the Henry James novel.

It is necessary to repeat Pound's insistence upon communication as a moral responsibility, in terms of the thing to be communicated, the artist's view of the thing, and the social circumstances in which the

[5] He wrote to Harriet Monroe (November 10, 1914) that "the arts, INCLUDING poetry and literature, should be taught by artists, by practicing artists, *not* by sterile professors."

communication is undertaken. At certain times expression will be more erratic, "rebellious," insistent, even repetitious, than at others.

The condition of the arts, as Pound and his fellows saw it immediately before the war, was such as to require a rather heavy program of manifesto, proclamation, debate, and editorial communiqué, with the object of forcing both reader and artist to a re-examination of fundamentals. In his survey of the opportunities for new work Pound thought America sadly lacking.[6] He was encouraged for a while to think that London was a better place, and from 1908 to 1920 lived there, engaging in many informal, casual activities with the aim of sponsoring, encouraging, and "purifying" the arts.[7] The war, especially the death of certain people in it, proved the culminating discouragement,[8] and in 1920 Pound left London for Paris. In 1924 he established permanent residence at Rapallo, Italy.

Whatever his dissatisfactions with Paris as he actually experienced it, Paris and the French nation and culture appealed to him as a great "laboratory of the spirit." Before he himself had left for Paris, he argued insistently that Americans should transfer their allegiance from England to France, and in February 1918 published a long critical introduction to French poetry in the *Little Review*. In the pages of the *Dial* he informed Americans concerning new French literature and his own views

[6] See *Patria Mia,* a group of essays written for the London magazine *The New Age* in 1912, collected and published in book form in 1950.

[7] Iris Barry describes "The Ezra Pound Period" in London during the war (*Bookman,* October 1931), suggesting some of its excitement and importance: "It was as though someone kept reminding us that the war was not perpetual (as it certainly seemed by then) and that it was in the long run more important that there should be new music and new and fresh writing and creative desire and passionate execution than that one should believe angels descended at Mons or that the population of Germany had from inherent vileness taken to consuming margarine decocted from boiled corpses. It was, for the hours of the gathering [at the weekly supper meetings] less important that so many were being killed and more that something lived; it was possible to recall that for every Blenheim there is a Voltaire and that the things that endure are not stupidity and fear."

[8] Both T. E. Hulme and Henri Gaudier-Brzeska had been killed in it (see *Hugh Selwyn Mauberley,* Poem V: "There died a myriad,/And of the best, among them . . ."). Yet Pound thought that the war had been fought for "civilization against barbarism," as he put it in an essay on Henry James (1918). Looking back in 1929 on what he had then said, he remarked: "I still believe that a Hohenzollern victory would have meant an intolerable postwar world. I think I write this without animus, and that I am quite aware of the German component indispensable to a complete civilization" (*Make It New,* 1934).

of old French literature.[9] Not only the literature but also the place, the "atmosphere" of Paris attracted, its tolerance and encouragement of the arts. In one of his several tributes to Rémy de Gourmont (*Fortnightly Review*, December 1915) Pound linked Paris with what he thought was indispensable to the health of the arts:

> But Paris is the laboratory of ideas; it is there that poisons can be tested, and new modes of sanity be discovered. It is there that the antiseptic conditions of the laboratory exist. That is the function of Paris.

From about 1910 the influence of French writing grew steadily; the war, which brought many Americans newly to France and encouraged numbers of them to stay, was perhaps the most important factor in the change from Anglo-Saxon to French influences upon American writing.[10] Much of the response to France was of course romanticized and sentimentalized. Many Americans did not discriminate in their choice of "enthusiasms"; and a moderate share of them were just generally enthusiastic about "the life of art" or *la vie de bohème*. But the image of Paris persisted as a "laboratory of the spirit," as the one place where, after the war, one might be most independent and receive the greatest help.

The first clearly defined development in experimental literature has now been classified in literary histories as Imagism. It began as

[9] He was not the only one, of course. Malcolm Cowley published a number of essays on French writers, and so did many other Americans and Englishmen. Amy Lowell's *Six French Poets* appeared in 1916, with considerations of Verhaeren, Samain, Gourmont, Régnier, Jammes, and Fort. While Eliot preferred to stay in London and (as he advanced beyond his early poems) moved back into the English literary past more often than into the French for his sources and inspiration, he did testify to the value, especially of Pound's greatest enthusiasm. See his use of Gourmont in "The Perfect Critic," *The Sacred Wood* (1920); and Edward J. H. Greene, *T. S. Eliot et la France* (Paris, 1951).

[10] There was, of course, not a little activity in the late nineteenth century; France had its American *symbolistes,* and both France and Italy were objectives of "passionate pilgrims." James Huneker advertised European literature in the early part of the century, and Arthur Symons' *The Symbolist Movement in Literature* (1899) was read eagerly by young men in America. Eliot claims that it was his first introduction to French literature: "we remember that book as an introduction to wholly new feelings, as a revelation. After we have read Verlaine and Laforgue and Rimbaud and return to Mr. Symons' book, we may find that our impressions dissent from his. The book has not, perhaps, a permanent value for the one reader, but it has led to results of permanent importance for him" (*The Sacred Wood*).

Imagisme, and the first collection of poetry illustrating its principles was called *Des Imagistes* (1914).[11] There were two important divisions in the career of Imagism: the "Pound Period," from 1909 to 1914, which began March 25, 1909, and featured informal supper meetings in Soho and in Regent Street, and occasional lectures by Pound and Hulme; and "Amygism," as Pound scornfully called it when he "turned it over" to Amy Lowell, from 1914 to about 1920. The most important document of the second phase was *Some Imagist Poets* (1915), edited by Miss Lowell and Richard Aldington, with a new "statement of principles" by both. Of this second stage Pound said (*Poetry*, April 1916): "At present its chief defects are sloppiness, lack of cohesion, lack of organic centre in individual poems, rhetoric, a conventional form of language to be found also in classical textbooks, and in some cases a tendency more than slight towards the futurist's cinematographic fluidity." The first phase concentrated on essentials, on the absolutely necessary objectives and disciplines; the second, while repeating the objectives of the first with some variation, allowed for a considerable expansion of the original assumptions, a loosening of the lines of demarcation, and a much freer range in the adaptation of "new ideas." [12]

The first phase of Imagism received its most cogent definition in a

[11] The following dates are of some importance for seeing the "new poetry" in historical perspective:

> 1908: Pound's arrival in England
> 1912 (to 1919): Pound's association with the Chicago *Poetry* (his active career with it lasted until 1917, but his name was carried on the masthead until 1919)
> 1913: Eliot in London
> 1913: *The New Freewoman* (became *The Egoist*, an "Individualist Review")
> 1917 (to 1921): Pound's association, as "Foreign Editor," with the *Little Review*
> 1918: Pound's *Pavannes and Divisions* (containing materials published as early as 1912 in various magazines)
> 1920: Eliot's *The Sacred Wood*
> 1924: Hulme's *Speculations* (edited by Herbert Read; essays written before 1917, many of them published in British magazines before then)

[12] As Stanley K. Coffman put it (*Imagism*, 1951), "Amygism" became "so inclusive that it was less a specific doctrine than a platform to win the approval of almost anyone interested in honest, sincere poetic technique." Eliot, looking back upon her work in 1950, said that Miss Lowell was a "kind of demon saleswoman; and unless my memory of her methods is at fault . . . they were more enthusiastic than critical" (*An Examination of Ezra Pound*, edited by Peter Russell).

statement of three principles agreed to by Pound, H. D., and Aldington in the spring or early summer of 1912. Since this statement, while frequently repeated and adapted, was never improved upon, it may serve as a basis for discussion of the aims and achievements of Imagism.[13] The first of these principles advocated "direct treatment of the 'thing' whether subjective or objective." This urged a basic economy of poetic expression. The "thing" was to be considered not a physical object, but a complex of emotional and intellectual details united in the imagination and as nearly identical with the artist's preconception of them as possible. Pound defined "an Image" (*Poetry,* March 1913) as the means by which the "thing" is represented in art, as "that which presents an intellectual and emotional complex in an instant of time."

This was an absolute minimum of art; anything not crucially related to the "complex" was considered irrelevant, dishonest, false (or at any rate marked an inferiority of perception and talent).[14] Several critical metaphors were used to indicate the nature of the directness, the degree of subjectivity and objectivity involved in creating the image. Not the least of these was found in Hulme's essay, "Romanticism and Classicism" (written in 1913 or 1914), his most important contribution to the critical background of Imagism. Speaking of "accurate, precise and definite description," Hulme employed a metaphor of curve to define that precision:

> You know what I call architect's curves—flat pieces of wood with all different kinds of curvature. . . . Suppose that instead of your curved pieces of wood you have a springy piece of steel of the same types of curvature as the wood. Now the state of tension or concentration of mind, if he is doing anything really good in this struggle against the

[13] See Coffman, Chapters II and VII, for a discussion of the second phase, together with a treatment of the "principles" as given in 1915 by Amy Lowell and Aldington.

[14] Most relevant here is a statement made by Pound in a lettter to Harriet Monroe (January 1915), which deserves a prominent place among critical documents of our century: "objectivity, and again objectivity, and expression: no hindside-beforeness, no straddled adjectives (as 'addled mosses dank'), no Tennysonianness of speech; nothing—nothing that you couldn't, in some circumstance, in the stress of some emotion, actually say. Every literaryism, every book word, fritters away a scrap of the reader's patience, a scrap of his sense of your sincerity. When one really feels and thinks, one stammers with simple speech; it is only in the flurry, the shallow frothy excitement of writing or the inebriety of a metre, that one falls into the easy—oh, how easy!—speech of books and poems that one has read."

ingrained habit of the technique, may be represented by a man employing all his fingers to bend the steel out of its own curve and into the exact curve which you want. Something different to what it would assume naturally.

This metaphor and the first principle of Imagism ("direct treatment") try to probe the genuine mystery of "exactness"—the word "direct" indicates a desire to make the expression resemble the "object" as closely as art can make it. Hulme's view of poetry is almost entirely visual, pictorial; Pound's includes and often emphasizes music, rhythms learned from poetries of languages other than one's native tongue, and sculpture.[15] Perhaps the best illustration of this first principle and its implications is Pound's two-line poem "In a Station of the Métro" (*Poetry,* April 1913):

> The apparition of these faces in a crowd;
> Petals on a wet, black bough.

Here are the minimal necessities stressed in the Imagist statement. The object is an observation that must be rendered exactly: faces in a Métro station turned variously toward the light and the darkness. The "image" used to support and intensify the impression is that of flower petals which are half absorbed by, half resist the texture of wetness and the darkness of a bough. The word "apparition" clearly binds the two aspects of the observation—in its being both an appearance (a thing to be observed) and an experience not quite real (that is, not sharply outlined, the darkness of the scene partly dulling and shading the scene observed).

The second of the three principles in the 1912 statement served primarily to reinforce the first: "To use absolutely no word that does not contribute to the presentation." This phrase contained the essence of the Imagists' urgent appeal for concentration and economy of expression. It was stimulated chiefly by a strong reaction against late nineteenth-century verse, what was variously called "cosmic utterance," "Tennysonianness of speech," philosophical "padding" to meet the needs of both the meter and the genteel reader. In accepting his position with Harriet Monroe's magazine, Pound put the phrase in another way:

Can you teach [the American poet] that it is not a pentametic echo

---

[15] The "vortex" is primarily a version of the image given a three-dimensional, sculptural quality. In his *Gaudier-Brzeska* (1916), Pound discusses vorticism at some length, in connection with a study of the sculpture of his friend.

of the sociological dogma in last year's magazines? Maybe. Anyhow you have work before you.

Any unnecessary word, whatever the incentive (metrical, sentimental, or otherwise) for including it, interfered with the "directness" of the "treatment" and was by that much a loss of precision, a moral and artistic defection.

Finally, "As regarding rhythm, to compose in the sequence of the musical phrase, not in the sequence of the metronome." Whatever Pound may have meant by this, he did *not* mean a wholesale sponsorship of "free verse"; nor did Eliot believe that there was such a thing as *vers libre,* in spite of the fact that the most lively controversy in modern poetry had to do with the question of free verse.[16] In his essay on "Arnold Dolmetsch" (*New Age,* January 1915), Pound made his position on this matter clear: "Any work of art is a compound of freedom and order. It is perfectly obvious that art hangs between chaos on one side and mechanics on the other. A pedantic insistence on detail tends to drive out 'major form.' A firm hold on major form makes for a freedom of detail." [17] Pound did mean, however, that poetry ought not to be a result of mere accent counting, a ticktock rhythm in the adjustment of individual detail. He was much interested in the interrelationships of verse and music and maintained that thematically and texturally poetry had much formally to learn from musical composition —as indeed it did from the practice of translating, adapting from, or merely reading verse written in foreign languages.

These were the beginnings of the "new poetry," and a genuine attention to their full meanings marked the beginning of the "new criticism." A great variety of changes were rung upon these original statements: by F. S. Flint, John Gould Fletcher, May Sinclair, Ford Madox Ford, Amy Lowell, and others. From precisely stating what poetry should

[16] See Glenn Hughes, *Imagism and the Imagists* (1931), Chapters I–IV, and especially Chapter III, "The Critical Reaction." Miss Lowell, in Point Two of her Preface to *Some Imagist Poets* (1915), stated her position as follows: "To create new rhythms—as the expression of new moods—and not to copy old rhythms, which merely echo old moods. We do not insist upon 'free-verse' as the only method of writing poetry. We fight for it as a principle of liberty. We believe that the individuality of a poet may often be better expressed in free-verse than in conventional forms. In poetry, a new cadence means a new idea."

[17] See Eliot, "Reflections on Vers Libre" (*New Statesman,* March 3, 1917): "*Vers libre* does not exist, and it is time that this preposterous fiction followed the *élan vital* and the eighty thousand Russians into oblivion. . . . There is no escape from metre; there is only mastery."

at the least aspire to do, Imagism moved into a kind of competition regarding the varieties of "new poetry" that might be admitted and
allowed.

A similar variety and confusion marked the acceptance of French
influences and models. The sponsorship of French poets in English
and American magazines increased substantially during and after the
war years. In general, all critics agreed with Aldington's remark (*Little
Review,* 1915) that "French poetry is the foremost in our age for
fertility, originality, and general poetic charm." The major nineteenth-
century French poetic development, *symbolisme,* had little specifically
to do with Imagism, strictly defined; in a sense it was really opposed to
it. Symbolism did, however, influence a wide range of American poets
in one way or another: Cummings, Stevens, Crane, Miss Lowell,
Fletcher, among them.[18] At least in its first stages, Imagism was at an
opposite pole from the *symboliste* objective, especially in Mallarmé's
formulation of it.[19] His best-known statement marks well the dividing
line between the two:

> *Nommer* un objet, c'est supprimer les trois-quarts de la jouissance du
> poème qui est faite du bonheur de deviner peu à peu; le suggérer, voilà
> le rêve. C'est le parfait usage de ce mystère qui constitue le symbole.[20]

In spite of the differences, French symbolism was not a negligible
factor in the formation of modern American poetry. Both symbolism
and Imagism were concerned with a poetry that vividly expresses states
of consciousness; both were variously opposed to the idea that literature gains its value only as a servant of other disciplines; both were
inspired by the belief that the artist is a significant, responsible, and
valuable member of a community. As Imagism expanded, as the influence of French poetry and poetic increased, the two came closer together; and in individual cases certain French poets had significant roles
in the formation of certain American poets.[21] Supplementary influences

---

[18] See René Taupin, *L'influence du symbolisme français sur la poésie américaine de 1910 à 1920* (Paris, 1929).

[19] Cf. A. G. Lehmann, *The Symbolist Aesthetic in France, 1885–1895* (1950),
especially Chapters I, II, and VI.

[20] "*To name* an object is to suppress three-fourths of the enjoyment of the
poem, which comes from the pleasure in understanding it little by little, in thinking of it for what it suggests of the dream. The ideal practice of this mystery is the
essence of the symbol."

[21] Pound's interests in French poetry was almost entirely non-symbolist. See
his letter to René Taupin (May 1928), for his summary of the relationship
(*Letters*).

were those of Théophile Gautier, whose *Émaux et Camées* was of great importance for Pound's early work; and Tristan Corbière and Jules Laforgue, both of whom helped to influence the special kinds of irony found in the early verse of Pound and Eliot.

The scope of experiment in modern American poetry can perhaps best be understood if we examine five "experimental forms of order." The first of these is "pure imagery," with little or no attempt to "intrude" a meaning upon an isolated imagistic statement (H.D., Hulme, some few of Pound's verses). Beyond that form of simplicity or purity, there is the poetry which "adds on to" or imposes upon the image an indication of attitude or an external "use" of the imagery: William Carlos Williams' occasional adjurations ("These things are important"; "These things astonish me"; "So much depends . . ."), or H.D.'s "Spare us from loveliness." More complicated and elaborate, and an advance in structure as well, is the "image cluster" (what Randall Jarrell has called the "mosaic"): an accumulation of images, with spatial and temporal orders of varying complexity. Eliot's "Preludes" are perhaps the best illustration of this form, as indeed they are the finest examples of what the Imagist disciplines were able to do for modern poetry.

The fourth form of "order" is symbolic in an elementary sense. Such a poem as Miss Lowell's "Patterns" is complex only because its images are given as symbols and provide its narrative unity. They are *explicitly* symbols or symbolic "tags," and they are symbolic precisely and only because the poem's development depends on them rather than on a more "rational" order.

The final class may be called "forms of symbolic order." The most important modern poetry belongs to this class. The simplest variation of it is the poem in which the substance *is* the symbolism contained within it; the order is implicit within the location, the action, and the modulation of the symbols. Such poems as Marianne Moore's "The Grave," Williams' "The Yachts," Wallace Stevens' "Sea-Surface Full of Clouds," are examples. Fletcher's "Symphonies" and his "Irradiations" are so overcome by richness of imagery and nervous textural effects that the symbolism often fails of realization. Most complex are the poems of symbolic structure or symbolic progression; [22] the great demonstrations are *The Waste Land* and the *Cantos*. Another example is Hart Crane's *The Bridge,* in which the continuity of the poem as a whole comes from symbols that reveal a mythology personally invented

---

[22] What Kenneth Burke has called "qualitative progression."

and fashioned. The development in each of the poems depends upon a repetition of symbolic motifs, with qualitative changes in dramatic, lyrical, and thematic value.

"Experiment" in modern American poetry was not merely the result of a desire for eccentricity or willful obscurity. It was motivated first of all by the need for a review of communication in the arts; it was an attempt both to clear modern poetry of open didacticism and sentimentality and to mark the absolute minimal needs for exactness in poetic expression.

2. Some "Imaginary Gardens with Real Toads in Them"

IN HIS autobiography, *Troubadour* (1925), Alfred Kreymborg described meetings in his home at Grantwood, New Jersey, of a group of poets who were subsequently published in his short-lived magazine *Others* (1915–1919). The group included William Carlos Williams, Marianne Moore, and Wallace Stevens. "They enjoyed talking shop most of all, but their discussions spread an evasive levity over the serious current of their actual thought. Like almost every other cultural activity of the new soil, the intercourse of these people was a novel experience. . . . It was not a lack of self-confidence which dictated so shy a contact, but a joyous bewilderment in the discovery that other men and women were working in a field they themselves felt they had chosen in solitude."

While the major instruments of the "new poetry" had been those magazines to which Pound had frequent access (*Poetry,* the *Little Review,* the *Egoist*), other "little" magazines rose and fell, were born and died in quick succession. The *Pagan* ("a magazine for eudaemonists," 1916–1922) and Guido Bruno's several magazines tried to continue the 1890s into the twentieth century; *Others* gave a place to such poetic individualists as Kreymborg describes in *Troubadour.*[23]

---

[23] It had itself been preceded by an even shorter-lived Greenwich Village sheet, the *Rogue,* March to September, 1915. Pound's *Des Imagistes* received its American publication in the first issue of another Kreymborg-sponsored magazine, *Glebe.* (See the bibliography of *The Little Magazine,* by F. J. Hoffman, Charles Allen, and Carolyn Ulrich, for more titles pertinent to this matter.)

Here there was little enough of the proud manifesto or proclamation of the "new" literature, such as characterized some of the American magazines published abroad; rather, a serious excitement in the discovery of poets by editors, poets by themselves. For these men and women the little magazines were essential to the new American poetry, an opportunity for genuine and self-confident beginnings. The range of their interests varied widely; each one was influenced by what was going on in Europe (as reported in *Poetry* and the *Little Review*), but none consciously "followed a school" or wrote according to the dictates or the manifesto of a new movement. They were interested in themselves as poets, in poetry as a form (a new form, almost independent of history), in the *status* of poetry in America. They were, in brief, aestheticians native-grown, freshly original, and naïve.

For these writers, poetry was experimental in its very nature; the writing of it was a continuous experience of discovery. Miss Moore, Williams, and Stevens were all preoccupied with the question of what poetry could do, or might do, by way of elevating mere "things" to the level of imaginative reality. In their own way they contributed to the new poetry, to the discussion of an artist's role and value, and to the defense and definition of an artist's original talent. A glance at some of the titles published by them testifies to the exploratory, tentative character of their offerings in the 1920s: Williams' *Al Que Quiere* (1917), *Kora in Hell: Improvisations* (1920), *Sour Grapes* (1921), *Spring and All* (1922); Miss Moore's *Observations* (1924); Stevens' *Harmonium* (1923).

Miss Moore is, in many ways, the "moralist," the witty rational commentator. Her vivid pictorial sense, her sharp powers of observation with respect to small things and narrow perspectives, unite with a conversational shrewdness, a sense of the values of fable and analogy, an incisive insight into the eccentricities and comical absurdities of the human tribe. Her talent is in a subtle sense forensic and admonitory. Her *Observations* are just that: observations of the human and natural world in strange but significant conjunction; observations of both amusing and profound varieties in human relationships. "There is a great amount of poetry in unconscious/fastidiousness," she says in "Critics and Connoisseurs"; and she discovers "poetry" where it is not customarily found—in many poses and attitudes, in creatures small and great. The brave and rather pathetic posturing of her "Apish Cousins" is an occasion for zoological commentary upon one kind of human frailty:

> I recall their magnificence, now not more magnificent
> than it is dim. It is difficult to recall the ornament,
>   speech, and precise manner of what one might
>   call the minor acquaintances twenty
>   years back; . . .[24]

An admirable example of her method of compressing much shrewd thought within a small space, as well as of her talent for inferring much from the perfection of a small object is the poem "To a Snail":

> If 'compression is the first grace of style,'
> you have it. Contractility is a virtue
> as modesty is a virtue.
> It is not the acquisition of any one thing
> that is able to adorn,
> or the incidental quality that occurs
> as a concomitant of something well said,
> that we value in style,
> but the principle that is hid:
> in the absence of feet, 'a method of conclusions';
> 'a knowledge of principles,'
> in the curious phenomenon of your occipital horn.[25]

Literature, the arts (especially poetry), are matters of the first importance for her. The primary warning in her poetry is against abusing the privilege that art grants. It is an index of a larger abuse, the abuse and misunderstanding of life itself. She says in "Picking and Choosing":

> Literature is a phase of life. If
>   one is afraid of it, the situation is irremediable; if
> one approaches it familiarly
>   what one says of it is worthless. Words are constructive
> when they are true; the opaque allusion—the simulated flight
>
> upward—accomplishes nothing. . . .

The key to a proper attitude toward poetry is a genuine " 'accessibility to experience,' " as she puts it in "New York." There is much to be said for those who protest that poetry is obscure or vague, that it does not fully and sharply realize the experience. So, in "Poetry" she begins with a disarming admission: "I, too, dislike it: there are things

[24] This is as stated in the second version of the poem, called "The Monkeys," in *Selected Poems* (1935).

[25] See excerpts from her *Notebooks* (*Tiger's Eye*, October 1947) for a view of Miss Moore's preparations for the writing of this form of poetry.

that are important beyond all this fiddle." [26] While this statement is meant to be taken as literally true, it cleverly prepares for a thorough reconsideration of the terms of distaste. What *sort* of "fiddle" is objectionable? Reading poetry, she goes on, "with a perfect contempt for it" (with no illusions that it is acceptable sight unseen), one finds in it "after all, a place for the genuine." This "genuine" is the crucial test: the genuine experience, gesture, fact, however odd, small, out of the line of what one usually thinks is poetic, belongs in poetry:

> Hands that can grasp, eyes
> that can dilate, hair that can rise
> if it must . . .

These things "are important" not because they are available to one form or another of "cosmic" inference, but simply "because they are useful." The danger is that in poetry their usefulness is obscured, is lost in the verbiage. If "the genuine" is translated into poetry, *anything* is (or becomes in the translation) poetic; all "phenomena are important." But this does not mean that they will easily be made into poetry; "the result is not poetry" if the poets are only "half poets." The "raw material of poetry" must be re-formed by poets who are

> 'literalists of
> the imagination' [27]—above
> insolence and triviality and can present

> for inspection, imaginary gardens with real toads in them . . .

This is one of the fullest (as it is one of the most persuasive) accounts of the necessities of poetry, as these had earlier been set down by the Imagists. The "genuine," what the poet has originally to go on, is spoiled by spiritual faking, by deliberate obfuscation, by distortion for any number of reasons. The true poet will have so correct, so astute a sense of his art that he will be a "literalist of the imagination." [28] The objects, the "raw material . . . in all its rawness," will persuasively

[26] The original version of "Poetry," published in *Observations,* was only thirteen lines; in *Selected Poems* (1935) it was expanded to twenty-nine lines and much enriched. The early version is without the meticulously careful and relevant stanzaic plan, lacks a clear use of its examples, and above all does not have the two most important phrases of the revised poem—"literalists of the imagination" and "imaginary gardens with real toads in them."

[27] Quotation from *Ideas of Good and Evil* (1897) by Yeats (Miss Moore's "Note"). Yeats is speaking here of Blake.

[28] Cf. Pound's "The Serious Artist."

remain, but they will dwell (as "real toads") in an "imaginary garden"
—will assume a new reality in both the texture and the structure of
the poem, enhancing the original and yet giving us its vitality reshaped.

From 1925 to 1929 Miss Moore was "Acting Editor" of the *Dial,*
really (according to one of the magazine's sponsors) very much in
charge of its editorial activities. If conversation may be considered
"editorial," hers was the editorial sensibility of the decade; her reviews were a neat pastiche of what her authors had said, monitored by
the most polite of syntaxes and conjunctions.

The editorial conviction revealed here and in *Observations* is not unlike the statements made in the 1920s by other American poets. What
she called the "genuine" was described by Williams in another and
simpler context, but one fully as persuasive:

> so much depends
> upon
>
> a red wheel
> barrow
>
> glazed with rain
> water
>
> beside the white
> chickens.[29]

Here the material objects are reduced almost to the level of plain
factual statement. But this is not a list; it is an "arrangement" of objects,
a still life of a special kind.

Williams stresses again and again, in a variety of ways, the need
for "direct treatment of the 'thing,' whether subjective or objective."
His ideal poetic manner depends resolutely upon factual integrity;
he feels the grain of the experience, records the gnarled, drab, cool,
windy, sweet, sour, dusty, pungent, cluttered, serene, distraught facts of
his observation: the "blackbirds in the rain/. . . notate the dawn";
colors and shapes of flowers and leaves "in their bowl/in violent dis-
array/. . . remain composed";

> Coolly their colloquy continues
> above the coffee and loud talk
> grown frail as vaudeville.

[29] In *Spring and All* (1922), one of the most important volumes of modern
poetry published in the 1920s. It is a veritable "book of examples" of the principles (implicit and explicit) that governed the making of it.

As winter approaches,

> The half stripped trees
> struck by a wind together,
> bending all,
> the leaves flutter drily
> and refuse to let go . . .[30]

A tree on the top of a "little grey-black hillock" is bent from a lifetime misery of winds:

> Bent as you are from straining
> against the bitter horizontals of
> a north wind . . .

While the poplars below, protected from the wind, are "secure" in their design,

> . . . you alone
> warp yourself passionately to one side
> in your eagerness.[31]

The best example of Williams' skillful development of "things" into forms is the opening poem of *Spring and All*.[32] The slow, painful arrival of the spring season, together with the universal meaning of such an event, is brilliantly suggested through objects, natural things, which slowly respond to the early invitation of the season. The observer travels along "the road to the contagious hospital," and he notes the transition from winter to spring: the "blue mottled clouds" driven by "a cold wind." [33] Beyond, evidences of the waste revealed by the departure of the winter: the "waste of broad, muddy fields/brown with dried weeds."

> All along the road the reddish
> purplish, forked, upstanding, twiggy
> stuff of bushes and small trees
> with dead, brown leaves under them
> leafless vines—

[30] This and preceding quotations from *Sour Grapes* (1921).

[31] From *Al Que Quiere* (1917).

[32] There are other poems in which progress is clearly seen either in spatial and temporal movement or in symbolic pattern; see, for example, "Overture to a Dance of Locomotives" and "Queen Anne's-Lace" in *Spring and All*.

[33] Contrast the rather coyly informal statement of the same transition in Robert Frost's "Two Tramps in Mud-Time," stanza 3 (from *A Further Range*, 1936).

Their entrance into the new world is attended by uncertainty; they are sure only "that they enter," and the entrance is the key to the change, growth, rejuvenation, that the spring symbolizes:

> Now the grass, tomorrow
> the stiff curl of wildcarrot leaf

"One by one the objects are defined—" Gradually the objective fact of spring is fully seen and defined, in terms of an awakening of life:

> But now the stark dignity of
> entrance—Still, the profound change
> has come upon them: rooted they
> grip down and begin to awaken

The essential for Williams is not to violate the integrity of these "things," since they are reality itself and need only to be encouraged to offer (in their *being* objects) the most natural kind of commentary upon themselves. Ideas are, then, in things; there are no ideas *but* in things. This does not mean that ideas do not belong in poetry; only that they do not *overtly* belong there but should be developed from the particulars talking among themselves.

Williams is concerned with the basic poetic difficulty of communicating this reality without distortion. While such communication is not ideally possible, there are degrees of success and failure. Williams defines in various ways the reasons for the failure: things are after all abundant—there are a great many of them; they exist in natural profusion, and to this is added the artificial confusion of man-made (or half-made) objects, conditions, situations. To name an object, to classify things in scientific orders, to generalize with respect to the societies and histories of things—these are not enough; though all men are ambitious, if not to master this reality, at least to assert themselves in relation to it.

In his career as poet Williams has considered all the barriers to communication, including the task of the poet himself, who is confused, silenced, all but paralyzed by the rush and roar of things. It is a matter of utmost importance, however, that he retain his loyalty to things as he sees them. This reality is local, particular in its attention to specific regional detail; it is the mundane, quotidian, contemporary detail of Rutherford, Paterson, and northeastern New Jersey. The problem of what to make of this detail, how best to signify its importance, how to *order* it without losing sight of it, has preoccupied Williams throughout his life. It is both a formal and a moral problem: as a formal problem, it involves a choice of poetic means; as a moral problem, it considers the behavior of man (and his history) in terms of the barriers he has set, unwittingly or maliciously, to natural communication and understanding.

Something of the same issue confronts Wallace Stevens, though he faces it in his own way. It is not only a question of objects but of their basic merits and their relationship to a universal order. The imagination serves (in its several mutations) as Stevens' metaphysical instrument. The poet, everyman, the "Comedian as the Letter C," [34] is forever concerned to fashion an aesthetic of order, an "explanation" of reality, that will help to define his place within it.

"Sunday Morning" [35] states the problem of order in dramatic terms. The woman to whose mind the reflections occur is both charmed by her circumstance and fearful that it will not continue. The fact of death qualifies her every pleasure:

> She dreams a little, and she feels the dark
> Encroachment of that old catastrophe . . .

She protests: why should she have to give up the things that please her? Of what value death if it be seen "Only in silent shadows and in dreams?" To these complaints the answer is that "Divinity must live within herself." If there is to be any significance, order, beauty, it must be found in the facts of her own experience:

> All pleasures and all pains, remembering
> The bough of summer and the winter branch.
> These are the measures destined for her soul.

There is no reality beyond the grave, nothing that will permit her "remembrance of awakened birds" to endure. Death is not only the end of life; it is "the mother of beauty." Through the fact, the inevitability, of death, things while they live acquire a quality, a beauty they would

---

[34] Title of a long discursive poem written in 1921 and 1922 and published in the first edition of *Harmonium*. Crispin is a "clown," an acrobat of the imagination, trying to adjust himself to a world of objects, which he has failed entirely to understand and place. Cf. "The Woman That Had More Babies Than That" in *Parts of a World* (1942).

[35] Five stanzas were published in *Poetry* (November 1915); three were added and the whole rearranged in the first edition of *Harmonium*.

not otherwise have. Mortality, in setting limits to life, also forces or encourages a mode of intense evaluation of experience:

> She makes the willow shiver in the sun
> For maidens who were wont to sit and gaze
> Upon the grass, relinquished to their feet.
> She causes boys to pile new plums and pears
> On disregarded plate. The maidens taste
> And stray impassioned in the littering leaves.

The most extreme statement is made in stanza 8, a final word concerning religion and death: Palestine is not the beginning but the end of life, not " 'the porch of spirits lingering' " but " 'the grave of Jesus where he lay.' " In this "old chaos of the sun" in which we live, we realize the beauty and pathos of impermanence:

> Deer walk upon our mountains, and the quail
> Whistle about us their spontaneous cries;
> Sweet berries ripen in the wilderness;
> And, in the isolation of the sky,
> At evening, casual flocks of pigeons make
> Ambiguous undulations as they sink,
> Downward to darkness, on extended wings.

This poem is a beginning for Stevens, not a conclusion. To say that "Death is the mother of beauty" is to leave major questions of beauty and order unanswered. Stevens' poems are in one sense a history of his attempts to answer these questions, to find the balance of reality and the gesture or "pose" of the artist who faces into their complexity. "The Comedian as the Letter C" is a travesty account of the artist as picaresque hero in a world of bewildering variety. A poem of six divisions, it describes the changes a person undergoes in his attempt to find an imaginative order for his experience. Crispin, the "comedian," has

> An eye most apt in gelatines and jupes,
> Berries of villages, a barber's eye,
> An eye of land, of simple salad-beds . . .

But, sensitive and alert as Crispin is to all forms and varieties of sense-impression, he is aware that these pleasant pictures are not vital:

> The whole of life that still remained in him
> Dwindled to one sound strumming in his ear,
> Ubiquitous concussion, slap and sigh,
> Polyphony beyond his baton's thrust.

In Part II, Crispin, more confident in the power of his imagination, searches for a suitable education of the senses. He finds "a new reality in parrot-squawks" and realizes

> That earth was like a jostling festival
> Of seeds grown fat, too juicily opulent,
> Expanding in the gold's maternal warmth.

His education is interrupted by a storm, whose "Tempestuous clarion" frightens him away from his new-found interest in the workings of his imagination. The storm proves another revelation:

> The storm was one
> Of many proclamations of the kind,
> Proclaiming something harsher than he learned
> From hearing signboards whimper in cold nights
> Or seeing the midsummer artifice
> Of heat upon his pane.

In Part III, "Approaching Carolina," the search for an aesthetic enters a new phase; the moonlight through which Crispin travels is the light of the imagination, the sun seems an undifferentiated and vibrant reality, and Crispin is not altogether sure about his choice. Perhaps the moonlight "really gave/The liaison, the blissful liaison,/Between himself and his environment," But

> It seemed
> Illusive, faint, more mist than moon, perverse,
> Wrong as a divagation to Peking,
>
> . . .
>
> Moonlight was an evasion, or, if not,
> A minor meeting, facile, delicate.

He decides finally against the moon; it is a pale reflection of reality, while the sun is the source of life. He has abandoned the practice of merely annotating reality and will now attempt fully to understand it. Part IV shows this new intelligence at work.

> What was the purpose of his pilgrimage,
> Whatever shape it took in Crispin's mind,
> If not, when all is said, to drive away
> The shadow of his fellows from the skies,
> And, from their stale intelligence released,
> To make a new intelligence prevail?

This decision, as we note in Part V, has drained him of his energies; the sun is a hard taskmaster, leaving him with "The blue infected will":

> For all it takes it gives a humped return
> Exchequering from piebald fiscs unkeyed.

So that (Part VI) Crispin, in risking a return to the sun, has had to abandon his project and has been left a victim of the reality he sought to understand. He decides that his experience is material enough for a "doctrine":

> The world, a turnip once so readily plucked,
> Sacked up and carried overseas, daubed out
> Of its ancient purple, pruned to the fertile main,
> And sown again by the stiffest realist,
> Came reproduced in purple, family font,
> The same insoluble lump.

The "Comedian" has been waylaid by his efforts to organize his senses and thus to minimize their confusion. In his failure he becomes a victim of their fate. The substance is slight, but the manner of presenting the rich range of sensation, the rhetorical exhibition of Crispin's sensuous life, are at once the essence of poetry and a plea for its value.

Stevens' many and varied attempts to define imagination remind us of the comparable preoccupation of the French symbolists. The lightness and grace of French poetry, he said in a letter to René Taupin, "its sound and color," had "upon me an undeniable influence and a precious one." Commenting on this letter, Taupin suggests that Stevens "profited from the subtleties of expression and the essays in pure poetry which came from France." [36] Stevens' poetry shows human life endlessly qualified and detained by the color and warmth of sensuous things —"complacencies of the peignoir," "the green freedom of the cockatoo," "the pungent oranges and bright, green wings." His love of color and the unusual vocabulary of his poetry were discussed by Gorham Munson in *Destinations* (1928) as evidences of "dandyism":

> Wallace Stevens gains elegance in large measure by his fastidiously chosen vocabulary and by the surprising aplomb and blandness of his images. He will say "harmonium" instead of "small organ," "lacustrine" instead of "lakeside," "sequin" instead of "spangle"; he will speak of "hibiscus," "panache," "fabliau," and "poor buffo." The whole tendency of his vocabulary is, in fact, toward the lightness and

[36] The late Hi Simons, who wrote a number of important criticisms of Stevens, published a study of Stevens and Mallarmé that makes the resemblances between the two poets quite convincing and significant. (See *Modern Philology*, May 1946).

coolness and transparency of French, into which tongue he sometimes glides with cultivated ease.

While Stevens is a master of the exceptional word and image, his use of them is part of his effort to find a defensible theory of the imagination; this quest for definition has affected many of his poems, especially the more recent "Notes toward a Supreme Fiction" and "Esthétique du Mal." "The poet refuses to allow his task to be set for him," he said in "The Noble Rider and the Sound of Words." [37] "He denies that he has a task and considers that the organization of materia poetica is a contradiction in terms. Yet the imagination gives to everything that it touches a peculiarity, and it seems to me that the peculiarity of the imagination is nobility, of which there are many degrees."

The poetry of Stevens, Williams, and Marianne Moore illustrates an important truth of the literature of the 1920s. Each wished to see the world in his own way and to evaluate it in his own terms; they sometimes preferred merely to present it, or those parts of it they actually knew. Working independently of the clichés, the traditional obligations of the past, they concerned themselves with problems of "the genuine," of communication, and of the imagination as a means of order. In modern poetry, experiment has been in essence a research into the resources of poetry, an appraisal of its values, and a demonstration of its own kind of viability and "truth."

3. The Color and Shape of the Thing Seen: Gertrude Stein

"IN THE summer of 1922, in Paris," said John Peale Bishop in his essay "The Missing All," "Ezra Pound told me about a young newspaper correspondent who had written some stories." Some of these Hemingway had written "lying on a bed in a roof-sharpened room which once had provided shelter for Verlaine in his last decrepit and drunken years." The phenomenon of this young American's living "up five flights of narrow winding stairs" on the rue Cardinal Lemoine was scarcely unusual. He had come, from Kansas City and from the Italian battlefront, so that he might learn to write fiction. Gertrude

[37] First published in a collection by several critics, *The Language of Poetry*, edited by Allen Tate (1942).

Stein, speaking through Alice B. Toklas, took the credit (with Sherwood Anderson) for teaching him:

> Gertrude Stein and Sherwood Anderson are very funny on the subject of Hemingway. The last time that Sherwood was in Paris they often talked about him. Hemingway had been formed by the two of them and they were both a little proud and a little ashamed of the work of their minds. . . . And then they both agreed that they have a weakness for Hemingway because he is such a good pupil. He is a rotten pupil, I [Miss Toklas] protested. You don't understand, they both said, it is so flattering to have a pupil who does it without understanding it, in other words he takes training and anybody who takes training is a favourite pupil.[38]

Whether or not Hemingway did it "without understanding it," the fact remains that he came to Paris convinced that it could help him to learn his art. Paris was a training ground for young writers, and in 1922 it was richly endowed with teachers of the craft. What could a young man learn? What did he need to learn, in these years following the war? Hemingway needed advice in a number of matters: simplicity of expression—the kind of simplicity not always learned in the career of a newspaper reporter; [39] economy—that is, what to do about adjectives, adverbs, metaphors (how *many* of each to use, and how much *weight* to put upon each word, in the total economy of the narrative); point of view: how to *locate* a narrative, in what kinds of intelligence to convey its meaning, how to establish the proper relationship of narrator to story; the very difficult problem of describing violence and action. As Hemingway phrased it in *Death in the Afternoon* (1932), he needed to learn how "to put down what really happened in action; what the actual things were which produced the emotion that you experienced . . . the real thing, the sequence of motion and fact which made the emotion. . . ."

There were, of course, several native resources to which the young writer had access. The most important was naturalism, partly because

[38] *The Autobiography of Alice B. Toklas,* 1933. The account of Hemingway in this book is colored by the fact that Miss Stein and Hemingway quarreled after a period of great friendship, and each claimed to be the major factor in the other's success.

[39] See Charles A. Fenton, who in Chapter II of *The Apprenticeship of Ernest Hemingway: The Early Years* (1954), claims that most of the "Hemingway manner" had already been achieved before he left Kansas City. See also Carlos Baker, *Hemingway: The Writer as Artist* (1952), Chapters 1 and 2, on the question of journalism as a training ground for fiction.

it often treated of violence, and especially because in the work of Stephen Crane there was evidence of an honest skill and artistry. Another was the "colloquial tradition" in American fiction, the colloquial point of view. The supreme instance, as Hemingway and many of his contemporaries readily acknowledged, was Mark Twain's *The Adventures of Huckleberry Finn.* Many of Sherwood Anderson's stories show an indebtedness to that novel; Hemingway's "My Old Man" (*In Our Time,* 1925) was directly influenced by Anderson, indirectly by Mark Twain.[40] The naturalists offered Hemingway and his generation of writers a sense of liberation from the limitations of subject matter; and they had at least begun the battle against the "genteel" critics at the turn of the century, had made the victory over them possible.[41]

More important was the naturalist's interest in violence, his experiments in the description of physical action. First, as to the physical action itself—as Hemingway put it, the problem of "the sequence of motion and fact which made the emotion": it was solved in several ways by the naturalists. Frank Norris, in the midst of McTeague's "big scene," the murder of Trina, halted the novel's progress to say simply and flatly: "Then it became abominable." Dreiser, challenged by the crucial scene of *An American Tragedy,* had recourse to a confusion of vocabularies and incentives: "At this cataclysmic moment, and in the face of the most urgent need of action, a sudden palsy of the will." [42] Dreiser was trying to describe a state of mind from which he hoped action could be inferred; Hemingway's usual method was to describe the action, to leave the state of mind for the reader to infer.

In many ways the naturalist pioneered in the portrayal of the *setting* of violence; or, as Hemingway called it, "The places, and how the weather was." The opening paragraphs of Crane's *The Red Badge of Courage* and of Hemingway's *A Farewell to Arms* testify to a happy coincidence of talents. It was not a difficult thing to describe a setting: Norris did many, some brilliantly; Dreiser was especially skillful in

[40] Hemingway said in *Green Hills of Africa* (1935): "All modern American literature comes from one book by Mark Twain called *Huckleberry Finn.* If you read it you must stop where the Nigger Jim is stolen from the boys. That is the real end. The rest is just cheating. But it's the best book we've had. All American writing comes from that. There was nothing before. There has been nothing as good since."

[41] See Grant C. Knight's *The Critical Period in American Literature, 1890–1900* (1951), for an excellent description of these events.

[42] The whole passage (end of Book II) is an object lesson in Dreiser's failure to come to grips with a crucial situation in his narratives.

portraying the scenes in which the most important events of his novels occurred. But the integration of setting and physical act, the interweaving of the pattern of static scene and physical movement, were entirely different matters, and, of all the naturalists, Stephen Crane was the only one who was entirely satisfactory. Finally, in the matter of a *perspective* upon violence, the naturalists had a contribution to make. The task of examining, understanding, representing personal reactions to immediate situations was performed in one way or another by Stendhal (in *The Charterhouse of Parma,* which Hemingway knew well), Ambrose Bierce, above all by Crane. The problem of reducing the scale of violence, keeping it consistently within the range of a single participant (or at most a few participants), was solved most happily in *The Red Badge of Courage.*

Hemingway encountered the formal problems peculiar to his own generation and circumstance. He engaged in an informal "course of reading" while he was in Paris,[43] but he especially needed an adequate means of interpreting contemporary facts, of translating immediate experience into art. Two American women had been in France during the war, Edith Wharton and Gertrude Stein; both were writers interested in the art of fiction. Mrs. Wharton's *The Writing of Fiction* appeared in 1925; Miss Stein's *Composition As Explanation* was published in 1926. Of the two, Mrs. Wharton had the longer, the more honorable career; yet no one was more remote than she from Hemingway's special circumstance, no one was closer to it than Gertrude Stein. She did not have his experience; her reaction to the war was primarily verbal, while his was personal, physical, direct, and immediate. She did, however, have "a method," a number of insights into what needed to be done to make immediacy formally and stylistically real. Hemingway went to her to find out what the twentieth century was all about and how it might be articulated and formalized. The twentieth century began, for both of them, in 1918, as it began in 1922 or thereabouts for Willa Cather. After the war, Miss Stein said, we had the twentieth century.

She had spent more years in France than Mrs. Wharton, having come there in 1903. She had written *Three Lives* (one of the earliest

[43] See Baker, *op. cit.* Among the men read by him in 1922–1923 were Turgenev, Chekhov, Tolstoi, Dostoevski, Stendhal, Balzac, Flaubert, W. H. Hudson, Mark Twain, Stephen Crane, Henry James, Thomas Mann, Joseph Conrad, and James Joyce. "Aside from the actual reading experience, which is something, when well done, involving all the artist's powers of observation, he seemed to be using the masters to test his own deepest critical convictions about the art of writing as it should be practiced."

truly modern works of American fiction) in 1905 and published it at her own expense in 1909. When Hemingway arrived she was working over the sheets of *The Making of Americans;* she had bought her Picassos and other paintings, and had sat for a Picasso portrait herself; her place at 27, rue de Fleurus was known as "the place to see," and she was considered the person to consult.

Pound was in Paris too. Having convinced some that poetry should be written as well as prose, he occasionally took time out to convince others that prose might be written as well as good poetry.[44] Ford Madox Ford was also there, as editor of the *transatlantic review,* and he availed himself of Hemingway's willingness to help with the magazine. In a very real sense, these three associates of Hemingway were all interested in the same thing, though each saw it in a different way.

The way for Gertrude Stein was closely allied with the forms of contemporaneity in art. She felt that only the present, the thing that was or that was in process of becoming, was valid and exciting.[45] It was not that "newness" fascinated her; she felt that the artist needed above all to make immediate experience real, to write in terms of and according to the nature of its immediacy. *Composition As Explanation* contained the essential principles of her aesthetic of fiction.[46] In it she spoke not only of the problems of writing but of the history of "generations" of writers in terms of "the thing seen." She felt that composition was essentially that and little more:

> The thing seen by every one living in the living they are doing, they are the composing of the composition that at the time they are living is the composition of the time in which they are living.

In order fully to grasp the thing seen, she wrote, a writer must possess an ideal time sense, a sense of living and composing at the same time; he must also be able to compose in such a way that his living of the thing seen is repeated in the composition. To accomplish this successfully, she proposed three "rules": maintaining a "continuous" or a

[44] This famous remark about Pound and Miss Stein was reportedly made later by Hemingway to John Peale Bishop: "Ezra was right half the time, and when he was wrong you were never in any doubt of it. Gertrude was always right." (See "Homage to Hemingway," *New Republic,* November 11, 1936.)

[45] She was interested in the past too, but only on her own terms. See Chapter IV: 3.

[46] There were other essays and books, of course: *Narration* (1935), *Lectures in America* (1935), and *How to Write* (1931) among them. But they did not add anything substantially new.

"prolonged" present, "beginning again and again," and "using everything." There must also be progress, which she defined as *narration:*

> And after that what changes what changes after that, after that what changes and what changes after that and after that and what changes and after that and what changes after that.

Progress in a narrative is the *distribution* of time, movement in terms of accretion, accumulation, essential sameness and subtle shades of difference. It does not simply occur, but is rather the result of a gradual change in the nuances of objects and meanings, expressed in terms of their slight differences and their essential relations. Style in composition is repetitious, as it needs to be. It repeats, it ranges its effects in terms of rather simple relational words, it returns again and again to its initial phrasing, it is careful to alter slightly each time the narrative moves toward its next phase. In short, it begins "again and again" and it "uses everything" in order to maintain a "continuous present."

Miss Stein had her difficulties with paragraphs. "A sentence is not emotional a paragraph is," she said in *How to Write* (1931). The sentence holds its line; a good sentence (one of Sherwood Anderson's, for example) answers the requirements of "composition as explanation." But once you move on to larger units of composition there is the risk of losing the order of your perceptions, of breaking their rhythm and dulling their sense of immediacy. But one *must* advance,[47] and does advance, from the sentence to the paragraph and to total structures. The great achievement is to move from one sentence to another and still retain a "continuous present." Similarly, syntax is an object of distrust. Syntax is logical; it forces a false and too rigid order upon the mind. The principal need is to *follow* an order of thought processes, not to *impose* an order upon them. If one *must* have syntax, make it as simple as possible.

Miss Stein's "composition" can best be explained by examining an example of it. The model of her writing, because it both contains a subject and follows her rules of composition, is "Melanctha," the sec-

---

[47] Miss Stein had great trouble with the paragraph in her own writings. *Tender Buttons* (1914) is really a collection of "sentences." When she was most self-conscious about method her writing seemed to collapse into such assortments. When she "had a subject," however, paragraphs gave her no difficulty; when the subject was herself (as in *The Autobiography of Alice B. Toklas*), the sequence of paragraphs took care of itself. But her method was pre-eminently a guide to the writing either of sentences or of successions of them that differ only slightly from one another.

ond of the *Three Lives.*[48] Melanctha Herbert "was always seeking rest and quiet, and always she could find new ways to be in trouble." She "always loved and wanted peace and gentleness and all her life for herself Melanctha could only find new ways to be in trouble." She searched for wisdom and she was afraid of what the wisdom would do to her. With Jane Harden, who drank and "wandered widely," she "had come to see very clear, and she had come to be very certain, what it was that gives the world its wisdom." The three motifs—her "always seeking rest and quiet," her getting into trouble, her desire for the experience that brings wisdom—are joined in Melanctha's relationship with Jeff Campbell. There is a succession of meetings in which they try to "talk it out"; there is a gradual change in the way they look at each other, until "Every day now more and more Melanctha would let out to Jeff her real, strong feeling." But the affair does not prosper; Jeff does not want to "go so fast," and as he tries to explain why he is so uneasy when he is with her, her impatience increases.

The torture of their trying to decide what they mean to each other, and what they mean by meaning it, and what they might have meant if they had not meant it, is too much; Melanctha begins "once more to wander." [49] Though they can now say "love" to each other, Melanctha is forced to admit that "I ain't got certainly no hot passion any more now in me." So "they never any more came close to one another," and Melanctha finds another man, one who is "fast enough" for her. But Jem Richards' affection for her depends on his luck with the horses, and he has very bad luck. This time Melanctha is deserted, and she "descends"—until she dies, lonely and disconsolate, in a home "for poor consumptives."

The narration is a texture of human understanding, desires to understand, failures to achieve understanding. As these situations develop, progress is indicated not so much in external event (there is a minimum of that) as in the gradual changes in what one person thinks of another; the narrative also advances in terms of groupings of persons as one relationship fades and is replaced by another. The complexity of this narration comes through as a consequence of a pattern of simplicities; complex states of mind are revealed to us in terms of the conscious-

[48] *Three Lives* is her version of Flaubert—the Flaubert of *Three Tales,* not of *Madame Bovary.* She was quite incapable of writing a *Madame Bovary.*

[49] At this point Miss Stein offers one of her rare generalizations upon the experience: Jeff is made to suffer from Melanctha's infidelity because "In tenderhearted natures, those that mostly never feel strong passion, suffering often comes to make them harder."

nesses that possess them. The style and rhythm of the sentences effectively secure the impression of a complex matter simply developed. There is a slow "beginning again and again"; changes are effected by repetition of word and phrase, with slight modulations ("what changes after that").[50]

It is difficult to measure Miss Stein's influence exactly. Many American writers must have had Sherwood Anderson's fascination for her "laying word against word, relating sound to sound, feeling for the taste, the smell, the rhythm of the individual word." [51] Others thought her something of a charlatan, who had made too much of too little talent.[52] Leo Stein, her brother, who had amiably tolerated her eccentricities for many years, eventually dismissed her as a woman of small competence.

Hemingway revised his estimate of her (as she did her view of him) toward the end of the 1920s; and *The Torrents of Spring* (1926) was a way of ridding himself of her, and of Anderson's, influence. But she had quite definitely helped him, at a crucial time in his career, to "see things in a contemporary way," had urged him to develop a style consistent with the nature of "the thing seen." As a result of her influence his style had been immersed in a "continuous present." In the fiction he wrote in the 1920s the time sense is often remarkably like that she had advised: not a sense of quick breaks of narrative or of "fill ins" of external event, but a flow of time, of which the style is an index. The time of *The Sun Also Rises,* for example, is given in terms of clusters of personalities, "subjective time." In the 1930s Hemingway once more returned to "public time," and his narratives became more closely associated with public events. The earlier grasp of immediacy is seen especially in the passages describing physical action. We may assume that—in consequence at least of Miss Stein's presence in Paris—Hemingway's description of action in the fiction of the 1920s was a refine-

---

[50] See *Things As They Are* (1950; originally called *Quod Erat Demonstrandum* when it was written in 1903) for a similar narrative style applied to sophisticated white consciousness.

[51] *Sherwood Anderson's Notebook* (1926).

[52] She published in *transition* from 1927 to 1935. Her *Autobiography of Alice B. Toklas* (1933) had displeased some members of the magazine's staff, and in 1935 *Testimony against Gertrude Stein* was published, signed by Henri Matisse and Georges Braque, among others. Eugene Jolas claimed that she had no "understanding of what really was happening about her," that she might "very well become one day the symbol of the decadence that hovers over contemporary literature."

ment of the naturalists', more exact, more in accordance with "the sequence of motion and fact which made the emotion."

The precise nature of that influence is clearly to be seen in three paragraphs at the end of Chapter 3, *A Farewell to Arms:*

Motif 1:

That night at the mess I sat next to the priest and he was disappointed and suddenly hurt that I had not gone to the Abruzzi. He had written to his father that I was coming and they had made preparations. I myself felt as badly as he did and could not understand why *I had not gone.*[53] It was *what I had wanted to do* and I tried to explain how one thing had led to another and finally *he saw it and understood that I had really wanted to go* and it was almost all right. I had drunk much wine and afterward coffee and Strega and I explained, winefully, *how we did not do the things we wanted to do; we never did such things.*

Development of Motif 1:

We two were talking while the others argued. *I had wanted to go* to Abruzzi. *I had gone to no place* where the roads were frozen and hard as iron, where it was clear cold and dry and the snow was dry and powdery and hare-tracks in the snow and the peasants took off their hats and called you Lord and there was good hunting. *I had gone to no such place*

Beginning of Motif 2: Anticipation of Motif 3:

but to the smoke of cafés and *nights* when the room whirled and you needed to look at the wall to make it stop, *nights* in bed, drunk, when you knew that that was all there was, and the strange excitement of waking and not *knowing* who it was with you, and the *world all unreal in the dark* and so exciting that you must resume again *unknowing* and *not caring in the night,* sure that *this was all and all and all* and not caring. . . .

Motif 3: (combining 1 and 2 on the level of "explanation")

I tried to tell *about the night* and *the difference between the night and the day* and how *the night was better* unless *the day was* very clean *and cold* and *I could not tell it; as I cannot tell it now.* But if you have it you know. He had not had it but he understood that *I had really wanted to go to* the Abruzzi but had not gone and we were still friends, with many tastes alike, but with the difference between us. *He had always known what I did not*

[53] The italics throughout these selections are mine.

> *know* and what, when I learned it, I was always able
> to forget. *But I did not know that then,* although I
> learned it later.

The progress seems deceptively easy, at first sight childishly repetitious. But it actually involves subtle gradations in the expression of two major ideas, symbolically given in terms of the two places Lieutenant Henry might have gone on his leave. As in Miss Stein's "Melanctha," the narrative progress comes through in gradual changes in the quality of knowledge and understanding: the priest knows that Lieutenant Henry wanted to go to the Abruzzi; Lieutenant Henry knows why he *had* to go to Milan instead, but thinks that the priest does not know; later he discovers that the priest *does* know. There are degrees of insight in all of this, as there are intimations of the quality given desires by the presence or absence of religious belief. The prose is rich in meanings; it is the process of "beginning again and again" that gives these meanings subtle degrees of intensity and importance.

This was in many ways a more significant "experiment" in American prose writing than that caused by the influence of the several variations of interior monologue in the prose of Dorothy Richardson, Joyce, and Virginia Woolf.[54] It was an experiment with economy of language, more "native to the grain" of the American experience. What Miss Stein did in the very beginning was to show the complexities that reside in the texture of simplicity; her "Melanctha" was an index of Negro subtleties totally different, for example, from Sherwood Anderson's brief and illusory auditing in *Dark Laughter.* Her method (and its occasionally successful demonstration in her work) was an experiment with the time sense as much (and with the same degree of intensity) as Imagism was an experiment with the spatial definition and limitation of the object. The major problem of most experimental fiction was the problem of time; its principal objective was drastically to revise the role of time in the narrative structure, to substitute metaphors of space or metaphors of flux for chronological or biographical timing.

In this sense, Miss Stein's influence has been more considerable than at first appeared. Perhaps because of the informality of her "teaching" (*Composition As Explanation* is her most formal organization of principle), because notoriety preceded fame in her case, and because she too often proclaimed her genius before others were ready to recognize it—for these reasons the nature of her influence has not been ade-

[54] See section v for a discussion of "stream-of-consciousness" fiction.

quately judged. Nor would it have been of much consequence, were it not for her contemporaries, who preached and practiced from their own points of view and from substantially different incentives. Her significant contributions were a sense of the immediate present and a fully documented discussion of the aesthetic strategies required to make immediacy functional within a prose text. These could not have been gained from the naturalists, who were (except for Stephen Crane) often handicapped by the most awkward and ambiguous notions of the novel as form, and were especially inadequate in their views of what was important subject matter for fiction.[55] Hemingway's style, at its best, successfully rendered gradations of awareness; and Gertrude Stein had much to do with his best in the 1920s.

4. "Cry I! I! I! Forever . . ."

"WITHOUT adultery, what would happen to imaginative writing?" asks Denis de Rougemont in his *Love in the Western World*. Commenting upon the great frequency of references to "lawless passion" in Western literature, he considers this preoccupation with adultery an important clue to modern morality: "Whether the subject is idealized by speaking of the divine rights of passion, refined away with the help of a psychology of social success, or mocked by the popularity which the eternal triangle enjoys in the theater, we are constantly *betraying* how widespread and disturbing is our obsession with the love that breaks the law." The word adultery "sums up one half of human unhappiness—renunciation, compromises, separations, neurasthenia, together with the irritating and petty confusions of dreams, obligations, and secret consents."

The general attitude toward marriage during the years 1915–1930 was one of free criticism; there was a search for alternative arrangements between the sexes, within and without marital bounds. In many respects the attacks upon marriage seemed a new variation upon female aggressiveness, a new demonstration of the woman's wish to free herself from her traditional status. "Women are demanding a reality in their relations with men that heretofore has been lacking," said Beatrice Hinkle in 1924, "and they refuse longer to cater to the tradi-

[55] Cf. *Green Hills of Africa:* "I cannot read other naturalists unless they are being extremely accurate and not literary. Naturalists should all work alone and some one else should correlate their findings for them."

tional notions of them created by men, in which their true feelings and personalities were disregarded and denied." A number of writers called the exploitation of the female by the male humanity's major error. In the opinion of one critic, monogamy had always been an illusion; it had never really existed in this world: "Our present custom is a partial monogamy for many women and some men, and divorce, remarriage, prostitution, and promiscuity for others."

The novels of the period were filled with debate and discussion of sexual morality. One character in Douglas Goldring's *Façade* suggested that though the "disease" of love still existed, "modern science has discovered it to be curable." Aldington's *Death of a Hero* spoke of "that rather hard efficiency of the war and postwar female," who concealed "the ancient predatory and possessive instincts of the sex under a skillful smoke barrage of Freudian and Havelock Ellis's theories." The slick romantic surfaces of Joseph Hergesheimer's essays on adultery offered marital unhappiness as an excuse for extramarital indulgence. Lee Randon of *Cytherea* (1922), for example, had what the world regarded as "an admirable existence, an admirable family," but from time to time "the desire, the determination swept over him to smash to irremediable atoms what was so well applauded." As for the long and faithful marriage, it was thought to demonstrate a lack of imagination or of courage. The elder Basines of Ben Hecht's *Gargoyles* had been married for twenty-seven years and had in that time achieved "an utter disregard for each other which both took pride in identifying as domestic happiness."

Scores of statements regarding the restrictions of the marital vow testified to the uncertainty of its value in the minds of the young men and women of the time. Women followed up their successful campaign for suffrage with additional demands that they be allowed to imitate men in appearance, in style, in freedom of movement, to extinguish forever the belief held by men that they were sweet, frail young things who needed to be coddled and pampered. This point of view was treated with some humor by Floyd Dell. In *Love in Greenwich Village* (1924), one of his modern women married, then rejected the marital status because her husband asked her to sew buttons on his shirts. "I've got a right to be *myself*," she said as she prepared to leave him. "That comes first of all. And if marriage prevents *that*, it's wrong. People can think what they like. They're all under the matrimonial illusion." There was the squeamishness of Edmund Wilson's Hugo Bamman (*I Thought of Daisy*, 1929), who was "invariably alienated from the types of emancipated women whom he encountered in the Village, by an un-confessed but ineradicable instinct which rejected them as not being ladies."

An insatiable curiosity about sex was one of the most obvious char-acteristics of these years. Frankness about sexual matters, together with an avid reading of books dealing with problems of sex, gave the subject an exaggerated importance. At the end of the decade Edwin Sapir sum-marized in the *American Mercury* the "anti-Puritan revolt" of the 1920s: "It is a generalized revolt against everything that is hard, nar-row, and intolerant in the old American life, and which sees in sex repression its most potent symbol of attack. Many young men and women of today who declare themselves sexually free are really revolt-ing against quite other than sex restrictions."

Lengthy, intimate, and rather tedious investigations of sex life, such as Havelock Ellis's *Psychology of Sex,* met with an eager and excited reception. Because of censorship, Ellis's monumental work was not distributed generally in America until 1936, but his position as an au-thority on sex had been established and accepted early in the century. He was a hero of the "new knowledge," suffering humiliation at the hands of the British censor, but victorious eventually in his fight for unlimited knowledge of all phases of sexual inversion and perversion, in all languages and in all places. Other leaders of the sexual revolution were Ellen Key and Edward Carpenter. Miss Key's books, *The Century of the Child* (1909) and *The Woman Movement* (1912), part of the feminist agitation, served the cause of rebellion against sex morality; they attacked marriage as an institution that held dogmatically to a misalliance of persons and often enforced by law a relationship origi-nally made ignorantly and in bad taste. The proper sex relationship, Miss Key maintained, could exist quite as well outside of as within marriage. Carpenter's *Love's Coming of Age* (1896) proved one of the most influential books of the scores that argued for a revision of sex morality.

These pioneers were popular in the second decade of our century, widely received, and much discussed. But they were all but replaced by a rival interpretation of the human mind and body, which avoided the vagueness and localism of Miss Key's feminism and Carpenter's liberal-ism, and provided what at least appeared to be a scientific thoroughness and sanction. The overwhelming popularity of psychoanalysis in the twentieth century affected not only the matter of sexual morality but the entire range of human activity and consciousness. It encouraged the exploration of man's subjective nature and often supplied an excellent substitute for social and economic motives in explaining his social behavior.

Psychoanalysis was mocked and burlesqued by its opponents, applauded eagerly by its sponsors. The Freudian jargon became part of the small change of popular journalism and was used to add a spurious scientific note to off-color stories about murders, divorces, and other newspaper fare. Figures from the political, sports, and religious worlds were given public analyses, their talents and their shortcomings subjected to a pseudo-psychoanalytic scrutiny. It was assumed that every feature-story journalist had a smattering of ignorance about psychoanalysis and that he could therefore explain why Gloria B. was now in Reno, why Ruth W. used an ax instead of a gun in the murder of her husband, why Calvin C. preferred wolfhounds to cocker spaniels, why thousands of fans shouted so vigorously when Babe R. stepped to the plate. An entire nation took the high road to the analyst's clinic, to be told that it was psychically starved, immature, repressed, or what-have-you.[56]

[56] The great game of psychoanalysis provided ample copy for the bright, slick journalists of *Vanity Fair* and other magazines designed for eager sophisticates. "Fish," one of *Vanity Fair's* artists, portrayed a series of analysis victims (May 1921) under the general caption "The Solace of Psychoanalysis: The only Polite and Painless Cure for Human Faults and Failings." In the same magazine (July 1925) John Peale Bishop offered a few Mother Goose rhymes brought up to date: little boys are made "Of Oedipus Rex and Infantile Sex," little girls, "of Iphigenia's incestuous desires"; and Mary's garden is no longer a mystery.

> Mary, Mary, wise and wary
> Who helps your garden grow?
> The tiny bees, with hairy knees,
> Tote pollen to and fro.

One of Alan Odle's sketches of "Members of the Learned Professions" (*Vanity Fair*, January 1926) pictures "Doctor Paul Ehrich, the popular New York psychoanalyst, . . . probing the complexes of a young lady who has been dreaming of red lights, boa constrictors, and caviar. Disregarding the fact that she had supped on Welsh rarebit, he will diagnose her case as agoraphobia and acute mania resulting from an Electra Complex." To the magazine's raillery E. E. Cummings contributed two essays—"The Tabloid Newspaper: An Investigation Involving Big Business, the Pilgrim Fathers, and Psychoanalysis" (December 1926) and "The Secrets of the Zoo Exposed: Proving That Our Fear of Wild Animals Is Done with the Aid of (Freudian) Mirrors" (March 1927). In May 1922 Heywood Broun offered a psychoanalytic explanation of Babe Ruth's great popularity, "Bambino the Maestro: the Suggestion of a Possible Freudian Interpretation of the Aesthetic Appeal of Babe Ruth": "We hope it will not be considered

Regarded seriously or frivolously, the new "depth psychology" attracted the attention of scores of writers, who sometimes blamed it for having caused the "modern psychic illness," sometimes credited it with having suggested the clue to all the defects of our civilization. By 1916 there were approximately five hundred so-called psychoanalysts in New York City alone; so Alfred Kuttner tells us in his contribution to Harold Stearns' symposium, *Civilization in the United States* (1922). In a great number of cases Freud's theories, presented usually in fragmentary form, were made over, "sweetened" and "refined," to suit the client's needs. Freud's admirers obscured or exaggerated him, and his enemies used his popularity to prove his reputation was based on sensationalism. In fact, Freud met with three fates: he was wildly embraced, rejected in toto with appropriate academic lynching, or accepted with "improvements." [57]

By 1920 there were hundreds of popular summaries, expositions, and distortions of Freud's original works, together with a growing number of works allegedly presenting the psychologies of Jung, Adler, and other psychoanalysts.[58] Perhaps the most successful popular "physician of the soul" was André Tridon. He wrote summaries of Freudian theory, with elaboration and adulteration of text, designed to bring what Bernard De Voto has called a "comfortably diluted version of Freud within the capacity of everyone." The *Nation's* announcement of his lectures in the issue of February 16, 1921, included a testimonial from H. L. Mencken: "Even a college professor or congressman can understand Tridon on 'Psychoanalysis.'" The five lectures included discussions of Freud, Jung, and other theorists.

Other successful popularizers were James Oppenheim and Harvey O'Higgins. O'Higgins offered the new psychology to the American pub-

---

extravagant if we suggest that the subconscious spectator tends to identify the pitcher with all the forces of negation throughout the world. As he winds up and puts upon the ball every ounce of repression which is in him, he becomes suddenly a little brother to Puritanism, Volstead, law and order, the Malthusian theory, and keep off the grass."

[57] See F. J. Hoffman, *Freudianism and the Literary Mind* (1945), Chapters 2 and 3, for a survey of Freud's reception in America.

[58] One evidence of the mature interest in psychoanalysis was the publication in 1924 of the Modern Library volume, *An Outline of Psychoanalysis,* edited by J. S. Van Teslaar. This included contributions by the psychoanalytic greats— Freud, Jung, Ferenczi, Stekel, and Jones. Another serious study, A. C. Tansley's *The New Psychology and Its Relation to Life,* was published in both London and New York and enjoyed nine printings between June 1920, and September 1924.

lic as a long-lost "secret spring" to the knowledge of self and salvation in modern terms. In *The Secret Springs* (1920), he offered a summary of Freudian discoveries, discussions of the unconscious mind, the "subliminal self," and the sexual life, and discussed the remarkable teaching of a "Dr. X" (Dr. Edward H. Reede of Washington, D.C.). O'Higgins claimed that Dr. X's interpretation was an improvement upon Freud's, since it "took the curse of excessive sexuality off the unconscious mind." Dr. X advised his patients to consider all impulses, however mean and evil they may appear to be: "If you drive them down into your secret cellar, they may end by tearing down the whole house. If you welcome them into your parlor, you may be surprised to see how quickly they will wash their faces and change their clothes and make themselves respectable." The book was typical of many popular estimates of psychoanalysis; it was enthusiastic, wide-eyed, and happy in the discovery of a psychological key to modern unhappiness; it exulted in having pioneered in a new brand of "healing"; it was proud to be the sponsor of a theory that had not as yet been accepted by traditional old fogies of the medical world. As in most popularizations, *The Secret Springs* assumed all psychoanalysis to be its province, and allowed the theories of one analyst to modify those of another if such a procedure was likely to prove more acceptable to the public.

One of the principal causes of the distortion of psychoanalysis was this care on the part of the popularizer to water down the "sensational discoveries" with assurances and qualifications of a non-scientific character. James Oppenheim's potboiler, *Behind Your Front* (1928), was an extreme form of dilution. The concepts of introversion and extraversion, which Jung had painstakingly developed and carefully qualified in *Psychological Types,* were made the substance of a popular parlor game, "Know Your Type"; a chart for analysis was provided in the book, and a list of forty questions, to enable the reader to label himself psychologically and compare himself with the celebrities whose personality charts were included. America as a whole, said Oppenheim, is "an over-extraverted nation. . . . The introverts in America are crushed, and because they are crushed they either try to twist themselves into extraverts with false fronts, or they instinctively and fanatically rebel." [59]

---

[59] In 1931 Oppenheim published another popular treatment of psychoanalysis, *American Types: A Preface to Analytic Psychology*—a more serious work, concerned primarily with the use of Jung's *Psychological Types* but containing also brief chapters on Freud and Adler. Oppenheim had prepared himself for this

Freud, in his discussions of the ego, its place in the conscious and the unconscious, and the gravity of its struggle for shape and form in a world of complex and hidden motive, provided a complete set of speculations about the modern soul. The literature of the 1920s offered many examples of the mind's turning in upon itself, examining, explaining, and excusing itself in psychological terms. Persistent diagnosis often figured as a substitute for traditional morality, and it most certainly provided a means of justifying the modernist's abandonment of his past. The key concepts of soul-searching in modern literature were not infrequently borrowed from psychoanalysis. The interest in self took the place, and argued the futility, of a sense of social responsibility; and one of the reasons politics, economics, and the idea of a social code did not especially interest the writers of the 1920s was this preoccupation with the nature of the self, separate from community and society.

In "Psychology and Art To-Day" (an essay published in *Arts To-Day,* 1935), W. H. Auden discussed what he called "The Implications of Freud" for the modern consciousness. "What we call evil was once good," said Auden, "but has been outgrown, and refused development by the conscious mind with its moral ideas." The real character of our moral interests and problems "depends on the nature of our relations

---

work, so the dust-jacket maintained, by three years of practicing analysis and eighteen years of study.

From the scores of references to psychoanalysis in the fiction of the 1920s, the following is a sampling of remarks made in one or another context:

It was curious to find even placid Laura facing a problem, and Campaspe wondered, half-amused, if Laura would consult a psychoanalyst regarding her enigma, as was the current fashion, rather than a priest. (Carl Van Vechten, *Firecrackers,* 1925)

Three psychoanalysis books are enough for any library. To hell with Sigmund. I begin to dislike him anyway. He's corrupted immorality. (Ben Hecht, *Humpty Dumpty,* 1924)

These things which foolish people speak of with grave-faced straining after objectivity, with uncouth scientific jargon and sudden lapses into pruriency, Sophronisba presents as a genuine revelation. . . . Her allegiance went, of course, quickly to Freud, and once, in a sudden summer flight to Jung in Zurich, she sat many hours absorbing the theories. (Randolph Bourne, "Portrait of Sophronisba," 1920)

"And my dear, have you heard about Tony Hunter's being straightened out by a psychoanalyst and now he's all sublimated and has gone on the vaudeville stage with a woman named California Jones." (John Dos Passos, *Manhattan Transfer,* 1925)

with our parents." The sense of guilt which we are used to calling *conscience* is associated intimately with this familial relationship. Many writers of the twenties took as their point of departure the early amoral, "libidinous" self, and described its development thereafter as a ceaseless and rather painful struggle for simple satisfaction. The self in this estimate rarely "broke through" or developed naturally; it was hindered at every turn by repressive moral agencies concerned with "what was good for it." Conformity was therefore considered a primary evil, for it indicated a maximum surrender to these agencies of "the good" and a minimum development of the self. The clamor raised against convention was in part an expression of the need to acknowledge an individual sense of guilt, in some way actually to experience evil. "At the root of all disease and sin is a sense of guilt," said Auden, and the cure is a personal one; it "consists in taking away the guilt feeling, in the forgiveness of sins, by confession, the re-living of the experience, and absolution, the understanding of its significance."

This attitude is linked historically with the tradition of Baudelaire's *Flowers of Evil,* Rimbaud's *A Season in Hell,* Dostoevski's *Crime and Punishment* and *The Possessed.* The attractiveness of such literature is twofold: it makes of morality a very complex and an intimately personal responsibility, and it allows us to share the realization that salvation does not come quickly or easily. We often quite smugly feel that we need not fear the terrors of hell as described by evangelists; the more vivid the details, the greater is our assurance that if we are "good" we may avoid them. Religious exhortations are warnings that we must avoid evil if we wish to escape punishment; the writings of Baudelaire, Rimbaud, and Dostoevski warn us that we cannot understand punishment until we have experienced crime.

In this important sense the egoism of the 1920s was a highly moral preoccupation with the issue of personal involvement in evil. The great development in modern art of self-consciousness as both motive and subject had its sources in this personal realization of evil, this distrust of patent goodness. It was also characterized by a fundamental pessimism—a pessimism not entirely based upon the materialism of modern science or justified solely by the rational destruction of illusion, which seemed to be one of the tasks of Freudian psychoanalysis. It was a pessimism *faute de mieux:* there seemed no justification for optimism, an attitude apparently founded upon an evasion of psychological truth. There was no real acceptance of J. B. Watson's Behaviorism, for example, because Watson's psychology stopped at the very threshold of moral significance. It was a psychology for advertisers, for businessmen and statisticians, not for moralists.

The self-consciousness of modern writing was often ludicrous—not, however, because of its basis in pessimism, but because of its distortion of personality. Many novels of the twenties barely escaped the sentimentality of the jazz lyric because their interest in personality was so exaggerated as to deny them much insight into character. Their plots also suffered from a lack of depth and from a failure to correlate adequately external acts and motives. Particularly in the matter of form, they demonstrated an irresponsibility that was both moral and aesthetic. The so-called autobiographical novels were too often excuses for conduct rather than explanations of it. Characters were often grotesques, in that their actions possessed no reasonable consistency. Their journey through life was often circular. How many of these characters returned to the womb as a refuge from the cold, harsh reality of life itself! Their very reactions were often an acting-out of prenatal attitudes.

It is not so much their hatred of conventions that made these novels wearisome; it was their personal inadequacy, their failure to shape their own personal world and to live in it with some degree of mature confidence. In a sense these deficiencies were the result of a literal exploitation of psychoanalysis, or misappropriation of it, for personal interests.

Several of these novels enjoyed a temporary success, became bestsellers, and were widely discussed. They seemed to have described accurately an attitude that young people shared widely. Their attractiveness for the public can be explained by their free and open discussion of sex relations, their affectation of worldly cynicism (which made some of the novels a series of epigrams fashioned out of the paradoxes of contemporary society), and their timely use of the popular notions of the day. Usually these novels were portraits of young intellectuals who were very much aware of prevailing fashions in morality and used them quite cleverly to explain, defend, rationalize, and prepare a way for their conduct; for example, such works as Fitzgerald's *This Side of Paradise;* Ben Hecht's *Erik Dorn, Gargoyles,* and *Humpty-Dumpty;* Floyd Dell's *The Moon-Calf, The Briary-Bush,* and *Janet March;* Maxwell Bodenheim's *Blackguard;* Sherwood Anderson's *Windy McPherson's Son, Many Marriages,* and *Dark Laughter;* and Waldo Frank's *The Unwelcome Man, The Dark Mother, Rahab,* and *Chalk Face.* Frank's novels perhaps deserve special mention; they were not strictly autobiographical, but rather fictional applications of their author's philosophy: a mixture of spiritual prophecy, psychoanalysis, an earnest concern over the dilemma of modern man as he saw it. One is aware in the novels not so much of the author himself but of his grandiose analyses and suggestions for the treatment of modern ills.

These novels illustrate in one form or another the mood of the postwar intellectual, explain and justify it, and describe his behavior in a world in which conventional standards have been excluded or severely criticized. The heroes are usually outcasts by choice; they fashion their behavior along lines of personal resistance to prevailing codes; their lives touch upon the intellectual interests of the time. The novels are built consciously upon the war and upon the postwar manner; their code is therefore in the process of growing; it is being tested and qualified at every turn by some new and ingenuous experience, and in almost every novel it is left incomplete and inadequate.[60]

The mood of self-revelation combined despair over superficial realities with desire to bring all emotions immediately to the surface. Implicit in this mood was an imitation of the psychoanalyst's procedure; for psychoanalysis depends for its effectiveness upon the patient's willingness to bring disagreeable truths to the surface of consciousness. It was only this *practice* which the novelist imitated; the object was not to control but to display neuroses, to point to the inadequacy of the conventional world as a source of regulation and control of impulses.

> I'll swell my gullet,
> Leap in the common grave and like a cock
> Crow from the carrion. I'll tell the world.
> I'll make a book of it. I'll leave my rare
> Original uncopied dark heart pain
> To choke up volumes and among the rocks
> Cry I! I! I! forever.[61]

These are the words of the modern Hamlet, who would heal his wounds by exhibiting them, by making copies of them, for all to see.

> I'll tell you how I loved too, all my loves,
> My bed quilts, bolsters, blankets, my hot hands,
> My limbs, my rumps; my wretchedness: my lust,
> My weakness later and lascivious dreams.

[60] See Chapter III:2 for a detailed discussion of some of these.
[61] *The Hamlet of A. MacLeish* (1928).

The repressive ordinances of traditional morality and society had to be revealed for what they were. "There was a deep well within every man and woman," said Sherwood Anderson in *Many Marriages,* "and when life came in at the door of that house, that was the body, it reached down and tore the heavy iron lid off the well. Dark hidden things, festering in the well, came out and found expression for themselves, and the miracle was that, expressed, they became often very beautiful."

Demonstrations of "the new freedom" were many and curious; revolt against conventions often had the rather indecent suggestiveness of undressing in public. Repressions were thrown off in a joyous affirmation of a primitive life, in a bitter gesture against criminal tradition, in a spirit of argumentative opposition to a set of Victorian restraints. But, with all these gestures of daring release from tribal taboos, the general impression to be gained from this literature is of a pathetic sparring with shadows.[62] They are "spiritual quests" of a sort, but for the most part they announce not the quest of the spirit but the defeat of it.

5. "Pure Psychic Automatism": Some Extremes of Improvisation

"[Freud] has been misappropriated by irrationalists eager to escape their conscience," said W. H. Auden in "Psychology and Art To-Day." Perhaps he had the surrealists in mind, for they thoroughly exploited psychoanalysis. Surrealism was at the beginning almost entirely a Gallic idea. Its central figures were French, and since its capital was Paris, it belonged also to the expatriate Americans. Such little-maga-

---

[62] In Anderson's case especially, the work of D. H. Lawrence had an influence comparable with Freud's. Several of Lawrence's books were first published in America (*Women in Love* was printed in 1920 "for subscribers only"), and he often enjoyed a much greater sale here than in England. "Have just finished Lawrence's book [*Women in Love*]," Anderson wrote Paul Rosenfeld (January 1921). "It's tremendous . . . like a storm I once lived through. . . . Lawrence went after something—a feeling that in some queer way rides over all thought and he came very nearly pulling it off." *Many Marriages* and *Dark Laughter* seem especially to have been influenced by Lawrence. Both are inferior to Lawrence's work in grasp of situation as well as in their exploration of "primitive" alternatives to the "white, conscience-ridden world." (See Irving Howe, *Sherwood Anderson,* 1951, for a discussion of the relationship.)

zine personalities as Margaret Anderson and Eugene Jolas followed the movement closely and featured it from time to time in the *Little Review* and *transition*. Miss Anderson's interest was part of her willingness to exhibit the new in the arts, and the pages of the *Little Review* were open to the surrealists as to any other new school of writing and painting. Eugene Jolas had a more personal interest; it was one of the several sources of his theories of language and literature.

Surrealism began with dada; the setting was the Zurich of the war years. Along with Lenin, who was waiting for the right moment to cross Germany to Russia and the new political society, Zurich housed writers and artists who were to introduce the most extreme forms of experiment into the intellectual history of our century. In the Cabaret Voltaire, on the evening of February 8, 1916, dada was officially launched; it was a thorough-going attempt to dismiss the civilization then being fought over on the battlefields of Europe. The pioneers of dada included Tristan Tzara, its founder, a young Rumanian student of philosophy; Hans Arp, an Alsatian poet and artist; and several Germans, who were to establish dada in postwar Germany. From the office of Mouvement Dada, at Zeltweg 33, Zurich, the *Bulletin Dada* was issued from 1916 to the end of 1918. The "epigraphe," allegedly from Descartes, read: *"Je ne veux même pas savoir s'il y a eu des hommes avant moi."* (I do not wish even to know whether there have been men before me.) In June 1916 another review, *Cabaret Voltaire,* was started, named for the dadaist headquarters, where pictures were exhibited, poems read, and concerts given.[63]

Dadaist exhibitions, or "demonstrations," provided the key to their purpose. *La Matinée Dada,* held at the Salon des Indépendants, at the

---

[63] The poetry of dada was a mixture of startling imagery and pure sound effects, as in this example by Tzara:

> in your inside there are smoking lamps
> the swamp of blue honey
> cat crouched in the gold of a flemish inn
> boom boom
> lots of sand yellow bicyclist
> chateauneuf des papes
> manhattan there are tubes of excrement before you
> inbaze inbaze bazebaze inlegarga garoo
> you turn round rapidly inside me
> kangaroos in the boat's entrails

Dadaist poetry is not always as clear as this; usually it is a series of *effects* rather

Grand Palais des Champs Élysées, Paris, on February 5, 1920, was described by André Gide as a mixture of the most severe formality and the most outrageous tricks. Someone in the audience called out, *"Faites des gestes!"* and everyone laughed; but no one dared to stir, for fear of admitting bewilderment. In Cologne, where the German dadaists were headed by the painter Max Ernst, one of the more sensational exhibitions took place. David Gascoyne described it in *A Short Survey of Surrealism* (1935):

> In order to enter the gallery one had to pass through a public lavatory. Inside, the public was provided with hatchets with which, if they wanted to, they could attack the objects and paintings exhibited. At the end of the gallery a young girl, dressed in white for her first communion, stood reciting obscene poems.

These were gestures of rebellion against three cherished aspects of civilized decorum, neatly and exactly made: against civilized privacy, against the hush-hush reverence for art in conventional galleries, and against the purity of religion and morality.

Dadaism was a series of attacks upon decorum and convention of all sorts. The manifestoes of dadaists were expressions of nihilistic objection to all forms of affirmation. So too were the "definitions" of *Dada: "Voilà le mot qui mène idées à la chasse"; "DADA ne signifie rien"* (Tristan Tzara); *"Toute conviction est une maladie"* (Picabia); *"L'absence de système est encore un système, mais le plus sympathique"* (Tzara).[64]

Dadaism was a violent attempt to kill off Western civilization by

---

than a form or pattern. An extreme example, "Paroxysme," by Pierre Chapka-Bonnière, was published as late as 1921:

```
    ——; ——; ——o——O
    !!!  tsi—:—:—I
—et sam—et sam—sam— saM
—et sam—et sam—sam— saM
?  oha — keink —— tsi H.
   ! rrroor —— O
   —— atakak — af — oh — tzzi g
```

The poet was accused of plagiarism by one Nicolas Baudouin.

[64] As for their own ability to make definitions and distinctions, the dadaists prided themselves on their ignorance of dadaist significance; so that we have Francis Picabia making this speech in "explanation" of dada in February 1920: "You do not understand, of course, what we are doing! Well, my dear friends, we understand it still less. How wonderful, isn't it, that you are right! . . . You don't understand? Neither do I; how sad!"

ridicule and laughter. André Gide (*Nouvelle Revue Française,* April 1920) spoke of the physical ruin wrought by the war and suggested that "the mind has a right to some ruins too." Dadaism welcomed horrified indignation, enjoyed its reputation for violence, and took special pleasure in puzzling and outraging the respectable sponsors of Academy art and literature. The horror it inspired was in a sense a fulfillment of its purpose, which a Chicago critic called "a universally inclusive, desperately serious, supremely conscious hoax intended to undermine the whole fabric of decadent European society." Waldo Frank, while he admitted that dada might have been an appropriate expression of relief in "over-mature Europe," declared that Americans had no need for such explosions of ridicule: "A healthy reaction to our world must of course be the contrary of dada: it must be ordered and serious and thorough." To these remarks Malcolm Cowley, a visiting dadaist in Paris, replied, saying that dada was after all "a discovery: that nonsense may be the strongest form of ridicule; that writing is often worst when it is most profound, saintly, or devoted, and best when it is approached in a spirit of play; that associational processes of thought often have more force than the logical; that defiance carried to the extremes of bravado is more to be admired than a passive mysticism."

Dada was a joke, an all-inclusive hoax played upon wartime and postwar Europe. It was against all systems, defied all logic and reason; full of sound and fury, it stressed the absolute significance of nothing. It could not outlast its opportunity, but within its ranks were the founders and leaders of surrealism. André Breton, who joined forces with Tzara when the latter came to Paris in 1920, had already been working on a surrealist aesthetic. In his experiments in automatic writing, undertaken with Philippe Soupault, Breton covered "sheets with writing, feeling a praiseworthy contempt for whatever the literary result might be." From its beginnings as a simple experiment in associational writing, surrealism eventually became an aesthetic and a philosophy of revolution. Breton's first Manifesto underscored his objection to rationalism, which, he claimed, had served to put facts of primary importance beyond the reach of the personal consciousness. Logic and reason had barred all fantasy from the minds of men; "all uncustomary searching after truth has been proscribed." But Freud and psychoanalysis had only recently revealed the great hidden resources of the unconscious, "strange forces" in the depths of our mind, manifested in dreams, hallucinations, and all expressions of man's unconscious.

Breton's definition of surrealism [65] was given in the first Manifesto:

> Pure psychic automatism by which it is intended to express, verbally, in writing, or by other means, the real process of thought. Thought's dictation, in the absence of all control exercised by the reason and outside all aesthetic or moral preoccupations.

This simple definition referred entirely to the kind of free association with which psychoanalysts, following Freud's suggestions, tried to discover the causes of neuroses in their patients. Surrealism differed from psychoanalytic uses of free association in several ways, however: its purpose was not to interpret the results of free association but merely to present them; nor did it wish to exercise clinical control over the psychic illness which such reports usually revealed to the analyst; finally, it was a deliberate exploration of the artist's own unconscious by the artist himself, for the purpose of uncovering new resources of the poetic imagination. Breton in the beginning admitted that the poet's discoveries might later be given a rational order of some sort and that the success of surrealism would not necessarily "depend on the more or less capricious means that will be employed."

The mechanism of the dream became the most important source of all surrealist art; in its disguises one found remarkable associations of images and discordances of thought. These were also to be found in Freud's *Interpretation of Dreams,* as well as a careful discussion of the "logic" of the dream and its "syntax," for use by the analyst in deciphering the latent dream-thoughts. Surrealists were generally satisfied to find the images and the latent fantasies of the unconscious and to reproduce these in whatever form the artist seemed best qualified to give them.

From the beginning, however, surrealism was more than an experiment in the arts. Like dadaism, it developed a strategy of attack against the conventional world, wherever that world seemed to offend the surrealist taste. Its opposition to convention was as unrelenting as dada's, but it attempted an elaborate program, which included active protests against traditionalism in the arts and in society and an alignment with communism. [66] The moral purposes of surrealism emerged, in fact, from its original theory of art—for the surrealist use of the unconscious uniformly ridiculed the pretensions and forms of existing so-

---

[65] The word "surrealist" was used by Guillaume Apollinaire in 1917, in the subtitle of a play, *Les Mamelles de Tirésias: drame surréaliste.*

[66] Collaboration with the Communists was indicated both in the title and in

ciety. Breton's second Manifesto (1929) pointed up the importance of what he termed "moral asepsis," "the only chance of success for the surrealist operation," and called upon man to despise all prohibitions. Breton insisted on making the dialectic of Marxism adaptable to surrealism. "I really cannot see, despite the views of a few narrow-minded revolutionaries," he said in his second Manifesto, "why we should abstain from taking up the problems of love, of dreaming, of madness, of art, of religion, so long as we consider these problems from the same point of view as they, and we too, consider revolution."

Surrealism began in curiosity about the usefulness of psychoanalysis for modern writing, but the two were widely dissimilar approaches to the unconscious. There is a great difference between a scientific effort to *explore* and *control* the unconscious and the artist's attempt to *exploit* it. Surrealists were interested in the direct transference to paper or canvas of the imagery found in the unconscious; so that in the immediate and intimate view they offered of the unconscious, the analyst was deserted at the very beginning of his constructive work.

This difference of purpose can best be shown by juxtaposing two statements about the unconscious and its relationship to conscious life. The first is from Freud's *New Introductory Lectures on Psycho-Analysis*. The object of psychoanalytic procedures, he says, "is to strengthen the ego, to make it more independent of the super-ego, to widen its field of vision, and so to extend its organization that it can take over new positions of the id. Where id was, there shall ego be." The second is from André Breton's first Manifesto. Surrealism, he says, is "thought's dictation, in the absence of all control exercised by the reason and outside all aesthetic or moral preoccupations."

Here are two images of the unconscious life:

> The dreamer sees three lions in a desert, one of which is laughing, but she is not afraid of them. Then, however, she must have fled from

---

the contents of the surrealist magazine, *Le Surréalisme au service de la révolution,* the first number of which appeared in 1930. Several years before that surrealism had proclaimed its own kind of revolution by its attacks upon all guardians of the *status quo.* In August 1925 the fifth number of the magazine printed a manifesto in which the adherence of surrealism to communism was clarified, and the manner and degree of its association with political radicalism explained. The surrealists attacked all forms of official suppression and imperialism and agreed with the communist strategy of activity in capitalist countries. This active political program was, however, only accidentally related to the surrealist aesthetic; it was the specific form that surrealist humor assumed at the time, and the Communists were often embarrassed and not infrequently indignant over the alliance.

them, for she is trying to climb a tree, but she finds that her cousin,
who is a teacher of French, is already up in the tree.

Just before midnight close by the wharf.
Should a woman with loose-hanging hair pursue you pay no attention.
It is the sky color. You have nothing to fear from the sky color.
There will be a huge blond vase in a tree.
The steeple of the village of molten colors
Will serve as a landmark. Take your time,
Remember. The brown geyser sending skyward spurts of sprouting ferns
Greets you.

The first image is from Freud's *Interpretation of Dreams*. It is followed by an explanation of its curious sequence of incidents. The analysis is based chiefly upon a series of puns on the word "lion," which the
dreamer relates to past experience and the names of some of her acquaintances. In some such way as this the matter of dreams is brought
to light in psychoanalysis, straightened out in interpretation, and related to the dreamer's psychic difficulty. The roots of neurosis are
ferreted out, and a history of the patient's repressions is fitted together
from diverse sources. This leads to understanding and possibly to a
cure, which in all psychoanalytic cases has in part the character of re-
adjustment.

The second quotation is a fragment of André Breton's *Le Revolver
à cheveux·blancs,* called "Concerning Gods." The object is representation, not analysis. The imagery is derived from the errant ways of the
unconscious, but there is no attempt to explain or use it rationally. The
character of the imagery may be called almost accidental, though there
is always some creative opportunity in surrealist demonstrations.
"Language has been given to man," said Breton in his first Manifesto,
"that he may make a surrealist use of it." The results of such use may
be striking, as in Pierre Reverdy's "The day was folded like a white
cloth," or they may be simply eccentric and fugitive, no effort of the
imagination having been made to give them meaning or to suggest their
relationship to the total product of the surrealist's inspiration.

The most important single *formal* result of Freudian influence was
not surrealism but the "stream of consciousness" technique.[67] Joyce's
Ulysses (1922) was the major document. His *Finnegans Wake* also ap-

[67] See Hoffman, *Freudianism and the Literary Mind,* Chapter 1 and pp. 124–
131; Robert Humphrey, *Stream of Consciousness in The Modern Novel* (1954).

peared in the 1920s, as "Work in Progress," in *transition* and in the *transatlantic review*. Both works stimulated experiments in fictional prose, some successful, others (like those of A. Lincoln Gillespie in *transition*) wild and nonsensical. Joyce demonstrated in *Ulysses* the possibilities of the new method; he did not claim Freud as his master, though there are evidences in his two major books that he was more than aware of what the "dream work" might contribute to both form and matter.

Most conspicuously indebted to Joyce among American novelists was Conrad Aiken. "I decided very early," Aiken said in reply to a questionnaire (*New Verse,* 1934), "that Freud, and his co-workers and rivals and followers, were making the most important contribution of the century to the understanding of man and his consciousness; accordingly I made it my business to learn as much from them as I could." *Great Circle* (1933), *King Coffin* (1935), and *Blue Voyage* (1927) all testify to Aiken's interest in Joyce and his concern over the Freudian explanation of the human consciousness.

Blue Voyage is in many ways modeled on *Ulysses:* it has its Stephen Dedalus in Demarest, its Leopold Bloom in Silberstein, a merchant of "chewing sweets." The style and design follow clearly the descent of Demarest into the lowest regions of his unconscious and his final rise to the level of rational self-appraisal. As does Joyce in *Ulysses,* Aiken clearly indicates time and place, and allows for an indication of narrative progress in terms of both. Demarest is on a ship, sailing for England. His mind is absorbed by thoughts of his fiancée, Cynthia, whom he expects to see when he arrives. After he has discovered that Cynthia is on the same boat and after she has greeted him coldly, the narrative becomes for a while a monologue, an unconscious reverie. The rest of the novel is a record of Demarest's fight to return to full consciousness of his situation, a progress that is interrupted at one point by an extravagant fantasy, in which he quarrels with his "censor" (in this case, an analyst friend) about the worth of his life and art, and a hallucinatory vision of his shipmates discussing his life calmly and impudently but with penetrating accuracy. The style and subject matter both participate in the Freudian analysis of the dream world. But it is important to note that Aiken *uses* the psychoanalytic matter to his advantage, conscious that it must be ordered to some literary purpose, the examination of a neurotic state.

The most skillful use of the subconscious is to be found in William

Faulkner's *The Sound and the Fury* (1929). Less "literary" in tone than *Ulysses,* it is a more successful adaptation of states of consciousness to narrative purpose. This is partly because Faulkner directs his narrative very clearly in terms of a limited number of perspectives and facts. The central fact is the defection of Candace Compson. The novel is developed according to the four principal judgments of the act, in terms of her sin against moral, family, economic, and traditional proprieties. Faulkner presents the sin and its consequences through the minds of Caddy's three brothers, and finally in terms of the *public* world—the world of Jefferson itself, of the shrunken Compson estate, and of the moral and religious judgment of Dilsey, the Negro servant.

The perspective of the idiot brother Benjy is the most extreme of the four, but only because Faulkner must here articulate and give intelligible form to a mind that neither verbalizes nor discriminates past from present. Benjy's mind works through simple association and the identity of events that bear similarities, however widely separated in time. Since he does not know time, he cannot understand or tolerate change; his insights into Caddy's nature have therefore all been settled at a time before Caddy sinned. His is the moral order of an age of innocence; and that order is rigidly and eloquently upheld in his every response. He reacts by bellowing or whimpering to any suggestion— sight, smell, or movement—that the time of innocence has been changed in the slightest particular. He does not judge persons and acts in terms of a moral order arrived at by reason; he senses disorder, smells out evil, is sensitive to every threat to the family structure.

Like Benjy, Quentin is a monitor of Caddy's moral life. But Quentin's private world—to which Caddy is as essential as she is to Benjy's —is the product of obsessive formulation, ratiocination, conceptualizing. The world of the past is brought back by sensuous images of Caddy as a little girl; but Quentin's memory of the past is not the simple familial order Benjy has seen. He fixes it in terms of concepts of honor and virginity. For him, virginity is a condition of stasis, in which "nothing has happened," and if nothing has happened he can retain his moral design. Caddy's sin has destroyed this design; she has "made things happen" in losing her virginity, in marrying, in giving birth to an illegitimate child. Quentin tries to recover the design—first by an attempt on the life of her first lover, then by trying to fix the blame for the act on himself (incest, by confining the sin, will at least make guilt and atonement possible within the design),[68] finally by committing suicide. He tries to defeat time through death and thus to fix permanently his conceptions of family and personal honor. This is another kind of consciousness, and Faulkner gives it a style and vocabulary quite different from Benjy's. Benjy exists below the level of articulation; Quentin's mind is given excessively to abstracting and codifying, until he drives himself to the ultimate act of abstraction, death by suicide.

Jason's consciousness is totally different from that of either of his brothers. For Benjy, Caddy's sin is a violation of a world of sensation, for Quentin, a loss of honor; for Jason, it is a breach of contract, a legal matter for which legal restitution must be made. The section devoted to his view is liberally supplied with references to money, checks, agreements, investments, profit and loss. Jason is the comically rational character who lives in a common-sense world of calculable facts and figures. He is defeated on a legal technicality; in attempting to recover his "birthright," he appropriates money intended for Caddy's illegitimate daughter, who takes both it and Jason's other savings and escapes with a man from a traveling carnival. His rational world is in the end defeated by the irrational world, which he has never allowed for in his plans.

The prose of these three appraisals follows strictly the requirements of the narrative; there is no display of stylistics for their own sake, no overstepping the bounds of each consciousness. Faulkner neither exploits the unconscious mind for sensational effects nor imposes extraneous matters upon it. The reader is made ready, through the three private reconstructions of the novel's central event, for the final perspective upon the Compsons. It is the external world, the world of the present, as contrasted with Benjy's and Quentin's fixed pasts. Temporally this world is Easter Sunday, 1928, some thirty years after the significant moment of the past; spatially it is reduced to the now small and aging house, actually to Dilsey's kitchen, which is the only place where any genuine living takes place. The reader discovers, finally, that the affairs of the Compson family are not to be judged by any one of the three previous perspectives, but to be evaluated in the somber notes of an old Negro servant, who emerges from her cabin on a wet morning, her skeleton "draped loosely in unpadded skin that tightened again upon

[68] The debate (in Quentin's mind) on this matter between Quentin and his father is one of the most remarkable passages in modern fiction.

a paunch almost dropsical, as though muscle and tissue had been courage or fortitude which the days or the years had consumed."

The Sound and the Fury is a remarkably mature and restrained experiment with the possibilities of "stream-of-consciousness" techniques.
Other experimental writing in the decade did not have such successful
results. Experiment in so new a thing as the exploration of human consciousness *on its own terms* was handicapped by love of experiment
for its own sake: the excitement of innovation was quite often the only
incentive. Joyce testified to the brilliant range of improvisation possible in fictional prose, and Faulkner to the sound usefulness of explor-
ing human states and presenting them with insight and depth.

6. Mr. Zero and Other Ciphers: Experiments on the Stage

"I HAD THE curious experience with *The Great God Brown,*" said
Stark Young of the performance on January 23, 1926, "of
being moved with something that I felt behind the play, but almost always untouched by the play itself." It was an "interesting" play, and
there were moments when the restless experimenting with new theat-
rical devices succeeded. But these tricks were not in themselves wholly
admirable: "When once a device is adopted in a drama and the expressive meaning of it has become clear, the continued significance or suggestiveness of its use will depend on the artist's imagination."

The American theater in the 1920s was overwhelmed by experiment
of one kind and another: it tried to represent life more concretely
through abstractions, tried to moralize, satirize, lyricize in terms of new
manipulations of space and movement, new concepts and sequences
of dialogue, new versions of characterization. It performed brilliantly
in the matter of stage design; the settings in many cases proved more
revealing of theme and motivation than the characters themselves. The
newness was not exclusively a matter of techniques, but part of the
general stir of experimental activity in the arts. The imagination had
boundless opportunity to dramatize its imaginings.

When a group of strictly amateur playwrights gathered in a deserted
old fish house in Provincetown, Massachusetts, in the summer of 1915,
the "new theater" was launched. It was an act of defiance, to free the

stage from the "commercial manager's interpretation of public taste." [69]
With a firm conviction that creative imagination must be kept alive,
the leader of the group, George Cram Cook, sponsored whatever new
plays he could find, whatever old ones he thought were valuable. "Without [the creative imagination]," he affirmed, "the wreck of the world
cannot be cleared away and the new world shaped."

From Europe came the movement called most often *expressionism*.
It affected all the arts, was especially striking in its demonstrations in
German films and architecture. In the drama, as in the cinema and
painting and sculpture, expressionism demonstrated the artist's dissatisfaction with naturalism or realism, with the limitations set upon the
work of the artist by these schools. The aim of the expressionist was
to project in outer symbols a state of mind, an inner crisis, a psychological condition. This also involved expressions of the dream state.
One of the earliest expressionist dramas, Strindberg's *Dream Play*
(written 1901–1902), attempted, as Strindberg explained in the pro-
logue, to "imitate the disconnected but seemingly logical form of the
dream. . . . Time and space do not exist. . . . The characters split,
double, multiply, vanish, solidify, blur, clarify. But one consciousness
reigns above them all—that of the dreamer; and before it there are no
secrets, no incongruities, no scruples, no laws. There is neither judgment nor exoneration, but merely narration."

George H. Scheffauer, in *The New Vision in the German Arts*
(1924), showed great excitement over what he thought was primarily
a German art movement. He defined expressionism as *"direct action
in art*—the forthright naked impulse, delivered without intermediaries
from the imagination to the outer world—like a child from the womb."
Scheffauer analyzed the products of German expressionism—the film
Dr. Caligari, the plays of Max Reinhardt, Ernst Toller, and Georg
Kaiser, especially the latter's *Gas*—and he concluded by saying that
the movement, as headed by Kaiser, was "the American spirit idealized
by a European artist, purged of its slag, of the trivial, the cynical and
the ephemeral, and given power, voice, direction as an element in art."

Whatever the actual contribution of expressionism to "the American
spirit," there is no doubt that it encouraged a remarkable variety of
experiments, large and small, on the American stage. Some of its most
successful effects were found in comedy, where its exaggerations and

[69] See Helen Deutsch and Stella Hanau, *The Provincetown: A Story of the
Theatre* (1931).

arrangements of abstractions in motion were especially useful. Elmer Rice's *The Adding Machine* (1923) was the most remarkable illustration of expressionist comedy. Stereotypes of character and setting illustrated the native stereotypes which the comedy satirized.

The main character of *The Adding Machine* is Mr. Zero. In his home he is surrounded by the clichés of modern life: installment-plan furniture, walls papered "with sheets of foolscap covered with columns of figures," and so on. His wife, his friends, his opinions, his desires, are similarly cliché extensions of the reality. His office is abstracted from the obvious setting of a small-time bookkeeper's life; his uncharming assistant is given the most glamorous of Hollywood names, Daisy Diana Dorothea Devore. Zero must endlessly mark down figures as she calls them out, and add them, a function he has mechanically performed for many years.

In the play's first crisis, "the Boss," another stereotype ("middle-aged, stoutish, bald, well dressed") announces the installment of adding machines, regrets that "for business reasons" Zero will have to be fired; after which the stage itself acts out Zero's murder of the Boss, as the stage directions indicate:

> His voice is drowned by the music. The platform is revolving rapidly now. Zero and the Boss face each other. They are entirely motion-less save for the Boss's jaws, which open and close incessantly. But the words are inaudible. The music swells and swells. To it is added every offstage effect of the theater: the wind, the waves, the galloping horses, the locomotive whistle, the sleigh bells, the automobile siren, the glass-crash, New Year's Eve, Election Night, Armistice Day, and Mardi Gras. The noise is deafening, maddening, unendurable. Suddenly it culminates in a terrific peal of thunder. For an instant there is a flash of red and then everything is plunged into blackness.

This is violently comical, noisily "representative." *The Adding Machine,* in its expressionistic phases at least, abstracts from an abstraction. Mr. Zero, from birth a cipher, can give expression only to the limited variety of his cipherhood. Murdering the Boss is his rebellion; but after the interval of stereotyped bliss that follows the murder, Zero is put back on the track of his routine—again in an exaggerated form. In his next incarnation Zero operates a "super-hyper-adding machine" with "the great toe" of his right foot. In sum, the devices of repetition and abstraction all lead to the comic thesis of the play: that the soul of Zero is the soul of the small-time worker,[70] whose acts are duplicated

---

[70] "You're a failure, Zero, a failure. A waste product . . . the raw material of

a million times, in all phases of history, who doesn't grow at all but merely changes his work as mechanical progress dictates.

Expressionist comedy found an especially useful subject in the twin scapegoats of much criticism of the 1920s—the standardization of life in modern business and the standardization of morality in middle-class convention. *Beggar on Horseback* (1924), by George S. Kaufman and Marc Connelly, exploited both themes. The plot is as conventional as slick comedy can provide; it is the stage that makes the play. Undecided whether to marry a vulgar rich girl or a sensitive poor one, the hero takes time out to dream. The expressionist dream outlines his future life, should he choose the grossly wealthy Miss Cady; in his dream-exasperation he murders the entire family, is given a comic-opera trial, and is sentenced to hard labor in the Cady Consolidated Art factory, where he is forced to produce jingles in great numbers. The dream convinces him, and he is presumably doomed at the play's conclusion to live happily ever after with the poor but sensitive Cynthia.

This is vaudeville given an expressionist streamlining. Similar effects are gained in John Howard Lawson's *Roger Bloomer* (1923).[71] The Bloomer family at dinner—in Excelsior, Iowa—reiterate banal lines and gestures as they consume their food. In New York, to which Bloomer flees to escape the banality, he discovers that it persists; and his discovery is suitably externalized in a monotonously precise repetition of stage props. Lawson is in more deadly earnest than Rice or Kaufman and Connelly; Bloomer doesn't solve his problem easily. Aware that he is not for Wall Street, he tries suicide but fails; his sensitive companion tries and succeeds; and in the concluding dream scene she returns to him, encouraging him to continue "fighting through."

Parody and criticism of the economic order lent themselves remarkably well to the use of expressionist effects. Rice combined these again and again. In *The Subway* (1929), Mr. Zero has become George, who takes a correspondence course in SUCCESS ("Capacity plus perseverance spells success"); in the subway, Sophie, the heroine, is sur-

---

slums and wars—the ready prey of the first jingo or demagogue or political adventurer who takes the trouble to play upon your ignorance and credulity and provincialism."

[71] See also Lawson's *Processional* (1925) and *The International* (1928): the first, an anticipation of the proletarian play of the 1930s, treats the strike theme with a mixture of expressionist devices and vaudeville satire; the second is an expressionist fantasy of proletarian situations and dogma.

rounded by men who wear identifying masks (a dog, a pig, a monkey, a wolf, a rat). Eugene, the sensitive one, plans a masterpiece, a "mad mechanistic dance" leading finally to the destruction of Western man; years later scientists, digging in the ruins, will find a few odds and ends (false teeth, a pair of jade earrings from the 5-and-10), "all that remains of Western civilization." In the final scene Sophie, dressed in nightgown and light coat, rushes to the subway station, is fascinated by the approaching train ("like the waves on the beach"), and jumps into its path.

The tendency, evident in the work of Rice and Lawson, to move from comedy to social tragedy was not uncommon in the history of expressionist drama. The Machine, implying "efficient" standardization of commercial life, was associated with class conflict in the plays of Kaiser, Reinhardt, and Toller. Toller's *Masse Mensch,*[72] Reinhardt's *The Machine-Stormers,* and Kaiser's *Gas* take advantage of the abstractions to be found in the life they criticize. The limitations of this type of drama lie in the very restricted use to which the abstractions can be put. Abstractions require an immense effort of the imagination to give them individuality and a meaning beyond the most generalized kind of cardboard editorial. Rice's characters are almost invariably fleeing from expressionistically defined circumstances; frequently they are victimized more by the stage setting than by life itself. The experiment has its own risks: in comedy it leads to a modernized kind of vaudeville sequence; in tragedy, the devices of the "new stage" get in the way of a proper consideration of the characters, even though they are there supposed to clarify and explain them.[73]

The most remarkable American experiment in the expressionist drama was E. E. Cummings' *Him* (1927). The two main characters, Him and Me, are types. Him is an artist-creator; Me is his mistress, an expressionist idealization of the Cummings *"Weiblichkeit."* They are surrounded, victimized, annoyed, by representatives of modern evils.

---

[72] See Scheffauer, *The New Vision in the German Arts* (1924): "The characters are nameless—Workmen, Workwomen, the Nameless One, Officer, Priest, Man, Bankers, Prisoners, Guards, Shadows. Only the heroine, Sonia Irene L., a woman of the caste of officials who makes common cause with the workers, is given a name—significantly Russian."

[73] Cf. Stark Young (*Immortal Shadows,* 1948): "You could take a knife and fork to represent a man and wife. But to achieve anything important there must then be imagination exercised in the use of these symbols, otherwise you have only the regular story, plus the knife and fork instead of man and wife, and have achieved nothing beyond the first device, the initial metaphor."

Him's great distinction is that he is not successful, "hasn't been favored by fate." He is the circus man, the acrobat, the clown: "an artist, a man, and a failure." The Man in the Mirror is an ideal representation of Him's bohemian nature; this man, this part of Him, puts on a play of nine scenes, drawn inconsequentially from aspects of the contemporary scene: Prohibition, soap-box oratory, nostrums and patent medicines, the business "unlife," the censorship ("Mr. John Rutter, President pro. tem. of the Society for the Contraception of Vice"), and fascism.

The individual scenes push hard (though often with extreme cleverness) the thesis of man's need to realize himself in spite of circumstance and his own fear of self-knowledge. The final act represents the positive values identified with Him and Me: their love for each other, her great gift of feeling, the way toward "honest" beauty and passion, the miracle of birth, the beauty of little children. Scene vi presents a great sideshow; Me, holding a newborn baby, shocks the crowd with this vision of life, and it turns away in disgust and terror. She is a freak in the sideshow, but the conclusion of the play is that the freaks are important; they are the elements of life put aside by the crowd. The dominating symbol of the circus acrobat and clown enforces this conclusion: the acrobat describes in his action the grace of movement which is expression in art; the clown is the humorist who gets his laughs because he is absurd and utterly unlike the conventional audience who laughs at him. It is a simple thesis, but it is particularized in brilliant dramatic fragments, which are interrelated in terms of what each adds to the sum of meaning. Perhaps this is the best that can be done with expressionism; at any rate, *Him* succeeds because of, rather than in spite of, its wealth of dramatic variations.

One may almost say that the American drama of the 1920s was O'Neill's drama: he was so valuable an asset to the Provincetown Players and subsequent groups; he seemed capable of so many new ideas for the theater; his plays were so much the expression of dramatic experiment and innovation. He had decided on the theater as a career after having read the plays of Strindberg, Wedekind, Kaiser, and other Europeans during a five-month convalescence in 1912–1913. He spent a semester at Harvard, working in George Pierce Baker's "Workshop 47" (fall of 1914). He was ready for the Provincetown Players when he joined them in the summer of 1916—with plays, most of them one-acters based on life at sea.

Expressionist effects were first made noticeably a part of his drama in *The Emperor Jones* (1920), a remarkably skillful projection of its hero's inner consciousness. From that point O'Neill moved to bolder and more varied experiments. In *The Hairy Ape* (1922), expressionist devices and settings combined with strictly naturalistic details, so that the "real" achieved a symbolic quality through formal repetition and exaggeration. In *The Great God Brown* (1926) he tried the addition of masks as an experiment in dramatic effects. They were the best way, he explained (*American Spectator,* November 1932), for the dramatist to express "those profound hidden conflicts of the mind which the probings of psychology continue to disclose to us." *Lazarus Laughed* (1928) carried the use of masks to an extreme of complication: seven masked choruses representing seven periods of life, each of which contained seven types of character. He also experimented with that unwritten agreement between audience and playwright concerning the play's tolerable length. The performance of *Strange Interlude* (1928) lasted from 5:30 until after 11:00, with an eighty-minute intermission; the trilogy, *Mourning Becomes Electra* (1931), was supposed to be performed in a single evening; and, in 1936, O'Neill wrote Barrett Clark that he was working on a series of nine plays to be produced on nine successive nights.

O'Neill was, in short, extremely versatile. The range of his plays, from a one-acter like *Before Breakfast* (1916), in which there is only one character on stage, to the complications of *Lazarus Laughed,* testifies to his great talent for surprise and innovation. There is scarcely a dramatic idea, device, trick that he did not try. While he borrowed from expressionism, he invented his own original variants.

A driving intellectual ambition to "get at the root" of human desires and frustrations was ever present in O'Neill. He tried to explore the complexes of the human spirit, the psychology of human motive and obsession (*Diff'rent,* 1920; *Desire under the Elms,* 1924; *Mourning Becomes Electra*); the tensions of race differences (*All God's Chillun' Got Wings,* 1924); the comedy of modern commercial life (*Marco Millions,* 1928). In 1929 he announced a new trilogy of "the human spirit," a "trilogy that will dig at the roots of the sickness of today as I feel it—the death of an old God and the failure of science and materialism to give any satisfactory new one for the surviving religious instinct to find a meaning for life in, and to comfort its fear of death with." Two plays were completed, *Dynamo* (1929) and *Days Without End* (1934).

Not only is O'Neill burdened with this sense of "profound mission," but his characters are almost invariably disturbed by it; not infrequently the disturbance and the stagecraft are all the play has to offer. Jim Harris of *All God's Chillun'*, for example, is troubled by the problem of his personal relationship with God. "Maybe He can forgive what you've done to me," he says to Ella, his wife, "and maybe He can forgive what I've done to you; but I don't see how He's going to forgive—Himself." There are numerous speeches of this kind in the most ambitious of O'Neill's plays. The characters share his perplexity about the human state—as the devices of the stage represent it—and are so often urged to comment upon it that the plays become entangled in the confusion and torture of explaining themselves. The experiments often get in the way of the drama; they give an impression of a depth and complexity they only infrequently possess. Occasionally, as in *The Emperor Jones,* the experiment and the theme are almost perfectly integrated. The hero does not become an amateur philosopher but remains a man victimized by his fears and struggling vainly to escape his danger; he grows in terms of, and as a result of, the skillful and controlled use of dramatic experiment. That balance O'Neill rarely achieved.

O'Neill's reputation was based upon his love of experiment; he kept his public in a state of excitement over his restless and clever experimenting. His failure as a dramatist may also be identified with the general failure of expressionism itself. In its effort to objectify inner states of mind and emotion, it forced the dramatist to devote too much of his attention, energy, and imagination to problems of new stage conventions, to the neglect of the essential concerns of any literature.

7. The Text: Hart Crane's *The Bridge:* The Crisis in Experiment

THE TRUE meaning of experiment in modern American literature may be found, after close study, in Hart Crane's fifteen-poem symbolic reading of America, *The Bridge* (1930). Crane was exposed to all the movements in modern literature that were of any consequence. Lacking a formal education, he improvised in his search for background; he read widely but on impulse, and along lines he set for himself. This is important only because it helps us to see how remote he was from any previously established order or discipline of perception, and therefore how extreme was his need to be self-sufficient.

That he possessed an extraordinary native lyrical power was indicated from the very beginning of his career. When his first volume of poems, *White Buildings,* appeared in 1926, that power was widely acknowledged, though no critic was unreserved in his admiration. Waldo Frank said that Crane "belongs to a group of poets who create their world, rather than arrange it" (*New Republic,* March 16, 1927). Yvor Winters hailed the volume as the work of "a poet who accepts his age in its entirety, accepts it with passion, and . . . has the equipment to explore it" (*Poetry,* April 1927).[74] Allen Tate considered *White Buildings* "probably the most distinguished first book ever issued in the country" and added that "Crane's blank verse is one of the few important contributions made by a contemporary to poetic style" (*Bookman,* January 1929). The fault was not in the gift itself, but in its abundance. There was "too much," and it lacked control, discipline, "a system of disciplined values" (Tate); Crane tried "to crowd more images into each poem—more symbols, perceptions, and implications—than any few stanzas could hold or convey" (Cowley, *New Republic,* April 23, 1930). Much was said about the crowding, the rich natural abundance, the romantic sensibility. This was a common complaint in the criticism of all his poetry. It was a matter that contemporary poets had much in mind, for many of them also sought to improvise new "forms of order" in which to contain their own perceptions.

Crane's mind was shaped by modern influences. Even his use of the past was *in extremis* a modern use; his search for a philosophy took him from Munson and Frank to Ouspensky, Spengler, and Whitehead; his effort to train his genius brought him to read and occasionally to translate French poets (Laforgue, Rimbaud, and Vildrac) and to Jacobean and metaphysical verse.[75] When he went to the past, it was to a past that his contemporaries approved, and he developed his talent

[74] Edmund Wilson thought that *White Buildings* pointed to future rather than achieved greatness: "His poetry is, as they say of French troops, a *disponible*. We are eagerly awaiting to see to which part of the front he will move it; just at present, it is killing time in the cafés behind the lines" (*New Republic,* May 11, 1927).

[75] See Philip Horton, *Hart Crane: The Life of an American Poet* (1937). Crane "read religiously" the *Dial,* the *Little Review,* and the London *Egoist,* "comparing the language and technique of the moderns with those of the Elizabethans, of Donne and Vaughan and Blake." In 1919 and 1920 he was reading Pound, Marlowe, and Webster. He translated the three "Locutions de Pierrot" of Laforgue, published in the *Double Dealer,* a New Orleans magazine in which Faulkner and Hemingway also appeared.

by turning to the examples of his contemporaries and to the literatures that most excited them. His life (in Manhattan, Brooklyn, Ohio, Europe) was a modern poet's progress, from one group of critics and creators to another, from one little magazine to another. The special contribution made by contemporary letters was his experience, his training, his education. From it he formulated his own theories of organic metaphor, revisions of poetic language, explanations of the contemporary world. As he was from the start a poet in the modern world, so he became in his life a living symbol of the "forms of dislocation" an extreme sensitivity to that world might produce.

Unlike many of his contemporaries, however, Crane did not want to give in to what he thought was the pessimism of his age—the *"maladie moderne,"* as he called it. Association with Gorham Munson in the early 1920s had convinced him of important positive qualities in the present, and especially in the age of machine and urban society as he had experienced it in Cleveland, Manhattan, and Brooklyn. One of his first ambitions was to become a "suitable Pindar for the dawn of the machine age, so-called." [76] He wanted to use the techniques of the moderns, but "toward a more positive, or (if [I] must put it so in a sceptical age) ecstatic goal." [77]

This decision to "set the moderns aright" was crucial. It was not easy for Crane, and at times became impossible, to adhere to it; and he had, after all, only his contemporaries and his own erratic initiative to use for the purpose. He faced in himself a form of the crisis in modern experimental literature. He was motivated first of all by an oversimplified view of what Eliot and his followers were actually doing; it was based on a simple emotional division of the motives for writing about the contemporary world (as either blandly optimistic or frankly pessimistic). Crane was not acquainted with any orderly or systematic body of knowledge through which he could translate his convictions

[76] Letter to Munson, March 2, 1923, in which he continues: "I have lost the last shreds of philosophical pessimism during the last months. O Yes, the 'background of life'—and all that is still there, but that is only three-dimensional. It is to the pulse of a greater dynamism that my work must revolve. Something terribly fierce and yet gentle." See Munson's book on *Waldo Frank* (1923) in which his formulation of the "machine-age" view is most fully given.

[77] Letter to Munson, January 5, 1923. He is speaking here of Eliot's great "erudition and technique," and he goes on to say: "I feel that Eliot ignores certain spiritual events and possibilities as real and powerful now as, say, in the time of Blake. Certainly the man has dug the ground and buried hope as deep and direfully as it can ever be done. He has outclassed Baudelaire with a devastating humor that the earlier poet lacked."

into art; most of all, such a body of knowledge was not available (except at considerable expense of contemporary interests, in the universities) to him as he prepared to write his "great affirmation." [78]

The writing of *The Bridge* took almost seven years, from early 1923 to late fall of 1929. The original idea was to present the "myth of America." [79] What that myth was, and how he planned to develop it, he explained in a long letter to his benefactor, Otto H. Kahn (September 12, 1927). He had already written versions of many of the poems, and he was aware of the line of progress he wanted the whole to take:

> What I am really handling, you see, is the Myth of America. Thousands of strands have had to be searched for, sorted and interwoven. In a sense I have had to do a great deal of pioneering myself. It has taken a great deal of energy—which has not been so difficult to summon as the necessary patience to wait, simply wait much of the time— until my instincts assured me that I had assembled my materials in proper order for a final welding into their natural form.[80]

Crane was also concerned with the problem of form, which in each section of the poem was unique, "not only in relation to the materials embodied within its separate confines, but also in relation to the other parts, *in series,* of the major design of the entire poem." The major symbol would have to be a modern object, one that combined the finest artistry of the machine age with the most significant suggestions of symbolic meaning.

In April 1924 he occupied a room at 110 Columbia Heights, Brooklyn, where John J. Roebling, the engineer who had designed and planned the bridge, had once lived. His window looked down upon the East River, the turmoil of business and shipping, and the Brooklyn

[78] Critics have often discussed this in reviewing *The Bridge.* See Allen Tate, *Hound and Horn,* July–September, 1930; Gorham Munson, *Saturday Review of Literature,* May 29, 1937.

[79] Several of Crane's contemporaries also attempted such a myth and ended by presenting a mythology taken from the available documents and folklore of the American past. The temptation to "realize America" in a single heroic or all-encompassing work has been a stumbling block for many an artist. Perhaps its original incentive was Whitman's suggestion (in his Preface to the 1855 edition of *Leaves of Grass*) that the United States "are essentially the greatest poem." Yvor Winters reported (*In Defense of Reason,* 1947) that "when Crane was writing ["The River"] he informed me that he was rewriting Sandburg in the way in which he ought to be written."

[80] The letter continues with a discussion of each of the sections as he then saw them shaping up.

Bridge itself. The choice of the bridge was therefore inevitable.[81] His first effort was a thirteen-line version of "Atlantis"; it is significant that he should have begun with this, the concluding section of the poem as finally published. It was the most emphatic of affirmations; in a sense the next six years were spent qualifying it and preparing himself and his readers for it.[82]

The poem "For the Marriage of Faustus and Helen," published in *Secession* (Winter 1924), was a preliminary test of the possibilities.[83] He was very much aware that it presented a "new consciousness," a temper that the "Eliotic pessimists" would not easily understand. At this time he also felt a great spiritual association with Whitman, who became the monitory spirit of *The Bridge*. No one thought so highly of Whitman in the 1920s; no one needed him so desperately. Through Crane's work, Whitman was placed in the very center of the experimental literature of the decade. From Crane's reading of *Democratic Vistas*, he knew that Whitman had not been a superficial optimist concerning America; he liked Whitman's desire and his will to transcend the evidences of evil he had seen, and especially his attempts to translate material things into spiritual values. In short, Whitman was Crane's guide through the inferno of the 1920s, and, more than that, became a

[81] See Tate's comment (*Hound and Horn*, July–September 1930): "The idea of bridgeship is an elaborate metaphor, a sentimental conceit, leaving the inner structure of the poem confused."

[82] These are the original lines, as sent to his friend Wilbur Underwood, February 1923 (quoted in Brom Weber, *Hart-Crane*, 1948):

> And midway on that structure I would stand
> One moment, not as diver, but with arms
> That open to project a disk's resilience
> Winding the sun and planets in its face.
> Water should not stem that disk nor weigh
> What holds its speed in vantage of all things
> That tarnish, creep, or wane; and in like laughter,
> Mobile yet posited beyond even that time
> The Pyramids shall falter, slough into sand,—
> And smooth and fierce above the claim of wings,
> And figured in that radiant field that rings
> The Universe:—I'd have as hold one consonance
> Kinetic to its poised and deathless dance.

[83] It was an attempt to find a modern synthesis in terms of the love of two mythical figures translated into a modern urban setting. Even here, however, the ecstatic speech of the poem's declaration is qualified by fear of war and violence and an awareness of "The nervosities that we are heir to." Crane speaks of the "intricate slain numbers that arise/In whispers, naked of steel."

divine and mythical spirit to lead him safely to "Atlantis"; Whitman took over from Columbus in the journey to Cathay.

In spite of the assistance Crane found in Whitman's own mythicizing and the satisfaction he felt in the "Faustus and Helen" poem, he encountered many difficulties in his effort to see his large work whole and clear. At times he lost his confidence in the vision of America he had proposed to formulate. He was held grudgingly to the reading of Spengler's *Decline of the West;* at Patterson, New York, in 1925, he argued through the night with the Allen Tates over the persuasions of Spengler and Eliot. In the winter spent in the lonely old house in Patterson, he read in preparation for *The Bridge* such books as Prescott's *Ferdinand and Isabella, The First Voyage of Columbus,* Melville's *White Jacket,* Whitman's *Specimen Days,* and Whitehead's *Science and the Modern World.* He had broken from the influence of Munson [84] and Frank in the spring of 1924, on the question of their all too somber adherence to an imperfectly understood religious mysticism. Yet he could not entirely accept the other group, which included Tate, Cowley, Josephson, and Burke; they were too closely identified in his mind with the insights into the modern world Eliot was providing.

In the summer of 1926, on the Isle of Pines, Crane made good progress. In an atmosphere as different from Brooklyn and Manhattan as any could have seen, he wrote quickly the "Proem," "Ave Maria," and first versions of "Cutty Sark" and "The Tunnel." Throughout, however, he was plagued by doubt that his original vision could be sustained: "If only America were half as worthy today to be spoken of as Whitman spoke of it fifty years ago there might be something for one to say—not that Whitman received or required any tangible proof of his intimations, but that time has shown how increasingly lonely and ineffectual his confidence stands." At times he lost his belief in the Bridge itself, which today, he said, "has no more significance beyond an economical approach to shorter hours, quicker lunches, behaviorism and toothpicks." But he was committed to Kahn, to his friends, to himself, to complete the work: "A bridge will be written in some kind of style and form; at worst it will be something as good as advertising copy." [85] The temporary success in the summer of 1926 halted; Crane's

[84] The break with Munson was made all but complete when Crane read, in March 1926, Munson's essay criticizing him for relying on "private feelings and associations and magnification." (See Weber, *op. cit.*)

[85] See Weber, *op. cit.:* "it is poignantly and tragically symbolic that, at the

misgivings over the validity of what he had done were magnified; [86] and it was not until early December 1929 that Crane, urged on by Harry and Caresse Crosby, his publishers, finished the last draft of the fifteenth poem.

This is the history of the writing; how much its erratic course affected the achievement it is difficult to say. At any rate, *The Bridge* grew out of Crane's imaginative experience with his subject; while he was writing it, the convictions with which he began were constantly being qualified by new improvisations of manner, insight, and inference from his reading and conversations. He moved back, from the initial conviction of the Bridge as symbol to the shades of historical and present meaning it should have; he was finally left with the entire corpus of a mythology he made from the materials he had found in the American tradition as he had learned it. The final product (published in 1930) was unified beyond the expectations of anyone even slightly familiar with the circumstances of its composition. It contains evidences of a desperate struggle to maintain his initial conviction; it is truly the record of a crisis of experiment in the literature of the decade.

The "Proem," "To Brooklyn Bridge," is more than a prefatory tribute; it contains all the essential metaphors through which the entire poem is unified.[87] It is necessary to begin here, in the present, in the big

very moment when Crane faltered and *The Bridge* might have passed into limbo unwritten, or at the very least have been written as a critical tragic poem, it was revivified by a debt of honor to a banker closely identified with the materialism which had destroyed Crane's faith."

[86] To Munson he wrote (April 1928): "The spiritual disintegration of our period becomes more painful to me every day, so much so that I now find myself baulked by doubt at the validity of practically every metaphor that I coin."

[87] Thematic anticipations in the "Proem":

Line	Phrase	Section	Reference
1	"how many dawns"	II,1	"The Harbor Dawn"
6	"as apparitional as sails"	III	"Cutty Sark"
9	"I think of cinemas"	II,3	"The River" (opening strophe)
14	"As though the sun took step of thee"	II,4	"The Dance"
15	"Some motion ever unspent in thy stride"	II,4 VIII	"The Dance" "Atlantis"
17	"Out of some subway scuttle"	II,2 VII	"Van Winkle" "The Tunnel"
20	"A jest falls from the speechless caravan"	VI	"Quaker Hill"
22	"Rip-tooth of the sky's acetylene"	IV	"Cape Hatteras"
29	"O harp and altar, of the fury fused"	VIII	"Atlantis"
31	"threshold of the prophet's pledge"	IV	"Cape Hatteras"

(*continued on page 230*)

city, with the bridge dominating the scene and giving it a symbolic fixation. The "curveship" of the bridge is repeated in images of curve throughout; [88] it is the most clearly *functional* imagery of the poem: the "seagull's wings shall dip and pivot him," "white rings of tumult," "inviolate curve," and so on. Posed against these indices of a fixed and repeated curve are the insights into aimless motion, not apparently governed by a design:

> I think of cinemas, panoramic sleights
> With multitudes bent toward some flashing scene
> Never disclosed, but hastened to again,
> Foretold to other eyes on the same screen.

The confusion of the scene is signified in the suicide of one of the crowd, who rushes to the Bridge and plunges into the river.[89]

As in almost every other part of *The Bridge,* the "Proem" contains a form of prayer: in this case to the Bridge as divine symbol, which grants "pardon" to those not held by any faith or spiritual confidence. The Bridge is both "harp and altar"; its design, the cable strands, its spiritual quality—all testify to its divine origins ("of the fury fused") as well as to Crane's conviction of the unity of material and spiritual energies. The prayer concludes on an appeal that the "curveship" be the central index of the myth: "And of the curveship lend a myth to God."

Once the specific location and meaning of the Bridge have been established, Crane moves for the first time into the past, in "Ave Maria." Here too the symbolic value of Columbus's journey to the New World is explored (as it was in Williams' *In the American Grain*). The prospect of a New World is both a romantic challenge to man and a prophecy of a new history.[90] Columbus, returning from his suc-

---

32	"Prayer of pariah"	I	"Ave Maria"
32	"The lover's cry"	V	"Three Songs"
35	"-condense eternity"	VIII	"Atlantis"
39	"The City's fiery parcels"	VII	"The Tunnel"
41	"O Sleepless as the river"	II,3	"The River"
42	"the prairies' dreaming sod"	II,5	"Indiana"

I am indebted to Mr. Saul Gottlieb for the preceding information.

[88] See Stanley K. Coffman, "Symbolism in *The Bridge*," *PMLA,* March 1951: "All nature writes the figure of the curve or, by extension, the circle."

[89] It is quite possible that the "bedlamite" here described is intended by Crane to be himself. The Bridge for him is an access to eternity; his intense view of it is not understood by the multitude ("A jest falls from the speechless caravan"). Cf. Eliot, *The Waste Land:* "Why then, I'll fit you . . ."

[90] The epigraph of "Ave Maria" is taken from Seneca's *Medea*, in which the

cessful journey, offers to those who had sponsored him (who had "reined my suit/Into the Queen's great heart that doubtful day") the rewards of their confidence: "I bring you back Cathay!" His stubborn belief and purpose are now justified; he has seen "The Chan's great continent." He warns them, however, that this has not been a search for plunder, that the discovery must not yield to materialistic ambitions:

> Take of that eastern shore, this western sea,
> Yet yield thy God's, thy Virgin's charity!
>
> —Rush down the plenitude, and you shall see
> Isaiah counting famine on this lee!

The vast new worlds opened by his voyage are frightening in their amplitude; they who will follow him there need God's aid, His "Hand of Fire," to guide them. He looks ahead to the time when they will be led,

> In holy rings all sails charged to the far
> Hushed gleaming fields and pendant seething wheat
> Of knowledge . . .

This vision of Columbus, as he estimates the consequences of his voyage, is a primary historical insight into the realization of America.[91] It is given in terms of the "curveship" of the earth, which is linked with God's universe in the images of "one sapphire wheel:/The orbic wake of thy once whirling feet." The curve, here of the universe, is to be identified with the curve of the Bridge itself, celebrated in all its symbolic intensities in "Atlantis."

In Part II "Powhatan's Daughter," Crane moves in time both to the present and to the historical American past. In all the devices used in this, the most fully developed of all the book's divisions, time past and time present are given in an interacting unity; the shifts of time and space are both necessary to represent the "myth of America," and geographical space—in the description of the Mississippi River—is identified with time. This unity is also essential to the symbol of the Bridge's "curveship," since it bestows an "accolade" of "anonymity time cannot raise" ("Proem").

---

chorus prophesies that a time will come "when Ocean shall unloose the bonds of things" and there will be new worlds. This is offered as a prediction of chaos, not of happy fulfillment, and of this fact Crane must have been aware.

[91] It is also a part of the American literary tradition, though Crane's use of Columbus contrasts in many ways with the prophetic and epic references to him in eighteenth-century American poetry. See Joel Barlow, *The Vision of Columbus* (1787) and *The Columbiad* (1807).

Part II begins with "The Harbor Dawn," with the poet himself in his room near the bridge and harbor; he is both modern man and Columbus returned some four hundred years after his original voyage. The noises of commerce and shipping crowd through his brain until they take his sleep away altogether. With him is Pocahontas, who represents the land in its purest form. Mastery of the American myth requires that the love of the two be consummated; but she eludes him, and he pursues her through the land and through the historical past. When the full light of the present has come, leaving only vagrant memories of the past, she has fled.

In "Van Winkle" the poet is faced with present reality:

> Macadam, gun-grey as the tunny's belt,
> Leaps from Far Rockaway to Golden Gate . . .

As he prepares to make his way to the subway, the sound of a hurdy-gurdy reminds him of his childhood, and thus of America's beginnings:

> You walked with Pizarro in a copybook,
> And Cortez rode up, reining tautly in . . .

These references to past dream visions and memories are indispensable to Crane's symbol of time and history: his own childhood, the childhood of the nation, the history of the white man's exploitation of the Indian lands, all suggest an appraisal of the past in terms of the Bridge and will eventually qualify its mystic value. So that, when he and his companion, Van Winkle, descend into the subway, the reader is prepared for the synoptic journey that occurs in "The River." [92] The subway, raucous and noisy reminder of modern life in confusing motion, is transformed into the 20th-Century Limited, and the protagonist is moved from a setting of jumbled advertisements and commercial promises to a lonely spot in the heart of America.

There follows a contrast between present and past in terms of the American hoboes, who have not been taken in by American progress, who have in turn been ignored by it, tolerated as "blind baggage." They reckon time and their lives, not in terms of "SCIENCE—COMMERCE and the HOLYGHOST," but "As final reckonings of fire and snow." They possess scraps of memory and folklore, talk about "watermelon days," the songs they've heard and sung, places for which they have a special

---

[92] The rhythm of the first lines, like that of "Cutty Sark," is deliberately erratic and "futuristic." Crane called these lines "an intentional burlesque on the cultural confusion of the present . . . the rhythm is Jazz."

affection. They are nobodies, of no consequence to that other world—
"Blind fists of nothing, humpty-dumpty clods." Yet they have insights
into human life ("something like a key perhaps"); they "lurk across"
the body of the land and know it; and he feels himself close to them,
desiring their kind of knowledge, "As I have trod the rumorous mid-
nights, too." Like Van Winkle, they are his clue to the search for
Pocahontas, in which the vast continent itself is both the setting and
the goal. Pocahontas is both the feminine spirit of fertility and the
actual American land; the land is therefore identified with the history
of her race. This is not a narrow view of history in terms of what the
white man did by way of abusing the Indian; rather, the Indian, as a
precivilized race, symbolizes the land for Crane, and the history of
both involves an appraisal of the entire American past.

The train (which had emerged from the commercal bedlam of Manhattan) is now symbolic of the ruin of the land's past ("their timber
torn/By iron, iron—always the iron dealt cleavage!"). It is a most
suitable device to make the railroad run parallel with the river: the
"glistening steel" covering the American space, "a dance of wheel on
wheel." The poet appeals to and warns the "Pullman breakfasters"
who ride to remember the past and their own mortality:

> Oh, lean from a window, if the train slows down,
> As though you touched hands with some ancient clown . . .

For they too "feed the River" endlessly; they will also become the
victims of time. "The River" concludes with a remarkable vision of
the Mississippi proceeding through both space and time, carrying with
it "Damp tonnage and alluvial march of days" until "No embrace
opens but the stinging sea." The sea is eternity for both Whitman and
Crane: the river, which obliterates individual lives, flows finally into
it; the Bridge points both westward to the land and eastward to the
sea; and on the sea (as "Ave Maria" demonstrates) the "Hand of
God" is our only security.

From the geographical symbol of time and eternity Crane turns to
the configuration of "The Dance." Once again he attempts to pose the
moral question of America's history in terms of the Indian and of the
unified image of Pocahontas as woman and land. The dance is given
in a setting of storm; it is a dance of death, the death of the Indian
warrior Maquokeeta. The poet identifies himself with the warrior, and
the dance becomes a ritual of restoration, an appeal for survival of the
land through the sacrificial death of individuals.

Dance, Maquokeeta! snake that lives before,
That casts his pelt, and lives beyond! Sprout, horn!
Spark, tooth! Medicine-man, relent, restore—
Lie to us,—dance us back the tribal morn!

In the death that arrives in these ritual circumstances, the warrior is
made immortal through his union with Pocahontas. This seems a frantic effort on Crane's part to force a change in the reading of the American myth; but it is actually, once again, an attempt to link the land
with the Bridge through a secular-inspired religious mysticism. "Lie to
us" is an appeal to the efficacy of the ritual chant and formal dance,
whose objective is to sustain myth against the ravages of fact. In a
sense, the "bedlamite" of the "Proem," in hastening to his death "Out
of some subway cell or loft," is trying for the same unification of himself with the eternity promised by the Bridge. This is not a rational endorsement of faith, but a participation in ritual for an objective defined
by symbolism created within the myth.

Part II concludes with an inferior, sentimental poem, "Indiana,"
which serves as a transition from the land to the sea, from the pioneer
West to the East and the commercial life of the coast. "Cutty Sark"
(Part III) celebrates the era of clipper ships, the vast American commerce on the sea, but with full ironic recognition of the defections of
which that commerce was guilty. Again the form of the poem is pur-
posely erratic; as Crane said, "meant to represent the hallucinations incident to rum-drinking in a South Street dive as well as reminiscent
lurchings of a boat in heavy seas, etc." The primary imagery is the
green of the sea itself (and of death), and the rose (religious color) that
is part of a song played in the "nickel-in-the-slot piano." The "Rose of
Stamboul" becomes, as the refrain grows in explicitness, the Queen of
a lost city, Atlantis, until she is called "Atlantis Rose."

The image is a terrifying one, as is the use of Poe's "The City in the
Sea" in "The Tunnel":

> teased remnants of the skeletons of cities—
> and galleries, galleries of watergutted lava
> snarling stone—green—drums—drown—

The green of death overwhelms the rose of hope; "Cutty Sark" portrays the inner terror with which Crane viewed the approach to the
modern setting of the Bridge; but once again the "crisis" in his knowledge is alleviated, as the poet walks upon the Bridge and there sees a
phantom procession of the great clipper ships, "Blithe Yankee vanities,

turreted sprites." The last word of "Cutty Sark" is *"Ariel?"*—apparently the name of a ship, actually (with its accompanying question mark) an appeal for salvation from defeat and chaos—an appeal to Ariel of *The Tempest* to help him find his way back.

"Cape Hatteras" (Part IV), one of the last, and least successful, poems Crane wrote, is a specific tribute to Whitman and an appeal to him to guide him in his journey:

> My hand
>   in yours,
>   Walt Whitman—
>   so—

It is crucial to the sequence, and it is full of frantic images and rhythms. It fails because Crane could not control its mass of perceptions. Whitman becomes a divine spirit (*Panis Angelicus*), a "Vedic Caesar," a projection into infinity of the Bridge symbol itself, in the language of the machine and industry.

The "Open Road" has become the air; the "nasal whine of power whips a new universe"; the idiom and the wisdom of the land are converted into "sharp ammoniac proverbs,/New verities":

> Power's script,—wound, bobbin-bound, refined—
> Is stropped to the slap of belts on booming spools, spurred
> Into the bulging bouillon, harnessed jelly of the stars.

"Towards what?" Crane asks, and speaks of planes, "the dragon's covey":

> While Iliads glimmer through eyes raised in pride
> Hell's belt springs wider into heaven's plumed side.

In a verse calculated to repeat the design of motions portrayed, he describes the crash of a plane "into mashed and shapeless debris."

The assistance of Whitman in sustaining his vision is badly, desperately needed, and Crane puts his considerable knowledge of Whitman's writing to use here. Whitman had observed war and death, had mourned the loss of life; yet he had come through, and the prophetic hope had not diminished. He it was who had first inspired Crane to his vision:

> And it was thou who on the boldest heel
> Stood up and flung the span on even wing
> Of that great Bridge, our Myth, whereof I sing!

No one can miss noting the strenuousness of this language, its frantic jumbling of past with present, and most of all the stridency of its appeal—as though Crane were saying, "You were responsible for this in the first place; I *must* believe in you and it if I am to be saved." Nor can one help noticing the suddenness with which, through the agency of his *"Panis Angelicus,"* peace and security settle down once again at the end:

> Vast engines outward veering with seraphic grace
> On clarion cylinders pass out of sight
> To course that span of consciousness thou'st named
> The Open Road—thy vision is reclaimed!

At first glance the "Three Songs" of Part V seem the least suitable of all the parts to the structure of the whole,[93] but they possess an important number of unifying signs. They are all concerned with women and with love. "Southern Cross" celebrates the "nameless Woman of the South," as Eliot was to appoint the "Lady" the guardian of his protagonist's struggle for conversion (*Ash-Wednesday,* 1930). The woman ("Eve! Magdalene!/or Mary, you?") is a symbol of immortality and, through her association with the sea and the heavens, a universal refuge. The primary index of this role is the "long wake of phosphor" cast upon the sea by the stars of the constellation referred to in the title.

The next song speaks of the uninhibited "commercial" lust of the "National Winter Garden"; from this "empty trapeze of your flesh," each man "comes back to die alone." The full ugliness of the body in naked display of its sensuality is the "burlesque of our lust." The strip-teaser of "National Winter Garden" is contrasted to the virtuous little stenographer of "Virginia," who may be taken to represent a twentieth-century Virgin Mary; but her virginity is as unsatisfactory as the cheap, bawdy suggestiveness of the dance: Mary is an ordinary conventional woman, who does her work, picks up her check, and keeps "smiling the boss away." The poet appeals to her, as did the hero-prince of *Rapunzel,* to "Let down your golden hair!" The false brightness of the city routine is equated with the absurdities of ornamental architecture: if Mary is the Virgin, the Woolworth Tower is her cathedral; both falsify religious meaning and make it useless in a world in which "Crap-shooting gangs in Bleecker reign."

[93] Winters reports (*In Defense of Reason*) that Crane "wanted to include the songs because he liked them but that he was not sure the inclusion would be justified."

Crane never came closer to imitating the superficialities of Eliot's manner than in "Quaker Hill"; the ironies of Eliot's early poems and the deeper ironies of *The Waste Land* are here more or less crudely transcribed. Quaker Hill is itself a primary irony: formerly a meeting house, it is now a resort hotel to which come "the Czars/Of golf, by twos and threes in plaid plusfours/Alight with sticks abristle and cigars." The "Promised Land" has become a place of "bootleg road-houses where the gin fizz/Bubbles in time to Hollywood's new love-nest pageant." This is tired writing; it was finished shortly before deadline. Yet even here the major conflict is maintained, though it is certainly forced: these vulgar successors to our past are pathetic reminders of the nation's "sundered parentage." [94] The cheap amusements and preoccupations of the resort hotel are contrasted with the genuine artistry of Emily Dickinson and Isadora Duncan, to whom the poet finally appeals that they may shield "Love from despair."

The final passage to "Atlantis" needs still to await Crane's journey through the *Inferno;* and in "The Tunnel" he presents us with a remarkable evocation of the "terrestrial Hell." The self is finally and totally isolated, in full and dreadful consciousness of its isolation. The subway becomes in every detail a place of death, despair, and woe. The sound is a monotone punctuated by fragments of speech, disconnected and vagrant:

> In the car
> the overtone of motion
> underground, the monotone
> of motion is the sound
> of other faces, also underground—

To this terror Crane brings a vision of Poe, for whose sufferings as artist Crane felt an affinity. The head and body of Poe are victimized by the subterranean hell. The total effect of industry is signified by the subway as demon, "Whose hideous laughter is a bellows mirth," and men are "caught like pennies beneath soot and steam." In this description Crane employs the full resources of the poem as it has thus far been presented: the kiss of agony of "Ave Maria," the hope of immortality of "The Dance," the reminders of death and eternity of "The River."

[94] The "sundered parentage" undoubtedly also refers to the marital difficulties of Crane's own parents, which were ever present in his mind as he wrote *The Bridge.* But it is important to read the phrase in the context of the poem's design and its symbolic as well as its cultural meanings.

He finally rescues himself from the agony by a return to the Bridge itself and to "the River that is East."

He has at last returned to his beginnings—the Bridge itself, and the full measure of its symbolic and mystical figuration. The cables radiating from the towers (the "harp"), the shape of the surface (the "altar"), and the curve of the span are all drawn in, to describe the "myth" which is America. They are also symbolic, in their unity and their geometric design, of the pattern of the turning world, as previous sections of the poem have led us to anticipate. The Bridge is "synoptic" of "all tides below"; it incorporates all pasts, not only America's but those of Tyre and Troy; it is the Logos, the "multitudinous Verb": "O Love, thy white, pervasive Paradigm . . . !"

It is the ultimate knowledge, "steeled Cognizance," whose "curve-ship" unites all patterns of curve, mundane and celestial:

> O Thou steeled Cognizance whose leap commits
> The agile precincts of the lark's return;
> Within whose lariat sweep encinctured sing
> In single chrysalis the many twain,—

It presents the one absolute "intrinsic Myth," in its "Swift peal of secular light." It is therefore the culmination of Crane's search for a secular myth, not dependent upon past dogmas but "intrinsic," containing its certainties and its symbology within itself. As a product of the "fury fused" of science, it is constantly renewed and strengthened as science adds "fresh chemistry" to its song. To it Crane addresses his final prayer—the Bridge now stands where the "Hand of God" once was. The prayer is not unqualifiedly rapturous; it is burdened with a final expression of doubt and humility: "Thy pardon for this history, whitest Flower." And the poem concludes with questioning and doubt. *Is* this Cathay? *Does* "this history" lead without doubt or fear to this worship? *Are* we certain that time has been conquered and immortality assured: "The serpent with the eagle in the leaves . . . ?" *The Bridge* thus concludes on the note of unease and uncertainty with which it began.

The elements of experiment and improvisation in modern letters induced and forced Crane to consider the possibility of a positive myth that might avail itself of the techniques of modern poetry and at the same time to make through them an assertion that would differ from other applications. The poem itself testifies to the great difficulty Crane had in sustaining his vision, how often he was in danger of committing himself not only to the methods but to the points of view of his contemporaries. In the tension set up between an oversimplified vision and a tortured awareness of realistic circumstance, the poem demonstrates the very mood of experiment in the literature of the 1920s: its complexities, its untraditional modes of approach to the uses of poetry, its attempts to force a new idiom and to utilize a new range of subject matter, and above all, its moral concern over the special value and function of poetry itself. The poet of *The Bridge* is a man alienated from his community because of (and in the very act of) his search for an acceptable, believable synthesis of that community.

VI

SCIENCE AND
THE "PRECIOUS OBJECT"

1. The Problem

OF THE hundreds of books and essays published in the 1920s on the matter of science and its gifts to man, two stand out as especially pertinent: Bertrand Russell's "A Free Man's Worship" (1918) and Joseph Wood Krutch's *The Modern Temper* (1929). The first emphasized the challenge offered by a scientific reading of the modern world; the second spoke with almost unrelieved pessimism of a generation's loss of belief and illusion.

The "dilemma of modern youth," said Krutch, as he surveyed the postwar decade, was a consequence of our no longer being able to sustain either an unreasoning faith or a rational doubt. "Unlike their grandfathers, those who are its victims do not and never expect to believe in God; but unlike their spiritual fathers, the philosophers and scientists of the nineteenth century, they have begun to doubt that rationality and knowledge have any promised land into which they may be led." In the past man was supported by myth and illusion, but he has now been relieved of them. "His teleological concepts molded [his world] into a form which he could appreciate and he gave to it moral laws which would make it meaningful, but step by step the outlines of nature have thrust themselves upon him, and for the dream which he made is substituted a reality devoid of any pattern which he can understand."

For the most part, science has been responsible for this sharp division between feeling and thought: "Try as he may, the two halves of his soul can hardly be made to coalesce, and he cannot either feel as his intelligence tells him that he should feel or think as his emotions would have him think, and thus he is reduced to mocking his torn and divided soul." Man is capable of an apparently endless extension of his intelligence, but he is not happy in the knowledge. This is the prevailing mood. So long as man accepts it and acts in terms of it, he will be incapable of belief in anything that his intellect is forced to reject.

With this apparently hopeless division in mind, Krutch examined several of the "illusions" men are forced to reject. Humanism, he said, offers no solution of the dilemma, for its confident assumptions are also disproved by the scientist, or they are hard to accept. Perhaps, if we cannot accept formulations of value by non-scientific minds, we can work with confidence in the laboratory of the scientist? We have long since been disabused of this hope; though scientific knowledge has greatly increased, "Science has always promised two things not necessarily related—an increase first in our powers, second in our happiness or wisdom, and we have come to realize that it is the first and less important of the two promises which it has kept most abundantly." We have discovered that faith does not come from knowledge, that knowledge is more likely to destroy faith or to make its exercise all but impossible. "We are disillusioned with the laboratory not because we have lost faith in the truth of its findings, but because we have lost faith in the power of those findings to help us as generally as we had once hoped they might help."

Krutch next considered the hope that love may prove a substantial source of happiness. The idea of sex as possessing somehow a key to happiness and stability, the idea put forward by the advocates of free, uninhibited love, has failed of its obligation, chiefly because the modern attitude has led only to "a certain lessened sense of the importance of the passions that are thus freely indulged; and, if love has come to be less often a sin, it has come also to be less often a supreme privilege." This fact is brought home to us in the novels of Aldous Huxley, Ernest Hemingway, and others, for whom "love is at times a sort of obscene joke." The mysteries of sex once removed, we are wearied by the monotonies of boudoir and barn loft; "the world is no longer well lost for love."

As for literature, Krutch maintained that it was no longer possible to write genuine tragedy. Great tragedy requires a certain naïve faith in the nobility of man and in the genuineness of his suffering, a willingness to suspend current fashions in disbelief and to entertain the illusion that man can act heroically. An educated society cannot give itself to such play-acting; it has "neither fairy tales to assure it that all is always right in the end nor tragedies to make it believe that it rises superior in soul to the outward calamities which befall it." The drama we call tragedy is a depressing reiteration of man's helplessness in a hostile universe. The only kind of tragedy we are temperamentally disposed to tolerate, it produces in the audience "a sense of depression which is the exact opposite of that elation generated when the spirit of a Shakespeare rises joyously superior to the outward casualties which he recounts." The "tragic fallacy" is no longer possible: the illusion that makes great tragedy effective in an age willing to believe in it. "Our cosmos may be farcical or it may be pathetic, but it has not the dignity of tragedy and we cannot accept it as such."

Aesthetic principles cannot give society the stability it needs "because, though the human mind may be made to work in accordance with them, external nature will not, and the ultimate dilemma may be stated thus: the proposition that life is a science is intellectually indefensible; the proposition that life is an art is pragmatically impossible." Similarly, the hope for certitude in a world of maneuverable fact is futile, for this world has been purchased at a sacrifice of other certainties it is now incapable of bringing back. It is true that recent developments in science have suggested a release from the tyranny of materialism, but the scientists have as yet not agreed upon what inferences may be drawn for metaphysics and religion from these new interpretations of the physical universe. The work of the physicists has been too well done to be easily undone; it is doubtful that we may ever return to a belief in what has been so effectively refuted.

Krutch ended his book on a note of resignation but of no comfort. We shall have to make "such peace with [our world] as we may." There is a melancholy satisfaction in having knowingly made our choice and accepted our fate: "we know at least that we have discovered the trick which has been played on us and that whatever else we may be we are no longer dupes."

That we were no longer dupes Bertrand Russell would have agreed. He advised a kind of despairing courage in view of our awareness of an indifferent universe. In his writings on ethics, politics, and government he suggested that the intelligence is its own means of advance in a world indifferent to human wishes. There is a kind of courage that prevents suicide, but on this side of suicide there are infinite variations of human resourcefulness. Man may make of himself what he wishes, either as an individual or in cooperation with his fellows, but he had better not expect any support from the prophets of a beneficent

God, for the idea of a world order that smiles on man's desires is an illusion.

Russell's essay, "A Free Man's Worship," first published in *Mysticism and Logic* (1918), remained for many intellectuals a challenging statement of the only attitude it seemed possible for modern man to assume. Science has given us a description of a meaningless world, Russell said, a world in which belief is not possible. Man must recognize that he is of no importance in such a world; unless he realizes his insignificance, he will not adjust himself intelligently to the world. The dispiriting facts of that world, revealed by science, must be faced and accepted:

> That Man is the product of causes which had no prevision of the end they were achieving; that his origin, his growth, his hopes and fears, his loves and his beliefs, are but the outcome of accidental collocations of atoms; that no fire, no heroism, no intensity of thought and feeling, can preserve an individual life beyond the grave; that all the labors of the ages, all the devotion, all the inspiration, all the noonday brightness of human genius, are destined to extinction in the vast death of the solar system, and that the whole temple of man's achievement must inevitably be buried beneath the débris of a universe in ruins—all these things, if not quite beyond dispute, are yet so nearly certain, that no philosophy which rejects them can hope to stand. Only within the scaffolding of these truths, only on the firm foundation of unyielding despair, can the soul's habitation henceforth be safely built.

Not only the conviction of this passage attracted the writers of the 1920s, but its rhetoric, a rhetoric of prayer, whose rhythms were all but guaranteed to persuade the reader of its wisdom and its earnestness. The essay became a naturalist prayer; it appealed to the gloomy, self-conscious vision of a universe indifferent to human endeavor. But Russell followed this announcement of a purposeless universe by an appeal to the intelligence of men to reject the advocates of Power and Force, who, he claimed, have failed to maintain their ideals against a hostile universe. "In this lies Man's true freedom: in determination to worship only the God created by our own love of the good, to respect only the heaven which inspires the insight of our best moments." Though we must often submit "to the tyranny of outside forces," we can remain free "in thought, in aspiration," if we will keep ever before us "the vision of the good."

It is not that good will alter in any way the nature of our world, but that we may make either a heaven or a hell out of our lives, and ought to choose the way that will best utilize our intelligence, with least harm to ourselves. We must endure the insults offered our intelligence by a hostile universe and find a certain glory in preserving liberty for our time and for ourselves. "Brief and powerless is Man's life," Russell concluded; "on him and all his race the slow, sure doom falls pitiless and dark." Man can preserve his dignity and strength only if he is fully aware of the indifference of "omnipotent matter":

> . . . disdaining the coward terrors of the slave of Fate, to worship at the shrine that his own hands have built; undismayed by the empire of chance, to preserve a mind free from the wanton tyranny that rules his outward life; proudly defiant of the irresistible forces that tolerate, for a moment, his knowledge and his condemnation, to sustain alone, a weary but unyielding Atlas, the world that his own ideals have fashioned despite the trampling march of unconscious power.

In many other essays Russell showed a lively interest in the actual physical and intellectual problems of a world dominated by a scientific point of view; he was interested chiefly in the effects of science upon the industrial and economic worlds. The technical achievements of science, he said in "Causes of the Present Chaos" (1923), are responsible for both industrialism and nationalism; and, though science is non-political, it controls all political occurrences. "It is science, ultimately, that makes our age different, for good or evil, from the ages that have gone before. And science, whatever harm it may cause by the way, is capable of bringing mankind ultimately into a far happier condition than any that has been known in the past."

In the little volume *What I Believe* (1925), in Dutton's Today and Tomorrow Series, Russell weighed the value of religion and science. The notions of good and evil, he said, are made of man's own wishes and of their clash with society. The danger lies in their having been read into nature, as somehow antedating and governing human acts. "Optimism and pessimism, as cosmic philosophies, show the same naïve humanism: the great world, so far as we know it from the philosophy of nature, is neither good nor bad, and is not concerned to make us either happy or unhappy. All such philosophies spring from self-importance, and are best corrected by a little astronomy." Religion has erred by inspiring fear in men, fear of death especially, though all fear is bad and works great harm when it is used as a religious sanction for human acts. The man with a "scientific outlook on life" will not be frightened by either the Scriptures or the Church. "He will not be content to say 'such-and-such an act is sinful, and that ends the matter.'

He will inquire whether it does any harm, or whether, on the contrary, the belief that it is sinful does harm."

The exercise of intelligence in such matters will help to cut away from our way of life the superstitious and harmful notions of sexual decorum, for example, and will replace them with the two motivating forces of "a good life"—love and knowledge. Specific knowledge of facts is a good deterrent to excessive and irrational behavior. "All moral rules must be tested by examining whether they tend to realize ends that we desire." Russell assumed intelligence as an indispensable accompaniment of desire, for without intelligence we are led to one excess or another, and ultimately the exhaustion of all hope. The fetish of sin is a superstition which has held on to man's habits with a strange tenacity. It can inflict on man "preventable suffering," and Russell described a cradle-to-grave portrait of its effects. "In all stages of education the influence of superstition is disastrous." It prevents the child from learning the normal facts necessary to his intelligent living, and worse, suggests that such facts as have to do with the sex life are sinful. "Moral rules ought not to be such as to make instinctive happiness impossible."

According to Russell, science has both a quantitative and a qualitative gift to make to modern civilization. In the matter of technics, its quantitative gift has already been bestowed to the point of abuse. Man does not possess enough inner stability to take intelligent advantage of it. If he had adequate resources for the intelligent control of this gift, it would never be used to excess. But, as Russell remarked in another Today and Tomorrow essay, *Icarus* (1924), "The sudden change produced by science has upset the balance between our instincts and our circumstances, but in directions not sufficiently noticed. Overeating is not a serious danger, but over-fighting is."

The real danger is that man, freed from the moral superstitions of the past, which have at least theoretically been disproved, will no longer wish to control his life and will give in to his passions in frightening and destructive measure. If man controls himself, he can use the quantitative gift of science to fullest advantage; if he will not, then science is a danger multiplied a thousand times by technics. "And so we come back to the old dilemma: only kindliness can save the world, and even if we knew how to produce kindliness we should not do so unless we were already kindly. Failing that, it seems that the solution which the Houyhnhnms adopted toward the Yahoos, namely extermination, is the only one; apparently the Yahoos are bent on applying it to each other."

The history of science between the dates of Russell's essay and Krutch's book is full of surprises and quick changes in point of view. During the decade important changes in modern physics were antici- pated in Einstein's *Theory of Relativity* (1920), and they also had some effect on the philosophical views presented in Whitehead's *Science and the Modern World* (1925). The work of the American pragmatist, John Dewey, proceeded apace with every new development in science, and it formed the very basis of the liberal theory in politics, economics, and morality: for Dewey's examination of all three in terms of conse- quences, in the light of a psychology of act and a metaphysic of fact, provided a thorough summary of liberal hope for "intelligence in the modern world." Of all the intellectuals of the decade the men most enthusiastic about science were the Communists; they reasoned that the practical results of science held promise for any organization of the body politic and might (*vide* Russia) be most successfully pro- duced, distributed, and used in a Communist state. They were the optimists of the scientific world and were accordingly scornful of the cynics, the doubters, and the escapists. In the opinion of the Com- munists, all thinking was escapist that did not contribute positively to the hastening of the "new world" or to its liberal stocking of goods.

The persons whom they called pessimists, doubters, and escapists— in short, a considerable body of writers and artists who were convinced neither of the disastrous menace of science nor of its bright promise— regarded with a suspicious reserve the achievements of science and its method. In a world that offered the promise of abundance for all, they held firmly to the view that somehow science had failed to gain its ob- jectives. To begin with, they doubted the validity of a method that so cleverly excluded the concrete details of individual experience and sought only for a norm of experience, a manageable commonalty in things and events. They refused to believe that scientific language was accurate, or at least they could not agree with the suggestion of Max Eastman (*The Literary Mind,* 1931) that poetic language, being in- accurate, had lost its real function and should be banished from serious consideration.

They were, of course, not easily swayed by liberal pragmatic visions of a world happily adjusted and smoothly run by a community of reasonable men. Some of them followed the fashion of sophisticated despair, indulged in the luxury of futility, often to great excess. But the more substantial of them (like John Crowe Ransom, Allen Tate, Pound, and Eliot) worked with precision and confidence on the formulation of a group of aesthetic principles, which had for the most part been neglected in the history of American literature. These were concerned with questions of the precise nature and meaning of literature, its language, its form, and its extent. They availed themselves of whatever suggestions science and philosophy might offer; in consequence, they helped to establish a complex body of criticism, quite without parallel in the previous history of American culture. They were influenced by science in some form or other, but this influence worked chiefly through a medium of opposition—that is, the suggestions science offered were assimilated in an unscientific way and used for unscientific ends.

There were many attempts in the 1920s to establish a "scientific ethic"—that is, a point of view based on intelligence, as Russell had described the term. One would be too naïvely optimistic to believe that the extraordinary advances could be matched by a corresponding refinement of the intelligence applied to their uses. From the pens of prominent scientists of the day came detailed suggestions for this practical achievement in morality. One of the first requirements was that the theological concept of sin be discarded. In the opinion of both Russell and J. B. S. Haldane, the religious sanctions against sin had become unhealthful, because they prevented men from doing what they could do for the advancement of their own happiness. This was a plea not for license but for a wider application of intelligence.

These men said in effect that all the skills required for the perfection of man's state on this earth are available, and that man needs only to use a small share of the scientist's intelligence. Haldane, in speaking of the deterrent effects of religions upon progress in morality, said in 1924 that the only kind of religion scientists could accept was one that "will frankly admit that its mythology and morals are provisional." Kirtley F. Mather (*New Republic,* September 9, 1925) admitted that modern science was destructive to faith in a God "whose chief mode of demonstrating his presence is by the breaking of natural laws" and to the childish belief that mankind would some day be saved by "some extra-terrestrial force aided only by the prayers of the elect." But there is another kind of religion, one "based on facts and experiences, a religion developed by rigidly scientific methods of thought." Mather believed that the scientists should have the responsibility of establishing and promoting such a religion. Though the scientist is usually indifferent to moral evaluations, when "his attention is called to illogical moral implications or erroneous spiritual by-products with which his truths are cloaked by others, surely he should be expected to point out what he considers the correct deductions to be."

This was the modern scientist's contribution to ethics. The suggestions of Mather, Haldane, Russell, and others added up to an appeal for an intelligence that would check the abuses of both fundamentalist morality and industrialism, establish a kind of moral discrimination that had never before been the property of more than a very small minority, and reinterpret basic desires in terms of the capacity of science reasonably to satisfy them.

One of the more interesting of the effects of science upon the thought of the twenties was the modernist view of religion. In its extensive application to all liberal thought, it had a bearing upon most of the reformation of religious ideas; and it acted with vigor and confidence in the interests of establishing its principles among the laymen who assumed important positions in the modernist church.

Herbert Croly, editor of the *New Republic* from the year of its founding to 1930, strongly advocated an intelligent revision of religious attitudes. In the issue of June 9, 1920, he spoke of "a new body of authoritative knowledge which would bind humanity together and save it from falling a victim to its prepossessions, aberrations, and distempers." Science had thus far failed to provide such an authority. In fact, "Its achievements have only intensified that moral chaos, of which the war with its barren victory, its peace without appeasement, and the ominous Bolshevist menace, are different but closely connected expressions." If science could only inspire man with its power of organization and its intelligence, then the effective reconciliation of science and religion would take place and "human nature would unfold itself with unprecedented momentum."

Such a reconciliation must proceed along lines laid down by Croly in another essay (*New Republic,* January 27, 1926): "Scientific inquiry must posit the existence of a world which the human mind is capable, after a fashion, of understanding. The religious life must posit the existence of a world in which human purposes can, after a fashion, get themselves realized." The experimental method of science must be applied to the phenomenon of human consciousness—each person, in other words, needs to examine himself with the same kind of discriminating and analytic thoroughness as the experimental scientist uses in his researches. This form of self-analysis is impossible in traditional religions; the paraphernalia of religious ceremony and ritual,

Croly maintained, "are devices for preventing the immature from straying rather than positive clues to the true way."

Other suggestions for the scientific renovation of human nature included one from William Pepperell Montague, professor of philosophy at Columbia University. In "The Promethean Challenge to Religion" (*New Republic,* August 6, 1924), Montague portrayed a desirable new religion. In its streamlined temple "there would be the welcome and luminous absence of sacrosanct authority. Such dogmas as remained, and there would be many, would be transformed into hypotheses. The most fantastic theory of the supernatural, if held as a hypothesis, is honorable, and belief in it is honest and to be expected." The ethic accompanying this religion would resemble it in having discarded the bugaboo of authority, "and with it the great clutter of prohibitions and taboos—rules taken as ends in themselves rather than as means to happiness." We need above all to abandon authority and asceticism; if we can do this, human ethics will for the first time in history be brought into "active partnership with human science." This Promethean adventure will succeed in preserving "the old supernatural hope for God and immortality," but it will also be united with an equally pressing demand for the use of creative intelligence.

What Montague's suggestion amounts to is a request that God be allowed in the modern temple on probation, that His attributes and the terms of belief in Him be accepted as hypotheses, presumably hypotheses that might never be pressed for evidence nor embarrassed by the need of verification; unless, of course, the immortality of the soul and the existence of a supernatural being can eventually be proved as "highly probable" through some extension either of science or of religion as yet not proposed.

These were the questions raised because of the position of science in the 1920s: what moral disposition to take with respect to its achievements; how to discriminate between the very effective strategies of its *method* and the not altogether satisfactory consequences of its applications to human affairs; what to do, either to restore to the human vision the illusions driven out by it, or to reinterpret religious schemata to make them acceptable to a scientific view. They were problems not peculiar to the decade; they had existed for many decades, and they would persist (and become aggravated) in the years to follow. But in no comparable period of time were there such extremes of view among those who tried to solve them.

2. The Technological Fallacy

I N 1918 the Massachusetts Historical Society published *The Education of Henry Adams*, which in 1907 had had a private printing of
one hundred copies. Its general distribution in the twenties gave it a
prestige and popularity among thinking Americans much greater, perhaps, than Adams had intended. The *Education* was, among other
things, the record of an attempt to find certain basic principles from
which Adams might appraise the new century. He felt that the machine had radically altered the pace and values of history; it had outmoded the rational politics of an earlier time and, in conjunction with
capitalism, had made the Washington of Adams's earlier education
seem inept and futile. He spoke of "the whole mechanical consolida-
tion of force, which ruthlessly stamped out the life of the class into
which Adams was born, but created monopolies capable of controlling
the new energies that America adored."

In 1900, at the Great Exposition of Paris, Adams had attended the
displays of machinery, "aching to absorb knowledge, and helpless to
find it." But under the guidance of the scientist Samuel P. Langley, he
was initiated into the mysteries of the dynamo, which became a symbol
of infinity to him:

> As he grew accustomed to the great gallery of machines, he began to
> feel the forty-foot dynamo as a moral force, much as the early Chris-
> tians felt the Cross. The planet itself seemed less impressive, in its
> old-fashioned, deliberate, annual or daily revolution, than this huge
> wheel, revolving within arm's length at some vertiginous speed, and
> barely murmuring—scarcely humming an audible warning to stand
> a hair's-breadth further for respect of power—while it would not wake
> the baby lying close against its frame. Before the end, one began to
> pray to it; inherited instinct taught the natural expression of man be-
> fore silent and infinite force. Among the thousand symbols of ultimate
> energy, the dynamo was not so human as some, but it was the most
> expressive.

This was the world a child born in 1900 would see, a world "which
would not be a unity but a multiple." The new American was going
to be "the child of steam and the brother of the dynamo," a product of
"so much mechanical power, and bearing no distinctive marks but

that of its pressure." It seemed to Adams that the language of this force was money, that through it the force could be manipulated, expanded, and controlled. The machines bought with money abolished the distinctions of time and place, made a confusion of all the things hitherto kept safely within a historical and metaphysical form. Adams's experiences with the machine, and his observations of it, helped him to move toward a new "dynamic theory of history," a theory that "defines Progress as the development and economy of Forces."

A dynamic theory, assigning attractive force to opposing bodies in proportion to the law of mass, takes for granted that the forces of nature capture man. The sum of force attracts: the feeble atom or molecule called man is attracted; he suffers education or growth; he is the sum of the forces that attract him; his body and his thought are alike their product; the movement of the forces controls the progress of his mind, since he can know nothing but the motions which impinge on his senses, whose sum makes education.

Adams noted that historical changes were primarily shifts in the process of symbolizing force; as the Virgin is the central symbol of medieval thought, so the dynamo is the symbol of twentieth-century thought. But the former had represented man's search for unity, while the latter seemed destined to stand for the multiplicity of modern life. "The movement from unity into multiplicity, between 1200 and 1900, was unbroken in sequence, and rapid in acceleration." The effect of the dynamo upon Adams's thinking was therefore not only that of discovery; it was to alter his conception of history, not as a mere event but as a new symbol of the development of man's relationship to nature and her laws. The machine had properties which, while they might be considered the result of man's inventiveness, were yet independent of them—as though at its birth the machine had assumed a form powerful and forbidding, and indifferent to man's mind and emotion, except insofar as these might perfect its form or diversify its function.

Nothing excited man so much as, or puzzled him more than, this belief in the dynamo as the most exact and exacting demonstration of science's long experiment with the abstract laws of physics. The great problem of the mechanical age, of which the 1920s were an important expression, had to do with his assimilation of the machine. It was made even more difficult by the machine's indifference to his worship. Emotional complexities entered into the history of the machine only as consequences of the part it played in man's life. During the 1920s there were efforts to understand the machine, to assimilate it, and to record it as cultural fact; but it remained, stolid and obtuse, as a mechanical fact, scarcely available to man's poetic sense. This is not to say that he did not write poetry about it, but such poetry was almost inevitably written in terms of a compromise with the mechanism itself. The fact remained, though it inspired a thousand responses, lyrical, halting, and mechanomorphic.

Writers of the 1920s, whenever they took account of the machine, saw it either as the perfect concrete demonstration of man's ingenious mind or as the last desperate symbol of the evil science had wrought upon his vain efforts to achieve a rational life. To break the machine upon the wheel of poetry seemed a futile aim; yet it was attempted again and again. Some poets saw in the machine a happy symbol of energy completely freed from the inhibitions and disintegrative imbalance of the errant human personality: obedient power, operating within the limits of natural energy, assimilating and using that energy with apparent ease, delicacy of movement, and precision, such as man himself could never hope to achieve in similar degree or fashion.

Few poets hoped to realize a similar balance and efficiency, but many were nevertheless impressed by the machine and sometimes paid clumsy tribute to it in their poems. "I am a modern," says Dinhard of John Cournos's *Miranda Masters* (1926). "I am not frightened of the thunder of Zeus. Our poems are dynamos, railway engineers, cranes, ocean liners, wireless, aeroplanes: everything that moves, and with speed. I translate that into terms of art. That is, I gather the essence of machine structure, the mechanism of life, in abstract terms suited to its nature." Such a point of view would sacrifice many, if not all, of the properties that, in their unmechanical and imprecise nature, belonged to the whole man, complex and self-defeating though he might be.

The movement called futurism had an important influence upon literature and the arts. It was begun in 1909 by Filippo Tommaso Marinetti, who maintained that the new age of movement and the machine had wrought a comparable change in our attitudes toward the arts: "Literature has hitherto glorified thoughtful immobility, ecstasy of sleep; we shall extol aggressive movement, feverish insomnia, the double-quick step, the somersault, the box on the ear, the fisticuff." Futurism attempted a language and grammar modeled upon the pace and tempo of an age of machinery, and proposed certain vital changes in the human personality, a closer resemblance than had previously been admitted between the men and women of modern society and the machinery they had created and were using.

"The wise men have spoken," Marinetti declaimed in one of his poems. "What of that? Their science is vain./Watch their old Syllogisms, gawks with white hair,/which flaunt the white clouds." In the same issue of *Poetry and Drama* (September 1913) appeared Marinetti's "New Futurist Manifesto," subtitled "Wireless Imagination and Words at Liberty." Futurism, he wrote, is based on "that complete renewal of human sensibility which has taken place since the great scientific discoveries." Those who use the new discoveries—telegraphs, telephones, gramophones, and so on—do not realize the decisive influence these are having upon their psychic nature. The inventions that have accelerated the pace of modern communication have also affected our sensibilities and made useless and out of date most of the linguistic and syntactic ordering of our minds with which we have up to now been satisfied.

Marinetti listed some fifteen ways in which our sensibilities have been affected by scientific discoveries. They have led to an "acceleration of life" and have made us despise the old and welcome "the new and the unforeseen." We now scorn the prospect of a quiet life; we are attracted toward danger. Further, we no longer subscribe to a theory of personal immortality and are therefore much more interested in ourselves and in increased possibilities for a "full life." Human desires have correspondingly been multiplied, and we no longer regard them sentimentally. Romantic love has disappeared and the sex life has become enormously more important because of the "greater erotic facility and liberty of women." Man's capacities have been multiplied by the machine, and he is by way of developing a "New mechanical sense, fusion of instinct with horse-power and with chained forces." His "new sensibility" expresses a horror of the curved line, of slowness and "of prolix analysis," loves the straight line, speed, abbreviation, and synthesis.

The new world, since it has so radically altered man's activities and outlook, requires, of course, a new language. "Disregarding syntax, he will waste no time in constructing sentences. Chucking adjectives and punctuation overboard, he will despise all mannerism or preciosity of style, and will seek to stir you by hurling a confused medley of sensations and impressions at your head." The "wireless imagination" is therefore adapted to man's increased needs; he must meet an acceleration of his external life with a corresponding speeding up of his powers of attention and perception.

Marinetti predicted "an entire freedom of images and analogies, expressed by disjointed words and without the connecting wires of syntax." With respect to the different parts of speech, adjectives ought to be considered "as railway or semaphoric signals of style, which serve to regulate the speed and pace of the race of analogies." The infinitive mood of the verb will prove indispensable in "violent and dynamic lyrical expression." It is "round and true as a wheel," while the other moods and tenses "are either triangular, square, or oval." Together with this radical revision of syntactic usage, Marinetti advises a "typographic revolution," advocates a free and expressive orthography. "We are . . . substituting the use of *words at liberty* for the old forms. Moreover, our lyrical intoxication must freely unmake words and make them anew, cutting them down and lengthening them, strengthening their centers or their extremities, augmenting or diminishing the number of their vowels and consonants." In an effort to keep pace with the speeding world of the machine, "It matters little if the actual word itself so deformed becomes equivocal." It must reach some form of onomatopoetic equivalence with the reality it attempts to describe, until eventually we shall "attain the *psycho-onomatopoetic chord,* a sonorous yet abstract expression of an emotion or of pure thought."

Though Marinetti's futurism never became (in exactly the form in which he proposed it) a widely accepted doctrine, the effect of his aesthetic upon the arts was pronounced. There was certainly some alignment of cubism and expressionism with the futurist aesthetic. And the Revolution of the Word that he proposed had some small influence upon the linguistic habits of experimentalists in literature. Experiment in free verse and free typography, while it had several other sources, in some ways respected the wishes of the futurist manifesto regarding the closer equivalence of pace and sound of language with meaning. It was an attempt to adapt the pace of writing—to vary its form in such a way that it revealed a change in tempo—to the industrial and urban milieu of the machine age.

Matthew Josephson suggested, for example, that we ought "to plunge hardily into that effervescent, revolving, cacophonous milieu . . . where the Billposters enunciate their wisdom, the cinema transports us, the newspapers intone their gaudy jargon" (*Broom,* November 1922). This is what John Dos Passos did, in *Manhattan Transfer* and more particularly in the newsreel experiments of his trilogy, *U. S. A.* Other experiments with the pace of the language, the attempt to hasten or retard the speed of visual and imaginative attention, occur in the poetry of E. E. Cummings. But to assume that Cummings' typographical and syntactic experiments pay more than superficial heed to the futurist credo is to mistake what is really a complex poetic strategy for a mere surface working with analogies in space and time.

Whatever else one can say of Marinetti's proposed revolution in literary style, its superficiality must be admitted; and the major experiments in literature of the twenties were not satisfied by mere analogy with external motion and pace, but found more profound inner relationships between language and the psyche. Marinetti's futurist manifestoes were symptomatic, however, of the influence of machinery (of the phenomenon of speed, particularly) upon the modern consciousness.

The problem of the machine as poetic subject was discussed in the decade in several interesting ways. On the one hand, the machine was a fact of modern life that the modern poet could scarcely ignore; on the other, it seemed that no genuine exercise of the poetic imagination could properly use it, because of its complete separation from the vocabulary of the emotions. The danger of the machine age to poetry, said Babette Deutsch (*New Republic,* August 21, 1929), was "not that it hurries us along too fast, or that it shrinks our horizons, or that it robs us of a comprehensive philosophy, but that it forces us to live in a world as empty of emotional values as the algebraic letter X." Miss Deutsch doubted the value of most poetry of the machine, because machines "are too complex to be understood except by a very few of us." The poems that attempt to realize the machine in poetic terms usually fail because they remake it into an object that can be directly and emotionally appreciated. The poems that despair of the machine suggest the human consequence of machinery, but even here the machine "enters into our lives and into our poetry in an oblique, indirect, tangential fashion."

"It's about time," Dos Passos said (*New Republic,* December 18, 1929), "that American writers showed up in the industrial field where something is really going on, instead of tackling the tattered strawmen of art and culture." Genevieve Taggard, reviewing the Machine Age Exposition in New York (*New Masses,* July 1927), spoke scornfully of "The Ruskinian boys and girls," who "are opposed to even the discipline of the elements; they are indignant that free souls should have the limitations of sun, wind, light, darkness, cold and heat. I am very fond of seeing such people up against it. And when they come back to bath tubs and hot water, transportation and an eight-hour day, they don't have so much to say." The artist should not oppose modern fact or look for a way to escape it; he ought to master that fact, to make it a vital part of his art. Quoting from Louis Lozowick, Miss Taggard said that the artist needs above all to *"Objectify the dominant experience of our epoch in plastic terms that possess value for more than this epoch alone."*

In January 1927 the *New Masses* published several answers to a series of questions, two of which related directly to the problem of the machine and the place of literature in a machine age. Question five read, "Does the advent of the machine mean the death of art and culture?" Typical answers included such remarks as these: "If machine-made wars continue, there will be no new culture, and no old culture" (Sinclair Lewis); "I think the tendency to worship the machine, or even reflect it, passively but admiringly as in pictorial art, is destructive of life" (Van Wyck Brooks). Question six, "How should the artist adapt himself to the machine age?" elicited these replies: "By not running away from it, and by trying to understand its complexities" (Babette Deutsch); "Let the artist attend to his art and the age will attend to his adaptation" (Edmund Wilson); "He can't. Unless he is of it, born deep in it, with complete identification of himself with its structure" (Genevieve Taggard).

In 1930 Oliver Sayler edited *Revolt in the Arts,* a collection of essays on the place of the machine in modern arts. The most noteworthy contribution was Hart Crane's "Modern Poetry," a discussion of the specific nature of the machine's vocabulary and of its adaptability to poetic expression. The poet's concern, said Crane, is "self-discipline toward a formal integration of experience." This self-discipline includes "all readjustments incident to science and other shifting factors related to that consciousness." The poet needs to absorb the machine, that is, to *"acclimatize* it as naturally and casually as trees, cattle, galleons, castles, and all other human associations of the past." The present difficulties of such absorption are the result of the machine's novelty, which will eventually be overcome by "continual poetic allusion." As for the familiar contention that science and the machine are hostile to poetic expression, Crane thought it untenable. But poetry must capture the significance of the machine without losing, in the process, any of its own significance.

In another essay, written in 1925 but unpublished until its inclusion in Philip Horton's biography of Crane (1937), Crane discussed further the problem of the poet who attempts to approximate the character and pace of modern life. "It seems to me that a poet will accidentally define his time well enough simply by reacting honestly and to the full extent of his sensibilities to the states of passion, experience, and rumination that fate forces on him, first hand." But mere *reference* to the facts of modern observation and experience is not equivalent to a poetic assimilation of them: "to fool one's self that definitions are being reached by merely referring to skyscrapers, radio antennae, steam whistles, or other surface phenomena of our time is merely to paint a photograph." The "logic of the metaphor" can succeed in changing what is merely a dead listing of mechanical things into poetic language; the metaphor will, however, adopt whatever there is in modern experience that requires a changed vocabulary. New *things* within the range of our experience require a changed form of metaphoric presentation: "I realize . . . that the voice of the present must be caught at the risk of speaking in idioms and circumlocutions sometimes shocking to the scholar and historians of logic. Language has built towers and bridges, but itself is inevitably as fluid as always."

The machine had had several effects upon the vocabulary of human experience. In the 1920s there was no really successful attempt to assimilate, without either sentimentality or fear, its offering to the modern sensibility, because the machine was twice removed from the complex nature of that sensibility. It was essentially the product of a scientific method whose success depended upon severe abstraction and consistency of operation. Such a method excluded emotional differences from the laboratory and from the mind. Further, the machine was the happy combination of certain elements in nature—the content of metals, the properties of electrical energy, the successful nourishment of that energy by coal, itself a product of the processes and history of the earth. In each case, whatever the nature of any of the machine's parts or the quality of its operation, its success depended on its being free of any interference from the complex emotional nature of man. The machine was therefore twice abstracted—and the shifting passions of man could have only an incidental part in its operation.

How, then, could the poet expect to write verses about the machine? Only by refusing to consider it as merely an efficient and abstract *modus operandi,* by endowing it with the very qualities most conscientiously omitted in its construction, or by speaking of it only in terms of its *effect* upon human experience. The poetry written about the machine in the 1920s shows in varying degrees all the faults that come from a naïveté or a blindness concerning the machine's position and function in modern life. In some cases the poet looked at the machine in an attitude of respectful incomprehension, trying to find in it a kind of emotionless utopia of the spirit, but endowing it nevertheless with the language of emotion. In other cases the machine was personified—or at least some of its functions were translated into an analogy with human nature. In still other poems the machine became a symbol, as it was for a time for Henry Adams, of the metaphysical force or forces whose energies it presumably channeled and controlled.

The sentimental utopian reaction—the push-button religion of machine-worship—the whimsical use of analogy, and the use of symbolism were the three states of poetic response the machine inspired. In one way or another they exhibited and illustrated the technological fallacy. Harriet Monroe's "The Turbine" shows a confusion of sentiment and a failure of comprehension not untypical of its kind of poetry. The turbine is personified, has the whims and the temperament of a woman, who at one moment "sits upon her throne/As ladylike and quiet as a nun," yet reacts violently to any crossing of her wishes. The fallacy is consistently demonstrated. It is a failure to grasp emotionally the meaning implicit in a machine's purpose and nature.

> I do her will
> And dare not disobey, for her right hand
> Is power, her left is terror, and her anger
> Is havoc. Look—if I but lay a wire
> Across the terminals of yonder switch
> She'll burst her windings, rip her casings off,
> And shriek till envious Hell shoots up its flames,
> Shattering her very throne.[1]

[1] A precedent for this approach and for that of Miss Tietjens' poem (p. 260) can be seen in Emily Dickinson's "I Like to See It Lap the Miles." Miss Dickinson reduces the size of her machine and of its setting so that they are manageable, in the same way a toy train must appear manageable to a child. Indeed, Miss Dickinson's machine may be said to be like many others of her poetic objects; it is translated into an idiom and discussed on a scale that provide for an easy, convenient attitude within the range of her sensibility and taste. The power of any locomotive depends in large part on its size as a moving, disciplined mechanism. Though the metaphoric resemblance to a playful animal is not exceptional, in this poem it is used in such a way as to reduce the size and significance of both the machine and the animal. In short, Miss Dickinson's poem can easily be understood as a convenient basis for an illustrated children's book. Both Miss Monroe and Miss Tietjens, though personifying their machine (and committing the technological fallacy), prefer their machines full size, and the emotional effect is in consequence quite different.

Carl Sandburg's lines from *Smoke and Steel* (1920) represent another extension of the technological fallacy—this time, quite close to the poet's expression of the cultural and economic place of the machine in modern life. Sandburg portrays the human energy, time, and blood that have gone into the production of the machine's body. No matter the shape of a bar of steel, there will always be

> Smoke at the heart of it, smoke and the blood of a man.
> A runner of fire ran in it, ran out, ran somewhere else,
> And left smoke and the blood of a man
> And the finished steel, chilled and blue.[2]

The industrial efficiency of America, Sandburg tells us, is purchased at a cost of human blood; he means actual blood spilled in accidents, and most of all the emotional effects of working conditions upon the men responsible for the finished bar of steel. Sandburg's steel-mill poems are in the nature of an appeal to those who use the machine not to forget that it is after all the product of human sacrifice, and that human beings have something to do with its mechanical perfection, will in fact survive its breakdown, and will eventually triumph over the economic conditions under which they suffer in its manufacture. "Prayers of Steel" carries this idea—of man's intimate relationship with the very being of steel—to its furthest extreme:

> Lay me on an anvil, O God.
> Beat me and hammer me into a steel spike.

[2] Walt Whitman's "To a Locomotive in Winter" (1876), though in many respects different from Sandburg's steel-mill poems, nevertheless illustrates the poetic treatment of the machine as part of a cultural complex. Whitman's treatment alternates between the specific and the symbolic, as well as between dry precision and vague personification. That he is thinking of the locomotive as a worshipful symbol of America's cultural strength and promise is suggested by the archaism of address. The poem shows the kind of confusion so often found in Whitman's poetry when he attempts to specify objects as supporting evidence for his semiphilosophic generalizations about American culture. The locomotive as machine has an appearance quite often precisely given ("black cylindric body," "parallel and connecting rods," etc.); at other times, the poet speaks of it as a "Fierce-throated beauty!" whose power and noise assert its domination over hills, prairies, and lakes. There are at least three points of view in the poem, and they are not unified; nor are they given in an arrangement that allows one to anticipate a shift from one to another. It should be pointed out, however, that this and other Whitman poems provided the incentive and the inspiration for some of Sandburg's work and for Hart Crane's puzzled optimism concerning the machine in modern American civilization.

Drive me into the girders that hold a skyscraper together.
Take red-hot rivets and fasten me into the central girders.
Let me be the great nail holding a skyscraper through blue nights into
    white stars.

The mood in poetry of the machine shifted from sympathy to exaltation to despair. Frank Ernest Hill, who wrote for the *Nation* some of the earliest verse on the subject of man's mechanical conquest of the air, spoke of aviators as "the children of Science that mated a Vision":

Sons of a song that was wedded to furnace and wheel;
We are riders of vapor and vastness Elysian—
Oceans impalpable dying in light at our keel . . .
The paths of Icarus over an earth engirdled
With rail of iron and rope of copper and steel!

And he appeals to "Ye that are cheated of life by the toil that sustains you," to seek

The wine of speed and the great-sailed galleys
Riding the road of gods till the paths ye follow
Shall wake the god that sleeps in the dust of your soul!

"The Steam Shovel" by Eunice Tietjens pictures the Frankenstein product of man's industry as "a creature huge and grim/And only half believed." The steam shovel is a "thwarted monster,"

A lap-dog dragon, eating from his hand
And doomed to fetch and carry at command . . .

and Miss Tietjens expresses wonder at his compliance:

Have you no longing ever to be free?
In warm electric days to run a-muck,
Ranging like some mad dinosaur,
Your fiery heart at war
With this strange world, the city's restless ruck,
Where all drab things that toil, save you alone,
Have life;
And you the semblance only, and the strife?

She feels pity for the "Poor helpless creature of a half-grown god," particularly for his having to work without a wage!

For day, no joy of night,
For toil, no ecstasy of primal rage.

Another form of personal response to the machine, Marianne Moore's "To a Steam Roller," impresses, in contrast with Miss Tietjens' pity, by its quality of whimsicality and its deliberate, playful use of the machine as a personified symbol of brutish existence. "You lack half wit," she tells the steam roller. "You crush all the particles down/into close conformity, and then walk back and forth on them."

Were not 'impersonal judgment in aesthetic
matters, a metaphysical impossibility,' you

might fairly achieve
it.

The attempt to capture the nature of machinery within the limits of poetry is well illustrated in the work of an obscure Philadelphia poet, MacKnight Black, whose volume of poems, *Machinery,* was published by Horace Liveright in 1929. Black's early, unpublished poems are conventional imitations of the rhythms and sentiments of Swinburne, much the worse for having been written in immature parroting of late-Victorian clichés. There is nothing in them to suggest that he would eventually change his interests and adopt the Corliss engine as the object of his poetic love, but the circumstances of his career may have had much to do with it. His association with the advertising concern that carried a Ford account, his trips to the River Rouge plant, and his acquaintance with Charles Demuth and Charles Sheeler, American painters, combined to stimulate his interest in the abstract lines of the American machine.

Black chose machinery as the subject of his poetry because of its simplicity and because it seemed free of the complications of human lives. He suggested that it was the principal object of American pride, almost the only product of American culture to which he might point with unqualified respect. Preferring the machine, he neglected both the economic objection to industrial oppression and the complaints against the machine offered by such writers as D. H. Lawrence and Sherwood Anderson. Black isolated the machine from its economic and its cultural contexts, enjoyed it, and described it as a single poetic object. At the same time he burdened the machine with the voluptuous and sensuous imagery that had survived the Imagists' onslaught upon Victorian platitudes. In *Machinery* one finds examples of the extremes to which the technological fallacy can go.

The machine represents "Thought as clean as the soul's unthinking labor/As sure, as far-off from fear and hope," which has yielded a harvest "Beautiful and bare from the dreamless ground." In the machine "is the same clarity as in the wheel-swung universe," the clearest translation of the physical energy in the universe into terms man can understand: ". . . shaped by our hands from the world's stuff, this wheel/Is like a word our ears have taken from the sky." Captured within the trim lines and the faultless movement of a Corliss engine are "The swift and meaningless designs/Of power scattered through a universe," and these are held in steel, "Remote and changed and beautiful."

Black demonstrates the technological fallacy at work: machinery is born of "virgin steel"; the machine is a new religious symbol:

> The mystic body of a Christ of power
> Is come to earth—
> And finds no worshippers
> Or star.

Similarly, a reciprocating engine inspires him to the image of matter "Brought to beauty/Carved in moving steel," and man born "of lightnings," "Man absolute/Compacted in a wheel."

In general, and except for occasional lines in Hart Crane's *The Bridge,* writers of the 1920s viewed the machine in several distortions of its nature. It was, first of all, the product of an artificially simple process, which neglected or deliberately excluded the complex nature of man; and though it might be complicated in its structure, the careful explication of many intricate scientific formulas, it appeared, superficially at least, to be remarkably uncomplex. This impression led to the kind of sentimental mechanomorphism of Harriet Monroe's poem, and Miss Tietjens'. Or it offered an inducement, to a poet like Black, to abandon personal complexity for the symbolic peace of the machine. In the steel poems of Carl Sandburg the technological fallacy assumed the form of an intimate blending of human spirit and effort with the physical ingredients of the earth, so that the human remnant in steel gave it a teleological and personal reference.

3. The Pre-Industrial Illusion

OPPOSITION to the machine took many forms in the 1920s. As the product of modern industry, it was held responsible for almost all the evils of the modern city [3]—for the ugliness, the congestion, the

[3] Samuel Butler's *Erewhon* (1872) set the pattern for criticism of machinery. In one scene the citizens of Erewhon decide, after some persuasion by "one of the most learned professors of hypothetics," that machines "were ultimately

ludicrous restriction of man's physical activities, and, above all, his spiritual frustration. For D. H. Lawrence the machine madness was another of the distortions of modern civilization, caused by the dominance of the intellect over the body: "The industrial England blots out the agricultural England. One meaning blots out another. The new England blots out the old England. And the continuity is not organic, but mechanical." In *Women in Love* (1920), Lawrence described the effect of an industrial passion for profit upon the human personality, its disastrous murder of the will. The God was the machine:

> Each man claimed equality in the Godhead of the great productive machine. Every man equally was part of this Godhead. But somehow, somewhere, Thomas Crich knew this was false. When the machine is the Godhead, and production or work is worship, then the most mechanical mind is purest and highest, the representative of God on earth. And the rest are subordinate, each according to his degree.

Speaking of the difference between machine work and handcraft, Lewis Mumford pointed out (*New Republic,* June 6, 1923) that the qualities of good machine work are "precision, economy, finish, geometric perfection." It is impossible for the workman to leave his mark upon the product of machine work. "Indeed, could the workman express anything in the course of the machine process, fatigue, depression —or his lack of imagination—or his desire to escape?" In other essays Mumford complained about the distortions caused by the artificial values of an industrial age. Debating with Genevieve Taggard on the subject of "That Monster—the Machine" (*New Masses,* September 1927), Mumford discussed the skyscraper as a "thing of beauty" and distinctively the product of a modern economy. "It would be foolish to say that the skyscraper could not, on occasion, be aesthetically interesting, because it has grown out of the price system; but it is far more stupid to tolerate the congestion and the land speculation because they produce an occasional Shelton." The industrial revolution, Mumford wrote (*Freeman,* December 1, 1920), "was obviously the product of

---

destined to supplant the race of man, and to become instinct with a vitality as different from, and superior to, that of animals, as animal to vegetable life." The idea has been repeated often in fantasies of one kind or another since the publication of *Erewhon.* The danger the professor anticipated was that machines might develop a consciousness superior in kind and degree to that possessed by humans. Will not the slave eventually become the master? The professor advocated that as many machines be destroyed as could safely be done away with, "lest they should tyrannize over us even more completely."

energetic, immature minds" that desired and hastened the progress of an industrial system with little regard to its consequences upon the beauty of the landscape or the security of personal life. The very existence of suburbia, Mumford argued (*New Republic,* September 7, 1921), proved that men wished to escape the urban monster they had created. The real danger of our industrial system was not its brutalizing effect upon the worker or the economic danger of concentration of power, but

> the fact that the greater part of the labor exacted in a Ford plant could be performed by a healthy imbecile; the fact that by care for their health and by a nice adjustment of wages to prices and by organized luxury campaigns which tether the worker to vacuum cleaners and elaborate radio sets and snobberies of one sort or another he can be kept docile and contented with a servile status, quite unable to shake off the chains on his manhood because he has literally been "sold" on all the pleasures that the chains bring him. Similarly, in the distribution of power, it is not personal autocracy so much as anonymity that is dangerous; in every large organization the equipment for passing the buck is polished and inspected every day.

Several writers predicted that man would finally be destroyed by the monster he had created. In 1925 and 1926 a little magazine called *The Pilgrims Almanach* appeared in New York; its object was to point out the deterioration of the human personality in an age of machinery and industry. "Our minds are so contaminated by the consciousness of utility," the magazine editorialized in its fourth issue, "that we cannot grasp the ideal motives of the men of the past who laid the groundwork for our civilization, simply because their conception of life was so much nobler than ours." The chief sources of beauty and faith in the past were now commercialized: "Instead of the traditional trinity of art, stage, and altar we have come to the prosaic trinity of machine, money, and majority rule."

In the next issue of the magazine "Ivan Narodny" predicted "The Revolt of Man against the Machine." "We can see the irony of American individualism from the mechanical aspect of New York streets," he wrote, "where a man looks nothing but a miserable troglodyte in some enchanted world of steel and concrete. Money here and machines there —that is the nightmare of tomorrow." The revolution will come in the form of a thorough strike against the machine: "One beautiful morning all the machines in New York will stand still: there will be neither running water nor steam, gas or electricity—and the masses will lift their hands for any relief." The revolution will be headed by "a futuristic Rainbow Regiment of intelligentsia—a handful of great individuals"—who will employ, not the barricades and rifles of past revolutions, but "the latest invention in every field of science and art."

Certain works of the decade—Karel Çapek's *R.U.R.*, Rice's *The Adding Machine*, Eugene O'Neill's *Dynamo*—asked: To what extent are we beginning to resemble the machine, becoming mechanical beings, and losing the last shreds of human dignity and individuality? "We flounder before the machine and are features more or less groveling of its external life," said Waldo Frank (*New Republic*, November 18, 1925), "because we lack an instinctive metaphysical consciousness to make us master and absorb it—to fuse the machine with all its elements of will and act into our own expression." So long as we are passive servants of the machine, we shall lose our own wills and allow the machine and its owners to dictate every term of our lives. Freedom of the will in these circumstances, Frank concluded, is absolutely indispensable to our survival as thinking and willing persons.

The fight against standardization was part of the general reaction to the machine's effect upon modern life. Sherwood Anderson, who had discussed this problem in an essay in *Vanity Fair* (November 1926), published *Perhaps Women* in 1931, a study of the effects of factory life upon men. Visiting several factories, he felt that workers genuinely suffered from the pressures of the assembly line. "You feel it when you go in. You feel rigid lines. You feel movement. You feel a strange tension in the air. There is a quiet, terrible intensity." Much of "the old mystery" in life is gone; for men need direct contact with nature in their work. "They need to touch materials with their hands." Instead, they seem to have lost their strength, to have given in to the machine. He offered as a solution the proposal that woman take man's place in the factories; she is and will remain "untouched by the machine." She has a quiet power that the machine cannot touch. For Anderson, modern industrial life seemed degrading, humiliating, and dispiriting. His heroes end by withdrawing from it, by walking away from it (as he himself had once done), moving toward some vague horizon, looking for the chance somehow of renewing their spirits.

Nowhere in the work of Anderson is the problem of the machine, of the entire complex pattern of industrialism, put with such force as in *Poor White* (1920). It is a novel of transition: transition from a comparatively simple economy to a complex one; from a moderately peaceful society to one shot through with intrigue and venality; from a Lincolnesque hero to a bewildered half-villain of a dawning industrial age. The years of the novel are 1870–1910, the crucial decades of industrialism in the Midwest; the setting is the small town of Bidwell, Ohio. The hero is Hugh McVey, half folk hero, half industrial genius. In the beginning he has "a dreamy detached outlook on life," prefers sleeping to progress, suffers the "curse of indolence." Like the widow Douglas and Miss Watson of *Huckleberry Finn,* Sarah Shepard, a transplanted New Englander, determines that she will reform Hugh, root out his ignorance (as her father had rooted out stumps from pioneer land), save him from the worst of all Puritan sins (his being "dreamy and worthless").[4]

When his father is killed in a drunken brawl (the same fate suffered by Huckleberry Finn's "pap"), Hugh McVey is finally persuaded that he must make something of himself. He leaves the forlorn town of Mudcat Landing, travels eastward to Ohio. But making something of himself requires that he discover in himself a skill that he can develop, exploit, and eventually give to the world. That skill is calculation, a restless mathematical urge to count, figure, estimate:

> Hugh went into one of the residence streets of the town and counted the pickets on the fences before the houses. He returned to the hotel and made a calculation as to the number of pickets in all the fences in town. Then he got a rule at the hardware store and carefully measured the pickets. He tried to estimate the number of pickets that could be cut out of certain sized trees.

From then on his life is filled with such movements, gestures, strings of calculation. His great contribution is a talent for abstracting from the life about him, rearranging it in mechanical terms, making an abstract imitation of it that will work; he is the genius of the machine.

He brings his gift to Bidwell, Ohio, a sleepy farming community (with its wise old men, its halfwit, its miser, its annoying gogetters), which is just beginning to stir with frontier energy and enterprise. Here the energy will take the form of industrial progress. Hugh McVey becomes the folk hero of this phase of the frontier epic. Hungry for recognition, anxious to prove himself, he turns to his calculations, is seen working over drawings and figures. He has his first chance to prove his good will when he observes the people in the fields, at work planting cabbages. Immediately he begins work on a mechanical sub-

---

[4] There is more than a hint here of a division of personalities along geographical lines: the Missouri-Southern *versus* the New Englander; the two seem (at least in McVey's case) to have gone into the making of a modern folk hero.

stitute, reducing the act of planting to a gesture that can be duplicated by a machine.

> After the impulse to try to invent a plant-setting machine came to him, he went every evening to conceal himself in the fence corner and watch the French family at their labors. Absorbed in watching the mechanical movements of the men who crawled across the fields in the moonlight, he forgot they were human. . . . Certain intricate mechanical problems, that had already come into his mind in connection with the proposed machine, he thought could be better understood if he could get the movements necessary to plant-setting into his own body. . . . He tried to relate his arms to the mechanical arms of the machine that was being created in his mind.

He becomes a grotesque of the age of industry, banks, cities, strikes, and slums. The busy entrepreneur, Steve Hunter, soon persuades him that he is important to the town's economy. After an initial failure Hugh's inventions begin the magic process of transforming Bidwell. Gone are "poetry and vague thoughts"; in their place, restless planning, building, expansion, organization. Only a few citizens resent the change: Ezra French cries out that the machine is contrary to God's will; Joe Wainsworth, skilled maker of harness, becomes "a silent and disgruntled man." Most of the townspeople pray to God to protect Hugh's machines and their investments. For Hugh the changes are puzzling and disillusioning; the machine, instead of bringing him closer to the town, has changed the town into an industrial maze, fast becoming a waste land.

The real crisis in Anderson's novel, however, is neither economic nor industrial but sexual. His criticism of the age is most incisively given in terms of sex balance: men who become involved in "calculations" (inventing, business organization, assembly-line disciplines) lose their potency. The heroine of the novel, Clara Butterworth, is a symbol of the neglected earth. She is the goddess of fertility, seeking recognition in the industrial waste land, offering her gift to men who are "too busy to attend to it." "She wanted to draw near to something young, strong, gentle, insistent, beautiful." But this desire is insulted, ignored; there is no one to "communicate" with her. Hugh McVey strikes her as the only great man she will ever know—a latter-day Lincoln or Grant, a hero, a "creative force." When he proposes marriage, she seizes the opportunity "like a wild animal seeking prey." The marriage begins most inauspiciously; shoes in hand, Hugh escapes via the bedroom window. Back in the safety of his workshop, he expresses the fury of his disappointment by smashing a part of his latest invention, as a "protest against the grotesque position into which he had been thrown by his marriage to Clara."

The crisis in Hugh's life occurs in his relationship with Clara; sex is not easily understood, cannot be mastered through "calculation." The "gladness" of the body is somehow different from industrial achievement. The scapegoat, Joe Wainsworth, must help resolve the issue. The novel moves toward its melodramatic and symbolic climax: Wainsworth, goaded by his assistant into a frenzy of mechanophobia, destroys his employee with his harness knife, cuts the sets of mail-order harness into a thousand pieces, and rushes out of the shop, gun in hand. Clara, her father, and Hugh are out driving in their new car. When Clara hears about Wainsworth's act, she admires him for it: he stood "for all the men and women in the world who were in secret revolt against the absorption of the age in machines and the products of machines." Wainsworth, captured, is taken into town in the Butterworth car; as he is being led to the jail, he turns to Hugh and attacks him; springing forward, he "sank his fingers and teeth into Hugh's neck." This attack persuades Clara; she comes to Hugh's defense. A few minutes' violence has apparently resolved years of tension and hatred, has united Hugh and Clara, and has restored virility to Hugh. The novel concludes in a haze of resolution. Wainsworth, the tragic figure in this society, has in his act of violent repudiation unwittingly brought the two heroic forces of the novel into satisfactory union.

This is a typically Andersonian vision. The solitary, quiet, half-inarticulate folk hero, in his search for self-identity, turns to his single talent; the talent is foreshortened, grotesque; in consequence of its exercise, business and slums come to the town. The "natural life" is the pre-industrial illusion, symbolized by the sluggish Mississippi, on whose banks Hugh once dreamed; the "artificial" life, the disciplined life, is a product of New England energy and Old Testament conscience. The two forms of life *must* be united, their tensions resolved; and their resolution is portrayed in the long, tortuous progress of the marriage. For its happy conclusion, the sacrifice of the artisan, the worn-out, old-fashioned, pre-industrial scapegoat, is essential.

Anderson did not deny the industrial age, but he regretted its influence in destroying the "poetry and vague thoughts" available to a pre-industrial sensibility. In his other fiction there are men who avoid the complications of industrial society, or who live serenely in the midst of it without allowing it to touch them, or who climactically renounce it.

Against the neurosis and fever of this complicated and pointless world, there are the examples of the Negroes whose "dark laughter" provokes a scornful commentary upon it. The Negroes have somehow come through almost untouched and unharmed; their vital, primitive wisdom is rural, pre-industrial, "Southern" (as temperamentally opposed to New England), simple, and of the earth earthy. This simplification of racial and human personality was of some importance as an exemplum in the critical text of the 1920s. Waldo Frank's *Holiday* (1923) used it to define the white consciousness in contrast with the black. Carl Van Vechten allowed it to give particular stress to his portrayal of *Nigger Heaven* (1926).[5] This kind of primitivism, at best a convenient distortion of racial realities, was quite significantly a part of the widely expressed opposition to the world allegedly created by "white" ingenuity and its disciplined commercial drive. Not only the Negro personality, but his music, his art, and the figurations (described by popular anthropologists) of his "pure," pre-industrial life, were exploited by those who needed to define their rebellion against the "machine."

The primitivism of the 1920s was in many respects a reaction against the standardization caused by modern science in all its social applications. The noble savage of Huxley's *Brave New World* (1932) was but one of the many rebels against this standardization. Writers referred often to more primitive societies, pointed out their customs, rites, and habits, and suggested by invidious contrast that the modern, sophisticated, and civilized white man was losing out in strength and happiness. Neo-primitivism was the animating spirit of several religious cults, which were an attempt either to escape the enervating pace of modern life or to recapture in a moment's release from consciousness some semblance of the spiritual order the cultists professed to have missed from their ordinary lives.

Many artists expressed their primitivism by taking up American jazz.

[5] See also Ronald Firbank's *Prancing Nigger* (published in America in 1924), another book that emphasizes the simple racial division. The Negro is the provincial naïf who is violated in the corrupt and decadent city; he suffers shame, denigration, when he takes part in city life; he exercises a moral judgment upon what has lowered him.

The ships that carried hundreds of Americans to Paris in the twenties almost invariably had their complements of Negro jazz musicians; and Negro performers were the toast of the Parisian night clubs. But much of the sophisticate's attachment to jazz was just an excuse, a fashionable way of securing himself against monotony and boredom. Except for the genuine students of Negro jazz, intellectuals were likely to consider Paul Whiteman's sweetened, carefully orchestrated "white" jazz the real thing.[6]

Interest in jazz was part of the general interest in African culture and art, which André Gide and others helped to foster—Gide by his reports from North Africa and the Congo, anthropologists by their investigations of primitive cultures, and artists by their discovery of Negro sculpture. The lines and forms of African sculpture, the frankness and improvisation of original jazz music, the apparent naïveté and simplicity of Negro performers and Negro athletes captured the attention of Europeans curious about "native" American culture. For many of the Europeans especially, these evidences of a pre-industrial culture were a serious matter for study, a source of new forms and ideas in the arts. Generally, however, their interest took the lines of emphasizing simplicities against the complications of the world in which they were living. The usual evaluation was that *this* was something not white, that it was pre-civilized and therefore worthy of enthusiastic attachment.[7]

The study of Negro arts and societies (by Europeans, Americans abroad, and Americans who stayed at home), while it was not neces-

[6] Celebrities of American jazz made frequent tours of Europe: "The Original Dixieland Jazz Band" was in England in 1919 and 1921; Sidney Bechet came to Europe with a Negro revue in 1925 and toured Paris, Brussels, Berlin, and Moscow; Josephine Baker made her debut on this occasion. Paul Whiteman, who took his orchestra to England in 1926, was *not* received favorably there. His kind of music was quickly identified as a "white" sophistication of the original jazz music.

[7] Note the serious consideration shown jazz, as suggested in the following sampling of European titles: Ernest Ansermet, "On a Negro Orchestra," *Revue Romande* (October 1919); Marion Bauer, "L'Influence du 'Jazz-Band,' " *La Revue Musicale* (April 1924); M. Ladoche, "Musique Américaine," *Revue Politique et Littéraire* (June 5, 1926); Constant Lambert, "Jazz," *Life and Letters* (1928); Darius Milhaud, "Jazz Band and Negro Music," *Der Querschnitt* (Summer 1924); W. J. Turner, "Jazz Music," *New Statesman* (February 5, 1921). Among the books on the subject were titles by Clive Bell (in *Since Cezanne,* 1929), Stephen Chauvet (*La Musique Nègre,* 1929), Jean Cocteau (*Le Coq et l'Arlequin,* 1918). The most important French study was Hugues Panassié's *Le Jazz Hot* (1934; translated into English in 1936).

sarily associated with the problem of living in a machine age, nevertheless pointed up an almost obsessive concern of the decade. A phase of American culture and history (variously called Puritan, industrial, commercial) was repudiated and scorned; in its place, writers, artists, critics sought for aspects of the American scene that had (or were alleged to have) escaped involvement in the worst disasters of that culture. Since the Negro lived differently, seemed to have reserves of wisdom not available to the white consciousness, his life, art, and society were given special examination and praise. His was a free, uninhibited, un-mechanized soul, and his "dark laughter" provided an interesting commentary on the fretful, petty obsessions of the white man. Superficial as all this was,[8] it was definitely a part of the self-examination of the decade, the search for causes of social failure.

4. The Affair of Dayton, Tennessee

ONE OF the tasks assumed by the scientist was that of re-educating the public concerning the background of its beliefs. Most men were willing to accept the accomplished facts of their daily lives and were aware that, in the world of *things,* many remarkable changes had taken place. *Things* were the real proof of science's victory over the past. Robert A. Millikan, Nobel Professor of Physics, in an address to the New York Chamber of Commerce (November 1928), said of the relationship of pure science to industry that "the one is the child of the other. You may apply any blood-test you wish and you will at once establish the relationship. Pure science begat modern industry." The public was aware of that relationship, appreciative of it, and was ready to consider any argument that advised a comparable change in their religious and moral attitudes. Science enjoyed the distinction of having succeeded in a way that could be seen, touched, tasted, and experienced. The popular mind, therefore, pronounced science valid in view of its ever-present practical achievement. The usefulness of the motor, its capacity for accelerating the pace of life and for reducing distance

[8] Contrast the oversimplification of the Negro as exemplum in the work of Anderson and Frank with this brief but significant glimpse of the Negro mind in Faulkner's *The Sound and the Fury:* "They come into white people's lives like that in sudden sharp black trickles that isolate white facts for an instant in unarguable truth like under a microscope; the rest of the time just voices that laugh when you see nothing to laugh at, tears when no reason for tears."

to a minor inconvenience, made possible a life more complicated, open to a wider range of experience. And the advances in medical science produced the illusion of safety against illness and accident —in fact, made accident less hazardous and the risk of it easier to take.

In a world of uncertainties and half-certainties the awesome discipline, the monastic regimen, of the scientist gave the public a feeling of confidence almost like that inspired by the priest in an earlier time. Scientists were represented as a group of selfless workers; their discoveries were dramatized in the popular imagination as landmarks in the creation of a paradise of comfortable life, from which all fear of sickness, ugliness, and other forms of secular evil would at some time in the future be forever banished.

If we define a religion as the organization of truths and the strategy of dramatizing them in a way to enlist the interest, the devotion, and the energy of a people, it follows that the genuinely popular religion in America in the 1920s was the religion of practical consequences—in short, science as it was known through its results, multiplied by efficient industrial means, and distributed over the extensive reaches of a democratic population. There was no lack of men eager to spread the new gospel—in books, in pamphlets, in almost every newspaper and magazine published in the country. The difficult and the complex were made easy to distinguish and understand. People wanted information with a minimum interference of theory and abstraction. They were also impressed by the adventures of scientists—their selfless devotion to the cause of scientific proof, the dignity with which they assumed the role of laboratory pioneers.

The wish to know the details of scientific research was on the whole a healthy one; but for the most part it amounted to a desire for easy synthesis, a plausible substitute for the simplicity of the Sunday sermon, an interpretation of reality at once convincing and easy to grasp. Popularizers tried to extend the boundaries of folk metaphor, to relate the complex unknown to the simple and familiar. The common man developed a passion for fragments of information, held together quite loosely by attempts at harmless synthesis. The greater, though more hazardous, syntheses provided by religion were less respected—though custom prevented their being openly discarded—and in their place was an accumulation of fragments of new information gathered from scientific experiments and followed by halfhearted generalizations about their significance.

Most popular of the methods of imparting information was the "outline," which acted as a secular guide to a universe freed from the mystery of religion and the unknown of philosophy. The devotee of the outline "wants his learning not only condensed but quick," said Isaac Goldberg (*American Mercury,* June 1925). "No time for frills, for hesitant speculation, for adumbration. Give it to him in neat packages, in laws laid squarely down, in clear-cut outlines. Nor is this enough. He must be flattered in his conceit."

In 1927 David Starr Jordan published his indictment of the "get-wise-quick" schemes, *The Higher Foolishness;* he appealed for a reinstatement of the "plodding honesty of the scientific method." Robert Littell, speaking of the outline habit (*New Republic,* October 20, 1926), accused the public of defaulting in its serious responsibility to the scientific disciplines: "We are too lazy to rediscover the whole and too hungry to accept fragments," and are therefore gulled by all of the medicine men of the modern popularization racket. The outline habit was parodied by Donald Ogden Stewart, Robert Benchley, James Thurber, and E. B. White. Satirical portraits of the salesmen of popular knowledge abounded. John Riddell offered a parody of Will Durant's omnibus mind, accompanied by a Covarrubias caricature of Durant, a stained-glass window with the head of the master popularizer surrounded by dollar signs. Edmund Wilson (*New Republic,* October 27, 1926) published a mock review of an outline of science, claiming that "Mr. Doakes tells you in three minutes what it takes a scholar a lifetime to learn." In 1923 appeared a book called *The Outline of Everything,* to which was attached "A Critical Survey of the World's Knowledge by Sir J. Arthur Wellswater, with an Introduction by Hughe Jawpole." The master "outline" was of course H. G. Wells's *An Outline of History* (1920).

There were many men who saw the dangers of oversimplification and of presenting a fake picture of science. C. E. Ayres, in *Science, the False Messiah* (1927), deplored the public's habit of accepting the assurances of science with too much reverence. Science, said Ayres, has become "the object of our devout belief. It is the great constant, superstition, in another guise." We are attracted to it because we know it deals with the truth; but we have not been wise or curious enough to realize the precise limits of that truth. One of the worst consequences of this is that we are losing respect for religion, are condescending toward it, and saying with exasperating smugness that religious truths need only be verified and proved to be accepted. This misguided attitude confuses two specific and different kinds of truth-seeking and subordinates the one (religious truth) to the other (scientific truth). "What civilization needs is protection against every conceivable scientific theory," said Ayres, "a reconciliation between all possible religion and all possible science. Such a general reconciliation must be couched in very general terms—philosophical terms. It is likely also to result in a reconciliation so general, so philosophical, that, for those who succeed in making it at all, reconciliation becomes an end in itself, in which both science and religion have disappeared."

The scientists warned against the misapplication of their aims, insisted that the terms of their method ruled out a consideration of authority, and stated precisely the limits of their intention and of the usefulness of their results. But the popular reception of these results was so confused by an appreciation of tangible consequences that the public was only slightly interested in the limits and discipline of scientific method. The stage was therefore set for a struggle between those who read science out of the schools in an effort to protect the Bible and those who misread science as a conqueror of all superstition and religion.

Popularization of science—presenting it as an exaggerated world scheme and a guaranteed cure-all—gave the public an opportunity for easy belief, for shifting its belief from large intangibles to a great number of tangibles. It was ready, therefore, to accept the miraculous every day; the sole qualification for acceptance was that the miracle should *work*—that is, it should be demonstrably efficient. The proof was in the things that resulted: practical, useful, maneuverable symbols of the success of science.

This success, however, left large areas of the human disposition unaccounted for. Man had always believed in some kind of supernatural order; could he now discard all myths of the supernatural and be satisfied that science had made them unnecessary? In the history of science, the question remained a really vital one: to what extent can belief be explained or explained away by the scientific mind? A practical situation can be met, judged, and acted upon by reference to the truth or falsity of one's knowledge of it. We can assent to a judgment regarding common elements in the behavior of things. We can label a statement as "true" or "false," but our having done so will not inform us of our attitude toward any fact in any given complex of facts at any given time. If we assume all of nature, including ourselves, as something quite settled, or remaining to be settled, by the investigations of scientifically minded men, then we apparently have to give up a belief in the super-natural, to substitute for it a common understanding of the coherence of any fact within a system of other facts, omitting from our acceptance a personal attitude toward any of them.

The lines of opposition were drawn between what were known as the modernist and the fundamentalist camps. The modernist was generally assumed to be the enlightened one, the liberal, who, if he accepted the religious text at all, thought of it as "poetry" or "myth," neither of which should seriously interfere with the progress of enlightenment. Modernists were aware of strong opposition from the ranks of the "unenlightened clergy," who insisted on a literal interpretation of the Bible and resisted all the persuasions and arguments of their intelligent but heathenish opponents. The quarrel between modernism and fundamentalism had a long history before the 1920s, but during that decade it was highlighted by a series of bitter controversies climaxed by the Scopes trial in Dayton, Tennessee.

The Scopes trial took place in the summer of 1925. As a spectacle for the curious and as newspaper copy it excelled such other sensations of the decade as the Leopold-Loeb murder trial and Lindbergh's flight to Paris. It was the result of a bill passed by the Tennessee legislature, forbidding the teaching of any theory that denied "the story of the Divine creation of man as taught in the Bible" and that in any way suggested that "man has descended from a lower order of animals." Such a law was not a new event, not even a rare one. Nor was it unusual for a college to make its biology courses conform to fundamentalist ideas. Maynard Shipley, in his documentary *The War on Modern Science* (1927), cited numerous examples of similar restrictive action. Somewhat in the manner of H. L. Mencken's *Mercury,* Shipley relied on an accumulation of evidence derived from speeches in state legislatures and college chapels and from news clippings to make his case against the fundamentalists clear.

The fundamentalist objective, he warned, was "subjugation of our state and national governments, a virtual union of church and state under sectarian—fundamentalist—domination." The Ku Klux Klan, in alliance with fundamentalism, he said, wanted to set up a National Klan Church, which would eventually control the political life of the nation. The principles of fundamentalism, as Shipley gave them, were five:

1. The inerrancy and infallibility of the Bible.
2. The Virgin Birth and the complete Deity of Jesus Christ.

3. The resurrection of the same body of Jesus which was three days buried.
4. The substitutionary atonement of Jesus for the sins of the world.
5. The second coming of Jesus in bodily form, according to the Scriptures.

The "shame of Tennessee," Shipley said, had begun before the twentieth century with the dismissal of a professor of genetics from Vanderbilt University. The law under which Scopes was tried had been passed in 1920, with only eleven dissenting votes. Another bill, requiring all teachers employed by the state to "swear allegiance to the Divinity of Christ," had been defeated. Since the textbooks in use in state schools accepted evolution "as a recognized process of nature," four young teachers decided to make a test case. John T. Scopes, a biology teacher, agreed to teach the evolution theory and thereby give cause for indictment, in order to test the validity of the law. He was arrested on May 9, 1925, and tried from July 10 to 21 before Judge Raulston, a practicing evangelist. He was convicted and given the minimum fine of a hundred dollars.

These were the facts of the trial. But it was more than a mere violation case; it became a crisis in the struggle of modernists and liberals against fundamentalists, represented at the trial by Clarence Darrow on one side and William Jennings Bryan on the other. "Who won at Dayton?" asked C. E. Ayres (*New Republic,* May 12, 1926). In his opinion, the trial had proved that the "scientists" were far more friends of God and protectors of the faith than crusaders against fundamentalism. H. L. Mencken, industrious compiler of the aberrations of the average American citizen, presented what amounted to a defense of the Daytonians: "No principle is at stake save the principle that schoolteachers, like plumbers, should stick to the job that is set before them, and not go roving about the house, breaking windows, raiding the cellar, and demoralizing the children" (*Nation,* July 1, 1925).

Walter Lippmann offered a reasoned interpretation of the trial in *American Inquisitors: A Commentary on Dayton and Chicago* (1928). Men do not ordinarily prefer the privilege of speculation to the security of belief, he began; rather, they want ideas they can count on, sure cures, absolute promises. When a man accepts the limits of scientific thought, Lippmann argued, he has learned to live without the support of any creed.

Lippmann presented the issue in terms of a debate between modernist and fundamentalist. The fundamentalist begins by saying that mod-

ernism destroys the moral initiative of the young, who end by disbeliev-
ing the whole religion and morality of their fathers. Worst of all, the
modernist provides no incentive for moral decisions, to replace the
ones it has forced men to give up. Each young man and woman must
face "the temptations and the perplexities of the world with nothing
more than a tentative moral code, which he is at liberty to revise as he
sees fit."

Modernism pretends that man at every turn of events is capable of
choosing wisely for himself, without harm either to himself or to his
fellows. This is impossible, says the fundamentalist, because only a
very few men have been able to live "without supernatural sanction."
It is even less likely that the masses of men will be equipped intellec-
ually or psychologically to embrace what modernists call "the scientific
spirit," because that means "that men must learn to act with certainty
upon premises which are uncertain." The dangers of scientific training
are twofold: in the first place, it destroys respect for the religious doctrines that have been the single moral support of most men; second,
the training itself is fragmentary and presents at best a partial view. The
scraps of learning are morally worthless, and the result is chaos and
confusion.

Lippmann's hypothetical defendant of fundamentalism said quite
flatly that modernism had destroyed a genuine basis of belief with
scarcely a hope of offering man any equivalent of religion; that such a
change in belief happened gradually, if indeed it was possible at all;
finally, that one could not force people to choose uncertainty in preference to spiritual security. The moderns were floundering because they
had lost their sense of security; they should not be too disappointed if a
great number of people did not want to be like them.

5. Science, Poetry, and Belief

IN A SCIENTIFIC age, what role might literature serve? Perhaps it
could still be read "for enjoyment," or unemployed writers might
be assigned the task of polishing the prose of scientific treatises. But
poets would have to mend their ways; they were altogether too obscure,
too precious, too narrow in their attitude toward audience, and too
self-centered about their responsibilities to the public. At any rate,
these were the views of Max Eastman, in whose The Literary Mind:

Its Place in an Age of Science (1931) such advice and more was offered:

> Literature, then, as a thing distinct from science, may be a pure communication of experience; it may interpret experience in spheres as yet untouched by science; it may offer interpretations as intellectual things to be enjoyed without a tense regard to their validity. . . . To which we must add that in these spirited activities, serious and yet set free from the tether of verification, new ideas and suggestions of infinite value to science may be born.

Eastman's condescending program for unemployed writers was not an unusual one for a certain brand of critic—who, having thought all his lifetime that art had a serious function to perform, came to the conclusion that science was really taking better care of it, with the inevitable result that art would very soon be reduced to a less than minor role. It was the old theory of the bard, the poet as seer, in a new guise. And, after all, as Eastman's own excursions to the haunts of modern literature testified, writers were deliberately, wantonly evading their responsibilities. "They have abandoned meanings and at the same time ignored the strategy of communication, as though these two things were one and the same." So science is "pushing poetry out," upsetting its once proud role in the communication of human meaning. There is no doubt about it: "Poetry is compelled by its very nature to yield up to science the task of interpreting experience, of finding out what we call truth, of giving men reliable guidance in the conduct of their lives."

The role of literature in an age of science was posed and debated with varying seriousness and stridency. Against the contention that science was more accurate than poetry, critics urged an examination of the differences in range of discourse, in type of matter, in use of language. Against the confident assumption that science had fairly well settled most moral and religious issues and would shortly get round to verifying the rest, artists asserted their superiority in the matter of identifying and specifying the individual qualities of the aesthetic object. The suggestion that religion and art were somehow inferior readings of the human condition, since they could not be verified or proved, was not considered tenable by those who defended religion and practiced art.

The important questions debated in criticism were these: *Is* there a poetic as opposed to a scientific discourse? In what ways do they differ and what are their separate functions and knowledges? Is there an

ssociation between art and religion? In what ways does the problem of
belief enter into the creation and appreciation of art? Dominating
these, perhaps, was the major question of the certainties posed by
science itself: *Was* science as sure of itself as it sometimes appeared to
be? Could it afford to condescend, to reduce other interpretations and
valuations of experience to minor, negligible roles, or dismiss them as
either "superstitions," or as "intellectual things to be enjoyed without
a tense regard to their validity," as Eastman had put it?

I. A. Richards, a British psychologist who taught poetry at Cambridge University, addressed his attention to these questions; his *Principles of Literary Criticism* (1924), *Science and Poetry* (1926), and
Practical Criticism (1929) were essential documents in American
criticism of the decade; the second of these especially attended to the
question of the separate roles and fields of scientific and poetic discourse. Richards was, in this short book, disturbed by much the same
concerns as had caused Eastman to dismiss poetry as no longer of much
importance; but his consideration of the problem was less smug and
better informed. Science *had* made significant changes in our ideas, he
said; the way to adjust to them is not to discard but to re-examine our
ideas, beliefs, and tastes.

"How is our estimate of poetry going to be affected by science? And
how will poetry be influenced?" Richards replied by summarizing the
essential "findings" of his *Principles of Literary Criticism*. Literature
provides for "a state of readiness for action"; it "tests" and contributes
a pattern of experience, makes one more subtly "organized," capable
therefore of a richer and more complex experience. It is essential, of
course, that it be itself good literature, that it should not make appeals
to "stock responses" and thus merely postpone or destroy the possibility
of mature experiencing. In these respects literature has a role quite
distinct from science: science appeals to and commands the intelligence;
poetry appeals to man's "interests," to the constitution of his attitudes
and emotional dispositions:

> In its use of words poetry is just the reverse of science. Very definite
> thoughts do occur, but not because the words are chosen as logically
> to bar out all possibilities but one. No. But because the manner, the
> tone of voice, the cadence and the rhythm play upon our interests
> and make *them* pick out from among an indefinite number of possi-
> bilities the precise particular thought which they need.

The crucial task is to consider what poetry can do for the human
sensibility; the worst mistakes for man are that he not live fully, that

his experience be too narrow, or that he waste opportunities to organize his entire emotional and experiential nature. For this reason, the status of poetry (and especially its apparent loss of position) is of the utmost importance:

> The best kind of life then which we can wish for our friend will be one in which as much as possible of himself is engaged (as many of his impulses as possible). And this with as little conflict, as little mutual interference between different sub-systems of his activities as can be. . . . And if it is asked, what does such life feel like, how is it to live through? the answer is that it feels like and is the experience of poetry.

But the modern world has steadily removed major responsibilities and major subject matters from poetry. No longer can poets identify themselves with the "world of Spirits and Powers which control events"; the "Magical View" of the world has been replaced by the scientific. There is the serious danger that poetry, which "arose with this Magical View," will pass away with it. In its place we have the universe of the mathematician, the abstractions of the scientist, which cannot tell us anything about the nature of things in any *ultimate* sense. Science makes *statements* about man and his place in the universe; it depends for its success upon the verifiability of these statements. Poetry makes "pseudo-statements," "emotive utterance, where 'truth' is primarily acceptability by some attitude." It is not the poet's task to make true statements. In this way, by identifying truth with verification, Richards separates the discourses of science and poetry; the one to appeal to the intelligence, the other to affect feelings and attitudes.

The really serious problem emerges from the past history of pseudo-statement: poetry has in the past been linked with belief; but men no longer find it possible to accept these pseudo-statements as true (as verifiable):

> Countless pseudo-statements—about God, about the universe, about human nature, the relations of mind to mind, about the soul, its rank and destiny—pseudo-statements which are pivotal points in the organization of the mind, vital to its well-being, have suddenly become, for sincere, honest, and informed minds, impossible to believe. For centuries they have been believed; now they are gone, irrevocably; and the knowledge which has killed them is not of a kind upon which an equally firm organization of the mind can be based.

This is the crisis: man can no longer believe, but he desperately needs more than the gifts science offers him; he is not merely a physical being, and no amount of mechanical improvement in the externals of his life will compensate for the loss of belief. The solution, as Richards sees it, is to free pseudo-statements from belief, to acknowledge that the value of any attitude lies not in its attachment to a belief but in "its serviceableness to the whole personality," to believe that experience is its own justification. Degrees of value in poetry will therefore no longer depend upon their attachment to beliefs, but upon their success or failure in contributing to the mature organization of the personality.

Since science has proved that what was once believed is now no longer "true" (in the sense that it cannot be scientifically verified), belief can no longer in itself be a satisfactory means of governing our lives; we fall back upon the ordering of our personalities, and to this task poetry must address itself. Poets mislead themselves if they think they can defy science by inventing their own forms of order:

> Mr. De la Mare takes shelter in the dreamworld of the child. Mr. Yeats retires into black velvet curtains and the visions of the Hermetist, and Mr. Lawrence makes a magnificent attempt to reconstruct in himself the mentality of the Bushman.

One does not replace old beliefs by inventing new ones. It is necessary to think of a poetry that is independent of all beliefs.

Richards concludes on an almost hysterically earnest note:

> It is very probable that the Hindenburg Line to which the defence of our traditions retired as a result of the onslaughts of the last century will be blown up in the near future.

Poetry *can* "save us"; "it is a perfectly possible means of overcoming chaos." But this can happen only if man "can loosen in time the entanglement with belief which now takes from poetry half its power."

Much in the tone of this essay suggested a loss of confidence in poetry; the advantage of science was stressed to the point of its taking over everything of importance; such phrases as "pseudo-statement," however qualified, were disparaging and denigrating. Other critics refused to believe that science had so fully usurped all significant fields of knowledge, or had reduced the problem of truth to such an unbending criterion as "verifiability." They also suggested that scientists were not nearly so convinced of their reading of the universe as they were alleged to be. Further, they felt that frequently artists and critics who were dominated by "value systems" were as a result poor artists and imperceptive critics. The arts are *not* philosophy or sociology, and they should not pretend to be; *as* arts they may (and should) in their special ways communicate significant truths either ignored or disparaged by science. This conviction led to various definitions of the discourse of poetry; they were unanimous in concluding that the information given by poetry was different from that offered by science, in being more concrete, more accurate, more complex. The data of poetry were closer to the particulars of human experience and were therefore more pertinently moral.

The most vigorous attack upon science concerned the very issue Richards had raised, in discussing the loss of belief in what he called "pseudo-statements." Science not only disproved important myths; it did not permit the serious consideration of them, explaining them away as illusions and superstitions.[9] But the entertainment of myths, the act of "legislating Gods," was essential to the moral order. It did no good to say that man might have his Gods if he could not also sustain his belief in them. Scientists were themselves uncertain about their substitute explanations of matter and the universe; they had always hedged on the question of a "Force" or "Prime Mover," were embarrassedly concerned to "keep God in the universe" while stripping him of most of His powers. What *was* the scientific explanation of the universe? Was there a metaphysic to replace the myth of Creation and the biblical story? If all this was mere "literature" or the history of an unimportant people in Asia Minor, how could "the truth" satisfy man's wish to place himself within the earth's history? In the fields of practical affairs, science was brightly optimistic; but when it became a matter of providing a replacement for the metaphysic and myths it had encouraged men to discard, it was confused and contradictory.

The confusion was especially evident in the responses to Einstein's newly advanced theories; critics and artists both eagerly tried to take advantage of the "opening" these theories apparently offered. "Relativity" became a key word in discussions of individualism, of liberation from the prison of science. "We find in relativity a strange and literal confirmation of the egoistic assertion that man is the measure of all things," said one reviewer (*Freeman*, April 27, 1921). Claude Bragdon asked, "Are we on the point of discovering that the only reality is thought—consciousness?" The theory of relativity, he concluded, may well take the measure of things away from physics alto-

---

[9] Cf. Yeats: "Locke fell into a swoon, the garden died;/God took a spinning jenney out of his side."

gether and restore it to consciousness, "for the world-secret dwells not in the world, but in the self" (*Dial,* January 1920). J. W. N. Sullivan, commenting upon the popularizations of Einstein that had flooded the market, cautioned his readers: "There was never a time when hearty dogmatism and loud confidence were more out of place." All we can truthfully say at the present is "that the mind lives in a universe largely of its own creation, and that the universe, together with the mind, will change in ways we cannot foresee" (*Galileo, or the Tyranny of Science,* 1928).

Sullivan admitted that the "physical subjectivity" of the universe— its dependence upon individual measurement and calculations suitable to the terms of each event—might have its effect upon the attitudes of the artist and philosopher. "Professor Eddington has even hinted that these phenomena may indicate that the universe is finally irrational, that is, that the attempt to describe nature mathematically will have to be given up." This apparent disproof of the old physical laws of absolute space and time was, however, considered a declaration of independence from the tyranny of classical physics. What men did with such a declaration depended chiefly upon the point of view of each of them.

It was possible to consider Einstein's theory simply as an indication of the inadequacy of classical mathematics, or to assume that, as a result of it, physics and mathematics were both incompetent to describe and deal with what was fundamentally an irrational universe. The changes in physical theory might also be regarded as an act of "heroism" on the part of science. As Edmund Wilson suggested, science at the time might be considered "not abject, but, just at present, particularly heroic. . . . In the last century it was often literature which magnified humanity and almost invariably science which made us feel insignificant. Today, the situation seems reversed: it is science which restores us to importance and fiction and poetry which very often makes us feel like worms" (*New Republic,* January 26, 1927).

All these readings of relativity depended upon the use of the term *observer.* If we suggest that the observer is a subjective being whose will, and perhaps his whim, alters and dominates the description of nature—that he can make of it what he wishes—then, of course, the instruments and suppositions of science have to be discarded altogether. It was one of the fortunes of intellectual history that this became not only the popular notion but the general rationalization— the suggestion being that this latest lesson from science had thrown all absolutes into the discard, including moral absolutes. "There has been a tendency to give an extreme subjectivist interpretation to this new doctrine," said Whitehead (*Science and the Modern World*, 1926). "I mean that the relativity of space and time has been construed as though it were dependent on the choice of the observer, if he facilitates explanations. But it is the observer's body that we want and not his mind. Even his body is only useful as an example of a very familiar form of apparatus."

This caution was disregarded in all but severely scientific circles. The theory of relativity had freed us from notions of a fixed space and time; therefore we could exercise at will whatever new and arcanic interpretations of time we wished. Time was equated with spirit, with the subjective control of human consciousness over reality. The spirit of the time philosophers reached the level of mystic insights into the nature of reality. The "new dimension," governing the specific nature and value of the other three, was allied with human consciousness, and eventually with the unconscious, as that is portrayed in dreams.

The *Tertium Organum* of Ouspensky (first published in 1920 and translated into English in 1922) carried the mystic view of subjective time to its furthest extreme. "Ouspensky presents a new logic," said Claude Bragdon (Introduction to the 1922 edition), "or rather, he presents anew an ancient logic—the logic of intuition—removing at a stroke all of the nightmare aspects, the preposterous paradoxes of the new mathematics, which by reason of its extraordinary development has shattered the old logic, as a growing oak shatters the containing jar." Ouspensky maintained that the understanding of objects in space depends upon the conceptualizing power of the human mind. It is this which distinguishes us from the other animals, who have only a limited capacity for grasping the nature of objects. Three-dimensional vision is dependent upon "the properties of our psychic apparatus," but the mastery of the fourth dimension demands a still greater exercise of the human consciousness.

We are therefore right in being dissatisfied with the fumblings of the physical sciences, Ouspensky continued, "because science has really entered a *cul de sac* out of which there is no escape, and the official recognition of the fact that the direction it has taken is entirely the wrong one is only a question of time." Through the "higher consciousness" we are able to sense the spiritual nature of man, to assimilate and synthesize experience which, in a three-dimensional world, is merely a confusion of spatial and limited objects. We can exercise intuition where both perception and cognition fail. Our senses and our concepts "are too crude, for that fine differentiation of phenomena which must unfold itself to us in higher space." For these reasons the importance of science is rapidly diminishing, and the artist must henceforth take the scientist's place; for art "sees vastly more than the most perfect apparatus can discover; and it senses the infinite invisible facets of that crystal, one facet of which we call man." Beginning with the Kantian notion of the power of the mind to give shape to perceptions, Ouspensky proceeded to define the absolute control of the mind over nature through its "higher" power of intuition.

Ouspensky's was an extreme use of the opportunity modern science had afforded for extravagant valuations of the observer in the new physics. It amounted to the contention that science had disproved itself and had left the major task of reintegrating reality, which it had forfeited when it found its instruments inadequate, to the mystic and his entourage. One of the most important literary consequences of relativity was the interpretation of the "time sense" in terms of human consciousness. Once instruments seemed inadequate to the task of measuring reality, it could be proved that measurement was in itself a mistaken and overly simple device of comprehending it. The "time sense," which amounted to an intuition of flux, was then the only hope one had of going beyond the certainties of measurable, three-dimensional things and uniting them in a "higher space." [10]

[10] Such a critic as Wyndham Lewis asserted (in *Time and Western Man*, 1927) that the consequence of Einstein's theory of relativity was nothing less than disastrous. Einstein and Bergson have combined, Lewis said, to ruin the hope of an ordered and comprehensible world. Lewis feared a philosophy of fluid concepts subject to the vagaries and intuitions of whatever quacks might set themselves up as sages and seers. Most of all, he saw in this philosophy the death of art as "the civilized *substitute* for magic" and the revival of a "time-saturated" aesthetic that will "lead us down and back to the plane of magic, or of mystical, specifically religious experience." Instead of the classical reliance upon the capacity of the mind for order, the theories of Einstein and Bergson, and the extension of them by Whitehead, threaten to wave a magic wand over dead matter, give souls to things, and ultimately force upon the human mind a universe over which he can exercise no control other than a kind of sympathy or "spiritual agreement." In Lewis's opinion, the writing of Proust and Joyce had already demonstrated the disastrous effects of this change of view. For neither of them, he maintained, is the serious problem of aesthetic form—that is, the realization in the mind of orderly process, intelligent and intelligible—a major consideration. Joyce's *Ulysses* is flooded by the "einsteinian flux," and it shows equally the influence of Bergson and of the psychology of "that old magician, Sigmund Freud." This is the danger Lewis sees in the consequences of Einstein's discoveries: the "purely

Einstein's theory of relativity, as it was presented in popularizations at one level of understanding or another, impressed the experimentalists as somehow important for their revisions in the space-time continuum, which had been the basis for traditional fiction. But there was no genuine attempt to write an "Einsteinian" novel. The theory was taken up quite superficially, made an easy device for the shifting of scene, as in some of the novels of H. G. Wells and J. B. Priestley, and in general used as an additional justification for what had already been established in experimental writing.

Though there was no writing in the twenties that directly attempted to exploit the suggestions made in the theory of relativity, a great amount of experimental writing can be explained in part by reference to it. By transferring the theory from the spheres of mathematics and physics to the world of "subjective relativity," it was possible to add it to the several other philosophical and psychological revisions made in twentieth-century attitudes toward the nature of reality. Freud's analysis of the unconscious—particularly of its "logic" and physical nature—Bergson's theory of *durée* and his description of the nature of memory, Whitehead's explanation of reality in terms of space-time "events," and Nietzsche's pioneering work in the study of subconscious motive—all contributed to a new psychological attitude toward the material and form of art. They combined with Einstein's theory of the relativity of space-time conceptions and measurements to contribute (quite often by an unusual reading of what these men had actually said) to an aesthetic of disintegration, in which space and time were made dependent upon the psychic disposition of a personality rather than assumed as stage properties.

The really opportunist exploitation of Einstein, however, came in the popular skepticism about all human knowledge—what Herbert Muller has called "the cocktail chatter about relativity and uncertainty," which assumed that the revolution in modern science had really amounted to suicide. The theory of relativity, to quote Muller once more, "does not limit these relations to our *consciousness,* make them a purely subjective affair; it refers them to the velocity of the physical system we inhabit, makes them still more objective" (*Science and Criticism,* 1943). The incautious reading of relativity acknowl-

---

physical theory of Einstein" has given us such a radical change in our view of matter that even though "it sets out to banish the mental factor altogether and to arrive at a purely physical truth, it nevertheless cannot prevent itself turning into a psychological or spiritual account of things, like Bergson's."

edged only an admission of defeat and impotence, a signal that science was no longer able to hold the human personality in bondage or to inform us, without the extensive assistance of religion and art, about reality and its laws.

In 1929 Archibald MacLeish published the poem "Einstein," in which he used Einstein as the symbol of the self-defeating speculations of modern science. The burden of the poem is that science in its final incarnation has left us a hopeless and uncertain world. The figure of Einstein also symbolizes the attitude that a man who has accepted his theory must have toward the universe—an attitude of pathetic and futile defiance:

> But it seems assured he ends
> Precisely at his shoes in proof whereof
> He can revolve in orbits opposite
> The orbit of the earth and so refuse
> All planetary converse.

The lone figure, "provisionally before a mirror," examines the world as subjectively contained:

> Decorticate
> The petals of the enfolding world and leave
> A world in reason which is in himself
> And has his own dimensions.

He cannot grasp or understand the *qualities* of things, so familiar to the eye and ear of the poet. For "there is no speech that can resolve/ Their texture to clear thought and enter them." They resist his attempts to control them, and he tries then to "Break them to reason."

> He lies upon his bed
> Exerting on Arcturus and the moon
> Forces proportional inversely to
> The squares of their remoteness and conceives
> The universe.

He will reduce events to atoms, remove the incomprehensible qualities from them: "If they will not speak/Let them be silent in their particles." With his mind he "relaxes the stiff forms/Of all he sees . . ." until all things "Sweep ever into movement and dissolve/All differences in the indifferent flux!"

This solitary figure of the scientist is the end result of modern physical theory. The scientist has control of the universe, but all of its parts, its qualities, must be reduced to abstractions his mind can understand and receive. In his effort to comprehend them, he eliminates from each its individual quality, and he destroys "All differences in the indifferent flux!"

Repercussions of the Scopes affair in many ways highlighted the rebellion against scientific confidence; it involved, in various readings of its meaning, the significant role of religion, the viability of the religious myth, and, by implication, the role of both the artist and the theologian in crediting the value of "objects" mundane and biblical. No book sums up so thoroughly the issues contained in the controversy between science and religion over control of the "precious object" as John Crowe Ransom's *God Without Thunder* (1930). In his dedicatory letter to Sidney Hirsch, Ransom identified himself as "the son of a theologian and the grandson of another," and ranged himself on the side of the fundamentalists. Modernism was, he said, "a comparatively poor kind of religion"; it was *"Hamlet* without the Prince of Denmark."

God Without Thunder offered a number of perspectives on the problems of science and belief; it was at once a "fundamentalist," an "Agrarian," and a "new critical" document. Its primary objective was to prove that scientific discourse was empty of significant truth, that scientists were egregiously and unjustifiedly self-confident, that the myth of God or gods to superintend the moral universe was indispensable, and that the modernist God was a pallid substitute for the God of the Old Testament, allowed to exist only on sufferance. The "orthodox" faith is the religion of the Old Testament; in the history of Christianity it has gradually been lost. Even the Christ of the New Testament, who had announced his intentions with a most gratifying humility, had had his message and his meaning distorted. The "old God" was mysterious, but the modernists have simplified and "clarified" him; he was worshiped according to certain ritual patterns, but advocates of the "new God" consider such ritual trivial and childish. The "old God" was "the author of evil as well as of good," but the modernists prefer a God wholly benevolent:

> They will do nothing about [evil]. They will pretend that it is not there. They are not necessarily Christian Scientists in the technical sense, for they do acknowledge some evil, of a kind which is now or prospectively curable by the secular sciences. . . . They represent evil in general as a temporary incidental, negligible, and slightly uncomfortable phenomenon, which hardly deserves an entry in the theological ledger. They have no God for it.

The major issue is the refusal of science to accept myth. Since all religion and theology may upon examination be proved "mythical" and therefore fictional ("lies"), science leads to the discrediting of a significant body of human thought and belief. This is an unfortunate result of intellectual arrogance and shortsightedness; for if scientific assertions are examined closely they also prove to have their myths. They are myths of an abstracting imagination, but they are no less "fabulous" than the myths of religion. To the mind of man these myths are essential:

> The myth of an object is its proper name, private, unique, untranslatable, overflowing, of a demonic energy that cannot be reduced to the poverty of the class-concept. The myth of an event is a story, which invests the natural with a supernatural background, and with a more-than-historical history.

Myths are not available to proof, but they fulfill a role in satisfying man's need to believe in a supernatural sanction and governance of "the natural." But they must be "appropriate": the God at their center must be strong; the myth must vividly dramatize His moral universe; it must be in keeping with our taste; it must "be institutionalized, or become a social possession." The acceptance of a myth with a God at its center is an act both aesthetic and practical. The man who enacts a myth ("legislates a God" from Principles) is giving vigorous concrete detail to abstract law and thus enforcing his adherence to Principle. It is an act of the imagination, which strengthens the rational admission of moral law by concretely dramatizing it and retaining it within a context of imaginative and cogent particulars.

The value of this activity is not that of mere play-acting, or entertaining the tired scientist when he wishes to relax from "the tense regard for validity." Ransom firmly subscribes to the conviction that the arts and religion are essential for the creation of codes, rituals, forms; through them a natural scientific lust for objects may be postponed, and the objects themselves enriched in value through the postponement:

> Religion is an order of experience under which we indulge the compound attitude of fear, respect, enjoyment, and love for the external nature in the midst of which we are forced to live. . . . Science is an order of experience in which we mutilate and prey upon nature; we seek our practical objectives at any cost, and always at the cost of not appreciating the setting from which we have to take them.

If we look closely at one of Ransom's remarks, we may see that the myth-making tendency of religion has an aesthetic advantage: "Love is the esthetic and lust is the science of sex." Lust is an incentive for the "efficient" satisfaction of the sex desire; love, however, sets its standards, formulates its "manners" with respect to its object. In making the object of desire a "precious object," accessible only through *forms* of attention and desire, love becomes a religious attention to it, desiring it but sensitive to the complex formal order of courtship. Man is both a creature of instincts and a creator of formal codes; science has stressed only instinctive man, and religion and art have as their task to restore formality to the drama of his behavior. "Culture consists essentially in having and defending a delicate sensibility even while we are engaged upon the stern drive of the practical life."

All this has an important bearing upon the question of available knowledge. Ransom would restore to us the privilege of contemplating precious objects. Although science has occupied itself with exact comparisons and measurements, it cannot give us an adequate knowledge of the concrete thing. Science defines the truth, and it is truth of a kind, but it is not the whole truth. And this is the basic difference between poetry (as well as religion) and science. We can understand an object by defining it scientifically, but in doing so we leave out much that is in the object and its intimate relations to other objects; even these relations, when scientifically measured, are not the whole truth. The talent for looking beyond definition is the aesthetic gift.

If we consider, therefore, the range of abstraction science has introduced into life, the effect on religion may be clearly seen: it is an extension of the scientific tendency to reduce objects to measurable dimensions. God is no longer a concrete or a precious object; myths are no longer morally useful; belief is reduced to the mere acceptance of abstract principle. But if the desire for belief is not satisfied by the suggestion that science and religion are working in partnership, that our God is a God of natural law progressively defined and clarified by science, then one major incentive for moral action has been destroyed. Ransom concludes by offering a program for the restoration of orthodoxy: "Let [modern man] insist on a virile and concrete God, and accept no Principle as a substitute"; in short, "Let him restore to God the thunder."

Whatever the distortions evident in this and other attacks upon scientific confidence, it brilliantly summarized a genuine and urgent need. Throughout the decade writers struggled with problems created by the scientific reading of man and universe. The dreadful suggestion that science, having long since reduced man's significance in the universe, was now in the process of destroying God as well (or weakening Him and making Him all but morally useless) forced them to one of several strategies: they had to find the kind of "glory" that Russell recommended in courageously accepting the universe as science had revealed it; they had to take advantage of every loss of scientific confidence; they had to hold firmly to a fundamentalist position, with such defenses of religion and myth as Ransom provided; or they had to distinguish between scientific and aesthetic orders of perception, either to destroy the confidence in the scientific or to restore the aesthetic to the level of useful supplementary knowledge. The tragedy for many of these men and women was that there could scarcely be a tragic or heroic act without a structure of myth and an acceptable mode of belief within it. This was a genuine dilemma; symbolically it might be considered the condition of a spiritual waste land. The agony of a spiritual quest in a world that regarded spiritual matters with indifference was one of the most profound emotional experiences of the 1920s.

6. The Text: T. S. Eliot's *The Waste Land*

The Waste Land [11] contains a single unified metaphor, variously given and dramatically developed. It can be seen in at least two realizations: the fable of the land itself (and of its King); the situation of love in its profane, sacred, and mystic forms. [12] These are unified in terms of analogies involving the cultural and personal meanings of fertility. The fertility of the land has been directly associated many times with both religious and sexual rites; in the legends of the Fisher King, the King and his land suffer analogous wounds, which make fertility impossible. There are gradations in the dramatic treatment of love: lust,

[11] Published in the English *Criterion*, October 1922; in the American *Dial*, November 1922; and in the same year by the New York publishers Boni and Liveright.

[12] Discussions of Eliot's indebtedness to Jessie Weston's *From Ritual to Romance* (1920) and to J. G. Frazer's *The Golden Bough* (1890 to 1915) are so abundant that I have not made more than a few references to it. See Eliot's "head note" to *The Waste Land;* Cleanth Brooks, in Leonard Unger (ed.), *T. S. Eliot: A Selected Critique* (1948). For a detailed explanation of the allusions in the poem, see Kimon Friar and J. M. Brinnin, *Modern Poetry* (1951).

indifference, perverted love, the love of man for woman, divine love; these are associated throughout with religious legends, ceremonials, rites, so that we can assume an identity of love with *faith,* or *belief.* A failure of love is a failure of belief; the struggle for a meaningful sexual experience is identical with the search for a satisfactory religious experience. The major images of these spiritual-physical analogies are fire and water: the lack of water is the physical characteristic of spiritual loss; it is fire in the sense that living things cannot survive because of it. But there are two kinds of water, as there are two kinds of fire: water as the source of the land's recovery or of the seasonal resumption of its fertility, and water as the source and place of death, inspiring a fear in the protagonist that haunts him throughout the first three sections of the poem; fire as a sterile burning lust, and fire as a means of purification.

These elementary matters comprise the underlying meaning of *The Waste Land;* they provide a kind of thematic security as the poem advances through many mutations of particular reference. Eliot has brought to them a great number of variations: allusive, topical, dramatic, and lyrical. The texture of allusion is especially fine and complex; in some ways an allusion becomes a shorthand reference to an entire body of literature, or to an entire work, or to a situation available in many literatures and religions. A single word or phrase, a line adapted from another work or directly borrowed from it; the rhythms of another work either imitated or parodied to meet his specific needs. Consequently *The Waste Land* becomes a universal metaphor, not confined to specific locales or personalities but relevant wherever or whenever its condition obtains. The thought of the poem is never abstract but concretely or dramatically contained within a poetic substance. *The Waste Land,* therefore, is the acting out, the concrete bodying forth, of a human and cultural situation to be discovered in many forms in human history and legend. It is modern only in the sense that the poem is written with its modern coordinates present (as well as in the ways in which it was accepted by readers and reviewers as a version of the modern condition).

Since the land has been laid waste, the conventional, legendary references to fertility and to the promise of it inspire fear rather than hope (Part I, "The Burial of the Dead"); life and the beginnings of new life are fearful things, and the season that breaks from the "security" of death reminds us cruelly that the cycle of living is to resume. The great relevance of the opening lines is to this reversal of the ordinary ritual emotion: April, the beginning of spring, is "the cruellest month" because it forces life where death had been and where it had been preferred to life. The great majority of religious rites convey and encourage the opposite emotion—the Easter season, the fertility rites, the celebrations of renewed life. In *The Waste Land* these rites are introduced to individualize the fear, the wish to remain free of the complications of life, the "living death" that has stricken all who inhabit the land; "roots that clutch," branches that grow "Out of this stony rubbish," are a frightening anomaly. Here there is only "A heap of broken images," a chaos of life destroyed, meaning shattered. Over all the sun beats, no longer a source of life but, without water, a relentless destroyer of it. This is the setting of certain sections of the Old Testament; it is also one of the settings of the *Inferno*. Fear is imaged in "a handful of dust."

Dramatically *The Waste Land* identifies its general circumstance in terms of a failure of great love, of sexual communion and spiritual communication. The protagonist of the waste land can neither accept the "gift" of the woman nor face the "light" of divine love. Immediately following the description of the waste land there is a garden scene. The hyacinth flowers, the images of love and beauty, are all invitations to share a great love; but the invitation is not accepted; the protagonist cannot respond:

> . . . I could not
> Speak, and my eyes failed, I was neither
> Living nor dead, and I knew nothing,
> Looking into the heart of light, the silence.

This initial failure is a paradigm of the essential failure of physical and spiritual communication throughout the poem. The circumstances leading to the failure form a large part of the poem's texture. For one, in all religious interpretations love has been identified with faith, with belief. The woman of the waste land is for a moment a "blessèd lady," a reminder of the Virgin, of Dante's Beatrice; but the scene fades, with the commentary from *Tristan und Isolde:* "Vast and empty is the sea."

The waste land also has its reminders of religious messengers, oracles; these too have lost much of their power and insight. That Eliot should have introduced the substance of the poem through such a figure as Madame Sosostris, who "Had a bad cold, nevertheless/Is known to be the wisest woman in Europe," is a clear indication of the reduction in religious significance of these religious functionaries.

Through her "wicked pack of cards" (the Tarot pack), the *personae* of the poem are given, the "you" and "I" of the hyacinth passage are individualized. The "drowned Phoenician Sailor" signifies the efforts toward deliverance in the poem, efforts that will fail because Madame Sosostris' advice is to "Fear death by water," not to welcome it as an essential sacrifice. "Belladonna, the Lady of the Rocks,/The lady of situations," represents the several forms the woman of the waste land takes: in each case her role is a perversion of love, a deadening of the spirit; she is a poison; she is not the Lady of "Dry Salvages" but the Lady who will draw men on to their destruction; she is the lady not of great loves but merely of "situations," aimless routine affairs. The "man with the three staves" is the Fisher King himself, whose three "staves" of Part V are the poem's major religious and moral directive. The "one-eyed merchant" appears later in Mr. Eugenides. The "Hanged Man" cannot be seen, as the crucified Man was not recognized on the way to Emmaus; His sacrifice cannot be recognized in the waste land.

To complete the reading of the cards, Madame Sosostris says, "I see crowds of people, walking round in a ring." They are the inhabitants of the waste land, and in the next passage the protagonist views them in the context of an "Unreal City," specifically London but also Baudelaire's *fourmillante cité* and that "city" of lost souls, the Limbo of Dante's *Inferno*. It is necessary to appreciate that, in Eliot's specifying of *personae* in the poem, all persons are one person and all details are integral parts of one situation. The "I" is both an observer of these "crowds" and a member; he is both victim and participant.[13] He quite understandably recognizes one among the crowd—that is, he identifies and names himself: "There I saw one I knew, and stopped him, crying:/ 'Stetson!' " Which is to say, "Everyman," the crowd named but still not individualized, singled out momentarily from the crowd so that its situation can be defined and discussed in individual terms. Stetson is not only one of the crowd that "flowed over London Bridge" and one of those "many" whom "death had undone"; he is also one of those who fought in the Punic Wars ("You who were with me in the ships at Mylae!").

[13] This form of identification is also present in other Eliot poems; perhaps the primary distinction is that the protagonist is singled out from the mass as a man *aware,* however dimly, of the situation of which the others, "Assured of certain certainties," cannot become aware. Their failure of awareness is the blight of which the protagonist is aware.

Part I concludes, as it begins, with an expression of fear at the threat of life renewed; the single advance is that the fear is now expressed dramatically, in terms of a *persona* addressing another *persona* (both of whom are at once identical and individualized). The protagonist asks if the god who had been buried has now begun to encourage the land to bring forth life; he fears that it might have done so. He begs that the Dog "that's friend to men" be kept from digging up the corpse, hastening the process of renewal. Stetson merges finally not only with the crowd out of which he had been specified, but also with the reader himself, who is a part of the waste land too: "You! hypocrite lecteur!— mon semblable,—mon frère!"

Ironically the "Burial of the Dead" is presented in two forms: of the god symbolically "planted" to insure a renewal of fertility; of the death of the waste land itself, from which the protagonist fears to rescue it because he can do so only at the cost of a heroic realization and sacrifice. These ambiguities, so brilliantly imaged and dramatized in Part I, are an essential texture of the waste-land generalization. They stress the inhibiting and defeating fears that paralyze the will to deliver the land from its death. A major dramatic signification of that failure is, of course, the sexual failure, which is given expression in several waste-land scenes.

Not the least of these is found in Part II, "A Game of Chess." There are several indications of this defeat of love; sexual "play" has declined to the level of a "good time," or a routine place on the daily calendar of engagements, or "a game of chess." The opening lines of Part II are rich reminders of the past: Cleopatra, who gave "all for love"; Dido, whose grief over losing her loved one caused her to destroy herself. The voluptuous setting of the first scene is offered in poetry rich in sensuous and sensual qualities; but these are confined, part of a room, and almost immediately suggest a decadence of great love rather than the full emotion itself. This claustrophobia is precisely indicated in the listing of cosmetics:

> In vials of ivory and coloured glass
> Unstoppered, lurked her strange synthetic perfumes,
> Unguent, powdered, or liquid—troubled, confused
> And drowned the sense in odours; . . .

The "glitter" and the "rich profusion" are after all "synthetic," and the richness troubles and confuses rather than enhances the scene. The emotion of love is overcome by a "rich profusion" of sensuous effects, which distract from the object, drawing attention only to themselves. Among them is the carving of a scene from Ovid, the myth of Tereus and Philomela; and in this myth the transition from the rich suggestiveness of the past to the present is given. Every effect in the passage contributes to the change: the rhythm of the lines breaks; the language changes to indicate brutality and rape; the tense shifts from past to present (with past contained in present and united by the two verbs "cried" and "pursues").

We are now in the unrelieved waste-land present, and the woman no longer reminds us of Cleopatra but resumes her role as the "lady of situations," speaking out in neurotic tones to the protagonist, who cannot (for fear and dread of his dimly sensed "mission") answer her. The gift offered in the hyacinth garden is hysterically pressed upon him; she senses his fear and shares it, aware that he is incapable of rescuing them from it:

> "What is that noise?"
> The wind under the door.
> "What is that noise now? What is the wind doing?"
> Nothing again nothing.
> "Do
> "You know nothing? Do you see nothing? Do you remember
> "Nothing?"

He remembers only the echo of the warning given him by Madame Sosostris, the line from *The Tempest* ("Those are pearls that were his eyes"), which recalls a death by water. It is "that Shakespeherian Rag," a designation which reminds one again that the tempo of Part II is syncopated throughout; this part of the poem is a poetic representation of neurasthenia. Since the protagonist "knows" nothing, "sees" nothing, has nothing in his head, there is nothing to do except to follow the routine, mechanic gestures of a life that, deprived of meaning, is a living death:

> The hot water at ten.
> And if it rains, a closed car at four.
> And we shall play a game of chess,
> Pressing lidless eyes and waiting for a knock upon the door.

The "knock" is a signal for a change of scene—or, rather, a melting of one scene into another; for substantially the situations are identical, the despair is fully as great and comes from the same causes. The second scene is a London pub, near closing time, the barman setting the limits of the "good time" ("HURRY UP PLEASE ITS TIME"). This is a "Sweeney" world; the lines are written in a rapid, gossipy, colloquial tone. A woman rattles on to her companion about her friend Lil, whose husband has just "got demobbed." Lil, worn out with childbearing, has taken the money her husband gave her "To get yourself some teeth" and bought pills to prevent another birth. The comment upon this act is put with colloquial abruptness: "What you get married for if you don't want children?" The gathering is broken up by the barman, who rushes them out into the street, where they exchange perfunctory good nights, which lead finally to the ironic farewell of Ophelia: "Good night, ladies, good night, sweet ladies, good/night, good night."

The two scenes together portray the defeat of love in all situations, whatever the particulars of setting or allusion: both Cleopatra and Dido failed to win their lovers; the woman of the waste land cannot break through the fears of her companion to arrange a union more meaningful than "a closed car at four" would suggest; and Lil, overcome by the pointless biological insistencies of her body, refuses to permit another life to come from it. Frustration, neurosis, abortion: these are the variations upon the "game of chess." Because religious incentive is lacking, belief fails of a divine purpose, love has no real opportunity for issuing either in a meaningful sexual relationship or in life itself. The full terror of this situation is presented in terms of a dramatic analogy of faith and love—given a concrete, social, human meaning.

It is a text for a sermon, and Part III is that sermon, drawing upon many texts and offering many exempla. The sexual failure of Part II is greatly expanded in detail of setting and incident; the metaphorical association with the failure of belief is clearly given; the protagonist is presented in a number of *personae,* associated through allusion and concrete incident with the plight of the land itself. Nowhere in modern poetry is there a comparably brilliant shifting of scene and reference, though the line of development remains clear and sharply relevant.

The opening lines of "The Fire Sermon" introduce the Thames maidens in a melancholy scene, which yet recalls the wedding hymn of Spenser's "Prothalamion." The river itself—a source of life, as the legends investing the history of the Nile testify—is seen in the last days of fall, but it is also the "dull canal" of the waste land:

> The river's tent is broken: the last fingers of leaf
> Clutch and sink into the wet bank. The wind
> Crosses the brown land, unheard.

From this scene "The nymphs are departed"; no tokens of their loves are left:

> The river bears no empty bottles, sandwich papers,
> Silk handkerchiefs, cardboard boxes, cigarette ends
> Or other testimony of summer nights.

But, in the role of "nymphs" preparing the way for blessed ceremonial, they have never actually been there at all. They are companions in spiritless affairs with "the loitering heirs of city directors" who "have left no addresses." Love is not love if it cannot be identified with "addresses," with the circumstances of home, the responsibilities of a human continuity; it is only an "incident," something quickly indulged in and forgotten, a source of boredom.[14] In this setting the protagonist sits down to weep; he is an exile in his own land, now become a strange land. Around him are reminders of the terror:

> The rattle of the bones, and chuckle spread from ear to ear.
> A rat crept softly through the vegetation
> Dragging its slimy belly on the bank.

In his mind are vague memories of the past, echoes of the Ferdinand to whom Ariel's song was addressed; but these are violated by the vision of death and decay associated with the waste land.

It is important to see that the "Grail Knight," suggested from time to time in this poem (especially in Eliot's notes), is never really free to contemplate the task of deliverance; he is forever haunted by

> White bodies naked on the low damp ground
> And bones cast in a little low dry garret,
> Rattled by the rat's foot only, year to year.

He is therefore quite incapable of heeding the echoes of another world, of giving them another meaning; every suggestion of a placid, fruitful, credible, and divinely sanctioned world is canceled by the reductive terror that intrudes upon his thoughts. The textural irony of the lines plays with a remarkable grace upon these terrible ambiguities of the human spirit: the "sound of horns" becomes the sound of "motors, which shall bring/Sweeney to Mrs. Porter in the spring"; the ritual

[14] Cf. Eliot's remarks in his essay "Baudelaire" (1930): "Having an imperfect, vague romantic conception of Good, he was at least able to understand that the sexual act as evil is more dignified, less boring, than as the natural, 'life-giving,' cheery automatism of the modern world. For Baudelaire, sexual operation is at least something not analogous to Kruschen Salts." (*Selected Essays, 1917–1932.*)

washing of the feet (part of the New Testament story and of the Grail legend) becomes an accompaniment to Sweeney's affair with one of Mrs. Porter's prostitute "daughters"; the song of children singing in the chapel (of Verlaine's *Parsifal*) becomes a reminder of the myth of Philomela, sounding "in dirty ears."

These "defeated echoes" bring the protagonist back to the vision of the "Unreal City" in which (in Part I) the waste-land situation was first specified. Here, "Under the brown fog of a winter noon," he meets another waste-land figure, who, like Madame Sosostris, is a degeneration of ancient religious ritual: "Mr. Eugenides, the Smyrna merchant/ Unshaven, with a pocket full of currants," who suggests a homosexual affair, "luncheon at the Cannon Street Hotel/Followed by a weekend at the Metropole." As he is a decadent member of a religious cult, so his proposal is a perversion of the sex with which religious grace is analogically identified.

His offer is succeeded by the most fully developed of all the exempla in "The Fire Sermon": the affair of the typist and "the young man carbuncular," which is superintended, though not controlled, by the figure of Tiresias, who combines all the *personae* of the waste land, male and female:

> I Tiresias, though blind, throbbing between two lives,
> Old man with wrinkled female breasts . . .

The dread pathos of the scene is texturally enriched by an ironic play of meanings and allusions: the evening hour is "the violet hour" (the hour of prayer and of homecoming), but it is also the hour "when the human engine waits/Like a taxi throbbing waiting"; [15] the typist, home, prepares her meal ("lays out food in tins"), while "Out of the window perilously spread/Her drying combinations touched by the sun's last rays"; her "divan" is a daybed bought at Selfridge's or Macy's, and on it no great romantic triumphs will be won; she awaits the "expected guest," who turns out to be

> A small house agent's clerk, with one bold stare,
> One of the low on whom assurance sits
> As a silk hat on a Bradford millionaire.

[15] Cf. Eliot's "Preludes," IV:

> His soul stretched tight across the skies
> That fade behind a city block,
> Or trampled by insistent feet
> At four and five and six o'clock; . . .

The seduction is played out in an atmosphere empty of all genuine meaning or feeling; even the rhetoric and the rhythms are a mockery of serious logical form; there is a false, ironic formality of language. His "endeavours" to "engage her in caresses," though "undesired," are "unreproved." He does not make of her a "precious object" to whom he might address a formal ritual appeal, but "Flushed and decided, he assaults at once." He is not opposed, he is not wanted; and the affair is consummated in the most indifferent terms. In the end he "Bestows one final patronising kiss,/And gropes his way, finding the stairs unlit." For her part, she "allows one half-formed thought to pass:/'Well now that's done: and I'm glad it's over.' " This terrible scene of absolute indifference, foreseen by Tiresias, concludes with her "automatic" gesture: "She smoothes her hair with automatic hand,/And puts a record on the gramophone."

No act could more definitively underscore the mechanical, routine nature of the seduction. It is the "Shakespeherian rag" reduced to its naturalistic extreme. And, as the protagonist hears "This music," there is no doubt about the meaning of the songs that follow; they are the songs of the Thames maidens, who have been violated, destroyed, their love reduced to a casual assault. Prefacing these songs is another glimpse of a failure of love—that of Elizabeth and Leicester, the luxury of whose life does not conceal the emptiness of their passion. "The Fire Sermon" concludes with a play upon the two meanings of fire:

> To Carthage then I came
> Burning burning burning burning
> O Lord thou pluckest me out
> O Lord thou pluckest . . .[16]

As everywhere else in *The Waste Land,* these references are to a religious state of sacrifice and purgation, which has not been achieved and will not be achieved in the waste land itself. This failure is again dramatically revealed in Part IV, "Death by Water." If we recall the insistent refrain in the protagonist's mind, "Fear death by water," and realize with what terror he contemplates the warning, Part IV can be understood as death from insufficient cause. The "deliverer" surrenders his body to the water; this is no heroic act of sacrifice, but a death such as comes to all of us.

[16] See Eliot's "Notes." The first line is from St. Augustine's *Confessions:* "to Carthage then I came, where a cauldron of unholy loves sang all about mine ears." The last three lines are from Buddha's Fire Sermon.

Gentile or Jew
O you who turn the wheel and look to windward,
Consider Phlebas, who was once handsome and tall as you.

The last section of *The Waste Land,* "What the Thunder Said,"
must be viewed as a series of culminating reflections. The setting has
not changed; its details are merely intensified. The Fisher King, alone
and moving toward a degenerated "Chapel Perilous" through an ultimate chaos, receives the "message" of the thunder and reflects upon
its meaning for himself. The protagonist has now reached the final
stage of his awareness; he is fully conscious of the distraught circumstance, and for the first time he considers a decision with respect to it.

Part V is full of the reminders of physical and spiritual dying; it is
a complex pattern of the forms of dying: the death of Jesus, the living
death of those who have failed to recognize its meaning, the spiritual
meaning of life as a preparation for dying. The loss, the desperate
need, of faith, is expressed in the most brilliant of expressive passages,
utilizing the images of drought already offered in "The Burial of the
Dead":

> Here is no water but only rock
> Rock and no water and the sandy road
> The road winding above among the mountains
> Which are mountains of rock without water
>
> .   .   .
>
> And no rock
> If there were rock
> And also water
> And water
> A spring
> A pool among the rock
> If there were the sound of water only
>
> .   .   .
>
> But there is no water

The scene becomes inhabited by "hooded hordes swarming/Over
endless plains," and it is transformed into an almost surrealist halluci-
nation of Old Testament lamentation and prophecy.

Finally, in the empty chapel, "Over the tumbled graves," the mes-
sage of the thunder comes "In a flash of lightning. Then a damp gust/
Bringing rain." The message, given in three Sanskrit words from the
Upanishads, is not a deliverance but a precise setting of limits upon

the moral life for those who will and can "redeem the time"—that is, redeem themselves until the time of spiritual renewal should come. In each case the advice given is qualified by a statement of its violation: *Give* ("The awful daring of a moment's surrender"); but we have seen that that daring was not present and that surrender did not occur in "an age of prudence"; this has not been an age of heroic, selfless acts. *Sympathize:* but each man exists in his own prison; "Thinking of the key, each confirms a prison." *Control:* but the image of the boat responding "Gaily, to the hand expert with sail and oar" is finally qualified by the verb "would":

> . . . your heart would have responded
> Gaily, when invited, beating obedient
> To controlling hands

The Fisher King is left alone, "Fishing, with the arid plain behind me"; and he asks if he ought not "at least set my lands in order?" Appealing to three fragments of verse in other languages (they *are* fragments, not faiths or religious structures, and they offer only a minimum of hope), he considers their evocation of penitence (the purifying fire), regeneration (the swallow), and resignation (the ruined tower) as exemplars of his own condition and resolve. "Why then Ile fit you," the poet says—put these fragments together, "shore" them "against my ruins"; and this even though, like Hieronymo, he may appear "mad againe" to those incapable of a like decision. The words of the thunder recur, and the poem concludes with the Sanskrit word "peace":

> Shantih shantih shantih

The Waste Land is not a poem for any one given time; it not merely describes a local circumstance but reveals a universal dilemma. The essential emotions of the poem are the terror and agony that accompany a loss of belief, of the *capacity to believe,* to enter absolutely into a communication with the spiritual and moral life. Its value to the 1920s was that it pointed up the problem of belief, as it was debated in the 1920s, and as it was associated with the influence of science on the mood of religious acceptance and on the formations of "industrial waste land" observed and commented upon by scores of writers.

That Eliot should have presented his waste land largely in terms of the irony of a perverted myth, a defeated ritual, a spiritually inhibited and uninformed people, gave the poem a special relevance; for the confidence of both modernist and fundamentalist with respect either to the scientific or to the religious "bible" was shallow and imperceptive. Meanwhile the "automatic" gestures, the meaningless routine, the planned abortion of life, which constitute a few of the exempla of this poem, were also matters of great concern to those who considered the consequences of an age organized along almost purely secular lines. *The Waste Land,* while it was many other things as well, was in some respects at least a concrete, dramatic realization (given a universal and therefore also a "contemporary" form) of a world in which the strength of belief was hard to achieve, even more difficult to sustain.

VII

CRITIQUES OF
THE MIDDLE CLASS

1. The Booboisie

ON TWO occasions *Vanity Fair* honored H. L. Mencken with membership in its "Hall of Fame": in February 1921, "Because he wrote one of the first and best books on Nietzsche in English"; in January 1924, "Because he has contributed more to the popular understanding of Nietzsche than any other American." This recognition was for a number of Mencken's efforts in behalf of the German philosopher: *The Philosophy of Friedrich Nietzsche,* published in 1908; the little volume of selections from Nietzsche, called *The Gist of Nietzsche* (1910); his editorship of "The Free Lance Series of Books," published from 1919 to 1922; his translation of and introduction to Nietzsche's *The Antichrist,* one of the Free Lance series, published in 1920; and finally, his comments on, quotations from, and use of Nietzsche during most of his career as journalist and provincial philosopher.

In 1907, when he began working on *The Philosophy of Friedrich Nietzsche,* only five of Nietzsche's works had been translated into English, and there was no American exposition of his ideas. Mencken undertook the task of reading Nietzsche in the German. "Characteristically," says Isaac Goldberg, in *The Man Mencken* (1925), "having tackled the job, he plowed through the man complete in the original, read the biography by his sister, as well as everything available on the man in English." The result was not a learned, objective exposition of Nietzsche's thought, but a stimulating discussion of what Mencken decided was valuable in it. It was Mencken's Nietzsche, and not Nietzsche's, that came through to the reading public, a selective and highly prejudiced study of his ideas.[1] On his own terms and with his own views of contemporary society in mind, Mencken brought to the American a "popular understanding of Nietzsche." This is perhaps the reason so many Americans thought of Nietzsche as a hard-hitting, sharpshooting enemy of "boobocracy" and of the type of stuffed-shirtism current in American politics and morals in the 1920s.

The association with Nietzsche is best seen in the light of Mencken's two major activities: the formation of an anti-democratic philosophy of government and an unceasing attack upon the stupidities of the *"Herdenmoral"* (morality of the "herd" or mob). In 1910 Mencken and Robert Rives La Monte published a series of letters, called *Men*

[1] "In the vast extent and variety of Nietzsche's writings there are texts to suit many purposes," said Ernest Boyd in 1925. "Nothing could be more natural than that this particular commentator, at that particular time, should emphasize that element in Nietzsche's work which fitted both his purpose and his own temperament. Mencken created Nietzsche in his own image, hence the affecting superstition that he is a Nietzschean."

Mencken imposed his belief in what he called "efficiency" upon Nietzsche's view of the Dionysian spirit, so that we have "a new aristocracy of efficiency" emerging from Nietzsche's works. The "unreasonable, emotional faith in the invariable truth of moral regulations" was "a curse to the human race and the chief cause of its degeneration, inefficiency, and unhappiness." Nietzsche was made the sponsor of an aristocracy of free and efficient minds, who scorned the slaves of convention and lived as they pleased. There is very little of the poetic, Dionysian ecstasy in Mencken's Nietzsche. In the opinion of his American sponsor, Nietzsche had preached the philosophy of the elite; but this elite was not a group of supermen but a group of men who lived leisurely lives and amused themselves by observing the foibles of the booboisie.

The superman of Mencken's view, in being prudently selfish, will be much less apocalyptic in his fight against the evils of the Christian and humanitarian world. He will make renunciations, but they "will be the child, not of faith or of charity, but of expediency. . . . The ideal superman . . . is merely a man in whom instinct works without interference—a man who feels that it is right to live and that the only knowledge worth while is that which makes life longer and more bearable."

Together with this localized version of the superman, Mencken offered Nietzsche as the foe of Christianity, democracy, and socialism. The ideal laboring class, he explained Nietzsche as saying, is "a class content to obey without fear or question." Socialism had simply made the masses envious, resentful, and bothersome. Similarly, in his remarks on Nietzsche's opinions of women, Mencken adapted them to local circumstances. Though Nietzsche did not despise women, "he was constitutionally suspicious of all who walked in skirts," and he would certainly not have countenanced "the sentimental fashion of those virtuosi of illusion who pass for lawgivers in the United States," and who insist upon making goddesses of their women.

Versus the Man, supposedly a debate on socialism. The socialist theory
contained several serious threats to Mencken's form of "absolute individualism." The mob, he said, "is inert and moves ahead only when
it is dragged or driven. It clings to its delusions with a pertinacity that
is appalling." To attempt equality of privilege and opportunity, to raise
the economic position of this mob, will only result in bringing "the
first-caste man" down to the dismal level of the mob. The life of this
first-caste man, whose survival in a democracy is one of Mencken's
primary concerns, must be kept free of democratic and socialist "im-
pedimenta."

> Briefly, I demand that he possess, to an unusual and striking degree,
> all of those qualities, or most of them, which most obviously dis-
> tinguish the average man from the baboon. . . . The chief of these
> qualities is a sort of restless impatience with things as they are—a sort
> of insatiable desire to help along the evolutionary process. The man
> who possesses this quality is ceaselessly eager to increase and fortify
> his mastery of his environment. He has a vast curiosity and a vast
> passion for solving the problems it unfolds before him.[2]

In the series of *Prejudices* (1919–1927), in essays published in
the *Freeman,* the *Nation,* and the *New Republic,* and in his own *American Mercury,* Mencken elaborated upon his anti-democratic position. Nor was his support of radicals in danger of attack from patriotic
societies a contradiction; it proved only that he was interested in *any*
form of individualism, however wrong-headed and ill-guided it seemed.
Generally he disliked both political radicals and conservatives. Far
from being supermen, capitalists seemed to him merely economic op-
portunists; "their intolerable hoggishness threatens to raise the boobery
in revolt and bring about a reign of terror from which the strongest
will emerge."

The book *Notes on Democracy* (1926) throws into clear relief all
of Mencken's scattered remarks upon the inefficiency and fraudulence
of democratic life.[3] Here he portrayed democratic man plagued by

---

[2] This aristocrat of taste does not necessarily belong to a favored economic
class. Some of the wealthiest Americans have the worst manners. For example,
Mencken commends John D. Rockefeller for his work in the improvement of
capitalism's distributing power. But "his belief, as a good Baptist, that total im-
mersion in water is a necessary prerequisite for entry into heaven, places him
quite unmistakably in the lowest class of superstitious barbarians."

[3] As Edmund Wilson said in a review, it "is the same old melodrama, with the
gentleman, the man of honor, pitted against the peasant and the boob." Wilson

fear and greed, grossly envious of his superiors. Incapable of realizing the true meaning of liberty, ignoring the merits of the elite, he tries his best to interfere with the liberties of exceptional men. The story of democracy "is a history of efforts to force successive minorities to be untrue to their nature." Law, custom, and concepts of right and wrong are all designed to make the average man safe and to reduce the superior man to his own level. For his moral security, democratic man sets up the Puritan as his dictator of taste and decency. "This irreconcilable antagonism between democratic Puritanism and common decency is probably responsible for the uneasiness and unhappiness that are so marked in American life, despite the great material prosperity of the United States."

To the question, "If you find so much to complain of in the United States, why do you live here?" Mencken replied (*Mercury,* September 1924), "Why do men go to Zoos?" If democracy has any genuine merit, he said, "it is the merit and virtue of being continuously amusing, of offering the plain people a ribald and endless show."

The contradictions between virtue announced and vice committed, the somberly stupid affection for the law, the one-hundred-per-centism of the American Legion and the Ku Klux Klan, the naïve pride in locality and region, the unwitting irony of middle-class behavior, the resistance to enlightenment and novelty—all these, and many more demonstrations of democratic man's mastery of the rules for vaudeville entertainment, Mencken described elaborately in the newspaper columns and the magazines he edited during most of his career. *The American Mercury* gave Mencken his most extensive opportunity to catalogue democratic activities, but it was not his first. From 1911 until the autumn of 1915 he conducted the "Free Lance" column of the *Baltimore Evening Sun.* The general aim of the column, wrote Ernest Boyd, was "to combat, chiefly by ridicule, American piety, stupidity, tin-pot morality, cheap chauvinism, in all their forms." The four years of raillery against the booboisie resulted in two million words of copy, for which he was "attacked in probably ten thousand letters to the

admitted, however, that Mencken's portrait of the democratic man had impressed itself upon the consciousness of American readers more deeply than any other notion, with the possible exception of Fitzgerald's flapper. "Sinclair Lewis's Babbitt and the inhabitants of his Main Street are merely particular incarnations of the great American boob, evidently inspired by Mencken." To have made Americans see themselves in Mencken's portraits of the "super-boor," Wilson agreed, is no mean achievement. (*New Republic,* December 15, 1926.)

editor. Resolutions were passed against me by all religious and uplifting organizations save Catholic and Jewish."

In December 1914 he began almost ten years as co-editor (with George Jean Nathan) of the *Smart Set,* a magazine for which he had been writing articles and reviews since 1908. During this period, which lasted until the *Smart Set* was sold to the Hearst interests in December 1923, Mencken sponsored the writing of Theodore Dreiser and Frank Norris, was responsible for the first appearance in America of poetry and prose by James Joyce. Other Europeans whom he sponsored, in the *Smart Set* and elsewhere, were Havelock Ellis, Lord Dunsany, Henrik Ibsen, Gerhart Hauptmann, and, of course, Nietzsche and Shaw. American names that had been all but unknown in 1908 had become established by 1923, partly through Mencken's efforts. He could say, in closing that part of his career, that modern American literature, as well as the appreciation of it, had had some help from him in growing up. "Today," he said in 1923, "it seems to me, the American imaginative writer, whether he be novelist, poet, or dramatist, is quite as free as he deserves to be. He is free to depict the life about him precisely as he sees it, and to interpret it in any manner he pleases." In subsequent years he lost interest in creative literature, showing an especial obtuseness in the matter of experimental writing and demonstrating little or no understanding of poetry. His time was taken up almost entirely with prose, chiefly with sociological and cultural studies of contemporary America.

The *Mercury,* begun in January 1924, was almost wholly a prose commentary upon the native scene, revealing every nook and cranny of democratic life and belaboring with a heavy stick the sins of taste and credulity of the American middle class. Its monthly issues are a storehouse of evidence to support the Mencken point of view.

In its announcement the *Mercury* promised to "devote itself pleasantly to exposing the nonsensicality of all such hallucinations [as Marxism, Bryanism, Prohibition, etc.], particularly when they show a certain apparent plausibility." The editors—Nathan was co-editor for one year—were "committed to nothing save this: to keep to common sense as fast as they can, to belabor sham as agreeably as possible, to give a civilized entertainment." The magazine had especially in mind its audience of "The Forgotten Man: that is, the small group of intelligent citizens who are harassed by cumulative executive, legislative, and judicial follies, and bedeviled by Socialist fol-de-rol, and who do not subscribe to either." There were many of these intelligent citizens, though Mencken was probably a bit surprised to find that as many as sixty thousand of them could afford subscriptions.

One of the *Mercury*'s major achievements was its prolonged investigation of the strange cults and manners of "the hinterland"—particularly the Bible Belt, the Midwest, and the Middle Southern regions. The leaders of thought in these regions were inept and narrow expositors of the gospel of convention; the spiritual and intellectual leaders of the mob were dull, narrow-minded, unintelligent; and the political leaders were worse.

Reports on the nature of the country's cultural terrain described it for the most part as a desert. Of the pedagogue, James Cain reported (May 1924) that his chief peculiarity was "his incurable hankering for the posture of wisdom." He was, moreover, extremely timid in his discussion of issues, loved "the delicate balancing of one side against the other side. That delicious, teetering moment before it becomes apparent that both sides (in the last analysis) are right!" T. N. Gillespie (May 1927) marveled at the efficient sales movement in education: "Once the concern of eminent and puissant philosophers, pedagogy in the Republic is today sold over the counter as well as *via* the mails and radio by the scintillating salesmen of super-efficient educational rolling mills." Granville Hicks (October 1928), discussing the academic gentleman of letters, used for his target Hamilton Wright Mabie, the "Christian Literatus," "the finest flower of that lovely era in American letters when substantially the only qualities required for success in the field of literary criticism were church membership and an honest face."

In this portrayal of bourgeois types the clergy also suffered—both the dignified gentlemen of the Protestant churches and the rabble rousers of religious way stations in the hills. The clergyman is not religious, Mencken said in his "Clinical Notes" of June 1924. "I doubt gravely that the sorceries he engages in professionally every day awaken in him any emotion more lofty than boredom." The young men are attracted to the profession not because of their dedication or piety, but because, being "excessively realistic," they are convinced that genuine faith "is far more apt to keep a youth out of the pulpit than to take him into it." Naturally enough, the *Mercury* underscored the alliance of the church with American business; the indispensable function of religion was to provide an easy Christian surface for business activity and to furnish sanctity at a very reasonable cost to Christian endeavor in a capitalist economy. The "Gospel of Service" (James

Cain, November 1925) was considered an evangelical support of the idea of Progress. "That is, humanity is conceived to be moving toward a goal in accordance with God's holy law, and this goal is the millennium."

The politicians were more evidently stupid than the clergy because their errors of taste and intelligence were more glaringly public. The favorite target was the silent sage of the White House, Calvin Coolidge. Reviewing a volume of Coolidge's speeches, which had appeared at election time in 1924, Mencken remarked: "The whole repertory of Rotary Club ideas is rehearsed and exhausted; the wisdom of an entire race is boiled down to a series of apothegms, all indubitable, all freely granted by every right-thinking man." In other appearances as scapegoat, Coolidge was described (by Frank R. Kent) as "a thoroughly commonplace, colorless person with a neat little one-cylinder intellect and a thoroughly precinct mind." His election in 1924 was noted by Mencken in the December issue: "It is as if a hungry man, set before a banquet prepared by master cooks and covering a table an acre in area, should turn his back upon the feast and stay his stomach by catching and eating flies." Harding was spared only because his death had preceded the founding of the *Mercury;* but his contributions to American speech were annotated and classified as "Gamalielese," the new form of statesmanlike speech.[4]

Social commentaries on the political scene also remarked the activities of one-hundred-per-cent patriots. Though the *Mercury* had no sympathy with what one contributor called the "Communist Hoax," it noted and analyzed the Red-baiting of the decade. Harvey O' Higgins (March 1929) gave the Red scare his very best psychoanalytic treatment. The American businessman's fear of bolshevism, he said, was "a

---

[4] Cf. this Cummings poem, published in *Viva* (1931):

the first president to be loved by his
 bitterest enemies" is dead

the only man woman or child who wrote
 a simple declarative sentence with seven grammatical
errors "is dead"
beautiful Warren Gamaliel Harding
"is" dead
he's
"dead"
if he wouldn't have eaten them Yapanese Craps

somebody might hardly never not have been unsorry, perhaps

popular mania that has had no equal in America since the early Puritans went wild about witchcraft and saw a torturable witch in every old woman who had lost her teeth"; and he explained the current fear as a psychic projection of the ever-present fear of failure, the "sin of the American business world."

Mencken, in his reflections on the law as an image of democratic social manners, selected the Prohibition amendment as the greatest of all blunders committed by the "virtuosi of virtue." This law was always in his mind and under his skin: he published gratefully the statistical and scientific papers of his Johns Hopkins University friends, which proved the harmlessness of liquor; he commissioned sketches by revenue agents to show their own resistance to the mockery they were asked to enforce; he raged in scores of editorials and "Clinical Notes" over the antics of Prohibitionists. This event in our legal history seemed to him to have demonstrated once and forever the incredibly stupid attitude toward law in a democracy. The Puritan strategy was first to get it on the books, as a constitutional fact; after that, the normal reverence for law as law was sufficient to keep it there, for democratic man is superstitious about legal statutes. "The principle is set up that there is a mystical virtue in law *per se.*" Law does not need to be obeyed, but merely worshiped.

Exhaustive evidence of the down-at-the-heel culture of Mencken's booboisie was presented in the section of the *Mercury* called "Americana"; in 1926 a full-length book of selections from the monthly column was published. "Americana" was a collection of quotations from newspapers, public speeches, advertisements, and various other sources, arranged alphabetically by state of origin, so that each reader might easily find his place in it. The strategy of "Americana" was to present as distorted a picture of the American intelligence as was possible, by culling diligently the worst blunders and reaching far into the provincial and cultural hinterland for grotesque examples of somber idiocy. It was the "enlightened man's" jokebook; he turned to it first, as the tired workingman turned to the comic page or the sports section of his daily newspaper.

Most frequently cited were extravagant statements by ministers, politicians, and chamber-of-commerce boosters, oddities in city and state laws, expressions of faith in the American flag, threats against alien dissenters, attempts to link the history of American business with Old and New Testament celebrities and events, and other alignments of gold with God and culture with gilt-edge securities.

From an address in Waterloo, Iowa:

Men elected as presidents of Rotary are put there to think. Men have sought to define what Rotary is—what is the secret of its hold upon men. I say Rotary is a manifestation of the divine.

Announcement made by a Harvey, North Dakota, pastor:

Next Sunday Night—at 7:30 o'clock sharp, I am going to preach the plainest, straightest, and hottest sermon about the sins of Harvey that I know how to preach.

An advertising circular, distributed in New York City:

Each $100 contributed constitutes one share and when paid entitles the donor to *an engraved certificate of investment in preferred capital stock in the Kingdom of God.*

Statement made by a Kentucky politician:

If Governor Fields is right, I am going to stand by him because he is right. If he is wrong, I am going to stand by him because he is a Democrat.

An ordinance, passed by "the Christian legislators" of Long Beach, California:

No person shall indulge in caresses, hugging, fondling, embracing, spooning, kissing, or wrestling with any person or persons of the opposite sex . . . and no person shall sit or lie with his or her head, or any other portion of his or her person, upon any portion of a person or persons upon or near any of the said public places in the city of Long Beach.

Statement by the advertising director of Colgate and Co.:

I challenge you to find a boy with a clean mouth and a dirty heart. The boy who washes his teeth doesn't go wrong. He can't.

Announcement of a sermon in Owensboro, Kentucky:

"Solomon, a Six-Cylinder Sport."

Statement about the biblical origin of Rotary:

Rotary began 'way back there when Abraham told Lot to take his choice of cattle lands, in the interests of harmony, Abraham taking what was left.

A scientific report from Yakima, Washington:

The source of man's wickedness is "a torrid zone" in the brain, an inch and a half thick from the ears up.

Further information about Jesus:

The first president of Lions International was Jesus Christ. I quote you from the Bible: He was "Lion of the tribe of Judah."

These statements demonstrated to Mencken the full nature of the democratic sensibility: its false optimism and enthusiasm, its grotesque affirmation of political and religious allegiance, its hostility to all differences of thought, color, or sentiment. Such an extensive display of incriminating evidence seemed to him more than enough to merit the maximum penalty for democratic man. But "Americana," far from demonstrating the failure of democracy as a political idea, merely describes in detail the abuse of democratic privilege, the failure to realize it intelligently. The items quoted are no more laughable than the fumbling gestures of Helen Hokinson's women's-club characters in the *New Yorker.* As comedy, the gestures transcribed from life in "Americana" mark the worst form of social and intellectual error of which a democratic people are capable. They are grotesque extremes.

It was a strange America that Mencken presented. Since he had no party commitments, he was often engaged in controversies with those who held more strictly to a doctrinaire indictment or defense of American civilization. The *New Masses* group thought of him as a fuming reactionary whose lick-spittle tactics served merely to depress his followers and enrage his enemies. A cartoon (*New Masses,* December 1926) showed him, dressed as a Madonna, in a Baltimore stable, bottle-feeding a child who wears only mortarboard and horn-rimmed spectacles. The drawing celebrated what its artist called "The Immaculate Conception of the Superman." *New Republic* and *Nation* liberals were alternately amused by his wit and distressed by his political obstinacy. The world he had described struck one *Nation* critic as "a vast, mysterious continent, as strange and perilous to civilized men as the remote reaches of Tibet or Siberia. The swarming population, as incomprehensible as the fabulous peoples in books of imaginary voyages, is perpetually engaged in all manner of incredible barbarities, follies, stupidities, cruelties, blasphemies—an unending spectacle of a life as terrible as it is futile. Individually each incident is trivial or even ludicrous; in the aggregate they become a gigantic panorama, at once lurid and somber, of the pride, stupidity, and folly of mankind" (December 9, 1925).

Mencken's portrayal of the American middle class was curiously paradoxical. The product of diligent, industrious, almost obsessive research, it had its basis in fact—in journalistic truth of the kind that we see and read about day after day. But, because of the forms Mencken gave this fact, it was translated into a fantasy of human life. Mencken began his investigation with a few simple principles or prejudices, many of them borrowed from his reading of Nietzsche. His survey of American culture was motivated entirely by an urgent necessity to prove himself right in these original assumptions. He discovered an inexhaustible mine of documentation in the daily press; he arranged his exhibits in an artificial order and threw glaring light upon the sensational extremes of evidence. As a result the booboisie emerged as a fantastic caricature of humanity, a figure who has always existed but has never really been alive, a type superficially true but profoundly unreal. Mencken was neither a sociologist nor a moral scientist. He was a theorist of the comic, whose interest in the absurd was essentially that of some fantastic research scholar working from the narrowest of assumptions toward the most improbable of conclusions. He never lied; he never actually told the truth. He worked slowly, painstakingly, to fit fragments of reality into a gigantic parody of the social metaphor.

2. Philistine and Puritan

LIKE many another term in our intellectual history, puritanism was used in a special sense in the American twenties. The historical Puritan who inhabited and regulated seventeenth-century New England became both the unhistorical victim and villain of popular journalism, even of the avant-garde version of American culture. This was one of the notorious examples of historical distortion practiced by Harold Stearns' "Young Intellectual." As in most distortions, there was a dim and more than misunderstood outline of truth in it—more than misunderstood because ignored, as much of American tradition was ignored in the attempt of the 1920s to justify its revolt against convention.

The young man who began to write during or shortly after World War I grew up to the custom of attacking the cultural *status quo;* it became fashionable for him to refer loosely to scientific studies that seemed to him to disprove convention or to make it appear ridiculous. He was inclined to make inferences from science that were either not there or were applicable in a very limited sense. More than that, he saw no place (or very little) for what he regarded as "orthodox" religious doctrine, or "fundamentalism." Since religion had gone out of fashion he needed a scapegoat, a substantial "enemy," to whom he

could attach responsibility for the absurdity of an outmoded, impractical morality. The name Puritan occurred to him happily and almost
without effort. This much he thought he knew: the Puritan had been
associated with grim, stark, colonial reality; he was a pre-scientific personality, a man ignorant and rudely affirmative, who forced his religion
and its strait-laced moral code upon a growing country. Having been
forbidden a natural life, he made the artificial, repressed one all the
more effective; his energy was directed fanatically toward a single,
limited purpose. As the country prospered, he regarded the increase of
material goods as a sign of the rightness of his purpose and the efficiency
of his means.

Charles Beard (*New Republic,* December 1, 1920) discussed the
great variety of distortions that had been visited upon the term puritanism as a result of the anti-Puritan crusade. Once the term had had
a fairly definite meaning, he said, but now it has lost any sharpness of
definition. "By the critics it is used as a term of opprobrium applicable
to anything that interferes with the new freedom, free verse, psychoanalysis, or even the double entendre." The Puritan's historical importance has been exaggerated, Beard maintained; and since he is
needed as a symbolic scapegoat, he has become so vague in outline as
to be all but unrecognizable. Among the definitions listed by Beard
there were such unpleasant attributes as "sour-faced fanaticism, supreme hypocrisy, intellectual tyranny, brutal intolerance, religious
persecution, sullenness, stinginess, conceit, and bombast."

Beard had pointed to a gross misappropriation of historical truth.
The seventeenth-century Puritan described in documents and scholarly
biography "sinned" chiefly in being an earnest and self-committed doctrinaire. The principal reason for his being so greatly misunderstood
was the wide range of cultural difference between his century and
ours. That he regulated social behavior and interfered with the private
lives of his fellows is undeniably true. He also seemed unjust to some
of his contemporaries and ridiculous to others. But the striking feature
of his life was his sense of theological responsibility, his awareness of
a superintending and implacable God, whose control over the American conscience had diminished considerably by the end of the nineteenth century. The young men of the early twentieth century were
able to appreciate this God scarcely at all. Their conception of the historical Puritan (if they had any) was of a man who had behaved ob-
noxiously without cause and who had served not God but himself. It
was impossible for them to distinguish between the social judgment

of Samuel Sewall and that of John Sumner. Where there was some knowledge of past Puritan history (as in the case of Mencken), that knowledge was obscured by a polemical devotion to more recent philosophies of history and society.

Several suggestions awaited the young intellectual for completing his false analysis of the moral and cultural ills of his country. Of these the new Freudian psychology and the slightly older Nietzschean philosophy were most readily at hand: Freud had been introduced to America early enough in the century to warrant considerable misuse by 1920; Nietzsche's attack upon democratic middle-class European society had been given an American revision of emphasis and application by Mencken in 1908. Though these two men were scarcely responsible entirely for the Puritan-baiting of the 1920s, their statements—revised, maneuvered, and distorted—formed a substantial portion of its background.

The principal contribution made by Freud to the terminology of anti-puritanism was the term "repression." For the young men and women of the period the word served as a convenient label for all their grievances against society. It was their feeling that the absurd, exorbitant moral demands society had made upon its victims had culminated in a national neurosis. Repression became the American illness. With little or no thought of personal responsibility—that is, the ever-present conflict between ego and id, which, Freud insists, antedates any precise formulation of conventions—they decided that any force was evil that stood in the way of a full, wholesome, primitive expression of natural impulses. Repression stood for all the social formulas that prevented the natural expression of life impulses.

The idea of repression was soon enough applied in the popular mind to American history and sociology. If repression was a national illness, then all the social and moral forces that had led to the neurosis of an entire people must have had this object: to repress the natural life of a people, to shut off the natural satisfaction of healthy desires as the price paid for achieving economic and industrial success. The Puritan pioneer had stood in the corridors of heaven, hat in hand, unsmiling and ungracious, waiting his turn for reward of his unrelenting pursuit of the moral ideal. A people so earnestly engaged in Puritan good works had not learned how to laugh, how to live graciously; they had invented words and phrases designed at every turn to avoid mention of any natural act; they had made courtship and marriage polite but arduous formalities, had taken from them every last joy and pleasure. This was the verdict of many Americans of the twenties, who interpreted their past history as part of a national malaise resulting from continuous distortion of native impulse.

Such books as Frank's *Our America* (1919) and Harvey O' Higgins' *The American Mind in Action* (1920) read like lengthy case histories of the Puritan as the archetype of all neurotics. O' Higgins accused the Puritan of having continuously repressed "the most potent instincts of ordinary healthy life," the sex instinct principally of course. "The instincts were not merely to be prevented from impelling to sinful action; they were to be stopped from getting into the conscious mind, as sinful thoughts; they were to be dammed up in the subconscious mind, with all their undrained energy and all their unrelieved tension."

The American Mind in Action is a study of several American figures; in each case the effect of the national repression is demonstrated. Mark Twain, for example, suffered from a repressed hatred of his mother and the awful biblical God whom she had used to thwart his desires. His humor, like all American humor, "is an outlet for repressed emotions in disguise." Both *Huckleberry Finn* and *Tom Sawyer* are disguised expressions of filial impiety, and "the typical American" reads them because he too "retains in his subconscious mind a dynamic, repressed, and undrained emotion of filial revolt, caused by his hatred of the Calvinistic puritanism of his parents."

Criticism of Puritan society assumed many forms, but the majority of it insisted on a clear-cut division between natural desires and the social forces acting on every hand to frustrate them. The baiters of puritanism protested against the institutions that had codified morality and regulated conduct, and accused them of having been responsible for repression. In this fashion social critics in some degree excused the individual from the responsibility of control by demonstrating that the existing agencies of control were interfering with the natural development of human life. In so doing they were forced to exaggerate and distort their description of these agencies, to offer a caricature of the American Puritan as an unholy agent of repression, and to blame him for the sad state of cultural frustration from which they believed the country as a whole was suffering.

The attack upon society as an agent of repression was most vigorous in the matter of sexual morality. The Puritan was often pictured as a stern, austere figure whose body was so carefully guarded against exposure that it is difficult to imagine by what means he succeeded in reproducing his kind. The proper reaction to him, of course, was to defy his code, to act in deliberate scorn of it, and to experiment as much as possible with sexual manners prohibited by it. In some cases this defiance acquired the characteristics of a primitivism in its attempt to point out the great happiness of people who were not brought up in terror of sex and therefore lived normal, happy, casual lives. The "paleface" attitude, as Wyndham Lewis called it, expressed itself in such novels as Sherwood Anderson's *Dark Laughter* and Waldo Frank's *Holiday*. In the former the Negro servants are a chorus laughing its disapproval of the conventional stupidities of their masters; in the latter the Negroes and white men live in adjoining parts of a city owned and dominated by the whites, but only the Negroes seem happy. "White folks wanting, white folks shutting down, white world hungering and a cold hard hate, a hating poison from its hungering love."

In other examples the white folks don't stay in their town, wanting and hating, but flee to the city, where life is easier and it is more difficult for the code to work successfully. Many of them make the pilgrimage to Greenwich Village, pursuing some vague ideal of adventure, of beauty, of joy, of freedom. The harsh repression of natural wishes often issues in violence, in which the all but inarticulate person becomes briefly, violently articulate and repressions are thrown off with an almost insane abandon. The little people who inhabit Anderson's Midwestern villages often live dull, inhibited lives; then with emotional violence they free themselves of their burden of repression. In Anderson's stories there is often an occasion for walking away from the responsibilities of the code—as happens in the case of John Webster of *Many Marriages,* who finds his position as a Midwestern manufacturer intolerable and who abandons his office and his family in consequence.

Freud's explanation of the psychic mechanism of repression was a convenient device, a label, an easy means of organizing cultural protest about a central concept. The opposite of puritanism was not only anti-puritanism but sensuality, experiment in sexual matters, and tolerance of all oddities of sexual behavior.

Most literary portraits of the middle class were drawn by disinherited sons and daughters from that class. The intelligentsia for the most part belonged economically to the middle class; culturally they took pride in repudiating it. Their criticism was an all-out attack upon the customs and manners, the native cultural disposition, of the bourgeoisie. The vigor of anti-bourgeois criticism in the 1920s came, not from the proletarian critics, but from the middle-class men and women who were disgusted with their cultural heritage and viewed the guardians of middle-class morality and culture as hopelessly stupid and comical parodies of human nature. For the most part this reaction was not economic or political in its nature; it was cultural and moral. The burghers offended in a thousand ways and made countless errors of taste.

What distressed their critics more than anything else was the religious intensity with which they exploited what had originally been chiefly an economic convenience. The bourgeoisie were condemned, not for having made money, but for having turned the making of it into a religion and a morality. Out of this concept of the conventional man grew the portrait of conventional virtues. The cardinal virtues ascribed to the class were dullness, stupidity, aggressiveness in commerce, conformity to the remnants of traditional morality, and a moral opportunism, linked with certain blind convictions about the economic *status quo*. Their critics felt that money was not an adequate determinant of other values, that money was a value of a kind so totally different from these others that it was bound to kill them or distort them beyond recognition. Convention corrupts taste; and absolute adherence to convention corrupts absolutely.

This criticism of the middle class was almost wholly an urban thing; the critics were augmented from time to time by numbers of refugees from the Midwest. And, though they scattered to various parts of the world, they seemed agreed about the broad outlines of their attack. These outlines, whether they were presented in caricature or satire or polemic, were unified under the characterizations of two terms, each of them applicable to its separate sphere of interest: the cultural bourgeoisie were termed Philistine, the moral were dubbed Puritan. The predominating motif was not so much the consequences of their actions as the *manner* in which they acted. Thus the errors of narrowness and stupidity were condemned in the Puritan; he was a moral Philistine whose sins of taste were the product of his cultural helplessness, his refusal to consider the arts as having values independent of the moral setting in which they were considered.

During the twenties attacks upon the ramparts of Philistia differed widely in detail but almost never in general strategy. To the intellectuals the Philistine appeared to be searching constantly and nervously for a respectable culture, for a culture of outward form, which would soften the harsh outlines of bourgeois economic primitivism. In some instances the notion of respectability served cleverly to conceal an inner emptiness; the "Cambridge ladies who live in furnished souls" of Cummings' poem "are unbeautiful and have comfortable minds" (in *Tulips and Chimneys*, 1923); their vision is cut off entirely from a life not prescribed by their conventions:

> While permanent faces coyly bandy
> scandal of Mrs. N and Professor D
> . . . . the Cambridge ladies do not care, above
> Cambridge if sometimes in its box of
> sky lavender and cornerless, the
> moon rattles like a fragment of angry candy

The suburban mind also wore a protective coloration. "In the suburbs," wrote Maxwell Bodenheim (*Chicago Literary Times,* June 1, 1924), "life wards off the partial reproaches of Nature with hosts of moral and material activities, and preserves the weakened connection with the heart of the city, and dodges into the city now and then for a relieving evening's spree." Culture for these people is something one has acquired as an additional display, a possession one boasts of because of the class distinction it demonstrates. "The whole atmosphere of the concert hall," said the *New Republic* (April 8, 1925), "is heavy with the miasma of community coercion."

The culture of the Philistine was portrayed as a patchwork quilt of easy knowledge, affectations of the graces, and utilitarian aesthetics. The easy knowledge was gained from Chautauqua meetings, from the lecture platform of women's clubs, from the popular debasements of the intellectual coin. When the middle class imitated the practices of Greenwich Village, as that place had been described in the *Saturday Evening Post* and the popular press, the fake freedom and strained casualness impressed the intellectual as another violence done upon his sincerity and good taste. There was a certain civic pride in this matter of sinning à la bohemia, said Marquis Childs (*American Mercury,* October 1928). It is "the expression of a dim conviction that the vices of Paris, France, really haven't much on those of Paris, Illinois." This amateur "villaging" of the middle class struck Childs as a rather pathetic demonstration of self-consciousness. "What really exists is a preoccupation with certain bright, new toys, a preoccupation for which there is available plenty of leisure and energy. This is commonly coupled with a pleasurable sense of wrongdoing, the challenging stimulation of having accepted a dare of long standing."

The debasement of popular literature was similarly commented upon as a cheapening of the literary talent for purposes of entertaining the middle class, without disturbing too much its sense of comfort and security. This pressure upon the literary conscience limited the value of literature so that it became, in a society dominated by middle-class taste, merely "useful," in the sense of engaging the senses and securing the sentiment against any violation of its conventional habits. "The truth of the matter," said Lewis Mumford (*Freeman,* April 18, 1923), "is that almost all our literature and art is produced by the public, by people, that is to say, whose education, whose mental bias, whose intellectual discipline, does not differ by so much as the contents of a spelling book from the great body of readers who enjoy their work." They have made a literature which echoes the dullness and fails forever to break through the limitations of their own world. This narrowness of literary approach produces best-sellers that are either escapes from bourgeois routine or pathetic and detailed portraits of it; in neither case is the literature illuminated or relieved by any imaginative transcendence of the environment in which it is written.

The diversions offered the shopgirl and the clerk were a composite of lurid sensationalism and the inept, pious platitude that kept actual immorality conveniently beyond reach. The sensation seekers had little trouble finding an ample supply of printed thrills; the tabloid newspaper, the cheap magazine, the motion picture, provided a capsule form of immorality, to be taken as often as required but always with a Christian, bourgeois antidote. The lower classes might enjoy the vicarious sensation of murder, rape, and kidnaping, in much the same way as the middle classes enjoyed the sensation of art. Thus was the Christian morality of intention, so strongly ridiculed by Nietzsche, safely circumvented.

The unfortunate few who, like Leopold and Loeb, translated intention into action provided both spectacle and lesson for the others. Their trial, one of several lurid spectacles for the tabloid-hungry public, was a constant source of thrills; Leopold and Loeb had themselves acted in an effort to demonstrate violently their boredom with bourgeois life and in doing so provided millions of their compatriots with an easy and safe diversion. "Both were romantically bored by their luxurious bourgeois life," said Robert Morss Lovett (*New Republic,* June 25, 1924), "and they recognized in crime the most powerful means of escape, of setting the individual free from social bonds, of putting him *jenseits von Gut und Böse*"—that is, beyond Good and Evil.

To the devastating attack upon the tastes and manners of the Philistine was added the criticism of his moral brother, the Puritan. It was the Puritan who provided religious protection against violations of the code, who determined the limits of middle-class behavior, and who with a clumsy hand censored the literature it enjoyed and set the limits of respectability in the arts. Randolph Bourne's famous essay on "The Puritan's Will to Power" (*Seven Arts,* April 1917) and Mencken's description of the Puritan influence on American literature in *A Book of Prefaces* (1917) established the tone of anti-puritanism for the 1920s.

The Puritan loves virtue, said Bourne, not for its own sake but for the power his affectation of it will give him. He is passionately in favor of moral righteousness, but this point of view is actually a matter of power strategy, "an instrument of his terrorism." Mencken discussed the "almost unbearable burden" which the Puritan's "unbreakable belief in his own bleak and narrow views" and his "lust for relentless and barbarous persecution" had put upon the intellectual life in America. That the Puritan forces were strong Mencken was obliged to admit; he described them as in ceaseless and bitter struggle "against the rise of that dionysian spirit, that joyful acquiescence in life, that philosophy of the *Ja-sager* [the yea-sayer] which offers to puritanism as in times past, its chief and perhaps only antagonism."

The Puritan scored one conspicuous victory in the 1920s, that historical example of virtuous triumph over reality, Prohibition. One other victory it was proud to announce, but it could scarcely claim absolute success in its struggle for it—the censorship of entertainment, the decade-long struggle by Watch-and-Warders all over the nation to "keep it clean," which forced Hollywood, in self-defense, to set up a czar of morality in the films, the Will Hays office of countercensorship.

The conspicuous victory of the Puritan over the drinking habits of a nation at large was called by Herbert Hoover "an experiment noble in purpose," in one of his numerous campaign expressions in the interests of caution and safety. That Prohibition had been a farce from the word go was the opinion of all those who attacked its effect upon the nation's manners and morals. Clarence Darrow commented several times on the futility of trying to enforce a law fundamentally at variance with American life and tastes. Heywood Broun, in one of several articles on this omnipresent joke, spoke "in praise of Prohibition," maintaining that it had "furthered the amenities as well as the hazards of drinking"

(*Vanity Fair,* October 1928). In similar spirit one of the characters of
Elmer Davis's novel, *Friends of Mr. Sweeney* (1925), explained why
"a nation starved for excitement tolerated the Volstead Act. It made any
place at all that contained liquor look like a wild café." Sherwood Anderson commented on the effect of bootleg liquor on American taste;
the drinking of liquor of dubious origin will help the general degeneration of American taste in all other matters, he maintained (*Vanity
Fair,* February 1927). And E. B. White suggested that the government
take over and run the speakeasies. "In that manner the citizenry would
be assured liquor of a uniformly high quality, and the enormous cost
of dry enforcement could be met by the profits from the sale of drinks"
(*New Yorker,* January 1, 1927).

The reformist aspect of middle-class morality included the suppression of other freedoms as well. The bourgeois reformer was perhaps
best symbolized by the spare, thin face, the white hair, the thin fingers,
and the formless, ankle-length gown of the tea- and water-drinking
matron of the W. C. T. U. But she was far exceeded in popularity as a
subject of caricature by her male companion, the censor of middle-
class entertainment. The war against "Sumner Volstead Christ and
Co." gave the public some of its most entertaining moments during
"the epoch of Mann's righteousness/the age of dollars and no sense"
(Cummings, in *IS 5*). An unsigned poem in the *Nation* (July 20,
1921), brought "Torquemada up to Date":

> Old Mississippi claps in jail
> The man who utters cusses
> In Utah smoking cigarettes
> Is worse than cutting purses.
>
> "To mention man's mammalian ways,"
> Says Comstock, "is not nice, sir;
> And if you do you'll share the fate
> Of Cabell and of Dreiser."

The battle over the censorship was bitter and prolonged, as well as
enormously amusing. One of the censor's most laughable characteristics
was the ineptness with which he handled the blue pencil. Because of his
naïveté, he forced the letter of immorality out of textbooks, while
leaving the spirit in. The true censor, said Francis Hackett (*New Republic,* December 3, 1919), is "so often not taste or conscience in any
clear condition but an uninstructed agency of herd instinct, an institu-
tional bully." The censor serves not beauty but moral "edification" and

decorum. Joseph Wood Krutch, considering the matter of decency and censorship (*Nation,* February 16, 1927), maintained that it was impossible "to set any legal standard of decency," simply because decency was a matter that relied upon prevailing convention, and convention is not a fixed social form. If censorship would be effective, it would have to control "an emotional reaction on the part of a spectator, which, being purely subjective, is not subject to regulation." The general result of censorship is to encourage indecency rather than prevent it. "I am certain," Krutch concluded, "that the inanities blessed by Mr. Hays are more genuinely corrupting than any pornography."

The battle to protect the middle class from the Anglo-Saxon four-letter word lost on all fronts. It lost ground because it was stupidly managed, untimely, and offered the reading public the dullest of all possible choices. The Puritan censor condemned all literal references to biological realities as well as every "suggestive" reference to the "baser senses." This strenuous effort to keep immorality out of sight and to shut the mind and senses to all immodesty was often diagnosed as a neurotic reaction to instincts so well repressed by the Puritan that they could reissue only in violent upheavals of insanely evangelical crusading. Puritanism, said F. B. Kaye (*New Republic,* December 15, 1920), is a point of view based on a fundamental distrust of human nature, and not confined to the anti-vice crusaders:

> Wherever you find a mother imbued with the idea that the will of her child should be broken, there you find a Puritan. Wherever you see a legislator obsessed with the idea that the slightest relaxation in the rigidity of the laws and the heaviness of the punishments restraining action will lead to a violent anarchy, there you see a Puritan. Wherever you discover a man who despises himself because his healthy normal feelings do not measure up to the conventions he has been taught to believe in, there you have a Puritan. Distrust of normal human life does not now take the form of a belief in infant damnation; it takes the more subtle forms of rigid conventions, of a sense of sin, and of cramping legislation.

The positive contribution made by the middle class to democratic culture, according to its critics, was the religion, the morality, and the manner of modern business. Many intellectuals followed the example of R. H. Tawney, who in his *Religion and the Rise of Capitalism* linked Puritan morality with business efficiency. There was a shift in morality and religion in the American business life which was observed by a number of these critics, and it was noted in perhaps its most extreme form in an advertisement discussed in an article by Gilbert Seldes (*New Republic*, September 9, 1925). It had promised "Salvation and five per cent," and proposed the construction of a mammoth skyscraper on the corner of 173rd Street and Broadway in Manhattan, dedicated to Christianity and business good will.

> The significant thing about the advertisement is that it is not offensive. "Salvation and 5 per cent" is brash, but not hypocritical. "Business and Christianity will be housed under one roof" is, after all, a statement of fact; and the investment in your fellow man's salvation is preceded by the promise of 5 per cent. . . .
>
> The 5 per cent based on ethical Christian grounds implies a great deal; above all that the 5 per cent will be earned in such a way that there will be no conflict with the ethics of Christianity.

The advertisement put into bold relief the actual relationship of Christianity to business and was therefore refreshing as a frank announcement of the final safe incorporation of security in this world with happiness in the next.

The marriage of business and religion was celebrated in various ways. The bank was of course the actual temple of modern business; its exterior and interior architecture conveyed a more intimate and a closer relationship of modern man with the rituals of religion than did the churches themselves. There was certainly a more sincere following of the ritual—it was less remote from everyone's interests—than could be found in the patently artificial following of Sunday's creed in Sunday's church. The full cycle of religious rite was followed in the business world, in the opinion of Virgil Jordan, who offered this interpretation of the Ford-Babson-Coolidge trinity (*Freeman*, December 5, 1923):

> In their temple of Venus, the devotees of the rainfall and the crop-cycle re-enact the mystery of the reproduction of the seven-year boom. In the catacombs of Wall Street, followers of the one true Chart kneel about mystic circles and crosses; and in the colosseums of collegiate "economic services," primitive statisticians are being led to the lions. From the tops of skyscrapers the mathematical muezzins watch industrial productivity wax and wane, and summon the faithful to sell short. The mendicant friars of Fra Roger preach the new gospel on the highways and by-ways among the Kiwanis and the Rotarians.

All that we need now is a Cathedral of Saint Index, "with stained-glass windows bearing graphs of money-rates, volume of production, wages, and the cost of living." We already have our demonology in the anti-bolshevist code and our ancestor worship in the respect for the names, deeds, and philanthropies of the robber barons of old.

This linking of religion with business was a rather important and serious transference of loyalties, from the simple, life-denying, charitable acts of the medieval saint to the aggressive counterimages of the modern salesman, banker, and economist. The new religion used the Christian text for the most part as window dressing, and with condescension masquerading as piety presented the celebrities of biblical history with honorary membership in the new religious fraternity. The new biblical exegesis was Bruce Barton's *The Man Nobody Knows*, published in 1924 when the faith was making new records in direct and satisfying rewards for shrewd works. The "real Jesus" whom Mr. Barton purported to have uncovered from the biblical text had proved his skill as a business organizer by having brought twelve obscure men from their inefficient pasts and "welded them" into the greatest organization of all time. Jesus had known and followed "every one of the principles of modern salesmanship," Barton averred. The parables were among the most powerful advertisements of all time. And as for Jesus' having been the founder of modern business, Barton pointed simply to the words of the master himself: "Wist ye not that I must be about my father's *business?*"

Never in our history was the power of the middle class so strongly entrenched; never did its rituals seem so convincing; and never were its heretics, the anti-bourgeois intellectuals, so loud in disclaiming its virtues. The portrait of the middle-class man, in the dark gray of his moral business suit, humbly worshiping the golden calf, gave the impression of having come from the most improbable of fantasies. Money is the symbol of value, said Richard Roberts in discussing two books by priests of the new religion, "and value is created by the expenditure of the priceless stuff of life. A coin is so much minted life, a holy thing, neither common nor unclean; a sacramental thing like the bread and wine of the Communion, the symbol of life fruitfully expended. That is why the banker should be as a priest, and a bank a holy place." Merchandise is "so much congealed life," continued Roberts; anyone involved in a crooked trade is therefore "defiling the Temple no less than the hucksters and money changers in Jerusalem long ago" (*Nation*, February 16, 1921). And in philosophic terms, Harold Loeb spoke of "the mysticism of money," which is replacing the theology of the past. It may prove to be "like the Christian religion in the early centuries, a revitalizing force to most aesthetic expressions" (*Broom,* September 1922).

What pained most anti-bourgeois writers was not the apparent economic efficiency of the middle class, but its arrogance in assuming that economic success gave it cultural privilege and moral immunity from criticism. It was this smugness, this complete and self-contained satisfaction, that Mencken underscored in his "Americana" and Sinclair Lewis pointed out in his middle-class extravaganza, *The Man Who Knew Coolidge.* The great, complacent, practical man of Mencken's "Americana," for example, is sure of himself, and he laughs at the feeble efforts to find chinks in the armor of his self-confidence. On Park Avenue lives his successful brother of the faith. "Here the American dollar reaches its dizziest point," said Stuart Chase in one of his portraits of the false economic man. "To the towering and relentless rectangles of the street, the richest nation which the world has ever seen consecrates its cash balance, develops its personality in ten easy lessons, reads the confessions of those who have climbed to the stars from one suspender, improves its table manners, consolidates button factories, makes the sign of the cross with Mr. Bruce Barton, buys for a raise, and dedicates its life" (*New Republic,* May 25, 1927).

3. The Midwest as Metaphor

FORD MADOX FORD, in his Preface to *Transatlantic Stories* (1926), spoke of "Middle Westishness," which, he said, was "in fact a world movement, the symptom of an enormous disillusionment . . . and an enormous awakening." It was as prevalent in Cardiff, Wales, as in Lincoln, Nebraska, in Birmingham, England, as in the outskirts of Indianapolis. In the United States it was produced by "a sudden conviction that the world—even the world as seen in the central western states of North America—is a humdrum affair, and bound to be a humdrum affair for all humanity in *saeculum saeculorum.*" This conclusion was forced upon him when he realized that the Midwest had taken over Paris in the 1920s, in the final stage of a restless, nomadic move.

Why did so many of these young men and women write so many manuscripts on the same subject? The progress of the American had now apparently been reversed; the long journey across to New England, then to the "Western Reserve" and beyond, had in a half-century or less been turned about. The Middle West had become a metaphor of abuse; it was on the one hand a rural metaphor, of farms, villages, and small towns; on the other, a middle-class metaphor, of conventions, piety and hypocrisy, tastelessness and spiritual poverty. The young man or woman had to go east instead of west: in search of freedom (Floyd Dell), a "style" (Glenway Wescott), culture and sophistication (Willa Cather, Carl Van Vechten, Ruth Suckow), or moral maturity (Wescott, Sherwood Anderson).

Evidence, large and small, of the strength of the metaphor abounds in the novels and the short stories: the hero grows up ("is reared") on a farm, in a village, in a colorless, monotonous small town of merchants and ministers, or, at best, in a small commercial city, a provincial metropolis. In one way or another he discovers his parents, realizes them as an alien, elder generation, who have been taught to adhere firmly to a code that seems inappropriate to the circumstances of their living. The hero proceeds along two lines of education; his parents (or so he thinks) have had only one. He is forced to obey the tradition of the fathers; he searches for another tradition. Books, music, the arts, become valuable sources of the new—the real—education; but good literature and good art are hard to come by. There are "sympathetic souls": a school teacher perhaps, an aging or defeated musician or sculptor; an "intellectual" (often a lawyer, a doctor, a professional of some sort, rarely a minister); or a girl who is vaguely dissatisfied with the choices available to her.

As the second education grows in importance, the young man sharpens his talent for moral classification; he rejects the pattern of the community—as tedious, hypocritically moral, without taste or love of beauty, life-defeating, timid and resentful; he chooses instead an imaginary world (a pattern of fictions made out of what he has read, heard, imagined of a non-Midwestern society), and his growth consists chiefly of his effort to translate this second world into an actual occasion. At this point there are several possibilities: the hero may be frustrated in his efforts to break away, may suffer the fate of a "trapped sensibility"; he *may* try to sustain the second world within the first; he may simply lose his awareness of the second, or forget his earlier zeal for it, become the second-rate citizen he despised in others; or he may (and frequently does) get away—in which case, he begins his journey east. A little money, carefully saved by a loving mother, a will or an insurance policy from an unexpected source, an accommodating countess, a scholarship: the means of escape are various, but the impulse to leave is invariable.[5]

For various reasons the image of the middle class was most appropriately identified with the Midwest as metaphor. All the criticisms of the middle class seemed especially adaptable to the geographical and cultural facts of the "middle-border" provincial life. There was a gray dull tone of uniform dreariness: the happy, vital life of the farm was stifled in moral prohibitions and commercial greed; the townsfolk were either without a spark of insight and understanding or viciously hypocritical in the conduct of their affairs; the landscape was not beautiful, the townscape was tediously uniform or hideously vulgar, the social life was timid and ludicrous. Men went to Cleveland or Chicago or Omaha for their "affairs," returning to resume their moral lives. A traveling salesman, a carnival or sideshow, a broken-down stock company (playing *Topsy and Eva* or *East Lynne*), the annual "elocutionary" competition—these were the cultural opportunities available to the young.

There were a limited number of variations on the theme, and the fiction quickly hardened into a very few designs. It was either monotonously realistic or obviously satiric. Robert McAlmon's novel, *Village: As It Happened Through a Fifteen Year Period* (1924), published by his own press in Paris, offered a succession of illustrations of the monotony of village life, with its refrain of pointless violence. The setting is a North Dakota village; the people are uniformly dull or desperately unhappy. The men drink, the women gossip; they try to forget their own bad luck or are comforted by the memory of the bad luck of others. The inference is that a Midwesterner is "neither a savage nor a civilized man," but "a roughneck who's a little too refined."

Glenway Wescott's testimony is much more subtly given. He was truly the Midwesterner become expatriate, at once exploiting and condemning his Midwest in the work written en route to his second country or in it. His novel *The Apple of the Eye* (1924) marks the break from the Midwest and defines life in two ways: the simple, unconscious, beautiful life of farm creatures and "nature"; the mature life of the human soul, who has had to fight his way to a complex insight into simple nature and human society. The simplest life of all is represented

---

[5] Almost without exception, the railroad station is drab, gross, vulgar, covered with dust and soot, when men or women return after their ambitions have failed—glamorous, when it first invites them to leave. Cf. D. H. Lawrence's short stories.

by Hannah Modoc, who possesses the charm and passive goodness of Dreiser's Jennie Gerhardt and suffers exile in a brothel in consequence. The most complete indictment of the Puritan life-denial is given in a burial ceremony; here "talk of fear and punishment," of death and preparation for death, disgusts the young hero as the worst extreme of Midwestern decorum. The people suppress life, fear death, inwardly hate the morality they practice outwardly. "The animals in their nuptials offered the only clue," but he is frightened by the brutality and resolved to suppress the "beast" in himself. He will be "pure," and turns to his mother's puritanism ("that architecture of chastity") for refuge.

His young friend explains the complex of puritanism: "It has beauty. . . . To live in the spirit instead of the flesh. The flesh nothing but candlewax under the flame. Then you feel that you're Christ and all the saints. Puritanism appeals to the imagination, but it makes people sick." This appeal to the moral imagination is a challenge to human dignity and pride; men desperately want to be thought superior to the coupling beasts, so they become overweeningly moral and drive out natural impulse and sicken from the effort. The truth is that sex is *not* bad; it is only the brutality of lust or the frenzy of suppression that is harmful. "There are a great many ways of doing harm. But if you love life and love people, instead of hating them, it isn't so hard to keep from hurting others." This simple balance of feeling and desire must be understood in terms of a maturing experience; and the young man, growing up, must adjust his estimate of "doing harm" and "loving life" before he can say that he has finally understood. The harm done life may come as easily from a Puritan denial of life as it does from a brutal assault upon it. After this lesson has been brought home fully to him, in a series of experiences that are closely associated with the natural world, he is ready to leave the farm, to find a way of adding sophistication to his knowledge of natural and human good and evil. In his mind the two forms of life are clearly seen: the life of "religious people," who are never satisfied because "Life's not perfect"; the life of Hannah ("Bad Han"), who "took what came" and never subjected her acts to puritanic analysis. "Something's wrong," and he will go to the university, and beyond, to find out what it is. The novel is a model expression of the attitude of the 1920s toward the metaphor of the Midwest.

In the short stories of *Good-Bye Wisconsin* (1928), Wescott speaks of the nomadic Midwesterners, "a sort of vagrant chosen race like the

Jews." They are abroad in the world because the land from which they have fled is morally, aesthetically incomplete, rich in its "output of food, men, and manufactured articles; loyal to none of its many creeds, prohibitions, fads, hypocrisies." The Midwest is a label for a state of mind, a condition, which was first experienced and observed in a geographical region, then became a place of "no fixed boundaries." As for the actual Wisconsin, those who could not say "good-bye" to it— who remained on the farms or in the little college town—were bitterly unhappy, envious of the nomads for their apparent moral emancipation, their "pocket money, literal and otherwise," their gaiety. The Wisconsin town of the title story is a thorough realization of the Midwestern metaphor: "there is the sluggish emotional atmosphere, the suavity of its tedium, the morbid grandeur of its meanest predicaments." There are the Calvinist church ("helping itself cease to be a religion at all"); the denominational college, which depends for its revenue upon a strict, tyrannically Puritan appearance; the motion-picture palace ("imagination's chapel in the town"); everywhere, dissatisfaction with life, a vague sense that it is graceless and without charm, that something is missing from it, something that can be found elsewhere, "to the East."

Like any other, this metaphor can easily become trite through constant repetition. However deeply felt, the emotional repudiation of a set of human circumstances like these wears thin. Many portrayals of the Midwest were either unwitting or actual parodies of whatever reality they exploited.[6] Carl Van Vechten's *The Tattooed Countess* (1924) presents the provincial metropolis of Maple Valley, Iowa, to which its most distinguished citizen, the Countess Nattatorini, returns after twenty years abroad. After a succession of balls, operas, concerts, and the company of distinguished men and women, now "a succession of lonely suppers with her austere sister, a series of euchre-parties and receptions." The countess, now fifty, meets the sensitive young man Gareth Johns (still seventeen). He is unhappy, desperate, vainly fighting his father's wish to make him a businessman, "starved for culture." The unformed young and the overformed old meet in a communion of spiritual, aesthetic interests and commiserate over the "narrow prejudices of this town, based on a complete ignorance of life." They conclude that, in Iowa, people worried about "surfaces" but "wore hidden scars."

[6] See John Riddell's parody of the gloomy "Midwestern Story," *Vanity Fair* (April 1929): "She broke her arm at the elbow, just to hear it snap."

> Life is inverted here in Maple Valley [the Countess decides]. . . .
> Everybody is busy trying to conceal his vices or his amiable faults, or
> what others consider vices or amiable faults; one only tells the public
> how good one is, how intelligent, how charitable. These people . . .
> have their love affairs . . . but they have them behind closed doors
> and make clothes for the orphan out in the open.

In Europe, especially in Italy and France, things are different. To
Europe the two plan to go—he to escape the tedium and exasperation
of the metaphor, she to feed upon his youth. The scandal thus brought
to Maple Valley is considered at length in the colloquial idiom of the
rocking-chair "Parcae"; as the novel closes, Missus Bierbauer speaks
of it to her neighbor: good riddance of "bad rubbidge," she says.
"Iowa's a pure, one hundred per cent American state, an' it's lookin'
up!"

No more extreme distortion of the metaphor is found in American
literature than in the writings of Edith Wharton. She was convinced
that the barbarians of Apex City and Euphoria were entirely without
intelligence or taste. In the hero of *Hudson River Bracketed* (1929)
she presented a simple representative of that hinterland to which only
her imagination had given her access. It is not only that she considered
the Midwest tedious, unmannerly, vulgar; she did not know it at all
and created a fantasy of "what it seemed," which was more improbable
than any parody of an imitation of a Sinclair Lewis novel. The names
of her towns (not Maple Valley, but Euphoria and Agamemnon) and
of her characters (Mabel Blitch, Indiana Frusk, Undine Spragg, Ora
Prance Chettle, Elmer Moffatt), showed her distaste. The forces that,
in her opinion, were destroying the society she respected seemed always to have come nakedly from the Midwest, where apparently all
commercial drives, all cultural stupidity, existed in a pure, abstract
form, waiting merely the impetus to move them eastward. In *Hudson
River Bracketed* she tried, perhaps for the only time, to come to grips
with the Midwestern character; though even here, in the naming of
the hero (Advance G. Weston), her dislike of the task is clear. Vance
Weston (named by his father after a real-estate development in
Euphoria, Illinois) comes East from the worst of cultural waste lands,
a land of bad cooking, execrably bad architecture, dullness, tedium,
and a petty, mean commercial go-getting spirit.[7] He seeks his salvation in the East and in the past; specifically, he goes to Paul's Landing,

[7] "I was always vaguely frightened by ugliness," Mrs. Wharton wrote in *A
Backward Glance*.

CRITIQUES OF THE MIDDLE CLASS   333

on the Hudson River, with its charming old architecture, its surviving evidences of an aristocracy of taste, and the presence of a woman who, unhappy in her own life, tries hard to help him recover his. But Vance is not only a Midwesterner fleeing in space and time into the past; he is also a member of the "new generation" and suffers the great disadvantage of both urgencies. It's a "bad time for a creator of any sort to be born," his literary adviser tells him, "in this after-war welter, with its new recipe for immortality every morning."

Whatever the difficulty of the time, there is no doubt that Mrs. Wharton thought the source of the malaise lay in a hypothetical hinterland or cultural waste land, which had neither the saving graces of her Lawrence Selden and Paul Marvell nor the saving integrity of her Ethan Frome. Willa Cather was also affected by this dislike of the Midwest, though in her case it was not a Midwest she did not know, but rather one she knew too well. Her repudiation of the Midwest was essentially a rejection of its gadgets and its commercial sense, which had ruined the happy pioneer balance of man and nature, or man *versus* nature. Her violinists, sculptors, singers either suffer violent defeat and debasement in the small towns where they grow up or flee to the big cities, in which, after all, the garage had replaced the gracious drawing room. Neither the Midwestern town nor the grossly vulgar city could save her people; only the culture of France or the simplicities of landscape and inscape of an unspoiled Southwest.

Only Zona Gale may honestly be said to have loved the Midwestern metaphor. To her, Portage, Wisconsin, was a romantic place, a place of quiet homes and "small lawns, sloping to lilacs and willows," on one bank of a river; if there was no great abundance of cultural events, one could at least remember that the Ballet Russe had momentarily stopped on its way to Minneapolis from Chicago.[8] The church festivals, the recipes, the Christmas entertainments, the "funeral lore," were all treasured as evidences of a quiet, inconspicuous, but genuine smalltown culture. But Miss Gale's fiction, like that of others, participated in the general task of developing the metaphor. Perhaps, in her case, it was more in the nature of associating it with a human metaphor, not especially linked to its regional origins. Miss Lulu Bett (1920) is, after all, victimized by a narrow-minded, selfish community, as Bad

---

[8] See *Portage, Wisconsin, and Other Essays* (1928). Ruth Suckow (*The Odyssey of a Nice Girl*, 1925) honestly posed the Midwest against the East, found Buena Vista, Iowa, sane and sound after Boston, and thought that it provided a quiet cricket-laden context for the eternal verities, Midwestern style.

Han, and the lesser unfortunates of Van Vechten's novel, had been. And in the fabulous *Preface to a Life* (1926) the hero is driven to an appearance of insanity in order to complete his renunciation of a provincial life. He has had his choice: he could have gone to Europe with his beloved (using her money); but he remained to advance the fortunes of his lumber business, inherited from his father, whose death had come about after an outburst of anger over his son's obstinate decision to flee the small town for a better life. Eleven years and three children later, he suddenly breaks down, has the kind of experience which (after Anderson's *Many Marriages*) no one, confronting it in American literature, can quite confidently define as either insanity or a new awareness of life. He had "got sick" of lumber and business and coffee and bacon, and he "went delirious and escaped . . . into something real." He sees through, around, and into people, is given to strange inappropriateness of speech and laughter, and has generally changed from an upstanding success into an insufferable nuisance.

The hero whose mind awakens to the emptiness of his world is the scourge of the Midwestern locale; through him, its Puritan hypocrisies are uncomfortably divulged, its failure of manners and taste advertised. Sherwood Anderson's *Winesburg, Ohio* (1919) provided the myth from which the metaphor's most impressive definitions have been derived. It is a myth of strange, inarticulate, unhappy creatures, who force their way into open expression of their gnarled, warped, suppressed lives. They suffer primarily from a basic failure of communication; and the failure is the result not only of their own essential diffidence, but also of moral and cultural circumstance. The sensitive young man serves in the role of critic, catalyst, judge. But it is because of his youth, because he seems at least both sensitive and communicative, that the grotesques of the village assert themselves in his presence and all but force themselves upon him, in the vain hope that identifying themselves with his personality will somehow save their own. George Willard is, for this and for other reasons, an exceptional center of the Midwestern metaphor. The consequences of his influence upon the community are neither so simple nor so one-sided as are those of other young heroes. He draws from his fellows not a simple indictment of Puritan hypocrisies but a series of revelations concerning their own natures. They are not pure victims of community dullness or suppression; the fault lies in themselves as often as in the community manner; it is the incapacity for feeling, for thinking, and for expressing themselves in public that Willard causes to be revealed. When he finally bows out of Winesburg, headed apparently for the big city where he will become a writer, he leaves much human wreckage behind him. But he is not there merely to document a thesis; Anderson suggests, not that the small town has driven its citizens into either despair or subterfuge, but that the citizens have themselves brought to the surface the tortured lives they had but imperfectly suppressed before.

From these varied demonstrations of one form of middle-class failure a type of criticism was fashioned. The personalities involved were not always mean, hypocritical, evasive, fearful individuals; frequently they were afflicted by a kind of frustrated pride, more often by an excessive narrowness of cultural experience, a lack of the *opportunity* to educate themselves. Nevertheless the principal motifs of this criticism were the puritanic moral code and the empty commercial drive, which, in terms of the metaphor, dominated these people: the one blinded them to natural virtue, the other made it impossible for them to entertain any suggestion of the beautiful, sensitive world beyond. Like the historical metaphor of puritanism, the Midwestern metaphor suffered a variety of distortions in its literary applications, whether for polemical or for purely satirical purposes.

4. The Liberals and the Public Life of the Middle Class

FROM all the evidence of its journals, the power and influence of American liberalism suffered a serious decline in the years following the war. In the first twenty years of the century the progressives had been a strong and effective political and moral force. It had been the age of reformers and muckrakers; in the magazines and newspapers such journalists as Ida Tarbell and Lincoln Steffens had described the shame of the cities and of Standard Oil. There had been a reformist zeal, an effort at honest appraisal of capitalist democracy, with the aim not of disturbing the effectiveness of capitalism but of reducing the incidence of corruption in government and business.

This activity all but disappeared in the 1920s. Liberals were resigned to observing the triumphant display of power on the part of business, a resignation prompted chiefly by the overwhelming public endorsement of successive Republican administrations.[9] One of the reasons for the retreat of liberalism in the twenties was the sudden collapse of the popularity of Woodrow Wilson, whose program of international cooperation had been effectively sabotaged and whose mistakes at Versailles added up to confusion and disappointment in the minds of most Wilsonian liberals. Liberalism was thus a sort of casualty of World War I. It did not, after the end of hostilities, regain its prestige or its popular following until the early days of the Roosevelt New Deal. There were a few men who carried on the progressive tradition —in their books and pamphlets and at the ballot box. Upton Sinclair, a persistent and energetic reformer, continued his criticism of democratic institutions. Robert M. La Follette, Sr., was a candidate for President in 1924, on a third-party ticket, and managed to poll almost five million votes. The *New Republic* and the *Nation* continued bravely in the 1920s, announcing, defending, and utilizing the liberal position in American politics and economics.

To the young men and women of the postwar decade, Wilson's association with the war was enough to discredit him; for those who wished to explain their disappointment, there was enough discussion in the press of Wilson's inconsistencies to justify their break from his progressive-liberal program. No fair-minded person could deny, Harry E. Barnes maintained (*American Mercury,* April 1924), "that Woodrow Wilson produced more cynics than any other figure in modern history." Harold Stearns said (*Freeman,* October 6, 1920), that the young men's "universal attitude towards President Wilson is simply

[9] In the issue of February 1, 1926, the *Survey* published a series of statements in answer to its question, "Where Are the Pre-War Radicals?" For the most part the contributors, many of them graduates of the progressive movement of the 1910s, admitted that progressivism was either no longer needed (having accomplished its purpose) or inadequate for the liberal requirements of the 1920s. Morris Hillquit, Right-Wing Socialist, went further and condemned the progressives as inept and confused. The "motley radicalism" of the second decade, he said, "had neither coherence nor substance, neither program nor material foundation. When it was put to the test in the soul-trying period of war hysteria and terror, it also proved itself wtihout conviction and courage." Norman Thomas answered the question in this way: "The old reformer has become the Tired Radical, and his sons and daughters drink at the fountain of the *American Mercury.* They have no illusions but one. And that is that they can live like Babbitt and think like Mencken." Frederick C. Howe, whose book, *Confessions of a Reformer,* had been the occasion for the symposium, admitted simply (in the April 1926 issue) that "his kind" of reformer would probably never again appear, "because the conditions that made us what we were have gone."

contempt, tempered only by pity for his illness," and went on to maintain that the postwar generation no longer believed "a word about the ostensible aims for which the war was waged." The failure of the war to realize the promises of its leaders in concrete political terms provided a form of rationalization for the indifference shown in the postwar years.

The *Nation,* which had opposed Wilson's war policies, remarked: "We are paying the price for the falsities and hypocrisies which are the inevitable accompaniment of any war, but which, in the great struggle just ended, were raised to a pitch never before deemed possible" (July 5, 1919). Wilson's "befuddling liberalism" had made it "impossible for American radicals to know where they stand"; he had succeeded "in 'putting over' the most complete sabotage of our ideals and traditions that this republic has suffered in 144 years of its national existence" (March 23, 1919). The election of Harding in 1920 seemed the direct result of Wilson's policies; their unpopularity made the return to Republican conservatism inevitable.

The decline of liberalism followed naturally upon the failure of the peace to convince intelligent men that the war had in any way fulfilled the promises of its progressive and liberal backers. They felt they had been deluded, and reacted with a feeling of embarrassment and indignation. This gave the cue—if one was needed—to the younger people, who wished in any case not to have their minds disturbed by optimistic visions of a disciplined progress toward a liberal utopia. But the *Nation* and the *New Republic* went on, insisting on the need of liberal thinking as a means of preserving the democratic process. "Liberalism is a theory of compromise and adjustment," said Benedetto Croce (*New Republic,* April 29, 1925). "To actuate its ideals requires experience, meditation, a sense of history, and an appreciation of the complexities and complications of life." Liberalism requires of men more inner discipline than any other political doctrine, a greater sensitivity to contemporary problems. "As a party, it is characteristically the party of learning and education. Socialism and Reaction are, in contrast, parties of extremes, and, as such, they tend to abstractions and simple formulae. That is why they appeal so particularly to young minds and warm hearts, ever bearing, as a result, the marks of scant or unilateral education."

The skepticism of liberalism and its sense of moderation combined to make it unattractive to these "young minds." Its hope of acceptance was founded on a belief in a disciplined human progress. If men were

capable of exercising their minds, of keeping their passions within
reasonable bounds, and of resisting appeals to prejudices, they would
eventually make their own good society. The liberal theory assumed
that man was slowly, but surely and without violence, progressing
toward a safe and rational world. This had been the philosophical
motivation of Edward Bellamy's utopian novel, *Looking Backward*
(1889), and it had served to encourage and direct the thinking of most
Christian Socialists in the late nineteenth and early twentieth centuries.
It was a Christian doctrine of gradual improvement combined with a
theory of progress that looked toward the evolution of science and a
disciplined, steady improvement in human affairs. For J. B. Bury, *The
Idea of Progress* (1920) meant "that civilization has moved, is moving,
and will move in a desirable direction."

To the man writing for liberal journals, ignorance was the worst
enemy, knowledge man's only defense against abuse of power. Liberal
behavior was also necessarily self-disciplined; not to resist the temptations of extremists could cause irrevocable damage to human society.
Education of the mind meant both development of factual knowledge
and a classical disciplining of the will, in an intelligent and aggressive
campaign against ignorance and prejudice. In this last respect liberal
expression in the 1920s worked in an uneasy partnership with the
Marxists, the aesthetic radicals, and the readers of Mr. Mencken's
Mercury. The liberals thought criticism of present weaknesses in society an indispensable part of their program of educating the democratic public toward a realization of its aims. For liberal spokesmen
ignorance and prejudice were synonymous with evil; wherever these
were found, they must be expelled.

The great philosophic mentor of American liberalism in the twentieth
century was John Dewey. It was he who pointed out most effectively
the dangers of *a priori* thinking in morality and advocated the adoption
of an experimental attitude in politics. The "experimental" ethic, he
said, "implies that reflective morality demands observation of particular situations, rather than fixed adherence to *a priori* principles; that
free inquiry and freedom of publication and discussion must be encouraged and not merely grudgingly tolerated; that opportunity at
different times and places must be given for trying different measures
so that their effects may be capable of observation and of comparison
with one another." This was, in brief, the method of a functional democracy, in which the governing of human affairs most nearly followed
the lines of scientific thought. The authoritarian doctrine, on the other

hand, insisted "that there is some voice so authoritative as to preclude the need of inquiry."

Dewey advised against an inflexible use of authority, spoke for an intelligent use of scientific method; for, after all, it follows precedent "only as long *as no evidence is presented calling for a re-examination of their findings and theories.*" Above all, Dewey defined human growth as *process,* gradual adjustment to new conditions, to material and moral changes in society. Ideals "must themselves be framed out of the possibilities of existing conditions, even if these be the conditions that constitute a corporate and industrial age. The ideals take shape and gain a content as they operate in remaking conditions." A program of ends and ideals, if it does not allow for intelligent modification in answer to changing requirements, "becomes an encumbrance. For its hard and rigid character assumes a fixed world and a static individual; and neither of these things exists" (*Ethics,* 1908).

In the *New Republic,* which published his observations throughout the decade, Dewey gave a profession of liberal faith: "belief in the conclusions of intelligence as the final directive force in life; in freedom of thought and expression as a condition needed in order to realize this power of direction by thought, and in the experimental character of life and thought." Dewey agreed that this was at present an unpopular position: "To believe in mind as power even in the midst of a world which has been what it is by thought devoted to physical matters, is said to evince an incredible naïveté." Yet the mind does work, even in such times as these; and Dewey pointed to the work of Justice Holmes as a supreme example of the functioning intelligence in the modern world. Holmes had been for years the great example of the mind at work interpreting the law, as La Follette had been the liberal personality in public life. Both had sought a reasonable use of the principles of democracy, protection from abuses of privilege, and the progress of intelligent government.

In the decade the liberals devoted themselves to defining and defending their position. The serious division of liberal opinion over the matter of America's entry into the war took years to heal. The democratic assumption of the worth and dignity of man had been questioned throughout the world, said George Boas, in a review of Alphonse Daudet's book *Le Stupide XIXe Siècle.* Criticism of these assumptions, of liberals themselves, was much in evidence; in the *New Masses,* for example, William Gropper (December 1928) described the American liberal as "the funniest clown in American life"; his ludicrous behavior comes from his "trying to steer a dignified middle course in American politics, at the same time preserving the balance of his Olympian Soul. . . . He voted for Al Smith, but when any fundamental social change is suggested, he whispers, 'But oh dear, the facts are not all in yet.' "

The career of the liberal *Nation* during the decade followed the line of caustic, skeptical, and indignant commentary upon the national scene; underlying this was anxious appraisal of the weaknesses of the liberal position, its unhappiness over what seemed a wholesale reversion in the country to reactionary policies and prejudices. During the 1920 elections the *Nation* predicted the defeat of the Democratic candidate, because the issue was chiefly Wilson and the American people had already repudiated his foreign policy. The election of Harding, "a triumph of reaction," proved that "for liberals there is a long road ahead before the United States can be ranked as a politically progressive nation." During the Harding administration the *Nation* regarded Herbert Hoover as the sole liberal hope in the Cabinet and suggested that many who were dissatisfied with both Republican and Democratic policies should turn to him.

The journal spoke ironically about political sideshows, such as Attorney General Palmer's singlehanded rescue of the country from the "Red menace." It remarked that Palmer was to be credited with saving the country from a menace that he had himself created. The Harding Cabinet was "a good, old-fashioned Big Business Cabinet, without a woman in it, without a representative of the masses of the laboring people, without anyone whose name at once suggests liberalism and democracy" (March 9, 1921). The inauguration address of Mr. Harding brought forth the following comment: " 'Forward March— straight to the rear!' This is the inaugural command of our new Commander-in-Chief, President Harding. We are not even to be allowed to stand still, but are to advance backwards just as rapidly as possible—to normalcy by way of stability!" (March 16, 1921).

A series of articles by Arthur Warner gave "The Truth about the American Legion" and characterized that organization's activities as dominated by "the spirit of repression and coercion, of prejudice and unreason, which the war nourished; but it had to heed the cry of 'Back to normal!' which the rest of the community is raising, and is beginning to clothe the nakedness of its purposes in peacetime garments" (July 13, 1921). The Legion's aggressive intolerance toward liberal and socialist groups had continued since May Day of 1919, said Warner.

To the *Nation,* the Klan closely resembled Italian fascism; after printing the *fascisti* oath (November 22, 1922), it suggested that "we Americans have [fascists] in a cruder and less developed form in the Legion and the Klan." [10] Revival of the Klan's power was considered one of the real dangers to a liberal democracy. Though the Klansmen were themselves rather ridiculous creatures ("Solemn but Undignified Penguins"), their activities and their influence could not be taken lightly. The Klan was "in its expressions, as 100-per-cent American as Mussolini's cohorts were 100-per-cent Italian" (January 3, 1923).

There were several indications throughout the world that men were getting impatient with the orderly processes of democratic government. Do not listen, the magazine warned, to the advice of fascist-minded men. "A skillful despot may give an outward appearance of efficiency for a time, but in the end he leaves worse ruin behind him The broader the base of government, the surer its results. Democracy works poorly enough, but there is no substitute for it" (July 2, 1924). Efficiency in itself could not be assumed as the aim of government; it could only be an adjunct to a humanitarian program. The faltering, hesitant, stumbling operation of democratic processes may rouse men to indignation and impatience at times, but we had rather accept them than take the consequences of undemocratic and authoritarian efficiency.

Of the threat to the democracies that was to develop some ten or twelve years later in Germany, the *Nation* exhibited a momentary awareness, and it published a brief note on the beer-hall putsch in Munich, in the issue of November 21, 1923. "Hitler, firing melodramatically into the air to force attention from a feverish crowd, and escaping from an unheroic encounter with the police, wounded

---

[10] The *Nation's* vigorous campaign against the Klan elicited the following letter from an indignant Kluxer, which was printed in the issue of November 8, 1922. The Ku Klux Klan, said the white-sheeted gentleman, is for 100-per-cent Americanism and for making this "a Christian country, free, clean, and democratic; we want clean politics; we want the elimination of the bootlegger, prostitute, gambler, niggers, Mexicans, Irish, Jews, Germans, Huns, and in fact all foreigners, so they will not be able to appropriate to themselves the policies and destinies of this *Great and Glorious American Republic."* The letter concluded with the warning: "Take our advice, shut your mug, and keep your vituperations to yourself."

only by the violence with which he threw himself on the ground when the firing began, has lost his glamour. . . ." Though the *Nation* dismissed Hitler as another postwar opportunist whose loss of face in the Munich failure meant the end of his political career, it was otherwise astute in pointing to the general effect of impatience with democratic processes and the appearance in many parts of the world of various kinds of authoritarian and fascist activity. This was an important function for a liberal paper to fulfill, as was its comparison between fascism in Europe and the apparently ludicrous but potentially dangerous demonstrations of undemocratic belief in America.

The *Nation* had some opportunity for comedy and much for serious thought in its attention to the country's political affairs. The middle class was enthroned in public life, its leader the Vermont "Puritan in Babylon," Calvin Coolidge. The long desert of Republican control stretched as far as the 1928 horizon, and liberals saw little hope for a change even then. Meanwhile their journals relaxed occasionally and enjoyed the comedy of the solemn, thrifty, New England Puritan, whose administration easily survived the La Follette opposition in 1924. His speeches were derided as empty and tiresome, full of the ifs and buts of a cautious man groping his way in a world he scarcely understood.

Sinclair Lewis's "The Man Who Knew Coolidge," printed first in Mencken's *American Mercury* (January 1928), quite effectively caricatured the President, through Lowell Schmaltz, his enthusiastic Zenith sponsor. Mr. Coolidge "is the President for real honest-to-God Americans like us," says Schmaltz to his Pullman-car friends. Of course, "You can bet your sweet life he isn't popular with the bums or yeggs or anarchists or highbrows or cynics." Schmaltz had gone to school with Coolidge. "I can remember just's well as if it was yesterday, Cal and me happened to come out of a class together, and I said 'Well, it's going to be a cold winter,' and he came right back, 'Yep.' Didn't waste a lot of time arguing and discussing! He *knew!*"

In a more serious vein Harold J. Laski, British socialist, pointed out (*New Republic,* January 18, 1928) that the accidental appearance on the political scene of a man like Coolidge indicated a great weakness in American political method. Bruce Bliven (*New Republic,* June 18, 1924) saw no reason "why we should not face the facts and recognize that Coolidge is in no sense a genuine choice either of his party or of the people in general; that he is conspicuously lacking in those qualities which ought to be required of any aspirant to such high office." As for his silence, which some commentators had pointed to as a shrewd Yankee trait, Bliven explained that "Coolidge was saying little a year ago solely and simply because he had little to say. What was true then is true now; and the fact is not concealed by causing him to say his little in more words." Coolidge's world (*New Republic*, December 15, 1926) has the attraction of seeming safe, sane, and sure. "It provides no excuse for surprises and no pretexts for adventures. It ignores all mysteries except those which are officially recognized and labeled. It is laid out in uniform, rectangular blocks which have all been meticulously surveyed and in which every important place and object is located."

This was the heavenly city of the Republican myth. A vision of cleanliness and godliness, with its great comfort and its freedom from doubt and fear, it kept the loyalties of the voters throughout the decade. So long as Coolidge and his advisers convinced the middle class of this image he might stay in the White House if he cared to. The "spotless town" did not actually exist, but it advertised well. The *New Republic* (October 24, 1928) pointed out the success of the Republican party in getting votes even though "its political stock in trade has come to consist exclusively of provoking mechanical popular responses to a few sacred phrases, and of avoiding as it would the devil any effort to give to those phrases a fresh and a living meaning."

At no time in the country's history was there less interest in a careful, intelligent discussion and analysis of vital issues. Voters were lulled to sleep by promises of continuing prosperity. It was no wonder, then, that the liberals failed to impress the public. "Economy is idealism in its most practical form," said the caption under Miguel Covarrubias' caricature of Coolidge (*New Yorker*, March 14, 1925); and it seemed the slogan of most businessmen, who liked the idea of a thrifty, careful President who allowed his constituents economic *carte blanche* while he himself checked carefully his household budget and eliminated the "nonsense" and "frills" from his administration.

The liberals were not only puzzled by this *"status quo* or chaos" form of electioneering; they also regretted the amazing apathy toward public affairs. Political education seemed almost at a standstill; men were for the most part bored with politics. Viewing this disinterest in political matters in the light of fascist regimes in Europe, the Ku Klux Klan, the dishonesty and profiteering of Harding's associates, and the serious defection of democracy in the Sacco-Vanzetti case, the liberals had just cause for their fears. Our democracy, they felt, had failed to exercise its franchise with even the slightest intelligence. "The shabbiest American citizen is the voter who is disgusted with politics and abuses the politicians in power and is indifferent or blind to the public aspects of his professional or economic activity. It is he who is doing most to make American politics sick" (*New Republic,* July 23, 1924).

Midway in the decade, in 1926, two books surveyed democracy from extremes of judgment: H. L. Mencken's *Notes on Democracy* and T. V. Smith's *The Democratic Way of Life.* The first, as we have seen, analyzed democracy from the point of view of a Nietzschean journalist and found that it lacked the primary advantage of a "civilized aristocracy." The second was convinced of the value of democracy. It was one of the ironies of the liberal reputation that Mencken's book was well distributed and Smith's almost not at all. Smith was convinced of the democratic value, Mencken was disabused of it.

A democratic society, Smith said, gives men the chance to "seek the good life in their own way." He insisted that the democratic political machinery came much closer than any other to satisfying the sensible wishes and suiting the habits of intelligent men. To the essential question "How ought we to treat one another in order to achieve the good life?" Smith answered that equality involves an honest sharing of political privilege as well as a fairly even distribution of goods. He hoped to achieve this equality through "compulsion"—that is, legislation and encouragement to union organization. The most intelligent use of machinery and invention, the widest distribution of goods, and the development of the most acceptable kind of social environment are the basic essentials for a practical modern democracy. "We must, therefore, explore the power of social stimulation for mechanical invention and of social prestige for investing otherwise unpleasant work with meaning, and on the other hand we must exploit to the full the potency of machines for banishing both drudgery and monotony."

The two books contained the most radically opposed interpretations of democratic promise. While the economy functioned well, the average American subscribed to neither one; the incompetence of the leaders or suspicions of their dishonesty meant very little to him. The Doheny oil scandals, the revelations concerning the operations of Harding's "Ohio Gang," offered good press copy for liberal magazines and newspapers, but they could not upset the general complacency or affect the election results in 1924. Nothing defeats liberalism so thoroughly as a conservative government that seems to have fulfilled its economic guarantees. The people generally wished no relations with Europe except those that would bring a profit; they wanted no tampering with government so long as the business index remained comfortably high.

The Republican myth was powerful in the 1920s. It was begun as campaign strategy, and as the years of the decade proved at least superficially prosperous, the myth prospered also, so that even hardened politicians began to believe in it; even some liberal critics thought it might be true. Though astute readers of economics thought the economy must sometime crack and statisticians pointed to a constant of unemployment in even the best years of the decade, no persuasive or prophetic voices disturbed the tranquillity of the electorate. The major issue of the 1928 campaign, less than a year before the Wall Street crash, was Prohibition, with the Catholic Church a strong second. The liberal papers had good reason to fear that democracy might die from sheer lack of effective education in its uses.

At the same time writers were losing their belief in the liberal theory of progress. They had ceased to admire H. G. Wells, who was described as "The Last of the Great Parlor Socialists" (*Liberator,* September 1923). Wells's *The Outline of History,* most popular of all non-fiction best-sellers in the twenties, proclaimed and documented the theory of progress in typical Wellsian fashion. He did his best to exorcise the devils of war from the caves of history; blow upon sturdy blow fell upon the bruised shoulders of the Martians. Science, on the other hand, was the liberal angel, laying the ghosts of superstition, working unceasingly at the task of preparing the heavenly city of the future. In the last book of the *Outline,* Wells turned prophet; he predicted the coming of a new order that would be free of all martial and nationalistic taint, blessed by peace and prosperity. Despite the revenues the best-selling *Outline* gave Wells, his confident reading of history had little appeal for the intellectuals. It was too simple, too easy to believe; it seemed another example of liberal wishful thinking.

Another interpretation of history had more persuasiveness. It offered novelties of method and organization, and it was pessimistic to the core. The introduction to Oswald Spengler's *Decline of the West* had been translated by Kenneth Burke for the *Dial.* (The complete English translation, by Charles F. Atkinson, appeared in two volumes, in 1926 and 1928.) This complex book disconcerted the theorists of progress by rejecting their linear view of history and substituting for it a concept of cyclical change, in which civilizations were described as developing according to a definite morphological pattern, and social growth was limited therefore to a repetition of cultural states. If Spengler was correct, the enormous advances of science and the less impressive development of social utilitarianism were aspects of the last stage of Western culture. Such a view of history ran counter to the hopes of both liberals and Marxist radicals. But for many who distrusted the optimistic views of progress-theorists and were not willing to accept the aggressive remaking of history sponsored by the Communists, Spengler seemed interesting, novel, almost plausible.

The cautious optimism of liberalism, its demands upon human intelligence and patience, its failure to offer any immediate reward for the stresses and strains of intelligent political behavior, all vexed the men and women of the twenties, who either wished for no involvement in political action or preferred the more melodramatic ways of the Communists. As for the liberals themselves, they scoffed at campaign promises much as did their fellow journalists to the left and right of their center. They too laughed at the antics of the middle class in public control; but unlike Mencken and his followers, they ceased to laugh when they considered the implications of such control for the future of the economy. They were especially displeased with the apathy shown by a great majority of fellow intellectuals, who refused to listen to liberal reiterations of a prewar political philosophy and who blindly accepted the economy as a self-operating machine that would continue to run with a minimum of watching or with none at all.

5. The Anarchist and the Radical Hope

S PEAKING in 1925 of the *Masses* and of the men and women who had worked for it, Genevieve Taggard called the second decade of the century "a holiday"—compared, that is, to what had happened since. "There was zealous social work, backed by optimistic social theory; humanitarian crusades abounded, gracious amateur movements made a mushroom growth. This activity was never ruthless or bitter, but earnest, idealistic,—always Christian." The "holiday" had begun with the first issue of Emma Goldman's *Mother Earth,* in March 1906; [11] it came to an end with the suspension by the United States

[11] *Mother Earth* was founded a few months after the Revolution of 1905 in

government of Max Eastman's and Floyd Dell's magazine, the *Masses,* in November 1917. Though there was animated debate over proper guiding principles, as these might be inferred from a reading of Karl Marx, Kropotkin, Max Stirner, Nietzsche, and others, radicals before the advent of World War I did not usually expect or desire a sudden defeat of the capitalist system. The philosophy "which underlay our movement," said Floyd Dell "forbade us to believe that the Great Change was to be effected by a sweeping conversion of men's minds, or that the gradual conversion in which we were assisting was any other than the reflection of an economic process. We were bringing this process and its effects into the general consciousness. But it was the Process itself which was really to be trusted to realize our desires" (*Intellectual Vagabondage,* 1926).

In the years before 1917 there were several radical strains, which complemented one another with very little conflict. The anarchist movement had its roots, at least in part, in the American tradition of individualism, but it was also indebted to foreign ideological interpretations, brought over by emigrants from Russia and Italy. The Marxist interpretation of history was applied by a few intellectuals to the growing drive toward trade unionism. But the divisions between Marxists of one persuasion and those of another were not clearly or effectively drawn; socialists of the right mingled with socialists of the left, who in turn saw no inconsistency in their sympathetic alliance with Emma

---

Russia had come to a disastrous end, because the revolutionaries had failed to gain control of military power. Emma Goldman, its editor and publisher, had migrated to America from Russia in 1886. Her subsequent study of anarchism convinced her that its highest expression was to be found in the best work of America's intellectual history, in Emerson, Thoreau, and Whitman. In 1911 Miss Goldman published a collection of essays in which she explained the anarchist position. Anarchism, she said then, is "the philosophy of a new social order based on liberty unrestricted by man-made law; the theory that all forms of government rest on violence, and are therefore wrong and harmful, as well as unnecessary." In her lecture appearances and in her articles and editorials, she spoke of the "anarchist necessity" in a society badgered and restricted by social law and political practice, cited gratefully the tradition of Thoreau in this country, defended and derived support from the doctrines of Max Stirner and Nietzsche, and in general recommended an alliance of philosophical anarchism with practical support of current labor activities. Anarchism, she affirmed, is the only philosophy that gives to man a "consciousness of himself," and therefore assures him of a protection of his liberty against the encroachments of politics and religion. It is the only doctrine that insists upon the value of the individual and therefore "maintains that God, the State, and Society are non-existent, that their promises are null and void, since they can be fulfilled only through Man's subordination."

Goldman's anarchism. The real crisis of interpretation came when the smoke of the Russian Revolution had cleared, when its events and its example demanded doctrinal exposition and clarification. From 1918 to 1924 the battle for supremacy of doctrine took place, and the harmony of liberals, radicals, and anarchists ceased to obtain.

In the years before World War I, Bill Haywood was a hero of the New York radicals, the knight-errant of labor, the toast of the fellow travelers in the salons and at Greenwich Village parties. A veteran of court trials and imprisonment, Haywood fought in the front ranks of the I.W.W. in its struggle with capitalists.[12] In 1913 he was in New Jersey and New York, helping the strikers in Paterson, New Jersey. On one of Mabel Dodge's "Evenings," Haywood spoke for the labor cause and also discussed the place of art in the socialist state. It was an exciting occasion, Mabel Dodge tells us in her *Movers and Shakers* (1936). "Bill was at his best, with Dasberg flashing and witty, and Arthur Lee, with terrific earnestness, trying to pound out his somewhat reluctant thoughts, and others cutting in, several talking at once, until in the end we really had General Conversation and the air was vibrant with intellectual excitement, and electrical with the appearance of new ideas and dawning changes." In many ways this meeting illustrates the disposition of intellectual radicals at this time: the leisurely manner of the conversation, the fact that it was an "Evening," characterized by tolerance and politeness.[13]

[12] The Industrial Workers of the World was established in 1905 chiefly with the object of making union organization more effective, of ridding it of its outworn organizational forms. The new labor movement advocated an international union of workers, which might work on a major scale, and provided as well for local craft autonomy. Its aim was also to work for an eventual defeat of capitalist power, through various means, particularly that of giving labor political and economic strength. In his country-wide activities during the early years of the twentieth century Haywood suffered imprisonment and unfair trials, and denunciation by the capitalist press. In 1913 Haywood went East to defend Ettor and Giovannitti in the trials there, which anticipated the arrests of Sacco and Vanzetti some years later. The trial of Ettor and Giovannitti touched off "a mad wave of patriotism" among the businessmen of Lawrence, Massachusetts, "and for a time they all wore little American flags in their button-holes, to the great satisfaction of the flag manufacturers" (*Bill Haywood's Book*, 1929). Ettor and Giovannitti were acquitted, but their successors to the chair of martyrdom, Sacco and Vanzetti, were not to succeed as well in defeating the pressures of patriotism and business in the 1920s.

[13] In his novel *Venture* (1927), Max Eastman has preserved a picture of that evening, and has used the clashes of personalities and ideas as parts of an intellectual drama. The chairman of the meeting, says Eastman, was a "philosophical

The atmosphere of the salon, the informal "club," the *Masses* editorial conference, was fairly representative of political radicalism in the 1910s. These intellectuals entertained radical proposals in much the same way that they entertained views on other matters. Political issues and economic questions were—like birth control, woman's suffrage, psychoanalysis, and vegetarianism—subjects of debate. For the leader of the salon the great merit of ideas lay in their daring and novelty and the feeling stimulated by discussion of them. There was an atmosphere of pageantry in Mabel Dodge's "Evenings"—a parade of ideas and feelings, the display of which counted for more than clarity or precision of expression. Certainly those Wednesday displays of

---

anarchist," the kind of man who, "like the 'socialist in idea,' wants to enjoy the little thrill attending an extreme belief without taking the social consequences or doing any of the work." Haywood talked briefly upon the subject of a proletarian art; he was apparently aware of this assignment as a job he needed to do, in order to raise funds and arouse the sympathies of the New York intellectuals for the Paterson strike. His speech was brief and without any concessions to the devotees of art. There is no time now, he said, for the teaching of art to the proletariat. They need to be organized and trained to fight for their rights, for an eventual triumph over their oppressors. But when all this has been accomplished and the socialist state has arrived, then everyone will have an opportunity to learn and practice the art. What kind of art will they have? "I think it will be very much kindlier than your art. There will be a social spirit in it. Not so much boasting about personality. Artists won't be so egotistical." The response to Haywood's remarks was varied. One of the questioners agreed with Haywood in principle, but was afraid that socialist art might be controlled art, and he was anxious to retain the gifts of his own personality and to use them in his own way. The psychoanalysts were represented by two persons, one of whom analyzed Haywood: "Mr. Haywood might sincerely think he was interested in the proletariat, but his real interest was in overthrowing the tyranny of the father image." A socialist spoke next; she believed in socialism, she explained, but distrusted class fighting and class hatred. "I base my socialism on Darwin and not Marx, on evolution and not revolution. I am in no hurry. I can wait for human intelligence to evolve to that point where it will be able to organize in a rational way the distribution of the good things of life." A woman rose next to dispute Haywood's slighting references to the unimportance of art in the socialist state. "It takes twenty years to make an artist!" she said indignantly. "Aht, my deah man, requiahs yeahs of consecrated effort. Do you suppose I would be an artist today if I had been standing ovah the tubs all these yeahs? Do you mean to say that I could wash my own clothes and get my own meals and yet make sculptuh that would find a place in the Metropolitan Museum of Aht?" These questions were parried by Haywood with such deliberate humor that the lady's husband was moved to protest that the entire meeting was an insult to his and to his wife's intelligence: "In the absence of the police, I voice my protest by leaving the room."

conversation, though only a fragment of the intellectual life, were symptomatic of a general, polite confusion in the matter of objectives. The guests were agreed upon the general need of reform in contemporary mores and institutions, but they were not anxious either for a revolution or for the sudden collapse of a society they found delightfully amusing.

A more complete view of the radical mind of the 1910s may be found in the career of the *Masses* after Max Eastman took over the editorship, from December 1912 to November 1917. The political cartoons by Art Young, Boardman Robinson, and others emphasized the native quality and temperament of the editors' radicalism. These drawings, much of the poetry, the essays of Floyd Dell on free love, marriage, and sex—all argued a non-doctrinal form of radicalism, which Eastman's somber editorials on "Knowledge and Revolution" almost alone tried to correct. It was as though the editorial in each issue was a kind of formularized ritual of identification, which was got through in haste, before the playful and discursive activities of the magazine could begin.

No single contribution to the cause of radicalism, no matter what its form or variant of intent, was ignored by the *Masses* editors. Eastman on several occasions, after the *Masses* had ceased publication, defended the place of the artist in a radical magazine; the professor of philosophy, the student of Marxism, was also a poet, a man sensitive to the needs of the artist. "We are distinguished, we literary and artistic people," he said (*Liberator*, June 1921) "by our ability to realize, to feel and express, the qualities of things. We experience vividly the existing facts, and the revolutionary ideal, and the bitterly wonderful long days of the struggle that lies between these two. All the way along we are dealing as experts in experience. . . . And this faculty of vivid living—besides the ultimate and absolute value it has in itself—contributes something indispensable to the practical movement. It contributes something that we might call *inspiration*."

In the pages of the *Masses* the love poetry of Eastman, Dell, and E. E. Cummings was printed beside the rough-hewn lines of the Italian labor agitator Arturo Giovannitti. The cartoons, alternately serious and gay, satirized immediate conditions and the cultural status of American institutions. The poetry was varied in intent and quality; its selection was not governed by political message or content. The reportage, especially the articles of Mary Heaton Vorse and John Reed, gave a running account of industrial and labor conditions.

This harmony of many radical points of view gave Max Eastman his best argument when he came to the defense of the *Masses* in the two government trials. After having banned the magazine from newsstand sales (January 1916) and from the mails (August 1917), the government finally brought charges against Eastman, Dell, Art Young, and the business manager, Merrill Rogers, for "conspiracy against the government" and "interfering with enlistment." The first trial, in April 1918, resulted in jury disagreement; a second was called, and it ended with eight of the jurors for acquittal, four against. But the magazine itself gave up publication in December 1917. In March 1918 its successor, the *Liberator,* appeared.

Eastman's long summary of the *Masses'* stand was made on October 4, 1918. As published by the Liberator Publishing Company, the speech rested its argument on the question of intent. There was no evidence of deliberate intention on the part of the *Masses* editors to obstruct recruiting or enlistment, Eastman said. "On the contrary, our intention was to issue into the general current of public opinion our satirical and argumentative and poetic and pictorial comments upon the general policy of the Government from a socialist point of view." Eastman asked the jury to notice that "we never adopted any policy toward this war. We never adopted any policy toward anything. We simply continued to express, each in his own chosen way, his own opinion and emotion about the policies of our Government."

Russian events were in themselves sufficient to put a temporary end to the satisfactions of speculative radicalism. The Revolution was not a thing one could merely watch from the vantage point of the bourgeois intellectual or contribute to with money or creative talent. The *Liberator* (1918–1924), with Eastman and Dell as editors, realized this altered fact of radical history. The magazine was apparently a continuation of the *Masses:* the similarities of format, contribution, and editorial were obvious enough. The real difference was the Russian point of reference, a genuine opportunity for endowing political theory with evidence and substance.

There was, of course, the possibility of a world revolution, or at least one seemed possible, if one could trust reports from Germany, Hungary, and elsewhere. "Truly, the Communist International is ready for its great task," said Max Bedacht (March 1923). "It will prove its readiness when the masses rise to deal tottering capitalism its fatal blow. It will prove its readiness no less in the preparation of the masses for that great rising." John Pepper (November 1923) said that the world revolution, once put down by the capitalists, was again rising.

"The bourgeoisie is economically and politically bankrupt. It can no longer lead mankind. The might of the workers is growing." When George Bernard Shaw was asked what he thought of the possibility of a general European revolution, he replied, "Europe is too big, and not sufficiently integrated and organized, to be capable of any single simultaneous operation; but I have seen her shake off three super-empires and replace them with republics; so that she is now predominantly republican and only apologetically and shakily dynastic-monarchical. Surely that is enough for one lifetime" (November-December 1922).

To some extent, the tendency to exaggerate the significance of revolutionary events was an attempt to protect the hope against a too early disillusion. Speaking of the program adopted in Chicago in 1919 by the new American Communist party, Eastman called it "a vital, simple and realistic application of the theories of Marx, and the policies of Lenin, to present conditions in America. . . . It is written in a more American idiom, it is written in the language of action rather than of historic theory, it is not abstractly didactic in its attitude toward organized labor, but somewhat humbly instructive and promising of concrete help" (October 1919).[14]

In spite of the *Liberator*'s joy in proclaiming the revolution, there was very little actual interest in sponsoring radical activities in the 1920s. The *Liberator* was, after all, a small magazine, less influential even than the *Masses*. The intellectuals were quite generally as indifferent to Marxist ideas as to liberal theory.

The Red scare led in 1919 to wholesale arrests and deportations of aliens, suspected aliens, persons whose accent was suspiciously un-American, and persons with a labor record one inch to the left of the Gompers center. On December 21, 1919, the *Buford* sailed from New York with 249 "aliens" aboard, whom the press (according to Louis Post) described as "249 blasphemous creatures who not only rejected American hospitality and assailed her institutions, but also sought by a campaign of assassination and terrorism to ruin her as a nation of free men."

The government had previously defined two classes of anarchist:

---

[14] In 1923 Eastman left the *Liberator*, to see the Revolution for himself. Robert Minor took over the editorship, with Joseph Freeman as his managing editor and a number of associate editors. Though Eastman contributed reports from Russia, his influence upon the magazine waned. In November 1924 the *Liberator* was offered directly to the American Communist party and was merged with the *Labor Herald* and the *Soviet Pictorial*, to form the *Worker's Monthly*.

the "destructive revolutionists," who carried bombs in cheap suitcases and were trained in revolutionary ballistics; and the philosophical anarchists, who wished harm to no one except themselves. The Act of Congress of October 16, 1918, obliterated the distinction, and Americans were deported for being anarchists of any kind. The Attorney General, seeing a destructive and explosive revolution directly around the corner of history, was out to stop it. In the words of Louis Post, who as Assistant Secretary of the Interior judged numerous cases of unfair arrest and imprisonment, the "Red crusade" was "saturated with 'labor spy' interests—the interests, that is, of private detective agencies, which, in the secret service of masterful corporations, were engaged in generating and intensifying industrial suspicions and hatreds" (*The Deportations Delirium of Nineteen-Twenty*, 1923).

The Red scare helped to draw the lines sharply between active political radicals and speculative radicals, whose interests were not altogether bound up with the fate of labor or the future of the Communist party. The happy union of radicals of all shades of political and philosophical belief was finally dissipated by these events. The Communist party, formed from the left wing of American Socialists, worked on the problem of strengthening the labor movement and developed along the lines of watchful and opportunistic waiting for the next demonstration of capitalist "maturity." The liberal papers adopted a cautious but generally sympathetic attitude toward radical events in both Russia and America; they were interested, as always, in the guarantee of personal rights and liberties within constitutional limits, and they judged Russia from the vantage point of a democratic society that preserved legal and cultural forms.

Friend and foe alike kept a watchful eye on events in Russia. One thing changed profoundly: debates about theoretical Marxism were replaced by discussions of Russia; the ideological soundness of Marxist doctrine was always measured in terms of that immediate revolutionary fact. Some few intellectuals felt the need to travel to Russia, to see the Marxist philosophy of history in actual operation. On October 19, 1927, Theodore Dreiser sailed from New York. He spent eleven weeks in Moscow and in the interior of Russia, and approved of much of what he saw. It was true that in the schools only communism was taught; but, said Dreiser, "at any rate it can be said for communistic dogma [that] it seeks to give every living human being an equal start in the life race and afterwards to help him as much as possible in his struggle to sustain himself and the race." The theater, he thought, was dull, because of the repetitious use of the Communist-hero *versus* capitalist-villain theme. As for the Russian rulers, he granted their autocratic hold upon human rights, but they were nevertheless sincere and honest; and the dictatorship he felt, was only "a weapon for a particular end—the bringing of that classless, brother-loving society in which no dictatorship will be needed."

Dreiser's sensitivity to the needs and hopes of the proletariat qualified every remark he had to make about the imperfections of both rule and economic conditions in Russia. All such weaknesses must be endured; at least they ought not be used in support of disaffection. The faith that moved so many who watched the internal struggles of the first modern communist state held Dreiser's anger and irritation in check. The propaganda, for example, distressed him—the ceaseless and repetitious instruction in communist aims, the myriad pamphlets, the garish posters; yet Dreiser called this, not lying, but pardonable exaggeration of a hoped-for reality. Both art and knowledge, he noticed, "are for one purpose, and one purpose only—the conformation and so establishment of communism." He recalled a revised version of *Uncle Tom's Cabin,* in which Little Eva had been omitted from the cast of characters and Simon Legree was triumphantly liquidated by a young Negro's gun. Dreiser was not unaware of the planned distortions of fact that formed part of the *modus operandi* of Russian propaganda. And he noticed also "the inescapable atmosphere of espionage and mental as well as social regulation." The G.P.U. was to be found "at every railway station and dock throughout Russia, by night as well as by day"; and he had always the same explanation: "counter-revolution, brought about by foreign intervention, is their justification for maintaining this large body of men."

At the end of his visit Dreiser remained convinced not only of the vitality of the Russian Revolution but also of its fundamental correctness, in terms of human values. Consider, he said, the differences between Fifth Avenue and the Bowery in a single city of capitalist America. "You cannot walk the streets of any city anywhere in Russia . . . and gather a suggestion of that difference between classes and conditions that so haunted you in your childhood. It is not possible. Do you sense the import of this?"

Commentators found evidence in Russia for whatever position they wished to take. The liberal journals contrasted practical fact in a revolutionary state with the liberties guaranteed by a liberal conscience. Businessmen saw nothing to cheer about in Russian affairs, except for one incident in its early history, the declaration by Lenin of a "New Economic Policy," which to American capitalists meant the end of a communist economy and a return to private enterprise. Americans, liberals and reactionaries alike, could view the revolution from a distance, make comparisons, invidious or flattering, with democratic policies and institutions. They were privileged to subscribe to whatever stereotype of classification suited their fancy or fear.[15]

The majority of intellectuals were political negativists. They enjoyed pointing out the absurdities of Harding, Coolidge, Hoover, and Company; they were quite happy to describe the bad manners of the middle class, but they were not much interested in attacking the economy supported by that class. Most of them, at any rate, were quite ignorant of economics and quite indifferent to the science of revolution. As Malcolm Cowley put it, in *Exile's Return,* "Society was either regarded as a sort of self-operating, self-repairing, self-perpetuating machine, or else it was not regarded."

This attitude toward the imperatives of society set in motion by the revolution was roundly condemned by liberals and Communists alike. To the latter, literature and art were vitiated by self-indulgence. The liberals of the *Freeman* resented what seemed a defeatist attitude, the use of the war as an excuse for abdicating one's proper role and duty. One of the Marxist critics of American culture, V. F. Calverton, was shocked by this tendency of the literary radical to play 'possum in a critical time. To what extent are our modernists radical? he asked

[15] Scores of articles on Russia by businessmen and their apologists testified to their preoccupation with this fascinating and fearsome subject. "It is the doctrine of strife and hatred among men," wrote one. "It is the doctrine of chaos, and opposed to the Fatherhood of God and the Brotherhood of man" (Peter W. Collins, *Current Opinion,* March 1920). The *Literary Digest,* of course, carried an account of "the world revolution" almost every week, accompanied usually by a cartoon of the bearded, bomb-carrying, wild-eyed radical. What seemed to please the apologists for business more than anything else was the evidence (particularly in the early years of the decade) that Russia was dangerously near economic collapse. But the conservatives were also anxious to point to the collapse of religion and morality in Russia, and to the complete absence of civil liberties.
When the news came through of Trotsky's fall from official grace, conservatives collected all information they could find and offered numerous interpretations of this sign of revolutionary failure. "The revolution," said one, "is obviously approaching some crisis, perhaps the second greatest of its existence" (Lancelot Lawton, *Contemporary Review,* March 1925). In the opinion of another, the "pendulum of the Russian Revolution, after touching the extreme of bolshevism, is gradually but irresistibly swinging back to the middle course of democratic development" (A. J. Sack, *Current History,* May 1925).

(*Modern Quarterly*, September-December 1926). "Their technique reveals radical change, expressive of profound causation, but does their substance disclose a corresponding radicalism of ideas? If we mean by radicalism a desire and a demand for a new social order, our answer must be in the negative." The young men *are* critical of "our acquisitive civilization," but "there is but a small group of all our modern poets who are genuinely radical also in their social philosophy." Calverton described an America well advanced in capitalism but with "no social lyric and no revolutionary satire. We are playboys in a social world which, in its whirling anarchies of rotation, threatens to engulf and devour us in another cataclysm at any moment." [16]

One of the most vigorous critics of this negativism was Mike Gold. As book reviewer and critic for the *Liberator*, as reporter and polemicist in the cause of Sacco and Vanzetti, and finally as policy-maker of the *New Masses*, he repeated and underscored his simple critical thesis. Young man, go left! he advised and pointed to Soviet Russia, where the only hope of humanity and model for action appeared to reside. As for his own country, his autobiographical novel *Jews Without Money* (1930) showed what he thought was wrong. The reasoning of the aesthete seemed to him trivial and absurd. There was once a genuine literary radicalism in this country, he argued, but it has died. The product of the little theater, the little magazine, and the Village was cruelly disappointing. Writers of the Village, though they occasionally looked at vital issues and sometimes wrote well, were all too often merely sophisticates of despair. "They believed in nothing but the empiric of sensation, or in the undisciplined chaos of the subconscious" (*New Masses*, September 1928).

[16] One of these "playboys," E. E. Cummings, traveled to Russia in 1931 to see the revolution for himself. In the record of that trip, published as *Eimi* in 1933, his impressions gave full support to his feeling that the single, isolated being had been overwhelmingly defeated by the state—the mass of unpalatable detail

> . . . guarded by
> a helplessly handsome implausibly
> immaculate soldier . . .

The geometric solidity of the Russia that made him feel its power to destroy the eccentric, the personal, in man was symbolized by Lenin's tomb:

> a rigid pyramidal composition of blocks; an impurely mathematical game of edges: not quite cruelly a cubic cerebration—equally glamourless and emphatic, withal childish . . . perhaps the architectural equivalent for "boo!—I scared you that time!" (hard by are buried martyrs)

6. Sacco and Vanzetti as Leftist Heroes

ONLY one event of the 1920s succeeded in arousing intellectuals of every kind of political loyalty: the arrest, trial, and execution of two Italian anarchists, Nicola Sacco and Bartolomeo Vanzetti.

It began at three p.m. on April 15, 1920, when the paymaster of the Slater and Morrill shoe company and his guard were shot and killed by two men in front of the company's office building in South Braintree, Massachusetts. Since the crime was committed in the middle of the afternoon and on the main street of the town, many persons were attracted to the scene and several caught a fleeting glimpse of the murderers' car as it sped through the town. Two days later the car was found abandoned in a wood some distance from the scene of the crime.

Sacco and Vanzetti, arrested on May 5, were among the leaders of the Italian laborers in eastern Massachusetts factories. To the jury that listened to the prosecuting attorney's skillful use of this information, the radical association became the principal issue, and the jurors were all the more anxious to believe in the circumstantial evidence offered in court.[17] It was inevitable that the Red hysteria, which had reached new heights in the Boston area, should have affected the nature of the prosecuting attorney's approach to the trial. In so framing his questions that they related directly or indirectly to political beliefs, he played upon the prejudices and sympathies of the jury. The practice of introducing irrelevant matters for the purpose of working upon the prejudices of the jury was, of course, contrary to proper criminal procedure, as Felix Frankfurter and his colleagues in the legal and academic professions pointed out. "By systematic exploitation of the defendants' alien blood," Frankfurter said, "their imperfect knowledge of English, their unpopular social views, and their opposition to the war, the District Attorney invoked against them a riot of political passion and patriotic sentiment; and the trial judge connived at—one had almost written, cooperated in—the process" (*The Case of Sacco and Vanzetti*, 1927).

After several months of testimony and questioning in the courthouse

---

[17] That Sacco and Vanzetti had fled to Mexico during the war, to escape the draft, was also strongly emphasized at the trial.

at Dedham, Sacco and Vanzetti were convicted of the South Braintree crimes on July 14, 1921. Throughout the trial they were defended by Fred Moore, an experienced labor attorney whose record of defending radicals gave him useful knowledge of procedures in such cases but also served to antagonize the prosecution and the public. On October 1, 1923, the case was taken over by William G. Thompson, a conservative lawyer of considerable reputation and standing in the Massachusetts courts. On that date a hearing was held regarding five motions for a new trial, based on affidavits collected from various persons by the Defense Committee. Judge Thayer refused the appeal for a new trial, as he had earlier dismissed other motions. The next attack was upon Thayer's ability as trial judge. The Supreme Judicial Court of Massachusetts ruled on May 12, 1926, that it could find "no error" in any of Thayer's rulings, so the verdicts were allowed to stand.

On November 18, 1925, Celestino F. Madeiros, a young Portuguese criminal, in prison on a conviction for murder, submitted the following confession to the jailer: "I hear by confess to being in the South Braintree shoe company crime and Sacco and Vanzetti was not in said crime." The Defense Committee, convinced it had "a sure thing," worked furiously to build its case. Madeiros, who confessed because he felt sorry for Sacco and "the kids," provided further details; he told the story of the holdup and the murders, but refused to reveal the identity of other participants. Everything pointed, however, to their having been members of a professional gang of criminals. The defense linked Madeiros' description with confederates of the Morelli gang, known to police all over the area for a series of robberies. The prosecution maintained that Madeiros had made the confession in the hope of receiving money from the Defense Committee; but the state finally admitted that there was no evidence that the Defense Committee had offered Madeiros any promise of financial aid. Judge Thayer did not change his mind; in an opinion of twenty-five thousand words he denied the motion for a new trial.[18]

After each new refusal the Defense Committee worked with renewed energy. Until the very hour of the executions and beyond, it was busy with appeals, searches for new evidence, petitions, and meet-

---

[18] In Charles E. S. Wood's own heaven, to which Sacco and Vanzetti reported immediately after their deaths, they were given a new trial, this time with God as judge and with Jesus offering testimony by way of historical analogy. They were acquitted without difficulty. See "Heavenly Discourse," *New Masses,* September 1928.

CRITIQUES OF THE MIDDLE CLASS

ings. The defense had started with only the Italian friends of the two
defendants, but it was not long before labor leaders and labor lawyers
moved into Massachusetts to take part in the proceedings. To Sacco
and Vanzetti, schooled by experience in such matters, the case was
evidence of class hatred: they were being persecuted because they were
an anarchist threat to the wealthy people of Massachusetts. The anarchists who served on the committee soon quarreled with the leftists of
other parties. As Upton Sinclair put it in *Boston* (1928), "a committee of anarchists was a contradiction in terms; it was not a committee, but a number of impermeable and unassimilable units, and anybody who ever did anything was sure to be regarded as a dictator or
meddler."

During their seven years of imprisonment Sacco and Vanzetti became the heroes of radicals all over the world, the dramatic center
of vigorous and desperate efforts to fight the forces ultimately responsible for the official crime against their persons.[19] The affair threw into
dramatic relief all the revolutionary, anarchist, and liberal efforts to
define justice and to clarify left-wing policy. It was a *cause célèbre,* followed by all men who were not simple reactionaries or merely indifferent to problems of justice and law. It became a critical struggle between right and left, caused explosions in Paris and in Zurich, parades
and protests in Europe and in South America; [20] it inspired poems,
plays, and novels; it served as a crucial test of liberal and radical loyalties. For almost the only time in the 1920s, liberals, anarchists, Communists, and Harvard professors joined in political action and dra-

[19] From France came an appeal "To the American People," published in the
Nation, November 23, 1921, and republished frequently thereafter by the Defense Committee. Anatole France begged the Americans to "Save Sacco and
Vanzetti. Save them for your honor, for the honor of your children and of all
the generations yet unborn." It is horrible to think, he said, that men should be
condemned for "a crime of opinion," should have to "pay with their lives for the
exercise of that most sacred right, the right which we ought all to defend, to
whatever party we may belong."

[20] Violent reactions against the trial and executions began in October 1921. In
its December 10, 1921, issue the *Literary Digest* expressed and quoted the
indignation of the conservative press over the world-wide bombings and parades.
There were reports of protest meetings, demonstrations in front of American
embassy and consulate offices, and bombings. The French reaction took the form
of a demand for an immediate boycott of American goods. In Rome the "Radical
members" of the Chamber of Deputies demanded intercession by the Italian government. In Lima, Peru, the American Embassy received a letter stating: "If
these two innocent beings are put to death, you will pay with your lives."

matically fought the hands of the clock on the night of the executions.

At midnight of August 22, 1927, Sacco and Vanzetti went to the chair. Efforts of liberals, radicals, professional men of good conscience, had all failed. The State House grounds in Boston and the streets nearby were a riot of protesting parades and speeches, which were illegal but in which participated a host of men and women who had watched out the affair to the last bitter minute: Edna St. Vincent Millay, John Dos Passos, Powers Hapgood, Lola Ridge, and many laborers and friends of Sacco and Vanzetti. In Union Square the scene was duplicated. In Europe, American consuls were threatened; there were parades and protest meetings in many capitals; expatriate Americans were treated with open hostility or scrupulously ignored.

Out of all this came a flood of protest literature. The melodramatic potential for the revolutionary cause was soon realized. Poetry, struck from the red-hot fires of social indignation, crowded the pages of the *New Republic,* the *Nation,* the *New Masses.* A collection of Sacco-Vanzetti poems was published under the title of *America Arraigned.* In New York, Maxwell Anderson and Harold Hickerson collaborated in the writing of *Gods of the Lightning* (1928), which, although banned in Boston, appeared on the New York stage. Upton Sinclair's two-volume novel *Boston* appeared first in the *Bookman,* then was published by Albert and Charles Boni in 1928. Edna St. Vincent Millay brooded over "Justice Denied in Massachusetts." Dos Passos, Malcolm Cowley, Kathleen Millay, Babette Deutsch, and Witter Bynner wrote poems for the first anniversary.

Cowley's tribute to Vanzetti, "For St. Bartholomew's Day," was published in the *Nation* (August 22, 1928):

> A doctor sneezes, a chaplain maps
> the streets of heaven, you mount the chair,
> two jailors buckle tight the straps
> like those which aviators wear,
> the surgeon makes a signal.
> > Die!
> lost symbols of our liberty.
>
> Beyond the chair, beyond the bars
> of day and night your path lies free.
> Yours is an avenue of stars.
>
> March on, O dago Christs, while we
> march on to spread your name abroad
> like ashes in the winds of God.

Dos Passos' " 'They Are Dead Now—,' " published in the *New Masses* (October 1927), began with the words, "Sacco and Vanzetti have been executed./This isn't a poem," and described the act of execution:

> The warden strapped these men into the electric chair
> the executioner threw the switch
> and set them free into the wind
> they are free of the dreams now
> free of the greasy prison denim
>
> their voices blow back in a thousand lingoes
>   singing one song
>
> to burst the eardrums of Massachusetts.
> Make a poem of that if you dare!

Perhaps the most effective and most widely quoted work of literature came from Vanzetti himself, the words he had spoken to Judge Thayer. This simple speech found its way into almost every anthology of leftist literature in the 1930s:

If it had not been for these things, I might have live out my life, talking at street corners to scorning men. I might have die, unmarked, unknown, a failure. Now we are not a failure. This is our career and our triumph. Never in our full life can we hope to do such work for tolerance, for joostice, for man's understanding of man, as now we do by an accident. Our words—our lives—pains—nothing! The taking of our lives—lives of a good shoemaker and a poor fish peddler—all! That last moment belong to us—that agony is our triumph.

The Sacco-Vanzetti case provided the dynamics of crisis in a decade in which there were few other occasions to stir the public mind. The radical affiliations of the two men were with the anarchists, and these affiliations reverted to the days of the second decade, the years of Emma Goldman's *Mother Earth,* of the I.W.W. and Bill Haywood, and of Arturo Giovannitti. It was not the fact of their being anarchists, however, that made them important for radicalism in the twenties. As anarchists, Sacco and Vanzetti were the heroes of their immediate friends and the terror of the bogey-ridden public whose stereotyped notions of the anarchist had been formed from a long history of journalistic misrepresentation. But as victims of a smooth-working machine of oppression, they were anybody's and everybody's heroes, and their fate was a challenge to leftist movements of all shades.

The liberals insisted that the affair was merely a case at law and should be treated as such; that the trial was a challenge to the effectiveness and validity of democratic legal processes. Felix Frankfurter and William Thompson, who viewed the case with considerable sympathy for the defendants, nevertheless thought of it as a bitter test of the workability of the Anglo-American system of criminal justice. "All systems of law, however wise, are administered through men, and therefore may occasionally disclose the frailties of men," said Frankfurter in his book on the case. "Perfection may not be demanded of law, but the capacity to correct errors of inevitable frailty is the mark of a civilized legal machine."

In a larger sense, not only the legal system but all liberal principle was at stake. "One of the most sinister events which have as yet taken place in the life of the American nation," the *New Republic* remarked (August 31, 1927). The men responsible for it were "the spokesmen of a community which is afraid of being destroyed by the impact of alien agitations and peoples, and which, for that reason, is peculiarly disposed to assert against such people the full rigor of a presumably offended law." Of the nation and of themselves the liberals asked this question: Was the law, following the Sacco-Vanzetti precedent, to be used to implement the fears of the community, to destroy those who fell out of favor with the ruling interests; or could it remain as a means of impartial protection of human rights? But the unity brought to liberal ranks by the Sacco-Vanzetti case did not have the desired results; it ended in defeat. Liberals failed to interest more than a few of the "middle-minded people who fill important administrative positions in American political, professional, and business life."

For the Communists, the affair was an opportunity to stimulate public protest against the reactionaries of the state of Massachusetts, to take the case outside of Dedham and proclaim it to the nation and the world. They were not the sort to miss this chance to offer proof of the advanced state of capitalist corruption and injustice. "There is no white virgin of Platonic perfection living in this bad world and named 'justice,'" said Mike Gold in the *New Masses* (October 1927). "There is a bloody battle between classes, and one side wins, or the other, and the victory is Class Justice." In view of their propaganda value for "the cause," Sacco and Vanzetti were already heroes:

To become a legend for millions of fishermen, coolies, peasants, miners, steel workers, house-mothers, Red Soldiers, pick-and-shovel men, war cripples, hounded girl prostitutes, prisoners, Negro slaves, poets, Ein-

stein, Barbusse, able-bodied seamen and Jewish tailors: to be their
battlecry, their red flag:

that is a beautiful fate, it cheats the grave of darkness, it makes sweet
even those last leaping, fiery minutes in the electric chair! [21]

The dramatic urgency and simplicity of the case appealed to the Communists and fellow travelers who saw political doctrine in dramatistic terms. The propaganda value of the situation was enormous. In substance, Communists summed up the case in this way: Look at the simple, puzzled, saintly men, holding firmly to their radical creed, powerless to fight against a force which had murdered and tortured their friends, eloquent both in their silences and in their halting, accent-laden speeches in court! Look next at the men of law—hideous, treacherous, cunning, yet frightened at the purity of their enemies and at the enormity of their guilt! Never had American capitalism fallen so easily into a revolutionary trap, which their greed and hatred had helped to build! To consider the case as a test of law, as the Harvard professors wished to, or as a challenge to the working of liberal reason, seemed to the Communists a crime of strategic blundering. It was not merely a case of criminal law, but a moment in history, of which the chosen actors of the Marxist drama ought to take the fullest advantage.

It was natural enough, therefore, that writers for the New Masses should have objected to the cautious and polite disturbance among liberals, condemning them once again for their failure to take full advantage of the melodrama in the affair. They found cautious Bostonians irritating, anarchists obstructive, and liberals too slow-moving for the pace of events. "Liberals sit apart in the manner of a setting hen on her eggs," said John Dos Passos. "When something happens that threatens their routine they peck out anxiously and little gurgles of distress come from their throats" (New Masses, November 1927).

In these ways, the fates of two obscure Italian workingmen became a crisis in the liberal and leftist consideration of democratic law, economics, and politics. However interpreted, the case and the executions were a challenge to the political and moral consciences of many men and women of democratic good will. It was a crucial event in the formation of Dos Passos' aesthetic position and influenced the writing of the trilogy U.S.A. more than anything else that happened in the 1920s. It

[21] In the May 1929 issue of the New Masses, Gold composed "a worker's Recitation," almost every line of which was a verbatim extract from the public speeches and letters of Vanzetti.

was remembered for many years after its conclusion as a dramatic crisis in political thought. For this time only, in the activity associated with the trial, liberal, anarchist, and radical feeling was directed toward a common object.

7. The Text: Sinclair Lewis's *Babbitt*

IN HIS novels of the 1920s, Sinclair Lewis assumed every possible role with respect to the middle class. He was its critic and judge, its satirist and parodist, minister to its victims, Balzacian commentator upon its many-sided life, and "liberal" guardian of its political activities. *Main Street* (1920) treated the Midwestern metaphor of the small town, trying to discover, as Lewis said, how "much of Gopher Prairie's eleven miles of cement walks" was "made out of the tombstones of John Keatses." [22] With *Babbitt* (1922) he began a full-scale investigation of the small Midwestern city, the "Zenith" city with 250,000 to 300,000 inhabitants, and growing steadily. He searched indefatigably for every kind of venality, corruption, stupidity, and demagoguery, every tendency toward fascism in middle-class society, every pressure upon the "man of good will" to abandon his rights as a democratic citizen. He was so successful in accumulating evidence, so fond of echoing and parodying the grandiose absurdities of his subject, that his novels became (or threatened to become) fantasies woven from the kind of facts that Mencken reported in his "Americana."

Lewis's portrait is at once a skillful organization of middle-class detail, a series of caricatures of middle-class types, a parody of middle-class habits, forms of speech, gestures, and a fantasy world, derived from the real but unreal in its actual effect. His interest is primarily anthropological; he is the student of a strange tribe that exists in a world (Winnemac) that includes all states of the Midwest but is none of them, behaves in a way that resembles the behavior of the actual middle-class world, but in vigor and extreme of gesture transcends it. As an analyst of this half-real, half-fantasy world, Lewis gives it all forms of attitude, belief, faith, gesture: a "piety of things"; a full complement of rituals (together with totem signs and magic slogans); a metaphysic ("Service and Boosterism"); an ethic ("Gotta hustle"); a religion (Dr. John Jennison Drew's "Salvation and 5 per cent" church,

[22] See also the portrayal of Wheatsylvania in *Arrowsmith* (1925).

where "everything zips"); an aesthetic (red-blooded, efficient, senti-mental "Poemulations" by Chum Frink); and a fully articulated politi-cal philosophy (Republicanism and the wisdom of Harding and Coo-lidge).

The Zenith setting is itself an architectural and religious symbol of the faith, a temple dedicated to the religion of business. Its Athletic Club is a masterpiece of eclectic display: the entrance lobby "Gothic, the washroom Roman Imperial, the lounge Spanish Mission, and the reading-room in Chinese Chippendale." [23] In this world, in the Floral Heights residential region, lives Babbitt, the symbolic hero, scapegoat, and prodigal son. His religious faith is associated almost entirely with "things"—gadgets, automatic and mechanical and efficient instruments of a busy man's life. To maintain his morale he has to buy more things, whether he needs them or not: their "thinginess," quite apart from need or practicality, sustains him.[24] His outward expression of "the faith" is "hustle," which gives the appearance of absorption and di-rection and quiets the suspicions of the tribe; any attempt to remain iso-lated from it is a form of backsliding. In a noisy confraternity lies the best resort of orthodoxy.

Babbitt wears the uniform of the solid citizen, as his mind wears uni-form opinions. The "standard suit" is a gray business suit, and in its pockets he carries certain badges of his loyalty: a fountain pen and silver pencil, a gold penknife, a silver cigar-cutter, "a large yellowish elk's-tooth," a loose-leaf pocket notebook (containing, among other things, verses of C. Cholmondely Frink [25] and newspaper editorials), and the Boosters' Club button ("his V.C., his Legion of Honor ribbon, his Phi Beta Kappa key").

The Babbitt "program" involves a dedication to Unselfish Public Service ("a thing called Ethics . . . if you had it you were a High-Class Realtor"), a proper reverence for the "spiritual value of things,"

[23] ". . . but the gem of the club was the dining-room, the masterpiece of Ferdinand Reitman, Zenith's busiest architect. It was lofty, and half-timbered, with Tudor leaded casements, an oriel, a somewhat musicianless musicians' gal-lery, and tapestries believed to illustrate the granting of Magna Charta."

[24] "He had enormous and poetic admiration, though very little understanding, of all mechanical devices. They were his symbols of truth and beauty."

[25] For example: "I sat alone and groused and thunk, and scratched my head and sighed and wunk, and groaned, 'There still are boobs, alack, who'd like the old-time ginmill back; that den that makes a sage a loon, the vile and smelly old saloon!' I'll never miss their poison booze, whilst I the bubbling spring can use, that leaves my head at merry morn as clear as any babe new-born."

and intellectual stimulus from "rubbing up against high-class hustlers every day and getting jam full of ginger." It demands the right kind of political activity: campaigning for the "right kind" of loyal Americans, warning against the "Red professors" in the university, guarding the local political scene against its enemies. Most of all, it requires a tribal solidarity with "the boys": Vergil Gunch, Professor Joseph K. Pumphrey (of the Riteway Business College, instructor in Business English, Scenario Writing, and Commercial Law), Orville Jones (owner of the Lily White Laundry, the "biggest, busiest, bulliest cleanerie shoppe in Zenith"), Chum Frink, Dr. Howard Littlefield, Ph.D., and the rest.

At the peak of his success as a tribal Booster, Babbitt delivers the annual address before the Zenith Real-Estate Board. This is a summing up of the "parody Babbitt" and of his stock-in-trade of tribal opinions and evaluations. It is a literary ordering of Mencken's accumulations of what "the booboisie" thinks. Its substance is contained in Babbitt's description of "Our Ideal Citizen": he is "first and foremost" busy ("busier than a bird-dog"), and he has no time for daydreaming "or going to sassiety teas or kicking about things that are none of his business," but spends all his time "putting the zip into some store or profession or art." The slang puts the daydreamers in their place; the warning that no one should "kick about things that are none of his business" identifies the solidarity of the group, jealously guarded. Our citizen is also a "he-man," [26] an extrovert, a conscientious family man; for entertainment he plays "a few fists of bridge, or reads the evening newspaper, and a chapter or two of some good lively Western novel if he has a taste for literature." He is a good, sound, efficient man in his taste for the arts; nothing of the bohemian about him—"in America the successful writer or picture-painter is indistinguishable from any other decent businessman"—and he should be properly rewarded, have his chance "to drag down his fifty thousand bucks a year."

The middle-class stereotype is a hundred-per-cent standardized American, a full-blooded, he-man, native American citizen:

Here's the specifications of the Standardized American Citizen! Here's the new generation of Americans: fellows with hair on their chests and smiles in their eyes and adding machines in their offices. We're not doing any boasting, but we like ourselves first-rate, and if you don't like us, look out—better get under cover before the cyclone hits town!

[26] Gertrude Stein once called "he-man" a vulgar redundancy.

There are those who "don't like us"; but one advantage of Zenith over big cities like New York is that there are very few "foreign-born" people in it, with their "foreign ideas and communism."

The "Regular Guys" are creating a new civilization of vital, standardized living, which is the great hope of the future and must be protected from "the long-haired gentry who call themselves 'liberals' and 'radicals' and 'non-partisan' and 'intelligentsia' and God only knows how many other trick names!" There are certain instructors "over at the U" (of which "I am proud to be known as an alumni") who "seem to think we ought to turn the conduct of the nation over to hoboes and roustabouts." These are the men to watch; if we're going to pay them our good money, "they've got to help us by selling efficiency and whooping it up for national prosperity!" Only when they are set right, and the communist-socialist foreigners are locked up, can this he-man tribe of Moose, Elks, Lions, and other right thinkers proceed on the road to a glorious standardized civilization, a paradise of gadgets and standardized proprieties.

This is, of course, as far as the parody Babbitt can go. But *Babbitt* is a novel as well, and its hero is a personality; Lewis had the choice of making him simply a mouthpiece of middle-class views (as is Lowell Schmaltz of *The Man Who Knew Coolidge*) or of breaking into the pattern of his gestures and appearance to give him a sensitivity, make him a doubter of his own loud confidence. Lewis was careful to plant suspicion of a "complex" Babbitt from the start: the businessman Babbitt does not seem the same person when the very latest alarm clock with its cathedral chime and its phosphorescent dial rouses him from dreams of the "fairy child." Further, he has a friend, Paul Riesling, who is not a mixer, who sits apart from "the boys," and encourages Babbitt to doubt the whole tribal structure. Riesling is obviously the "criminal type," and his friendship is a great risk to Babbitt; when Riesling tries to kill his wife and is given a three-year sentence, Babbitt loses confidence and morale. This is the beginning of his treachery, his flirtation with "alien" ideas. It is the novel as distinguished from the parody.

It is interesting that Lewis should have made the two Babbitts so very distinct from each other. The doubting Babbitt, upon yielding to his temptations, becomes an anti-Babbitt, a rebel and scapegrace, violating the social, political, and sexual taboos, and for a while taking pleasure in his defiance. He associates with the bohemian "Bunch" instead of with the Athletic Club boys or regular guys; he refuses to join any more Booster organizations; he is unfaithful to his wife, neglects his family, sneers at the architectural harmony and social stability of Floral Heights, openly flouts Prohibition.[27] Worst of all, Babbitt begins to defend his friend, Seneca Doane, who remembers him from the university as "an unusually sensitive chap." He begins to play the role of the liberal, argues against those who condemn Doane's middle-of-the-road liberalism, defends the strikers and admires men who march with them in a protest parade. Lewis has saved Babbitt from himself, has given him this "fling" of sanity and intelligence, and has thus revealed his own private confidence in the soundness and the fundamental decency of the extracurricular Babbitt.

Lewis's own position was that of a liberal humanist; in a "Self-Portrait" (1927) he admitted that the parody-artist was not his real self:

> All his respect for learning, for integrity, for accuracy, and for the possibilities of human achievement are to be found not in the rather hectic and exaggerative man as his intimates see him, but in his portrait of Professor Max Gottlieb, in *Arrowsmith*. Most of the fellow's capacity for loyalty and friendship has gone into Leora in that same novel and into the account of George F. Babbitt's affection for his son and for his friend Paul.

Lewis saves his greatest respect and affection for the man and woman of integrity, of an instinctive sense of decency. The double view of Babbitt is thus a consequence of Lewis's mixed emotion concerning the middle class. Its most hideous extremes of boasting, vulgarity, and cheapness of mind are fully given in the parody figure of Babbitt in the "gotta-hustle" public world; but Babbitt is himself saved from the parody. In the end one discovers he is only weak—not malicious, illiberal, ungenerous, and fascistic, but sentimental and basically decent. In so revising the portrait of Babbitt, Lewis has to shift the center of his characterizations. Babbitt, who is in the beginning the epitome of all the violations of decorum that Lewis hates, must—because of his revolt—move downstage. The really villainous incarnation of the middle-class evil is not Babbitt but Vergil Gunch. His hostile eyes follow Babbitt as he moves from one petty defiance of the tribe to another; he proposes that Babbitt join the Good Citizens League as a testament of

[27] Drinking is a secret rite for "the boys"; it is not forbidden but must be attended by a proper ceremonial rationalization regarding "the law" and class proprieties in keeping and breaking it. When Babbitt drinks outside the tribe his act becomes a crime against it.

renewal of the faith; he leads the move toward extradition, which strikes fear in Babbitt's heart.

Vergil Gunch succeeds finally in convincing Babbitt that his extra-tribal spree is sinful. "The independence seeped out of him, and he walked the streets alone, afraid of men's cynical eyes and the incessant hiss of whispering." A minor family crisis helps to solve the major tribal crisis. Myra Babbitt is stricken, and at once he reacts with all tribal and family correctness; he drops all his "inner dramas" and asks his wife's forgiveness for them. "The boys" return, with fulsome gestures of regular-guy affection; and Babbitt, almost in tears because he can now stop fighting them, is restored to full membership. He moves quickly to resume his status; as a newly accepted member of the Good Citizens League, he is "fired up" over "the wickedness of Seneca Doane, the crimes of labor unions, the perils of immigration, the delights of golf, morality, and bank-accounts." He goes to the efficient Reverend Doctor Drew, who efficiently prays with him (watch in hand) for five minutes, after which he must rush off to a meeting of the Don't-Make-Prohibition-a-Joke-Association. And now Babbitt knows he is safe from the terror of being alone, outside the tribe, isolated "from the Clan of Good Fellows."

The crucial fact about *Babbitt* is that it is two novels—or two types of literary exposition poorly combined in one work. The Babbitt of the address before the Real-Estate Board is one character, a perfect representation of its limited kind; but Lewis creates another, a sensitive, humane Babbitt, who in his person and in his behavior cancels the validity and nullifies the success of the other. The parody Babbitt is so irrevocably the imaginative product of the Lewis-Mencken view of the middle class that he cannot also be an anti-Babbitt, a Babbitt conspiring against himself. In order to humanize a parody figure, Lewis must make him over into a person with at least some of the sensitivity of a Seneca Doane. Babbitt must become a complex man in order that "something happen." What happens to the parody Babbitt is within its own context merely a succession of "Americana" incidents; the novel demands more of crisis, a stronger narrative line. Besides, Lewis does not want to leave us with a pure caricature; he likes the middle class and would only point up its absurdities and follies. So, midway in the novel, Babbitt changes from a raucous, naïve Booster to a vaguely resentful doubter; and the center of the criticism shifts from Babbitt to "the boys" and especially to Vergil Gunch. The middle class is saved from its worst sins, and its worst sins have at the same time provided high comedy.

Lewis touched upon every critical image applied to the middle class in the 1920s. The chief of these is, of course, Mencken's image of an inverted business mythology; but there is also—and perhaps underlying it—the liberal humanistic position of Seneca Doane, which, in Babbitt's brief flirtation with his ideas, is drawn into the range of a possible middle-class self-criticism. Babbitt briefly recognizes the heroism of strikes and the selflessness of sympathizers who put their "alien, red notions" on public display. But all of this is dominated throughout by the great middle-class tribal fantasy, to which the extremes of standardization of thought, ownership, and belief contribute. This, the dominating motif of middle-class criticism in the 1920s, is by all odds the most memorable quality of the novel. Because of it, *Babbitt* is especially representative of one phase of thinking and writing in the decade.

VIII

SOME PERSPECTIVES
ON THE 1920S

1. The Snow of 1929

Not long after October 1929 people began to regret the 1920s, to renounce the sins of a "wasted decade"; they admitted they had had a good time while "the gaudiest spree in history" had lasted, but they were ready now to assume the roles of adult, mature persons. No more pathetic reminder of the reformed playboy exists than Charlie Wales of Fitzgerald's story, "Babylon Revisited" (written in 1931). Wales returns to Paris, after an exile, to reclaim his life. He is properly humble, regretful, resolved; he has become "a new man," learned his lesson, and will his sister-in-law please restore his daughter Honoria to him? He will now be able to take care of her: sober, restrained, solvent, and anxious to identify himself with the human race, he feels that she will secure him in his new conviction. He now believes "in character"; he wants "to jump back a whole generation and trust in character again as the eternally valuable element."

Paris, the Babylon to which he has made his journey of contrition, is itself suffering a depression of the spirit. The streets are almost empty of tourists, where a few months before they had been gay and colorful. "The Poet's Cave had disappeared, but the two great mouths of the Café of Heaven and the Café of Hell still yawned—even devoured, as he watched, the meager contents of a tourist bus—a German, a Japanese, and an American couple who glanced at him with frightened eyes." Looking upon the waste, reflecting upon the pathos, Charlie Wales suddenly realizes "the meaning of the word 'dissipate'—to dissipate into thin air; to make nothing out of something."

The "waste" is both a moral and a dramatic problem. There are those who soberly endured the antics of their American contemporaries during the 1920s; now they have become their judges. But the morally correct do not enjoy their role; they have a sense not so much of wickedness resisted as of their having been cheated out of something. Marion Peters, the sister-in-law who has kept Charlie's daughter from him, "was a tall woman with worried eyes, who had once possessed a fresh American loveliness." Between the two a quiet but intense struggle develops, a struggle of two equally strong determinations, for Honoria, the prize. If he should prove that one can morally survive the 1920s, the prize is his; if not, if there is the slightest doubt of his having fully reformed, Honoria remains with the "good woman," the woman who has sacrificed her "American loveliness" so that character might return to the American personality after an absence of at least ten years. Slowly, arduously, Wales works to regain her confidence. But the stain of the 1920s is hard to remove. Two of his friends reappear from out of the past; and, though Wales tries to keep them away, to prevent their violating the temple of his humble resolve, they do just that. The 1920s cannot be put away. The terrible crime of irresponsibility, which had led to the death of his wife, haunts the atonement at the very moment of forgiveness, and Wales is once more back at the beginning, without the reward he had wished for his patient efforts to redefine himself as a responsible human being:

> Again the memory of those days swept over him like a nightmare —the people they had met traveling; then people who couldn't add a row of figures or speak a coherent sentence. The little man Helen had consented to dance with at the ship's party, who had insulted her ten feet from the table; the women and girls carried screaming with drink or drugs out of public places—
> —The men who locked their wives out in the snow, because the snow of twenty-nine wasn't real snow. If you didn't want it to be snow, you just paid some money.

On January 2, 1950, *Life* magazine summarized the five decades of our century in one hundred pages of pictures and comment. As is usual on such occasions, the 1920s figured prominently, and there was nothing new or unexpected in the display. From Gilda Gray to Grover Whalen, the celebrities of the time were exhibited; and the brief preface reflected upon their meaning:

> When the 1920s ended in the crash it became fashionable (and merciful) to forget them, and they have been buried beneath recovery,

war, and a new boom. It is startling to find the old headliners still looking as chipper as they do in these pictures taken in the past few months—startling, and pleasant. They were the life of the party and everyone loves them, even though it was not a party that the nation can afford to throw again.

What distinguishes this quotation from the Luce "capsule" is the quality of its metaphor; the 1920s were a "party" that resulted in a serious hangover. We still talk about the party but are properly repentant and resolved not to have another. The same metaphor is encountered in a collection called *The Pleasures of the Jazz Age* (1948), edited by William Hoddap: "Here is a ten-year-long weekend party in which they all participated and whose hangover never really started till the stock-market crash." These people had founded "an uncharted colony of freedom—even license—for refugees from reality." In other characterizations the 1920s were called "The Era of Wonderful Nonsense," the time of the "lost generation," the "Jazz Age," the age of Freud, Ziegfeld, and Coolidge.[1]

In a very real sense Fitzgerald, who had been in the vanguard of those establishing this image of the twenties, helped to make it a permanent view. When the decade died in the last months of 1929 Fitzgerald "tightened his belt"; and in subsequent years he wrote a series of pieces, for *Scribner's, Esquire,* and other magazines, in which he described both the pleasures and the agonies of atonement since undergone. Fitzgerald's Charlie Wales perhaps best symbolizes the crowd who "went to the party" and had to pay the check.[2]

The "golden boom," the "gaudiest spree in history," required in 1931 "the proper expression of horror as we look back at our wasted youth." In the 1930s Fitzgerald wrote about his "wasted youth," dwell-

---

[1] See a recent "handbook" (*Backgrounds of American Literary Thought* by Rod W. Horton and Herbert W. Edwards, 1952): The 1920s "in reality . . . presented the rather sad spectacle of irresponsible youth having its last fling." Elsewhere it speaks of "the whoopie mentality of the happy-talking twenties" and employs the usual clichés concerning "national adolescence" and other reflections that recall Fitzgerald's remarks in the early 1930s. The authors do admit that there was talent in those years, that the young men "gave the nation the liveliest, freshest, most stimulating writing in its literary experience."

[2] Since the Depression had followed immediately upon the end of the decade, "perspectives" upon it were quickly achieved. But Fitzgerald had his personal reasons for looking back in such a way. It is of some interest to note that Nick Carraway, in the midst of the wild clamor of charge and countercharge at the Plaza Hotel, suddenly and sadly remembers that he has reached "the thirtieth year of his age."

ing again and again upon its glamour and its misguided energy. The
pages of *Tender Is the Night* (1934) are filled with judgments delivered
upon the waste, the triviality, the pathetic effort to realize what in the
decade had seemed hopelessly beyond realization.[3] The hero, Dr.
Dick Diver, sacrifices his every talent, his last ounce of energy, to
keep alive an illusion that has been doomed from the start. His struggle
is not with the 1920s but with a complex of enemies who, in Fitzgerald's view, had made the decade what it was: easy wealth; the
falsely sentimental view of life symbolized in the Rosemary Hoyt of the
film *Daddy's Girl;* the inner weaknesses and tensions of its most gifted
persons; above all, its indifference to human responsibility—its inability to define the terms on which men *become* responsible. In the
end Diver, on his "way out," his wife gone away with another man,
pauses for a final "benediction" of that "prayer-rug" of Riviera beach
that had been the scene of his greatest triumphs and his most painful
defeats:

> "I must go," he said. As he stood up he swayed a little; he did not
> feel well any more—his blood raced slow. He raised his right hand
> and with a papal cross he blessed the beach from the high terrace.

In the quiet blasphemy of this gesture Diver dismisses the decade and
himself; he had been identified with it and his talents and charm were
exhausted to preserve in it a quality it had not wanted. He is through
with it, and it with him.

In spite of the indifferent reception of *Tender Is the Night,* Fitzgerald's identification with the 1920s persisted. The two were indistinguishable in the public mind. A man of great talent, he had fought
a losing battle with the temptations and the frivolities of the time. In
loving them for their own sakes, he had forfeited his full right to judge
them incisively. But Dr. Diver's final gesture is ironically a farewell
to something pathetically lost when the decade ended. "Now once more
the belt is tight," he said in November 1931 (*Scribner's Magazine*),

---

[3] If one examines the history of the composition of this novel (begun almost
immediately after *The Great Gatsby* was published in 1925), one can understand
its pertinence as a commentary upon the decade. It began as an account of
planned murder, in essentials exploiting the most sensational contemporary
"copy." Gradually this quality of American life was toned down; and Fitzgerald
moved toward the use of a hero who is endowed with the most affectingly
"charming" good will and is (in his profession) a scientific minister to the decade's
ills as well. See Arthur Mizener's *The Far Side of Paradise* for the story of the
several plans that led to the novel of 1934.

"and we summon the proper expression of horror as we look back at our wasted youth."

> Sometimes, though, there is a ghostly rumble among the drums, an asthmatic whisper in the trombones that swings me back into the early twenties when we drank wood alcohol and every day in every way grew better and better, and there was a first abortive shortening of the skirts, and girls all looked alike in sweater dresses, and people you didn't want to know said 'Yes, we have no bananas,' and it seemed only a question of a few years before the older people would step aside and let the world be run by those who saw things as they were—and it all seems rosy and romantic to us who were young then, because we will never feel quite so intensely about our surroundings any more.[4]

Nevertheless the image of the twenties that remained most clearly in the public mind in 1950 was that established by Fitzgerald in 1920, exploited and all but exhausted by him in the following years, and then reassimilated in terms of a moral view of wistful regret in the 1930s.

It required more than Fitzgerald, however, to fix that impression upon the public mind. The crash of 1929 was, after all, not only a sign of moral collapse. It was a fact of economic history, and in the 1930s economic facts were also moral facts. The sturdy and persistent men of Marx watched the collapse of Wall Street with ill-concealed pleasure and began the 1930s with a determination to wipe the previous decade entirely off the record. "Social responsibility," all but absent from the American scene for ten years, according to the leftists, now became the major concern. The sad young men were welcomed back to America, on probation, and were asked to renounce their sinful past and promised reward for their assumption of doc-

[4] Fitzgerald's wife, Zelda, gave her own version of the 1920s in her only novel, *Save Me the Waltz* (1932). The heroine has to suffer the disadvantages of marriage to a celebrity; she turns to ballet dancing for salvation, as Mabel Dodge Luhan might have turned to Gurdjieff's rhythmic ceremonials. This tedious novel is valuable only for its annotations upon the Fitzgerald perspective: "They were having the bread line at the Ritz that year"; "People were tired of the proletariat—everybody was famous"; "Nobody knew the words to 'The Star-Spangled Banner'"; the expatriates sought "stimulation in the church and asceticism in sex." These are *New Yorker* captions; the conflict in "Alabama's" soul concerning allegiances and loyalties is patently contrived. The strongest impression one gets from reading this novel in 1953 is that the Fitzgeralds did have a "rough time" and that the violence of their hysterias must have disturbed his every paragraph and altered the punctuation of his every sentence.

trinal saintliness. The men who had made a pilgrimage to Moscow instead of indulging themselves in Babylon-on-the-Seine prepared themselves for the roles of moral spokesmen. A haunting sense of missed opportunities for "social good" overwhelmed the men and women of the 1930s, who looked back upon the "nation that for a decade had wanted only to be entertained." The apostles of social responsibility used the decade as a grim reminder: there but for the grace of Marx go I. The antics of the 1920s were "cute but horrible." Never had a more suitable demonstration appeared of the tragedy of social and moral dissipation. It was ideally suited to the Marxist text, which exploited it with great ease and convincing persuasion.

Mr. Roosevelt's liberals toned down the criticism a bit, but only because they wanted it to be less Marxist, more native to the grain of American social thought. The *New Republic* and the *Nation* regained their confidence and addressed themselves to the review of a tradition they thought had been lost when Sacco and Vanzetti were destroyed. The men who had begun their careers in the 1920s revised their points of view, addressing themselves eagerly and respectfully to great "social forces." John Dos Passos, whose John Andrews had risked and suffered all for art, now, in *U.S.A.*, relegated the aesthetic conscience to that corner of his trilogy called "The Camera Eye." Hemingway sought and found a social objective in the streets of Madrid, and later had his Robert Jordan defend the line that Lieutenant Henry had deserted. They were cured, or seemed to be. They came back to see what they had earlier ignored; and what they had previously seen they now ignored.

It was the leftists of the 1930s who were the first to count the cost, and they outlined the terms of payment in phrases of economic liability, which invariably had overtones of moral judgment. The early years of the *New Masses* (1926–1929) had anticipated the pattern of criticism: a pitiful waste of great talent and promise, because these people had not the slightest respect for society. They were pathetically unable to go beyond a childish "revolution" against the bad taste of their elders, ignoring in their rebellion the really disastrous sins committed by the older generation, the sins of capitalism. There was no doubt about it: the failure to understand the social economy was a consequence of the disrespect for any sensible tradition, American or Russian.

This view of the 1920s has not yet been entirely corrected or revised. In the 1940s the perspective was changed a bit, but it was just as much distorted by current moral and social urgencies. To the men who fought in World War II and survived it, the 1920s seemed either a period of amusing but stupid gaiety or a horrible and expensive example of what the "irresponsibles" could cost a nation with moral and military commitments to the world. In the 1950 reviews of the half-century provided in radio broadcasts and popular magazines, the 1920s appeared a grotesque world, remembered for sophomoric behavior and ingenious evasions of serious responsibility. The popular mind saw the decade only in the figure of the musical revue, in Hollywood's strange version of Jay Gatsby, or in the revival of Anita Loos's Lorelei.

The work of Van Wyck Brooks, Archibald MacLeish, Bernard De Voto, and the editors of the *Saturday Review of Literature* sounded another kind of alarm. Their arguments combined a search for a creditable American past and an appeal for a sensible atomic future: according to them, the irresponsibles of the 1920s had either not known or not respected the American tradition. A simple formula was set up: personal responsibility is above all responsibility to one's neighbor, to one's group, and to the world at large. An explosion at Hiroshima, or anywhere, accelerates that sense of responsibility, should make man more vitally concerned than ever over the men who killed and the men who were killed. Isolationism of any kind was immoral. The historical event must hereafter be the constant locus of literary reference. Above all, one must respect one's America, as had Whittier and Twain and Whitman. There was no such respect in the 1920s; writers had given a distorted view of American life, mocking what was pardonable in it, ignoring what was admirable. When they dismissed H. G. Wells as a "Fabian schoolma'arm," spoke condescendingly of John Dewey, and welcomed the dismal historical metaphors of Spengler, they were committed to a grievous violation of literary proprieties—a violation that could lead only to the fascism of Ezra Pound and the solemnly obedient acceptance and defense of his unhappy views.

Such a judgment of the 1920s was a complex of both leftist and liberal views; the "Marxist" condemnation, relieved of its economic emphasis, became wholly moral and wholly traditional. Perhaps we could no longer claim that the writers of the twenties were responsible for the collapse of the American economy, but we could accuse them of having failed to provide a sufficient moral "readiness" for World War II; and we could also say that they gave us no clue to the awful responsibilities of the "atomic age."

Invariably these attacks upon the decade were the product of one form or another of moral disposition and prejudice. Fitzgerald's Charlie Wales recognized only the difficulties of atonement for serious human errors; Mike Gold described the "hollow men" (1941) as guilty entirely on the grounds of their indifference to the "right" issues or the right interpretation of them; Brooks, having earlier condemned the American past for its failure to meet his moral demands, in the late 1930s and the 1940s condemned those who had thus renounced the past; De Voto accused writers of having committed the unpardonable sin of attending to their writing, to the neglect of certain subject matters that he thought indispensable to a proper understanding of our tradition; MacLeish called his own fellow writers of the 1920s irresponsibles for similar reasons. These critics, in their emphasis on what they thought was primarily important, in their insistence upon *their* reading of human nature and of its relationship to literature, almost invariably shared the special moral dispositions of their age.

In his lectures at Indiana University (*The Literary Fallacy,* 1944), De Voto passed many remarkable judgments upon the literature of the twenties. The principal accusation was contained in the phrase "the literary fallacy"; that is, the notion that evaluations of American life "as a whole" can be seen and realized exclusively in literary terms. Most of the writers whom De Voto condemned "begin with the study of literature; most of them employ literary data exclusively. Practically all of them who extend their inquiry beyond literary data extend it by means of primarily literary ideas." This would not be a serious error, were it not that they also speak of such matters as "culture" and "civilization." But they do not know what these terms mean; they have confined their interests to form, to a narrow reading of human and cultural matters, and they have not studied the "things that matter." As a result they commit the error of assuming that what they have found within the range of their limited interests is generally or exclusively true. This is why we need not, or should not, take them seriously; their literature lacks a "basic acknowledgment of the dignity of man. That is why it is a trivial literature—why the Waste Land of Mr. Eliot and the solutrean swamp of Mr. Hemingway are less than tragedy, smaller than tragedy."

None of these critics showed respect for the values of literature, only a persistent attempt to command and direct the perceptions of literary artists in terms of an "extra-literary" set of moral imperatives. This was in part due to the "emergency" in which much of this criticism was written; during World War II almost nothing mattered but a "literature of crisis," a literature that reaffirmed what Brooks called "primary" values; and they found little or none of this "primary" literature in the 1920s. Having discovered that the writers of the 1920s were "indifferent" to the causes that led to World War II, they accused them of being irresponsible: that is, of having neglected their roles as spokesmen of a culture and thus having encouraged the public to remain indifferent and irresponsible.

All these critics were able to cite texts. The flapper of Fitzgerald's novels and stories, for example, repeated endlessly and apparently without variation her gestures of tired sophistication. " 'You see I think everything's terrible anyhow,' " Daisy Buchanan says in *The Great Gatsby,* "in a convinced way. 'Everybody thinks so—the most advanced people. And I *know.* I've been everywhere and seen everything and done everything.' " Through Fitzgerald and his imitators, every place seemed to take on the character of an undergraduate campus, and every person either to be living on one or in the memory of his having lived there.

Another text might be found in the pose of bright cynicism affected by Ben Hecht's newspaperman, Erik Dorn. The business of bootlegging, in which fortunes were quickly made by evading the law, was a background of *The Great Gatsby* and Dos Passos' *Manhattan Transfer.* Daisy's "advanced people" also wrote and published gloomy estimates of the melancholy results of World War I for a nation that had won it. Americans were better out of the "international gamble," which had been so patently exposed by the war (Dos Passos' *One Man's Initiation* and *Three Soldiers;* Hemingway's *A Farewell to Arms*). It was best to make "a separate peace"; desertion from public affairs was the only means of salvaging private dignity (*Three Soldiers, A Farewell to Arms, In Our Time*). Since the war had proved that the men in charge could not command respect, one was left with a problem of personal adjustment, deprived of past securities (*The Sun Also Rises*).

But no real tragic insight into the nature of man was possible in a time when the war had destroyed certain necessary illusions and the march of science had served to reduce all remaining ones. Beginning with Harold Stearns' *America and the Young Intellectual* (1921) and ending with Joseph Wood Krutch's *The Modern Temper* (1929), the decade offered one "proof" after another of moral and social incapacity. Both the village and the small city were riddled by prejudice, stupidity, callousness (Sinclair Lewis's *Main Street* and *Babbitt;* Carl Van Vechten's *The Tattooed Countess*). The clergy were transparently ridiculous and ungodly (Lewis's *Elmer Gantry;* Mencken's "Americana"). Political morality and intelligence had never reached so low a level, at least not since Mark Twain's Gilded Age (Lewis's *The Man Who Knew Coolidge;* weekly editorials in the *Nation,* the *New Republic;* Walter Lippmann in *Vanity Fair*). Numerous suggestions were offered for easy solutions of the human distress. Doctor Coué performed his "miracles" on one level of human response with as much effectiveness as Doctor Freud did on another. Edith Wharton's Mrs. Manford (*Twilight Sleep*) enjoyed an almost daily change of cult and "vision"; and the middle-aged ladies of Lewis's Zenith vied with Helen Hokinson's suburbanites in their search for the very latest word from the decade's multiple heaven.

The new social symbolism included many strangely acute designations of the period of adjustment: what Malcolm Cowley described as "significant gesture" became in the eyes of Hemingway's Count Mippipopolous the "values" of the good life, for his Nick Adams the right restraint in the use of the senses, for Jake Barnes the "pure line" of the matador artist. Fitzgerald's brooding ex-Yale man, Tom Buchanan, nibbled "at the edge of stale ideas" and invoked white supremacy as a means of explaining his own boredom and tension. His more sensitive and pathetic Abe North had "a code": he was against the burning of witches. The more articulate of the expatriates believed their social behavior to be closely associated with art, even when it was concerned entirely with the destruction of art. Dada was significantly concerned with destruction—the most vulgar gesture might be the most significant or the most effective. The aim was to invert the scale of decorum, to exalt vulgarity and explode convention. Mr. Babbitt was found daily in a thousand pieces in Montparnasse and Greenwich Village.

2. "Spirits Grown Eliotic"

O F THE general images the literature of the decade impressed upon us, two are especially vivid as "classical" reminders of the time: the "pathos of the adolescent" and the "unregenerate bohemian." For the first there is the evidence of many occasions. It is contained usually in a gesture, the very vagueness of which served to thrill its readers. Undoubtedly the great early success of Fitzgerald's *This Side of Para-*

dise was due to its appeals to the mind of the younger generation. Its most popular gesture comes in the last two pages: Amory Blaine speaks up for the new generation, endowing it with the privileges of its immaturity. This new generation, "grown up to find all Gods dead, all wars fought, all faiths in man shaken," was to be more brilliantly and more fully characterized in other texts; but no other work was able to endow it with quite the glamour of lonely defiance to be found in the novel's last lines:

> He stretched out his arms to the crystalline, radiant sky. "I know myself," he cried, "but that is all."

Again, at the beginning of the decade, the moment of adolescent awareness was shown in Sherwood Anderson's *Winesburg, Ohio,* whose George Willard experiences for the first time "the sadness of sophistication":

> With a little gasp he sees himself as merely a leaf blown by the wind through the streets of his village. He knows that in spite of all the stout talk of his fellows he must live and die in uncertainty, a thing blown by the winds, a thing destined like corn to wilt in the sun.

This shock of realization is like a birth into a new world. Cynicism has not set in, nor has a philosophy grown. The protections accorded normal experience are removed, and the young man is forced into a world he can never really understand. This insistence upon the youth of the generation, upon its perilous freedom, proved a strong incentive to those who could claim to belong to the generation; it made those who didn't qualify wish to belong as well. In its many variations, it sounded a note of individual rebellion, of a determination to work outside conventional securities: Hemingway's Nick Adams makes a "separate peace"; Dos Passos' John Andrews calmly accepts the penalties of desertion; Floyd Dell's heroes and heroines run the gamut, from Iowa to Chicago to Greenwich Village; and Lieutenant Henry speaks for them all:

> That was what you did. You died. You did not know what it was about. You never had time to learn. They threw you in and told you the rules and the first time they caught you off base they killed you.

The range of experience varies, the definition achieves different shades and degrees of meaning. But the prevailing impression is that of the very young, frightened and puzzled and defeated at the start, but determined to formulate a code that both justifies and utilizes that defeat. This was part of the tone of the 1920s: a rhetorical quality quite different from the gestures made by Frank Norris's trapped superman or Theodore Dreiser's Hurstwood. It was a pathos realized too early, with neither the setting nor the incentive to give it the quality usually associated with "tragedy."

As for the attitude of the "unregenerate bohemian," it was even more roundly condemned by those who later criticized the decade, because it apparently ignored altogether what was usually recognized as "social experience." Far from being depressed by the period of his birth, the bohemian preferred to ignore it, except in satirical acknowledgment of its absurdity. The individual became an uncompromising anarchist, a radical of a kind that has almost vanished from the American scene since 1930. There were two variations of this attitude: one assumed that the aesthetic and the social conscience were the same; the other assumed there was no such thing as a social conscience, that there was no history but only persons. It was natural enough that this latter view should condemn the type of middle-class person Cummings had scornfully called the "official." Upton Sinclair proved to be the sole active survivor of progressive liberalism in the twenties, and Cummings was almost alone in his active sponsorship of aesthetic radicalism in the thirties. To affirm the value of the non-social personality was a difficult and unpopular task after 1929; even Maxwell Bodenheim marched in proletarian parades up Fifth Avenue in the thirties. But the basic point of view stated and dramatized in *The Enormous Room* was never altered thereafter by Cummings, except in details and kinds of reference.

Throughout the twenties writers shifted their ground uncomfortably with respect to the question of their debt to society. Of this maneuvering we have abundant evidence in Joseph Freeman's *An American Testament* and in the early history of the *New Masses*. But the position taken by Cummings is a partial sign of what in the decade was thought to be a most important privilege: that of aesthetic self-determination. From this point of view, most attacks were launched, trivial or profound or both, upon the restrictions and conventions of the world. The aesthetic radical retained a free and independent mind, refusing to permit any interference with his freedom. He was flattered to think that his views might be explained "scientifically," but he rejected without qualification the basic requirements of a scientific method. More often than not the "unregenerate bohemian" rejected philosophy as such altogether, thought himself possessed of finer instincts than the "prurient philosophers" of Cummings' poem.

The unregenerate bohemian was an extreme form of what has been an important contribution to modern culture: the emphasis, the *insistence,* upon the value of personal vision. The 1920s were one of a very few times when one could be respected for having a private view of public affairs. This private view applied not only to actual headline copy but to systems of philosophical thought, to scientific discoveries, to investigations of the nature of man and his world, and to theories of the writing and value of literature.

Much of the activity thus sponsored was of course reckless and irresponsible in its neglect of logic and in its sporadic enthusiasms. Nevertheless the literary activity of the decade stressed the very defensible assumption that the artist's sensibility is a legitimate means of gaining insight and knowledge that are indispensable to our total view of a culture. Since the artists of the decade realized the importance of their gift, they gave a special quality of insight into facts often unchallenged or misunderstood by others. For one thing, they pointed, not to the gifts of science, but to its dangers. They risked being called frivolous and ignorant, so that they might point out that science was not wholly good, that material progress may even be quite harmful, that an entirely satisfactory religious experience was all but impossible in a world that had "educated" itself beyond the need of it.

Perhaps their strongest (at any rate their loudest) activity consisted of their documentation of human absurdities. This criticism of the modern world, in spite of its frequent triviality, was both a profound and a necessary contribution to the knowledge we must have of our society. We realize now that for the most part it was correct and shrewd. Its value can be seen in several ways. One is its treatment of history, the act of taking the straight line of liberal prophecy and twisting it— rejecting the linear view of H. G. Wells for the cyclical view of Spengler. Another is the valuable distinction often drawn between scientific data and aesthetic—which suggested that mere science omitted much from what Ransom called "the world's body," and warned that a too narrow concern with abstract principle is almost as bad for life as it is for art. Again, this generation of critics described what they called a loss of taste in contemporary life. Vulgarity was clearly defined as a frantic and amoral desire to accumulate and to own goods; further, as the feeling that taste might be bought and did not need to be a responsible part of experience as a whole. The absurdities of the bourgeois mind and soul, the deformities of its architecture and its conscience, were never so fully documented. Perhaps the most valuable criticisms of the decade, and the most profound, were those which made it clear that defections of taste were not merely surface phenomena but betrayed an underlying inadequacy in our tradition and our culture.

These criticisms could not, after all, have remained effective had they pointed merely to superficial issues. The 1920s could make no more important contribution than is contained in their most jealously guarded thesis: that history and society are and remain abstractions until they are associated with personal experience. As Arthur Mizener has said (*Kenyon Review,* Winter 1950):

> . . . the situation, the moment in history, is not in itself tragic; it only provides the occasion on which the aware individual suffers the experience of unavoidable moral choices. No matter what the occasion, there is no tragedy where the forces of circumstance are not transmuted into personal experience.

If the twenties in America can be condemned seriously for a fault, it is not for their vulgarity (there is vulgarity of some sort in any time) or for their immorality (immorality in any period is ordinarily a characteristic of the move toward moral redefinition). The greatest fault was their naïveté. Men and women were often quite literally and self-avowedly ignorant of tradition. They had chosen to be; they had rejected both sound and unsound generalities and thought. As a result they were open to every new influence that came along; in most cases there was no intellectual experience to use as a measure of validity. That is undoubtedly the reason so much of the discussion of ideas in the decade seemed the talk of an undergraduate newly and overly impressed by his introductory course in philosophy.

Perhaps the young men and women of the 1950s are immensely more sophisticated, learned, and disingenuous. The theories of Freud have been greatly extended, and the attitude toward them lacks the naïve enthusiasm of an earlier generation. The French masters of literature are now not only thoroughly known; they are being revaluated and their influence upon a handful of American poets now seems a part of ancient literary history. The mood in which bulletins from Moscow were received in the offices of the *Liberator* now seems incredibly naïve. Marxism has not only undergone numerous shifts in interpretation; there have been great changes of heart regarding the "crusade that failed." It is no longer possible to imagine (one no longer has the naïve expectancy to await) a doctrine's role in saving the world. The new generation is much wiser, much less likely to be taken in—one may say, less *capable* of being taken in. But in a very real sense the assertions so often made in the twenties now seem more sensible than they did in their own time. Certainly in our own postwar world we now are convinced (and not especially shocked to find) that evil actually does exist. We are aware of the peculiar failures of scientific research and suspicious of its direct application to human affairs.

It is perhaps unfortunate that we know so much and are so helpless at the same time. In looking back upon the 1920s perhaps we ought not to be worried about the "party we cannot afford to throw again," but rather about our loss of confidence in free, if erratic, inquiry, which we seem to have abandoned along with our naïveté. Our knowledge seems to lack the strength of will that accompanied the ignorance and the errantry of the 1920s. We become more sophisticated and more inflexible with each passing year. We are competent scholars, writers, thinkers, voters; we are properly shocked when one of our fellows commits an especially noticeable error against good taste and good manners. Why, then, are we restless, uncertain, and unhappy? Why is our literature not first-rate? Why are the majority of our critical essays written about the literature of the 1920s and not about that of our own time? Something must be true of that decade that has nothing to do with the big party they were supposed to have had. Perhaps they were more sane, less frivolous, than we have been led to believe.

The most intelligent and the most sensible attitude we can have toward the 1920s, as well as toward our own time, is to accept the saving grace of an irony directed at both. They are, both of them, times of war and of the effects of war. In neither time is it possible unqualifiedly to admire or simply to repudiate man's responsibility for what has happened. That irony is expressed with an especial relevance in Allen Tate's "Ode to Our Young Pro-Consuls of the Air" (1943), the concluding text of our survey. The times, the poet says, have once more come round to war; and each citizen is again called upon "to take/His modest stake." We have responded to the call with full patriotism and with angry mechanical force. Once again humanity is simply divided into friend and foe; the enemy is "The puny Japanese" and "the German toad." Observing these demonstrations of moral and military might, the poet reflects upon what he had done (or might have done) to prevent these "enemies of mind" from resuming their quarrel.

There follows an ironic survey of the attacks upon the irresponsibles. The poet tries to recall past wars to present memory: the "Toy sword, three-cornered hat" of "York and Lexington"; the "Toy rifle, leather hat/Above the boyish beard" of the Civil War; then the "disorder" of Versailles, when

> Proud Wilson yielded ground
>   To franc and pound,
>   Made pilgrimage
>   In the wake of Henry James

and its aftermath, when France "Opened the gate/To Hitler—at Compiègne." "In this bad time" the poet had no role, nor took any responsibility:

> He studied Swift and Donne,
>   Ignored the Hun,
>   While with faint heart
>   Proust caused the fall of France.

Literature thus irresponsibly caused, or permitted, the disaster to happen. Yet, when our fortunes were most desperate, the critics rushed to the rescue of a faltering republic:

> Yet all that feeble time
>   Brave Brooks and lithe MacLeish
>   Had sworn to thresh
>   Our flagging spirit
>   With literature made Prime!

And, in response, our culture has revived, sprung to the defense of American ideals:

> Nursing the blague that dulls
>   Spirits grown Eliotic,
>   Now patriotic
>   Are: we follow
>   *The Irresponsibles!*

This is the spectacle of a nation aroused from its "Eliotic" sloth, cured of "the blague that dulls," transformed almost as if overnight by the magic of the "responsible word" from "Spirits grown Eliotic" to efficient and confirmed patriots. The poet ironically salutes the young men who have gone off to "win the world" on such short notice and after such a treacherous, defeatist past: with "zeal pro-consular," these "partisans/Of liberty unfurled!" will (once reminded of their duty) resume the task of civilizing the world.

The "Ode" concludes with a vision of the "saviors," the young men

who have (because of "Brave Brooks and lithe MacLeish") thrown
aside their indifference and resumed the traditional role, with the aid
of "literature made Prime." The planes in which they travel on their
liberating missions impress the poet with their "animal excellence,"
and he bids them success in finding their targets:

> Swear you to keep
> Faith with imperial eye:
>
> .   .   .
>
> Upon the Tibetan plain
> A limping caravan,
>   Dive, and exterminate
>   The Lama, late
> Survival of old pain.
> Go kill the dying swan.

The full, rich irony of this message to the "Young Pro-Consuls"
comes simply from a shrewd penetration of certain falsely moral readings of American culture: first, that there is necessarily a direct relationship between literature and public life; second, that the moral responsibility for a present emergency can quickly and easily be ascribed
to a literature that had not anticipated or prepared for the crisis; further,
that the crisis can be met by searching for a "literature made Prime,"
by ignoring the totality of a culture and selecting only that part of it
that is suitable to the occasion; finally, that the instruments of a war,
which are the consequences of a total history and not just servants of
an "ideal," can be used to return the world to sanity and rescue it from
"the puny Japanese" and "the German toad."

The irony is addressed primarily to those who accused the writers
of the 1920s of "the literary fallacy"—the critics who have been guilty
of a larger "moral fallacy." For, as the poem suggests, literature is
not maneuverable; a culture cannot be one thing at one time and its
opposite immediately thereafter. An extreme neurosis of "social conscience" has led the judges of the 1920s into a trap of false criticism;
it has assumed that the literature produced in the decade was cynically
or irresponsibly (and thus dishonestly) engaged in corrupting an entire nation. These judgments suffer from a serious loss of perspective.
The critics who made them have chosen to make what they need (what
they will) out of the 1920s. They have insisted that literature should
serve a moral objective of an extraordinarily narrow and limited kind.
Since it has not seemed to do so, they have condemned it for not meet-

ing their terms. This is not the way to a just or accurate estimate; it is a victim of its own narrowness of vision, and it cannot or should not endure beyond the limits of its occasion.

3. The Uses of Innocence

THE POSITIVE values of the 1920s may perhaps best be suggested in the phrase "useful innocence." In the decade two generations collaborated in an exhaustive review of America's past greatness and present status. The one, the "old generation," contemporary with the Old Gang, surveyed the weaknesses of a tradition that had culminated in a war and an uneasy peace. The other generation, young in 1920 but old enough to have attended or participated in the ceremonies of 1914–1918, assumed the task of renewing that culture, of making it over according to new principles and what seemed newly acquired insights into human nature.

Of necessity, many of the writings of the decade were either important variants of old forms or new and original forms. No one can overemphasize the value of formal experiment in the 1920s. De Voto and Brooks have complained about "moral failure" and the "literary fallacy." The truth is that the writers of the 1920s, finding a world that seemed cut free of the past, had to invent new combinations of spirit and matter and new forms of expressing the human drama. They were not aided by any secure ordering of social or religious systems. They were novelists of manners in a society distrustful of past definitions, poets of formalized insight into moral chaos. Their restless desire for the new was always motivated by their distrust of the old. *Form,* then, was a major concern, a major necessity. The careers of all important writers who began publishing in the decade are marked by a restless concern with literary form. Since the forms of the past had been generally associated with a tradition now abhorred, the new forms had perforce to be different, newly inspired, and newly seen.

When Gertrude Stein lectured on method, when Ezra Pound fulminated against softness and weakness of speech, they were speaking for a formal revolution that was also a moral revolution. The concern with form was basically a concern over the need to provide an aesthetic order for moral revisions. It is true that the best of our writers were preoccupied with literature; they were "whole men" in the genuine sense of being profoundly concerned with the moral value of literary form. Essential to the enlightenment the decade gave us was that sense of the significance of the aesthetic, of its essential nature. Such a preoccupation appears on the surface to be morally irresponsible; actually it is truly moral in the sense of its earnest desire to communicate the variants of the modern condition.

The great strength of the decade lay in its useful and deliberate innocence. Ideas habitually lose their vitality as the employment of them alters or is too closely aligned with social expediency. Naïve, innocent demonstrations of wrath over smugness, indolence, or hypocrisy are outward expressions of moral revision. The language communicates these ideas; when they descend from the level of genuine moral judgment to that of comfortable journalism, the language and the forms must be changed. The writers of the 1920s, concentrating on literary form, went about the business of morally redefining the function of the language and its association with present realities. To begin with the "new"—which is to say, the raw, unformed, unsupported, and unexplained present literary condition—is to begin innocently afresh, to explore "the thing seen" in terms of the "way it is seen."

Having rejected all precedents, the writers of the 1920s themselves became precedents for the literature of future decades. But it was in their literary, their aesthetic, successes that future writers saw merit. The narrator of Budd Schulberg's *The Disenchanted* (1950) wishes that he could accept the brilliant literary successes of Halliday and ignore the *man* who had achieved them. This narrator is a *naïf* of another decade, unable to see the tragic artist whole or judge him from any point of view other than the documentary morality of the 1930s. It is almost beyond the capacity of those who look at the 1920s, however carefully, to understand the close rapport between literary concentration and moral insight. The writers of the 1920s—or many of them—had both to *see* a world as it frankly was and to *re-establish* that world in their literary formulations. The very matter of Fitzgerald's moral extravagances (which are the substance of Halliday's past) is incorporated into his art; however imperfectly, that art formalized what would otherwise have been merely a series of sensational and superficial dissipations. The writers of the 1920s believed in everything, those of the 1930s in only one thing, those of the 1940s in nothing. The second and third groups borrowed from the first the means of formulating their one thing and their nothing. This fact startlingly, enduringly remains: the 1920s were an opportunity and a challenge offered to a group of persons who were freshly and naïvely talented, anxious to learn *how* to restate and redramatize the human condition, morally preoccupied with the basic problem of communicating their insights into their present world.

But the weight of tradition is always heavy upon the individual talent. The important truth of the decade is not that its artists rejected the past but that they looked at the past from an orientation psychologically different from that of previous decades. They did not borrow from tradition so much as they forced tradition to give to them precisely what they needed from it. They refused to accept without question the formal systems of judging and dramatizing the moral values of the human race, preferred to select what they would, and on their own terms, from what the past had to offer. As a result the literary history of the decade, like its moral history, is a mélange of contrivance, experiment, and revolt.

Invariably didactic precedent interferes with a genuine moral appraisal of such a time and such a phenomenon. The literary heroes of the time assist in perpetuating the confusion: they recant, they are "converted," they rebel against their rebellion, they grow old and do not dare to face impeachment. They cannot see, or do not wish to see, that what they did and were at one time was of the utmost importance for the state of their own health and of that of society at large.

This fact, that they do not now wish to see and that no one cares truly to see for them, remains of all the important positive legacies of the decade: the fact of useful innocence. They were truly, recklessly, innocently, rawly, tenaciously naïve. The emperor had worn no clothes after all. The world had not been saved. The health of society was not after all good. The Bridge did not lead us to Cathay. They therefore made—formally, aesthetically, and morally—what they could of the thing that they had seen. They often crossed the Atlantic in an attempt to see it from another perspective, to disengage themselves from its immediate nature only to see it more closely. They went to masters of French poetry, of seventeenth-century British drama, of nineteenth-century German philosophy and psychology, and took from them what "influences" they needed. But the best of them were from the beginning, and remained, endowed with talent, with reserves of irony, satire, and intelligent respect for the "right word." The best of them preserved in their work the exact *rapprochement* of experience with the act of experiencing, of action with the moral comedy of man acting.

When, as almost always, men complain of the 1920s that there was no steady adherence to the morally proper, they are narrowly right but fundamentally wrong. This was no time for Edith Wharton, as she admitted; in a genuine sense the opportunity for a formalized comedy of social manners had passed, and with it the opportunity to employ a fixed, traditional mode of moral examination. François Mauriac once said that if one were asked what is the most genuinely real human experience of personal agony, he would have to answer that it is the time immediately preceding his death, when the full weight of tradition and personal past bears upon an uncertain future, immediately foreseen. The moment of one's death is of such primary importance that the history of an entire culture can be relevant to it. This crisis in human experience requires all moral strength to meet it. But no one has sufficiently explored the role that form plays at such a time. The "comforts" that a culture offers then are either extremely reassuring or vaguely disturbing. When, as occurs so often in the literature of the 1920s, men say that "it does not mean anything to die," they would like to suggest that the agony of death is not attended by the solaces of a public moral security. It is indispensable to the health of any culture that this security be constantly examined, naïvely questioned, explosively rejected, and finally re-established and re-formed.

The "best of them" who did not die in 1914–1918, who came back to "frankness as never before," were possessed of a useful innocence in their approach to the world that was left them. They explored the corridors of history, inspected the meaning of a religion temporarily discredited; they formulated in several brilliant ways the most important of all symbolic figurations of our century—that of isolation, of the single, dispossessed soul whose life needs to be re-established in terms specifically new and unencumbered. They did not always succeed in defining this symbol, for themselves or for others. Many of their works suffered from intellectual colloquialism—which, like all other forms of colloquialism, loses its value as it loses its fresh relevance. But the great contributions to our ways of speaking about our ways of feeling have—in a manner still and always valuable—preoccupied themselves with the proper answers to the question Eliot's Gerontion put to himself at the beginning of the decade: "After such knowledge, what forgiveness?" After such experiences, what forms remain of meeting, defining, and sensibly tolerating the human condition?

BIOGRAPHIES

CHRONOLOGY, 1915–1932

SELECTED BIBLIOGRAPHY

TEXT OF *HUGH SELWYN MAUBERLEY*
BY EZRA POUND

BIOGRAPHIES

ADAMS, Henry (1838–1918)

American scholar, teacher, historian. Born in Boston, Mass., of an illustrious family, which included the country's second and sixth Presidents. Accompanied his father to England (1861–1868), where the latter served as American minister. Served as assistant professor of history at Harvard (1870–1877); editor of the *North American Review* (1870–1876). Though *The Education of Henry Adams* (privately printed, 1907) is his best-known work, other important books are *Mont-Saint-Michel and Chartres* (1904), a study of medieval religion and culture, and the nine-volume *History of the United States during the Administrations of Jefferson and Madison* (1889–1891). He also published, anonymously and pseudonymously, two novels, *Democracy* (1880) and *Esther* (1884).

AIKEN, Conrad (1889–)

American novelist, poet, critic. Born, Savannah, Ga.; spent most of his youth and college years in and near Cambridge, Mass.; also lived some time in Italy and England. His writing shows considerable sensitivity to modern experiments in style and structure; the novel *Blue Voyage* (1927) is in some respects an adaptation of the method employed by Joyce in *Ulysses*. Among his works are novels: *Great Circle* (1933), *King Coffin* (1935), *Conversation* (1940); short stories: *Bring! Bring!* (1925), *Costumes by Eros* (1928), *Among the Lost People* (1934); poetry: *The Jig of Forslin* (1916), *The Charnel Rose* (1919), *The Coming Forth by Day of Osiris Jones* (1931), *Time in the Rock* (1936), *The Soldier* (1944), *The Kid* (1947); criticism: *Scepticisms* (1919). *The Collected Poems* was published in 1953. *Ushant* (1952), an autobiography, is of literary interest because of its reminiscences of contemporaries as well as its method and style.

ALDINGTON, Richard (1892–)

British novelist, poet, critic; associated with *The Egoist* and other magazines and with the Imagist movement in modern poetry, about which he helped to formulate several statements. Married American poet, Hilda Doolittle, 1913. Among his works are poetry: *Images Old and New* (1915), *Exile and Other Poems* (1923), *Collected Poems* (1928); novels: *Death of a Hero* (1929), *All Men Are Enemies* (1933); autobiography: *Life for Life's Sake* (1941).

ANDERSON, Margaret (1893?–)
American editor, sponsor of new literature; known especially for her editorship of *The Little Review* (1914–1929), which began in Chicago and was published thereafter in New York and Paris. Her career in modern literature and the arts is described with enthusiasm in her autobiography, *My Thirty Years War* (1930); a second volume of reminiscences, *The Fiery Fountains* (1951), discusses her life since the end of *The Little Review*.

ANDERSON, Maxwell (1888–)
American playwright and critic of the drama, known especially for his attempts to write verse drama on both historical and modern themes. Of the latter, *Winterset* (1935; critics' award) is the best known and proved most successful on the stage. The Sacco-Vanzetti case, which forms the background of that play, was more directly and crudely treated earlier, in *Gods of the Lightning* (1928), written with Harold Hickerson. With Laurence Stallings, Anderson collaborated in the successful war play *What Price Glory* (produced 1924). Other notable plays include *Saturday's Children* (1927), *Elizabeth the Queen* (1930), *Both Your Houses* (1933; Pulitzer Prize), *Valley Forge* (1934), *High Tor* (1936; Critics' award), *Key Largo* (1939), *Joan of Lorraine* (1946). *Off Broadway* (1947) contains his essays on the theater.

ANDERSON, Sherwood (1876–1941)
American novelist, short-story writer, journalist. Born, Camden, Ohio. After serving in the Spanish-American War (1898) he became a businessman in Elyria, Ohio; he left there in 1912 for a career of writing in Chicago. The early novels, *Windy McPherson's Son* (1916) and *Marching Men* (1917), were not successful, but *Winesburg, Ohio* (1919) brought him distinction. Among his later works are stories: *The Triumph of the Egg* (1921; *Dial* award), *Horses and Men* (1923); autobiography: *A Story-Teller's Story* (1925), *Tar* (1926); novels: *Dark Laughter* (1925), *Beyond Desire* (1932), *Kit Brandon* (1936). *Perhaps Women* (1931) was an essay on the problems of the machine age. As his autobiographies and his *Letters* (1953) reveal, he was very active in the discussion and formation of modern writing. At one time or another he knew and influenced Hemingway, Gertrude Stein, Faulkner; the persons closest to him in the formative years were Van Wyck Brooks, Waldo Frank, and Gorham Munson.

AUDEN, Wystan Hugh (1907–)

British-born poet, dramatist, critic. Educated, Christ Church, Oxford; taught in Malvern, England (1930–1935) and later in several American colleges and universities. Became an American citizen in 1939. The early *Poems* (1930) established him as one of England's most promising poets. His later works include the poetry: *The Orators* (1932), *Spain* (1937), *On This Island* (1937), *Another Time* (1940), *The Double Man* (1941), *For the Time Being* (1944), *The Age of Anxiety* (1948); verse plays: *The Dance of Death* (1933) and, with Christopher Isherwood, *The Dog Beneath the Skin* (1935), *The Ascent of F6* (1936). His critical essays reveal several modern intellectual interests, such as psychoanalysis, Kierkegaard, Kafka; the originality and liveliness of his critical prose is clearly evident in *The Enchafèd Flood* (1950).

BABBITT, Irving (1865–1933)

American Humanist critic. Born, Dayton, Ohio; educated, Harvard and the Sorbonne. From 1894 until his death (except for a year at Williams) he taught French literature at Harvard. He and Paul Elmer More were the leading spokesmen of American Humanism in modern criticism. His principal works include *Literature and the American College* (1908), *The New Laokoon* (1910), *Rousseau and Romanticism* (1919), *Democracy and Leadership* (1924).

BARTON, Bruce (1886–)

American authority on advertising, writer of popular interpretations of business, religion, and their interrelationships. Member of Congress, 1937–39 and 1939–41. Among his most successful books are *The Man Nobody Knows* (1925), *The Book Nobody Knows* (1926), and *What Can a Man Believe* (1927).

BAUDELAIRE, Charles (1821–1867)

French poet, critic. His volume *Les Fleurs du Mal* (1857) has had a profound influence on poetry in France, other European countries, and America. One of the principal sponsors of the work of Edgar Allan Poe in France, he translated the *Tales* into French and was in other ways largely responsible for Poe's considerable reputation in Europe in the nineteenth and twentieth centuries. His prose volumes include *Les Paradis artificiels* (1860), *Curiosités esthétiques* (1869), and *L'Art romantique* (1869).

BEACH, Sylvia (?–)

American editor and publisher. She went to France around 1915, to learn French literature. Opened a bookshop in Paris on the rue de l'Odéon, near the one managed by Adrienne Monnier. Under the imprint Shakespeare and Company, she brought out the first edition of Joyce's *Ulysses*. In the 1920s she was a friend and counselor of many American expatriates, for whom her shop, and the French bookshop of Adrienne Monnier nearby, served as informal headquarters.

BEARD, Charles A. (1874–1948)

American historian, teacher. Born, Indiana; educated, DePauw University, Oxford, Columbia; instructor in and professor of politics, Columbia (1904–1917), from which he resigned in 1917 as a protest against the dismissals of pacifist teachers. His important books include *An Economic Interpretation of the Constitution* (1913), *Economic Origins of Jeffersonian Democracy* (1915), *The Economic Basis of Politics* (1922); with Mary R. Beard, *The Rise of American Civilization* (1927), *America in Midpassage* (1939).

BENÉT, Stephen Vincent (1898–1943)

American novelist, short-story writer, poet. Born, Bethlehem, Pa.; educated, Yale. His best-known work is the historical poem *John Brown's Body* (1928); among his other works are novels: *The Beginning of Wisdom* (1921), *James Shore's Daughter* (1934); short stories: *The Devil and Daniel Webster* (1937), *Thirteen O'Clock* (1937), *Last Circle* (1936); poetry: *The Ballad of William Sycamore* (1923), *Burning City* (1936), *Western Star* (1943).

BISHOP, John Peale (1899–1944)

American critic, poet, novelist. Born, West Virginia; educated, Princeton, where he was a contemporary of F. Scott Fitzgerald and Edmund Wilson; later became literary journalist and reviewer for *Vanity Fair* and other publications. The critical and other prose was collected by Edmund Wilson (1948); the *Collected Poems* (1948) were gathered and edited by Allen Tate. His fiction includes a novel, *Act of Darkness* (1935), and a collection of short stories, *Many Thousands Gone* (1931). An excellent poet in his own right, whose talent has only recently been recognized, he was known in his lifetime chiefly for his penetrating studies of contemporary literature.

BLACK, MacKnight (1897–1931)

American poet. Born, Philadelphia, Pa. His poems about machinery were published in *The New Masses* and elsewhere. His poetry was published in *Machinery* (1929) and *Thrust at the Sky* (1932), the latter edited by Marcus Goodrich and published posthumously.

BODENHEIM, Maxwell (1892–1954)

American novelist, poet. Born, Mississippi; moved to Chicago, then to New York, where he was prominent in bohemian circles. His volumes of poetry include *Introducing Irony* (1922), *Against This Age* (1923), *Bring-*

ing Jazz (1930); novels: *Replenishing Jessica* (1925), *Crazy Man* (1924), *Naked on Roller Skates* (1931).

BOURNE, Randolph (1886–1918)
American critic. Born, Bloomfield, N.J.; educated, Columbia University; traveled in Europe on a Gilder Fellowship (1913–1914). One of the most promising younger critics, Bourne contributed his essays (on education, politics, literature, and the arts) to the *New Republic, The Seven Arts* (1917), and *The Dial* (1917–1918). His books include *Youth and Life* (1913), *The Gary Schools* (1916), and *Education and Living* (1917); two volumes were published posthumously: *Untimely Papers* (edited by James Oppenheim, 1919) and *The History of a Literary Radical* (edited by Van Wyck Brooks, 1920).

BOYD, Ernest (1887–1946)
Irish-born critic; first came to America in 1913, lived in United States after 1920. He was a prominent figure in criticism and journalism, a contributor to the *American Mercury* and other magazines. Criticism includes *Appreciations and Depreciations* (1918; studies of Irish literature), *Portraits, Real and Imaginary* (1924), *H. L. Mencken* (1925), *Literary Blasphemies* (1927).

BOYD, Thomas (1898–1935)
American novelist and short-story writer. Born, Ohio. Gained temporary prominence with the novel *Through the Wheat* (1923) and the short stories *Points of Honour* (1925), which show an obvious indebtedness to Stephen Crane's stories of the Civil and Spanish-American Wars. Before his death Boyd identified his fiction with the prevailing leftist interpretation of war and munitions-makers (*In Time of Peace*, 1935).

BOYLE, Kay (1903–)
American novelist, short-story writer, poet. Born, St. Paul, Minn.; since 1922 has spent many years in Europe, which serves as setting of much of her fiction. Her fiction includes the novels *Plagued by the Nightingale* (1931), *Year Before Last* (1932), and *Monday Night* (1938); the short stories *Wedding Day and Other Stories* (1930), *The First Lover and Other Stories* (1933), *The White Horses of Vienna and Other Stories* (1936).

BRETON, André (1896–)
French poet, critic; one of the most important of the founders of surrealism, which was widely discussed and influential in America during the late 1920s; later, chief of the school. Two surrealist manifestoes (1924, 1930) sum up his view of the role the movement played in the arts and in politics.

BROOKS, Van Wyck (1886–)

American critic. Born, Plainfield, N.J.; educated, Harvard. Served as editor of *The Seven Arts* (1916–1917) and *The Freeman* (1920–1924). His essay *America's Coming-of-Age* (1915) exerted a considerable influence on his generation of writers, as did *Letters and Leadership* (1918) and a number of biographical studies, among them *The Ordeal of Mark Twain* (1920; revised, 1932). In 1936 he began an informal history of American letters, with *The Flowering of New England;* the fifth and final volume was *The Confident Years* (1952). In recent years he has spent much time disavowing his earlier critical position; *The Writer in America* (1953) is the most specific statement of this change of view, though the change probably dates as early as *Emerson and Others* (1927) and the revised edition of *The Ordeal of Mark Twain.*

BROUN, Heywood (1888–1939)

American critic, journalist, fighter for social causes in his contributions to the *New York Tribune, New York World, The Nation, New Republic.* Drama critic, general reviewer in the 1920s. His criticism includes *Seeing Things at Night* (1921), *Anthony Comstock* (1927, with Margaret Leech); novels: *The Boy Grew Older* (1922), *Gandle Follows His Nose* (1926); journalism: *Pieces of Hate and Other Enthusiasms* (1922), *Sitting on the World* (1924).

BRUNO, Guido (1884–)

Greenwich Village editor and celebrity; edited several slight magazines and chapbooks, in which he featured his friends and the works of writers of the English 1890s.

BURKE, Kenneth (1897–)

American critic. Born, Pittsburgh, Pa.; educated, Ohio State and Columbia; taught at University of Chicago (1939, 1949–50) and Bennington College (since 1943). Has translated from Thomas Mann, Oswald Spengler, others. A frequent contributor to *The Dial* (1922–1929). Most important criticism includes *Counter-Statement* (1931), *Attitudes Towards History* (1937), *Permanence and Change* (1935), *The Philosophy of Literary Form* (1941), *A Grammar of Motives* (1945), *A Rhetoric of Motives* (1950).

CALVERTON, Victor F. (1900–1940)

American critic; applied Marxist criteria to American literary and political history in such volumes as *The Newer Spirit: A Sociological Criticism of Literature* (1925) and *The Liberation of American Literature* (1932). Editor, *The Modern Quarterly* (also called *The Modern Monthly;* 1923–1940).

CARPENTER, Edward (1844–1929)

British author of widely read, controversial studies of sex and family life, examinations of democracy and social reform. Most popular of his books in America, *Love's Coming of Age* (1896), was much discussed in the 1920s.

CATHER, Willa (1876–1947)

American novelist, short-story writer, poet. Born near Winchester, Va.; moved (1883 or 1884) to farm near Red Cloud, Neb.; educated, University of Nebraska; worked as drama editor, Pittsburgh, then as managing editor of *McClure's*. After her first novel, *Alexander's Bridge* (1912), she returned to Nebraska, where several of her important works of fiction have their setting. Among the most influential of her novels are *O Pioneers!* (1913), *The Song of the Lark* (1915), *My Ántonia* (1918), *One of Ours* (1922; Pulitzer Prize), *A Lost Lady* (1923),· *The Professor's House* (1925), *Death Comes for the Archbishop* (1927), *Shadows on the Rock* (1931). Short stories and nouvelles are included in *The Troll Garden* (1905), *Youth and the Bright Medusa* (1920), and *Obscure Destinies* (1932). *April Twilights* (1903) is a volume of poems, and *Not Under Forty* (1936) is a collection of essays. After her death a selection from her essays on writers and writing was published (*Willa Cather on Writing*, 1949).

COOK, George Cram (1873–1924)

American dramatist, founder and leader of the Provincetown Players, which he left shortly before his death to make a pilgrimage to Greece. Collaborated with third wife, Susan Glaspell (whose *The Road to the Temple*, 1926, is his biography), in writing of one-act plays, *Suppressed Desires* (1914), *Tickless Time* (1918).

CORBIÈRE, Tristan (1845–1875)

French poet; famous for the harsh satire and mockery in his poems (*Les Amours jaunes,* 1873), which interested and influenced Ezra Pound and T. S. Eliot.

COURNOS, John (1881–)

Russian-born novelist, critic; has lived in America since 1891 (except for residence in England, 1912–1930). Novels include *Babel* (1922), *The New Candide* (1924; satire of American society), *Miranda Masters* (1926); other prose: *A Modern Plutarch* (1928; biographical sketches), *Autobiography* (1935).

COWLEY, Malcolm (1898–)

American critic and poet. Born, Belsano, Pa.; educated, Harvard and University of Montpellier, France (American Field Service Fellowship).

He has translated books by Paul Valéry, Maurice Barrès, André Gide, and others. Associate editor, *New Republic* (1929–1944), contributing editor since 1944. Poetry: *Blue Juniata* (1929) and *The Dry Season* (1941). *Exile's Return* (1934; revised edition, 1951) is an important study of his generation of writers; *The Literary Situation* (1954) is a survey of the writing profession in the 1950s. In addition, he has done outstanding editorial work with *After the Genteel Tradition* (1937), *Books That Changed Our Minds* (1939), *The Portable Hemingway* (1944), *The Portable Faulkner* (1948).

CRANE, Hart (1899–1932)

American poet. Born, Garrettsville, Ohio; moved to New York in 1916, and after that alternated between the Midwest and the East. With financial assistance from Otto Kahn, he began planning and writing of *The Bridge,* a complex sequence of poems on what he called "the Myth of America." *White Buildings,* a collection of early poems, was published in 1926; *The Bridge* appeared in 1930, first in Paris, later in America. In 1932 (April 26), on return voyage from Mexico (where he had spent the previous year under Guggenheim auspices), he committed suicide. *The Collected Poems,* edited by Waldo Frank (1933) and *The Letters, 1916–1932,* edited by Brom Weber, complete the list of his publications.

CRANE, Stephen (1871–1900)

American novelist, short-story writer, poet. Born, Newark, N.J.; spent one year at Syracuse University, after which he left for New York City, where he began his career as a journalist. *Maggie* (1893) is one of the earliest naturalist works of fiction; *The Red Badge of Courage* (1895) has had a profound influence on twentieth-century American writing. His imaginative reconstruction of war scenes in that novel was later supplemented by his stories based upon events in the Spanish-American War, which he saw as correspondent *(Wounds in the Rain,* 1900). Other collections of stories are *The Monster* (1899), *The Open Boat* (1898), *Whilomville Stories* (1900). The poems are included in *The Black Riders and Other Lines* (1895) and *War Is Kind* (1899).

CROCE, Benedetto (1866–1952)

Italian philosopher, critic, historian; very influential especially in development of aesthetic theory, in association of art with history, theories of expressionism in the arts. Works important in this sense: *Aesthetic as Science of Expression and General Linguistic* (1922), *The Poetry of Dante* (1922), *The Conduct of Life* (1924), *The Defense of Poetry* (1933).

CROLY, Herbert (1869–1930)

American journalist, founder and editor-in-chief of the *New Republic;* known especially for *The Promise of American Life* (1909), an important examination of the nation's intellectual and moral resources from a liberal, progressive point of view.

CROSBY, Harry (1898–1929)

American writer, editor. Born, Boston, Mass.; educated, Harvard. Served as an ambulance driver in World War I. With his wife, Caresse, founded the Black Sun Press in Paris. Assistant editor, *transition* magazine, 1929. Committed suicide, New York, 1929. Among his works: *Sonnets for Caresse* (1926), *Red Skeletons* (1927), *Chariot of the Sun* (1927), *Transit of Venus* (1929), and *Shadows of the Sun* (diary, 1922–1929). His press published the first edition of Hart Crane's *The Bridge* (1930).

CUMMINGS, E. E. (1894–)

American poet, dramatist. Born, Cambridge, Mass.; educated, Harvard. Served in Norton-Harjes Ambulance Corps, France, where he was arrested (1917) and held in detention camp at La Ferté Macé; an account, partly fictionalized, of this experience appears in *The Enormous Room* (1922). Poetry: *Tulips and Chimneys* (1923), *XLI Poems* (1925; *Dial* award), *IS 5* (1926), *No Thanks* (1935), *50 Poems* (1940), *1 × 1* (1944); play: *Him* (1927); *Eimi* (1933), a report of his visit to Soviet Russia.

DAVIDSON, Donald (1893–)

American poet, critic, teacher. Born, Tennessee; educated, Vanderbilt University. Member of original "Fugitive" group at Vanderbilt (*The Fugitive* magazine, 1922–1925); one of the Twelve Southerners of the symposium *I'll Take My Stand* (1930); edited another symposium, *The Attack on Leviathan* (1938). Poetry: *The Tall Men* (1927), *Lee in the Mountains* (1938), and other volumes.

DELL, Floyd (1887–)

American novelist, critic, journalist. Born, Illinois; worked on newspapers, Davenport, Iowa, then Chicago. Moved to New York City (1914), where he helped to edit *The Masses* magazine with Max Eastman (1914–1917), then was on the staff of the *Liberator* (1918–1924). A series of novels—*Moon-Calf* (1920), *The Briary-Bush* (1921), *Janet March* (1923), and others—marked him as a popular minor novelist of the young generation, a reputation he continued to exploit through the 1920s and beyond. Among his prose works, in part the result of his editorial experiences, the most important are *Were You Ever a Child?* (1919), *Intellectual Vagabondage* (1926; a study of the intellectual interests, 1910–1920), and *Love in the Machine Age* (1930).

DEUTSCH, Babette (1895–)

American poet, novelist, critic. Born, New York, N.Y.; educated, Barnard, Columbia. Among her works are poetry: *Honey out of the Rock*

(1925), *Fire for the Night* (1930), *One Part Love* (1939), *Take Them, Stranger* (1944); novels: *A Brittle Heaven* (1926), *In Such a Night* (1927); criticism: *This Modern Poetry* (1935), *Poetry in Our Time* (1952).

DE VOTO, Bernard (1897–)

American critic, historian, teacher, novelist. Born, Utah; educated, University of Utah, Harvard. Known especially for his study of the westward movement (*The Course of Empire*, 1952) and for his attacks upon Van Wyck Brooks and the 1920s (*Mark Twain's America*, 1932; *The Literary Fallacy*, 1944); has written some distinguished studies of the life and work of Mark Twain (the above and *Mark Twain at Work*, 1942). Occasional journalistic estimates of literature included in *Forays and Rebuttals* (1936) and *Minority Report* (1940).

DEWEY, John (1859–1952)

American philosopher, educator. Born, Vermont; educated, University of Vermont, Johns Hopkins; taught at Universities of Minnesota, Michigan, Chicago, and Columbia. Wrote several volumes on philosophy of education, pragmatism: *Psychology* (1887), *The School and Society* (1899), *Experience and Education* (1938), *Problems of Men* (1946); among his other works are *How We Think* (1909), *Reconstruction in Philosophy* (1920), *Human Nature and Conduct* (1922), *Experience and Nature* (1925), *The Quest for Certainty* (1929), *Art as Experience* (1934), *Logic: The Theory of Inquiry* (1938).

DOOLITTLE, Hilda (1886–)

American poet. Born, Pennsylvania; went abroad, 1911; married Richard Aldington, 1913. She participated in literary and critical activities in London, 1910–1915; was sponsored by Ezra Pound as "H. D., Imagiste." Poems and verse plays: *Sea Garden* (1916), *Hymen* (1921), *Heliodora* (1924), *Hippolytus Temporizes* (1927), *The Walls Do Not Fall* (1944), others.

DOS PASSOS, John (1896–)

American novelist, dramatist, author of prose studies and reportage. Born, Chicago, Ill.; educated, Harvard. Novels based on World War I include *One Man's Initiation* (1920), *Three Soldiers* (1921), *1919* (1932). *Manhattan Transfer* (1925), an impressionistic novel of New York, was a turning point, the beginning of a method that he expanded and elaborated in the trilogy *U. S. A.*, which includes *The 42nd Parallel* (1930), *1919* (1932), and *The Big Money* (1936). A second trilogy, *District of Columbia* (1952), includes *Adventures of a Young Man* (1939), *Number One* (1943), and *The Grand Design* (1948). Journalistic prose (ranging from *New Masses* to *Life*) has been collected in *In All Countries* (1934), *The Ground We Stand On* (1941), *State of the Nation* (1944), others.

DREISER, Theodore (1871–1945)

American novelist; one of the important early naturalists. Born, Terre Haute, Ind.; educated, Indiana public schools, one year at the University of Indiana. Experience as journalist in Chicago, St. Louis, Toledo, Pittsburgh, New York. Most important novels are *Sister Carrie* (1900), *The Financier* (1912), *The Titan* (1914)—these last two, with *The Stoic* (1947), form the "Frank Cowperwood" trilogy—and *An American Tragedy* (1925). He became a *cause célèbre* for H. L. Mencken and others when attempts were made to suppress *The "Genius"* (1915). His interest in social and political matters took many forms, including joining the Communist party and a trip to the Soviet Union, recorded in *Dreiser Looks at Russia* (1928). Also wrote autobiographical works of much interest: *Dawn* (1931), *A Book about Myself* (1922), *A Hoosier Holiday* (1916); short stories: *Free and Other Stories* (1918), others; plays: *Plays of the Natural and Supernatural* (1916); a kind of verse: *Moods, Cadenced and Declaimed* (1926).

EASTMAN, Max (1883–)

American journalist, critic; editor, *The Masses* (1912–1917), other magazines. In the 1920s a trip to Europe and Russia disabused him of Soviet interests; became one of the most prominent anti-Communists. Among his prose works are *The Literary Mind* (1931), *Art and the Life of Action* (1934), and *The Enjoyment of Laughter* (1936).

EINSTEIN, Albert (1879–)

German-born physicist, mathematician. Born, Ulm; emigrated to America, 1933, and became American citizen, 1940. Nobel Prize for physics, 1921. Author of many important works on physics and mathematics. *The Meaning of Relativity* (translated, 1923) caused much discussion in the 1920s and influenced several levels of American thought. Archibald MacLeish's *Einstein* (1929) is an example of literary reaction.

ELIOT, T. S. (1888–)

American-born poet, dramatist, critic. Born, St. Louis, Mo.; educated, Harvard, the Sorbonne, Oxford; has lived in England since 1914; a British subject since 1927. Assistant editor, *The Egotist* (1917–1919); founder and editor, *The Criterion* (1922–1939). Nobel Prize for literature, 1948. *The Waste Land* (1922) is the most famous of his poems; other influential volumes are *Prufrock and Other Observations* (1917), *Poems* (1920), *Ash Wednesday* (1930), *Four Quartets* (1943). Verse plays include *Murder in the Cathedral* (1935), *The Family Reunion* (1939), *The Cocktail Party* (1950), *The Confidential Clerk* (1953). Most important criticism: *The Sacred Wood* (1920), *Selected Essays, 1917–1932* (1932; new edition with additional essays, 1950), *The Use of Poetry and the Use of Criticism* (1933), *After Strange Gods* (1934).

ELLIS, Havelock (1859–1939)

British psychologist, teacher, critic; author of such literary and critical studies as *The New Spirit* (1890), *Affirmations* (1898; Nietzsche, Zola), *The Soul of Spain* (1908). His *Studies in the Psychology of Sex* (1897–1910), which led to prosecution in England, was widely read in America.

FAULKNER, William (1897–)

American novelist, short-story writer. Born, New Albany, Miss.; educated, University of Mississippi; enlisted Royal Canadian Air Force, World War I. After some years in Oxford, Miss., and New Orleans (where he met Sherwood Anderson), he published *The Marble Faun* (poems, 1924); *Soldiers' Pay* (1926), his first published novel. His fictional history of Yoknapatawpha County begins with the novels *Sartoris* (1929) and *The Sound and the Fury* (1929); other books with this setting include the novels *As I Lay Dying* (1930), *Sanctuary* (1931), *Light in August* (1932), *Absalom, Absalom!* (1936), *The Hamlet* (1940), *Intruder in the Dust* (1948), *Requiem for a Nun* (1951), and two cycles of stories, *The Unvanquished* (1938) and *Go Down, Moses* (1942). Short stories: *These 13* (1931), *Doctor Martino* (1934). *The Collected Stories* were published in 1950. Nobel Prize for literature, 1949.

FISHER, Dorothy Canfield (1879–)

American novelist. Born, Kansas; has lived in Vermont since 1907; educated, Ohio State University, Columbia, the Sorbonne. Her most popular novels are *The Bent Twig* (1915), *The Brimming Cup* (1921), *The Deepening Stream* (1930).

FITZGERALD, F. Scott (1896–1940)

American novelist, short-story writer. Born, St. Paul, Minn.; educated, Princeton. His first novel, *This Side of Paradise* (1920), was a great popular success, which was furthered by a second, *The Beautiful and Damned* (1922). *The Great Gatsby* (1925) is his most important novel. Other works include volumes of short stories: *Flappers and Philosophers* (1920), *Tales of the Jazz Age* (1922), *All the Sad Young Men* (1926), *Taps at Reveille* (1935); and novels: *Tender Is the Night* (1934; about expatriate Americans), *The Last Tycoon* (1941; unfinished story about Hollywood, published posthumously).

FLETCHER, John Gould (1886–)

American poet. Born, Arkansas; educated, Harvard; spent some years in Europe, especially in France and England. His poetry was at one time influenced by nineteenth-century French rhythms. As a Southern writer, contributed to symposium *I'll Take My Stand* (1930). Most important early volumes: *The Dominant City* (1913), *Irradiations—Sand and Spray*

(1915). More recent volumes: *South Star* (1941), *Burning Mountain* (1946). His autobiography, *Life Is My Song* (1937), contains much information about the activities of American poets in London, 1910–1920. Pulitzer Prize, 1939, for *Selected Poems* (1938).

FOERSTER, Norman (1887–)
American critic, teacher. Born, Pittsburgh, Pa.; educated, Harvard, University of Wisconsin; taught, Universities of Wisconsin, North Carolina, Iowa. Influential in teaching Humanist critical doctrine, editing textbooks and symposiums (among which, *Humanism in America*, 1930). Most important works: *American Criticism* (1928), *The American Scholar* (1929), *Toward Standards* (1930).

FORD, Ford Madox (1873–1939)
British novelist, critic, poet, editor; of great interest for his friendships with Conrad, Pound, Hemingway, others; sponsored new writers as editor of *transatlantic review* and other magazines. Novels include his tetralogy of World War I: *Some Do Not* (1924), *No More Parades* (1925), *A Man Could Stand Up* (1926), *The Last Post* (1928). Author of critical studies of Joseph Conrad—with whom he collaborated in *The Inheritors* (1901), *Romance* (1903)—and Henry James. Of several autobiographical studies, *It Was the Nightingale* (1933) is the most important and useful.

FRANK, Waldo (1889–)
American critic, novelist. Born, New Jersey; educated, Yale. Influential critic of American life and culture in the years following World War I; especially well known in France, Spain, South America. Best-known novels: *City Block* (1922), *Rahab* (1922), *Holiday* (1923), *The Death and Birth of David Markand* (1934). Among his critical works and collections of journalism are *Our America* (1919), *Salvos* (1924), *Virgin Spain* (1926), *The Rediscovery of America* (1929), *In the American Jungle* (1937).

FREEMAN, Joseph (1897–)
American critic, novelist, journalist. Educated, Columbia. Associated with *The Liberator, The New Masses,* as leftist critic, poet. *An American Testament* (1936), autobiography, describes his career. Wrote critical introduction for *Proletarian Literature in the United States* (1935); published novel, *Never Call Retreat* (1943).

FREUD, Sigmund (1856–1939)
Austrian psychologist, founder and pioneer interpreter of psychoanalysis, whose works influenced American thinking and writing on several levels. Born, Freiberg; educated, University of Vienna; studied in Paris under

Charcot. *The Interpretation of Dreams* (1900; translation, 1913), the first of his important works, offered a revolutionary description of man's psychic behavior. It was followed by *Three Contributions to a Theory of Sex* (1905; translation, 1910), *The Psychopathology of Everyday Life* (1904; translation, 1914), *Totem and Taboo* (1913; translation, 1918), and many other works. Among the American writers influenced either directly or indirectly by his theories were Conrad Aiken, Waldo Frank, Ludwig Lewisohn, Eugene O'Neill. He also influenced the writing of criticism, biography. A. A. Brill, Freud's most active American sponsor, translated many of his works into English.

GALE, Zona (1874–1938)

American novelist, short-story writer, essayist. Born, Wisconsin; educated, University of Wisconsin. Among her works are novels: *Miss Lulu Bett* (1920, the most popular), *Preface to a Life* (1926); short stories: *Friendship Village* (1908), *Neighborhood Stories* (1914), others. *Portage, Wisconsin, and Other Essays* (1928) is a defense of Midwest community life.

GAUTIER, Théophile (1811–1872)

French poet, novelist, critic, associated with the Parnassian poets and critics and their revolt against French romanticism. His most important collection of verse, *Émaux et Camées* (1852), influenced the work of Pound, Eliot, others.

GOLD, Mike (1896–)

American critic, journalist. Born, New York City's East Side, which he described in the semi-autobiographical *Jews Without Money* (1930). Editor for some years of the *New Masses,* beginning 1926. Studies of American society and politics include *120 Million* (1929), *Change the World!* (1937); *The Hollow Men* (1941) is a leftist survey and criticism of the literature of the 1920s. Plays include *La Fiesta* (1925), *Battle Hymn* (1936; with Michael Blankfort, on theme of John Brown).

GOLDMAN, Emma (1869–1940)

Russian-born exponent of anarchism; came to the United States in 1886. Lectured and wrote on anarchist subjects; editor, *Mother Earth* (magazine begun by her in 1906). Deported in 1919 to Russia, which she came to dislike; *My Disillusionment with Russia* (1924) describes the experience. Other prose: *Anarchism and Other Essays* (1911), *Living My Life* (1931; autobiography).

HAYWOOD, William (1869–1928)

American labor organizer. Born, Salt Lake City, Utah. One of the founders of the Industrial Workers of the World, 1905; participated in

Lawrence and Paterson textile workers strikes (1912, 1913); he was sentenced to imprisonment (1918); while awaiting a new trial he escaped to Russia (1921), where he lived until his death. A colorful hero of workers and artists, 1910–1920, he was featured in several novels, memoirs.

HECHT, Ben (1894–)
   American novelist, short-story writer, journalist; literary satirist and parodist. Editor, *Chicago Literary Times* (1923–1924); in recent years a script writer for the films and a director. Most popular of his satires on modern middle-class life, *Erik Dorn* (1920); others: *Gargoyles* (1922), *Humpty Dumpty* (1924). His autobiography, *A Child of the Century*, appeared in 1954.

HEMINGWAY, Ernest (1899–)
   American novelist, short-story writer, journalist. Born, Oak Park, Ill.; educated, Oak Park High School; training in journalism, Kansas City (1917). Enlisted in ambulance service, Italy; seriously wounded (July 8, 1918) on northern Italian front. After the war, served as journalist in various places; came to Paris (1922) to learn writing. *In Our Time* (1925), collection of short stories, was followed by novel *The Sun Also Rises* (1926). Other important novels: *A Farewell to Arms* (1929), *For Whom the Bell Tolls* (1940), *The Old Man and the Sea* (1952). Short stories: *Men Without Women* (1927), *Winner Take Nothing* (1933). Studies and reportage: *Death in the Afternoon* (1932; bullfighting and bullfighters), *Green Hills of Africa* (1935). His influence on modern American fictional prose is probably greater than that of any other figure in modern letters. He was awarded the Nobel Prize for literature in 1954.

HERGESHEIMER, Joseph (1880–1954)
   American novelist, short-story writer, author of historical novels and romantic portrayals of society. Most popular: *The Three Black Pennys* (1917), *Java Head* (1919), *Linda Condon* (1919), *Cytherea* (1922), *Balisand* (1924), *The Party Dress* (1930), *The Limestone Tree* (1931).

HOFFENSTEIN, Samuel (1890–1947)
   American poet, humorist; reporter and drama critic for New York newspapers. Volumes of humorous verse include *Poems in Praise of Practically Nothing* (1928), *Year In, You're Out* (1930).

HULME, Thomas E. (1883–1917)
   British critic, poet, philosopher. Translated Bergson's *Introduction to Metaphysics* (1912), Sorel's *Reflections on Violence*. His own critical writing (much of it essays first published in the *New Age* magazine, collected by Herbert Read as *Speculations,* 1924) reflects interest in Bergson but is more valuable for its statements concerning the nature of poetry. These

had much to do with the shaping of critical thought, 1910–1920, especially that of Pound, Wyndham Lewis, the Imagists. His few poems published as an appendix to Pound's *Ripostes* (1912).

HUXLEY, Aldous (1894–)
British novelist, poet, essayist, dramatist who lives in the United States, where his novels have been very successful. Best-known novels: *Crome Yellow* (1921), *Antic Hay* (1923), *Point Counter Point* (1928), *Brave New World* (1932). Friend of D. H. Lawrence; edited the Lawrence *Letters*.

INGERSOLL, Robert G. (1833–1899)
American orator, essayist, hero of many young intellectuals in the late nineteenth, early twentieth centuries because of his revolt against contemporary institutions; known as "the great agnostic" because of his campaign for free-thinking, his speeches criticizing established religion ("Superstition," "Some Mistakes of Moses," others).

JOSEPHSON, Matthew (1899–)
American biographer, critic, historian; editor or assistant editor in a number of little magazine ventures, such as *Broom* (1921–1924); student of, writer on, French literature. *Portrait of the Artist as American* (1930) was an important document in the appraisal of the literary life in America in the 1920s. Other works: *Zola and His Time* (1928), *The Robber Barons* (1934), *Victor Hugo* (1942), *Stendhal* (1946).

JOYCE, James (1882–1941)
Irish novelist, poet. His major experimental novels—*Ulysses* (1922; published by Sylvia Beach in Paris and banned in the United States until 1934) and *Finnegans Wake* (1939)—were important expansions of stream-of-consciousness or interior monologue, which influenced many American writers, critics. Other works: *Dubliners* (1914, short stories), *Portrait of the Artist as a Young Man* (1916, novel), *Chamber Music* (1907, poems), *Exiles* (1918, play).

JUNG, Carl Gustav (1875–)
Swiss psychologist, associated with Psychiatric Clinic, University of Zurich; in the beginning he was briefly in agreement with Freud, but soon differed with him, set up his own interpretation of depth psychology and psychiatry. His theories of the "collective unconscious" and his discussions of myth and the role of the artist had much influence on literature and criticism. Best-known works: *The Theory of Psychoanalysis* (1912), *Psychology of the Unconscious* (1916), *Psychological Types* (1923).

KEY, Ellen (1846–1926)

Swedish author, feminist. Her ideas of the role of women in society influenced social legislation in several countries and were widely discussed in America, along with those of Havelock Ellis and Edward Carpenter. Best-known works: *Love and Marriage* (1911; edited by Ellis, 1931), *The Century of the Child* (1909), *The Woman Movement* (1912).

KREYMBORG, Alfred (1883–)

American poet, critic. Sponsor and editor of such little magazines as *Others* (1915–1919), *Broom* (1921–1924). Among his books of poetry are *Mushrooms: A Book of Free Forms* (1916), *Manhattan Men* (1929), *The Selected Poems, 1912–1944* (1945). His autobiography, *Troubadour* (1925), contains much gossip of the period 1910–1920. *Our Singing Strength* (1929) is an attempt to sum up modern American poetry.

KRUTCH, Joseph Wood (1893–)

American critic, journalist. Born, Tennessee; educated, University of Tennessee, Columbia. Drama editor, *The Nation* (1924–1932); associate editor (1932–1937). Professor, Columbia. *The Modern Temper* (1929), a study of the influence of science on modern life, had a strong impact at time of publication. Other works: *Edgar Allan Poe* (1926; psychoanalytic study), *American Drama Since 1918* (1944), *Henry David Thoreau* (1948).

LAFORGUE, Jules (1860–1887)

French poet of special interest for his influence on several American poets, notably T. S. Eliot in such volumes as *Prufrock and Other Observations* (1917) and *Poems* (1920). Most important of Laforgue's works: *Complaintes* (1885), *Moralités légendaires* (1887, prose work), *Derniers vers* (1890).

LAWRENCE, D. H. (1885–1930)

Distinguished English novelist, poet, short-story writer, critic. Born, Eastwood, near Nottingham; educated, Nottingham University; lived in many parts of the world—Italy, Sicily, Australia, New Mexico, Mexico; died Vence, southern France. Works especially critical of modern "Puritan" attitudes toward sex, of ugliness of industrial communities; advanced his own theory of the sources of human life and energy in *Psychoanalysis and the Unconscious* (1921), *Fantasia of the Unconscious* (1922), other works. His contributions to the novel were widely influential, especially in America, where some of his works were first published. Most important novels: *Sons and Lovers* (1913), *The Rainbow* (1915), *Women in Love* (1920), *The Plumed Serpent* (1926), *Lady Chatterley's Lover* (1928).

Among his non-fictional prose works, *Studies in Classic American Literature* (1923) offered some interesting and original impressions of the American literary past.

LAWSON, John Howard (1895–)
American dramatist, interesting for his adaptation of expressionism to social comedy; wrote satirical plays of leftist point of view. Among his most successful plays are *Roger Bloomer* (1923), *Processional* (1925), *The International* (1927).

LEWIS, Sinclair (1885–1951)
American novelist, parodist of middle-class manners, whose *Main Street* (1920) and *Babbitt* (1922) were very popular in America and Europe. Nobel Prize for literature, 1930. Other popular novels: *Arrowsmith* (1925), *Elmer Gantry* (1927), *The Man Who Knew Coolidge* (1928), *Dodsworth* (1929), *It Can't Happen Here* (1935). Some of his letters have been selected and edited by Harrison Smith (*From Main Street to Stockholm: Letters of Sinclair Lewis, 1919–1930*).

LEWIS, Wyndham (1886–)
British artist, novelist, essayist, editor; associated with Pound in editing the magazine *Blast* (1914–1915) and in other ventures; also edited the magazines *Tyro* and *The Enemy*. Important works: *Tarr* (1918, novel), *Time and Western Man* (1927, criticism and philosophy), *The Childermass* (1938, novel), *Apes of God* (1930, novel), *Men Without Art* (1934, criticism).

LIPPMANN, Walter (1889–)
American journalist. Born, New York; educated, Harvard. Associated with the *New Republic* in its early days; has had varied career as writer of articles on politics, especially with the *New York World* and the *New York Herald Tribune* (since 1931). Among his important books are *A Preface to Morals* (1929), *A Preface to Politics* (1913), *Public Opinion* (1922), *The Good Society* (1937).

LOWELL, Amy (1874–1925)
American poet, critic. Sponsor of the "new verse"; took over the Imagists from Pound in 1914, became their principal sponsor and defender (1915–1925). Her own poetry showed interest in certain nineteenth-century French poets, Oriental art, experiments in lyrical prose, etc. Among her volumes of poetry: *A Dome of Many-Colored Glass* (1912), *Sword Blades and Poppy Seed* (1914), *Can Grande's Castle* (1918), *Men, Women, and Ghosts* (1922). Wrote one of the earliest studies of modern American poetry, *Tendencies in Modern American Poetry* (1917) and a similar volume on modern poetry in France, *Six French Poets* (1915).

LUHAN, Mabel Dodge (1879–)
American society woman at whose "evenings" in New York, from 1915 to 1920, young writers, artists, journalists, etc., discussed "new ideas." Her four volumes of *Intimate Memories* contain much gossip of the period 1910–1930. The most important of these is *Movers and Shakers* (1936).

MACKENZIE, Compton (1883–)
British writer, best known for such novels as *Sinister Street* (1913–1914) —which Scott Fitzgerald read and imitated to a degree in *This Side of Paradise—Carnival* (1912), *Extraordinary Women* (1928), *Our Street* (1931).

MacLEISH, Archibald (1892–)
American poet, dramatist, critic. Born, Illinois; educated Yale, Harvard Law School. Army captain in World War I; spent 1923–28 in France. His poetry of the 1920s reflects the prevailing literary and public interests: *The Happy Marriage* (1924), *The Pot of Earth* (1925), *The Hamlet of A. MacLeish* (1928), *Einstein* (1929). *Conquistador* (1932) is the most original and successful of his long poems. His satirical, "public" verse of the 1930s includes *Frescoes for Mr. Rockefeller's City* (1933), *Public Speech* (1936), *America Was Promises* (1939); verse plays, *Panic* (1935), *The Fall of the City* (1937), *Air Raid* (1938). During World War II he joined Van Wyck Brooks and Bernard De Voto in criticism of literature of 1920s (*The Irresponsibles,* 1940, an essay).

MALLARMÉ, Stéphane (1842–1898)
French poet, critic. Born, Paris; professor of English in lycées at Tournon, Besançon, Avignon; to Paris, 1871, where he became acknowledged leader of the symbolist movement; at his celebrated "Tuesdays" his important contemporaries gathered. His poetry was of great importance for illustration of aesthetic principles, generally grouped around label of *symboliste.* Translated verse of Poe, wrote much on the art of poetry, linking it with music and especially with work of Richard Wagner. He was an important influence on Eliot, Wallace Stevens, others. His volumes of poetry include *L'Après-midi d'un faune* (1876), *Poésies complètes* (1887), *Un coup de dès* . . . (1914).

MARINETTI, Filippo Tommaso (1876–1944)
Italian poet, critic. Founder (1909) of futurism, which was especially influential 1910–1920. For translations of some of his verse, see *Poet Lore* magazine, Volume 26 (1915).

McALMON, Robert (1896–)
American novelist, short-story writer. Born, Kansas; educated, University of Southern California. Spent much time abroad in England, France; estab-

lished own press in Paris, printed work of Hemingway, Gertrude Stein, others. He was also active as editor of and contributor to little magazines. His autobiography, *Being Geniuses Together* (1938), is a source of information concerning expatriate life, especially that of Paris in the 1920s.

MENCKEN, H. L. (1880–)

American journalist, critic. Born, Baltimore, Md. Popular spokesman of large group of critics and readers, especially during his editorship of *The American Mercury* (1924–1933). Among his more important works of critical prose are the six volumes of *Prejudices* (published from 1919 to 1927), *A Book of Prefaces* (1917), *In Defense of Women* (1918), *Notes on Democracy* (1926), *Treatise on the Gods* (1930), *Treatise on Right and Wrong* (1934). His work on *The American Language* (first edition, 1919; fourth edition, 1936) and on memoirs later all but replaced earlier polemical interests. Active in fighting literary censorship and in sponsoring certain writers of his generation. His *The Philosophy of Friedrich Nietzsche* (1908) was the first lengthy study of the German philosopher in America.

MONROE, Harriet (1860–1936)

American poet, critic, editor. Most important for her sponsorship of *Poetry* magazine, which she edited (1912–1936). With the help of such persons as Pound, she brought much new native and foreign poetry to the attention of the American public. Her work includes *Poets and Their Art* (1926, criticism), *The New Poetry* (1932, an anthology, with Alice Corbin Henderson), *A Poet's Life* (1937, autobiography).

MOORE, Marianne (1887–)

American poet, critic. Born, St. Louis; educated, Bryn Mawr; teacher, librarian. Acting editor, *The Dial* (1925–1929). Since the 1920s, she has been one of our most important poets, with a highly original poetic style and sensibility. Among her volumes are *Poems* (1921), *Observations* (1924; *Dial* award), *The Pangolin and Other Verse* (1936), *What Are Years* (1941), *Nevertheless* (1944). *The Collected Poems* were published in 1951 (Pulitzer Prize, 1952); her translations of the fables of La Fontaine appeared in 1954.

MORE, Paul Elmer (1864–1937)

American critic, lecturer, journalist; most important of the Humanist critics. Born, St. Louis; educated, Washington University, Harvard. Literary editor, *The Independent* (1901) and the *New York Evening Post* (1903); editor, *The Nation* (1909–1914). The *Shelburne Essays* (eleven volumes, 1904–1921) and the *New Shelburne Essays* (three volumes, 1928–1936) contain most of his critical writing; among them, these individual titles: *The Drift of Romanticism* (1913), *Aristocracy and Justice* (1915), *The Demon of the Absolute* (1928).

MUMFORD, Lewis (1895–)

American critic, journalist; especially important for his evaluations of American culture, architecture, the culture of the machine age. Among his volumes of criticism and cultural history are *Sticks and Stones* (1924), *The Golden Day* (1926), *Herman Melville* (1929), *The Brown Decades* (1931), *Technics and Civilization* (1934), *The Culture of Cities* (1938). Editor (with four others) of *America and Alfred Stieglitz* (1934), tributes to the photographic artist.

MUNSON, Gorham B. (1896–)

American critic, journalist; interested especially in modern literature, economics; friend of Sherwood Anderson, Hart Crane, Waldo Frank, and others. Among his books: *Waldo Frank* (1923), *Robert Frost* (1927), *Destinations* (1928), *Style and Form in American Prose* (1929).

NIETZSCHE, Friedrich Wilhelm (1844–1900)

German philosopher whose criticism of his own society, theories of the "superman" and the will to power, were important influences upon criticism and general thought from the time of his death through the 1920s; interpretations of him suffered many varieties of distortion in the popular press. The best-known popular study of him in America was H. L. Mencken's (1908). Among the works most widely known were *The Birth of Tragedy* (1872; translation, 1910), *Thus Spake Zarathustra* (1883–1884, 1891; translations, 1909, 1930), *Beyond Good and Evil* (1886; translation, 1907).

O'HIGGINS, Harvey (1876–1929)

Canadian-born novelist, journalist; especially well known for his popularizations of psychoanalysis, application of it to American literary and social scenes. *The American Mind in Action* (1924) was notable in this respect. His novels include *Julie Crane* (1924), *Clara Barron* (1926). He dramatized Sinclair Lewis's *Main Street* (1921).

O'NEILL, Eugene (1888–1953)

American dramatist. Born, New York, N.Y. After a year's training at Professor George Pierce Baker's "47 Workshop" at Harvard (1914–1915) he joined the Provincetown Players (1916), with whom (at Provincetown and in New York) he presented many of his most important plays. Most influential experimentalist in the drama in the 1920s, he was especially indebted to European expressionism but also very original in his adaptation of new ideas of stagecraft and dramatic representation. Among his more important plays are *The Emperor Jones* (1921), *Anna Christie* (1922), *The Hairy Ape* (1922), *Desire under the Elms* (1925), *The Great God Brown* (1926), *Strange Interlude* (1928), *Mourning Becomes Electra* (1931).

OPPENHEIM, James (1882–1932)

American essayist, poet, journalist; editor, *The Seven Arts* magazine (1916–1917). Poetry of *Songs for a New Age* (1914) shows conscious indebtedness to Whitman. *The Book of Self* (1917, poems) and his popularizations of Jung—*Behind Your Front* (1928), *American Types* (1931) —reveal his interest in psychoanalysis.

OUSPENSKY, Peter D. (1878–1947)

Mystic, writer on occult subjects; associated for a time with Gurdjieff. *Tertium Organum* (1922) influenced several poets in the 1920s, including Hart Crane; also published *A New Model of the Universe* (1931) and a novel, *The Strange Life of Ivan Osokin* (1947).

PARRINGTON, Vernon L. (1871–1929)

American critic, teacher. Born, Illinois; educated, Harvard. His *Main Currents in American Thought* (3 volumes, 1927–1930) was one of the most important studies of America's literary and social past produced in the 1920s. The third volume, published in unfinished form after his death, consists mainly of notes and paragraphs from lecture outlines.

PAUL, Elliot (1891–)

American novelist, journalist; served in World War I; spent much time in France and was associated with *transition*, other magazines. Novels include *Indelible* (1922), *Impromptu* (1923), *Concert Pitch* (1938). Popular journalism includes *The Life and Death of a Spanish Town* (1937), *The Last Time I Saw Paris* (1942).

POUND, Ezra (1885–)

American critic, poet, editor. Born, Hailey, Idaho; educated, Hamilton College, University of Pennsylvania. To Europe, 1908; in Spain, Italy, to 1912; England, 1912–1920; France (mainly Paris), 1920–1924; Rapallo, Italy, 1924–1945. Important not only for his own poetry and volumes of criticism but also for his advice to, and criticism of, other writers of his generation: Eliot (whose *The Waste Land* he helped to revise and cut), Hemingway, many others. European correspondent of *Poetry* (1912–1918) and *The Little Review* (1917–1919); contributor to or editor of many other magazines, including his own *The Exile* (1927–1928). Volumes of poetry include *A Lume Spento* (1908), *Personae* (1909), *Provença* (1910), *Riposte* (1912), *Hugh Selwyn Mauberley* (1920), and, beginning with 1925, a series of *Cantos*, which he is still engaged in writing (*Cantos*, complete edition to date, 1948). His criticism includes *The Spirit of Romance* (1910), *Gaudier-Brzeska* (1916), *Pavannes and Divisions* (1918), *How to Read* (1931), *Make It New* (1934), *Polite Essays* (1937), *Patria Mia* (1950; collection of essays given magazine publication in 1912).

RANSOM, John Crowe (1888–)

American poet, critic, teacher, editor. Born, Tennessee; educated, Vanderbilt, Oxford (Rhodes Scholar, 1913); teacher, Vanderbilt (1914–1937), Kenyon College (since 1937). One of the original editors of *The Fugitive* (1922–1925); one of the Twelve Southerners of the symposium *I'll Take My Stand* (1930). As editor of *The Kenyon Review,* he has exerted a considerable influence on the "new" criticism. Among his volumes of poetry are *Poems About God* (1919), *Chills and Fever* (1924), *Two Gentlemen in Bonds* (1926); *Selected Poems* (1945) contains a small group of poems, many of them considerably revised. Critical and speculative prose: *God Without Thunder* (1930), *The World's Body* (1938), *The New Criticism* (1941).

RICE, Elmer (1892–)

American dramatist; known especially for such plays as *The Adding Machine* (1923), *Street Scene* (1929), *The Subway* (1929), *Counsellor-at-Law* (1931), *The Left Bank* (1931), *Two on an Island* (1940), and *Dream Girl* (1945). Novels include *A Voyage to Purilia,* a fantasy (1930), and *Imperial City* (1937).

RICHARDS, I. A. (1893–)

British psychologist, critic; teacher at Cambridge University for many years; later at Harvard. Of great importance in the development of modern criticism; influenced William Empson, T. S. Eliot, John Crowe Ransom, others. *The Principles of Literary Criticism* (1924) was a primary critical document in the formation of a modern poetic. The essay, "Science and Poetry," was the basis for much discussion in the years following its publication (1926). Other important critical volumes are *The Meaning of Meaning* (1923, with C. K. Ogden), *Practical Criticism* (1929), *Coleridge on Imagination* (1934), *The Philosophy of Rhetoric* (1936).

RIMBAUD, Arthur (1854–1891)

French poet whose revolutionary verse and spectacular career held the interest and influenced the work of several modern American poets, Hart Crane among them. The poem "Le Bateau Ivre," among the *Poésies complètes* (1895) was especially influential, as were the prose poems *Illuminations* (1886) and *Une saison en enfer* (printed but not distributed, 1873; reissued, 1892). Especially important for critics and poets of the 1920s was the "Lettre d'un voyant" (written to Paul Demeny, 1871), the basis of much critical discussion concerning the occult sources of creation.

ROBINSON, James Harvey (1863–1936)

American historian, teacher. Born, Illinois; educated, Harvard, University of Freiburg; professor of history, Columbia (1895–1919); with the

New School for Social Research (1919–1921). Among his works on history the most important are *The Development of Modern Europe* (1907, with Charles Beard), *The New History* (1911), *The Mind in the Making* (1921); the last two widely influenced thinking about the past and its relationships with modern cultural experience.

ROSENFELD, Paul (1890–1946)

American critic, journalist; especially interested in music and literature, friend and counselor of Sherwood Anderson (whom he took on latter's first trip to Europe), Waldo Frank, others. Most important literary studies, *Port of New York* (1924) and *Men Seen* (1925). Also published a novel, *The Boy in the Sun* (1928).

RUSSELL, Bertrand (1872–)

English philosopher, mathematician; author of books on science, modern society; great philosophical work, *Principia Mathematica* (1910–1913, with Alfred North Whitehead). Essays of considerable interest to American intellectuals, 1915–1930: *Mysticism and Logic and Other Essays* (1918), *Icarus: or, the Future of Science* (1924); *The ABC of Relativity* (1928), *The Conquest of Happiness* (1930).

SANDBURG, Carl (1878–)

American poet, biographer. Born, Galesburg, Ill.; educated, Knox College. First gained prominence as poet in *Poetry* magazine. Among his volumes of poetry are *Chicago Poems* (1916), *Cornhuskers* (1918), *Smoke and Steel* (1920), *The People, Yes* (1936). Published much on Abraham Lincoln, of which the most important is the extensive biography, *Abraham Lincoln: The Prairie Years* (1926) and *Abraham Lincoln: The War Years* (1939). Interested in ballads and folksongs, published *The American Songbag* (1927).

SHERMAN, Stuart Pratt (1881–1926)

American critic, teacher, journalist; the most popular for a while of the Humanist school of critics, as reviewer for *The Nation* and as professor of English literature, University of Illinois. Among his critical volumes are *On Contemporary Literature* (1917), *Americans* (1922), *The Genius of America* (1923), *Critical Woodcuts* (1926), *The Main Stream* (1927), *The Emotional Discovery of America and Other Essays* (1932).

SINCLAIR, Upton (1878–)

American novelist, writer of prose tracts, journalist; one of the oldest and most consistent of the liberal, left-wing critics of American institutions; for many years conspicuous for his sponsorship of causes, his writing in behalf of them. Among his most important novels in this connection are *The Jungle* (1906), *The Metropolis* (1908), *Oil!* (1927), *Boston* (1928). He has lately been writing a series of novels, whose major figure, Lanny Budd, races to keep abreast of contemporary affairs. Most important journalistic prose and criticism: *The Brass Check* (1919; on journalism), *The Goose-Step* (1923; education), *Mammonart* (1925; fate of the arts in a business society).

SMITH, Thomas Vernon (1890–)
American professor of philosophy (University of Chicago, Syracuse University); author of several semipopular books on philosophy and public life, the most important of which, for the 1920s, were *The Democratic Way of Life* (1925) and *American Philosophy of Equality* (1926).

STALLINGS, Laurence (1894–)
American playwright; best known for his collaboration with Maxwell Anderson on the box-office success *What Price Glory* (1924); also collaborated with Anderson in production of *First Flight* (1925) and *The Buccaneer* (1925), and adapted Hemingway's *A Farewell to Arms* to the stage (1930).

STEARNS, Harold (1891–1943)
American essayist, editor of, contributor to, *The Dial, The Freeman,* other magazines. *America and the Young Intellectual* (1921) described what he thought were the major ills of American culture; edited the symposium *Civilization in the United States* (1922); spent the years 1922 to 1934 in France as reporter, free-lance writer; on his return, published his autobiography, *The Street I Knew* (1935), and edited another symposium, *America: A Re-Appraisal* (1937).

STEIN, Gertrude (1874–1946)
American novelist, poet, writer of memoirs. Born, Allegheny, Pa.; educated, Radcliffe, Johns Hopkins; to France in 1903, where she spent most of the remainder of her life. Her home in Paris was the center of discussion of modern writing and the arts; to her came Hemingway, Sherwood Anderson, many others. Her somewhat prejudiced account of those days is contained in *The Autobiography of Alice B. Toklas* (1933). Other works include *Three Lives* (1909), one of the most influential fictional works of the century; *Tender Buttons,* experimental writing (1914); *The Making of Americans* (1925), part of which Hemingway edited for publication in the *transatlantic review; Composition As Explanation* (1926), the lecture given at Oxford and Cambridge Universities; *How to Write* (1931), *Narration* (1935), and *Lectures in America* (1935), criticism; *Four Saints in Three Acts* (1934, play); *Picasso* (1938) and *Paris France* (1940), prose studies; and the books about World War II, *Wars I Have Seen* (1945) and *Brewsie and Willie* (1946).

STEVENS, Wallace (1879–)

American poet. Born, Reading, Pa.; educated, Harvard. First published in such little magazines as *Poetry* (1914), *Others* (1915). First book of poems *Harmonium* (1923; second edition with new poems, 1931); others include *Ideas of Order* (1935), *Owl's Clover* (1936), *The Man with the Blue Guitar and Other Poems* (1937), *Parts of a World* (1942), *Notes toward a Supreme Fiction* (1942), *Esthétique du Mal* (1945), *Transport to Summer* (1947), *The Auroras of Autumn* (1950), *Collected Poems* (1954).

STEWART, Donald Ogden (1894–)

American humorist; well known for his parodies of contemporary popularizations, such as *A Parody Outline of History* (1921) and *Aunt Polly's Story of Mankind* (1923). Other examples of his work include *Mr. and Mrs. Haddock Abroad* (1924), *The Crazy Fool* (1925), *Father William* (1929).

SUCKOW, Ruth (1892–)

American novelist, short-story writer, treating for the most part of middle-class farm people and townspeople of Iowa and the Midwest. Most popular of her books are *Country People* (1924), *The Odyssey of a Nice Girl* (1925), *The Bonney Family* (1928), *The Folks* (1934).

SULLIVAN, J. W. N. (1886–1937)

British writer on science, music; widely read in England and America in the 1920s for his balanced account of the role of science in modern thought. Among his works are *Aspects of Science* (1923), *Three Men Discuss Relativity* (1926), *The Bases of Modern Science* (1928), *The Limitations of Science* (1933).

TAGGARD, Genevieve (1894–1948)

American poet, critic. Among her volumes of poetry are *For Eager Lovers* (1922), *Travelling Standing Still* (1928), *Calling Western Union* (1936), *Slow Music* (1946). Editor of *May Days* (1925), anthology of pieces from *The Masses*, 1911–1917.

TATE, Allen (1899–)

American critic, poet, teacher. Born, Winchester, Ky.; educated, Vanderbilt. One of the original editors of *The Fugitive* (1922–1925); one of the Twelve Southerners of *I'll Take My Stand* (1930). Professor and lecturer, several colleges and universities, currently University of Minnesota; editor, *The Sewanee Review* (1944–1946). Among his volumes of poetry are *Mr. Pope and Other Poems* (1928), *Poems, 1928–1931* (1932), *Selected Poems* (1937), *Poems, 1922–1947* (1948). His criticism includes *Reactionary Essays on Poetry and Ideas* (1936), *Reason in Madness* (1941), *On the*

Limits of Poetry: Selected Essays 1928–1948 (1948), *The Hovering Fly* (1949), *The Forlorn Demon: Didactic and Critical Essays* (1953).

TZARA, Tristan (1896–)
 Rumanian-born poet and critic; educated, France and Switzerland. One of the initiators of dadaism, about which he wrote many manifestoes and explanations for French and American periodicals. Among his works are *Vingt-cinq et un poèmes* (1918), *Sept manifestes dada* (1924), *De nos oiseaux* (1929), *L'Homme approximatif* (1930), *Grains et issues* (1935), *Le signe de ma vie* (1946).

VAN VECHTEN, Carl (1880–)
 American novelist, critic. Much of his popular work touched on and exploited the fashionable interests of the 1920s. Among the novels that proved most popular are *Peter Whiffle* (1922), *The Blind Bow-Boy* (1923), *The Tattooed Countess* (1924), *Nigger Heaven* (1926), *Spider Boy* (1928), *Parties* (1930). Criticism, principally in field of music: *Interpreters and Interpretations* (1917), *Red* (1925), *Excavations* (1926).

WALSH, Ernest J. (1895–1926)
 American writer, editor. Born, Detroit, Mich. Joined air corps in World War I and was seriously injured in a plane crash, which left him an invalid. From 1922 until his death he traveled in Europe. With Ethel Moorhead, he was responsible for first issues of *This Quarter,* an important little magazine that featured writings of postwar generation. One volume of his poems, with a memoir by Ethel Moorhead, was published after his death (*Poems and Sonnets,* 1934).

WARREN, Robert Penn (1905–)
 American novelist, short-story writer, poet, critic. Born, Guthrie, Ky.; educated, Vanderbilt, University of California, Yale, Oxford (Rhodes Scholar, 1930). Teacher in several American universities, currently at Yale. Editor of *The Southern Review* (1935–1942), contributor to many reviews. One of the Twelve Southerners of *I'll Take My Stand* (1930). Among his works are novels: *Night Rider* (1939), *At Heaven's Gate* (1943), *All the King's Men* (1946; Pulitzer Prize, 1947), *World Enough and Time* (1950); poetry: *Eleven Poems on the Same Theme* (1942), *Selected Poems* (1944), *Brother to Dragons: A Tale in Verse and Voices* (1953); and short fiction: *Blackberry Winter* (1946), *The Circus in the Attic and Other Stories* (1947).

WELLS, H. G. (1866–1946)
 British novelist, essayist, professional man of letters, Fabian Socialist, popularizer of science. Known especially for a number of novels in which

the influence of science on the future is portrayed: *The Time Machine* (1895), *The War of the Worlds* (1898), others. Other novels are social and political: *Ann Veronica* (1909), *The History of Mr. Polly* (1910), *Tono-Bungay* (1909), *The World of William Clissold* (1926). Perhaps his influence on American thinking, 1915–1930, is best indicated by the success of *The Outline of History* (1920), which continued to be sold in several reprint editions through the decade.

WESCOTT, Glenway (1901–)

American novelist, short-story writer, poet, critic, translator. Born, Wisconsin; spent some years in Europe, living principally in France. Best-known works are the novels *The Grandmothers* (1927) and *Apartment in Athens* (1945), the short novel, *The Pilgrim Hawk* (1940), the short stories in *Good-Bye, Wisconsin* (1929). His autobiographical *Fear and Trembling* (1932) is, among other things, a discussion of the meaning of expatriation for his generation.

WHARTON, Edith (1862–1937)

American novelist, writer of short fiction, poet, critic. Born, New York, N.Y.; lived in France much of the time after 1907. Influenced by Henry James, but possessed her own original perspective upon American and international themes. Her most important novels are *The House of Mirth* (1905), *Ethan Frome* (1911), *The Reef* (1912), *The Custom of the Country* (1913), *The Age of Innocence* (1920). She wrote travel books on Italy and France, and a study of taste in houses and decoration (*The Decoration of Houses,* with Ogden Codman, Jr., 1897). During World War I, she worked in Paris with the Red Cross and other organizations, and subsequently wrote several war novels, the most important of which is *A Son at the Front* (1923). Among her short fiction are *Xingu and Other Stories* (1916), *Old New York* (1924). *The Writing of Fiction* (1925) is a study of James's fiction, her own, and that of others. *A Backward Glance* (1934) is a rambling autobiography, of value for glimpses of James and her own family background.

WILLIAMS, William Carlos (1883–)

American poet, novelist, short-story writer, critic. Born, Rutherford, N.J., where he practiced medicine after 1910; educated, Horace Mann High School, University of Pennsylvania Medical School, in Europe. Active as editor of, and contributor to, many little magazines. His volumes of poetry include *Al Que Quiere* (1917), *Kora in Hell* (1920), *Spring and All* (1922), *The Complete Collected Poems* (1938), *Paterson* (1946–1951). Among his other works are novels: *A Voyage to Pagany* (1928), *White Mule* (1937), *In the Money* (1940); short stories: *The Knife of the Times* (1932), *Life Along the Passaic River* (1938). *In the American Grain* (1925) is a lyrical and influential series of impressions of the American past.

WILSON, Edmund (1895–)

American critic, novelist, poet, dramatist. Born, New Jersey; educated, Princeton. Notable especially for his critical volumes and his essays in the *New Republic* (1926–1940), *The New Yorker,* elsewhere. Managing editor, *Vanity Fair* (1920–1921). His important critical works are *Discordant Encounters* (1927), *Axel's Castle* (1931), *The Triple Thinkers* (1938), *The Wound and the Bow* (1941). Among his other prose works are *I Thought of Daisy* (1929), novel; *The American Jitters* (1932) and *Travels in Two Democracies* (1936), journalism; *To the Finland Station* (1940), intellectual history.

WINTERS, Yvor (1900–)

American critic, poet, teacher; born, Chicago, Ill.; educated, University of Chicago, University of Colorado, Stanford University; teacher at Stanford since 1927. Editorial activities with *The Hound and Horn* (1932–1934), *The Gyroscope* (1928–1929), others. His volumes of poems include *The Immobile Wind* (1921), *The Bare Hills* (1927), *The Proof* (1930), *The Journey* (1931), *The Giant Weapon* (1943). Criticism: *Primitivism and Decadence* (1937), *Maule's Curse* (1938), *The Anatomy of Nonsense* (1943), *In Defense of Reason* (1947).

CHRONOLOGY, 1915-1932

This chronology provides a few dates of political importance as well as some publication dates of significance for the decade. It is not intended to be exhaustive in either case, but it should help the reader to see the text in some historical perspective. Some events (such as the Sacco and Vanzetti case) which do not ordinarily merit more than simple notice in political histories are here given because of their influence upon literature. Events of more or less importance to political history may have been omitted because of their negligible role in literature.

1915   Second year of World War I; third year of Woodrow Wilson's first term as President.
S.S. *Lusitania* sunk by a German submarine (May 7).

Others magazine (to 1919).
Founding of Provincetown Players, Provincetown, Mass.

Van Wyck Brooks, *America's Coming-of-Age*
Willa Cather, *The Song of the Lark*
Theodore Dreiser, *The 'Genius'*
Robert Frost, *North of Boston*
Amy Lowell and Richard Aldington, editors, *Some Imagist Poets*
Edgar Lee Masters, *Spoon River Anthology*
Ernest Poole, *The Harbor*

1916   Woodrow Wilson re-elected to second term
San Francisco Preparedness Day bombing
American punitive expedition in Mexico

The Seven Arts magazine (to 1917)
Theatre Arts Magazine
Witter Bynner and A. D. Ficke, The *Spectrist* hoax

Robert Frost, *Mountain Interval*
Vachel Lindsay, *General William Booth Enters Heaven* . . .
Eugene O'Neill, *Bound East for Cardiff*
E. A. Robinson, *The Man Against the Sky*
Carl Sandburg, *Chicago Poems*

1917 The United States enters the War (April 6)
Italian disaster at Caporetto
Proclamation of Russian Republic; capture of power by the Bolsheviki (March–November)

The Masses magazine suspended (begun 1911)
Ezra Pound becomes Foreign Correspondent of *The Little Review*
First awarding of Pulitzer Prizes

James Branch Cabell, *Cream of the Jest*
T. S. Eliot, *Ezra Pound: His Metric and Poetry; Prufrock and Other Observations*
Hamlin Garland, *Son of the Middle Border*
H. L. Mencken, *A Book of Prefaces*
Edna St. Vincent Millay, *Renascence*
W. G. Phillips, *Susan Lenox*

1918 Battles of Belleau Wood and Château-Thierry; Argonne and St. Mihiel offensives; second battle of the Marne
Armistice declared in World War I (November 11)
Wilson submits "Fourteen Points"

The Liberator magazine (to 1924)
Ernest Hemingway seriously wounded on northern Italian front (July 8)
Theatre Guild founded

Willa Cather, *My Ántonia*
Ezra Pound, *Pavannes and Divisions*
Carl Sandburg, *Cornhuskers*

1919 Versailles Peace Conference (January 18–June 28)
League of Nations set up
United States Senate rejects Versailles Treaty (November 19)
Prohibition Amendment (XVIII) adopted, to become effective January 1, 1920 (repealed, 1933)
Socialist party, in meeting at Chicago, splits into right and left wings
Attorney General Palmer's "anti-Red" campaign
Founding of American Legion

Sherwood Anderson, *Winesburg, Ohio*
James Branch Cabell, *Jurgen*
H. L. Mencken, *Prejudices,* First Series
John Reed, *Ten Days That Shook the World*

1920 Warren G. Harding elected to the presidency
National Woman's Suffrage Amendment (XIX) goes into effect

Nicolo Sacco and Bartolomeo Vanzetti arrested (April 15)
First commercial radio broadcasting

The Dial magazine, under editorship of Scofield Thayer (to 1929)
The Freeman magazine (to 1924)
Ezra Pound leaves London for France (to 1924)

Sherwood Anderson, *Poor White*
Van Wyck Brooks, *The Ordeal of Mark Twain*
John Dos Passos, *One Man's Initiation*
T. S. Eliot, *The Sacred Wood*
F. Scott Fitzgerald, *Flappers and Philosophers; This Side of Paradise*
Sinclair Lewis, *Main Street*
Eugene O'Neill, *Emperor Jones*
Ezra Pound, *Hugh Selwyn Mauberley*
Carl Sandburg, *Smoke and Steel*
George Santayana, *Character and Opinion in the United States*
Edith Wharton, *The Age of Innocence*

1921 Founding of Fascist party in Italy
Washington Armament Conference
New Economic Policy announced by Lenin
First trial of Sacco and Vanzetti (May 21)

Broom magazine (to 1924)
The Double Dealer magazine (to 1926)

Sherwood Anderson, *The Triumph of the Egg*
John Dos Passos, *Three Soldiers*
Ben Hecht, *Erik Dorn*
Eugene O'Neill, *Anna Christie*
Ezra Pound, *Poems, 1918–1921* (including first four Cantos)
E. A. Robinson, *Collected Poems*

1922 Coal and railway strikes
Fordney-McCumber Tariff Act
Mussolini becomes dictator of Italy
U.S.S.R. created

The Criterion magazine (to 1939), T. S. Eliot editor
The Fugitive magazine (to 1925)
Secession magazine (to 1924)

E. E. Cummings, *The Enormous Room*
T. S. Eliot, *The Waste Land*
F. Scott Fitzgerald, *The Beautiful and Damned; Tales of the Jazz Age*
Sinclair Lewis, *Babbitt*
Eugene O'Neill, *The Hairy Ape*
Harold Stearns, editor, *Civilization in the United States*

1923 Death of President Harding (August 2)
Calvin Coolidge succeeds him, begins administration (to March, 1929)

Hitler's abortive "Beerhall Putsch," Munich, Germany
Teapot Dome scandal (to 1924)

Time magazine

Willa Cather, *A Lost Lady*
E. E. Cummings, *Tulips and Chimneys*
Robert Frost, *New Hampshire*
D. H. Lawrence, *Studies in Classic American Literature*
Elmer Rice, *The Adding Machine*
Wallace Stevens, *Harmonium*
William Carlos Williams, *Spring and All*

1924   Investigation of scandals in Harding regime
New immigration quotas, with total exclusion of Japanese
Coolidge elected to the presidency
Second Progressive party, with Robert La Follette as its presidential candidate

The American Mercury magazine (H. L. Mencken editor until 1934)
The Saturday Review of Literature magazine
The transatlantic review (to 1925)
Ezra Pound to Rapallo, Italy

Maxwell Anderson and Laurence Stallings, *What Price Glory?*
Ernest Hemingway, *in our time* (Paris)
T. E. Hulme, *Speculations,* edited by Herbert Read
George Kaufman and Marc Connelly, *Beggar on Horseback*
Ring Lardner, *How to Write Short Stories*
Herman Melville, *Billy Budd*
Marianne Moore, *Observations*
Eugene O'Neill, *Desire Under the Elms*
John Crowe Ransom, *Chills and Fever*

1925   Scopes trial, Dayton, Tennessee

The New Yorker magazine
This Quarter magazine (to 1932; early issues edited by Ernest J. Walsh)
Guggenheim Fellowships begun

Sherwood Anderson, *Dark Laughter*
Irving Babbitt, *Democracy and Leadership*
Willa Cather, *The Professor's House*
H. D., *Collected Poems*
John Dos Passos, *Manhattan Transfer*
Theodore Dreiser, *An American Tragedy*
T. S. Eliot, *Poems, 1909–1925*
F. Scott Fitzgerald, *The Great Gatsby*
Ellen Glasgow, *Barren Ground*
Ernest Hemingway, *in our time*
Robinson Jeffers, *Roan Stallion*
Sinclair Lewis, *Arrowsmith*

Gertrude Stein, *The Making of Americans*
William Carlos Williams, *In the American Grain*

1926   General Strike in Great Britain
Byrd flies over North Pole
Transatlantic wireless telephone

The New Masses magazine (to 1948)
Book-of-the-Month Club founded

Hart Crane, *White Buildings*
Paul de Kruif, *Microbe Hunters*
William Faulkner, *Soldiers' Pay*
F. Scott Fitzgerald, *All the Sad Young Men*
Ernest Hemingway, *The Sun Also Rises*
Sidney Howard, *The Silver Cord*
Anita Loos, *Gentlemen Prefer Blondes*
H. L. Mencken, *Notes on Democracy*
Eugene O'Neill, *The Great God Brown*
Elizabeth Madox Roberts, *The Time of Man*
Gertrude Stein, *Composition As Explanation*

1927   Charles Lindbergh's non-stop solo flight to Paris
Sacco and Vanzetti executed (August 22)
First sound film shown in New York: *The Jazz Singer* with Al Jolson
U.S. Marines in Nicaragua (to 1933)

The Hound and Horn magazine (to 1934)
transition magazine (irregular after 1930)
American Caravan annual (to 1936)
Literary Guild founded

Charles Beard, *The Rise of American Civilization*
Willa Cather, *Death Comes for the Archbishop*
E. E. Cummings, *Him*
Ernest Hemingway, *Men without Women*
Eugene O'Neill, *Marco Millions*
Vernon L. Parrington, *Main Currents in American Thought*, Volumes I
    and II
John Crowe Ransom, *Two Gentlemen in Bonds*
E. A. Robinson, *Tristram*
O. E. Rölvaag, *Giants in the Earth*
Glenway Wescott, *The Grandmothers*
Thornton Wilder, *The Bridge of San Luis Rey*

1928   Pan-American Conference; Kellogg-Briand Pact
Herbert Hoover defeats Al Smith in presidential campaign
Trotsky and his followers exiled from Russia

American Literature journal

Maxwell Anderson and Harold Hickerson, *Gods of the Lightning*

Stephen Vincent Benét, *John Brown's Body*
Robert Frost, *West-Running Brook*
Archibald MacLeish, *The Hamlet of A. MacLeish*
Paul Elmer More, *The Demon of the Absolute*
Eugene O'Neill, *Strange Interlude*
Upton Sinclair, *Boston*
Allen Tate, *Mr. Pope and Other Poems*

1929   Stock-market crash (October 29); beginning of "The Great Depression";
          Gastonia strike
       Five-Year Plan begun in Russia

       Museum of Modern Art founded
       End of *The Little Review* (begun, 1914)
       Suicide of Harry Crosby

       William Faulkner, *The Sound and the Fury; Sartoris*
       Ellen Glasgow, *They Stooped to Folly*
       Ernest Hemingway, *A Farewell to Arms*
       Joseph Wood Krutch, *The Modern Temper*
       Ring Lardner, *Round Up*
       Sinclair Lewis, *Dodsworth*
       Elmer Rice, *Street Scene*
       Thomas Wolfe, *Look Homeward, Angel*

1930   Smoot-Hawley Tariff Act passed
       Hoover plan for relief of increasing unemployment

       Sinclair Lewis receives Nobel Prize

       Marc Connelly, *Green Pastures*
       Hart Crane, *The Bridge* (Black Sun Press, Paris)
       John Dos Passos, *The 42nd Parallel* (first of trilogy, *U.S.A.*)
       T. S. Eliot, *Ash Wednesday*
       William Faulkner, *As I Lay Dying*
       Norman Foerster, editor, *Humanism in America*
       Mike Gold, *Jews Without Money*
       C. Hartley Grattan, editor, *Critique of Humanism*
       Matthew Josephson, *Portrait of the Artist as American*
       Katherine Anne Porter, *Flowering Judas*
       John Crowe Ransom, *God without Thunder*
       Twelve Southerners, *I'll Take My Stand*

1931   Invasion of Manchuria by Japan
       Proclamation of the Spanish Republic
       Scottsboro trial

       The Group Theatre begun (to 1941)
       Story magazine

       Pearl Buck, *The Good Earth*
       Kenneth Burke, *Counter-Statement*

Willa Cather, *Shadows on the Rock*
William Faulkner, *Sanctuary*
Eugene O'Neill, *Mourning Becomes Electra*
Lincoln Steffens, *Autobiography*
Edmund Wilson, *Axel's Castle*

1932   Franklin D. Roosevelt defeats Hoover for first of four terms in White
        House
        March of "Bonus Army" on Washington
        Lindbergh kidnaping case
        Scottsboro case before the Supreme Court

        Scrutiny magazine (to 1953)
        Suicide of Hart Crane

        Erskine Caldwell, *Tobacco Road*
        Bernard De Voto, *Mark Twain's America*
        John Dos Passos, *1919* (second of trilogy, *U.S.A.*)
        James T. Farrell, *Young Lonigan* (first of trilogy, *Studs Lonigan*)
        William Faulkner, *Light in August*
        Ellen Glasgow, *The Sheltered Life*
        Robinson Jeffers, *Thurso's Landing*
        Archibald MacLeish, *Conquistador*

SELECTED BIBLIOGRAPHY

The following titles are offered as a selection from the great number of documents, studies, and histories which have helped me in the preparation of this book. Since it is quite impossible to list every one of the hundreds of books and essays, the books given below are merely suggestions for supplementary reading. The annotations attempt to point out the special value, scope, and limitations of each. Anyone wishing to make an exhaustive study of any of the authors or subjects discussed in this book can turn to the following reference works:

Hoffman, Frederick J., Allen, Charles, and Ulrich, Carolyn. *The Little Magazine: A History and a Bibliography*. Princeton, N.J.: Princeton University Press, 1946, 1947.

Leary, Lewis. *Articles on American Literature Appearing in Current Periodicals, 1920–1945*. Durham, N.C.: Duke University Press, 1947.

Millett, Fred B. *Contemporary American Authors*. New York: Harcourt, Brace, 1940.

Spiller, Robert, *et. al. Literary History of the United States,* Volume III. New York: Macmillan, 1948.

Allen, Frederick Lewis. *Only Yesterday*. New York: Harper's, 1931.
A classic of popularization and oversimplification, clever, interesting; provides a minimum of information. The most obvious of the facts are here presented with a proper appreciation of their value as entertainment, but the book gives only a superficial view of the decade.

Anderson, Sherwood. *The Letters* . . . , edited by Howard Mumford Jones and Walter Rideout. Boston: Little, Brown, 1953.
A generous selection of the letters now in the Newberry Library, Chicago. Those published here are mainly concerned with Anderson's ambitions as writer, his problems of writing, his literary theories and attitudes. Like the Pound and the Crane volumes, a valuable source book.

Bishop, John Peale. *The Collected Essays* . . . , edited by Edmund Wilson. New York: Scribner's, 1948.
There is much here of value, many insights and evaluations by a critic of sensitivity who had first-hand acquaintance with the writing and the writers.

Brooks, Van Wyck. *The Confident Years, 1885–1915.* New York: Dutton, 1952.
Though this work is not intended to include a discussion of the decade, there
is much of Brooks's special kind of interpretation in the concluding chapters.
Of Brooks's own role in modern criticism, nothing is said.

Cargill, Oscar. *Intellectual America: Ideas on the March.* New York: Macmillan,
1941.
A study chiefly of the sources of modern American literary thought in
nineteenth-century European literary and philosophical developments. The
judgments upon modern American writers are richly documented but suffer
from a narrow and prejudiced reading.

Cleaton, Irene and Allen. *Books and Battles: American Literature, 1920–1930.*
Boston: Houghton, Mifflin, 1937.
A superficial account, mostly concerned with an exploitation of the most sen-
sational events of literary censorship and publicity.

Cowley, Malcolm, editor. *After the Genteel Tradition.* New York: W. W. Nor-
ton, 1937.
Essays and appraisals of generally high quality by Cowley, Robert Cantwell,
Lionel Trilling, Newton Arvin, John Peale Bishop, others.

———. *Exile's Return: A Narrative of Ideas.* New York: W. W. Norton, 1934;
revised edition, Viking, 1951.
This remains the best, the most lively, in many ways the wisest estimate of the
decade. The revised edition contains some interesting new information and perspectives.

Crane, Hart. *The Letters . . . ,* edited by Brom Weber. New York: Hermitage
House, 1952.
A mine of information concerning Crane's life, the writing of his poetry, the
literary life of the 1920s, and the special problems of the writer in the decade.

Daiches, David. *Willa Cather.* Ithaca, N.Y.: Cornell University Press, 1951.
A perceptive study of the art of Miss Cather's fiction, which gives it a proper
analysis without either exaggerating or underrating its importance.

Fitzgerald, F. Scott. *The Crack-Up,* edited by Edmund Wilson. Norfolk, Conn.:
New Directions, 1945.
This important document contains, among other things, Fitzgerald's impressions of the decade (published mostly in magazines in the early 1930s), excerpts
from his Notebooks, some letters, and some critical essays on his work.

Freeman, Joseph. *An American Testament: A Narrative of Rebels and Romantics.*
New York: Farrar and Rinehart, 1936.
A curious document which often reads like a novelized version of its subject,
but an interesting self-examination by a member of the leftist group of writers
and critics during the 1920s.

Geismar, Maxwell. *The Last of the Provincials: The American Novel Between
Two Wars.* Boston: Houghton, Mifflin, 1948.
Long studies of H. L. Mencken, Willa Cather, F. Scott Fitzgerald, and Sinclair
Lewis.

———. *Writers in Crisis: The American Novel Between Two Wars.* Boston:
Houghton, Mifflin, 1942.
Studies of Hemingway, Dos Passos, Faulkner, Ring Lardner, others.

Hoffman, Frederick J. *Freudianism and the Literary Mind*. Baton Rouge, La.: Louisiana State University Press, 1945.
Discussions of Freud's theories as they influenced modern literature, followed by studies of the influence on several novelists.
──────. *The Modern Novel in America, 1900–1950*. Chicago: Henry Regnery, 1951.
A short introduction; chapters III, IV, and V of special value.
Horton, Philip. *Hart Crane: The Life of an American Poet*. New York, W. W. Norton, 1937.
The most perceptive study of Crane and his times.
Howe, Irving. *Sherwood Anderson*. New York: William Sloane Associates, 1951.
An intelligent and reasonable attempt to place and evaluate Anderson.
Jones, Howard Mumford. *The Bright Medusa*. Urbana, Ill.: University of Illinois Press, 1952.
A short account of a few aspects of the 1920s, mainly of the developments immediately before the beginning of the decade. Lectures given at the University of Illinois.
──────. *The Theory of American Literature*. Ithaca, N.Y.: Cornell University Press, 1948.
A survey of literary histories, critical attitudes toward American literature, in the nineteenth and twentieth centuries.
Joughin, G. Louis, and Morgan, Edmund M. *The Legacy of Sacco and Vanzetti*. New York: Harcourt, Brace, 1948.
A valuable study of the trial and the executions, and of their influence on literature.
Kazin, Alfred. *On Native Grounds: An Interpretation of Modern American Prose Literature*. New York: Reynal and Hitchcock, 1942.
A brilliant reading of prose literature since Howells, with suggestive discussions of the 1920s.
Krutch, Joseph W. *The American Drama Since 1918: An Informal History*. New York: Random House, 1939.
Perhaps the most acceptable study of the drama, especially of O'Neill.
Luhan, Mabel Dodge. *Movers and Shakers*. New York: Harcourt, Brace, 1936.
One of Mrs. Luhan's volumes of "Intimate Memories"; contains much gossip, occasionally gives valuable suggestions regarding marginal matters.
Mizener, Arthur. *The Far Side of Paradise*. Boston: Houghton, Mifflin, 1951.
A thoroughly documented biographical study of F. Scott Fitzgerald, which, in its exhaustive concern with its subject, helps to put Fitzgerald in his place in the 1920s and incidentally offers a valuable interpretation of several aspects of the decade.
Munson, Gorham B. *Destinations: A Canvass of American Literature Since 1900*. New York: Sears, 1928.
Interesting only as a contemporary impression of writers, most of whom were just beginning to publish.
O'Connor, William Van. *An Age of Criticism, 1900–1950*. Chicago: Henry Regnery, 1952.
A useful short introduction.

O'Connor, William Van. *Sense and Sensibility in Modern Poetry*. Chicago: University of Chicago Press, 1948.

A convenient reading of, among other things, some important poems of the decade.

Pound, Ezra. *The Letters* . . . , edited by D. D. Paige. New York: Harcourt, Brace, 1950.

One of the most important books for an understanding of the special kinds of critical orientation of the decade.

Rosenfeld, Paul. *Men Seen: Twenty-Four Modern Authors*. New York: Dial, 1925.

————. *Port of New York: Essays on Fourteen American Moderns*. New York: Harcourt, Brace, 1924.

These two books, as contemporary accounts, reveal a remarkably acute critical mind, with several penetrating insights into writers of the decade.

Soule, George Henry. *Prosperity Decade, 1917–1929*. New York: Rinehart, 1947.

Study of the economic history of the decade.

Sullivan, Mark. *Our Times*, Volume VI. New York: Macmillan, 1935.

One of Sullivan's huge compilations of newspaper and magazine clippings, this book requires patient winnowing and sifting by the reader.

Taupin, René. *L'influence du symbolisme français sur la poésie américaine de 1910 à 1920*. Paris: Champion, 1929.

The only book of its type, this needs to be extended, altered, and translated, but it does contain some valuable information concerning an important subject.

Trilling, Lionel. *The Liberal Imagination: Essays on Literature and Society*. New York: Viking, 1950.

Included here are several suggestive readings of the work of the decade, Anderson's, Fitzgerald's, and that of others.

Unger, Leonard, editor. *T. S. Eliot: A Selected Critique*. New York: Rinehart, 1948.

The most complete collection of Eliot criticism thus far published.

Ware, Caroline F. *Greenwich Village, 1920–1930*. Boston: Houghton, Mifflin, 1935.

This exhaustive historical and sociological study of the Village contains much valuable information and not a few shrewd insights into, and evaluations of, the bohemian life. It is the only study of its kind relevant to the decade.

Whipple, T. K. *Spokesmen: Modern Writers and American Life*. New York: Appleton, 1928.

Another contemporary estimate of several writers of the decade, this book contains much of merely historical value, some insights of continuing worth.

Wilson, Edmund. *The Shores of Light: A Literary Chronicle of the Twenties and Thirties*. New York: Farrar, Straus and Young, 1952.

A collection, mostly of Wilson's magazine pieces and reviews, this book provides much that has value by way of an insight into Wilson's mind and into the special quality of the decade as he saw it.

Winters, Yvor. *Primitivism and Decadence: A Study of American Experimental Poetry*. New York: Arrow Editions, 1937.

A severe judgment upon such moderns as Hart Crane, Eliot, and Pound, with a suggestive organization of the forms of experiment in modern poetry.

HUGH SELWYN MAUBERLEY

BY EZRA POUND

(LIFE AND CONTACTS) [1]

"VOCAT ÆSTUS IN UMBRAM" [2]
Nemesianus, Ec. IV.

I

E. P. ODE POUR L'ELECTION DE SON SEPULCHRE [3]

For three years, out of key with his time,
He strove to resuscitate the dead art
Of poetry; to maintain "the sublime"
In the old sense. Wrong from the start—

No, hardly, but seeing he had been born
In a half savage country, out of date;

[1] In the 1926 edition of *Personae: The Collected Poems of Ezra Pound,* published by Horace Liveright, Pound added this note to the title page of *Hugh Selwyn Mauberley:* "The sequence is so distinctly a farewell to London that the reader who chooses to regard this as an exclusively American edition may as well omit it. . . ."
The poem was originally published in 1920 (London, Ovid Press), the year Pound left London for Paris. Poems I–VI were published in the *Dial,* September 1920. Poems VI, VII, VIII, and IX were not numbered originally, but are now numbered so that the reader may more conveniently follow the interpretation of them (see pp. 36–46). The text of the poem is included here by permission of New Directions, publishers of *Personae* (copyright 1926, 1954, by Ezra Pound).
[2] "The summer calls us into the shade." The quotations from foreign languages are translated and explained here. For notes on other allusions contained in the sequence, see Kimon Friar and J. M. Brinnin, *Modern Poetry,* pp. 527–31.
[3] E. P. Ode on the Choice of His Tomb.

Bent resolutely on wringing lilies from the acorn;
Capaneus; trout for factitious bait;

Ἴδμεν γάρ τοι πάνθ’, ὅσ’ ἐνὶ Τροίη [4]
Caught in the unstopped ear;
Giving the rocks small lee-way
The chopped seas held him, therefore, that year.

His true Penelope was Flaubert,
He fished by obstinate isles;
Observed the elegance of Circe's hair
Rather than the mottoes on sun-dials.

Unaffected by "the march of events,"
He passed from men's memory in *l'an trentiesme*
De son eage; [5] the case presents
No adjunct to the Muses' diadem.

II

The age demanded an image
Of its accelerated grimace,
Something for the modern stage,
Not, at any rate, an Attic grace;

Not, not certainly, the obscure reveries
Of the inward gaze;
Better mendacities
Than the classics in paraphrase!

The "age demanded" chiefly a mould in plaster,
Made with no loss of time,
A prose kinema, not, not assuredly, alabaster
Or the "sculpture" of rhyme.

III

The tea-rose tea-gown, etc.
Supplants the mousseline of Cos,
The pianola "replaces"
Sappho's barbitos.

[4] "For we know all the toils that in wide Troy"—*Odyssey*, XII, 189.
[5] The thirtieth year of his age.

Christ follows Dionysus,
Phallic and ambrosial
Made way for macerations;
Caliban casts out Ariel.

All things are a flowing,
Sage Heracleitus says;
But a tawdry cheapness
Shall outlast our days.

Even the Christian beauty
Defects—after Samothrace;
We see τὸ καλὸν [6]
Decreed in the market place.

Faun's flesh is not to us,
Nor the saint's vision.
We have the press for wafer;
Franchise for circumcision.

All men, in law, are equals.
Free of Pisistratus,
We choose a knave or an eunuch
To rule over us.

O bright Apollo,
τίν᾽ ἄνδρα, τίν᾽ ἥρωα, τίνα θεὸν, [7]
What god, man, or hero
Shall I place a tin wreath upon!

IV

These fought in any case,
and some believing,
            pro domo, in any case . . .
Some quick to arm,
some for adventure,
some from fear of weakness,
some from fear of censure,
some for love of slaughter, in imagination,
learning later . . .
some in fear, learning love of slaughter;

[6] The beautiful.
[7] "What man, what hero, what god"—line from Pindar's second Olympian ode,
which should read: "What god, what hero, what man shall we loudly praise?"

Died some, pro patria,
                    non "dulce" non "et decor" . . .[8]
walked eye-deep in hell
believing in old men's lies, then unbelieving
came home, home to a lie,
home to many deceits,
home to old lies and new infamy;
usury age-old and age-thick
and liars in public places.

Daring as never before, wastage as never before.
Young blood and high blood,
fair cheeks, and fine bodies;

fortitude as never before

frankness as never before,
disillusions as never told in the old days,
hysterias, trench confessions,
laughter out of dead bellies.

V

There died a myriad,
And of the best, among them,
For an old bitch gone in the teeth,
For a botched civilization,

Charm, smiling at the good mouth,
Quick eyes gone under earth's lid,

For two gross of broken statues,
For a few thousand battered books.

VI

YEUX GLAUQUES [9]

Gladstone was still respected,
When John Ruskin produced
"King's Treasuries"; Swinburne
And Rossetti still abused.

---

[8] Latin words and phrases from Horace, *Odes,* XII, ii, 13: *"Dulce et decorum est pro patria mori"*—"It is sweet and fitting to die for one's country."

[9] Glaucous eyes—a brilliant yellow-green.

Fœtid Buchanan lifted up his voice
When that faun's head of hers
Became a pastime for
Painters and adulterers.

The Burne-Jones cartons
Have preserved her eyes;
Still, at the Tate, they teach
Cophetua to rhapsodize;

Thin like brook-water,
With a vacant gaze.
The English Rubaiyat was still-born
In those days.

The thin, clear gaze, the same
Still darts out faun-like from the half-ruin'd face,
Questing and passive. . . .
"Ah, poor Jenny's case" . . .

Bewildered that a world
Shows no surprise
At her last maquero's
Adulteries.

VII

"SIENA MI FE'; DISFECEMI MAREMMA" [10]

Among the pickled fœtuses and bottled bones,
Engaged in perfecting the catalogue,
I found the last scion of the
Senatorial families of Strasbourg, Monsieur Verog.

For two hours he talked of Gallifet;
Of Dowson; of the Rhymers' Club;
Told me how Johnson (Lionel) died
By falling from a high stool in a pub . . .

But showed no trace of alcohol
At the autopsy, privately performed—
Tissue preserved—the pure mind
Arose toward Newman as the whiskey warmed.

[10] "Siena made me and Maremma unmade me"—Dante, *Purgatorio*, V, 133.

Dowson found harlots cheaper than hotels;
Headlam for uplift; Image impartially imbued
With raptures for Bacchus, Terpsichore and the Church.
So spoke the author of "The Dorian Mood,"

M. Verog, out of step with the decade,
Detached from his contemporaries,
Neglected by the young,
Because of these reveries.

VIII

BRENNBAUM

The sky-like limpid eyes,
The circular infant's face,
The stiffness from spats to collar
Never relaxing into grace;

The heavy memories of Horeb, Sinai and the forty years,
Showed only when the daylight fell
Level across the face
Of Brennbaum "The Impeccable."

IX

MR. NIXON

In the cream gilded cabin of his steam yacht
Mr. Nixon advised me kindly, to advance with fewer
Dangers of delay. "Consider
        "Carefully the reviewer.

"I was as poor as you are;
"When I began I got, of course,
"Advance on royalties, fifty at first," said Mr. Nixon,
"Follow me, and take a column,
"Even if you have to work free.

"Butter reviewers. From fifty to three hundred
"I rose in eighteen months;
"The hardest nut I had to crack
"Was Dr. Dundas.

"I never mentioned a man but with the view
"Of selling my own works.

"The tip's a good one, as for literature
"It gives no man a sinecure.

"And no one knows, at sight, a masterpiece.
"And give up verse, my boy,
"There's nothing in it."

  ·   ·   ·   ·   ·   ·   ·

Likewise a friend of Bloughram's once advised me:
Don't kick against the pricks,
Accept opinion. The "Nineties" tried your game
And died, there's nothing in it.

X

Beneath the sagging roof
The stylist has taken shelter,
Unpaid, uncelebrated,
At last from the world's welter

Nature receives him;
With a placid and uneducated mistress
He exercises his talents
And the soil meets his distress.

The haven from sophistications and contentions
Leaks through its thatch;
He offers succulent cooking;
The door has a creaking latch.

XI

"Conservatrix of Milésien" [11]
Habits of mind and feeling,
Possibly. But in Ealing
With the most bank-clerkly of Englishmen?

No, "Milésian" is an exaggeration.
No instinct has survived in her
Older than those her grandmother
Told her would fit her station.

XII

"Daphne with her thighs in bark
Stretches toward me her leafy hands,"—

[11] Lady curator of Milesian ware.

Subjectively. In the stuffed-satin drawing-room
I await The Lady Valentine's commands,

Knowing my coat has never been
Of precisely the fashion
To stimulate, in her,
A durable passion;

Doubtful, somewhat, of the value
Of well-gowned approbation
Of literary effort,
But never of The Lady Valentine's vocation:

Poetry, her border of ideas,
The edge, uncertain, but a means of blending
With other strata
Where the lower and higher have ending;

A hook to catch the Lady Jane's attention,
A modulation toward the theatre,
Also, in the case of revolution,
A possible friend and comforter

.   .   .   .

Conduct, on the other hand, the soul
"Which the highest cultures have nourished"
To Fleet St. where
Dr. Johnson flourished;

Beside this thoroughfare
The sale of half-hose has
Long since superseded the cultivation
Of Pierian roses.

ENVOI

(1919)

Go, dumb-born book,
Tell her that sang me once that song of Lawes:
Hadst thou but song
As thou hast subjects known,
Then were there cause in thee that should condone
Even my faults that heavy upon me lie,
And build her glories their longevity.

Tell her that sheds
Such treasure in the air,
Recking naught else but that her graces give
Life to the moment,
I would bid them live
As roses might, in magic amber laid,
Red overwrought with orange and all made
One substance and one colour
Braving time.

Tell her that goes
With song upon her lips
But sings not out the song, nor knows
The maker of it, some other mouth,
May be as fair as hers,
Might, in new ages, gain her worshippers,
When our two dusts with Waller's shall be laid,
Siftings on siftings in oblivion,
Till change hath broken down
All things save Beauty alone.

MAUBERLEY

1920

"Vacuos exercet aera morsus." [12]

I

Turned from the "eau-forte
Par Jacquemart"
To the strait head
Of Messalina:

"His true Penelope
Was Flaubert,"
And his tool
The engraver's.

Firmness,
Not the full smile,
His art, but an art
In profile;

[12] "He bites vacuously at the air"—Ovid, *Metamorphoses,* VII, 786.

> Colourless
> Pier Francesca,
> Pisanello lacking the skill
> To forge Achaia.

II

> *"Qu'est ce qu'ils savent de l'amour, et qu'est ce qu'ils*
> *peuvent comprendre?*
> > *"S'ils ne comprennent pas la poésie, s'ils ne sen-*
> > *tent pas la musique, qu'est ce qu'ils peuvent compren-*
> > *dre de cette passion en comparaison avec laquelle la*
> > *rose est grossière et le parfum des violettes un ton-*
> > *nerre?"* [13]

CAID ALI

For three years, diabolus in the scale,
He drank ambrosia,
All passes, ANANGKE [14] prevails,
Came end, at last, to that Arcadia.

He had moved amid her phantasmagoria,
Amid her galaxies,
NUKTIS 'AGALMA [15]

  .   .   .   .

Drifted . . . drifted precipitate,
Asking time to be rid of . . .
Of his bewilderment; to designate
His new found orchid. . . .

To be certain . . . certain . . .
(Amid aerial flowers) . . . time for arrangements—
Drifted on
To the final estrangement;

Unable in the supervening blankness
To sift TO AGATHON [16] from the chaff

[13] "What do they know of love, and what can they understand?
"If they don't understand poetry, if they don't feel music, what can they understand of this passion, compared to which the rose is coarse and the perfume
of violets a clap of thunder?" (According to Friar and Brinnin, Caid Ali is a
pseudonym for Pound.)

[14] Necessity.

[15] The ornament of night (probably: Nuktos' Agalma).

[16] The Good.

Until he found his sieve . . .
Ultimately, his seismograph:

—Given that is his "fundamental passion,"
This urge to convey the relation
Of eye-lid and cheek-bone
By verbal manifestations;

To present the series
Of curious heads in medallion—

He had passed, inconscient, full gaze,
The wide-banded irides
And botticellian sprays implied
In their diastasis;

Which anæthesis, noted a year late,
And weighed, revealed his great affect,
(Orchid), mandate
Of Eros, a retrospect.

.   .   .   .

Mouths biting empty air,
The still stone dogs,
Caught in metamorphosis, were
Left him as epilogues.

"THE AGE DEMANDED"

Vide Poem II. Page 436

For this agility chance found
Him of all men, unfit
As the red-beaked steeds of
The Cytheræan for a chain bit.

The glow of porcelain
Brought no reforming sense
To his perception
Of the social inconsequence.

Thus, if her colour
Came against his gaze,
Tempered as if
It were through a perfect glaze

He made no immediate application
Of this to relation of the state
To the individual, the month was more temperate
Because this beauty had been.

> The coral isle, the lion-coloured sand
> Burst in upon the porcelain revery:
> Impetuous troubling
> Of his imagery.

Mildness, amid the neo-Nietzschean clatter,
His sense of graduations,
Quite out of place amid
Resistance to current exacerbations,

Invitation, mere invitation to perceptivity
Gradually led him to the isolation
Which these presents place
Under a more tolerant, perhaps, examination.

By constant elimination
The manifest universe
Yielded an armour
Against utter consternation,

A Minoan undulation,
Seen, we admit, amid ambrosial circumstances
Strengthened him against
The discouraging doctrine of chances,

And his desire for survival,
Faint in the most strenuous moods,
Became an Olympian *apathein* [17]
In the presence of selected perceptions.

A pale gold, in the aforesaid pattern,
The unexpected palms
Destroying, certainly, the artist's urge,
Left him delighted with the imaginary
Audition of the phantasmal sea-surge,

Incapable of the least utterance or composition,
Emendation, conservation of the "better tradition,"

[17] Impassivity.

Refinement of medium, elimination of superfluities,
August attraction or concentration.

Nothing, in brief, but maudlin confession,
Irresponse to human aggression,
Amid the precipitation, down-float
Of insubstantial manna,
Lifting the faint susurrus
Of his subjective hosannah.

Ultimate affronts to
Human redundancies;

Non-esteem of self-styled "his betters"
Leading, as he well knew,
To his final
Exclusion from the world of letters.

IV

Scattered Moluccas
Not knowing, day to day,
The first day's end, in the next noon;
The placid water
Unbroken by the Simoon;

Thick foliage
Placid beneath warm suns,
Tawn fore-shores
Washed in the cobalt of oblivions

Or through dawn-mist
The grey and rose
Of the juridical
Flamingoes;

A consciousness disjunct,
Being but this overblotted
Series
Of intermittences;

Coracle of Pacific voyages,
The unforecasted beach:
Then on an oar
Read this:

"I was
And I no more exist;
Here drifted
An hedonist."

MEDALLION

Luini in porcelain!
The grand piano
Utters a profane
Protest with her clear soprano.

The sleek head emerges
From the gold-yellow frock
As Anadyomene in the opening
Pages of Reinach.

Honey-red, closing the face-oval,
A basket-work of braids which seem as if they were
Spun in King Minos' hall
From metal, or intractable amber;

The face-oval beneath the glaze,
Bright in its suave bounding-line, as,
Beneath half-watt rays,
The eyes turn topaz.

INDEX

INDEX

INDEX

451

Time, theory of, 132

Time and Western Man, by Wyndham Lewis, 285–86n.

"To a Snail," by Marianne Moore, 177

"To a Steam Roller," by Marianne Moore, 260–61

To Have and Have Not, by Ernest Hemingway, 74, 80

Toller, Ernst, 217, 220

Tom Sawyer, The Adventures of, by Mark Twain, 317

Torrents of Spring, The, by Ernest Hemingway, 193

Tradition, American, uses of, 121, 122–23, 127, 130–31, 390; impressionistic views of, 131–39; Humanists on, 139–46; Southern writers on, 145–53; Willa Cather on, 153–62; and Hart Crane, 231–35

"Tragic fallacy," 241–42

transatlantic review, 30, 131n., 213

Transatlantic Stories, ed. by Ford Madox Ford, 30–31

Transcendentalism, 121, 128

transition, 32, 193n., 207, 213

Tridon, André, 200

Trilling, Lionel, 145n.

Trotsky, Leon, 355n.

Troubadour, by Alfred Kreymborg, 175

Troy, William, 118–19

Tulips and Chimneys, by E. E. Cummings, 320

Tully, Jim, 87

"Turbine, The," by Harriet Monroe, 258

Twilight Sleep, by Edith Wharton, 380

Two Gentlemen in Bonds, by John Crowe Ransom, 150n.

Tzara, Tristan, 27, 86, 207, 208, 209, 421

Ulysses, by James Joyce, 212–13, 214, 285n.

Untermeyer, Louis, 126

Unwelcome Man, The, by Waldo Frank, 204

Upanishads, 301–302

U.S.A., by John Dos Passos, 254, 363, 376

Van Doren, Carl, 7

Vanity Fair, 86–92, 199–200n., 265, 304, 380

Van Vechten, Carl, 87, 98–99, 202n., 269, 328, 331–32, 334, 379–80, 421

Vanzetti, Bartolomeo, see Sacco-Vanzetti case

Veblen, Thorstein, 87, 93

Venture, by Max Eastman, 348–49n.

Verlaine, Paul, 299

Verse, free, 172

Village . . . , by Robert McAlmon, 329

Violence, and World War I, 54

Vision of Columbus, The, by Joel Barlow, 231n.

Vorse, Mary Heaton, 350

Vorticism, 163, 171n.

Walsh, Ernest J., 52, 421

War (1914–1918), and the older generation, 47–51; reasons for joining, 52; and the "unreasonable wound," 52–54, 66–75, 84; influence on language habits, 54–55, 59; portrayal of death, 55–56, 66–75; influence on literature, 57, 77–78, 122, 167, 379, 388, 391; and architecture, 57–58; the "separate peace," 59–60; prevailing images of in fiction, 61n.; mentioned, 36, 40, 42

War (1941–1945), 377, 379, 385–87

Ware, Caroline, 16–17

War Is Kind, by Stephen Crane, 55

War on Modern Science, The, by Maynard Shipley, 275–76

Warner, Arthur, 340–41

Warren, Robert Penn, 147, 149n., 150, 421

Waste Land, The, by T. S. Eliot, interpretation, 291–303; "The Burial of the Dead," 292–95, 301; "A Game of Chess," 295–97; "The Fire Sermon," 297–300; "Death by Water," 300–301; "What the Thunder Said," 301–302; mentioned, 87, 144, 147, 174, 230n., 378

Waste land symbol, in *The Sun Also Rises*, 81–82

Watson, J. B., 203–204

Wealth, Fitzgerald's appraisal of, 108–111, 117-18

Weaver, Richard, 147

Wedekind, Frank, 221